DISILLUSIONED

DISILLUSIONED

Five Families *and the* Unraveling
of America's Suburbs

BENJAMIN HEROLD

EPILOGUE BY BETHANY SMITH

PENGUIN PRESS
NEW YORK
2024

PENGUIN PRESS
An imprint of Penguin Random House LLC
penguinrandomhouse.com

Portions of this book appeared in different form in "How the Fight for America's Suburbs
Started in Public Schools," "Suburban Schools Are Majority-Nonwhite. The Backlash Has
Already Begun," and "A New Teacher at 50: Inside the Struggle to Rebuild America's Black
Teaching Workforce" in *Education Week*, copyright © Editorial Projects in Education.

Maps by Gerry Krieg

LIBRARY OF CONGRESS CATALOGING-IN-PUBLICATION DATA
Names: Herold, Benjamin, author.
Title: Disillusioned: five families and the unraveling of America's
suburbs / Benjamin Herold; epilogue by Bethany Smith.
Description: New York: Penguin Press, 2024. |
Includes bibliographical references and index.
Identifiers: LCCN 2023016076 (print) | LCCN 2023016077 (ebook) |
ISBN 9780593298183 (hardcover) | ISBN 9780593298190 (ebook)
Subjects: LCSH: Suburbs—United States—Case studies. | American
dream—Case studies. | Minority families—United States—Case studies. |
Suburban schools—United States—Case studies. | Social problems—United
States—Case studies. | United States—Race relations—Case studies.
Classification: LCC HN59.3 .H47 2024 (print) | LCC HN59.3 (ebook) |
DDC 307.760973—dc23/eng/20231026
LC record available at https://lccn.loc.gov/2023016076
LC ebook record available at https://lccn.loc.gov/2023016077

Printed in the United States of America
1st Printing

DESIGNED BY MEIGHAN CAVANAUGH

For my father,

whose wish for me

came true after all.

CONTENTS

PART I

STUCK

PART II

PROMISED LANDS

PART I

[STUCK]

PREFACE

In the suburb, one might live and die without marring the image of an innocent world, except when some shadow of evil fell over a column in the newspaper. Thus the suburb served as an asylum for the preservation of illusion.

Lewis Mumford,
The City in History, 1961

I was born into my American dream in a suburb called Penn Hills.

But growing up on a quiet street ten miles east of downtown Pittsburgh, in a middle-class white family that had no trouble accessing suburbia's bounty, especially from public schools that delivered hundreds of kids like me to state colleges each year, I often found myself on the receiving end of a cryptic message.

I just don't want you to end up stuck like me, my father might blurt out during a commercial or while I was helping him in the garage.

Then his attention would snap back to the Steelers game or whatever backyard do-it-yourself project he was fixated on that month, leaving me alone to puzzle over his words. Were they an order to be followed? A secret to be kept? I remained paralyzed with uncertainty right up until the end of high school, when I decided my dad had been trying to warn me. Driven by a dread I didn't understand, I resolved to escape from suburbia as fast as possible.

It was in Philadelphia that I found work as a journalist, writing about the spaces between this country's promises and its realities. Like so many others before me, I became obsessed with the ways our education system so often seemed to widen that gap, especially for families of color. Still blind to the suburbs' role in that story, I struck out for everywhere else, reporting from the boarded-up blocks of North Philly and the wide-open ranges of western New Mexico, from weary tumble-down buildings on the South Side of Chicago and the rutted sweet potato farms of central Mississippi. It seemed obvious that the country's social contract had been broken in the cities we'd abandoned and the rural outposts we'd forgotten. It never occurred to me that the heart of the problem might instead lie in the tidy ranch houses and solid SAT scores of places like my hometown.

But then, in 2015, a flood of devastating headlines began pouring out of Penn Hills. After running up a staggering $172 million debt, the same school district that had once served my family so well was on the verge of collapse. Teachers were being furloughed, services slashed, programs eliminated. Home values stagnated. Property taxes skyrocketed. The state auditor general described the district's finances as the worst he'd ever seen. A grand jury concluded that the "catastrophic" fallout would cast a pall over my hometown for "literally decades to come." And underlying all the bad news, I soon learned, was a surprising demographic shift. The public schools in Penn Hills, 72 percent white when I'd graduated back in 1994, were now 63 percent Black. Thousands of families of color had come to suburbia in search of their own American dreams, only to discover they'd been left holding the bag.

Suddenly, the humdrum little town I'd fled a quarter century earlier seemed to be sounding a dire warning. The opening of suburbia was supposed to be the culmination of the greatest mass movement in our nation's history, and experts were still pushing to move Black and Brown families into the suburbs and their "good" public schools. After all, that's where the country's foundational covenant—everyone is created equal, we all get a fair shot, success is determined by merit—was supposedly strongest.

But what if those families were discovering that their advanced degrees and carefully tended cul-de-sac lawns still didn't grant them access to all the country's benefits? That their children still weren't safe, even in the nation's most sought-after public schools? That they were now stuck, not just in some quiet personal crisis, but in a wider unraveling, one that threatened to undermine the civil-rights-era dreams of equal opportunity and harmonious integration that followed the deeply flawed vision upon which suburbia was built? America, with its long history of broken promises, might not hold.

It was this fear that ultimately drew me back home. On a blustery day in January 2020, I climbed into my station wagon and drove across the Pennsylvania Turnpike. I was forty-three, tired, with a to-do list already spilling off the page. But I desperately wanted to locate an American dream that wouldn't leave my own two children stuck, financially or emotionally or morally. And now, the path forward seemed clear: I first had to understand how the abundant opportunities my family extracted from Penn Hills a generation earlier were linked to the cratering fortunes of the families who lived there now.

My search for answers would eventually lead me on a journey across America's rapidly changing suburbs, from the McMansion-filled subdivisions sprouting up north of Dallas to the bungalow-lined blocks of long-blighted South Central Los Angeles. Connecting these far ends of the suburban spectrum, I learned, was a relentless cycle of racialized development and decline that took root after World War II, then sucked huge swaths of the country into a pattern of slash-and-burn development that functioned like a Ponzi scheme. Through massive public subsidies, exclusionary local policies, and a nasty habit of pushing the true costs of new infrastructure off onto future generations, our government had essentially paid millions of white families to run away from Black America, then encouraged us to cycle through a series of disposable communities with shelf lives just long enough to extract a little more opportunity before we moved out, stuck someone else with the bill, and restarted the cycle somewhere new.

But even as this pattern became ubiquitous, it remained mostly invisible. One big reason was described by philosopher Charles Mills as a willful racial ignorance that allows white people to protect ourselves from the truths we've "needed not to know" since the country's founding. Even today, elected officials and everyday Americans alike remain deeply committed to forgetting about the government-sponsored white flight that fueled suburbia's rise. To erasing from memory the burning crosses, racial real-estate covenants, and gerrymandered school boundaries that were used to keep everyone else out. To ignoring the scars left by the long-ago compromises of desegregation, and to dismissing the pain of whole neighborhoods that mass suburbanization helped undo. When an aging suburb began to teeter, we turned a blind eye, leaving ourselves unable to reconcile the vacant businesses, declining test scores, and dwindling property values with our vision of what that place was supposed to be. And after the community's tax base vanished, its school system capsized, and its residents were all Black and Brown, we promptly forgot that the hollowed-out place left behind had ever been a suburb at all.

Much attention has already been paid to how this cycle and its underlying ideology decimated America's cities. In their classic book *American Apartheid*, sociologists Douglas Massey and Nancy Denton found that by the late 1970s, roughly two thirds of the white people in the nation's major metropolises had already fled to suburbia, often on the strength of privileged access to cheap mortgage loans guaranteed by the Federal Housing Administration and Veterans Administration. This exodus led to a profound concentration of poverty in the mostly Black and Brown urban areas they left behind. Thanks to rising home values and a dizzying array of tax breaks, white suburbanites then saw our advantages multiply and ripple across generations: By 1989, the typical white family held more than ten times the wealth of the typical Black family, and white Americans were four times as likely as our Black counterparts to inherit money.

"The advantage that FHA and VA loans gave the white lower-middle class in the 1940s and '50s has become permanent," concluded economist Richard Rothstein in his 2017 book, *The Color of Law*.

By then, however, America was already entering a perilous new stage. The same cycle that had already devastated our cities was now churning through suburbia itself. Hundreds of aging inner-ring suburbs like Penn Hills were falling into debt and disrepair. Thousands of newer suburban communities found themselves in the path of the same gathering storm. And two major societal shifts were making the problem increasingly difficult to ignore.

The first was demographic. The U.S. Census Bureau began projecting that America will be majority nonwhite before midcentury, the result of a white population that began aging and declining just as the nation experienced an explosion of youthful diversity. Nowhere did these trends diverge more sharply than in the suburbs, where white people went from 79 percent of the population in 1990 to just 55 percent three decades later. Inside suburban public schools, white children are already a minority.

And all the while, the heart of America's middle class kept disappearing. Home prices soared. Water supplies dwindled. Upper-middle-income families began hoarding an ever-larger share of the country's opportunities. Millions of other Americans found they could no longer escape demographic change by simply moving to a newer community farther out in the countryside. By 2019, a profound pessimism had taken root: half the country expected their children to experience a lower standard of living than they'd enjoyed.

Soon to be outnumbered, with no more *away* to escape to, white America is suddenly face-to-face with its ghosts. It is this confrontation that will define the next few decades of American life. And the early skirmishes are already under way. Pick a suburb. Go to a school board meeting. Sit through some high school math classes. Soon enough, you'll see a painful truth being laid bare: The diversification of suburbia did not lead to a universal American dream, untethered from whiteness and extended equally to all. Instead, Black and Brown and white and Asian and rich and poor and immigrant and native born have all been left to craft separate variations on a theme. As a result, many white families are now consumed with anxiety about the erosion of long-standing advantages. Countless families of color have grown disillusioned by the suburbs' failure to deliver equally on America's promises. And nearly seventy years after *Brown v. Board of Education*, many of the parents, educators, and activists who long carried the dream of integration are demoralized and retreating. Suburbia is now home to a collision of competing dreams, each of which seems to be crumbling.

This book follows five families and five suburban communities caught up in this unraveling. Outside Dallas, a conservative white family named the Beckers have just left rapidly diversifying Plano to buy a 5,500-square-foot home in an exclusive enclave where they hope to recapture a lifestyle that seems to be vanishing. In the sprawling suburbs of Atlanta, the Robinsons, who are Black, thought they were buying into a promised land of their own, only to find themselves fighting the highly regarded Gwinnett County Public Schools, which seems intent on sending their teenage son to its notorious disciplinary school. In leafy Evanston, Illinois, a multiracial mom named Lauren Adesina has joined a group of ultraprogressive parent-activists determined to root out white supremacy in local public schools long hailed as a model of successful integration. After being displaced by the gentrification transforming Pittsburgh, a Black family named the Smiths has just purchased the house three doors down from my childhood home. And in Compton, California, the infamous Los Angeles bedroom community that collapsed under the weight of suburbia's contradictions decades ago, the Hernandez family has arrived from Mexico and pinned their hopes on a ramshackle little school called Jefferson Elementary.

The Beckers and the Robinsons, the Adesinas and the Smiths and the Hernandezes. Each family is living out a separate act in the same story of suburban change. Together, however, their journeys reveal something larger, about why our postwar American dreams are faltering, and about the new dreams trying to rise up in their place.

To tell this story, I'll start by taking you directly to suburbia's fault lines, into the center of the rising friction between families who thought they'd arrived and suburban communities on the brink.

Part II will then take you back to the beginning, tracing how each family's hopes for the future came to intersect with the histories of the suburbs where they eventually settled. In the process, I'll show how suburbia and its public schools came to serve as the repository for three main variations of the American dream—and how the development pattern that followed now threatens them all.

Part III focuses primarily on the 2018–19 and 2019–20 school years, when the flaws in suburbia's foundation burst into public view, throwing both families and school systems into crisis.

And Part IV explores the ensuing conflicts, each of which is illuminated and exacerbated by the COVID-19 pandemic and the protests prompted by the murder of George Floyd, compelling all of us to reckon with forces well beyond our control.

Throughout the book, you'll be crisscrossing the country, jumping from a PTA fundraiser in one community to a geometry lesson in another, sometimes within the same chapter. That's because I believe the best way to understand what's happening in suburbia is to consider these families' journeys side by side. Look closely at the forces that transformed Compton into a community of last resort for undocumented families like the Hernandezes, and you can see how the Beckers are unwittingly helping sow the same seeds in Lucas. Mass suburbanization may have left us fragmented and divided, but it didn't change a fundamental human truth: the best way to make sense of our world is still in relationship with each other.

That's why my story runs through the pages of this book too. Before I could fully grasp the disillusionment that mass suburbanization has wrought, and before I could recognize a version of the American dream that might keep us from getting stuck in the ensuing mess, I first had to peel back the many layers of my own need-not-to-know.

Take that cold winter day back in January 2020. After exiting the turnpike, I drove to Penn Hills, then parked outside the house where I grew up. To be sure, my family didn't lead a gilded life during our time on Princeton Drive. Five of us were squeezed into 1,001 square feet, making my parents' regular fights about money and their own neglected dreams impossible to avoid. Later, when I started meeting people who had grown up in fancier neighborhoods and attended more prestigious schools, I would grow deeply insecure, focusing my attention on every advantage I didn't receive.

Sitting there in my station wagon, however, I'd already started to see things differently. Penn Hills may not have guaranteed me a perch at the top of society. But it did provide a sturdy floor that kept me from ending up anywhere near the bottom. Consider my third-grade year back at Dible Elementary, where I developed the annoying habit of drawing on classroom furniture after I finished my work. Rather than punish me, Ms. Bauman brought in a typewriter and turned me loose. The result was my first newspaper gig, as publisher of "Up to Date with Room 38," a mimeographed one-sheet full of interviews with classmates and all the latest developments from the World Wrestling Federation. In hindsight, it was impossible not to see how the value of such opportunities had compounded over time, each newly opened door eventually leading to two more. After graduating from Penn Hills High, I transitioned seamlessly to the University of Delaware and then Temple University before starting my career in journalism.

Now, though, the asphalt on Princeton Drive was cracked and faded. I climbed out of my car, then started down the patchy gravel driveway where I used to play Wiffle ball. My family wasn't directly responsible for Penn Hills' downward spiral. But we'd left behind a family-size mess of our own that now seemed like a microcosm of the township's larger predicament. I wanted to see if it was still in our old backyard.

Over the course of my childhood, my father's endless do-it-yourself projects had turned our property into a maze of walls and fences that seemed designed to protect whatever it was he'd been afraid of losing. But after my brothers and my mom and I all left, his work had ground to a halt, and we'd all ignored the piles of junk he let accumulate out back. When my dad finally decided to leave Penn Hills in 2014, he approached the task like he was escaping a trap about to snap shut for good, selling the house to a guy he met through Craigslist for $27,000 in cash, roughly a quarter of what it was worth, on the condition the buyer take the property as it was.

Five years later, everything was just as my father had left it. Trash, debris, and bald rubber tires streamed down the wooded hillside at the end of our driveway. Stacks of rotting wood, sheets of pink foam board insulation, and wooden crates full of empty glass jars were strewn about everywhere. Punctuating the scene were two dozen 55-gallon blue plastic waste barrels lying half submerged in a thicket of weeds and dead leaves.

For decades, my family had extracted opportunity from Penn Hills, converting the publicly subsidized bounty of suburbia into the private gains that had allowed me to build a comfortable middle-class life somewhere else. The depressing tableau before me represented the waste product of that process. Eventually, I assumed, someone else would have to clean it up.

It's that mindset—highly racialized, profoundly damaging, passed down from one generation to the next, making all of us complicit—that caused the disillusionment now permeating suburbia. And only by disrupting it can we revive the belief that has long held America together: that for all this country's flaws and contradictions and outright lies, we can always dream and pray and strive and hustle our way out of *stuck*. If we are to reimagine the nation's social contract, to distribute its opportunities and burdens more fairly, to be free, the process will have to begin in places like Penn Hills, where the debate over the legitimacy of America's promises has grown most fraught, where poverty is rising at an alarming rate, where a resurgent right-wing movement is finding thousands of foot soldiers, where Trayvon Martin and Michael Brown and Ahmaud Arbery were shot dead in the street, where the achievement and opportunity gaps within our schools are most stark, where control of our government is decided, where our infrastructure is aging, and where old debts are coming due. The illusion that suburbia remains somehow separate from America's problems is no longer viable.

As I turned away from my family's mess and headed back out to Princeton Drive, I knew where my journey would begin. In my pocket, I had a list of all the properties on the street that had recently sold. One was the house three doors down. At the corner of its yard was a large concrete planter holding two flags. The first was American, red, white, and blue. The second was striped red, black, and green, the colors of Black liberation. Together, they flapped furiously in the wind.

I walked up the gently curved sidewalk and stood on the porch. The front door was open. Inside, I saw a gangly boy, dark skinned, with his hair in twists. He was sitting at a table, doing homework. His name, I would soon learn, was Jackson Smith. His mother's name was Bethany. She'd bought the house with her mom in the hopes of building some wealth for their family. She'd enrolled her son in the local public schools in the hopes he'd receive the special education supports he badly needed. Both ambitions were already in serious jeopardy. The Penn Hills school board would soon vote on whether to again raise property taxes and again slash services.

Whatever happened next, I knew, for the Smiths and the four other families featured in this book, would serve as a window onto America's future, helping determine if we're finally ready to "let America be America again, the land that has never been yet, and yet must be," as Langston Hughes once wrote. What I didn't anticipate was that along the way, Bethany would challenge me to confront my own racial ignorance and the damaging expectations that flowed from it, in the process becoming a crucial contributor to this book.

But all that would come later. The sky over Princeton Drive was beginning to darken. I took a deep breath, then knocked on the door.

AUTHOR'S NOTE

This is a work of nonfiction. All characters, places, and institutions described are real. The names of principals, superintendents, school board members, elected officials, and other public figures are their own. The names of parents, children, friends and family members, and teachers have been changed to protect their privacy. The exception is Bethany Smith, who chose to use her real name for reasons that will become evident.

In those instances where I have used dialogue, all direct quotations were either recorded or confirmed by multiple participants or witnesses. When such corroboration wasn't possible, I did not use quotation marks, and I indicated that the exchange is by necessity based on the account of one central person or family. Private thoughts and internal monologues are presented in italics. Some quotations have been lightly edited for clarity and readability.

When confronted with difficult decisions about which version of events to prioritize, I have given extra weight to the accounts of the featured families. How they make sense of their own experiences is paramount, and I trust their perspectives will challenge your expectations and assumptions about suburbia as profoundly as they challenged my own.

INTRODUCTION

I'm furious and disappointed.

—NIKA ROBINSON

THE ROBINSON FAMILY | GWINNETT COUNTY, GEORGIA

Nika Robinson loaded her Nissan Altima with all the jeans and sweatshirts and toys her children had outgrown during the past year. It was the kind of bright August morning when you couldn't help but feel good, with a rising summer sun already warming her dark brown arms. For months, everything had been a struggle, leaving Nika drained and irritable, a shadow of her usual bubbly self. But a looming change of season whispered on the breeze. The 2019–20 school year had just begun. So far, things had unfolded smoothly. A few hours earlier, Nika's husband and teenage son had headed out the door for work and for school, sleepy and cute as they mumbled goodbye. Carter and Cassidy, suddenly second and fourth graders, were happy and laughing as they ate their cereal at the kitchen island. Now, with her schedule free for the first time in forever, Nika felt almost relaxed. The end-of-summer consignment sale at the Gwinnett County Fairgrounds was about to start. It would be like a little reward for keeping everyone intact.

Nika climbed into the driver's seat and slid forward. At just over five feet tall, she stood a full twelve inches shorter than her husband, Anthony

Robinson, once a lean and powerful high school linebacker, now built more like a bulky defensive tackle. The two had met in 2003, when they were in their early twenties, back when nearby Atlanta still had space for all the pent-up hopes of America's booming Black middle class. At the time, she had just earned her master's degree in public health. He was working as a network engineer. After they got married, there wasn't much debate. Upwardly mobile families like theirs lived in the suburbs. By 2012, the Robinsons had settled in a six-bedroom, three-bathroom, $223,000 house in one of the whitest parts of northern Gwinnett, forty-five minutes from downtown.

Nika still wanted to believe it had been the right decision. Now in her early forties, it had become habit to push any nagging doubts about the life she'd built below the surface of her busy days, which were typically filled with work, parenting, and courses in the doctoral program she'd recently started at the University of Georgia. Just that morning, Nika had caught herself staring again at the dining-room walls, which remained the same neutral beige as the day they'd moved in. Weeks earlier, she and Anthony had bought several shades of blue paint in the small sample-size cans, then put a series of squares on the wall, one row running from Blueprint to Gentleman's Gray, another from Van Cortland to Indigo Batik. But even after hiring a color consultant to offer advice, Nika felt unable to commit.

It was a problem for another time, she thought as she backed her car out into the cul-de-sac, then passed her neighbors' homes, their still-skinny front-yard trees and empty concrete driveways spaced at regular intervals. The condominium complex for active adults scrolled by, followed by the community's gated pool and fenced-in tennis courts. Everything was calm.

As they so often did, Nika's thoughts circled back to her oldest son, Corey. Now fourteen, he was a bowling ball of a boy, short and stout, with a complexion like hers. A running back. He'd just started ninth grade at Mill Creek High, widely regarded as one of the best schools in the county. It was a big reason she and Anthony had picked the house and neighborhood they did.

A favorite daydream returned after a long absence. Where might her son go to college? What would he study? Where would he work, live, raise a family of his own? Nika let her mind roam over the possibilities. She'd grown up in Buffalo, New York, then gone to undergrad in Rochester before making the big jump to Emory University in Atlanta for her master's. Corey was more likely to go to a historically Black college, she figured. Just like his father, who studied math and physics at Clark Atlanta. Nika could already picture her baby boy in his gown, holding his degree, posing for pictures.

It was good to feel such ease again. For much of the summer, the Backpack Incident had been replaying on an endless loop in her mind. Thanks to Corey's adolescent relationship with the truth and her own contentious relationship with the Gwinnett County Public Schools, Nika had limited visibility into the details of what had actually happened. But it clearly signaled a dangerous escalation. The trouble had started soon after Corey began seventh grade at Jones Middle School. First, it was a series of citations and detentions handed out by white teachers who complained that he was disrespectful and took too long in the bathroom. Nika and Anthony weren't the type of parents to kid themselves. They knew their son was loud and liked to clown around. They got on him about moderating his volume, watching his manners, regulating his tone, tempering his physicality. But then Jones staff classified an accidental collision between Corey and another boy as "Behav phys inj," a code that fell under the district's rules for assault and battery. It was while trying unsuccessfully to get that removed from her son's record that Nika heard about the Backpack Incident. By now, the spotty details she'd pieced together fell like dominos in her mind. The white boy who had reported a missing necklace. The school police officer who had searched the bags of Corey and another Black student. The teachers who didn't bother to call home. The lack of an apology after the necklace couldn't be found.

Before things could get any worse, Nika had pulled Corey out of Jones Middle and sent him to live with Anthony's parents in neighboring DeKalb County for the rest of seventh grade. She also began researching a private

Christian academy that reminded her of the private school she'd attended as a teenager back in Buffalo. But Anthony was cautious about money, and Corey wanted to be with his friends for eighth grade, so Nika had let the matter drop.

During those first few months back at Jones, her daydreams of college were crowded out by fears that Corey might end up in Gwinnett County's notorious disciplinary school, the GIVE Center. If that happened, what would be next? Dropping out? Prison?

But the call never came.

Still, for much of the past summer, the family had argued again about private school. Nika wanted to make the transition for ninth grade, before Corey became attached to a new group of friends. She scheduled interviews with the school's academic adviser, even arranged for her son to work out with the football team. But Anthony was torn. They were already paying almost $4,000 a year in property taxes so they could send their children to the best public schools in Gwinnett County. How did paying more than $12,000 a year in tuition on top of that make sense? And what about Cassidy and Carter? Would they have to go to private school too?

Grudgingly, Nika had relented, again. Mill Creek High enrolled nearly 3,700 students. Three fourths scored proficient or advanced in both reading and math. The morning of Corey's first day, Nika had been worried sick.

To her relief, though, things seemed to be going great. Corey had already made the JV football team. He was also taking Geometry, putting him ahead of most other freshmen in the state. And he had quickly become Mr. Popularity, attracting a wide cross section of friends with his constant jokes. When her son came home from those first few days of school smiling and relaxed, Nika finally exhaled. Now she began to chastise herself just a bit. Perhaps she was being overprotective, Nika thought as she neared the turnoff for the Gwinnett County Fairgrounds. Too focused on the negative, ungrateful for the blessings her family enjoyed. Maybe the dots she'd been connecting into the shape of some systemic problem really were just a series of unrelated incidents.

She parked the Altima and climbed out of her seat. The midday sun wrapped her in a warm embrace. Back when Gwinnett was mostly rural and white, the sprawling fairgrounds complex had been home to rodeos and livestock competitions. Now it hosted a steady stream of craft fairs and dog shows.

Nika gathered her things and headed inside, joining a throng of middle-class moms who were African American and Korean American and Nigerian American and Mexican American and multiracial and white. She drifted through 9,600 square feet of floor space that filled up each year with Spider-Man T-shirts and Lego bins and a small army of *Frozen* snowmen who stared goofily at passersby. Nika found the smartly organized totems of childhood soothing. Everything where it belonged. Smiling, she began hanging her family's old clothing on the for-sale racks.

Then her phone buzzed in her purse. It was one of Mill Creek's assistant principals. He'd just handed Corey a long suspension. Nika would later learn that her son had been slap-boxing in the locker room with a teammate, more horsing around than trying to hurt each other. But someone had recorded the boys jumping around, and a bunch of laughing students had crowded around a cell phone to watch, drawing the attention of administrators who classified what happened as a fight. Nika heard the assistant principal say the harsh punishment he'd meted out was partly a result of her son's past disciplinary record, which included the prior "assault" charge she'd been unable to get expunged from his record. Everything mooring Nika to the present moment seemed to dissolve.

Inside the Gwinnett County Fairgrounds, surrounded by sneakers and strollers and exersaucers, she began to shake. A wave of anger crashed over her, then receded, only to be replaced by something like grief. She burst into tears. A stranger had to help her back to her car. Nika forgot all about the clothes and toys she'd come to sell, leaving them in a pile on the floor.

"I'm furious and disappointed," she told me later. "I should have sucked it up and paid to send him to the school I thought would be a better fit."

THE BECKER FAMILY | LUCAS, TEXAS

America's suburbs have long promised a brighter future to those willing to forget the past. That's the first illusion, as old as the nation itself: that we can always start over somewhere new, find freedom farther out on the frontier, stay forever a step ahead of history. After World War II, this sales pitch proved wildly successful: Between 1950 and 2020, the population of the country's suburbs grew from roughly 37 million to more than 170 million, representing one of the most sweeping reorganizations of people, space, and money in the country's history.

By the tail end of this era, however, suburbia was in the midst of an identity crisis. Millions of Americans remained deeply invested in their belief that the suburbs were the place where they could find peaceful neighborhoods, good schools, and a generous social compact. But the lived experiences of countless families like the Robinsons increasingly suggested otherwise.

It was the work of scholars like John Diamond at Brown University; Linn Posey-Maddox at the University of Wisconsin; Sonya Douglass at Teachers College, Columbia University; Decoteau J. Irby at the University of Chicago–Illinois; and R. L'Heureux Lewis-McCoy at New York University that first helped me make sense of this rising discontent. By 2019, these researchers noted, the popular imagery of *Leave It to Beaver*, *The Wonder Years*, and *Desperate Housewives* was woefully outdated. Nearly half of suburbia's Generation Z was already Black, Hispanic, Asian, or multiracial, part of a long-term demographic shift that was exposing the root problems with the suburbs. Especially their deep-seated history of white control, racial exclusion, and systematic forgetting, which together helped fuel a cycle of unsustainable outward expansion.

Metropolitan Atlanta sat squarely on the leading edge of these shifts. As recently as 1990, the population of Gwinnett had been 90 percent white. By 2019, however, the county was nearly two-thirds Black, Hispanic, Asian, and multiracial. The ensuing tensions had crept into every aspect of families' lives, from where they shopped to how much their homes were worth to whether they believed they could keep their children safe. And in the middle of it all was Gwinnett's public school system, a sprawling $2.3 billion bureaucracy still controlled by older white leaders adamant that any sudden change risked the loss of everything they'd built over the preceding decades. Stick with what had always worked, they pleaded. Otherwise, the county would slide down the same path followed by its neighbor a few miles closer to Atlanta, DeKalb County, once among the most sought-after suburban communities in the country, now struggling under the weight of rising poverty, soaring infrastructure costs, and a dwindling tax base.

All over the country, suburban communities found themselves in various stages of this same cycle. In Texas, the area north of Dallas had once been wide-open Blackland Prairie, acre upon acre of tall waving grass lit up each summer by magnificent sprays of wildflowers. By 2019, though, bustling suburbs spread out from the city's edge in concentric rings, like a tree, a new community added every twenty years. Plano was in the second ring out. Just as its white population began to decline, its Hispanic population had grown by 105 percent, its Black population by 127 percent, and its Asian population by 205 percent. And just as those demographic shifts took hold, Plano was hit with rising costs, for everything from road repairs to senior housing to Chinese-language materials at the local library. The town's leaders responded by adopting a new comprehensive plan that aimed to preserve Plano's suburban character while also embracing greater density and the high-rise apartment buildings, mass transit, and racial diversity that would follow. Dubbed "Plano Tomorrow," the plan won a prestigious national award as an example of how to make an aging suburb vibrant and sustainable. But a group of local residents had aggressively challenged anyone who backed it, filing lawsuits, accusing the Black mayor of "trying to turn Plano into another Harlem" and running for office under the banner "Keep Plano Suburban."

Consumed with their day-to-day lives, Susan and Jim Becker didn't really follow such fights. They were both white, with cheeks and forearms that changed color across the seasons, from pale straw to warm bronze and back again. She was in her late forties. He was in his early fifties. They'd fallen in love in 2002, back when they both worked as bankruptcy advisers at a large consulting firm. They moved to Plano shortly after, then started a family that came to include three children and a dog named Astro, added after Jim promised the kids they could finally get a pet if his beloved baseball team from Houston won the World Series.

By 2019, however, Susan was gripped with a mounting anxiety. The Beckers had sent their oldest son to the Plano public school down the street for a single year before pulling him out. In the half decade since, they'd embarked on what Jim jokingly called their "journey through Sinai," skipping through a series of private and charter schools in search of someplace that could meet the very different needs of Sean, a strong and passionate swimmer who could be painfully shy around other kids; Avery, who was cheery and outgoing, but hated math and had trouble paying attention; and Noah, the youngest, whom Susan and Jim believed was academically gifted.

That spring, just as the Robinsons began growing disillusioned with Gwinnett, where they'd moved expecting to find the same suburban dream enjoyed by generations of white families before them, the Beckers started searching for a way out of rapidly diversifying Plano, where they'd lost faith that the suburban dream they once took for granted was still possible.

A path forward had emerged during one of Susan's visits to her chiropractor. On top of a wide glass table in the spartan waiting room, local wellness providers advertised speech therapy services, neurofeedback reports, and customized bionutrition plans. Susan had never paid the piles much mind. That March, though, one of the business cards caught her eye. It featured a photo of a smiling white woman. She was a private educational consultant. Her job was to help Dallas-area families find the perfect schools for their children, especially those who happened to be gifted or dyslexic or have attention issues.

How interesting, Susan thought, sensing providence at work.

She called the number a few days later. The consultant engaged her in a long conversation about Jim's travel schedule and the horrors of Plano traffic, the kids' personalities and what wasn't working in their current schools. It felt like therapy.

Shortly afterward, Susan received a sixteen-page report titled "Becker Family School Summary." The document listed three public school districts, three area private schools, and three different homeschool-support options. Susan quickly zeroed in on the section about the Lovejoy Independent School District. It served the new exurbs still going up in the third and fourth rings outside Dallas, several miles farther from downtown. The district enrolled just 4,200 children, far fewer than Plano's 53,000. Ninety-seven percent of its students passed the state tests. What really drew Susan in, however, was the personalized attention and opportunities her children might receive. Lovejoy swimmers had won multiple state titles, and the intermediate school had its own natatorium, key considerations for Sean. As a fourth grader, Noah could get a few hours a day of accelerated coursework. Lovejoy also had a stellar reputation for serving students with ADHD and other special needs.

She called the district's administrative offices to learn more. A sunny woman named Stacey Dillon suggested she come out for a tour. Susan told Jim to clear his calendar.

The morning of their visit, the Beckers headed for the North Central Expressway, built with millions of federal dollars after World War II, making the suburbanization of North Dallas possible. First it was Richardson in the 1950s and '60s. Then Plano, during the 1970s and '80s. Allen, one ring farther out, had boomed in the 1990s and 2000s. This was the exit Susan and Jim took, zipping past the Target and CVS, then by Allen's residential neighborhoods, each packed tight with 3,000-square-foot homes hidden behind long brick privacy walls bearing names like Cottonwood Crossing. The landscape was barely distinguishable from the Plano streets they'd been driving for years.

Then the Beckers crossed out of Allen and into the town of Lucas. The traffic lights grew farther apart. Pockets of grassy ranchland started to reappear beside the road. Susan felt something in her chest let go. The new homes going up in Lucas stretched out to 5,000 square feet, sometimes more. Daytime traffic within the insular subdivisions was limited to the occasional

Amazon Prime van silently making its delivery rounds. At one of the town's main intersections, the Beckers came to a stoplight. On the corner stood a Conoco station and a quirky old country convenience store. Strips of bright red aluminum ran in vertical stripes along the top half of its exterior. In the center, LUCAS FOODS was spelled out in tall white letters. To the left, the word BAIT rested directly on top of the word SANDWICHES, conjuring a disgusting image that made Susan and Jim laugh.

The Lovejoy Independent School District's administrative headquarters were located a few miles away, on Country Club Road, in a small complex centered around a little red schoolhouse that had once been the community's sole educational facility. The district still had just three elementary schools, plus single intermediate, middle, and high schools that everyone attended together.

Dillon met the Beckers at Puster Elementary. She clutched a clipboard to her chest and talked in a rapid-fire burst of words, coming off more like a corporate concierge than a public school bureaucrat. As the group walked through the brightly decorated hallways, she rattled off a menu of offerings that left Noah's eyes wide. STEM classes were run through a partnership with a group called Project Lead the Way. It emphasized hands-on engineering projects, starting in the local elementary schools, which all had their own makerspaces. Robotics began in middle school, where students could also join band, color guard, orchestra, theater, and a dance team. Starting in ninth grade, Lovejoy offered thirty different Advanced Placement courses, including Statistics and 3-D Design. The high school had its own auditorium plus a separate black-box theater, a competition gym and separate practice gyms, one wing devoted to engineering and another to visual arts. Students were also encouraged to pursue independent study programs in whatever fields captured their imagination.

"It could be Arabic, it could be saving dolphins," members of the Lovejoy board liked to say.

Left unspoken were the dramatic demographic differences that distinguished Lovejoy from many nearby school districts. Back in Plano, for example, the student body was now just 34 percent white. Almost one third of the students were considered poor, and 15 percent were still learning English. Lovejoy schools, meanwhile, were 75 percent white. Fewer than 4 percent of its students were considered poor, and just 1 percent were still learning English.

Susan and Jim professed not to care about such figures. They thought of themselves as color-blind, concerned more with who people were as individuals than what groups they represented. During their tour, they didn't think to ask what was behind Lovejoy's homogeneity. But if they had, Dillon would have been ready with her stock answer.

Septic tanks.

It all came back to the local zoning codes, she'd explained after smiling at the confused look on my face when I'd taken the same tour. Lovejoy schools served parts of several municipalities, with most of its students coming from Lucas and Fairview, where local officials had taken numerous steps to manage the student population of the district. First, they'd designated nearly all the land within Lovejoy's 17-square-mile attendance zone for residential development only. Industry and retail—and the traffic, density, and service workers that came with them—had to locate elsewhere. Then the towns had stipulated that any home built within that 17-square-mile area had to be on a lot that was at least an acre large. By comparison, most lots in Plano and Allen covered just a quarter acre. Officials in Lucas and Fairview had also forsworn public sewers within the Lovejoy attendance zone, requiring instead that every private residence within Lovejoy boundaries run off its own private sewage-treatment system.

The net result of these policies, Dillon would explain during the tours she gave, dozens each year, to wealthy parents looking for public schools capable of competing with the elite private schools in Dallas, was that not a single child attending a Lovejoy public school lived in an apartment.

Other factors shaped the composition of Lovejoy schools too. The market for real estate in the area was notoriously tight, pushing the price per square foot up to forty dollars higher than in most surrounding communities. In a few subdivisions, houses on one side of the street were zoned to Lovejoy, while identical houses on the other side were part of a neighboring district;

the Lovejoy homes cost as much as $50,000 more. Furthermore, even the most well-to-do Black families generally didn't bother trying to buy homes in the area. When they did, banks denied their mortgage loan applications at a rate 23 percentage points higher than the denial rate for white families with the same income.

For the district, this invisible filtering system meant the ability to control costs. Instead of hiring teachers of English as a Second Language or paying for diversity training, Lovejoy had added an extra period to the school day so they could offer more electives. The wealth in the surrounding community also meant that Lovejoy had access to a deep well of unrestricted capital that most public schools could only dream of; each year, the Foundation for Lovejoy Schools raised more than $500,000 from local parents, extra money that came on top of local property-tax revenue and went to amenities like virtual-reality headsets, a rock-climbing wall, and a special sensory hallway for children with special needs.

For Lovejoy families, meanwhile, buying a home in the area still seemed like a surefire way to compound their wealth. For starters, they got a private-school-style education without having to pay tuition. Because the local zoning code guaranteed that only other expensive houses could be built nearby, the value of their homes seemed almost certain to appreciate. There were also significant tax benefits, available to homeowners everywhere, but especially pronounced for those able to buy into exclusive suburban enclaves like Lucas and Fairview. In 2016, for example, the few thousand households living in Lovejoy's attendance zone claimed federal deductions for mortgage interest and local real estate tax payments that totaled roughly $4 million, or about $1,500 per household, money that local families didn't really need, but were disinclined to relinquish. And when Lovejoy families eventually did sell their houses, the first $500,000 in profit was tax-free.

But such financial benefits weren't driving the Beckers' search, they told me. They just wanted to make sure their children were happy and well rounded. After their tour of Lovejoy schools was over, the couple tried to process the experience.

"She just spent two and a half hours with us, and we don't even live here," Susan said.

The next day, she called the Lovejoy administrative offices again. She asked Stacey Dillon if she could recommend any real estate agents who specialized in Lovejoy. Of course, Dillon said, passing along the number of a local agent who happened to have two children of his own in Lovejoy schools. He also served on the board of the foundation that raised all that money each year.

The real estate agent began showing the Beckers houses that weekend. Jim quickly became enamored with a five-bedroom, five-bathroom, 5,500-square-foot home on an acre lot in a subdivision off Country Club Road. The house had peaked roofs and a huge fireplace. The kitchen featured a walk-in butler's pantry. Out back were a putting green and a swimming pool surrounded by a stone patio with a built-in grill. A girl who would be in Avery's class lived in the house directly behind the property. A boy Sean's age lived in the house catty-corner across the street.

The Beckers said they didn't really notice that everyone in the neighborhood was white and well-to-do. What did register was how being in Lucas made them feel. Like they could breathe again. Less worried about having to constantly watch what they said. The little things, like the lack of streetlights, which allowed them to see all the stars in the night sky, reminding them of their own childhoods in small-town Texas. Just when the Beckers had started to think that maybe this version of suburbia and all the advantages it offered had disappeared, they'd found Lovejoy.

The price of entry was $850,000.

THE ADESINA FAMILY | EVANSTON, ILLINOIS

In America, the community organizer Saul Alinsky famously said, "integration" refers to the vanishingly short period of time between the first Black family moving into a neighborhood and the last white family leaving. That's certainly been the case across much of suburbia, so often built on a foundation of white exclusivity, only to later experience a rapid racial transition and then severe resegregation. America's suburbs, however, vary tremendously. Some are gritty inner-ring bedroom communities. Others are stately streetcar suburbs that still retain their nineteenth-century charm, or sprawling expanses of shopping centers and subdivisions. Included in this motley assemblage are a relative handful of suburbs where people of different races and backgrounds have fought for decades to live, work, and educate their children together. One such community was right in Alinsky's backyard, on the shores of Lake Michigan, fourteen miles north of downtown Chicago. Evanston, Illinois, was a college town of 73,000 people. Liberal middle-class white residents couldn't resist the way late-afternoon light filtered through the old-growth maple and elm trees lining the wide streets of the town, which they lovingly called "Heavenston." Black families had also built homes and businesses there for 150 years, laying as much claim to Evanston's history and culture as anyone. And by 2019, an influx of Latinx, immigrant, and gay and gender-nonconforming families had given the town a decidedly cosmopolitan feel, which much of its highly educated population viewed as a valuable amenity, right up there with the lakeside beaches.

Lauren Adesina first moved to Evanston in the mid-1990s. She was eleven at the time. Her father was originally from Nigeria; her mother, from Ecuador. Like everyone else, they were drawn by the quiet streets and the racial diversity. Above all, though, the Adesinas prized the highly regarded local public education system, which consisted of two separate bureaucracies: District 65, responsible for the town's elementary and middle schools, and District 202, responsible for Evanston Township High.

Smart, athletic, and sociable, with high cheekbones and a warm terracotta complexion, Lauren had no trouble making good grades and plenty of friends. By the end of high school, however, sneaking out of school for lunch dates at the local McDonald's had lost its thrill. After graduating in 2003, she went to Oakton Community College, then moved to Chicago, where she earned her degree in psychology and sociology.

In her late twenties, though, Lauren came back home. She began renting an apartment in the historically Black section of Evanston known as the Fifth Ward. The neighborhood's elementary school had been shuttered several decades earlier, when District 65 decided to integrate by busing the Black kids from the area into mostly white schools in other parts of town. That was one reason Lauren had started her young son at Dewey Elementary, a mile away.

Chris was a small boy, gentle and silly, with a grin that seemed to wrap all the way around to the back of his head, where his long black hair was often pulled back into a little puff. Since before he was born, Lauren had been afraid of inadvertently causing him harm. Her worst fears had materialized when he was one. After receiving his immunizations, Chris developed a lump on his arm. Then a high fever. Then he went into febrile seizures. During a weeklong stay in the hospital, he'd been intubated, leaving Lauren helpless and frightened. She'd emerged from the experience determined to protect her baby for as long as possible and convinced her suburban hometown was the best place to make that happen.

By late 2018, however, even the secure bubble of Evanston felt fragile. On a hectic Monday night after work, Lauren wound through the town's tucked-in residential streets, past the glowing dining-room windows that formed a checkerboard pattern against the chilly night sky. The public portion of the monthly school board meeting was set to start at 7:00 p.m. inside District 65's administrative offices. She made it in just as the proceedings were getting under way.

"Are there any comments from the public regarding the tax levy?" asked Suni Kartha, an Indian American woman who had recently been elevated to board president.

But none of the parents, teachers, and local activists in the overflow crowd had come to discuss tax rates. Kartha nodded in the direction of superintendent Paul Goren, a sixty-year-old white man with narrow shoulders and a searching gaze that skipped around the room.

Goren was the latest in a long line of remarkably liberal Evanston education leaders. Fifty years earlier, the town had become a national model for how to desegregate schools without prompting riots. Now, Goren was still working to keep the district racially balanced. He'd also embraced district-wide training around racial awareness and culturally responsive teaching, bringing to Evanston programs with names like Beyond Diversity and Seeking Educational Equity and Diversity, which everyone called SEED. Under Goren's watch, the district had also crafted a racial equity statement and adopted a new racial equity policy, begun overhauling its approach to discipline and dress-code enforcement, and pushed along an effort to "de-track" the district's eighth-grade Algebra classes, which historically enrolled a disproportionate number of white and Asian students.

"I want to start this evening's discussions with my personal and professional commitment to live and activate antiracism principles at every level of District 65," he began. "Tonight, I am here as a white leader in the district, to listen openly, so that I can be part of the efforts to address systemic racism and discrimination in our schools and our communities."

When Goren was done, Anya Tanyavutti cleared her throat and tugged on the stem of her microphone. The lone Black woman on the board, she had sad eyes and dark hair. Along with her husband, who was Asian American, Tanyavutti had moved to Evanston six years earlier. She'd since had three children. The oldest had come home from preschool mistakenly convinced they were white and that other kids had problems. In the years since, neighbors in Evanston had regularly questioned whether Tanyavutti really lived in her well-appointed home. She'd also been asked on several occasions if she was the nanny to her own children. During her first several months on the board, Tanyavutti had danced along with the unspoken choreography of how things had always been done. Then she'd said to hell with it. For months, she'd been prodding her colleagues to publicly address a spate of racist hate speech in Evanston's elementary schools.

"As a Black woman who was once a Black child, and who was called and told many of the same things that we've heard being said to children in our community today, and who subsequently was not protected, validated, or heard, it pains me deeply to hear of the harmful experiences that children and families have had," Tanyavutti told the crowd.

Kartha then recalled a similar meeting the board hosted several years earlier that had led to many of the changes Goren had already implemented. Sergio Hernandez, a Latino member of the board, wasn't present, but had submitted a lengthy statement in both English and Spanish. Candance Chow, a white woman and the board's previous chair, spoke about how her racial identity and Christian faith had shaped her notions of peace as "everything's quiet," teaching her to mute her response to injustice.

Public testimony finally began thirty minutes after the meeting opened. A procession of audience members marched to a podium placed in front of an expressionless gray wall. Each gave detailed accounts of the racist incidents they'd experienced in the local schools. Their stories stretched back decades, opening a window onto the tensions that had long been festering beneath Evanston's idyllic surface.

An older Black man named Albert wore a blue button-down shirt and told the board how as a child, he'd been excluded from events and performances at certain District 65 schools. Then, as a teen, he'd taken part in a massive 1968 protest led by Black students at the local high school. But decades later, he'd visited the school his young relatives attended, only to see firsthand that teachers were still withholding from Black children the affection and attention their white classmates took for granted. A timer went off, indicating that his three minutes of speaking time were up. He turned to the board and pressed on.

"You are perpetrating a fraud here tonight," he said. "We need to establish an elementary school in the Fifth Ward. Return the bused Black children home."

Several white speakers also addressed the board. The president of the local teachers' union described her members as "all-in" on antiracism. They'd recently partnered with District 65 to curate a "Black Lives Matter at School Week of Action" curriculum. Another woman with eggshell skin and dangly earrings also rose to speak.

"One of the things that I have realized, as I have been doing my own work to understand my whiteness, my identity as a white person, and white supremacy, to be able to say the words 'white supremacy,' and understand, even a little bit, what that means and how pervasive it is, is that I am finally beginning to understand, my understanding is evolving, about centering whiteness," she said.

The woman urged the school board to ignore anyone who didn't support their efforts to become antiracist.

"Don't listen to them," she said to a chorus of cheers. "If you know you are on the right side of history—and all of us here who have spoken really, truly believe you are—be brave. Don't be afraid. And don't center whiteness."

Also speaking was Heather Sweeney, a white woman who told the board about a collection of local white parents who had formed their own anti-racism affinity group. A multiracial collective of parents had also formed an entity called Next Steps, then organized a yearlong discussion series of a book called *Despite the Best Intentions: How Racial Inequality Thrives in Good Schools* that detailed how white parents often perpetuate racism by seeking to hoard opportunities for their own children.

Lauren was called to speak midway through the public testimony. She wore brown Uggs, gray sweats, and a black jacket she'd thrown on before the meeting. At the podium, she took a silent breath, then opened her journal. Long braids with silver beads fell to either side of her face.

"So, I just want to start off to say that racism is a form of trauma," she began, turning to the board. "Right?"

Lauren's job was to design workshops on racial equity for arts educators. She'd already gone through District 65's Beyond Diversity and SEED train-ings. At Dewey Elementary, where Chris was then in first grade, she'd be-come an active PTA leader. Now Lauren cleared her throat and squeezed the side of the podium.

"Since his time at Dewey, my son experienced several acts of racism," she began.

"The first incident, somebody told, a student told, a white student told my son that all Black students are monkeys," she then said, looking to the ceiling.

"The second incident was another student told my child they didn't want to play with him because they didn't like his skin color," she continued.

"And then, while unpacking that, he was also letting me know that he's being teased in class regularly because he's darker than everybody," she added.

It was difficult to speak publicly about such experiences, Lauren told the board. She didn't want to be crammed into anyone's stereotypes. But District 65 must do better.

"I'm grateful for all the positive strides the district is moving toward," Lauren finished. "But from my experience and the experience of other families of color, it's not enough."

As the discussion stretched into its third hour, a group of guest speakers took the floor. One was the Reverend Dr. Michael C. R. Nabors, senior pastor at one of the roughly two dozen Black churches in town. A proud man whose closely shaved goatee was flecked with silver, Nabors wore a dark suit and striped tie.

"I want to start by saying I wonder if you all really know what you're asking," he told the school board.

Eradicating racism in Evanston would require far-ranging steps, Reverend Nabors said. First, the board needed to acknowledge the problem was a community-wide epidemic. Then, all eight square miles of Evanston needed to be designated an Anti-Hate Zone. More trainings and workshops would be needed. Businesses, fraternities, and houses of worship would have to dedicate themselves to change. If any Evanston residents witnessed racist acts or words, he said, they should be encouraged to immediately report the incident to the authorities. Most of the room seemed to agree.

But then Reverend Nabors told a personal story. His children were fourteen and nine. They liked to give their dad a hard time for always wearing a jacket and tie. A year or so earlier, Nabors and his wife had taken the family on vacation. Waiting at the airport gate, Nabors said, the kids had started in on him again, teasing him for dressing so formally just to get on a plane. Later, he sat them down for a talk.

"Listen," he recalled telling his children. "I wear a suit and tie to protect you. If I have my hoodie on, or if I have a T-shirt and blue jeans on, people don't know me, they may treat me in a way that's just completely unacceptable."

Suddenly, the conflicts that would soon start tearing Evanston apart were on full display. Goren, the liberal white superintendent, shook his head in earnest sympathy. By the start of the following school year, he would be gone. Tanyavutti, meanwhile, listened impassively. The Black board vice president was determined to push Evanston beyond the type of respectability politics Nabors was describing. No longer would the town's children be told they had to dress, talk, or look a certain way in order to be safe, she'd vow later in the meeting.

"Children deserve to go to school and feel fully alive and feel fully present and fully loved," Tanyavutti said. "If we as adults have to get a little uncomfortable in order to do that, then I expect that we do it."

Lauren absorbed the back-and-forth. She was still wary about how much white families in Evanston were really willing to give up. And after what happened at Dewey, she knew she couldn't keep her son at the school. Still, she couldn't picture herself leaving her hometown altogether. Where else was there to go?

It was approaching 10:00 p.m. Reverend Nabors was concluding his remarks.

"What you all have to do, since you've started this," he told the District 65 board, "is you have to openly, and publicly, declare war on racism."

THE SMITH FAMILY | PENN HILLS, PENNSYLVANIA

Of course, a public war on racism is not a battle that most suburbs have embraced. Instead, residents and elected officials alike tend to get caught in slow wars of demographic and economic attrition, embracing magical thinking right up until the moment the changes they've been denying and resisting reveal the fundamental flaws in their community's foundation. The possibility of ending up in such a place ran counter to the dream Bethany Smith was raised in. But over time, the runaway gentrification transforming Pittsburgh had severely narrowed her options.

She'd grown up in Sugar Top, a proud middle-class Black community that sat like a stubborn crown atop the city's battered Hill District. Its streets, some still cobblestone, mixed modest row houses with majestic three-story homes set back atop steeply sloped lawns. There, Bethany's often-gregarious personality and medium-brown complexion fit right in. During her teens and twenties, however, an invisible current had swept the Smith family from the Hill and out through Pittsburgh's rapidly changing East End before eventually depositing them in Penn Hills, the aging bedroom community east of the city where I'd grown up. In 2018, Bethany and her mother pooled their resources and bought a 1,001-square-foot ranch house on Princeton Drive.

The street had once been nearly all white. But for decades, families like mine had been fleeing and dying off. All the while, municipal revenues kept falling, the cost of maintaining the town's infrastructure kept soaring, and an entrenched culture of political backscratching and can-kicking kept making the resulting problems worse. By the time Bethany arrived, Penn Hills' population was nearly 38 percent Black and no longer uniformly middle class, and the interests of the town's younger Black families were increasingly at odds with those of its aging white seniors. But local leaders seemed largely incapable of meeting the town's shifting needs. Foreclosures became a major problem, hitting Black homeowners hardest, but there was little the township could do. Sidewalks went unbuilt and unrepaired, but private property owners often declined to cooperate. Teachers of color went unhired, creating a massive cultural disconnect between the adults and the children in the local public schools, but collective-bargaining agreements made any wholesale changes difficult. Most residents kept muddling along, choosing to believe Penn Hills could remain the sought-after bedroom community it once had been. But the tensions and contradictions eating away at the town's foundation were increasingly impossible to ignore.

Bethany responded by keeping one foot planted in her old life. Even after moving to Penn Hills, she and her mom returned every weekend to Grace Memorial Presbyterian, their old church in the heart of Sugar Top, where they helped run a youth program on Saturdays and attended services on Sundays. And when it came time to enroll her own son in kindergarten, Bethany chose Urban Academy, a Black-run charter school back in the city.

By the fall of 2019, though, her grip on such touchstones was slipping, causing an old panic to gain new life every time she thought about her son's future. Jackson was a handsome boy, tall for his age, with puppy-dog eyes and shirts that never seemed to stay tucked in. He was smart and usually sweet. But dark clouds could gather around him in an instant, compacting his face into a scribble of anger and frustration, foretelling a storm that would dissipate only after tantrums and tears. Now in second grade, his regular outbursts had turned his life at Urban Academy miserable. But the only alternative Bethany saw was the Penn Hills public schools, which many middle-class Black parents in the area viewed as a toxic mix of racist white adults and unruly, poor Black children, and thus strove to avoid.

On a gray October morning, Bethany woke up and remembered the choice before her. After inhaling slowly, she granted herself an extra minute in bed, pulling the covers tight and swaddling herself inside one of her warmest childhood memories.

It was New Year's Eve 1992. Bethany was eleven. She and her best friends had tiptoed to the balcony of Grace Memorial. Outside, the last ribbons of dusk had disappeared, leaving nothing but cold night sky around the golden-bricked church. As the Watch Night service began inside, the smell of chicken, bacon, and eggs wafted up from the kitchen, where a midnight brunch was being prepared. From the balcony, the girls could see the church sanctuary rolling out below, a sea of crimson carpet giving way to the bald spots and wide-brimmed hats of the old people rocking in the pews. Their faces were turned toward the pulpit, where a new pastor stood framed against the majestic brass pipes of the organ. Rev. Johnnie Monroe had just begun his sermon. Bethany and her friends exchanged glances, savoring the deliciousness of the task they'd been assigned. Then, giggling, they grabbed the inflated balloons they'd carried up the stairs and tossed them over the railing, watching with glee as they floated down on the unsuspecting congregation below.

Bethany had hoped to raise Jackson in a place as warm as that. And long after she left Sugar Top, the ethos that permeated the neighborhood—Black community nurturing self-love and excellence in Black children, so they'd be prepared to navigate an unkind world—remained deeply ingrained. After graduating from high school in 2000, Bethany had joined both Job Corps and AmeriCorps. In exchange for a grant that covered the cost of tuition at the Community College of Allegheny County, she worked as an assistant teacher in a kindergarten classroom at Pittsburgh's first charter school, founded by the local Urban League. It was run by a Black principal, and the blue-and-white hallways were lined with African American artwork. Bethany loved helping eager six-year-olds sound out words, the same way she had learned back in Sugar Top. She even helped start an after-school step team, teaching the girls the same dance moves she and her friends had once practiced in the front yards of her old neighborhood. When her small protégés performed at the school's first graduation ceremony, Bethany beamed with pride.

If I ever have a child, she thought, *I want him to go here.*

Jackson was born ten years later. At the time, Bethany and her mom were sharing a two-bedroom apartment in Pittsburgh's East End. Bethany wanted a bigger place so her son could have his own bedroom. By then, though, the area was undergoing a dramatic transformation, embodied most clearly in efforts to convert a long-abandoned Nabisco factory into a new mixed-use complex called Bakery Square. The development soon became home to Google offices, a Panera Bread, an Anthropologie, and a specialty store selling high-end learning toys. Then it spread into a shuttered public school building and through a main commercial strip, leading rents to soar. Between 2009 and 2018, the number of people with a college degree living in the area rose by more than 40 percent. The number of Black people dropped by 23 percent. By the end of the decade, Pittsburgh had lost 9 percent of its entire Black population, nearly seven thousand people in all. Among them were Bethany and her mother. In 2014, they began renting a three-bedroom house in Penn Hills.

True to her earlier vow, Bethany enrolled Jackson in Urban Academy a few years later. When his behavior quickly became an issue, she reached out to the school's CEO, a Black man she had gone to high school with. Bethany said the CEO set up a meeting with Jackson's teacher, a special education expert, the school's principal, and the dean of students. She also said the group decided to screen Jackson to see if he was on the autism spectrum. When no signs were found, Bethany chalked her son's worsening behavior up to brattiness, which she figured must be her fault. She began visiting the school regularly and providing volunteer help for the musical he was taking part in.

Still, Bethany told me later, by the second week of first grade, Jackson's teacher was calling home almost daily. Usually, she'd raise concerns about him playing too rough or storming out of class. But that fall, the situation escalated dramatically. As Bethany relayed the story to me, Jackson complained to his teacher that his arm was hurting. The teacher sent him to the school nurse. She asked what happened. Jackson said Bethany had punched him. The nurse asked if his mom punched him every day. Jackson said yes.

Bethany told me she was at work when she got a call that morning. She recalled an Urban Academy administrator saying the school was required to refer the incident for investigation of possible child abuse. It was true that she had a temper, Bethany acknowledged, and she sometimes did get angry with Jackson, gripping him up by the shoulder as she herded him out the door. But such incidents hardly seemed to rise to the level of abuse. Bethany recalled saying she had nothing to hide and going back to work.

That same afternoon, however, her phone buzzed again. Jackson was acting up, his teacher said. Bethany was so outraged, she left her job and went straight to the school.

If I was an abuser, she recalled demanding of the principal and CEO, how would I react to getting that phone call?

In the moment, her primary concern had been whether Urban Academy was organized enough to keep her son safe. But that had quickly morphed into frustration at the school's inability to identify and address the root cause of Jackson's behavior problems. And snaking its way through the layers of emotion was a deeper, more personal hurt. The staff at Urban Academy was mostly Black. Bethany had long-standing personal relationships with several people there. And for more than a year, everyone had seen her volunteering at the school. But now, she believed, they were treating her and her son like strangers.

Bethany told me that by August 2019, social workers had cleared her of any wrongdoing. Jackson went back to Urban Academy for second grade. His bad behavior started right back up. Feeling trapped, Bethany took him to be independently evaluated. She told me a psychiatrist diagnosed her son with attention-deficit hyperactivity disorder and oppositional defiant disorder. But when she relayed the information to Jackson's teacher, Bethany said, the teacher implied she was making excuses, leading Bethany's heart to run dry.

"They *know* me," she said. "Why look at my son like he ain't shit? Like he don't deserve support?"

The final blow came a few weeks later. In early October, Bethany said, she got another call home. Jackson and another boy had apparently ripped pages from each other's workbooks, then gotten into a shoving match. The possibility of a suspension loomed.

Lying in bed, seeking comfort in her childhood memories, Bethany's thoughts kept coming back to her old pastor at Grace Memorial. Reverend Monroe had come to Sugar Top with a vision that home, church, and school should work together to spin a web of support and affection around the community's children. Bethany had experienced the benefits of that approach firsthand; when she and her friends started getting in trouble of their own, Reverend Monroe had responded by tapping them to become junior tutors in the church's after-school program.

"We called them little hellions," the pastor told me years later. "But the more bad they acted, the more we loved them. That's how I got Bethany and that group tamed. Loving them to death."

For more than twenty years, she'd fought to maintain connections to that kind of community. Now, though, Sugar Top was struggling. The gentrification of the city's East End was unrelenting. Urban Academy had felt like the last hope for a familiar rock upon which her anchor might catch, preventing her from being washed out into an unfamiliar suburban sea. Now it, too, had given way.

Bethany had heard about the troubles in Penn Hills public schools. The district was still reeling from the revelations of that monstrous $172 million debt. If it couldn't get its finances in order, the state was threatening to take it over.

She forced herself out of bed, then went to wake up Jackson. They'd have to make it work.

THE HERNANDEZ FAMILY | COMPTON, CALIFORNIA

Fifty years earlier and twenty-four hundred miles away, Compton, California, had hurtled down the same fraught path Penn Hills was now following. The devastation that resulted should have set off blinking red lights to warn the rest of America's suburbs about the fate that might await them. But the country had long since forgotten how Compton had risen out of the alfalfa fields fifteen miles south of downtown Los Angeles, then developed into a prototypical bedroom suburb, home to caravans of mostly poor and uneducated white migrants from the Midwest and the Dust Bowl, whom state and federal lawmakers lavished with good-paying jobs, heavily subsidized higher education, and brand-new single-family homes for as little as $200 down. The country had long since forgotten how Compton then became the largest Black-run community west of the Mississippi. And the country had certainly forgotten the brief window when Compton was on the cusp of real multiracial integration. Instead, we'd decided the town's history began with its collapse. By the 1980s, Compton's new reputation as a violent, gang-ridden, inner-city dystopia was being cemented by the rap group N.W.A. By the 1990s, neighboring communities were renaming the stretches of Compton Boulevard that ran through their jurisdictions to avoid the stain of the town's name. And as the new century dawned, the scope of Compton's failure was evident above all in its public schools, long considered the worst in California, still cycling through state-appointed administrators nearly a decade after almost going bankrupt. The first had announced he would save money by laying people off. He was shot at on his way to a school board meeting. Another tried to pass a $107 million bond measure to repair crumbling schools, only to see Compton's mayor vigorously campaign *against* the plan.

This was the version of suburbia into which Alberto Hernandez landed in early 2002. He'd been born on a farm in central Mexico, then gone off to the Benemérita Universidad Autónoma de Puebla to study computer science, giving himself a serious leg up. By his early twenties, though, Alberto had given up hope of ever getting ahead at home. Short and stocky with a weathered complexion, he'd come to the United States alone, without papers. He'd since gotten married and had kids, found work as a welder, been mugged and robbed, struggled to learn English, and lost his father back home. But he'd never left Compton. Like millions of others, he'd viewed the border between the U.S. and Mexico for what it historically was—a casual suggestion kept vague enough to accommodate the workers who'd been coming and going from the region's farms and factories for generations, since before the American Southwest was American at all. But when the U.S. militarized the border in response to rising insecurities about the nation's changing identity, Alberto had been marooned. Now in his midforties, one part of him longed to return to Mexico. The other felt obliged to keep chasing what remained of the American dream for those who slipped through the cracks in the country's foundational promises.

"If someone holds up a dollar and holds up a peso, of course you're going to choose the dollar," he told me.

By the end of 2019, however, beleaguered Compton was showing signs of rebirth. At the state level, California was bucking the national anti-immigrant wave, investing in services and opportunities for its two-million-plus undocumented residents, saying their youth, enterprise, and multicultural fluidity were necessary to revitalize the nation. Locally, the resulting changes had shown up first in the Compton Unified School District, where per-pupil spending was up, the percentage of children reading and doing math at grade level had nearly doubled, and graduation rates had risen nearly thirty points. The district's board, finally back under local control, had even passed a $350 million construction bond to turn decrepit Compton High into a state-of-the-art campus with a performing arts center named after N.W.A. cofounder Dr. Dre. And no place embodied the incipient sense of possibility more than Jefferson Elementary, located on the edge of Compton's historic barrio neighborhood. Though they lived just outside Jefferson's attendance zone, Alberto and his wife, Cristina, had plotted for months to enroll their two children in the school.

Now it was a week before Christmas. Alberto rose before dawn to get dressed for work, then slipped quietly into the small bedroom his two children shared in the Hernandezes' portion of a duplex that was owned by somebody else. A lone dresser stood against the wall. The drawers belonging to twelve-year-old Marisol hung open, spilling clothes onto the floor. Those belonging to nine-year-old Jacob were closed tight, protecting the treasures he kept within. Both were born on U.S. soil and therefore American citizens, legally entitled to whatever fresh promises the country was willing to make in places where the old suburban dream had disappeared. Jacob seemed especially eager to claim his share of the future. After kindergarten, he'd skipped directly to second grade, earning straight As despite being the youngest student in his class. More than anything, Alberto wanted his son to have the chance to pursue his many questions without hesitation. He kissed his children's heads, then backed into the kitchen, where he grabbed the lunch his wife had made, then left, his mind already blank in preparation for the workday ahead.

Cristina, however, had an empty hour to fill. She was also short, with straight black hair and a complexion a shade or two lighter than her husband's. Sharp lines ran from the edges of her thin nose down to the pinched corners of her mouth. Before getting pregnant, she'd worked as a quality control supervisor at a large produce packaging plant in South Los Angeles. But Alberto believed couples had fewer problems if someone was devoted full time to parenting. To be fair, their relationship was still strong. During these in-between times, however, Cristina increasingly found her thoughts drifting back to her native Puebla, where two decades earlier she had been pursuing a master's degree of her own. Her mother, rest in peace, had sacrificed greatly to support her studies. But Alberto had convinced her to join him in the U.S. before she could finish her thesis, leaving Cristina with her own set of regrets that she hoped to avoid passing on.

"At that time, I didn't think about the future," she said.

Outside, a bleary December sun fought its way through the thick haze hanging over the Los Angeles basin, bathing the dingy facades of the buildings across the street in warm orange light. Jefferson Elementary was located several blocks away, just off Alameda Street, an industrial artery lined with scrapyards and ancient warehouses. A half century earlier, the leadership of the newly formed Compton Unified School District had launched a trailblazing bilingual education program at the school. For a moment, it actually seemed possible that an overwhelmingly Black and Brown suburb had found a way to deliver opportunity to all its children. Even more surprising, the rest of the country briefly seemed willing to listen.

"There are indicators that this model may become a prototype for bilingual programs throughout the United States," Compton Unified officials had written confidently as 1970 came to a close.

But then the spiral had hit. Black leaders began systematically excluding the town's growing Latino community from the dwindling opportunities Compton still had to offer. The bilingual program at Jefferson fizzled. The notorious Bloods street gang was founded on Piru Street, which dead-ended into the back of the school. Thousands of poor, Spanish-speaking students had since passed through Jefferson, earning some of the lowest test scores in all of California.

Only recently had the school clawed its way back to a place of hope. Ninety percent of Jefferson's students were still living in poverty, and more than a third were still learning English. But in 2018–19, well over half had scored at grade level or above in both reading and math. Administrators were also bringing back art and music. A prestigious grant from Apple had allowed them to give every student a computer or an iPad. They'd even formed a partnership of their own with Project Lead the Way; kids from Compton's old barrio were now getting the same hands-on robotics and engineering education as the wealthy white kids who attended Lovejoy schools in Texas.

Such changes were why Alberto and Cristina had fought so hard to get their children into the school. Because they were both noncitizens, it would always be a struggle for the couple to access opportunities for their children. As a result, they had little choice but to find the best Compton Unified had to offer. That meant holding out hope for a kind of integration that America rarely discussed; at Jefferson Elementary, Jacob's future was in the hands of a Latino teacher, a Filipino American principal, and a Black superintendent, all of whom were hoping to move beyond the painful Black-Brown power struggle that had riven Compton for decades.

Breakfast finished, Cristina loaded the kids into the family's minivan. As they drove through the streets around Jefferson, backyard roosters announced the new day. Parents and children tumbled out of 900-square-foot homes and past the postage-stamp-size front yards where they parked cars, let Rottweilers roam, or grew rose bushes in gravel gardens. By 7:45 a.m., dozens of families were already gathered in front of the chain-link fence outside the school, woven with bright blue and gold letters reading "EXCELLENCE ABOVE AND BEYOND." Jefferson's annual holiday concert would begin shortly after students were counted in their classrooms. Cristina stood off to the side with Jacob at her hip. His pomaded bangs formed a canopy over his big brown eyes. When the gate to the school opened, he rushed in without hesitation.

Victor Moreno was already waiting inside his classroom. Now fifty-three, with a quarter century of teaching elementary school behind him, he carried his weariness like family. Less than two years earlier, he'd suffered a hemorrhagic stroke. Moreno still didn't have much feeling in his left hand, and he was under doctor's orders to pace himself. That meant arriving at school only an hour early. After planning out his day, Moreno had pulled a faded black guitar case from the corner of the room, then eased himself into a small plastic chair with tennis balls on the ends of its metal legs. The last time he'd tried to play for his class, he'd cut his fingers badly, but didn't notice the blood dripping onto the floor until one of the children pointed it out. Later that morning, though, the class would sing "Up on the Rooftop." Moreno had promised the children he would accompany them, and he wanted to keep his word.

The fourth graders came spilling in wearing sequined reindeer horns and Santa hats with bells. Jacob hung his satiny green jacket in a worn cubby. At his desk, he opened a small package of Cinnamon Toast Crunch, then showed a friend the comic book he'd been working on. It was the second volume of "Captain Pumkin & Captain Max." He'd modeled the superheroes after himself and his dog, Rebel, whom his family had rescued that summer from an empty swimming pool. In the comic, the protagonists were doing battle with an evil red lobster named Dr. Crawbler, whose secret weapon was a ray gun that made everyone speak Spanish—a device Jacob had introduced into the storyline so that his parents, whose English was halting, could follow along.

"Let's be heroes!" Captain Pumkin said upon discovering his superpowers.

"I'll make outfits!" Captain Max responded in the next frame.

The class had thirty-two students. Most had been born in the U.S., but nearly all had roots in Mexico or Central America. One boy had recently lost his father, Moreno said; he'd died shortly after being deported to Tijuana. Regardless, all were expected to pass the state exams at the end of the year. That came straight from charismatic Compton Unified board chair Micah Ali, a local-boy-made-good who had been touting "the Compton turnaround" to any media outlet that would listen. Superintendent Darin Brawley was charged with backing up Ali's sometimes audacious claims. A data fanatic, Brawley had begun his tenure by insisting on the ability to know with the stroke of a few computer keys what academic skills every one of Compton's 20,000 public school students had mastered. Now, though, his gaze was fixed further out on the horizon. The superintendent didn't just want Compton kids learning on iPads. He wanted to prepare them to design and build the technologies that would reshape the world again.

Moreno appreciated the ambition. But it was also giving him heartburn. Back when he was still young and idealistic, he'd built his entire classroom around using music to tap into his students' natural wonder. Every day he would play his guitar in class, opening spaces that the children filled with their own questions and imaginations and musical theater productions. But at the end of each school year, almost all the students at his school would score below grade level on state exams. Moreno started imagining children running through large buildings and having doors slammed in their faces because they'd failed Algebra.

Over time, he'd gradually made peace with focusing most of his energy on teaching basic academic skills. Then, at the start of the current school year, Jacob had marched up to him with a request. He wanted to create his own class newspaper, complete with investigations into what was happening behind the scenes at Jefferson. I want to know if there's any hidden secrets they haven't told us, the boy said. The earnestness had nearly caused Moreno's heart to burst. Against his better judgment, he told Jacob he'd support the project. Just give me a few weeks, he said.

Now it was four months into the school year. Work on the paper had yet to begin. Moreno told the children to line up single file as they headed out into Jefferson's courtyard. More than three hundred adults—moms pushing strollers, dads holding Styrofoam cups of steaming coffee, grandfathers in faded leather motorcycle jackets—had come to support them. Cristina handed Jacob a red Santa hat as he walked past. Behind him, Moreno carried his guitar and a small amplifier trailed by a long orange extension cord. Principal Aquino bounded onto a makeshift stage and led the children in a loud call-and-response.

"Be in school every single . . . ?" Aquino started.

"DAY!" the children answered.

"If you believe, you will . . . ?" the principal continued.

"ACHIEVE!" they yelled.

"Are you ready to be at home for the next two weeks?" he asked.

"YESSSSS!" the children roared.

"What about you parents? Are you ready for your children to be home for the next two weeks?" Aquino finished, drawing rueful laughter.

When it came time for the fourth grade to perform, Moreno rested his guitar on his knee and fumbled his way through the melody to "Up on the Rooftop." The children snapped their fingers to simulate the sound of reindeer hooves. Jacob sang along brightly, untroubled by the self-consciousness of some of his older classmates.

Soon it would be time for recess. Then it would be Christmas. After that would be a brand-new year. In 2020, Jacob trusted, he'd finally get the chance to start his newspaper.

"Mr. Moreno is strict," he said. "But he always does what he promises."

PART II

PROMISED LANDS

ONE RING FARTHER OUT

THE BECKER FAMILY | LUCAS, TEXAS

The shibboleth of newness contained the seeds of its
own destruction.

—KENNETH T. JACKSON,
*Crabgrass Frontier: The Suburbanization
of the United States,* 1985

Plano is located at the southern end of Collin County, an 848-square-mile area that for centuries was inhabited by Indigenous tribes that were part of what became the powerful Caddo Nation. The thick black soil beneath the prairie was excellent for growing maize. By 1500, the local population had swelled to roughly 200,000 people. Then four bedraggled foreigners, separated from a larger Spanish expedition seeking to colonize parts of present-day Florida, ended up lost in what is now East Texas. The quartet roamed for years, exposing Caddo trading partners to unfamiliar diseases that mushroomed into a catastrophic epidemic. By the late 1600s, the Indigenous population of the area was almost entirely wiped out. The land that would become Collin County was Spanish, then Mexican, then independent territory that sat mostly empty. When white officials from the newly minted state of Texas officially drew the place onto their maps in 1846, they counted just 150 people.

For more than a century, change came slowly, if at all. Into the 1950s, Plano remained a small agricultural community, home to just a few thousand peo-

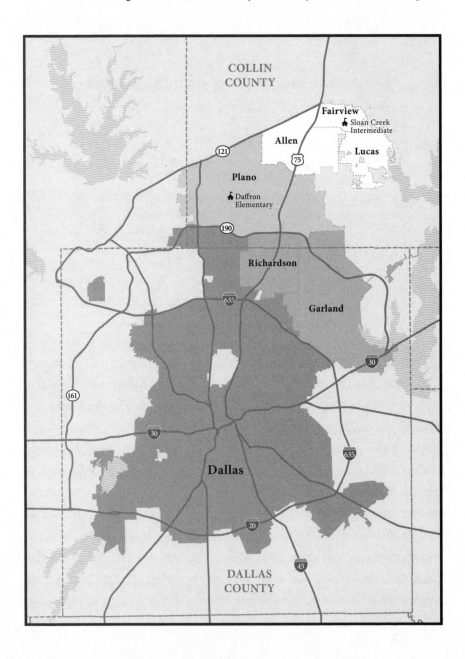

ple. Each fall, the local schools attended by Black children would close for a month so students could help with the cotton harvest. And each spring, the town's white high school would send its entire graduating class of thirty-five students on a field trip to a local ranch. There was downtown, some scattered residential neighborhoods, and the small Douglass community where Black families lived. Add it all up, and Plano's property-tax revenue was so limited the school district had to send its broken-down buses to a state penitentiary, where inmates could be forced to fix them for free.

By midcentury, though, a dizzying transformation was under way one ring closer toward the city. And when Plano's white mayor, city manager, and zoning commission gazed south toward the horizon, they saw nothing but bright, unspoiled future.

Dallas's first suburbs had started sprouting during the buildup to World War II. Worried about protecting critical industries from possible attack, federal defense officials pushed to locate key plants around the perimeters of cities in the Sunbelt that stretched across the country's southern half. In 1940, a large North American Aviation factory was built west of Dallas. The company soon employed more than thirty-five thousand workers, and the sleepy farming town of Grand Prairie was transformed by hastily erected tract homes. Other defense plants soon followed, leading to new development in towns like Richardson and Garland that formed a crescent around Dallas's northern perimeter. All told, the 1940s saw nearly one million people flock to the country's heavily subsidized and largely suburban "defense areas," including Dallas-Fort Worth.

Just as government helped spur this emerging migration pattern by directly intervening in the U.S. economy, federal agencies helped give that pattern shape. Especially significant was the Home Owners' Loan Corporation, which created insurance maps of hundreds of American cities, including one of Dallas in 1937. HOLC officials drew red lines around neighborhoods full of older dwellings that were occupied by mostly Black and poor residents. They drew yellow lines around neighborhoods that were "definitely declining" and often adjacent to redlined areas. "Still desirable" areas were circled in blue. And around the wealthier, all-white neighborhoods where single-family homes predominated, the federal government drew green lines, signaling they were the safest bets in the housing market. Over the next four decades, these maps and the principles they embodied would guide banks, private developers, and the new Federal Housing Administration as they made decisions on where to build homes, who should receive mortgage loans, and whether those loans would be insured. Implicit were the notions that neighborhood decline was closely tied to demographic change. Explicit was the belief that people of different races should be kept separate; the FHA not only embraced segregation, but for more than a decade required it, in many cases offering guarantees to developers only if they committed not to sell homes to Black buyers.

From the outset, the results were messy and violent. Thousands of Black people searching for factory jobs poured into Dallas during the 1940s. Many were unable to find suitable housing; at one point, 22,000 Black families were crammed into 12,500 dwellings. Some tried to move from one of the city's redlined Black neighborhoods into an adjacent white neighborhood. Determined to keep their street from turning "undesirable," white residents responded first with lawsuits, then with yard signs saying KEEP THIS NEIGHBORHOOD WHITE, then by organizing local housewives to throw stones through the windows of a Black family's house. When those strategies failed, they bombed the homes of their new Black neighbors roughly twenty times over a fifteen-month stretch, sometimes using dynamite believed to have been lifted from local construction sites.

Under pressure to stop the violence, Dallas's mayor proposed an interracial committee—but no Black members were appointed. A local congressman got involved, pushing the House Un-American Activities Committee to look into the situation—to determine whether communists had infiltrated the local NAACP.

Tensions remained high into the early 1950s, when Dallas officials began annexing land in West Dallas that was occupied by Black residents, seizing Black-owned homes in the Trinity River Bottoms, and razing a Black community in order to expand a new airport. Displaced residents again tried to push beyond the city's overcrowded redlined neighborhoods. Some local white residents again responded with terrorism, setting six fires and conducting eleven bombings.

Now, though, the federally financed North Central Expressway led out of Dallas and directly into its new northern suburbs. There, mortgage loans were cheap, thanks to millions of dollars in federal loan guarantees. For tens of thousands of white families living in Dallas's yellowlined neighborhoods, the message was clear. Instead of resisting demographic change, it paid to flee. The mass suburbanization of the country was under way.

Nineteen miles from downtown, Plano officials watched this process unfold with keen interest. In the early 1960s, they decided it was time to call Marvin R. Springer, the former Dallas planning director who would go on to advise dozens of suburban communities on how to accommodate the people, cars, and businesses now heading their way. It was his firm, Marvin R. Springer & Associates, that wrote Plano's first comprehensive plan, released in August 1963. The firm promised the town's leaders they could conjure an idyllic America, unbound by the burdens of the past.

"New growth offers an opportunity to create, through reasonable planning effort, a virtual new community," the plan stated. "There is opportunity to avoid many of the problems and ills which are apparent in existing communities."

Such a vision wouldn't materialize on its own, Springer & Associates cautioned. Almost 90 percent of the acreage the firm analyzed in Plano was farmland or vacant prairie. Major infrastructure would be necessary. Among the first orders of business was developing an expansive sewage system that cut across the creeks draining the prairie. An orderly grid of thoroughfares would also be needed to accommodate future traffic. At the center of each square, land would have to be set aside for parks and schools. None of this could wait, the planners stressed. On a chart showing the expected population growth of Dallas and its suburbs, the dotted line labeled Plano went almost straight up. By 1980, Springer & Associates projected, the number of people in the town could grow to 40,000.

Such pronouncements likely seemed a bit rosy at the time. Soon, though, it became apparent the planners had dramatically underestimated how popular Plano would be. By the early 1970s, officials in nearby Dallas were reporting the city had lost 100,000 residents to the suburbs. Legions of families were also migrating to the region from the Midwest and the Rust Belt, where the economies of old industrial cities like Buffalo were falling apart. To capture these new arrivals, Plano's business and civic leaders encouraged construction of new industrial parks, research centers, and single-family homes, turning the town into a prime destination for highly educated workers in fields like physics and molecular science.

In 1973, Plano's growth was further accelerated by more racial violence in Dallas. A white police officer named Darrell Cain shot and killed a twelve-year-old Mexican American boy named Santos Rodriguez during a game of Russian roulette intended to force a false burglary confession. News of the killing sent thousands of angry Black and Brown protesters into the Dallas streets, a development that was followed by even more white families fleeing to the suburbs.

Above all, though, what fueled the mass migration of white families to places like Plano were the changes taking place in America's public schools. In 1954, the U.S. Supreme Court had ruled in *Brown v. Board of Education* that segregated schooling was unconstitutional. The decision prompted a spike in right-wing ideology among some factions of white parents, many of whom viewed racially mixed schools and the interracial sex and marriage they believed would follow as an existential threat. For two decades, the Dallas Independent School District did its best to oblige their concerns, slow-walking every desegregation strategy that was suggested. By the early 1970s, however, a group of Black and Mexican American parents was gaining traction with a lawsuit that aimed to finally integrate Dallas's public schools for real. White parents responded by exiting the system en masse. Before the decade was out, the families of 52,000 white children—more than half of all the white students in Dallas—had left. Some vocally opposed integration of any kind. Others were more circumspect.

"We could just see all of these things happening," parent Claire Wood-chek told *D Magazine* in 1977, describing how court-ordered busing had prompted her son's Dallas elementary school to remove one of its libraries in preparation for an influx of new students.

"We got to thinking about private school for three boys," she said. "We figured it would be cheaper in the long run to move out."

By 1980, Plano's population had reached 72,000 people, nearly double what Springer & Associates had projected. The town got a new mall, followed by a rapid-fire succession of corporate relocations, from Frito-Lay to J.C. Penney to Electronic Data Systems, the tech behemoth founded by soon-to-be-presidential candidate H. Ross Perot. All told, nearly eighteen thousand acres were developed during those boom years, sending the value of the property that helped fund Plano's public schools soaring, to nearly $7 billion. In newspapers across the country, the once-sleepy agricultural community was now being described as "perfect."

Mostly left out of such stories, however, were suburbia's emerging racial politics. In Plano and across the nation, the benefits of mass suburbanization had for decades flowed mostly to white families, who time and again got the first—and often only—crack at new homes, cheap mortgages, big tax breaks, and high-quality public schools and services. The process amounted to a massive government-led redistribution of land, wealth, and opportunity. It also gave white families the chance to inscribe their values and priorities in the local institutions being built to accommodate their wants and needs. Rather than acknowledge this windfall, however, millions of white suburbanites chose instead systematic denial, fervently embracing the myth that they'd earned their suburban bounty solely through their own hard work and moral fiber. A resurgent conservatism took root, especially in Sunbelt suburbs around cities like Dallas, which became the epicenter of America's late-twentieth-century political realignment. It started with extreme right-wing ideologues like billionaire Texas oil baron H. L. Hunt, who reached millions with apocalyptic radio and television broadcasts detailing wild conspiracy theories about the communists burrowed deep within the State Department. Far-right groups like the John Birch Society found significant support among middle-class white professionals and homemakers who were showered with arguments that federally funded school milk pro-grams represented creeping socialism, the fluoridation of municipal water supplies was an elaborate mind-control plot, Chief Justice Earl Warren should be impeached or hanged for treason over the court's *Brown* decision, and control of local Parent Teacher Associations needed to be regained be-fore it was too late.

In 1964, the failed presidential campaign of Barry Goldwater showed conservatives what it would take to harness this energy in service of a somewhat more moderate agenda. Thanks to the advancing civil rights movement, millions of white suburbanites were already anxious that their new communities and schools and all they represented—the centrality of the nuclear family, the illusion of meritocracy, the supposed normalcy of middle-class white America—were in danger. To tap into this fear, the Re-publican Party crafted its "Southern Strategy," which amounted to promises to shrink the federal government before it could extend suburbia's generous social contract to racial and ethnic minorities. The approach proved wildly successful. By the early 1980s, a newly ascendant GOP controlled both the White House and the Senate, and the values and concerns of white Sunbelt suburbanites were squarely at the center of the nation's politics. If there were problems in America, President Ronald Reagan and his fellow conservative leaders insisted, they resided in the people and places that suburbanites had left behind, and that's where the blame and consequences would fall.

Such strategic amnesia found its way into the local politics of places like Plano too. Anytime the town's carefully burnished reputation was threatened—by Satanic graffiti in the tunnels under the Collin Creek Mall, by a rash of teen suicides, by a soaring divorce rate—a brief panic would ensue. Then a scapegoat would be found, local leaders and residents would get busy forgetting, and everything would go back to normal.

The most pronounced example came in the late 1990s, when a surge of teen heroin overdoses spoiled efforts by the local chamber of commerce to tout Plano as the fourth kid-friendliest city in America. Young people were copping in the parking lot of the local Starbucks, shooting up in the bath-room of a gas station across the street, then returning to buy a twelve-dollar crowbar with six shots of espresso to keep from nodding off. Inside Plano high schools, students asked their classmates-slash-dealers for "candy," which came in the form of a metal case of Altoids with a dose of heroin hidden below the paper wrapping. Nineteen local teens ultimately died. Dozens more survived overdose scares. If the victim was white, his friends tended to drive up to the doors of the local emergency room, push his limp body out of the car, and drive off. But when a Hispanic boy OD'd, his panicked friends kept his body hidden for almost two days, then dumped it in a church parking lot back in Grand Prairie.

By 1998, Plano's drug scourge was all over the news. Taking their cues from local police and school officials, the media framed the problem as innocent white teenagers who'd been targeted by Mexican drug cartels and Black dealers from Dallas. An *ABC World News Tonight* report titled "Heroin in Suburbia: It Can't Happen Here" made clear the assumption that the root of the problem must lie somewhere else.

"This week, the people of Plano, Texas, will meet to discuss a new enemy that has invaded their city and is threatening their children," anchor Carole Simpson told her audience. "It's an enemy no one expected would reach this quiet town."

Under pressure to avert the nation's gaze, local police set up an undercover sting inside Plano's high schools. "Operation Rockfest" yielded twenty-nine indictments, including eleven Mexican nationals described as the "kingpins" of local drug trafficking. None of these alleged kingpins could afford a private lawyer. Ten were convicted and handed lengthy prison terms, with two receiving life sentences. The remaining eighteen defendants were mostly white teenagers. They turned government witness against their Mexican counterparts in exchange for comparatively light sentences. The longest, for forty-eight months, went to a Black teen implicated in the death of a popular white football player.

PLANO'S WAR ON HEROIN PAYING OFF IN LIVES SAVED declared the local papers.

By the time Susan and Jim Becker arrived in town a few years later, the whole tawdry episode was just a hazy memory.

TOO GOOD TO BE TRUE

The fallout from Plano's history would eventually prompt the Beckers to flee farther north of Dallas, to a place where that same suburban cycle was starting anew. Back in late 2001, however, the couple's life together was just beginning.

That fall, giant energy trader Enron was exposed as a massive Ponzi scheme, imploding after revelations it had been using sketchy accounting techniques to hide massive losses. In early 2002, consultants from every corner of the country were being called in to administer the remnants of the company's sprawling business and make sure creditors got paid. Among them were Susan and Jim, then both working as bankruptcy experts. She was assigned to the small team he was leading.

Each morning, the two made their separate ways to Enron's glittering skyscraper in downtown Houston. Entering the lobby, Jim would look for Susan's long dark hair and strong Greek nose. Susan, who flew back and forth from Dallas each day, in turn hoped for a glimpse of the oddly angled grin that made Jim appear he knew something everyone else had missed. On lucky days, they'd ride the elevator up together, zooming past entire floors now eerily vacant. Huddled around a conference table on the fifteenth floor, they'd pore over balance sheets, attempting to make sense of balance sheets that Jim described as "fiction."

Over the course of twelve-hour days, their conversations gradually strayed beyond work. First, it was sports; in high school, Susan had been a state champion tennis player, while Jim was a sure-handed shortstop. Then it was their shared Methodist faith and conservative politics; both believed that God and family should be the driving forces in American life, with government somewhere much farther down the list. From there, it didn't take long to determine that their budding connection was rooted in their small-town Texas upbringings.

Susan had bounced around as a child, living in neighborhoods near whatever new high-end community her real estate developer father was helping build. By the time she was in high school, her family had settled just outside of Marble Falls, a small town of about three thousand people located in the lake country around Austin, where her father was helping build a nearby resort called Horseshoe Bay. Through tennis, Susan quickly made friends at her new school, mostly with the boys' team. When she supplanted the senior star, taking over the team's number-one singles slot, her alienation from the girls grew even more pronounced.

Jim, meanwhile, came from a tiny town called Weimar, which hung off Highway 10 halfway between Houston and San Antonio. His family lived on five acres, a half mile from their nearest neighbors. Many of the kids in his graduating class of forty-five had known one another since kindergarten. Weimar wasn't exactly agricultural anymore, and the Beckers were no longer farmers. Still, every winter, someone would take out the .22, slaughter a hog, and invite all the neighbors over for a cookout.

Ted Becker had worked as the general manager of a local trucking company. He died when Jim was ten. By high school, Jim was settling comfortably into the life his old man left behind, spending his weekends and summers bringing big rigs into the bay, then changing their tires and fixing the occasional trailer floor. No need for college, he figured. He could stay at Herder Truck Lines forever.

Mary Becker, though, had other ideas. Get your degree, she said. If you still want to come back to Weimar afterward, fine.

Jim's first lecture at Texas A&M had 250 students, more than his high school's entire enrollment. But he threw himself into his studies, graduating in 1990 with a double major in accounting and finance. Diploma in hand, Jim decided his mom had been right. Rather than return to Weimar, he went to work for Arthur Andersen, became chief financial officer for one of his clients, then headed off to grad school before finding his way back into consulting. Every six months or so, another company's shareholders or lenders would see a looming crisis, and Jim would jet off to oversee a big restructuring. Usually, the process involved layoffs. That part wasn't fun. But the work was never boring; Jim watched as employees from three consecutive clients were sent to prison.

Then came the Enron assignment, which gave him a front-row seat to the evisceration of America's middle class. A couple times a week, Jim would head up to the fiftieth floor to talk to the senior executives. A year earlier, their company had been valued at more than $60 billion. Now they couldn't say what accounts were being used to pay which vendors. Such mismanagement had resulted in some forty-five hundred lower-level workers losing their jobs. As a parting gift, the wealth they once had in the form of Enron stock also evaporated. It was crazy, if you thought about it.

Jim, however, was inclined to focus on things he could actually control. In that, he'd found a strong partner in Susan, who loved to game out scenarios and assess potential risks. Seeing the Enron disaster up close cemented in the pair a shared conviction. While many decried the ways deregulation had shifted so much risk onto ordinary Americans and wondered why no one had broken the spell of willful delusion that fueled the company's rise, Susan and Jim took home an additional lesson: If a situation started to go bad, it was best to get out while you still could.

Two summers later, the couple was living in Dallas and engaged to be married. More out of anticipation than any serious intent to buy, they asked a real estate agent friend to show them some places in Plano. Much of the town's housing stock was built in the 1970s and '80s and reflected the standards and tastes of that era. Susan and Jim considered these homes garbage, too old or dark or small. But when the real estate agent drove them around the newer parts of town, everything seemed to change. Just as Springer & Associates had advised, planners and developers had transformed the prairies of West Plano into a sensible grid of self-contained suburban neighborhoods. At the center of each was an elementary school, surrounded by a park, surrounded in turn by a protective maze of residential streets. To the Beckers, it felt as though the entire area had been designed to anticipate their needs.

When the real estate agent led them inside one of the newer properties, the implicit vision upon which Susan and Jim were about to stake their new life together seemed to materialize before their eyes. The house covered 3,700 square feet, with light-filled family spaces and big glass doors leading into the backyard. In front, the property flowed down to a protected sidewalk, which wound like a dry riverbed through a canyon of perfectly edged lawns to Daffron Elementary, just a quarter mile away. The fact that West Plano was still predominantly white provided silent comfort. What Susan and Jim actually talked about, though, were Daffron's test scores. Ninety percent of the school's students passed Texas state reading and math exams each year.

Reflexively, the Beckers pictured themselves walking hand in hand with their future children to Daffron each morning, then helping with homework at the granite-topped kitchen counter before dinner and peeking in on the kids as they studied in their brightly painted bedrooms at night. Susan and Jim saw themselves as hardworking and frugal, especially compared to their fellow corporate climbers, many of whom splurged on fancy private schools and expensive new cars. The Beckers had both attended Texas public schools, and they wanted their children to do the same. Still, the couple was determined that their kids would begin life with a head start. Without even trying, they seemed to have stumbled onto a direct path to all the opportunities the country had to offer; just a few days into their first house hunt, the Beckers had found a place that promised to deliver the American dream directly to their doorstep.

Half jokingly, Jim told the real estate agent he had a number in his head.

"If we could get it for this price," he said, "I'd take it today."

They bought the house in fall 2004 for $425,000, then moved in nine days before getting married.

"A DOWNWARD SPIRAL COULD RESULT"

Around that same time, a Transition and Revitalization Commission established within Plano's planning department was concluding the town was a ticking time bomb. Much of the infrastructure built during Plano's boom years would soon come due for repairs or upgrades, raising the prospect of big spikes in the town's operating costs. At the same time, Plano was expected to be almost entirely built out by 2020, which would sharply limit the new property-tax revenue and development-related fees the city could take in. Complicating matters, between 2000 and 2010, Plano would lose 158 white residents while gaining 8,500 Black residents, nearly 16,000 Hispanic residents, and more than 21,000 Asian residents. And when Plano officials looked toward the horizon now, their attention was no longer drawn south, toward Dallas, but to the north, where a new threat was rising: the region's fast-growing exurbs, busy attracting residents and businesses to newer communities thirty miles or more from downtown. Just months before the Beckers moved into their new home, the Transition and Revitalization Commission issued a blunt warning.

"As Plano's development, infrastructure, and facilities continue to age, and new development emerges in adjacent communities, Plano will be challenged to maintain and enhance the qualities that have attracted people to the city," the group's first report read. "A downward spiral could result."

Outside City Hall, however, the words had negligible short-term effect. Most Plano residents were far too busy and comfortable to notice the early stages of any transition from "outer" to "inner" suburb. The typical household income in the town was still above $80,000 per year. Voters were preparing to approve a $285 million school construction bond. Hell, Cowboys stars Troy Aikman and Deion Sanders even had homes in the area.

Slowly, though, an ambient urgency was starting to pervade the town. Susan and Jim first noticed the feeling in 2006, not long after Sean was born, the first of three kids in four years. Jim was still out of town for work every Monday through Friday. Susan, now a senior vice president at Bank of America, was determined to maintain her career. To make things work, the couple hired a Mexican woman in her sixties as a live-in nanny. But Lucia spoke little English, and the Beckers spoke zero Spanish, creating a gulf that Susan felt unable to bridge.

On weeknights, she slept alone in the first-floor master bedroom. Sean was on the second floor, not far from where Lucia slept. He'd start screaming. Susan would wake up sprinting. But when she arrived upstairs, Lucia would already be holding her baby. Struggling against the feeling she was losing something precious, Susan would resolve to get Sean first the following night, then simmer in her own resentment, silently blaming Lucia for providing help she was lucky to have but wasn't sure she actually wanted.

"I know there are probably some moms that would have been thankful and would have loved this," Susan said. "But I didn't."

By the time Sean was six months old, Susan was convinced he'd fallen behind, noting with alarm that he was slow to make eye contact and smiled less frequently than other babies. She began questioning everything, starting with Lucia. Was she talking enough to Sean during the day? Was her Spanish a problem? Was she making sure he spent enough time with other children? Susan started dropping Sean at day care a couple of times a week. When Avery was born in 2008, she tried a new nanny, then decided a more drastic step was necessary, stepping down from Bank of America.

The shift was jarring. Not because of money; the Beckers for years had devoted Susan's entire salary to savings, and Jim still made enough for them to buy a condo of their own in Horseshoe Bay. But the close-knit community the couple had envisioned in West Plano hadn't panned out. They were friendly with the retired couple next door, but that was about it. On Friday evenings, Jim would come home tired, wanting nothing more than to watch a ballgame and spend some time with the kids. Susan, fried from parenting solo all week, would alternate between wanting to talk corporate restructuring strategy and feeling obliged to justify how she'd spent her days, a tension that usually ended with her itemizing the diapers she'd changed.

"It wasn't anything with Jim, really. He got it, because he was a very hands-on dad," she said. "But it was definitely a struggle, an identity change. Because I was not Susan Becker anymore. I was Sean and Avery's mom."

Her worries about Sean only intensified the feeling. Nothing seemed to hold his attention. Doctors found a form of social anxiety, as well as some potential red flags to keep an eye on. Susan took this as her cue, pouring time and money into catching her son up.

First, she enrolled him in a program to help with his minor speech delays. To keep him active, she also started regular swimming lessons. Then she enrolled him in Canyon Creek Day School, one of the most expensive preschools in the Dallas area, where children were expected to work a year ahead, even prior to kindergarten. With a teacher plus an aide for every six-teen children, students received considerable personal attention; Sean's lead teacher, a white woman named Sharon Pennington, quickly homed in on his reluctance to talk in front of groups.

"By the time we got to the end of the year, there was never a more changed child," Pennington told me years later.

Watching their son blossom, Susan and Jim were so happy they decided to give him an extra year at the school. It was around this time that another Canyon Creek family recommended that Susan visit the chiropractor she'd soon come to trust and rely upon. Dr. Cavazos nodded knowingly as she shared her concerns about Sean, then ran a series of nutritional tests, look-ing for vitamin deficiencies, essential-fat imbalances, and digestive bacterial ratios that might be tied to developmental delays. Sean was never formally diagnosed with autism or any similar condition. But at Cavazos's urging, Susan started him on a new supplement regime and made his diet all-organic, eliminating gluten, dyes, and dairy in the process. She also began spending hours watching online videos about the dangers of childhood vac-cines.

A few months later, she and Jim took the kids for a getaway at Horseshoe Bay, where they stumbled upon a street fair. The couple watched slack-jawed as Sean sat calmly at a crafting table, coloring a pattern on a wooden snake for nearly an hour.

"All right, there's something to what we're doing," said Susan.

Then it came time to send Sean to Daffron Elementary.

In the nine years since the Beckers had bought the house on Carnation Lane, the public school down the street had gone from stirring their imagina-tions to a source of constant worry. Although Susan and Jim said they didn't really notice Plano's changing complexion, the demographic shifts were im-possible to miss at Daffron, which had gone from nearly two-thirds white when the Beckers moved in to 56 percent Asian, Hispanic, and Black now. One in four students were classified as English Language Learners. The school had also added a bilingual Spanish program, busing in nearly one hundred students who lived in other attendance zones. And thanks to a major renovation project, half the Daffron building was a construction site.

On the morning of Sean's first day, Susan was a nervous wreck. In front of the house, she posed her oldest son for a picture. His big red backpack hung below his rear end, and his smile revealed two missing teeth. *He's still so tiny*, Susan thought as she snapped the photo.

Then the moment was gone. It was already oppressively hot. Avery and Noah were fussing. Susan looked to the sidewalk, winding its way down the street to Daffron. Then she decided to load everyone in the car and drive.

Things were just as hectic inside the school. Sean was assigned to a temporary space too cramped even for a carpet that could fit all the children for read-alouds. That first day, a white boy left the makeshift classroom, went into the bathroom, entered a stall, pulled himself up into the window well, and tried to escape. Over the weeks and months that followed, Daffron's overwhelmed first-grade team took to calling the would-be escapee and his friends "the Dirty Dozen." In such an environment, Sean's teacher told me later, it was easy to lose track of the compliant kids. Even after the class moved to a bigger room, Ms. Campbell said, she'd sometimes look down during circle time and see Sean sitting crisscross, chin in his hands and eyes on the floor, waiting dejectedly for things to settle down.

Hoping to keep an eye on things, Susan started volunteering as a room mom. The extra assignments she'd hoped Sean might get to keep him working beyond grade level were few and far between. Her son was clearly unhappy. Rumors that the local middle school was even more chaotic led her to revisit Plano's demographics.

"That's a statistic you look at, the free and reduced lunches, right? I mean, that tells you. That doesn't mean there are going to be behaviors. But it can be an indicator, right? It can be," she said. "And it affects a lot of things. If the schools start to go down, which if you just look at the history of Plano, they have. Then it starts to affect your home values."

Throughout the year, Susan had remained in touch with Sean's old teacher back at Canyon Creek, who was involved in preparations to launch a new private elementary school. After the Beckers got word that the Guthrie School was a go, a decision came quickly. This was their children's education. They weren't inclined to wait around to see if things got worse.

On Sean's last day of first grade, Susan brought in Rubbermaid tubs full of snacks and supplies she'd organized neatly within. Outside, she watched the children run around, a happy blur of Crocs and T-shirts with the words "Daffron Second Grader" printed in black. She called Sean over for a picture. His front teeth now poked over his lower lip. Susan knelt down beside him. Saying good-bye to his first school was bittersweet.

"We sort of had a plan," Susan said. But "we didn't really understand big public schools and all the inherent things that go with that."

2

CHASING THE DREAM

THE ROBINSON FAMILY | GWINNETT COUNTY, GEORGIA

Many middle-class blacks remained hopeful that suburbia would serve as a buffer.

—R. L'HEUREUX LEWIS-MCCOY,
Inequality in the Promised Land, 2014

Ginikanwa Isah's journey to Atlanta started at Frank A. Sedita Elementary School in Buffalo, where the kids all called her Nika. She
was a bookish girl then, short and round, with an unrestrainable enthusiasm for learning. In class, her hand would shoot up freely, whether she
wanted it to or not. Then she'd pay the price at recess, toting one of her
Sweet Valley Highs out to the concrete playground, only to have her classmates call her an Oreo and snatch the book and play keep-away until the
bell rang.

The 1980s were a strange time to be a kid in the city. After resisting desegregation for nearly a quarter century, the Buffalo Public Schools had
started a citywide busing initiative and created a network of magnet programs open to families from all over the city. Local officials crowed about
the "velvet steamroller" they'd used to transform schools like Sedita from
overwhelmingly white to 60 percent Black and Brown. But the dream of all

Buffalo's children learning together proved fleeting. It didn't help that the Reagan administration slashed federal funding for school desegregation in the city. But even abundant resources would likely have been drowned out by the sound of people leaving, friends and neighbors and classmates with fathers who used to work in factories that made steel and cars and paper, now fleeing, not just from the city to its suburbs, but from the entire region to the Sunbelt. Even as a child, Nika couldn't help but notice the ambient decay that accrued on the streets surrounding her sagging low-rise apartment complex. Her mother saw the fallout up close; a case worker for the Buffalo Municipal Housing Authority, Amina Isah spent her days investigating complaints about the deplorable conditions in the city's public housing.

By eighth grade, Nika was a top student who dreamed of becoming a doctor. She was also bored, with a spark that was starting to dim. Not in a position to leave Buffalo altogether, her mother took on a second job cleaning office buildings and patched together a plan.

"You're going to school where there are lots of other smart people," Amina told her daughter before the start of ninth grade.

The Nichols School, however, presented an entirely new set of problems that extended well beyond tuition. The campus was far north of downtown, set on more than twenty acres, with big brick buildings and pristine walking paths that slashed diagonally across the close-cut lawns. Each morning, Nika would spend forty minutes on public transportation, two buses and a train, arriving at Nichols just as her new classmates pulled their Lexuses and BMWs into the student parking lot. And on weekends, when other kids went skiing or took private lessons or decamped to the houses and farms of Nichols faculty, where they swam in their teachers' pools and played with their dogs and drank their alcohol, Nika worked at her local McDonald's.

The isolation could be profound. Just a handful of other Black students were enrolled in her class. The white adults at Nichols still managed to mix them up. Nika and her best friend took to wearing name tags. "I'm Nika, not Jada" read hers. "I'm Jada, not Nika" read her friend's.

Junior year was the worst. Harboring quiet hopes she might be Harvard material, Nika walked into her counselor's office to talk about college.

How do you feel about cosmetology, the counselor asked.

Crushed, Nika held her tears in until she saw her mother that night.

I know, Amina said. I know. Just see if you can make it through one more semester.

By graduation, Nika figured she must be smart enough at least for a state school. She went off to the University of Rochester, where she started pre-med. Then she saw her first cadaver. A lifeline finally appeared sophomore year. The course was called Introduction to Community Medicine. An energetic white professor named Ted Brown turned the huge lecture hall into a kind of theater for his one-man performances. Imagine a doctor, he said. Every day, he drives the same route to work, parks in the same parking spot, and enters his office through the same door. Now imagine that day after day, this doctor treats an unending line of patients for the same injury, one lacerated leg after another. Don't you think he might eventually get curious, Brown asked. That he might change his routine, go out into the world, try to understand what was happening? What if our doctor went outside? And what if he saw an icy sidewalk with gaping cracks that kept causing people to fall and injure themselves?

The class rapt, Brown shifted to a British accent, assuming the persona of John Snow, the nineteenth-century English physician who birthed the field of epidemiology. A cholera outbreak in London was killing people by the hundreds. Snow responded not with medicine, but with graphs and maps, tracing the problem to a neighborhood water pump dug near a leaking cesspit. Brown acted out the interaction between the doctor and the mayor of London, playing both sides. "What should we do?" asked the mayor. "Remove the pump handle!" responded Snow.

The professor paused, letting the class consider the implications. Then, in a quiet voice, he delivered his climactic lines. You can't always treat people one by one, Brown said. Sometimes, you need to search for patterns across an entire population so you can find and eliminate the environmental condition that's causing the problem in the first place.

"I heard angels sing," Nika said. "This was my calling."

She graduated in 2000 with a degree in public health. Before she left Rochester, Brown gave her one more gift. Don't settle, he said one afternoon during office hours. Apply to all the best graduate schools. What about Emory University?

This was how Nika came to Atlanta, at the time the most powerful magnet in America for Black strivers.

Emory was located near the sweet spot where the western part of DeKalb County overlapped the eastern edge of Atlanta. Young, ambitious, highly educated Black people were everywhere. After earning her master's degree in Public Health, Nika landed a job providing technical assistance to community organizations working to prevent the spread of HIV. Weekday mornings, she would leave her apartment and head into the office, where she worked alongside one of her best friends, a Black fellow Emory grad named Imani Price. Over lunch, Imani would talk about her young son. "I don't do children," Nika would laugh in response. Family could come after she'd made her professional mark, she figured, perhaps as a county health commissioner. Until then, she would fully enjoy all that Atlanta had to offer.

After work, it was Emory networking events or shopping in Buckhead. Then, on weekends, Nika would get her hair done and pick up her friend Jasmine Boyd, another Emory grad. Together, the girlfriends would head downtown to Club 112, made famous by the Ludacris song "Welcome to Atlanta," or Level 3, which might host an NBA All-Star Weekend gala one Saturday, then a birthday party for singer Bobby Brown the next. An hour-long line would stretch around the block. No one cared. They had their own red-carpet party right there on the sidewalk, a bubbling anticipation carrying everyone toward whatever came next.

"We were very optimistic then, young and naive and getting our master's in our twenties," Boyd said. "Sky was the limit."

Then, in October 2003, fortune smiled on Nika again. Jasmine ran into an old classmate from Clark Atlanta, where she'd gone for undergrad. He's cute and nice *and* he has a good job, she told Nika. Can I give him your number?

Anthony Robinson was solidly built, with tawny beige skin and a splash of reddish freckles across the bridge of his nose. He took Nika to P.F. Chang's for their first date. As the two made small talk, his quiet confidence relieved the buzzing in Nika's brain. Anthony clearly valued family; he'd majored in math and physics, the same subjects his father had studied, and he worked now in telecommunications, the same field as his dad. And he seemed smart about money; his parents' search for the suburban good life had led them to a big house out in eastern DeKalb, and he'd already done them one better, buying a town house of his own one ring farther out from downtown.

But Anthony wasn't boastful. His gravity came instead from his calm. Nika felt herself being drawn into his orbit, her heart filling with ease as she fell. Everything about this man said security.

"He's such a yin to my yang," Nika said. "It was instantaneous."

BLACK ADVANCE, WHITE RETREAT

Long before that first date, Anthony's parents had joined a generations-long line of Black families who sought refuge on America's urban fringe. As far back as antebellum days, "suburb sheds" outside places like New Orleans represented an opportunity to live as far away from white enslavers as possible. And later, during the Great Migration of the early twentieth century, one in six Black people fleeing the Jim Crow South settled on the edge of a city, where they could find extra cushion in a spare bedroom to let or a dirt yard to raise chickens and vegetables. Theirs were not the mass-produced, heavily subsidized neighborhoods that would later come to define suburbia. But by the start of World War II, 20 percent of Black Americans were already suburbanites, largely united in their hope of finally being left alone.

From the beginning, though, this ambition sparked white retribution. Try to buy a home in many suburbs between 1920 and the mid-1950s, and you'd likely find the owners had inserted a racially restrictive covenant into the property's deed, making it illegal to sell to you. Try instead to build your own home on unclaimed land outside of town, and local white residents might put a pipe bomb under your porch. Persist, and your white neighbors were liable to incorporate the area, enact a new zoning code, and charge you with a crime. That's what happened in Woodmere, Ohio, about five miles outside Cleveland. In the early 1940s, a dozen or so Black families began building homes on land they owned. Almost immediately, their construction sites were destroyed by a suspicious fire. When the Black families had the temerity to rebuild, white residents responded by incorporating the Village of Woodmere, passing new building codes to restrict do-it-yourself construction, and arresting their Black neighbors for such offenses as "illegal use of used lumber" as subflooring in their homes.

With the advent of mass suburbanization, this dynamic would soon get repeated on a grand scale. Between 1960 and 1980, U.S. suburbs added about 3.5 million Black residents, including Anthony's parents. But those families' zigzagging paths were a testament to the countless barriers and roadblocks they encountered along the way, and their arrival often seemed to set off a chain reaction, eventually prompting their white neighbors to pack up and move out to some newer place where they could keep their tax dollars to themselves. Then, time and again, those older suburbs started falling apart shortly after a critical mass of Black families put down roots, driving home the precarity of the dreams they'd been chasing while reinscribing America's persistent racial inequality across vast new swaths of the country.

Because this pattern tended to unfold over decades and ripple across entire metropolitan areas, the effects could be difficult to see in real time. In Atlanta, however, a series of school desegregation suits condensed a half century of development, demographic change, and racial denial into a time-lapse account of the forces that would eventually shape Nika and Anthony's life together.

Back when *Brown v. Board of Education* was decided in 1954, DeKalb County was still mostly forest and rolling farmland. The local population included just a smattering of Black families, many of whom lived in fear of being flogged or shot by the police or the Ku Klux Klan, who were often indistinguishable. The local public schools remained rigidly segregated, a condition the county's white leadership was bent on maintaining. That May, on the very day the Supreme Court handed down its ruling in *Brown*, DeKalb schools superintendent Jim Cherry and the district's white leadership were busy breaking ground on a new segregated all-Black school building, one of several such schools the county would keep operating for over a decade. Such recalcitrance would be amply rewarded; between 1950 and 1970, the white population of DeKalb County grew by 193 percent, more than 235,000 people in all.

By 1968, however, the winds of change were blowing out of Washington, D.C. Facing fresh pressure from the civil rights movement following the assassination of Martin Luther King, Jr., Congress passed the Fair Housing Act, prohibiting discrimination in the sale and rental of most residential properties. The federal department of Housing and Urban Development—led by former Michigan governor George Romney, who famously described America's suburbs as a "high-income white noose" choking off opportunity in the nation's increasingly Black cities—launched an "Open Communities" program to pressure suburbs to integrate. And that same year, the liberal Warren Court reached a monumental decision in *Green v. County School Board of New Kent County*, a case that would help cement the courts as the locus of America's national conversation around race, suburbs, and education for a generation. Foot-dragging would no longer be tolerated, the court held. Instead, public schools must eliminate segregation "root and branch." Only when a system's student assignment patterns, faculty, staff, transportation, extracurriculars, and facilities were all integrated would it be free of federal oversight.

Inspired, a group of DeKalb families filed their own school-desegregation case just six weeks later. Superintendent Cherry was named as the defendant. In part because his surname would give the suit a memorable moniker, a Black student named Willie Eugene Pitts was named lead plaintiff. The complaint that launched *Cherry v. Pitts* pointed out that fifty-two of the county's seventy-seven elementary schools—including all-Black Lynwood Park Elementary, attended the previous year by Pitts—were still wholly segregated. And even in those schools that had begun mixing children of different races, plaintiffs claimed, Black children were subjected to "academic, disciplinary, and physical harassment by the white faculty and students." To remedy the situation, they sought the end of a system designed to keep tens of thousands of white DeKalb students apart from their 3,700 Black peers.

The case initially looked like a clear-cut win for the integrationists. After entering negotiations with the federal Department of Health, Education, and Welfare, the DeKalb school system agreed in 1969 to close its all-Black schools, desegregate its teaching force, and redraw attendance zones so that only one school in the county would be left with a majority-Black student body. Because the county's schools were still 94 percent white overall, it seemed a bearable price to pay; Cherry and the DeKalb board kept pouring millions into new buildings, fresh curricular materials, and a cutting-edge computer center where the enrollment forms of thousands of new white children could be processed each year.

What neither they nor the plaintiffs nor HEW accounted for, however, was how modernizing the DeKalb school system would become a major draw for the thousands of newly middle-class Black dentists, data processors, and Delta Airlines workers eager to snap up homes in the fast-multiplying DeKalb subdivisions closest to Atlanta. By the end of the 1970s, the Black population in western and southern DeKalb would increase eightfold, to nearly 88,000 people. Running like a seam through their communities was Memorial Drive, a 16-mile commercial corridor lined with a Kmart and Kroger and Rich's Department Store, a Red Lobster and a Shoney's and one of the busiest Pizza Huts in America. The street even laid claim to the country's first Home Depot, its location chosen after an exhaustive demographic analysis convinced the company's founders that DeKalb was the perfect place to start selling lumber, sinks, and socket wrenches to America's growing legion of suburban homeowners.

"Promising and profitable beyond our wildest dreams," chairman Bernie Marcus responded when asked that year how he thought the company's future might unfold.

It was during this period that Anthony's parents first began dreaming of a move to the Atlanta area, setting in motion the Robinson family's own multigenerational pursuit of the suburban dream. Hank and Danielle had grown up in different parts of New Orleans. Each had joined their friends in responding to crowds of white children who shouted "Two-four-six-eight, we don't want to integrate" with a chant of their own: "Two-four-six-eight, that's the shit you gotta take." After meeting in the math department at Dillard University, the pair got married in 1973, then decided to continue their studies together at Howard University. But before they could finish out their first semester, Danielle started waking up each morning with debilitating morning sickness. Six months after coming north, the Robinsons returned to Louisiana, where Anthony was born a few months later.

Not one to dwell on disappointments, Hank quickly landed a job designing telephone networks for AT&T. He reset his intentions, vowing to make vice president. But when a promotion offer eventually came, it was for a four-year rotation in Birmingham, Alabama.

That was in 1976. A decade after playing host to a series of bloody civil rights battles, the city was still riven with racial tensions. Hank was insulated from the worst of it; his new office was near the top of the thirty-story AT&T City Center. But Danielle wasn't so lucky. Her new job, also for AT&T, entailed long drives into Alabama's unreconstructed rural hinterlands, where she worked alone calculating the cost of running cables across vast fields full of God knows what. And her office, where everyone plainly believed she was an unqualified affirmative-action hire, wasn't much better. Things came to a head one weekday morning when Danielle walked over to a set of filing cabinets holding the thick binders of information she needed to run her estimates. On the way back to her desk, one of the drafters, a white man, slapped her hard on the ass. Livid, Danielle wheeled around and threw an armload of binders at him. The next day, Hank accompanied her to the office. After some debate, he'd reluctantly agreed to leave his gun at home.

"I don't want to hit you. But I will," he told the drafter. "We need to talk about what went on and see if we can nip this in the bud."

An apology was offered, and a formal reprimand followed. Still, in 1979, a year before Hank's four-year Birmingham tour was up, the Robinsons began looking to move. AT&T eventually offered two transfer options. The first was back in New Orleans and included moving expenses. The other was in Atlanta, where Hank and Danielle had friends who raved about DeKalb

County's excellent public schools and new subdivisions full of middle-class Black families.

At the time, it would have been difficult to imagine DeKalb's trajectory heading anywhere but up. In fact, planners were busy trying to spur even more construction in a crescent of farmland that swept from the southern end of the county up toward Stone Mountain in the Northeast. They'd soon dub the region "the New Frontier," chartering bus tours for developers and handing out brochures touting the area as the Southeast's next big suburban hot spot:

> The buyer profile includes middle management workers and professionals . . . Shopping is great . . . The DeKalb County School System is considered to be one of the best in the state of Georgia.

A trip to visit friends and check out houses in DeKalb left Danielle gushing.

"The mentality [there] was that the Caucasians would allow you to make a little something-something if it adds to their basket," she said. "Whereas in Louisiana and Birmingham, if it kept a dollar off your plate, they'd go without."

Beneath all the optimism, however, DeKalb was already in the midst of major change. As the Black population in the county's southwest exploded, white residents had begun moving, first to the county's north and east, then out to the newly suburbanizing areas one ring farther from the city. One of the most popular destinations was Gwinnett County. The area covered lands the U.S. government had forced the Creek Confederacy to cede 150 years earlier and had long been rural and overwhelmingly white. Now, though, suburbanization started turning the county even whiter; between 1940 and 1980, the Black share of Gwinnett's population would plunge from nearly 12 percent to less than 3 percent. A few years after *Cherry v. Pitts* (soon to be renamed *Freeman v. Pitts*) was initially decided, a group called Research Atlanta released a report showing that Gwinnett maintained the most segregated school system in the region. Five of its twenty-six public schools enrolled no Black students at all, and three more—including 1,355-student Berkmar High—enrolled a single Black child each.

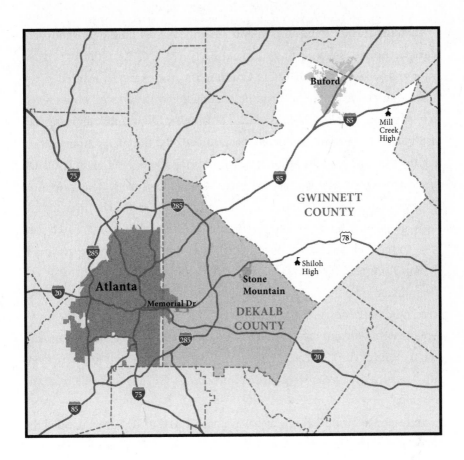

This pattern of Black advance and white retreat that was now spilling into Atlanta's outlying counties soon resulted in another court fight. In 1972, a lawyer representing a group of Black Atlanta families and working in conjunction with the American Civil Liberties Union filed a fresh desegregation lawsuit. The aim was a metro-wide desegregation order that would force the consolidation or merger of the city school system of Atlanta; the independent school districts serving nearby Buford, Decatur, and Marietta; and the county-wide districts in Clayton, Cobb, DeKalb, Fulton, and Gwinnett counties. All told, more than 324,000 students and their families would have been affected. When a handful of other outstanding school desegregation cases in the region were folded into the suit, the stage seemed set for an epic legal showdown.

In court filings, the ACLU lawyer sought to show how state-sponsored segregation was shaping those crucial early years of Atlanta's suburbanization. The Georgia Real Estate Commission, for example, was led at the time by an avowed white segregationist named Edwin Isakson, whose realty firm illegally refused to sell to Black homebuyers. New public housing had also been built almost exclusively back in the city, the ACLU noted, likely helping fuel the concentration of Black poverty there; even as 14,000 such units went up in Atlanta, just 290 were built in Gwinnett. And long after *Brown* was decided, both the state and several counties had continued funding segregated schools; in Gwinnett, nearly $200,000 in public funds had gone to the construction of one new all-Black school and the expansion of the all-Black Hooper-Renwick facility that would later house the district's disciplinary school. The net result was that even after Gwinnett schools were nominally desegregated, the county's long-standing racial hierarchy remained intact: during the 1976–77 school year, the ACLU eventually found, none of the 715 Black children in Gwinnett public schools were identified as gifted, but 104 were placed into classes for the "educable mentally retarded."

In response, white Georgia attorney general Arthur K. Bolton derided the ACLU's push for metro-wide busing as "monumental stupidity" and "grotesque from an educational viewpoint." Then he issued a thinly veiled threat:

> *Finally, we respectfully point out that among those things which our founding fathers considered to justify armed rebellion were the following actions of nonelected, life-tenured British officials: "... taking away our Charters, abolishing our most valuable laws, <u>and altering fundamentally the Forms of our Government</u>."*

As it turned out, however, the defendants needn't have worried, thanks again to shifting winds in Washington. By the mid-1970s, the dream of equal access to suburban opportunity that animated both *Armour v. Nix* and *Freeman v. Pitts* was colliding with the conservative legal establishment's dream of rolling back *Brown*.

"This effort began roughly after *Green* was decided and continued through the Reagan years, with the Republican Party using a host of different strategies to curtail and eventually end court-ordered desegregation," Georgia Tech historian Daniel Amsterdam told me.

This conservative agenda was aided greatly by the election of Richard Nixon. After sweeping to power on the strength of white Sunbelt suburbanites' fears of racial change, the Republican president moved quickly to undermine the Fair Housing Act and shut down HUD's Open Communities program. Then Nixon spent the rest of his first term appointing four new conservative justices to the Supreme Court. The liberal Earl Warren was replaced with strict-constructionist Warren Burger. Joining him were Harry Blackmun and William Rehnquist, a former Goldwater confidant who had once urged the court to uphold the segregationist doctrine of "separate but equal." And rounding out the group was Lewis Powell, a former school board member in Richmond, Virginia, who believed fervently in local control of public schools and worried that the push for equal education was the start of a slippery slope toward communism.

Over the next several years, these four justices would be at the center of three decisions that reinforced the racialized cycle of suburban development and decline that was by then starting to sweep the country. The first was in *San Antonio School District v. Rodriguez*, decided in 1973. Writing for the majority, Powell effectively said that affluent suburban school districts could not be compelled to share their property-tax wealth with poorer neighboring districts. Two years later, Powell led the court in declining to hear the case of *Warth v. Seldin*, in which a group of poor Black and Puerto Rican plaintiffs maintained that the zoning code of suburban Penfield, New York, unfairly excluded families like theirs. And in 1974, the court decided in *Milliken v. Bradley* to reverse a lower court order directing Michigan officials to craft a school desegregation plan that would have encompassed Detroit and fifty-three school districts serving its surrounding suburbs, affecting as many as 779,000 children. Justice Thurgood Marshall was adamant that Michigan had both the authority and the obligation to follow through on the plan. But Powell and the court's new conservative majority were unswayed,

ruling that suburban school districts were not to blame for regional segregation and thus bore no responsibility for fixing it.

Emboldened, the defendants in *Armour v. Nix* began showing their con-
tempt; in one motion, Gwinnett's lawyers acknowledged the county school
system disproportionately referred Black children to programs for students
with learning disabilities, but contended "this does not show anything except
an effort to provide the best education possible to Gwinnett students and a
sensitivity to individual needs." The claims against Gwinnett were dismissed
in 1978, opening the door for yet more middle-class white families to stam-
pede into the county, where they were greeted with 80,000 new single-family
homes and nearly three dozen new public schools. By 1990, Gwinnett would
be home to almost 353,000 people, 90 percent of whom were white.

DeKalb, meanwhile, kept speeding in the opposite direction. Just six years
after *Pitts* had ostensibly led to the desegregation of the local school district, the number of majority-Black schools in the county had ballooned from
one back up to fourteen. When the case landed back in court, a new question
was paramount: Was the resegregation of DeKalb primarily the result of
families' personal decisions about where they wanted to live and educate
their children? Or was it the result of school district policies?

The plaintiffs argued the latter, noting that DeKalb had launched a
"majority-to-minority" school transfer program, then barely publicized it
and failed to provide buses. As a result, only ninety-six students participated.
A federal judge agreed, ordering more changes.

By the mid-1980s, however, roughly three dozen more schools in southern and western parts of the county had turned majority Black. In response,
tens of thousands more white families fled the county. New superintendent
Robert Freeman insisted the DeKalb district was powerless to stop the shifts.

"You'd have a school eighty percent white, twenty percent Black in the
spring, and it would open in the fall eighty percent Black," he said.

Still, the plaintiffs kept filing fresh motions, leading Freeman to joke that
his snooze alarm had stopped playing music and instead said, "Will the defendant please rise." Tired of getting dragged before a judge, he and the
DeKalb board eventually decided to turn the tables. In 1986, they filed a

motion to eliminate court-ordered desegregation in DeKalb schools altogether. After a series of conflicting rulings and appeals, the case was sent to the Supreme Court.

By the time oral arguments began in October 1991, Chief Justice Rehnquist had been joined on the bench by Reagan appointees Anthony Kennedy, Sandra Day O'Connor, and Antonin Scalia, tilting the court even further right. Sensing an opportunity to land a decisive blow in a fight already turning their way, the country's conservative legal establishment detailed its top legal minds to represent the DeKalb school system. Leading the team was then-U.S. solicitor general Ken Starr and Brigham Young University president Rex Lee, himself a former solicitor general under Reagan. Also pitching in was Starr's deputy, future chief justice John Roberts.

The DeKalb parents, meanwhile, were represented by Christopher Hansen, a lawyer from New York who had been assistant director of the ACLU's children's-rights project. Hansen argued gamely, telling the court how the DeKalb school system had never fully dismantled racial imbalances in per-pupil funding or student and teacher assignment. Even more damning, Hansen said, the district had repeatedly closed existing schools in the center of the county, where integration would have been easiest, choosing instead to open new schools around DeKalb's segregated periphery. And when the justices pushed on one of Hansen's biggest weak spots, asking why the plaintiffs had expressed satisfaction with the changes instituted back in 1969, he had a ready retort.

"One swallow does not make a spring," Hansen said, quoting an argument made in a lower court that achieving temporary racial balance did not equal permanent desegregation.

The line drew the court's appreciative laughter, but no more. Especially after the lawyers representing DeKalb began hammering away at Hansen's arguments, saying the actual segregation in the county's schools wasn't what really mattered.

"The critical thing about the way this plan was carried out was that the school board was found by the District Court to be acting in good faith," contended Starr.

Lee, meanwhile, insisted it was time to stop trying to fix blame for ancient history, saying that it was "very easy at this point in time to suggest all kinds of things that should have been done in the past."

When the court's decision came down in 1992, it echoed those arguments. The mere passage of time had muted the impact of past segregation, Justice Kennedy wrote for the majority. And while it was true that DeKalb's "good-faith" attempt to prevent resegregation hadn't worked out, the effort was enough, and it was time for everyone to move on.

"Though we cannot escape our history, neither must we overstate its consequences in fixing legal responsibilities," Kennedy wrote.

Concerned the majority opinion didn't go far enough, Scalia issued a concurrence.

"At some time," he wrote, "we must acknowledge that it has become absurd to assume, without any further proof, that violations of the Constitution dating from the days when Lyndon Johnson was president, or earlier, continue to have an appreciable effect on current operation of schools."

Amsterdam, the Georgia Tech historian, later described these arguments as "historical erasure," writing that they "sent a clear message to federal judges across the country that a majority of Supreme Court justices would no longer expect particularly detailed scrutiny of the historical specifics of desegregation cases."

In the years that followed, federal judges would release DeKalb and more than two hundred other school districts around the country from desegregation orders. And something else profound was also lost. For decades, the courts had been the primary venue for whatever public reckoning America was willing to indulge over whites' refusal to share the suburbs and their schools. But now the highest court in the land had declared that conversation all but over.

WHAT OUR PARENTS DON'T TELL US

Hank and Danielle Robinson were too busy with their own lives to follow all the legal back-and-forth. Back in 1979, they'd reluctantly turned down AT&T's offer of an Atlanta transfer, which would have entailed paying their own moving expenses, instead returning to Louisiana so their aging parents could be closer to four-year-old Anthony. Life in the four-bedroom brick ranch house they bought in the New Orleans suburb of Harvey started off smoothly enough; it wasn't long before Anthony was hopping on his bike and pedaling toward the football field at the local playground, where he and the other neighborhood boys did their best to pound each other into the ground like star Saints linebacker Rickey Jackson. But just as would later happen for his own son, things began to change when Anthony started middle school.

At home, he was an introverted and analytical boy, with a mind that relentlessly broke problems down into their component parts, just like his father's. When Anthony sat with Hank at the kitchen table and worked through math problems, Danielle saw nothing if not another engineer in the making. At school, however, her son's teachers seemed to see something else. By eighth grade, getting them to recognize Anthony's gifts felt like a full-time job, leading Danielle to begin researching private schools.

It didn't take long to settle on St. Augustine's, a mostly Black Catholic boys' school back in New Orleans. Tuition was around $2,000 per year, which would have to come on top of the property taxes they were already paying. But St. Aug's regularly sent its boys on to top colleges and boasted storied football and debate teams, plus a legendary marching band that had performed for presidents at the Superdome and earned the school a reputation as the "Juilliard of the South." Anthony was reluctant at first, especially because he believed the football team at the local public high school had surpassed the St. Aug's squad. But the school turned out even better than advertised. Students wore button-down shirts and sweaters. The curriculum focused on Black history year-round. And discipline was administered with an oak paddle; when some of Anthony's football teammates got caught skipping classes, St. Aug's administrators lined the boys up and spanked them, a punishment the Robinsons took as a sign they were viewed as family.

"It wasn't something where they're looking to suspend you, put you out of school," Anthony noted years later. "But they got the point across."

The biggest revelation, however, came in the classroom.

Physics was taught by Lorenzo Williams, a Black man who'd graduated from St. Aug's two decades earlier and was still annoyed students were now allowed to talk in the hallways. He insisted that homework be turned in before the first-period bell. Then, when class started, Williams would conduct what he called "Ritual," reviewing each student's assignment to see if it was worthy of his attention. If a boy used the wrong kind of loose-leaf paper or left stray marks in the margins, his work was rejected. Dare to complain, and Mr. Williams would jump all over you, demanding to know what would happen if the assignment was a résumé submitted to a company hiring director.

"You don't have a shot! They're sitting down with their colleagues and laughing at you because you sent in a crappy résumé," the teacher would bellow. "I'm doing you a favor by telling you to your face that this is crap."

Hank and Danielle were thrilled. The problem, though, was they still had three more kids—one of their own, plus a niece and nephew they were also raising—to get through high school. It didn't take a math degree to figure out how quickly the tuition bills would pile up. And complicating matters, Hank was again feeling stymied at work.

So, in the early 1990s, the Robinsons began revisiting the idea of moving to DeKalb. Some of the older Black neighborhoods in the county's south and west were starting to teeter. Like most people, though, Hank and Danielle didn't really register the threat. Yes, test scores in the local public schools had slipped a smidge, but they were still high overall. And yes, 70-plus percent of the students in the county's public schools were now Black, but that was a feature, not a bug. Outside the school system, meanwhile, no one was cheering the county's recent budget shortfall or decisions by companies like

General Motors and Lockheed Aircraft to close or downsize their DeKalb operations, but the moves seemed more like isolated data points than evidence of any larger trend. Even the harder-to-miss signals were easy to explain away. Out on Memorial Drive, for example, places like Kmart and Kroger were getting replaced with discount stores and truck stops, but the resulting pockets of blight seemed far removed from the neighborhoods of the New Frontier.

Now in their midforties, Hank and Danielle finally decided to take the plunge, buying a 2,500-square-foot gray stucco house in a newish subdivision out near Stone Mountain. While he started a new position at BellSouth, she busied herself at the family's new church. Driving home, they'd smile as they passed the tulips and geraniums that marked the turnoff to their new street, which curved gently past the pool and tennis courts where neighborhood kids liked to play. But it soon became clear something wasn't right.

"It was mixed when we first moved in," Danielle said. "But they"—white folks—"were on the run."

It wasn't long before more of the good middle-class stores on Memorial Drive were replaced with pawn shops and fast-food spots; even the building that had once housed Home Depot #1 was turned into a flea market. During her long drives out to Gwinnett County, where Danielle now had to do most of her shopping, she found herself fighting back a bitterness whose source she struggled to name.

Then she got a call from Stone Mountain High. The voice on the other end of the line said Danielle's younger son had missed more than twenty days of math class. Confused and furious, she went straight to the school to figure out what was going on. It turned out that for weeks her son had been skipping class to goof around in the gym, but no one had thought to call home and let her know.

"The schools here were supposed to be number one," Danielle said of DeKalb. "But as soon as we got in, I ended up fighting the darn system again."

It was a crucial message. But it didn't get passed down to the next generation. By the early 2000s, *Armour v. Nix* and *Freeman v. Pitts* had long since been decided, leaving families like the Robinsons on their own to make sense of the shifting winds blowing through both DeKalb and the second-ring suburban counties beyond it. And Anthony was now a twentysomething single man in Atlanta with a good-paying job and a home of his own.

"Calls home weren't necessarily the first thing I was thinking about," he said.

Among the more pressing matters on his mind was the blind date his friend Jasmine had set him up with. After that first dinner at P.F. Chang's, Anthony invited Nika on a ski weekend with his Alpha Phi Alpha fraternity brothers. By January 2004, the budding couple were basically living together. Trips to Las Vegas and the Bahamas soon followed. Then, that winter, they got a surprise. Nika was pregnant.

It wasn't what she or Anthony had planned. But neither was particularly worried. They knew they wanted to be together. And the suburban dream was still right there for the taking. It just happened now to be found one ring farther outside the city.

3

A DOUBLE-SIDED LEGACY

THE ADESINA FAMILY | EVANSTON, ILLINOIS

There is, however, a striking difference in how race influences
one's optimism or cynicism for desegregation strategies.

—SONYA DOUGLASS,
Learning in a Burning House, 2011

As a child in the early 1990s, Lauren Adesina spent most of her time in Logan Square on Chicago's North Side. The neighborhood was largely Hispanic, as was her magnet elementary school, which boasted classes taught partly in Spanish and was located a stone's throw from the laundromat where her grandmother worked, all of which reinforced Lauren's connections to the Ecuadorian side of her family. Then her parents bought a yellow brick house in the suburbs three miles to the north, launching her into the complicated Black-white dynamics that shaped Evanston.

The Adesina family's new neighborhood was technically in the heavily Jewish community of Skokie, but it covered a racially mixed stretch of blocks whose children were zoned into Evanston public schools. For Lauren, not yet ten, it was like moving to another country.

Wow, she thought upon setting foot inside Walker Elementary. *There's people who have my skin color, or even darker.*

From the very beginning, hidden rules, invisible boundaries, and quiet assumptions helped order her days. Lauren's parents, for example, quickly made clear that she shouldn't ride her bike across the bridge that led over the Chicago Sanitary and Ship Canal and into Evanston's Fifth Ward, the historic Black neighborhood that many locals seemed to regard as almost haunted, designing elaborate detours to avoid even driving through the area. But Lauren took the directions in stride, especially after befriending two Black girls who began letting her tag along to the park. "You got to be one stupid motherfucker to get fired on your day off," one would say out of nowhere, quoting a favorite movie. "You got knocked the fuck out," the other would respond. Then they'd both fall out laughing while Lauren stood by awkwardly.

Eventually, she confessed her ignorance, and her new friends invited her over to watch and rewatch DVDs of *Friday*, *Menace II Society*, and *Crooklyn*. By the start of fifth grade, Lauren had also memorized the best lines and could bust them out on the Walker playground, where she quickly became popular among the Black kids with whom she felt a growing kinship.

It was at Chute Middle, however, that Lauren really began to feel herself. She was shy in accelerated math, which was nearly all white. But the hallways and lunchroom were full of Bulls jerseys, baggy overalls, and big hoop earrings; thanks to Evanston/Skokie School District 65's long-standing desegregation program, Black students made up over half of the school's enrollment, and the teaching staff reflected that mix. Lauren took history, for example, with Mr. Grimes, a Black man who called her "Miss Adesina" and told her parents how bright she was.

Then there was Ms. Underwood. Her science class was a ball. Kids would take jars of teeming water the teacher had collected from a local pond, then use eyedroppers to prepare slides for the microscope, turning millimeter-size scenes of tentacled hydra eating water fleas into epic battle sequences on par with anything in *Jurassic Park II*.

Ms. Underwood was also the mother of one of Lauren's close friends. They lived just a few blocks away, and Lauren regularly joined them for birthday parties, sleepovers, and trips to the grocery store. Sometimes, her father would take her to Evanston's public library, and there in the racks, they'd see Ms. Underwood, browsing for books on pond ecology, her face lighting up in a familiar smile when she saw them.

And the sense of connection went even deeper than that. Despite Chute Middle's diverse teaching staff, Ms. Underwood told me, elections for union rep were popularity contests usually won by someone white. Likewise with selecting grade-group leaders and informal department heads. By the late 1990s, Underwood said, she'd lost her stomach for the cliques and petty politics. Most days, she steered clear of the teachers' lounge, choosing instead to eat lunch alone in her classroom so she could prep for afternoon classes. But the recognition that many of the Black girls she taught felt similarly out of place, unseen, and constantly criticized was a source of frequent worry.

"Children need to feel like they have a hub where they can be themselves," Underwood said.

That was a big reason why she took over leadership of Chute's Dance Troupe. The group met twice a week after school. Sometimes, Underwood guided her students through the choreography of famous compositions, including *Revelations*, the modern Alvin Ailey ballet about Black grief and joy set to spirituals, gospel, and blues. But when the girls chafed at such serious material, saying they wanted to re-create their favorite R&B videos instead, Underwood didn't hesitate to give them her full support.

"I loved Brandy and Destiny's Child too," she said.

Lauren joined Dance Troupe in sixth grade. Most Mondays and Wednesdays after school, she and her friends would pull on matching turquoise T-shirts, warm up with some ballet exercises and jazzercise routines, then practice the moves that Beyoncé, Kelly Rowland, and Michelle Williams did in the "No, No, No" video. Stomping across the scuffed honey-colored wood floor of Chute's stage, the girls would rehearse their choreography for hours. Then, when they felt ready, Ms. Underwood would arrange for them to perform at student-of-the-month assemblies, local farmers markets and festivals, and the most significant venue the girls could imagine: the auditoriums of Evanston's other middle schools.

"We thought we were the shit," Lauren said. "It was just Black culture, unapologetically embraced and welcomed."

For all its power, though, Dance Troupe was only a shield. Evanston's wealth, connection to Northwestern University, and history of gradual development gave it many advantages relative to the suburban communities that emerged after World War II. But the work of integration remained half finished, and life in the town could quickly turn unpredictable and threatening. The summer before Lauren's ninth-grade year, for example, a white supremacist tore through Skokie during a multistate shooting rampage. He'd graduated from prestigious New Trier High in nearby Winnetka, then gotten "Sabbath Breaker" tattooed across his chest and joined the World Church of the Creator, which called for a race war because the white race was supposedly on the verge of extinction. After several months of distributing hate literature around the area yielded neither results nor serious sanction, he got behind the wheel of a blue Ford Taurus and began firing .22- and .38-caliber rounds at Orthodox Jews, Korean graduate students, and other supposed threats to white supremacy. One of his victims was Ricky Byrdsong, the former head basketball coach at Northwestern University, a Black man who was shot dead while jogging alongside his young children as they rode bikes just a few blocks from Walker Elementary.

And by the time Lauren started at Evanston Township High in 1999, less dramatic but still sharp racial cleavages belied the school's overall reputation for excellence. The cafeteria was balkanized, which wasn't really a surprise. But so were the school's entrances and exits; each afternoon, Lauren would leave with her Black and Brown friends out the front door onto Dodge Avenue, where they caught the bus, while most of their white classmates exited through the building's rear doors, which led to the student parking lot. Then there were the private school dances. Cotillion dated back to 1954, when several white parents decided their daughters should have a debutante ball. Membership on the board overseeing the event had since been handed from one group of Evanston Township High upperclassmen to another, creating a small group of mostly white, mostly wealthy families who got to decide which ETHS students were invited to pay hundreds of dollars to wear gloves and floor-length white gowns to a swanky affair at the private Evanston Golf Club. Tired of being excluded from the event, Black ETHS students eventually responded by launching the Ebony Ball, to which every Black kid at the school was automatically invited. But Lauren didn't really belong to either camp. Junior year, she finagled her way to both dances. A year later, she'd lost interest.

"I was just tired of high school drama," she said.

Allan Alson oversaw the high school. A link in the chain of liberal white Evanston superintendents that extended back to the 1960s and would reach forward into the 2010s, Alson spent years trying to create a more harmonious environment. In 1999, for example, he helped form an organization called the Minority Student Achievement Network, which soon included more than a dozen other racially diverse suburban school systems around the country. At the root of their troubles, Alson was convinced, was a combination of systemic racism and pervasive denial. And the fix, he believed, was an approach that his predecessors and successors would also embrace: documenting racial disparities as thoroughly as possible, then grappling with the results in public.

"The very first step is explicit honesty of where we stand," Alson told *The New York Times* in 1999. "Shame on us if we are not open in having the discussion."

To that end, the Minority Student Achievement Network soon began surveying 41,000 suburban high school students. When asked if they lived with both parents, three fourths of white respondents said yes, but two thirds of Black students said no. Those same Black students, meanwhile, were more likely to say their friends thought it was important to study hard—but also to say they didn't understand their teachers' lessons and assignments. Inside Evanston Township High, the net result was consistent thirty- to forty-percentage-point racial gaps on state tests.

A blizzard of Alson-led efforts to close those divides marked Lauren's tenure at ETHS. The superintendent changed the school's attendance and grading policies. He opened advanced classes to more students. He tried to stop guidance counselors from steering Black and Brown kids into the least challenging classes. He required all students to take at least one class on African, Asian, Latin American, or Middle Eastern history. He hung a world map over the school's entrance, then encouraged students to stick a pin in their family's country of origin. Twenty of ETHS's highest-performing Black students even began meeting in the wood-paneled rumpus rooms of their parents' basements to strategize about how to attract more nonwhite students into honors classes.

But none of it was enough to counter the invisible currents swirling beneath Evanston's tranquil surface. Throughout high school, Lauren's friends were Haitian and Jamaican and African American, Jewish and white, Mexican and Puerto Rican. After school, they'd all get together to hang out or work on a class project. Sometimes, they'd meet at the home of one of the rich white kids who lived in one of the big mansions over on Lake Michigan. Mostly it was fun; Lauren remembered feeling like a kid again when someone would turn off all the lights and her friends would spend hours playing hide-and-go-seek. But things sometimes took a meaner edge, with kids mimicking her father's heavy accent or making fun of his African heritage. And really, just being inside those lakefront houses was destabilizing in a way that Lauren struggled to put her finger on. Once, she and some friends were studying in a white girl's cavernous bedroom. Lauren had to use the bathroom. She walked down some hallways and around some turns. But she forgot to leave a trail of bread crumbs in her mind and got lost on her way back. For several minutes, Lauren wandered the white family's modern mansion, not making a sound, looking helplessly at the moon glowing through the wide skylights in the roof, her face flushing with an anger and shame that overwhelmed all her protective defenses.

"It just kind of made me feel small," she told me years later, when the feeling returned. "Like, Jesus Christ, what are we doing wrong, how come they have all of this and I don't?"

DESEGREGATED, BUT NOT INTEGRATED

Evanston's pattern of racism and reckoning, uneasy compromise and unresolved tensions dated back to before the Civil War. Illinois was ostensibly free then, and Black people were already living in the area. But the state's infamous "Black Codes" prevented them from voting, independently seeking employment, gathering in groups of more than three, and owning guns.

After the war, wealthy white businessmen began coming north from Chicago to build grand homes with sweeping views of Lake Michigan. Rail lines and a bustling downtown soon followed. Eager to keep up with the growth, local voters approved $50,000 in public funds for the construction of a new public school. In 1905, Foster Elementary opened on the west side of town, at the center of a small triangle of land bordered by railroad tracks, the Chicago Sanitation & Ship Canal, and Church Street. At the time, its faculty and student body were nearly all white.

But the increasing concentration of white money fueled demand for service work, leading many of the few hundred Black families living in Evanston around the turn of the twentieth century to send for friends and relatives still living in the Jim Crow South. By 1920, the town's Black population had swelled to more than 2,500 people. The men worked mostly as janitors, chauffeurs, or porters. And each morning, hundreds of Black women would leave their homes and fan out across the North Shore, where they cooked, cleaned, and cared for children in the white people's mansions.

Even as white Evanston grew increasingly dependent on Black labor, however, the town's political, civic, and business leaders began enacting an extraordinary range of measures to restrict their neighbors' mobility and limit their access to public amenities and prime real estate. In 1921, the town passed a new zoning ordinance that redesignated many of the town's Black residential neighborhoods for industrial use, forcing hundreds of families to relocate. Banks then refused to extend mortgage loans, especially if those Black families sought homes outside that small triangle of land on the town's west side. White residents banded together to buy homes on adjacent blocks to ensure they didn't fall into Black hands. Developers began inserting restrictive covenants into the deeds of new properties elsewhere in Evanston, stipulating that the homes "shall not be conveyed, leased to, or occupied by anyone not a Caucasian (servants excepted)." And the local school board got in on the action, too, shifting its attendance boundaries to force as many Black children as possible into Foster, the elementary school at the heart of the emerging Black residential district known as the Fifth Ward.

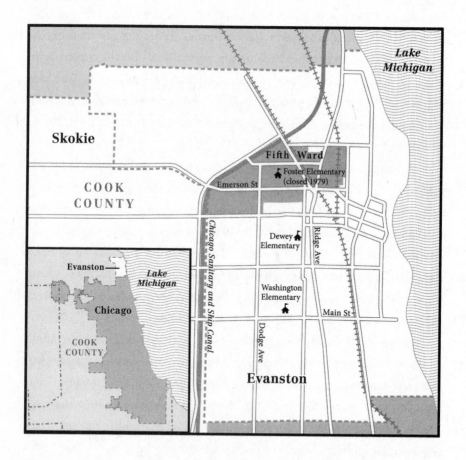

By the buildup to World War II, Foster's student body had flipped to 99 percent Black. Four of every five Black residents lived in the surrounding community. When the Home Owners' Loan Corporation redlined the area, federal officials noted without irony that the Fifth Ward was "overflowing" with Black families forced to double up in single homes. After trying and failing to find reasons other than race to downgrade the area, they warned white Evanston of a looming threat.

> *Altho the area is unattractive to other than the class of occupants already here, it is difficult to say that the section is declining, for it is in constant demand because of the limited number of areas available for negro occupancy in the north shore towns. . . .*
>
> *This concentration of Negroes in Evanston is quite a serious problem for the town as they seem to be growing steadily and en-croaching into adjoining neighborhoods.*

As Evanston's Black population kept swelling, Foster's hallways grew busy with children. Unhappy over slights like secondhand textbooks and a lack of field trips, many called the school "Red Rock Prison." But even back then, the Fifth Ward had complicated feelings about its segregated school. Black teachers had been working at Foster since 1942. Its students were mostly spared the racist indignities that were unavoidable for the handful of Black children who attended other elementary schools around town. And many Foster students could walk to school in the morning, head back home for hugs and hot tomato soup at lunch, and be back in time for afternoon classes. When a fire devastated the school in 1958, the local newspaper ran a photo of a dozen or so Black children sitting atop a nearby garage, solemnly watching the building burn, their faces full of loss.

Soon after Foster was rebuilt, Evanston became an important front in the desegregation battles sweeping the nation. Martin Luther King, Jr., began making regular appearances in the area, preaching in a local church and helping rally support for fair-housing campaigns. In 1965, a throng of more than 8,000 mostly white people gathered at a park in Winnetka to hear the civil rights leader speak. A handful of Nazi sympathizers tried to disrupt the event. But they were quickly drowned out and escorted away, energizing the speaker who'd been asked to warm up the crowd.

"Yesterday's white liberal must become today's white activist," implored Rev. Emory G. Davis of Evanston's Bethel AME Church. "We believe that those forces which stand in opposition to integrated, equal, quality education in Chicago, living out here in these plush suburbs, are the same forces that stand in support of maintaining the closed society that bars Negroes and Jews."

King arrived an hour late. He told the crowd in his sonorous preacher's voice that America suffered from a "schizophrenic personality," promising equality but practicing discrimination. For the good of the country, he said, it was time for white suburbanites to stop pretending they could be neutral on the two big issues of the day: separate schools and separate housing.

"Every white person does a great injury to his child if he allows that child to grow up in a world that is two-thirds colored and yet live in conditions where that child does not come into person-to-person contact with colored people," King preached.

At a time when suburban school systems outside cities like Atlanta and Dallas were digging in to fight for separate education, Evanston/Skokie School District 65 took King's message to heart, accelerating its efforts to desegregate the town's elementary schools. The work started with superintendent Oscar Chute, who launched a voluntary transfer program that allowed hundreds of Black children from the Fifth Ward to opt out of Foster and attend predominantly white schools in other parts of Evanston. The following year, the District 65 board adopted a resolution declaring segregated schooling detrimental to the well-being of all children, Black and white. Next came a commission charged with crafting a plan to eliminate separate schooling altogether. In 1966, an experimental mixed-race kindergarten program was started inside Foster. And that same year, Chute began personally recruiting his replacement, a balding, chain-smoking white educator from Connecticut who'd received kudos from King for showing civil rights speeches in social studies classes and launching a student-teacher exchange with schools in Harlem.

Gregory Coffin believed that public schools should shape society, not reflect it. Desegregation must therefore involve "more than mixing numbers," he maintained. It should also include "attitude training" that could help bring about "psychological integration." From the very outset of his tenure, the new superintendent made clear, he was in town to challenge white supremacy, which he believed the suburbs and their schools worked to uphold.

"All-white suburbia, especially in the big metropolitan areas, is where the power structure of tomorrow's generation is growing up today," Coffin said in a speech not long after he was hired. "If [their] attitudes are allowed to take the shape of those that created the all-white community in the first place, I don't think there is too much hope for tomorrow."

Such talk quickly earned the new superintendent enemies. His support for local Black leaders like the Reverend Jacob Blake, who would soon become pastor at Ebenezer AME Church and spearhead Evanston's open-housing movement, likely didn't help. The town's moderate white establishment wanted improved "race relations," but favored incremental change. Evanston's conservative white real estate agents and homeowners associations were more strident in their opposition, largely because their wealth depended on their ability to tout all-white neighborhoods and public schools to prospective homebuyers. Evanston's most extreme white parents, meanwhile, vehemently denounced what they saw as the attempted "Sovietization" of the town's public schools.

"The destruction of our neighborhood school system is part of a larger scheme to take children away from the influences of their parents" read one letter to the *Evanston Review*. "Russia has done it for years."

Keenly aware of such dynamics, Coffin chased his radical ideas with a pragmatic approach to policymaking. He wasn't sure he could persuade Evanston's mayor, city council, and business leaders to openly support integrated education. But the superintendent bet that a carefully calibrated proposal and the right mix of public pressure and private mollification could at least convince them to stay on the sidelines. This was the needle Coffin sought to thread in late 1966, when he submitted to the board his proposal to desegregate District 65 schools, a plan that would echo through Evanston for generations.

The primary goal was to ensure every elementary school in Evanston ended up with a student body that was between 17 and 25 percent Black. To make that happen, the superintendent wanted to close Foster and bus about 450 Black children to other predominantly white schools. Such one-way busing was "not totally fair," Coffin later acknowledged. So, as a kind of compensation, the experimental kindergarten program already inside Foster was expanded. Interested white families could have their children bused into the Fifth Ward at their own expense, and a lottery system would ensure that some Black families from the Fifth Ward still had access to the school.

Even before unveiling his proposal, the superintendent worried that white residents would view it as going too far; if successful, it would make Evanston the first northern city in the nation to desegregate all its elementary schools. His fears were borne out when a boisterous crowd of 800 people showed up to a school board meeting to demand the proposal be put to a public referendum. To avoid such a vote, Coffin unleashed a multifront public relations blitz. Knowing that Evanston's moderate establishment was key, the superintendent played to the values they prized: efficiency, order, and thrift. Computer experts from the Illinois Institute of Technology had analyzed reams of data to develop the optimal student-assignment plan, Coffin stressed. "Stability charts" showed just how few white children at each Evanston school would be directly affected. (Foster, which would be completely destabilized, was conveniently omitted.) And the total cost of new bus routes, Coffin told anyone who would listen, would be just $38,000 per year.

Winning the support of the Fifth Ward, however, required a different tack. Instead of a town-wide referendum, Coffin proposed to survey the families of the Black children who would actually have to be bused. Immediately upon winning approval for this strategy, the superintendent enlisted forty Black district staffers to administer the surveys—after they were trained on "survey techniques," including how to educate respondents on the plan's merits. To drum up additional support, Coffin also hosted a luncheon for clergy from all twenty-two of Evanston's Black churches, then met with the heads of several dozen Black civic and neighborhood groups. And a week before the survey went out, a flyer began circulating around town. It featured a photo of southern Black students surrounded by armed guards. A message read REMEMBER THE CHILDREN OF GRENADA, MISSISSIPPI WALKED TO SCHOOL IN SPITE OF ALL OPPOSITION. Below were detailed instructions on how to vote yes on Coffin's plan, plus a list of supporters that included the Foster PTA and the Evanston branch of the NAACP.

All the outreach worked. More than 90 percent of the Black Fifth Ward parents ultimately supported Coffin's desegregation plan. The District 65 board followed their lead, voting to implement the model for the 1967–68 school year. Coffin began receiving speaking invitations and glowing profiles in national newspapers and magazines. Still hoping to promote "psychological integration," the superintendent promptly sought to leverage the euphoria in service of his larger agenda.

First, District 65 flooded the experimental new LAB School at Foster with resources. On staff were a dedicated social worker, speech therapist, special-education teacher, reading tutor, nurse, and psychologist. Classrooms were also outfitted with space-age technology such as tape recorders, closed-circuit TVs, and a "teaching machine" that functioned as a cross between a View-Master and a voting booth. Experts from Northwestern, meanwhile, helped design a radical new instructional model in which classes contained children of different ages, taught by teams of teachers who led interdisciplinary projects and didn't give grades.

"It's just whatever you feel, and of course feelings are always right, they're never wrong," a white Creative Dramatics teacher in a sleeveless print dress told a multiracial group of eager children in a short documentary film about the school.

Coffin's new approach to training teachers showed just how far he was willing to go. In the summer of 1967, District 65 brought together three hundred Evanston educators—nearly half of District 65's teaching force—to learn about "the things that teachers do unwittingly which may perpetuate invidious racial distinctions." The so-called Integration Institute was such a hit that Coffin decided to expand it the following summer. Each Wednesday evening, an expert—legendary Black historian John Hope Franklin; sociologist James Coleman, who'd recently authored a seminal report on gaps in student achievement; Jonathon Kozol, a liberal educator from the Boston area who would soon find fame as a writer—gave a public lecture, open to parents from all over Evanston. Then, after the talks, each expert would work with District 65 to produce instructional manuals for teachers. The documents pulled few punches, especially the one titled "Black Power and Its Effects on Racial Interaction."

Black Americans would never achieve true equality if they had to "bargain with white supremacy," the manual advised, quoting civil rights activist J. Denis Jackson. Therefore, it was important that all students, Black and white, learn to "think Black." Suggested lessons included having students listen to soul music, study Black fashion trends, and "simulate an Alabama election" in their classrooms. The latter activity involved providing students with extra recess if they voted for the white candidate and detention if they voted for the Black candidate, then having the class role-play how organizers from the Student Nonviolent Coordinating Committee might respond. The "attitude training" Coffin had promised upon his arrival also focused on getting students to embrace the notion that "Black is beautiful," in part by holding class discussions of poems such as "I, Too" by Langston Hughes. It begins:

> I am the darker brother
> They send me to eat in the kitchen
> When company comes . . .

But after the poem's anonymous subject eats well and grows strong, nobody dares say such a thing.

> . . . They'll see how beautiful I am
> And be ashamed—
> I, too, am America.

The Integration Institute manual on Grouping Children in Integrated Schools ran well over sixty pages. When it came to discipline standards, District 65 teachers were urged to regularly take self-administered surveys.

Questions included "Do I discipline all students with the same tone of voice?" and "Do I embrace, hug, cuddle, or generally show affection to both white and black children?" Almost two years into his experiment, Coffin felt vindicated.

"We feel that we have started on the long road to real integration," the superintendent wrote.

But the reckoning he'd spurred would prove short-lived, and only a fraction of his reforms would take root. Urged on by the now-vocal displeasure being expressed by much of white Evanston, who felt Coffin was moving too fast and complained about Black classroom aides being promoted to teachers, the District 65 board voted in the summer of 1969 to end the superintendent's contract at the close of the coming academic year. A group called Citizens for Coffin responded by organizing a standing-room-only rally for one thousand supporters. The head of the local teachers' union threatened a strike. Reverend Blake at Ebenezer AME Church, whose fair-housing work the superintendent had vocally supported, now reciprocated, helping lead a petition drive that drew more than ten thousand signatures.

An apparent compromise was struck that fall. The final decision on Coffin's future would be delayed until after the regularly scheduled school board election the following spring. But the delay only made things worse. Some Evanston students began telling Coffin's own children that their father was a "n----- lover." His supporters countered by greeting conservative board member Marguerite Seyl with Nazi salutes, then denied her a speaking slot at a ceremony to rename the LAB School after Dr. King. District 65's local school board election quickly morphed into a referendum on the future of integrated suburbia.

"If Gregory Coffin is run out of progressive, enlightened Evanston, where can he survive?" the NAACP's national education director asked in a spring 1970 Op-Ed.

The election was held a few weeks later. A record 26,000 voters turned out. When their ballots were tallied, Evanston's moderate establishment had scored a narrow victory, shoring up the majority the board needed to send the superintendent packing.

More sobering news soon followed. In 1971, the Educational Testing Service released a study of the first three years of desegregation in District 65. Standardized test results showed little change in students' academic trajectories. The town's white children still tended to start out better prepared than both their local Black counterparts and other white children around the country, then perform well above the national average through eighth grade. The town's Black children still tended to start out in roughly the same place as Black children elsewhere in the country, then make modest gains, never closing the gap with their local white counterparts.

Even more disheartening were ETS's qualitative findings. Black students who'd gone from segregated classrooms at Foster to integrated classrooms elsewhere often felt worse about themselves, the researchers found. A review of thousands of student records also showed that teachers in newly integrated classrooms were twice as likely to refer Black boys to a psychologist as teachers had been back at Foster. Observations showed that Black children felt far less comfortable than their white classmates when it came to approaching their teachers. And most damning of all were the results of an extensive survey designed to gauge how more than four hundred Evanston elementary school teachers perceived the students in their classrooms. Despite the Integration Institute, District 65 educators described the Black children in their care as more hostile, indifferent, and aggressive than their white classmates, whom the teachers were more likely to consider friendly, cooperative, sensitive, and composed.

"It has been shown that the academic development of elementary school pupils was altered very little by desegregation," ETS concluded. "After desegregation, formerly segregated Black pupils were reported to decline in academic self-concept."

In the decades since, an extensive body of research has shown the many benefits of integrated schools. University of California, Berkeley, professor Rucker Johnson summarizes them in his 2019 book, *Children of the Dream*, which includes the results of a massive quantitative analysis comparing the life outcomes of children who were educated in desegregated schools and those who were not. Black children in the former group enjoyed smaller class sizes and greater per-pupil spending. They were less likely than their peers still in segregated schools to live in poverty or be incarcerated later in life. They were also more likely to attend college, graduate, live healthy lives, and make more money. Take pretty much any hard measure of life success you can imagine, Johnson argued, and the conclusion was clear: integration works.

But there's also a reason that Dr. King began privately fretting about the cause he would eventually be martyred for. Shortly before his assassination in 1968, he told confidants he'd "come to believe we're integrating into a burning house." A later generation of education scholars such as Columbia University Teachers College professor Sonya Douglass would expand on this notion, helping illuminate the damaging psychological and social effects that followed many school desegregation initiatives. As Douglass asked, what's the cost of having your gifts go unrecognized and unrewarded? How do we account for the price Black children pay when they are forced to sit in schools and classrooms that amount to "hells where they are ridiculed and hated," as W. E. B. Du Bois put it back in 1935? What about all that was lost during desegregation, including tens of thousands of talented Black teachers whose jobs disappeared when the schools they taught in were closed?

All were questions that became pertinent in Evanston. By 1979, the District 65 board was voting to move the King Arts academic program out of the Fifth Ward and shutter the old Foster building completely. The NAACP filed a lawsuit to prevent the closure, warning that the loss of another community anchor would leave the Fifth Ward even more vulnerable to creeping blight. But they lost. The Foster building sat vacant for six years. It was 1985 before a local social services organization finally bought the facility. The group's president was a Black woman named Delores Holmes. She had attended all-Black Foster in the 1940s, then sent her daughter to the integrated King Lab in the 1970s. Now, when she entered the badly deteriorated building, she saw windows covered with a thick layer of grime. Scrappers had stripped out all the copper pipe and wires. The water in the basement gymnasium was up to her knees. The school's empty hallways were littered with a dead dog and dozens of pigeon carcasses.

Inside and out, though, the walls of the old Red Rock Prison remained graffiti-free.

NO PLACE LIKE HOME

After graduating from Evanston Township High, Lauren Adesina went on to earn a degree in psychology from the University of Illinois–Chicago. Then she rented an apartment back on the city's North Side and started a job that paid $21 an hour. But there was a catch; the position was as an after-school counselor at Dawes Elementary back in Evanston, a place she had resolved not to return while she searched for bigger things. Thinking that becoming a math teacher would give her more options, Lauren started taking night classes in the fall of 2011. On a crisp November evening, she finished her shift at Dawes and prepared to head to Oakton Community College. The sun was already setting and the wind picking up as she rushed across the Dawes parking lot and reached for her keys. Then a sudden wave of nausea crashed over her insides, turning her knees wobbly and causing her to drop her purse. Crackling leaves swirled around her ankles as she tried to keep from vomiting on the asphalt.

Lauren learned she was pregnant a few days later. The timing couldn't have been worse. She'd just broken up with her boyfriend. She was already struggling to take care of her two Yorkie-Maltese mixes, named Ace and Rico after the Harlem gangsters in *Paid in Full*, one of her favorite movies. Now, watching her vague plans for the future evaporate, Lauren felt terrified. How the hell was she going to raise a child alone?

"As soon as I told my mom, the first thing out of her mouth was, 'Move back home,'" she said. "So I did."

The decision came with a heavy emotional cost. Lauren's parents had divorced when she was in high school, and the house her mother and two sisters now shared was volatile. Lauren soon found herself sleeping on a futon in the living room. After Chris was born, she came home one day to find all the locks had been changed. And despite everyone's promises, she told me, her family members were unreliable about helping out, even with little things, like watching her baby while she went for a walk. Before Lauren knew what was happening, she'd left her job, then stopped taking night classes, then reluctantly rehomed one of her dogs, then given up the other. Unsure how to regain control of her life, she was regularly overcome with heaving sobs.

Eventually, she decided to call her dad. Joel Adesina still lived nearby. Come over, he said. Let me watch Chris for a few hours. After greeting her at his front door, Lauren's father took the baby carrier from her arms and sent her straight to the local fitness center. They'd end up repeating the routine several times a week for the next eighteen months. *"Somebody said every day was gon' be sunny skies, only Marvin Gaye and lingerie,"* Lauren would whisper-sing to herself as she walked laps around the indoor track and listened to Tamar Braxton. *"I guess somebody lied."*

By early 2015, she'd found the space to imagine a new future. It started with renting her own apartment in Evanston. The place was located on Emerson Street, on the other side of the sanitation canal her parents had warned her not to cross as a child. Now, though, Lauren would look out her second-floor window over the tops of trees and see sturdy single-family homes surrounded by low hedges and neat fences. Walk a few steps west, and she'd end up at the park and greenway that lined the canal. A few blocks in the other direction, a small Christian private school had taken up residence on the second floor of the old Foster building and started bringing the playground outside back to life. Around this time, Lauren started a new job as the office manager at a nonprofit that provided arts education to Chicago public schools. Nothing felt settled yet, but the chaos seemed to be subsiding.

Except for when she thought about kindergarten. Chris was now four. Her tentative plan was to move back to the North Side and enroll him at Inter-American, the Chicago magnet school she'd once attended. It still had a good reputation, and Lauren thought the teachers there would help her son learn Spanish, which she'd been inconsistent about exposing him to at home.

One issue, though, was money. Finding an affordable place in Chicago was impossible, especially when you were also paying for childcare. Complicating matters, Inter-American still enrolled mostly white and Hispanic children. But Chris appeared Black to most people, leading Lauren to worry he'd never really feel at home. And an unexpected new problem arose when Lauren was promoted to the curriculum department at work. Every time she sat down to craft materials for a training workshop about racial equity, she'd come across some new data point detailing the funding shortfalls and alarming class sizes in Chicago. Then, in April 2016, Chicago teachers staged a walkout, followed by months of strike threats. The district responded with warnings about its spiraling budget deficit, which would eventually grow into the hundreds of millions of dollars. At work, Lauren would make plans with a district administrator one day, then get an email auto-reply that his position had been eliminated the next. When she imagined Chris trying to learn amid such instability, her heart filled with a creeping dread.

And the feeling was amplified by the unfolding presidential election. Lauren didn't much care for Hillary Clinton, whom she viewed as a corporate hack and neoliberal warmonger. But she recoiled in visceral disgust from Donald Trump, who'd alarmed her from the moment he'd announced his campaign by deriding Mexicans as criminals and rapists and describing the United States as a "dumping ground for everybody else's problems." At the height of the campaign, Lauren shared a ride home from an evening work event with a white colleague. He went on and on about why people needed to try to understand Trump. You can't just automatically assume that everyone who supports him is racist, the man said as Lauren sat frozen. Maybe he can shake things up.

"Would you honestly be comfortable with a reality TV star being commander in chief," she finally snapped.

It was amid all that uncertainty that Lauren began leaning toward starting Chris in District 65. As the decision took shape, her mind rushed to bathe her memories of growing up in Evanston in the warmest possible light. During Lauren's eighth-grade year, for example, Ms. Underwood had taken the girls from Dance Troupe to Evanston's YEA! Arts Festival, an annual event at which children exhibited and performed alongside established artists. Hundreds of people stood watching. The girls swayed their hips, dropped their shoulders, and popped their knees, bringing the house down.

Looking back, Lauren realized it was the first time she'd ever felt totally unafraid to be herself in public.

"At the time, I didn't even know what it was," she said. "It just felt comfortable."

When November 8 finally came, Lauren settled onto her sofa to watch the election results. By around 9:00 p.m., predictions of a Clinton landslide were starting to fall apart, but the needle on *The New York Times* website was still saying the Democrat would win. Lauren fell asleep on the couch. When she woke up around 3:00 a.m., it took a moment to register what had happened. Her phone was crowded with text messages, and the Electoral College map was somehow a sea of red. Seeing Trump's smirking face everywhere, Lauren screamed. Worried she'd woken Chris up, she then checked his bedroom. After allowing herself a quick cry, she locked in her decision to stay in Evanston. Whatever America's new president-elect might try, Lauren wanted to be someplace she could keep her family safe and still feel hopeful.

"Everything he'd been speaking on was basically anti-me and anti–my son," she said of Trump. "It's going to force people to really focus and make change."

4

AMBITION AND
DISAPPOINTMENT

I think, possibly, if we had had a little more foresight,
we would have done something about the sewers.

—FORMER PENN HILLS MAYOR ROY RITENOUR, 1994

Bethany Smith was tall for her age, with big feet and crooked teeth that crowded her mouth in overlapping rows, leading her sister to call her "shark mouth." But back in the late 1980s, such taunts rarely cut too deep or lingered too long, thanks to the loving web that the close-knit Black community of Sugar Top spun around its children. Bethany's house was just down the street from Madison Elementary, where her mom was active in the PTO. One of her teachers helped run a tutoring program at Grace Memorial Presbyterian Church, whose congregation included a couple of Bethany's best friends and several prominent movers and shakers in the Pittsburgh Public Schools. Summers were full of kickball at Williams Park, and every winter Sugar Top parents would pack Madison's cafetorium and smile along during the Christmas play. Put it all together, and Bethany had no trouble standing up for herself, speaking her mind, or digging into everybody else's business just like they dug into hers.

"It was *Stand by Me* meets *The Sandlot* meets *The Baby-Sitters Club*," she said. "That was our childhood."

Madison in particular was one of the city's best-kept secrets. Everything started with principal Vivian Williams, a Black woman who'd taken over in the early 1980s and immediately weeded out weak teachers, disloyal parent aides, and any program that wasn't focused on helping struggling students catch up. The school's teachers' union reps responded with an attempt to have Williams ousted. But with the support of a school board member whose own children attended Madison, the principal prevailed, and by the time Bethany started first grade, the school thoroughly reflected her no-nonsense manner. Especially when it came to discipline, which was treated as a family affair; for Madison students, nearly all of whom were Black, the prospect of getting called to the office to face a united front of Ms. Williams and a waiting parent was usually enough to deter serious trouble. And even when some knuckleheaded kid did roughhouse or run down the hallway, he was rarely sent home; at Madison, the suspension rate for Black boys was 0.6 percent.

The firm hand also worked in the classroom, where over three fourths of the school's students scored above the national norm in both reading and math, the result of a highly regimented form of direct instruction. Peek through the window in any first- or second-grade door, and you'd likely see students holding cards full of printed words. The teacher would make a sound, and the children would point to the letters that made that sound. Then they'd repeat it themselves and listen to a scratchy vinyl record with a voice reading out similar words. Such old-school phonics instruction had long since fallen out of vogue. But when the Pittsburgh Public Schools changed its curriculum, Madison kept right on using the old one. Researchers hoping to learn the secrets of the school's success quickly zeroed in on leadership.

"Moderately authoritarian," they noted in their reports.

Equally important, however, was how Madison reflected the best parts of kids like Bethany back to themselves, just like when her mom began teaching neighborhood parents how to start their preschoolers reading and Reverend Monroe directed that all the stained-glass windows at Grace Memorial be tinted so the biblical figures would have brown skin. Right up through fifth grade, Bethany acted in school plays, played violin in the concert band, and sang in Madison's chorus, falling in love with the leather boots and big 1980s hair of her white music teacher, who prepared her charges to sing carols for the businessmen and shoppers at Station Square each winter, then took everyone to celebrate at Roy Rogers when they were done.

"It would be the hardest, roughest students standing there singing," Bethany remembered. "And we sounded *good*."

So it was that the start of sixth grade hit with the force of betrayal. Instead of Milliones, the neighborhood middle school most of her friends were going to, Bethany's mom enrolled her at Schiller, a magnet school across the river on the city's North Side. The new girls on the school bus wasted no time ripping on her feet, lips, and natural hair, causing Bethany to retreat to the front seat and attempt to disappear. But the girls kept coming, homing in on her greatest vulnerability. Among family and friends back in Sugar Top, Bethany had met the taunts of "shark mouth" with attitude and volume. Now, though, she responded by sinking into silence, covering her mouth with her hands, and sucking her thumb.

"I wasn't strong enough to handle it or clap back," she told me later.

Her efforts to get kicked out of Schiller began before winter break. Some mornings, Bethany would miss the bus intentionally. Her mother responded by making her walk the two and a half miles to school. So Bethany started catching the bus, getting off with the other kids, then turning around and walking back to her house, dawdling beneath the golden steel beams of the Sixteenth Street Bridge to make sure she didn't arrive home before her mom left for work. When her grade point average dipped below one, her self-regard dropped even lower, leading Bethany to begin beating herself up with relentless vigor.

"I wanted to be happy-go-lucky," she said. "But I was just always searching for something. I just thought that was the way I was, and if I can't fix it, I just got to deal with it."

It didn't help that Sugar Top's protective cocoon was fraying too. Pittsburgh's Black strivers had long scraped and saved their way into the neighborhood. By midcentury, however, the second- and third-generation Greeks, Poles, and Italians who'd once shared parts of the Hill District were fleeing en masse for the new subdivisions popping up outside the city. The City of Pittsburgh responded by targeting the Hill for urban renewal, razing more than 1,300 buildings and displacing thousands of families, leaving behind a stretch of devastated blocks that the great American playwright August Wilson would later use as a backdrop to explore the struggles of twentieth-century Black life. There were self-inflicted wounds, too, like the period in the late 1960s when a faction of Grace Memorial's membership left Sugar Top for a new integrated congregation in the community next door, cleaving families and turning neighbors into rivals. Local residents didn't need to go to the theater to see the larger pattern they were caught up in; by 1990, Sugar Top had lost more than 15,000 residents.

Bethany and her old friends still had plenty of fun, especially after they began working as junior counselors at Grace Memorial and looking after a couple of younger kids from the neighborhood. Sometimes they'd get paid in food stamps, which they promptly blew on grape drink and freeze pops at the superette across from Bethany's house. Eventually, though, they'd cobble together enough money to take the PAT bus downtown, where they'd try on shoes at the Payless and stuff themselves with fries from McDonald's and gummy worms from the Candy-Rama. The freedom was sweet, and no serious trouble ever arose. But such outings did come with a menacing edge, in the form of snickers and sideways glances from strangers that pushed Bethany even further into her self-doubt.

"I was just the tall, weird one," she said.

It was around this time that Bethany made another Sugar Top memory that stuck into adulthood. She and her friends were hanging outside Grace

Memorial. An argument started. Someone went too far. Bethany felt a now-familiar flash of anger and hurt, then lashed out, leading Reverend Monroe to call her into his office.

Why are you acting this way, the pastor demanded.

"I am the way that I am," Bethany blurted out. "I can't change."

It was the first time she'd ever seen her pastor get mad.

I can abide a lot of things, he said. But thinking you can't change isn't one of them. When people from places like the Hill District start believing they're stuck, America will gladly prove them correct.

TEETERING BETWEEN POSSIBILITIES

Penn Hills had served as an outlet for the ambition and pain swirling around the Hill District since at least the Great Depression. Back then, a man named Gus Greenlee was the neighborhood's king. He owned the Crawford Grill, frequented by the likes of Duke Ellington, Lena Horne, and Billy Strayhorn. He also owned one of the greatest baseball teams ever assembled, the Pittsburgh Crawfords, who played their home games at Greenlee Field, a 7,500-seat brick stadium in the heart of Black Pittsburgh. But Greenlee's real money and influence came from running numbers; at its peak, his racket employed five hundred people and collected $25,000 a day in bets, making Greenlee and his cut-buddy William "Woogie" Harris rich enough to start looking for second homes in a more placid setting. Ten miles east of downtown Pittsburgh, they found a pocket of land that racially restrictive housing covenants hadn't placed off-limits. In the early 1930s, the pair bought stately Tudor homes that stood side by side in what later became Penn Hills, posing for pictures as their white-walled Cadillacs shimmered in the sun at the end of their long, shrub-lined driveways.

Perhaps because it was already home to a different dream when suburbanization began, the township never fully embodied the visions of white exclusivity, Black advance, or harmonious integration around which the suburbs chosen by the Beckers, Robinsons, and Adesinas coalesced. Instead,

Penn Hills always seemed to teeter on the brink of multiple futures, just as likely to go this way as that. The good news was this left the possibility of a better way always open. The bad news was most of Penn Hills' white residents and leaders never seemed to recognize or choose that better way, embracing instead the magical thinking that fueled suburbia's growth, then paying for it in subsequent generations.

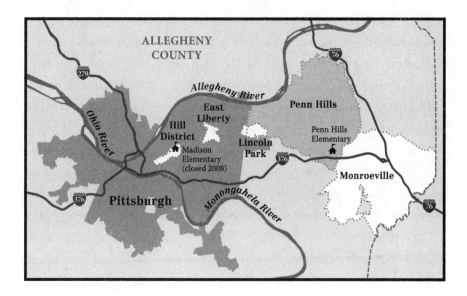

The township covered almost twenty square miles of steeply sloped terrain that was bordered on the north by the Allegheny River and on the west by the city of Pittsburgh. By the run-up to World War II, the farms, coal mines, limestone kilns, and cement factories that had once defined the area were disappearing, leaving in their wake sinkhole-scarred hillsides, a small Black community known as Lincoln Park, and a handful of scattered industrial neighborhoods that would soon become nodes in a suburban construction boom.

Developers were issued permits to build 912 new single-family homes in Penn Township in 1949, then more in each of the next two years. The local population hit 25,000 by midcentury, then doubled again over the next decade. Flush with new property-tax revenue, township leaders went on a building spree of their own, constructing seven new elementary schools and a new high school, many of which promptly required additions. But riven by sectional divisions and largely unable to keep up with developers, those same leaders remained perpetually behind when it came to coordinating the construction of other infrastructure, leaving the town to rely on a hodge-podge of patched-together systems that strained from the outset to keep up with the township's astronomical growth.

In the mid-1950s, Penn Township finally enlisted the Pittsburgh Regional Planning Association for help developing a comprehensive master plan. When the experts peeked under Penn Township's hood, they were aghast. Neither the municipal government nor the school district had any kind of long-term capital plan. The local roads were also a problem; many were too narrow and had been paved at unsafe grades, resulting in danger-ous intersections and traffic jams that backed up for miles. Businesses, meanwhile, huddled right on top of the clogged thoroughfares and made do without sidewalks or off-street parking, turning shopping into an experi-ence to be "endured rather than enjoyed." And one of the biggest red flags of all, the planners wrote, was the township's chaotic sewer system. Some neighborhoods lacked any sanitary sewers at all. Others had obsolete or shuttered treatment plants. Still others relied on septic systems and cess-pools, despite having grown far too dense for such setups to be used safely. And the township's storm sewers had a tendency to back up, too, regularly flooding local basements and washing out roads.

In response, the planners urged Penn Township to quickly raise a sum large enough to enact a comprehensive, township-wide series of sewer sys-tem improvements. The aim was not just to fix the existing problems, but to prevent their recurrence as more people moved in.

"The Board of Commissioners has proposed a bond issue of $1,500,000 to be placed before the voters in the spring of 1957," the planners wrote. "In view of the magnitude of the problem and the benefits to all parts of the Township that would be realized by the proposed improvements, it is rec-ommended that the proposed bond issue be passed."

But local voters shot down the bond measure that would have made implementing those recommendations possible, and roughly two more decades of haphazard growth followed. In the short term, the general affluence of the era obscured the spread of the problems the planners had tried to warn about. But in retrospect, the township's decision to back away from the recommendations of the 1957 master plan reflected a mindset that would later haunt Penn Hills—and countless other postwar suburbs that eventually got left behind by the slash-and-burn suburban growth machine.

"We don't know for sure why local voters didn't pass the 1957 bond," Alexandra Murphy, a sociologist at the University of Michigan who has studied poverty in Penn Hills, told me. "What we do know is that as suburbs in this era were growing, the idea took root that high-quality services could be offered while taxes were kept low. And over time, newer suburbs were able to use this same formula, often to the detriment of older communities like Penn Hills."

Amazingly, my hometown would soon get a second chance to recognize and correct the problems with its early infrastructure. But once again, the township would miss the opportunity to choose a better way. And this time, it was because the alarm was being raised by a group whose opinions many in Penn Hills apparently valued even less than those of regional planners: Black residents of Lincoln Park.

The neighborhood was full of often unpaved streets that wound through steep hillsides crowded with narrow homes, a substantial number of which lacked running water. And to the extent that Lincoln Park had a sewer system, it had long been a mess; in 1957, the planners explicitly warned that the sewage produced by the 3,500 or so people living in the area was going unprocessed because the township had abandoned a nearby treatment center, whose replacement a portion of the unrealized bond money was supposed to have funded.

Then, in the summer of 1965, everything got worse. The township rezoned a deep ravine that ran through Lincoln Park from residential to industrial use, and developers involved in the urban renewal projects sweeping through Pittsburgh decided the suburban neighborhood just outside the city's borders would be a good place to dump thousands of tons of construction debris. An enormous influx of rats and a series of underground fires soon followed, apparently causing multiple local homes to burn and creating an ungodly stench that settled over the area. As the piles of debris grew to fifty feet and higher, manholes also got covered up, a small brook running through the ravine got improperly dammed, and two terra-cotta sewer lines that had apparently been moving the community's untreated waste got smashed. Pools of stagnant sewage water soon began to form throughout the dump, first becoming a breeding ground for disease-carrying insects, then seeping back into the ground before making its way into the Allegheny River. A Lincoln Park doctor explicitly told the township the latter issue was a state and federal crime. He also warned of serious health hazards, not just to the 110 or so Lincoln Park children who reportedly lived within 50 yards of the ravine, but to everyone within a 13-mile radius.

As the fracas unfolded, Lincoln Park civic leaders organized protests and helped get a statewide Sewage Facilities Act passed. Neighborhood children also went door to door to collect money for a potential lawsuit, and county health officials ordered the township to develop a drainage plan. But Penn Hills leaders remained steadfast in their deflection and denial. Local police allegedly rounded up dozens of kids from Lincoln Park in the hopes of pinning the fires on them. Municipal officials reportedly blocked the Lincoln Park doctor from obtaining a copy of the public map of the township's sewer system. And instead of digging a ditch through the ravine to allow for immediate drainage, as neighborhood activists demanded, Penn Hills officials reportedly promised to finally build the treatment plant the planners had recommended a decade earlier—but said it would take at least two years to complete and cost more than four times what the planners had anticipated. During a tour of the ravine and several other dumping grounds in the area, representatives of the Penn Hills Association for Racial Equality (PHARE) and a community improvement association in the adjoining Black neighborhood of Homewood-Brushton tried to call attention to their plight.

What was happening in areas like Lincoln Park showed "an obvious absence of any capital investment," a PHARE representative told reporters. "There is only evidence of capital extraction."

Still, a profound need-not-to-know permeated much of Penn Hills. Many of the township's leaders and residents seemed to trust implicitly that the rapid growth upon which their new suburban lifestyle depended would continue indefinitely. Many also seemed content to ignore the ticking time bomb of the township's slapdash infrastructure, especially its sewers. And many seemed particularly disinclined to care about what was happening in Lincoln Park, dismissing not just the concerns about sewage and dumping, but also complaints about Lincoln Park Elementary and alleged abuses perpetrated by local police.

The latent tensions briefly erupted into public view in February 1971, when two white police officers found a nineteen-year-old Black man named Curtis Arnold stripping a stolen car in a cemetery. One of the officers shot Arnold in the back, killing him. Pickets by Black Penn Hills residents led to one of the officers being suspended. But township officials quickly reversed their decision, earning the applause of hundreds of white residents who showed up at meetings holding signs saying SUPPORT OUR LOCAL POLICE. By May, the ensuing anger had spilled into Linton Junior High, where a huge racial brawl broke out and several Black students accused teachers of roughing them up. Hoping to prevent additional trouble, Penn Hills' superintendent asked local Black parents to monitor the school's hallways. The parents reported that white kids were sneaking forks from the lunchroom and bending them around their fists to use as makeshift brass knuckles. School officials ordered Linton and the senior high school temporarily closed. But a few dozen pipe-wielding Black teens showed up the next day regardless. During the tumult that ensued, Black students again reported being brutalized, this time by the same white officer at the center of the Arnold shooting. The conflict reached its crescendo that weekend, when arsonists torched Lincoln Park Elementary and the garage of a Black family who'd lodged complaints against a Linton teacher.

But even then, the concerns of Black Penn Hills residents were quickly minimized and contained, allowing the underlying problems to fester for years and highlighting a second illusion that pervades American suburbia: that the needs and desires of community's Black and Brown sections can be neglected without causing damage to the larger whole.

The effects of this pattern on Penn Hills were often contradictory and difficult to discern in real time; decades later, *Ebony* magazine would still be lauding Penn Hills as a premier destination for Black families on the rise. But as early as the mid-1970s, some better-off Black families were already looking to buy nicer homes farther from downtown, a trend that made its way into August Wilson's first play about Pittsburgh. Set in 1977, *Jitney* includes a pivotal scene set on a Hill District block the city is set to raze. Youngblood is a twentysomething Black man from the Hill who's been working multiple jobs so he can surprise his girlfriend with a new house. Turnbo is older, nebby and bitter, constantly trying to undermine the younger man's ambitions. Also present are a hack cab driver named Doub and a numbers runner named Shealy:

DOUB: When you moving, Youngblood?

YOUNGBLOOD: Saturday.

SHEALY: I hear you bought a house in Penn Hills.

YOUNGBLOOD: Yeah.

SHEALY: They got some nice houses out there. Some of them boys play for the Steelers got houses out there. Them some nice houses.

TURNBO: They ain't as nice as the houses in Monroeville. Most people don't even buy houses in Penn Hills no more. They go out to Monroeville.

Such confusion was evident in the white parts of the township too. During the 1970s, Penn Hills would lose 15 percent of its white population, roughly 9,300 people in total. But white families like mine were also moving in and giving new life to the racial denial that had been shaping Penn Hills for decades.

My parents arrived on Princeton Drive in the spring of 1976. My father was in his midtwenties. Ecology was the closest thing he had to a passion; he'd spent the previous years trapping chipmunks out West and selling mountaineering gear at a camping store on Pittsburgh's East End. But after my older brother was born and news of my impending arrival soon followed, my paternal grandfather raised the possibility of a good-paying union job at the University of Pittsburgh, where he worked as an engineer. Though my dad was loath to accept his father's help and still held hazy ambitions of saving the planet with environmental-impact studies, he swallowed his pride and accepted the offer, choosing his hopes for his children over his dreams for himself. The job led to the house, which in turn led to the Penn Hills public schools.

But only after a detour. When it came time to enroll my older brother in kindergarten, my parents were shocked to learn he wouldn't be attending Dible Elementary, visible from our dining-room window. Instead, every kindergartner in the township was assigned to a program located in the old Lincoln Park Elementary, where they'd stay for a year before moving on to their neighborhood schools for first grade. Like many of their white counterparts on Princeton Drive, my parents were up in arms over this arrangement. Nap schedules were one concern. The length of the commute was another; a white mom from the neighborhood had already tailed the yellow school bus over to the Lincoln Park Kindergarten Center, growing alarmed as the drive stretched toward thirty minutes. But though my parents had never actually been to Lincoln Park, they viewed the neighborhood as a problem unto itself; it wasn't "our side of Penn Hills," my dad would tell me later, "but the other side, a Black area."

Despite still living paycheck to paycheck, he and my mom made a conscious and likely expensive decision to avoid Lincoln Park and absorb the cost of paying to enroll my brother at a school called St. Bernadette, where I soon joined him. For most of my life, I had no idea why I'd briefly attended Catholic school; it took me almost forty years to realize there was even a question to be asked. Then it took the decades-old writings of a white economist from Sweden and a Black social psychologist from Harlem to help me understand how my white family's silences and need-not-to-know both shaped my own trajectory and contributed to the larger forces already undermining Penn Hills' future.

Gunnar Myrdal and Kenneth B. Clark first began working together while researching the 1944 classic *An American Dilemma*. The massive multivolume tome has since received its share of criticism. But it remains unusual for analyzing how white racism affects white Americans, and it served as a precursor to Clark's groundbreaking research on the psychological effects of racism on children that Thurgood Marshall and the NAACP Legal Defense and Educational Fund used during arguments in *Brown v. Board of Education*.

Both Clark and Myrdal describe a pivotal moment in many white children's development. Sometime early in our lives, we find ourselves confronted for the first time with the realities of race in America. We get confused about the discrepancy between the ideals we've been taught and the world we see around us. But the adults we turn to for answers—parents, teachers, other white authority figures—by then tend to be deeply invested in their own need-not-to-know. As a result, they often fail to point us toward the truth, instead passing on their own penchants for denial, deflection, and willful ignorance, contributing mightily to the "great injury" to white children that Martin Luther King, Jr., highlighted in his speech outside Evanston. Clark described this as a silent rupture in many white children's sense of self. He also argued that our ill-fated efforts to resolve this rupture on our own often end up imbuing white children's personalities with "deep patterns of moral conflict, guilt, anxiety, and distortion of reality." Typically, the researchers maintained, this process unfolds unseen. But occasionally, a white child will catch a glimpse of the shadow that white America's pervasive need-not-to-know casts over his own life.

"Even the least sophisticated individual becomes aware of his own confusion and the contradiction in his attitudes," Myrdal wrote in a passage that brought me up out of my seat when I read it as an adult. "But most people, most of the time, suppress such threats to their moral integrity together with all of the confusion, the ambiguity, and inconsistency which lurks in the basement of man's soul."

Over time, I came to associate that suppression with my father's never-ending backyard projects. They didn't start out as the mess we'd later leave behind; by the mid-1980s, he'd built a stone retaining wall that could've withstood an earthquake, installed a jungle gym my brothers and I loved, and laid out beautiful wooden planter boxes already yielding tomatoes and flowers. I was about ten when he deemed me old enough to help. Down in our garage, he'd position me a few feet from his prized radial-arm saw, ask me to hold the end of the 4x4 he was cutting, and push a red button that brought the blades screaming to life. Then he'd make his cuts and throw the jagged ends of leftover lumber into one of the piles that would eventually grow out of control. Initially, it was thrilling to be invited into my dad's visions. But as the silent minutes stretched into silent hours, I'd stand there full of dumb hope that he might notice the questions swirling inside me, about why I wasn't allowed to wear suede Pumas to school and why I'd felt so awkward and exposed the first time I went to a classmate's birthday party in Lincoln Park. Over time, I became convinced that whatever it was I needed to fill that empty space inside myself was buried under my dad's growing pile of scrap wood. Only much later did I learn that Clark, Myrdal, and a subsequent generation of social scientists and psychologists had written about those feelings, too, describing them as part of the toll that white racism extracts from white Americans, by diminishing our capacity for intimacy, cutting off our ties to a shared past, and hampering our ability to accurately perceive the world around us.

What ultimately mattered most about my white family's need-not-to-know, however, was how it flowed into the larger denial and kick-the-can mentality that allowed the problems identified by the Pittsburgh Regional Planning Association and Lincoln Park residents to metastasize within Penn Hills' municipal infrastructure, leading to the township-wide mess that future residents would later inherit. It was the early 1990s when the Pennsylvania Department of Environmental Protection and the federal Environmental Protection Agency finally won an injunction against Penn Hills for illegally releasing raw sewage into the Allegheny and Monongahela rivers. After racking up more than thirteen thousand violations of the Clean Water Act, my suburban hometown became the first municipality in the country convicted of a federal environmental crime. Two municipal employees were found to have falsified treatment reports, and the township agreed to pay

$675,000 in fines. It also entered into a consent decree mandating repairs and upgrades that would ultimately total more than $60 million, costs that were promptly passed on to local residents, who saw their sewage bills sky-rocket. Even Roy Ritenour, the mayor of Penn Hills between 1984 and 1991, had to acknowledge that missed opportunities and the illusions that had shaped the township were now costing *all* Penn Hills residents direly.

"Every politician, myself included, tried to keep taxes down," Ritenour told the *Pittsburgh Post-Gazette* in 1994. "I think, possibly, if we had had a little more foresight, we would have done something about the sewers."

It would be more than two decades before I learned about the township's sewer problems. It turned out that Kenneth Clark and Gunnar Myrdal had written about this dynamic too. The process of internalizing America's need-not-to-know leads many white children to reproduce the same silences and racial ignorance that once injured us, a process of becoming complicit that leads us further into our own anxiety, guilt, and denial, creating a cycle that some researchers argue functions like an addiction.

"The escape mechanism works," Myrdal warned. "However, only to a point. Then it is no longer a question of escape. The conflict is raging out in the open."

Neither I nor Penn Hills was quite there yet; it would take a debacle in the local public schools even more disastrous than the sewer system shitshow for the full extent of the township's problems to become evident. But the stage was slowly being set. Penn Hills would lose an additional 16,000 white residents during the last two decades of the twentieth century. I joined the exodus in 1994. A year later, the Smith family moved out of Sugar Top, setting Bethany on a path that would eventually lead her to the troubled suburb I'd left behind.

"THIS CANNOT BE MY LIFE"

At her new house in Pittsburgh's Stanton Heights neighborhood, Bethany had her own bedroom and bathroom, both major pluses for a thirteen-year-old.

She could also return regularly to Grace Memorial. And after self-sabotaging her way out of Schiller, the magnet school where she'd been getting bullied, Bethany landed at Milliones Middle, the neighborhood school she'd wanted to attend all along, where she rebounded enough academically to get accepted into prestigious Schenley High. Her mom, aunts, uncles, brother, and sister were all devoted alums. She'd never imagined going anywhere else.

The school was housed in a gorgeous neoclassical limestone building tucked into the hillside below Sugar Top. The beloved Pittsburgh institution had once served as a gateway to opportunity for the children of immigrants, including Andy Warhol. Then it became a bastion of integration in an otherwise divided city. In the mid-1970s, Schenley transitioned into a predominantly Black basketball powerhouse. And by the time Bethany arrived for ninth grade, Schenley was reinventing itself yet again, this time as a collection of magnet programs with an ultradiverse student body that led Jesse Jackson to describe the school as a "little United Nations" during a visit in 1995.

Bethany, however, couldn't shake the sense that a void had opened between her and the world. For all its hype, Schenley systematically sorted students inside its walls. The highest-achieving kids, disproportionately white, were enrolled in the International Studies program upstairs. Bethany joined a diverse group of kids from across the city who studied topics like robotics and computer-aided design in the technology program on the floor below. The basement and first floor were reserved for Black kids from the Hill who were zoned into Schenley as their neighborhood school. Bethany would still see her old friends at lunch and Friday night basketball games. But she now felt further outside their circle than ever.

After graduating in 2000, she enrolled at the Community College of Allegheny County. Her first panic attack hit while sitting on campus. A clammy sweat covered her body and an unfamiliar pain filled her chest, forcing her to the hospital. Not long after, Bethany found herself on academic probation. She took a semester off, then came back for more classes, then landed on probation again. When CCAC placed her on academic probation a third time, she decided to drop out altogether.

By late 2006, she was nearing her nadir. Shortly before Christmas, she found herself at a Bible study. The discussion was typical, about Jesus dying for our sins and His love being the way to God, all messages Bethany had heard a million times before. But just as she was about to zone out, an epiphany hit: Since leaving Sugar Top, Bethany had assumed she had to fix whatever was broken inside her before she could receive God's love. Realizing the reverse was true felt like someone replacing a lightbulb she didn't know was out. And when it flashed on, what Bethany saw was the advice Reverend Monroe had imparted a decade before, still offering her the chance to change.

"I knew what to grasp on to, because it was already there," she said.

Her renewed faith couldn't stop the losses that mounted over the ensuing years. Pittsburgh's Board of Education closed both Madison Elementary and Milliones Middle, tearing huge new holes in the already fraying fabric of the neighborhood that had molded her. Then the board moved to shutter Schenley as well, claiming it would cost upward of $64 million to remediate the asbestos inside the building and pushing forward with their plan over the objections of students, alumni, and neighborhood activists who alleged that the costs of fixing the school were being wildly exaggerated to justify a real estate grab.

In the moment, Bethany didn't really have the luxury of dwelling on the bad news. She'd started a patient-care position on the surgical oncology floor of a local hospital, where she made small talk with cancer patients while emptying the J-P drains and ileostomy bags where their waste slowly pooled. Then, in 2009, she got a message from her father. An army veteran who'd been living in Detroit for years, he'd always been imposing and distant, around mostly for birthdays and graduations. Now he was sick too. When Bethany and her sister arrived at his home, their dad's once powerful body had been whittled down to ninety-five pounds and was tethered to oxygen tanks. They had to carry him to the car.

And the biggest blow came later that same year. Bethany learned that she was pregnant. But her water broke at four and a half months, leading her to give birth to a stillborn baby boy whose intestines were wrapped around the outside of his body. At first, her cascading grief crushed her capacity to do more than survive. Then it cemented her determination to fill the empty space between herself and the world with a wall. On the other side were all the uncontrollable forces causing her so much pain. On her side was God.

"It just made me grip on to Him harder," she said.

Bethany was thirty when she learned she was pregnant again. This time, her doctor diagnosed the issue that put her at elevated risk of complications. After putting her on bed rest, he suggested she eliminate as much stress from her life as possible. Bethany picked up the phone and broke up with her boyfriend on the spot.

Jackson was born happy and healthy, a miracle unto himself. After bringing him home to the apartment she shared with her mom, Bethany began talking to God even more than usual. Sometimes, she'd listen to herself, just to hear what she was saying. Over and over, she realized, she kept asking for the same thing. A little comfort. Some ease. Maybe a place where Jackson could have his own bedroom.

But she was already missing car payments to cover other bills, and the skyrocketing rents in Pittsburgh's East End made finding a bigger apartment increasingly unrealistic. At a loss, Bethany called her sister, who'd already been priced out of the area. When I asked her to reconstruct their conversation, Bethany's sister told me it had initially been exciting to see the long-abandoned buildings in East Liberty brought back to life. Then she'd gone shopping among the throngs who now flocked to Bakery Square. There wasn't a black-and-gold jacket, jersey, or hat in sight.

"They weren't even Steelers fans," she said in disbelief.

She'd moved to Penn Hills because she was already working in a hair salon there. She described her clients, mostly middle-class professional Black women, as snooty and dismissive, constantly deriding the aging suburb as "Homewood Extension," a reference to the struggling Black neighborhood next door.

Still, Bethany decided it couldn't hurt to look at the Penn Hills listings on Zillow. She quickly found an 1,150-square-foot Cape Cod for rent. It had three bedrooms, a porch, and a fenced-in backyard. At the open house, Jackson quickly claimed one of the bedrooms as his own, then dashed outside and ran in joyous circles around the big oak tree out front. Bethany and her mom signed the lease a day later.

Her prayers still weren't exactly answered. Money was still tight. Her depression still hovered, and she was still living life week to week. That Labor Day, Bethany decided on a whim to take Jackson to Lake Erie, two hours to the north. During the drive, she let slip that maybe they might stay the night at a hotel. Not one for words like "maybe" and "might," Jackson excitedly began making plans. But Bethany hadn't made a reservation, hadn't checked prices in advance, and wasn't sure she had enough money to cover both the room and gas for the drive home.

"This cannot be my life," she whispered to God as all her old self-doubts came roaring back. "I gotta get my shit together."

HOW QUICKLY WE FORGET

THE HERNANDEZ FAMILY | COMPTON, CALIFORNIA

The fear and the silence frustrate intelligent planning.

—WELFARE PLANNING COUNCIL,
Los Angeles Region, 1962

The founding families of Los Angeles included a Spaniard; eight Indigenous Indians; one mestizo who was mixed Indian-Spanish; ten adults of African descent, including eight identified as mulatto and one who was mixed African Indian; a woman who was Indian and either mulatto or mestizo; a man who was born in Manila and likely Filipino; an adult of Spanish descent born in Mexico; two Indian children; and nineteen children of mixed-race heritage. To be sure, their pueblo took shape within a landscape soon to be bloodstained by the colonial genocide of the Indigenous tribes who'd inhabited the area for millennia. But in those early days, the people of Los Angeles recognized no substantial hierarchies of race or class, working, playing, and marrying freely with each other and the Gabrielino Indians nearby, briefly creating a liminal world of multiracial and mestizaje possibility whose echoes would be heard in Compton 250 years later.

The town itself began as a part of Rancho San Pedro, granted by the Spanish Crown to Juan Jose Dominguez in 1784, just three years after the Pueblo de la Reina de Los Angeles was settled. Nearly four decades later, the land—along with the rest of California, plus all or parts of Arizona, Colorado, Kansas, Nevada, New Mexico, Oklahoma, Texas, and Utah—became part of the newly independent nation of Mexico. A quarter century after that, the United States declared war. The Mexican people living in and around the Rancho San Pedro fiercely resisted the ensuing invasion. But when the Treaty of Guadalupe Hidalgo was eventually signed in 1848, Mexico was forced to cede roughly half its territory and accept the annexation of Texas, losing more than 1.3 million square miles in the deal; had U.S. leaders not worried about the consequences of absorbing the vanquished country's "mongrel" population, they likely would have demanded even more. Instead, roughly 115,000 Mexican nationals living in the territories suddenly became temporary aliens on land they'd inhabited for generations.

California became the thirty-first state in the American union shortly after. Some of the men living in the area became U.S. citizens. Thanks to a kind of reverse "one-drop" rule, many were also considered white. But the state's rising Anglo ruling class quickly began consolidating power and land, especially around Los Angeles, where they segregated their neighbors in run-down barrios. The everyday people who lived in these communities were legally equal but socially second class, occupying a kind of in-between status that offered a regular reminder that America's most-cherished freedoms—to move, to control your own destiny, to invent your own future—were contingent on a belief in white supremacy that operated both within and above the strictures of law and citizenship.

It was against this backdrop that modern Compton took shape. In the 1860s, two pioneers purchased a huge tract carved from the old Rancho San Pedro for thirty-six cents an acre, then struck it rich a few years later by flipping the land to Methodist settlers willing to pay five dollars an acre so they could farm. For decades, the area remained a small agricultural community populated by a mix of people of European, Mexican, Japanese, and African descent.

Then oil was discovered nearby. The history that followed would unspool the entire arc of American suburbia, from government-subsidized white supremacy to profound Black yearning, a brief fling with multiracial integration to a short period of determined self-delusion. Then Compton would collapse and be left to struggle for nearly half a century, until a hint of the region's original diversity and spirit of cooperation began to shoot new sprouts.

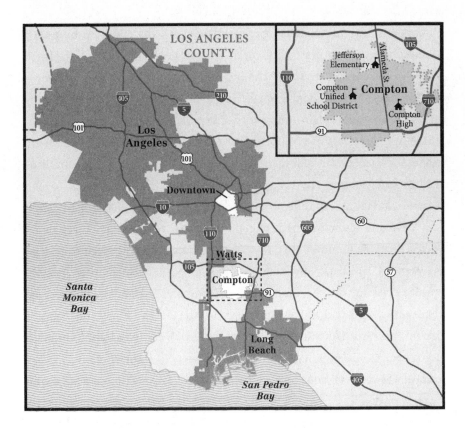

Just as with North Dallas, Compton's suburban transformation was kickstarted by massive government intervention. Between 1939 and 1945, $11 billion in federal defense contracts and millions more in guaranteed mortgages poured into the Los Angeles region. By the end of the decade, Compton had been transformed from a wide-open farming town to a booming bedroom community of more than 45,000 people. Among the migrants joining the swell was a young navy fighter pilot fresh out of Yale. Just twenty-five years old at the time, George Herbert Walker Bush came to sell oil-field drilling equipment for the Security Engineering Company, a subsidiary of Dresser Industries (later to be renamed Halliburton), whose board of directors included his father. Accompanying Bush were his pregnant wife, Barbara, and the couple's three-year-old son, George Walker, who settled comfortably into one of the A units in a sprawling new apartment complex called Santa Fe Gardens.

Certainly, the Bushes had more refined pedigrees than their working-class Compton neighbors, most of whom toiled out in the oil fields, or in small factories making pickles and bricks and rugs, or in one of the mighty defense plants powering the region's growth. But otherwise, they fit right in. Starting in 1921, Compton's Anglo leadership had begun pioneering the use of racially restrictive covenants in local property deeds, prohibiting homeowners and real estate agents from selling to Black families. Then, during the war, those leaders had watched the U.S. government's forcible relocation of several dozen local Japanese families to internment camps as far inland as Arkansas and passed a resolution opposing the families' release. And throughout, they'd kept one hundred or so Mexican American families headed by welders, cement finishers, and farm laborers mostly confined to a Spanish-speaking barrio. The net result was that Compton circa 1949 was bursting at the seams with Anglo whites who controlled the town's council and chamber of commerce, its police and fire departments, all three of its banks, two local newspapers, and a growing network of homeowners' associations.

Still, the conversations inside local bars and PTA meetings crackled with anxiety. A decade earlier, HOLC had yellowlined parts of Compton, warning the town was ripe for invasion by Black families living in the crowded Watts ghetto to the north. And just a year prior, the U.S. Supreme Court had declared racial covenants unenforceable, throwing Compton's system of racial exclusion into doubt. Now Black homebuyers were probing the town's boundaries, and sixteen Black children were already enrolled in the local elementary schools. White Comptonites responded to the changes with violence and vitriol. Just months before Bush settled his family into Santa Fe

Gardens, a Black man named Vernon Whitley purchased a home in the northwest section of town, near Watts. Nearby white residents greeted him, his wife, and their two young children by pouring oil across their lawn and scrawling "KEEP OUT NEGROES" in red paint that dripped down the brick exterior of their new home. At least ten other incidents of vandalism soon followed. But no arrests were made, the Black-run *Los Angeles Sentinel* reported.

"Compton Ku Kluxers, or their facsimiles, are busy as little bees trying to drive Negroes out of that community, and they are getting an effective assist from the police force," the paper opined.

The town's white-run newspapers, however, don't appear to have covered the incidents. Nor did they seem to recognize the other seeds of trouble by then burrowing into Compton's foundation. Middle-class white families were vocal in their demands for sewers, schools, streetlights, and police protection, all of which were expensive. But those same families were adamant about limiting development to new single-family homes, just like residents of places like Penn Hills and Lucas during the decades that followed. Such priorities meant forgoing revenue from the factories that located elsewhere in the region, leaving the town's already strained tax base stretched perilously thin. And the resulting financial problems were heightened by the rampant inefficiencies involved with maintaining segregation. Compton's public school system, for example, consisted of several distinct elementary districts that mostly kept Black and white children separated until they entered one of the local junior highs, high school, and community college, all of which together comprised yet another separate school district. Each had its own bureaucracy, and each was overcrowded. Faced with complaints from white families angry that rapid and poorly planned expansion was forcing their children to attend classes in portable army barracks, the districts responded by issuing more debt.

Compton residents couldn't see it yet. But by midcentury, their town was becoming a kaleidoscope of American change. Dreams of white separation, Black aspiration, and multiracial integration began to collide, foreshadowing the inflection point America as a whole would confront seventy years later. The Bush family left just before the storm began in earnest.

FOUR TEEN-AGERS SENTENCED, a headline screamed in the Black-run *California Eagle* in February 1953, a month after dozens of Black and white students brawled outside Enterprise Junior High.

VIGILANTES BRUTALLY BEAT MAN OVER SALE TO NEGROES read another headline later that month, after white Comptonites attacked a white neighbor who listed his home with a Black real estate broker.

In April, white vandals attacked the home of a Black couple on a formerly "forbidden" block of Reeve Street, leaving behind a violent threat written on lined paper from a child's notebook. Then, in May, on that same stretch of Reeve Street, all hell broke loose.

The block held sixty small bungalows, each of which covered roughly 750 square feet. When the houses had hit the market three years earlier, large signs saying HIGHLY RESTRICTED were everywhere.

Now, though, a Black shipyard worker and World War II veteran named Alfred Jackson had bought the house at 2318 Reeve for $11,500. He started moving his family in on a Saturday evening. Dozens of white people assembled on the lawn next door. Jackson tucked a Colt .45 into his pocket as he kept unloading furniture and his new white neighbors began hurling threats.

"Look at that damn TV set—that's a heap better than mine," said one man quoted by the *Eagle*.

"That house looks good now—it ain't going to look good in the morning!" said another.

"I feel sorry for your kids—they don't know what's going to happen to them," said a third.

As night fell, Jackson's neighbors began pelting his new house with rocks. When the Compton police finally arrived, the white residents of Reeve Street shrugged and said they were having a party.

Tensions flared again three days later when a Black real estate agent went door to door on Reeve Street, attracting a crowd of furious white people. The next day, angry white housewives began parading with banners and signs in front of the Jackson home. The crowd from Saturday night reassembled and started their threats anew. A front-page photo in the *Eagle* showed Luquella Jackson, Arthur's wife, in a white cotton dress, shotgun in hand, guarding the three small children at her side. The stakes of the paper's multipart series on "The Compton Story" couldn't have been clearer.

"It is the story of men and women, white and Negro, who are caught up in a population trend and who are bewildered by what is happening," the *Eagle*'s editors explained. "It is an important story, too, one that we must understand and solve if we are to escape trouble."

For the next fifteen years, Compton would struggle to rise to that challenge. Many of the white people who remained in the town continued to fight for racial separation. The all-white board of the local high school district, for example, had already responded to its precarious financial situation by cutting staff, shortening the school day, and further raising tax rates that were among the highest in LA County. But the board was not willing to curtail its increasingly costly investment in segregation. In response to overcrowding at Compton High, they decided to build *two* new high schools—one on either side of Alameda Street, the town's Maginot Line, separating white East Compton from increasingly Black West Compton.

At the same time, the town's fast-changing demographics were fueling a surge of Black ambition. Compton High's 1961 Senior Council featured several Black students. Two years later, local residents elected Douglas Dollarhide as Compton's first Black city council member. By 1969, Dollarhide would be mayor, and Compton would have three Black council members, a Black city manager, and soon its first Black superintendent.

And through it all, a third dream tugged at Compton. During that brief window between 1955 and 1970, when some in the town still held out hope for real integration, the local public schools began sending a steady stream of Black, Mexican American, and white students on to top universities and high-powered careers in academia, sports, entertainment, and government. Developers turned Santa Fe Gardens into the town's first condominiums, billing the change as a sign of hope for Compton's emerging Black and Brown middle class. The local police department even launched a new special services district, hanging a photograph of Malcolm X on the wall and inviting neighbors to come watch TV with plainclothes officers trained to provide social services.

"We're not powerful enough to create a police state," the town's white police chief said. "So consequently, we have got to work with the people."

But perhaps the most hopeful place in all of Compton during this period was Jefferson Elementary. More than 70 percent of the school's students were Hispanic. Hundreds enrolled each fall speaking little or no English. Many scored zero on the Peabody Picture Vocabulary Test, during which an adult read English words aloud and children were expected to point to the corresponding image. But prior to the 1969–70 school year, the Black leadership of the newly consolidated Compton Unified School District decided to launch an experimental new bilingual education program at the school.

Teachers began instructing Jefferson's youngest students primarily in Spanish. Classrooms began using custom textbooks that featured the unique lingo and syntax of the Compton barrio. Parents came inside Jefferson to teach traditional Mexican folk dances. A bilingual office was even established in the school's concrete courtyard, drawing a steady stream of families who congregated outside before and after school. As 1970 drew to a close, a report noted that the typical kindergartner at Jefferson went from identifying no English words on the Peabody Picture Vocabulary Test prior to the program to identifying more than fifty by the end of the year.

"A new spirit of community leadership and community destiny is developing," an evaluation of the program exclaimed.

But elsewhere in Compton, the wheels were already falling off.

As early as 1962, a few forward-thinking souls working inside a regional government agency called the Welfare Planning Council had tried to raise the alarm, just as their counterparts would later do in newer suburbs outside Pittsburgh, Dallas, and Atlanta. Middle-class families no longer wanted to shop in the 11-foot-wide shops on Main Street, the bureaucrats said. The town couldn't afford to improve the lighting in the dark alleys that made for most downtown parking. In the former willow sloughs beyond the town's borders, newer suburbs were already starting to drain Compton of the residents and businesses it needed. Although the youth population in predominantly Black and Hispanic parts of town was exploding, childcare services were still concentrated on the east side of town. And worst of all, the Welfare

Planning Council wrote, Compton's white leadership seemed profoundly committed to ignoring and denying the changes, mostly because they were worried about being "blackballed" by other white officials if they acknowledged the needs and concerns of Compton's families of color.

"The fear and the silence frustrate intelligent planning," the council concluded. "Conditions fostering the growth of a deteriorating slum ghetto are present, and a potentially 'explosive' situation is bound to develop if left unchecked."

Three years later, much of South Central Los Angeles went up in flames following an altercation sparked by the arrest of a Black motorist in Watts. For a moment, it appeared that Compton would be spared; even as thousands took to the streets of neighboring communities to protest, riot, and loot, leaving thirty-four dead and a thousand injured, a multiracial mix of residents stood together at Compton's borders with shotguns, successfully keeping the chaos at bay. But during the years that followed, those same residents who'd kept rioters out of their town proved unable to keep each other in. By 1969, one in five stores downtown was vacant. Just one new house was built. The average age of local residents would soon drop to an astonishing nineteen years old. As white and middle-class families kept fleeing, Compton was left with a surging population of poor Black and Brown children it couldn't afford to serve, creating a volatile swirl of thwarted dreams and unmet needs that fueled both anger and competition for increasingly scarce resources. The ensuing collapse was stunning and swift, starting in the local public schools.

In early 1970, a group of Black students beat some of their Mexican American classmates bloody. Then two students were murdered inside Compton school buildings. In September 1972, another student was murdered inside Compton High. Two months after that, a security guard shot and wounded a student inside Dominguez High, prompting a group of more than fifty teens to break windows and assault a teacher. Alarmed and afraid, some Compton Unified faculty and staff began deserting their posts.

"I am not going to die at Compton High after surviving Vietnam," said teacher Sydney Morrison.

The town's education leaders, meanwhile, stood by mostly helpless. Bloated and near broke, the new Compton Unified school system began running six-figure annual deficits. Promising efforts like Jefferson's bilingual program were shelved. Reports surfaced of exposed electrical wiring and flea infestations inside local schools. Compton High briefly went without running water or toilet paper. Atrocious working conditions led half the teachers at another school to call in sick in protest. Students responded by breaking windows, defacing classroom ceilings, and destroying their textbooks.

"What we're doing is putting iodine on a cancer," the city manager warned.

But more than two thousand additional students soon fled the district. Then teachers went on strike for sixteen days. Compton Unified's deficit grew to almost $2 million, forcing the district to take out an emergency loan to finish the school year.

By the mid-1970s, the entire town was in full-blown crisis. Unemployment hit 18 percent. Forty-six residents were murdered in a single year. Families gave up on the police, who seemed to have stopped even trying to respond to crimes like stolen bikes, instead barricading themselves in homes with bars on the windows and double locks on the doors. Unable to attract new businesses to replace the dozens of additional stores that closed, Compton's new Black leaders threw up their hands in public and began draining the town's already depleted coffers in private.

Over the next several years, cash advances were made to city staff without proper documentation. Two council members were convicted of extortion in a kickback scheme involving the local redevelopment agency. The school board and superintendent hired fifteen family members. Federal agents found that school officials had misspent $334,000, including thousands of dollars earmarked for poor students that were instead used to send district leaders to a six-day conference in Honolulu.

Hardest hit was Compton's growing Latino community, whose leaders complained that Spanish-speaking students were being improperly placed in classes for students with intellectual disabilities. The district, which claimed to have 163 bilingual classrooms, was found to have only 4 certified bilingual teachers.

The bottom never seemed to come. One year, arsonists and vandals did $750,000 worth of damage to Compton schools. Another, Compton High had to cancel shop classes because all the equipment got stolen. In 1980, district officials were accused of cheating on state tests by erasing and correcting wrong answers on 1,800 student answer sheets. Red flags were raised at the state education department because the results showed Compton schools going from the 6th percentile to the 99th in a single year. Confronted with the findings, Compton Unified superintendent Aaron Wade accused state officials of racism.

The RAND Corp. dubbed Compton one of fourteen suburban "disaster areas" around the country, saying it was caught in a vise of rising debt, declining revenue, and crumbling infrastructure. Between 1985 and 1990, local officials responded by cutting Compton's parks and recreation budget by 97 percent and raising the town's police budget by 195 percent, creating the police state they had once resisted. A group of local twentysomethings countered by forming N.W.A, becoming a national sensation by reflecting, magnifying, and commodifying the brutality and nihilism that had come to define the former bedroom suburb.

Nowhere was Compton's implosion more plainly visible than Santa Fe Gardens. For years, absentee slumlords ignored citations and demands they improve or close the crumbling complex. The residents who remained lived in fear, both of the gang members who hid in units after committing shootings and of the SWAT teams who came chasing in after them. In 1992, reporters found that just four of the twenty-four units in the Bush family's old building were legally occupied. Many of the rest had been taken over by squatters, sex workers, or drug users who left the landings covered in trash and feces. By then, George Herbert Walker Bush was president of the United States. A push to formally commemorate his time in Compton was greeted with derision by residents like Lorraine Cervantes, who first moved to Compton in 1952 and still lived in Santa Fe Gardens.

"I can't believe they want to make a historical landmark out of a crack house," she told reporters.

That spring, a jury acquitted four Los Angeles police officers caught on tape beating Black motorist Rodney King. South Central went up in flames again. This time, however, the rage came from inside Compton. Three local police officers were shot. Rioters set more than 130 fires and vandalized scores of buildings, resulting in some $100 million in property damage in Compton alone.

Across the country, President Bush was at a state dinner when the violence erupted. On May 1, 1992, he gave an address from the Oval Office, ordering thousands of federal troops and officers into the streets of Los Angeles while dispatching 250 U.S. Marines to quell the unrest in Compton. Framed by the American flag and pictures of his family, the president gave no indication of any lingering connection to the suburb he had once called home, instead going out of his way to deny the devastating forces that had begun wrecking Compton shortly after he left.

"What we saw last night and the night before in Los Angeles is not about civil rights. It's not about the great cause of equality that all Americans must uphold. It's not a message of protest," Bush told the nation. "It's been the brutality of a mob, pure and simple."

"A RARE DAREDEVIL MOMENT OF MINE"

That fall of 1992, Alberto Hernandez enrolled in the computer science program at the Benemérita Universidad Autónoma de Puebla in Mexico. He was eighteen.

BUAP's campus was located just ten miles from the dusty town where Alberto had grown up. But it felt much farther. San Juan Cuatalancingo was known mostly for its huge Volkswagen plant. Locals had been making Beetles there since 1967, pushing out millions of new cars and earning some of the highest manufacturing wages in Mexico. Alberto's family, however, were farmers. Both his parents and his grandparents had grown up working the same couple of dozen acres where he spent his childhood alongside a smattering of cattle, sheep, and horses. Because natural gas was a luxury to be used sparingly, Alberto spent his mornings and weekends chopping wood and milking cows, boring and backbreaking work that quickly had him dreaming about anywhere else.

By high school, he'd come to believe technology held the key to a better life. Only families with money had computers of their own, but Alberto enrolled in the computer science department at BUAP anyway. Fate seemed to smile on the decision. Shortly after he started, his sister won a raffle at work. The prize was a clunky machine that was powered by an old 16-bit Intel microprocesser and functioned more like a word processor than a PC. Still, when she gave it to him, Alberto was overcome with emotion. That first semester, as he pounded out assignments and sailed through his introductory classes in Algebra, Circuitry, and C++, a future seemed to take shape. He would work in IT.

Alberto's outlook got even better when the holidays arrived. He went to an end-of-semester celebration in a ballroom on campus. A pretty girl from the computer science department was there. She looked desperately uncomfortable. Fortified by his friends' encouragement, Alberto walked over and asked her for a dance.

"The truth is, I didn't know his name," Cristina said later. "I had never noticed him."

She also found his invitation rather forward. The youngest of nine children, Cristina still lived with her mother in a Puebla neighborhood known as Villa Posada. Her family had provided her with a rare opportunity to attend college full time without having to work. As Alberto tried to chat her up, Cristina heard her mother's voice in the back of her head, reminding her that she wasn't in school to meet boys.

"She did not want me to start school, then leave," Cristina said.

Still, the pair kept talking. Cristina found herself warming to Alberto's handsome face and dry humor. He detected the shift and latched on. Over the months that followed, he'd track Cristina around campus, striking up conversations whenever the chance arose. He learned that her father had passed away when she was nine. Her mother supported the family by managing rental properties on Villa Posada's crowded streets. And at school, she was focused on database architecture. But while Cristina also had a vague notion of becoming an IT professional, her plans rarely extended beyond earning the next A.

"I was just focused on studying and taking advantage of the opportunities my mom had given me," she said.

It took a year to introduce Alberto to her mother and brothers. They were not impressed. It wasn't just that he represented a drag on Cristina's commitment to school. It was also evident that he came from a farm. Then money grew tight, and Alberto's future prospects grew murky. He began bouncing between jobs, first as a bartender, then as a short-order cook. But the more time he spent trying to cover rent and tuition, the less time he had to study. By the mid-1990s, when he began watching his classmates graduate with degrees and licenses, but still struggle to find good jobs, Alberto was questioning whether paying for school remained a sound investment.

It didn't help that the country's minimum wage amounted to about $0.32 an hour, compared to $4.75 an hour in the United States. Or that Mexican cities like Puebla were flooded with young men who'd left their family farms in search of work, creating an oversupply of labor just as a financial crisis was causing manufacturers to cut their workforces. Still searching for a reliable income, Alberto picked up a job as a butcher in a small first-floor carnicería on a crowded street outside Puebla. The pay was decent, but the smells were terrible and the routine was always the same. He'd arrive early, then spend hours in a windowless back room, hacking away at an unceasing flow of 600-pound carcasses that hung from metal hooks. Then he'd wash down the bloody blades and do it all over again the following day. At twenty-three, five years removed from his family's farm, Alberto was back to wrestling with cows.

Ambition stifled, he took fresh interest in the stories of the people he knew who had gone north, including several of his uncles and one of his sisters. For generations, such migration had been regular and predictable, shaped primarily by the needs of U.S. employers, especially agricultural interests in the Southwest. Even back in 1924, when Congress had responded to concerns about waning Anglo-Saxon dominance by imposing a quota system that favored immigrants from Northern and Western Europe while banning entry from darker-skinned nations, Mexico had been exempted. During the decades that followed, there were periodic backlashes, one of which led to a major repatriation campaign. By World War II, however, American companies were back to recruiting, and Congress was back to mostly helping them, now via the Bracero Program, which granted temporary work visas to as many as half a million Mexican migrants a year, most of whom returned home when their seasonal work was completed.

In 1965, however, President Lyndon Johnson and Congress, filled with the spirit of liberal reform after passing the Civil Rights and Voting acts, decided to tackle immigration. The Hart-Celler Act eliminated the old quota system, opened the country to immigrants from the so-called Third World, and made it easier for naturalized citizens to sponsor relatives. At a bill-signing ceremony at the base of the Statue of Liberty, Johnson insisted the new legislation would have minimal impact on American life.

He was wrong. Between 1960 and 2000, the number of people of Mexican origin living in the U.S. soared from 1.75 million to more than 21 million. Because the new law coincided with the termination of the Bracero Program, many of those people no longer had temporary work permits and were instead undocumented. The result was the creation and dramatic expansion of a new underclass of people living in America without rights.

Again concerned about the nation's racial makeup, conservative leaders began militarizing the border in the mid-1980s. The result was a vicious cycle: More fear led to increased enforcement, which led to more apprehensions, which led to more fear. The ensuing billions of new dollars spent on border security did little to impact the flow of Mexicans into the U.S., but it did make the journey more dangerous and expensive. The migrants who made it north were thus deterred from ever returning home.

The shift transformed Compton. By the 1980s, a second generation of Black elected officials were busy protecting the patronage machines they'd fought so hard to gain control over. The town's growing Latino population, however, was beginning to gripe about being excluded from city jobs and contracts. Local baker and activist Pedro Pallan managed to wrangle a spot on Compton Unified's personnel commission, ostensibly to help promote Latino hiring. But his efforts were met with a deep disdain that mixed xenophobia with accusations that Compton's recently arrived Latino residents wanted handouts they hadn't earned. Affirmative action was about reparations for slavery, Black Compton school board member John Steward proclaimed in 1990, not "going back and forth across the border ten or fifteen times a year."

"This is America," Steward said. "Because a person does not speak English is not a reason to provide exceptional resources at public expense."

A détente seemed possible during the 1993 election season. The leading mayoral candidate was a Black councilman named Omar Bradley. Two years earlier, he'd soundly defeated Pallan. Now, though, Bradley oozed graciousness, publicly wrapping his arms around the baker's shoulders on the campaign trail. If Compton's Latino community helped him become mayor, Bradley promised, he'd personally recommend Pallan for his vacated council seat. Compton Latinos delivered, then came to the subsequent council meeting expecting a coronation. Pallan straightened his tie as he rose to accept the appointment. But when the name that came from the council president's mouth was that of another Black man, a stunned silence fell over the room. Power never concedes anything without a demand, Mayor Bradley would later tell reporters. Never has, never will.

"You know when someone hits you, and you see stars? That's how I felt," Pallan said.

Inside Compton Unified, meanwhile, Latino students regularly complained about being ridiculed, harassed, and even beaten by Black teachers and security guards. Many were taught by uncertified classroom aides. Activists called for boycotts. But their concerns were lost amid a bigger problem, revealed when district leaders were found to have filed a false budget with the state. Instead of a surplus, Compton Unified was $10 million in the red and owed $5 million in back taxes. That summer of 1993, Compton Unified became one of the first school districts in California to be taken over by the state.

Still, Black-Brown relations kept deteriorating. In 1994, Bradley and other Black leaders vocally defended Proposition 187, a ballot measure aimed at denying services to undocumented immigrants that would later be ruled unconstitutional. That same year, a Black Compton police officer was caught on tape brutally beating seventeen-year-old Felipe Soltero. Latino activists were outraged. Bradley responded by labeling them "agitators," prompting the activists to compare Compton's Black city government to the apartheid regime in South Africa. Latinos would soon account for well over half of Compton residents. But they'd never held a council seat, and as of 1990, nearly 80 percent of city workers, almost three fourths of Compton Unified teachers, and nine of every ten police officers in the town were Black.

"Have the oppressed become the oppressors?" Pallan asked.

Back in Puebla, however, none of that was part of the occasional conversations Alberto Hernandez had with his sister and friends north of the border. What they discussed was how much money they sent back home each month. Alberto was reluctant to follow in their footsteps, mostly because he wanted to marry Cristina, who was determined to finish her studies at home. But any path in Mexico felt blocked.

Then September 11 happened. Alberto heard rumors that the southern border had grown even more porous than usual. One of his friends in Compton said there might be an opening at the computer-parts recycling factory where he worked. Alberto knew if he asked Cristina to join him, she would say no, and he would lose his resolve. So at twenty-eight years old, he decided to just go, not telling anyone but his parents, getting on a plane for the first time in his life and flying to Tijuana. There, he met a coyote. After nightfall, the man drove a small group of people across the border. Once in

San Diego, it was just a matter of buying a train ticket. On his way to LA, Alberto had just one worry: How Cristina would react when she found out he'd left.

"I just believed we would be better off here," he told me later. "It was a rare daredevil moment of mine."

6

PROMISED LANDS

In a great dream of contentment, where all night long
The children sleep within tomorrow's peaceful arms
And the past is still

—JOHN KOETHE,
"In the Park," 2002

THE BECKER FAMILY | LUCAS, TEXAS

Just before the start of the 2019–20 school year, the Beckers took a vacation to Lake Tahoe in California. The trip was intended as a respite from a hectic week of packing the old house in Plano and moving to the new house in Lucas. But on their second morning away, Susan's phone buzzed as she was still waking up. It was an administrator from the Lovejoy Independent School District. Noah, the Beckers' youngest, had scored in the 94th percentile on the math portion of the district's placement test. That meant he'd missed the cutoff for Lovejoy's gifted program by just a couple of points.

"I mean, talk about your wind being knocked out of you," Susan said.

Now fully alert, her mind was already riffling through contingency plans. The main reason she and Jim had uprooted their old life was the promise that Lovejoy schools would provide each of their children a personalized glide path to the future. Years of pursuing that vision in a series of other schools across the North Dallas suburbs had yielded only disappointment.

The private Guthrie School, for example, often demanded hours of home-work a night from its second graders, leading Sean and Avery to bleed self-confidence and complain about hating school. The charter school Susan tried next had classrooms full of sofas and bouncy blue yoga balls and gave barely any homework at all. The kids loved it, but she and Jim feared they were falling behind; Avery, now in fourth grade, had such lackluster math scores that Susan felt obliged to sign her up for tutoring, which led to thrice-weekly screaming fights and complaints about being the only white kid at the local Mathnasium, followed by Susan getting the silent treatment for the duration of the nerve-destroying drive through Plano traffic. An ADHD diagnosis eventually led Susan to switch Avery to a $25,000-a-year private school for children with learning differences.

The move to Lucas had come just a few months later. The Beckers ini-tially planned to keep Avery at the private school while the boys started in Lovejoy. But the district made Susan and Jim an offer they couldn't refuse. First, they let Avery repeat fifth grade, even running a custom report to rule out the possibility she would be the oldest child in her grade. Then they ar-ranged for special classroom accommodations, stipulating that Avery could have her tests read aloud to her and receive twice-weekly thirty-minute sup-port sessions with one of her teachers, lifting from Susan's shoulders the burden of being the mean mom who dragged her daughter to tutoring while the other kids were out playing.

"Don't worry," Sloan Creek Intermediate principal Ray Winkler told her and Jim. "We got it."

Now, though, Susan was up and pacing the bedroom of the Marriott condo in Tahoe, searching for a way around Noah's scores. Before she could even get anxious, the Lovejoy administrator on the other end of the line po-litely interjected and began walking Susan through the process of reversing the district's own determination. Your son is really close, the woman said. You should appeal his results. Is there any other information that would show us he's ready? Susan set up a mini-mission-control center right there in the timeshare. By the end of the day, she'd secured commitments from three of Noah's former teachers to provide recommendation letters. He was accepted into Lovejoy's gifted program shortly after.

"It's like we were in the minors before, now we're in the big leagues," Jim said. "These guys know what they're doing, and they've got the system down."

Susan, however, knew from experience that it was still too early to let her guard down. And sure enough, in early September, another minicrisis sent her scrambling.

Each fall, Sloan Creek Intermediate took all its fifth graders on a three-day team-building trip to the Collin County Adventure Camp. A few weeks into the school year, Avery's teacher sent a message home asking for volunteer chaperones. Far more parents signed up than the camp could accommodate, leading the school to announce it would use randomization software to implement a lottery system and videotape the proceedings to ensure transparency. The results, however, spurred yet another flurry of communications, this time from parents who *were* selected to serve as chaperones but wanted to skip the orientation, because it conflicted with a Carrie Underwood concert or an older child's football game, and also from parents who *weren't* selected and now wanted a refund or to see if some special accommodations could be made.

Susan was in the latter group. An hour after getting the bad news, she composed her first email.

"This is really unfortunate," she wrote to the Sloan Creek counselor organizing the trip. "I would have thought parents to brand new kids might have gotten some sort of special lottery."

"I am so sorry!" the counselor promptly responded. "Please let me know if you would like me to talk with Avery about any concerns for the camp."

Susan then sent another message further explaining her family's situation.

> First let me say I can't begin to tell you how happy Jim and I have been with our transition into Lovejoy. Everyone from the top

down has been extremely welcoming and so helpful. We love the emphasis on community as that was what was missing from our Plano life.

As for the chaperone lottery, please know that Jim and I have never been ones to complain or raise issues with school policies because we have always empathized with how hard a job you all have and how impossible a task it is to make everyone happy. That said, we think not including new families on the first big trip of the year is a missed opportunity. . . .

Honestly, this was a letdown from the "high" we have been on since moving into the district. I hope this will be a process you will consider looking at in the future as I wouldn't want other new families to feel the same letdown we have.

This time, Sloan Creek's assistant principal responded. There may be some wiggle room as the trip got closer, she said. We would never want to add more hurdles to an already difficult race. Heartened, Susan began working the phones, talking first to her neighbors, then to other new Lovejoy parents facing the same problem. Soon enough, an extra bed opened up.

On the last Monday in September, Susan drove up I-75 and then out TX-121 through the far-exurban fringe north of Dallas, watching through the windows as workers cleared trees and prepared to widen the highway in anticipation of additional development to come. For now, the 435 acres covered by the adventure camp were still unspoiled. The caravan of cars and buses from Lovejoy bumped over a rocky road snaking through scrub-covered prairie. They were met by a young white woman with pigtails and bearded white guys in bucket hats who offered polite greetings, then exchanged private snickers as the group unpacked. Over the years, Lovejoy had earned a reputation for being "extra."

At Avery's cabin, a group of chaperone moms set about livening up their temporary new home, hanging streamers, Halloween decorations, and brightly colored lights while the kids unpacked. The next morning, the coffee in the mess hall was bitter and thin. But inside the education center, Avery handled a bearded dragon named Walter and a California king snake named Arcas.

At the lake, she plunged her arms into the muck-filled pools along the banks, pulling out crayfish and nymphs during an activity on pollution tolerance among aquatic organisms, then climbed into a canoe that Susan helped paddle through the calm blue water. The afternoon was for archery. Avery pulled her long, dark hair back with a hot pink bandanna, then stood tall and straight, her elbow cocked confidently behind her ear.

"Mommy, Mommy, watch, watch," she said.

For a moment, Susan felt torn. She was on the phone with Jim. He needed a notarized signature; to help ease the financials of moving to Lucas, the Beckers had decided to sell their vacation condo in Horseshoe Bay. But that would have to wait, Susan said, turning her phone instead to Avery, who sent an arrow whizzing into the target.

"You did it!" Susan said, winning a huge smile.

When she woke up the following morning, a few other parents were just returning from Buc-ee's, a roadside travel center known for its excellent coffee. Outside the cabins, they distributed steaming cups to grateful chaperones. When it was time to leave, Avery hung close to her new friends, filling Susan with a feeling she'd been hungering after for years. The Lovejoy Independent School District just kept passing test after test, and she finally seemed to have found a community that reflected her vision of what the suburbs should be.

"It all worked out," she said with a mix of surprise and delight. "Fortunately, we all had similar values."

THE ROBINSON FAMILY | GWINNETT COUNTY, GEORGIA

Corey Robinson settled into a crouch, eyes scanning the defense from his fullback position in the North Gwinnett Bulldogs' wishbone backfield. He was off at the snap, crashing through the line and squaring up a Lawrenceville linebacker. In his wake, a lanky boy cut into the newly opened space, his loping strides gobbling up sixty yards of shimmering green artificial turf at George Pierce Park before he scored.

"Touchdown by number nine, Elijah 'Flash' Williams!" the public address announcer cried.

In the stands, Corey's mother and siblings screamed their approval. His father, however, stood stoically on the sideline. Anthony Robinson was volunteering for the day, working the sticks in baggy black slacks and a bright red shirt that hung well below his generous waistline. After the touchdown, he ambled toward midfield and placed the first-down marker for the ensuing kickoff before allowing himself a satisfied nod.

"I try to keep some perspective," he said. "I mean, we're talking about ten-year-olds."

By 2015, youth football had become an all-consuming experience in Gwinnett County, the Robinsons' new home. The southern part of the county, long since built out, was increasingly dense with Black and Latino families. Nika and Anthony had bought a house farther north, where the population was still heavily white. To accommodate the ongoing frenzy of development in the area, the Gwinnett County Public Schools had recently created new academic clusters called Mill Creek and Mountain View. The Gwinnett Football League had followed suit, adding new teams in both regions. Still, Corey's North Gwinnett squad had to split into three separate teams so every child got a chance to play. All the growth meant the league was now as much business as recreation; a guy had apparently been making a killing by taping all the youth games, then selling access to the film to proud parents who wanted to compile their children's highlight clips and to ultra-competitive coaches who wanted to scout the third-down tendencies of the seven-year-old team they'd face the following week.

The Robinsons had taken a roundabout route to the area. After Corey was born in 2004, they'd rented out Anthony's town house in suburban Cobb County and lived for several years back in DeKalb, near Anthony's parents and just a ten-minute drive from the Centers for Disease Control and Prevention, the biggest client of the public health consulting group where Nika worked. Then, in the span of seven months, Nika had learned she was pregnant again, lost her mom, brought her teenage brother to live with her, and given birth to Cassidy. Overwhelmed and out of bedrooms, she and Anthony had reclaimed the town house in Cobb. When Corey started first grade, Nika quickly became a constant presence in his classroom, delighting in her son's teacher, who let her little chatterbox of a boy teach math lessons and tell jokes at the end of the day, just so he could feel special.

It was around that time that the dot-com layoffs finally reached Anthony. He pivoted quickly, getting a teaching certificate to pair with his math degree from Clark Atlanta, then starting work at a middle school in DeKalb, where he became an assistant football coach. A few years in, however, Anthony had a long conversation with the team's head coach. The older man lamented how the role had led him to miss much of his own children's athletic journey. That night, Anthony privately resolved to switch over to coaching youth football when his son eventually took up the game.

The move came when Corey started his second year of organized ball in Cobb County. Just six years old, the eager, energetic boy had already worked his way from the bottom of the depth chart to starting linebacker. Inside, Anthony was thrilled. But he did his best not to show it. Upon starting to coach his son, he laid down a foundational rule: Once you step on that field, there's no such thing as family anymore, because I'm damn sure not going to have these other parents accusing me of playing favorites.

"I remember I called him 'Daddy' *one time*," Corey told me later. "He called me over and was like, 'The next time you say that, I'm gonna make you run.'"

That was in 2011. Nika became pregnant with Carter shortly after. The Robinsons decided to move to a bigger home in Buford, a former farming town in northern Gwinnett that had boomed after the nearby Mall of Georgia opened in 1999. Families there sent their children to the public schools in the new Mill Creek cluster, which had a fantastic reputation. Ivy Creek Elementary, for example, had recently built a sparkling three-story addition with computer labs and a state-of-the-art media center and offered everything from an environmental club to mentoring programs pairing students with police officers and firefighters.

"We just looked at the numbers, test scores, percentage of kids eligible for free and reduced lunches, those kinds of things," Nika said. "I think what everyone wants. A good family environment, low crime, opportunities, the stereotypical American dream."

The house they ultimately bought was on a quarter-acre lot in a new subdivision where wild turkeys still sometimes roamed. It was just a half mile from Ivy Creek, two stories and 4,001 square feet, with a fireplace in the family room and granite countertops in the kitchen. The first-floor walls were the dullest possible beige, which Nika didn't love, but the builder let her pick the house's flooring and finishes, and the home office and finished basement offset the twinge of longing she still felt for her old life in DeKalb. Anthony, meanwhile, bought a new gas grill for the backyard, then set his sights on a riding mower that would make quick work of the lawn.

"That is my line in the sand," Nika joked. "Absolutely not."

Because registration for the local team in the Gwinnett Football League season had already closed, it took a few days of phone calls before Anthony found an open spot for Corey on one of the North Gwinnett squads. He began to have daydreams of his own; a tight end named Jared Cook had recently gone on from North Gwinnett High to the NFL, and the area was an increasingly fertile recruiting ground for colleges in the powerhouse Southeastern Conference. The great thing about football, Anthony believed, was that it was something you could control, one of the few areas of American life where talent reliably prevailed.

It came as a disappointment, then, when the Bulldogs provided something short of a real meritocracy. Parents went to extreme lengths to politick for their children, and coaches seemed intent on making sure their own sons got the majority of snaps at high-profile positions like quarterback and running back. *Daddy Ball*, Anthony snorted derisively. But he refused to step in, even when Corey was relegated to the offensive line and began to question why he seemed to be the only player on the team who didn't have someone speaking out for him.

"You've got to make your own way," Anthony told his son.

At first, the approach yielded mixed results, both on the field and at Ivy

Creek Elementary. Corey's second-grade teacher had been another dream, talking regularly with the Robinsons about how to keep their son focused by rewarding his considerable desire for attention. The following year, however, his teacher had seemed checked out from the start. Nothing particularly galling happened, but neither did anything particularly good; Nika and Anthony felt more tolerated than embraced, just as they did on the North Gwinnett football team.

Then, right before Corey started fourth grade, Anthony met Russell Rhodes, who coached a nine-year-old team in nearby Dacula that had won several recent GFL championships. Both men were from New Orleans. Both were Black. Both shared a decidedly old-school worldview. When Russ said he not only had an open spot on his squad, but was also looking for an assistant coach, the Robinsons wasted little time making the switch.

The drive to the new team's practice park took about twenty minutes, no small matter given that summer practices were held five days a week, two hours a day. But Nika and Anthony didn't mind. Coach Russ started Corey off at running back. The first week of camp, he saw the boy go through a drill at half speed. Russ pulled him off the field, loudly cursed him out, and put him with the offensive lineman. Then he said the magic words: I know you can do better. From his spot behind the defensive line, Anthony flushed with satisfaction. It was exactly what he would have done.

Dacula had six coaches altogether. Three were Black and three white. Every Sunday evening, the entire group would assemble in Russ's basement, where he had a big-screen TV and a whiteboard on wheels he used to diagram plays and track player snaps. Guys would show up early with some wings or potato salad, and Russ's wife would bring down jambalaya, and they'd start by watching the first half of a 4:00 game. Then they'd get to work, breaking down film of their own game from the previous day, followed by tape of their next opponent, debating how to best stop the college-style spread offenses some of the GFL's nine-year-old teams were already running. Discussions about playing time often grew heated, with the offensive and defensive coordinators arguing about whether a player like Corey was more valuable at running back or linebacker. Usually, the assistants worked it out on their own. But if a trusted arbiter was necessary, Russ would step in, reminding them of his guiding philosophy.

"We're gonna let these kids compete and put the better player in," he'd say.

By 8:00 p.m., all the disputes would be settled. Russ would turn on *Football Night in America*. By 9:00, the three Black coaches would be the only ones left. The conversation would turn to work and wives and how good they themselves might have been had they received the same coaching their kids were now getting. Two hours later, the men would still be shooting the bull, standing in Russ's driveway next to their SUVs and pickups, talking only now about what the future might hold for their own young sons, a chorus of crickets giving cover to their hopes and fears, the Sunday night game just a flickering glow through a window in the warm Georgia night, until someone would say shit, it's eleven o'clock, I got to work in the morning.

By Saturday, Nika would be back in the bleachers with the other coaches' families, laughing and not worrying when the younger kids went off somewhere to practice gymnastics or play tag. Sometimes, the moms would watch the game, and sometimes they'd swap stories and compare notes, giving Nika valuable tidbits of information about which teachers to avoid and how to handle the homeowners' association and where to get her nails done. Corey, now a starting running back and scoring touchdowns of his own, seemed to be settling in too. Their search had been long and full of surprises. But the Robinsons finally felt like they'd figured out how to make suburban Gwinnett their own.

"Having Anthony coach has really been helpful opening doors," Nika said. "People just looked at us different."

THE ADESINA FAMILY | EVANSTON, ILLINOIS

When did you first recognize racism in your own life?

The prompt hung in the air inside the Fleetwood Jourdain Community Center, located in the heart of Evanston's Fifth Ward. It was October 2017, just a few sessions into a new round of SEED, the District 65 program officially known as Seeking Educational Equity and Diversity. Each cohort included a couple dozen parents, teachers, and school district staff. They met once a month for three-hour discussions led by an anti-oppression consultant. Several of the people in the room now shifted uncomfortably in their brown metal folding chairs. Lauren Adesina, however, sat stone still. She was in her early thirties, with a son in kindergarten. But the question had transported her back to when she was a little girl getting stung for the first time by the colorism within her own family. She'd been at her grandmother's apartment in Logan Square with six or seven of her cousins on her mom's side. Her estranged grandfather called to announce he was coming over for a visit. What happened next was something that Lauren had only talked about previously with a few close friends. But *fuck it*, she thought. *Let these people see me as I really am.*

"My mom's dad comes over," Lauren began, her voice even at first. "And he specifically said that he didn't want to talk to the dark-skinned kids. And so my grandma facilitated it, and put my three cousins that were very fair-skinned, basically white, with green or blue eyes, in the living room, with him, so that he can give them gifts and love all on them. And had the rest of us in the back, in the kitchen, hidden away because he didn't want to see us."

Lauren paused to gather herself. The few times she'd told the story before, she told the group, she'd focused on her grandfather, like screw that racist prick, I don't care about him anyway. This time, though, she was thinking about her grandmother.

"I *know* she loved me," Lauren said. "But she didn't protect us."

At that, a few of the white women in the circle choked up. One began to cry. Lauren reflexively disregarded the spill of her own emotions. Don't cry, she said in a soothing voice. It's okay, I'm all right, you don't have to cry.

It was the crying white woman's response that had been the real surprise that evening. Please don't comfort me, she said. This is your story. You don't need to worry about my feelings.

The trust that bloomed afterward was just part of what had filled Lauren with a feeling of security after she settled back in her old suburban hometown. Each afternoon, Chris came home happy from Dewey Elementary, full of songs and stories about making Mexican hot chocolate. The school's dual-language immersion program was also working wonders; when Lauren took her son to visit, he would charm his great-grandmother by pointing to objects around the house and naming them in Spanish.

"What I wanted to happen was happening," she said.

The same was true at work, where her job at the arts-education nonprofit was opening her eyes in unexpected ways. First, she'd started attending evening talks on topics such as the history of housing segregation in Chicagoland. Then she'd started reading books like *The New Jim Crow*, which detailed how institutions like America's sprawling prison system furthered racial oppression without being explicitly racist.

All over Evanston, people seemed to be waking up to similar views, creating a kind of cross-pollination of ideas and campaigns that had the town buzzing. Just days after Donald Trump was inaugurated, hundreds of students had walked out of Evanston Township High and held a protest that was supported by school administrators and local police alike. Later that year, the town council had voted to create an Equity and Empowerment Commission, tasked with identifying and eradicating inequities in Evanston's official services and programs. Suni Kartha and Anya Tanyavutti had gained control of the District 65 board, replacing the two white women who preceded them as president and vice president and vowing to push racial justice to the center of the school system's agenda. And the energy wasn't just coming from above. At the urging of parent organizers, Washington Elementary had canceled its traditional Pioneer Day, which for decades had featured students dressing up and square dancing to celebrate white settlers. Principal Kate Ellison had also instituted race-based affinity groups for faculty and parents, then launched a school-wide study of *Culturally Responsive Teaching & the Brain*, written by self-described writing teacher turned equity freedom fighter Zaretta Hammond. Inspired, a woman named Katie Logan was working to bring similar initiatives to Dewey Elementary. It was a big change from 2012, when she'd first joined the school's PTA.

"I was the typical white person," Logan told me, recalling how she used to wonder, "Why aren't the Black and Hispanic parents coming to anything?"

But instead of complaining and blaming, Logan had started listening and building relationships. Over the course of several years, the stories of parents who felt frustrated or alienated at Dewey began to nag at her. All four of Logan's own children were having great experiences at the school. Why wasn't that true for everyone? After taking a fresh look at the PTA's written materials, she'd joined a group to discuss a book called *Waking Up White* that relayed the story of a white woman realizing she was part of the problem. Then Logan had signed up for SEED, where she was placed in Lauren's group.

Their first session had been iffy, with an elementary school–style arts and crafts project involving paper plates and the things that make us who we are. But the conversations had deepened over the subsequent weeks. At one point, the facilitators presented a timeline of the U.S. government's official support for racial discrimination. They tried to wrap up by pointing out how far America had since come. But Lauren and a couple of other parents of color interjected, saying, Um yeah no, you get the ending wrong, this stuff is still going on, just look at how many Black men have been incarcerated for minor drug violations and denied the right to vote. Logan told me later that such moments had made her feel like Neo at the beginning of *The Matrix*.

"I learned that there was a totally different reality," she said. "Not just for everybody else, but also for me."

It was after the SEED conversation about first encounters with racism that Logan and Lauren had formed a real friendship. They began by talking about their kids and childhoods and the politics of Evanston, where the new Equity and Empowerment Commission was mulling reparations to local Black families who been impacted by government-sanctioned discrimination. Increasingly self-conscious about the perception that the Dewey PTA functioned as a kind of sorority for white stay-at-home moms, Logan began nudging Lauren to get involved.

Who wants to join the PTA? Lauren thought. *It seems like* Mean Girls *for adults.*

But then, in early March 2018, parent activists arranged for sociologists

John Diamond and Amanda Lewis to give a book talk in Evanston. A few years earlier, the pair had published *Despite the Best Intentions: How Racial Inequality Thrives in Good Schools.* Two hundred people listened as the authors explained the concept of "opportunity hoarding," in which dominant groups restrict other people's access to goods such as public education, often by advocating for what's best for their own families without considering or caring how they might be hurting other families. In a suburb like Evanston, Diamond and Lewis said, that might look like white parents demanding their children have greater access to accelerated math programs or Advanced Placement courses. Racist outcomes could result even if the push was not explicitly racial; Black and Brown students might get tracked into less rigorous courses, or their parents might be blamed for not being involved.

"It was what we were all experiencing," said Heather Sweeney, one of the event's organizers.

She and Tanyavutti soon hosted a series of follow-up discussions. When Logan saw the flyer, she urged Lauren to come.

"It got to the point where it was like, 'Well, we've built this relationship, and I don't think she'd invite me somewhere I'll be harmed,'" Lauren said.

The meeting was held in the library on Dewey's second floor. Low shelves topped with children's books ran perpendicular to cinder-block walls painted turquoise. Lauren joined a group of Black parents seated at a wooden table. A mom named Lila Anyango-Hill promptly struck up a conversation, making her feel at home. Then Tanyavutti walked in, moving gingerly because she was thirty-eight weeks pregnant. She and Lauren shared a smile; they'd taken a mommy-and-me swimming class together back when Chris was still a toddler.

Since the start of her tenure on the District 65 board, Tanyavutti had become something of a lightning rod. After being appointed to fill a vacant seat, Tanyavutti had initially felt out of place; she'd be out at a local coffee shop and see board colleagues talking with some Evanston civic leader, but when she walked over and said hello, an invisible record would skip and everyone would get super squirrelly. But after Trump won the presidency,

Tanyavutti decided to run for a full term on the board and stop playing nice. Her relationship with white board president Candance Chow had since grown particularly strained, especially after Chow received a gentle slap on the wrist when the person managing her campaign for state representative was found to have used a work account to email Superintendent Goren's executive assistant to ask for volunteers.

"All she had to say was, 'Oops,' and she was all clear," Tanyavutti told me. "When I look at our data, we see replication of that. Black and Brown children and children with IEPs at the time were getting disciplined at five times the rate of white children."

Now, though, talking about opportunity hoarding in the Dewey library, Tanyavutti was in her element. To illustrate the difference between the *ostentative* and *performative* aspects of school policies, she and Sweeney presented several real-life scenarios from Evanston. One local school, for example, had required teachers to wait outside for ten minutes after school each day. Ostensibly, the purpose was to ensure that parents who might not be able to attend evening meetings had equal access to their children's teachers. In practice, though, white parents had used the time to deepen their existing bonds with the school's mostly white teaching staff, leaving Black and Brown parents feeling even more excluded. Lauren's mind was blown.

"Anya has this way of just connecting the dots for people," she said.

Fortunately, Tanyavutti and Sweeney continued, there were resources that could help. The pair distributed copies of a two-page document titled "Equity Impact Assessment Tool." It listed five questions that anyone taking action for or about Evanston schools—the board, the superintendent, a principal, a PTA—could incorporate into their decision-making process.

1. How does the proposed action (policy, budget, etc.) impact racial and economic disparities in Evanston?

2. How does the proposed action support and advance racial and economic equity?

3. Have voices of groups affected by the proposal or budget been involved with its development? Who's missing and how can they be engaged? . . .

4. What resources, what timelines, and what monitoring will help ensure success for achieving racial and economic equity?

5. What adverse impacts or unintended consequences could result from this policy? . . .

The subsequent discussion had been exhilarating. Afterward, everything happened quickly. Lauren joined the Dewey PTA, then became one of the group's coleaders along with her new friend, Lila Anyango-Hill, who said right off the bat that she wanted to zero out the line in the PTA budget for supporting Pioneer Day.

"That was like a breath of fresh air for me," Lauren said. "There was always this culture of everyone being polite and nice or not saying anything that might hurt somebody's feelings. But Lila was like, 'Nope, this is how I feel, take it or leave it.'"

Their next target was the PTA's bylaws. All executive committee members would be required to complete ten hours of racial equity training. The Equity Impact Assessment Tool was also made a formal part of the group's decision-making process.

The first big opportunity to test the new way of doing business came during the planning of Dewey's spring Fun Run. It was the PTA's biggest fundraiser. Students solicited sponsors to donate money, then ran laps around the school's field. When Lauren, Anyango-Hill, and the other parents began asking each other, *Who is being excluded? What are the unintended consequences?* the answers quickly became obvious. The Fun Run was usually held in the evening, making it difficult for some families to attend. Prizes went not just to the children who ran the farthest and fastest, but to those who raised the most money. And while the majority of Dewey students bought wristbands that entitled them to food and games, children who couldn't afford the bands often had to get theirs from the school social worker, creating what some considered a significant stigma.

In response, the Dewey PTA decided to run a free shuttle to help more families attend. They ended prizes altogether. And they made sure Dewey staff distributed the wristbands the same way to every student, regardless of how much money they'd raised.

When the event finally happened, attendance was up. More money was raised. Fewer kids felt excluded. Everyone still had fun. Other PTAs even began reaching out for advice. *Oh my God*, Lauren thought. *We can actually do this.*

"I was just like, 'Wow,'" she said. "The PTA has so much power."

THE SMITH FAMILY | PENN HILLS, PENNSYLVANIA

Bethany Smith gripped the steering wheel as she sat at the light on Bennett Street in one of the mostly Black communities on the edge of Pittsburgh that the city's aging eastern suburbs were now struggling to outrun. Despite renting the house in Penn Hills, she'd enrolled her son in the pre-K program at the Homewood YWCA, where the classrooms were sunny and colorful and the head teacher was a Black woman with a master's degree. Jackson was doing great. Bethany, however, needed a better job. Her most promising lead had been with a large health insurance provider where her friend was a manager. But she'd gotten radio silence since her interview.

The light was taking forever. Trying to calm herself, Bethany let her gaze wander down the intersection and over to the two-story building that housed the Homewood-Brushton branch of the Community College of Allegheny County. It had been nearly a decade since she'd landed on academic probation for that third and final time, and Bethany certainly hadn't been planning on reenrolling today; she was wearing flip-flops and a sundress, and the unpredictable Chihuahua named Cash she was babysitting sat beside her on the front seat. Still, when the light turned green, she hung the right instead of heading straight toward home.

"You know how they're like, 'Let your haters be your motivation?'" Bethany said. "People piss me off, and then that's when I go and do shit."

After parking, she cracked the car window for Cash, walked through a set of double glass doors, signed in, and took a seat by the copy machine. Before she could change her mind, an upbeat light-skinned woman of mixed racial heritage called her name.

Helena Liddle was an adjunct professor in CCAC's English Department who also worked part time in academic advising. Every day, it seemed, someone who'd been knocked down and then gotten back up would walk in off the streets of Homewood and tell her their story. We'll get you all set up, Liddle would tell them, pulling their checkered transcripts up on her computer. Don't you worry. This is absolutely fixable. Bethany responded to the encouragement by sharing everything, from her past academic probations to the challenges of being a single mom, the buckets of grief she was still carrying to her worries about money. Then she said she wasn't even sure she wanted to do school again. And besides, she couldn't stay now because she had a dog sitting outside in the car.

"Bring him in!" Liddle replied, already moving to fill up a plastic bowl with water.

Bethany had left CCAC with a 0.9 GPA. To get back on track, she would have to start part time and get permission from the dean to reenroll. Seeing her shoulders droop, Liddle wrote out a to-do list, complete with directions to the dean's office, the name of someone in the financial aid department, and copies of the forms Bethany had to submit. Liddle also added her own phone number, which she told Bethany to call if she ran into any trouble.

"Just because you made a mistake or had some issues or something happened to you in the past, it's not something that's going to damage you forever," she said.

By midafternoon, Bethany was registered for two new classes. A few days later, she got the call she'd been waiting for, offering her the job with the health insurance company. Sorry, Bethany told the person on the phone. I'm going back to school.

For the next seven semesters, she balanced her job as a home health aide with her coursework, which soon came to include classes in IT. In the midst of it all, she was called for extended duty on a grand jury, where she struck up a series of strange little friendships, including one with an older white man who explained how to flip properties and coached Bethany on how to improve her credit score. When he suggested that she pay off one of her out-standing $500 bills, she was too embarrassed to say she didn't have the money. But at home, Bethany looked up the sales history on the house she and her mom were renting in Penn Hills. The owner had bought it roughly fifteen years earlier for around $53,000. That meant he was likely clearing at least $600 a month from her rental payments.

"I'm making somebody else rich," Bethany told her mother. "It's time for me to start building my own wealth."

Their conversations about buying a house started off more as a wish than a plan. Jackson, now five years old, was becoming a handful, full of energy and emotion. And school was capturing Bethany's energy in surprising ways. Her first semester, she'd signed up for English 115, a literature course taught by Liddle, who'd thrown out the old syllabus and replaced it with readings by authors like James Baldwin, Jamaica Kincaid, and Zora Neale Hurston. The chance to dive into serious literature with complicated, deeply flawed Black characters who spoke, thought, and fought in the same ver-nacular she had used growing up started out thrilling. Early in the semester, the class read a poem called "Mother to Son" by Langston Hughes. It begins:

> Well, son, I'll tell you:
> Life for me ain't been no crystal stair.
> It had tacks in it,
> And splinters,
> And boards torn up,
> And places with no carpet on the floor—
> Bare.

Bethany loved the poem, mostly because the unnamed mother refused to give up or stop climbing, even through the darkness and danger of life, all while still finding ways to give her son the unvarnished truth. Her response paper came back with an A. Best writer in the class, Liddle said.

Several weeks later, however, Liddle had the class read *Fences*, the most famous of August Wilson's Hill District plays. Set in the 1950s, it revolves around Troy Maxson, a middle-aged Black man burdened by memories of a father he hated and his own thwarted dreams of playing big-league baseball. Now he's doing the same things to his family that were done to him as a child. Bethany felt a deep connection to the character of Rose, Maxson's wife, who constantly sings "Jesus Be a Fence Around Me," a prayer for protection against unfamiliar forces. But the story, its conflicts, and the intimately familiar dialects in which the characters spoke encroached on a place inside Bethany that still felt raw and vulnerable. When we talked years later about why she'd never finished the "Fences" response paper she was supposed to write, Bethany would tell me she'd been raised to wear two faces, cussing and getting loud and being herself behind closed doors, then being told to speak the Queen's English when she stepped outside. It was supposed to make white people accept her, she said. But all it had really done was make her doubt herself.

Hunting for houses, meanwhile, didn't exactly make her feel better. The first humiliation came when Bethany didn't realize she would need to get preapproved for a mortgage loan, leading to a brutal exchange with her real estate agent. Then the bank officer took one look at her credit score and said all future communications would have to run through her mother. Of the first twenty-two houses she and her mom looked at in Penn Hills, Bethany liked only one, which she dubbed the party house, because it had a finished basement with paneled doors that slid back to reveal a full bar and an old-school hi-fi stereo cabinet.

"It reminded me of my grandparents' house, nostalgic as hell," she said. "But my mom was like, 'Nuh-uh.'"

Somehow, though, everything came together that spring. Jackson finished kindergarten at Urban Academy, the charter school where Bethany had once worked, wearing a crisp gray suit and shiny brown loafers to his graduation ceremony. Bethany graduated from CCAC a few weeks later with a grade point average well above 3.0. To celebrate, she bought herself a new white dress, got her hair done, and glued sparkling gold letters that spelled

MOVE CONFIDENTLY IN THE WAY OF YOUR DREAMS onto the top of her mortarboard. When her name was called, Bethany bounded onto the stage, waved to her mother and Jackson in the stands, then gave Helena Liddle a big hug as she descended the stairs.

And that spring, the real estate agent called about a 1,001-square-foot ranch house on Princeton Drive that was about to hit the market. It had three bedrooms, a finished basement, and a new wooden deck out back. As ever, Penn Hills was a place that was hard to pin down; where some people might've seen a community in decline, Bethany saw an opportunity to finally go from surviving to thriving. On closing day, she and her mother took their seats on their side of a long mahogany table. Papers began flying back and forth for signatures, filling Bethany's insides with a curious mix of butterflies and pride. Then the money started changing hands. Thousands of dollars went to the seller, the real estate agent, the bank, and the notary. Then a mousy woman who'd sat silently for more than an hour cleared her throat.

"Even her ass got a check," Bethany said. "I'm like, 'What'd she do?'"

Someday soon, she resolved, she'd be on the other side of such transactions.

THE HERNANDEZ FAMILY | COMPTON, CALIFORNIA

In February 2003, Alberto Hernandez sat on the concrete curb outside a Mobil station in Compton, waiting. A row of squat single-family homes from the 1950s and a series of more recently constructed apartment buildings lined the block, hinting at the stages of development and decline that his adopted American home had already gone through. His eyes bounced from frame to frame, searching for Cristina, who was supposed to arrive soon.

The man driving her up from the border would only agree to meet at a busy gas station at a major intersection. Alberto wasn't sure of the make, model, or color of the car he'd be driving. Nor did he know what to expect from

Cristina. It had been fourteen months since he'd seen her. Those first several weeks after he arrived in the United States, she'd still been smarting that he'd left Puebla without telling her, forcing her to call his family's home and pry the details of his plan from his father.

"Not very good," Cristina said when I asked about her reaction.

For a time, she'd turned inward, focusing on her own family and on finishing her graduate program at BUAP. Her thesis involved coding databases in Oracle that could query information from multiple computers. The work was more satisfying than exciting.

Eventually, though, affection, loneliness, and curiosity got the best of her. Alberto kept calling, and Cristina started picking up, listening as he talked about the friends he'd made and the money he was sending home, the Mexican bakeries along Rosecrans Avenue and the Saturday soccer games at a park over in Carson City. They already had so many years invested in their relationship, Alberto said. He could barely stand how much he missed her. A familiar warmth soon began to creep into Cristina's replies.

Afraid of undoing such progress, Alberto kept the other 90 percent of his life in Compton to himself. For months, he'd been sharing part of a small house on Long Beach Boulevard with a few other men from Mexico, including the friend who helped convince him to come north. Six days a week, the group was out the door before dawn, praying that neither of the beat-up sedans they shared had been broken into the night before, then heading off to work together at a small factory. From six in the morning until six in the evening, Alberto tore open old toner cartridges, cleaned out the clotted ink, and passed them down the line to be refilled.

Early on, he'd decided it would be a good idea to learn English. He went so far as to sign up for an evening course within walking distance of the house. But on the way to his first class, he was robbed, so he never went back. It was all part of living in Compton, he'd learned, just like tiptoeing around the Black people who parked their cars in the middle of the street and yelled furiously at anyone who asked them to move, or swallowing your pride and looking at the floor when a teenager cut in front of you at the line in McDonald's.

"It was hard to convince her to come," he said of Cristina. "I didn't want her to know it wasn't safe."

It took more than a year for Cristina to finally decide to leave Puebla. I can't afford an entire apartment yet, Alberto told her. But don't worry. There was a room for rent in the home of a family his friend knew. It was spacious, 25 feet by 20 feet. And it would be all theirs.

A truck eased into the Mobil station, passing by the pumps and the haggard palm trees rising from small strips of grass and pulling up to the curb. Cristina stumbled out looking dazed. Alberto couldn't tell if she was happy, confused, exhausted, or all three. But it didn't matter; they were finally together, in a place where they could pursue the future.

A few weeks after her arrival, Alberto took Cristina to Universal Studios, outside Hollywood. Inside, a tram car took tourists past the Bates Motel from *Psycho* and the sleepy seaside town from *Jaws*. A set called Old Mexico, complete with a manufactured flash flood that swept over an artificially dusty street, had recently been featured in *Pirates of the Caribbean*. This is how you know you're in America, Alberto said during the hour-long bus ride. But they arrived late, then discovered that admission was $49.75 per person. So instead of entering the park, Alberto and Cristina contented themselves with strolling the streets of the outdoor tourist mall nearby. They couldn't afford anything from the swanky stores. Out on the sidewalk, though, you didn't have to pay to just be.

"It was about sharing time," Alberto said. "Things weren't hard."

The blur of years that followed quickly turned into a decade. Cristina started at the produce processing plant, and Alberto landed the job at the furniture factory, where he welded metal legs for tables and chairs, usually via an ancient touch-panel control system that made him feel like he was using at least some of what he'd learned in college. Together, they earned enough to send a little money back home. And they continued to go on adventures, including a 2005 trip to Las Vegas that started as a trip to visit friends from Puebla and ended with Alberto and Cristina getting married. Now in their early thirties, they soon began talking about kids, a dream that was starting to feel especially urgent for Alberto.

"I'm going to be Grandpa, not Dad," he said half jokingly.

Marisol was born in 2007. Jacob came three years later. Alberto couldn't get health insurance, food stamps, or a driver's license. But he could work, so he considered himself lucky.

"My mother always told us, if you are born without a hand or a foot, then you have a motive to struggle," Alberto said. By comparison, his situation was "like removing a hangnail."

The good news was that Jacob and Marisol were citizens. That meant they could travel freely back and forth to Mexico, a limitation on his own autonomy that Alberto had long since resigned himself to.

It briefly looked like things might change in 2013, when Jacob was three. Led by Democrats Chuck Schumer and Dick Durbin and Republicans John McCain and Lindsey Graham, the U.S. Senate passed a bipartisan immigration bill that included a path to citizenship or permanent legal status for the roughly 11 million undocumented people living in America, a change that would have dramatically expanded the nation's sense of who belonged and deserved a chance to succeed. But the GOP-controlled House of Representatives, where "Boxcar" Republicans who preferred mass deportations held sway, blocked the legislation for more than a year. Frustrated, Democratic president Barack Obama decided to act unilaterally, issuing conjoined executive orders aimed at granting nearly half the nation's undocumented residents formal work authorizations while shielding them from deportation. The first order expanded a Department of Homeland Security policy known as DACA that applied to undocumented residents who had been brought to the United States as children. It went into effect and withstood a series of legal challenges. The second order was known as DAPA, short for Deferred Action for Parents of Americans. It would have applied to Alberto and Cristina and roughly 3.7 million other people who had lived in the U.S. since 2010 or earlier, had a child who was an American citizen or lawful permanent resident, and maintained a clean criminal record. But congressional Republicans went berserk. Texas and twenty-five other mostly red states sued the White House, and the case eventually went to the Supreme Court, which was still in turmoil several months after the death of Justice Antonin Scalia. Thanks to the Republican-led Senate's blockade of Merrick Garland, the court deadlocked at 4–4, effectively killing DAPA and consigning Alberto and Cristina to continued limbo.

But their dreams for their children were still strong. Jacob was a bright and curious boy with a seemingly photographic recall of past events. Alberto and Cristina bought him Leapfrog videos and hit the book section first during their trips to Target so he could flip through the pages in the cart while the rest of the family shopped. Jacob started kindergarten at Foster Elementary in Compton already advanced. When he came home saying he was bored after three days, Alberto asked to speak to his teacher during afternoon pickup.

"My son has a higher aptitude than you are using right now," he said. "It's like he has a V8 engine, but you are treating him like a four-cylinder."

The staff at Foster proved accommodating, allowing Jacob to sit in on first-grade classes and giving him a battery of assessments to see how advanced he really was. At the end of the year, they allowed him to skip directly to second grade.

That year, however, would be Marisol's last at the school, which only went through fifth grade. Alberto was determined to keep his two children together. When two different Foster teachers pointed out that the nearby Jefferson Elementary went through eighth grade and was one of the best schools in the area, he and Cristina began staying up late to craft a plan. But their first visit to the administrative headquarters of the Compton Unified School District didn't go well. A woman greeted them in Spanish, which was encouraging. But it quickly became evident that she either didn't know what she was talking about or was trying to get rid of them. Unlike Jim Becker, Alberto definitely did not feel like he'd made it to the big leagues.

"We were being helped by rookies," he said. "It was like going to the DMV."

A second trip to district headquarters yielded an opening at Jefferson, but only for Jacob. The Hernandezes decided to take it. On their son's first day of third grade, he was greeted outside the school by Principal Aquino and the staff at Jefferson, who rolled out a hundred yards of bright red paper on the sidewalk, then barraged the line of sheepish kids with enthusiastic greetings as they filed past. It was enough to convince Alberto and Cristina to start calling the school's assistant principal, asking if Marisol couldn't be transferred too. A month into the 2018–19 school year, the whole family was settled into Jefferson. Jacob began returning home each day with a bag full of library books, plus a stash of pencils, necklaces, erasers, and drawings that he'd collected.

"Anything is a treasure for him," Alberto said.

Most exciting of all, though, was Project Lead the Way. One afternoon a week, Jacob and the rest of Jefferson's third graders would walk across the school's courtyard to the STEAM Lab, where they got to sit on a big over-stuffed black sofa and play with electronics kits called Makey Makeys that let you turn bananas into pianos and Play-Doh into video game controllers. The space was run by Mary Grace Santiago, a native of the Philippines who'd come to the district a decade earlier. She would soon be named one of Project Lead the Way's National Teachers of the Year. One of the first challenges she'd given to Jefferson's third graders involved designing and building a compound machine that could rescue a toy tiger trapped in a zoo. When Santiago turned the students loose, Jacob immediately began peppering his team with questions, pulling ideas from the other children's minds like brightly colored scarves from a magician's sleeve. Then, when things started to get a little crazy, the self-possessed nine-year-old calmly redirected the group's energy, encouraging everyone to sketch out their plans on large sheets of butcher paper.

Oh my God, Santiago thought. *This child has serious leadership potential.* At pickup the next day, she cornered Alberto and Cristina near the chain-link fence.

"Okay," she said. "Your kid and his sister, I really encourage them to participate in science pentathlon, in robotics, any activities." She also suggested that Jacob be tested for Jefferson's gifted and talented program.

Thank you, thank you so much, that's very kind, the Hernandezes responded politely. We will think about it.

Undeterred, Santiago kept after them. And in the spring of 2019, she tapped Jacob to help prepare the school's presentation for Compton Unified's third annual STEAMfest, a massive citywide science fair on steroids.

The event featured an extraordinary range of student-led projects, from solar ovens to holographic Millennium Falcons. As part of one challenge about decoding trauma and fostering community healing, students from Dominguez High designed mobile apps that could detect signs of anxiety and respond by offering meditation exercises or chats with crisis counselors. The team from Bunche Middle built a full-scale replica of an interstellar shuttle's command center. One boy crafted his own cardboard soda fountain, handing out cups of Coke and Orange Fanta to passersby, while another girl went the more traditional route, creating a Styrofoam solar system.

"Don't you think this is a beautiful event?" asked school board chair Micah Ali, decked out in a blue paisley shirt with matching pocket square.

"Yes?" the girl managed meekly.

"And she knows that it is, because she has an opportunity to look at some experiments, do some cross-collaboration, learn from industry leaders in the area of technology," Ali responded, talking now to everyone and no one and flashing a peace sign as he walked away.

Jefferson's booth was focused on space exploration. Jacob helped produce the hype video. Inside the STEAM Lab, he and three classmates had written a script, then used iPads to film each other against a green-screen wall.

"Helllloooooo," said a sweet girl in a pink onesie who opened the video. "Anybody out there?"

Jacob appeared in a long white lab coat with a popped collar.

"Yes! I am Dr. Academics!" he said. "Is there anything I can do for you?"

"I heard you and your brothers are participating in STEAMfest?" the girl responded.

"Yes! We are!" Jacob exclaimed. "Our booth will be innovative"—he circled his arms like an air-traffic controller—"and unique."

Alberto and Cristina laughed with joy when they saw what their son produced. Compton still didn't feel quite like home. But getting their children into Jefferson appeared to have been a winning play.

"At least now he's using maybe six of his cylinders," Alberto said.

PART III

THINGS FALL APART

"GOD'S HONEST TRUTH"

THE SMITH FAMILY | PENN HILLS, PENNSYLVANIA

> I don't think history is the past. If it were the past, it
> would not matter.
>
> —JAMES BALDWIN,
> *A Rap on Race*, 1970

The golden era of my own suburban childhood came during the mid-1980s. Back then, Dible Elementary was a sea of Starter jackets, Sebago Docksiders, and Iron Maiden back patches. With my obscure sports T-shirts and last year's Nikes, I had no natural clan. So my father did his best to bridge the distance already separating us, offering me a lifeline I'd cling to for years: Even if money is tight, my dad told me, he would always find me things to read. It was an offer I embraced enthusiastically, spending my days with the Hardy Boys and Encyclopedia Brown; with all my favorite athletes, whose biographies I consumed in an endless buffet; and with the columnists of *Sports Illustrated* and *The Pittsburgh Press*, back issues of which were by then accumulating in geologic strata around the sagging blue couch in our small living room.

Fortunately, my teachers also tended to my loneliness and nurtured my love of words. In second grade, for example, I was identified as a candidate for Dible's gifted program. But our family's beagle was run over by a car just before I was to be tested. Upon seeing my puffy eyes and hollow expression the morning of the exam, Ms. Dristas sprang into action, moving to have the test rescheduled so I wouldn't be at any disadvantage.

And it was the following year that Ms. Bauman brought in that type-writer for me to use, a gift that remains among the most extraordinary I've ever received. With the launch of my class newspaper, which I dubbed "Up to Date with Room 38," I suddenly had a reason to talk to the girl I was smitten with, interviewing her with Terry Gross–level attention about her burgeoning gymnastics career and the intricacies of the back walkover. Flush with my newfound power, I even sponsored a series of reader contests and began running weekly opinion polls, determining with scientific precision that Hulk Hogan was in fact the most popular athlete in room 38.

The benefits of such experiences accrued like interest. By fifth grade, I was being invited to special events like Authors Day, which pulled together promising writers from all the elementary schools then scattered around Penn Hills. I can't remember much about the actual writing workshops. But I did learn an important lesson. Lunch was outside. I sat by myself on the jungle gym. Lost in my little fantasies, I missed the call to head back inside. When I eventually looked up, I saw the playground was empty except for a forgotten purse left lying in the grass. With all the nonchalance I could muster, I walked over, picked the purse up, took out all the money, and stuffed the bills deep into my pocket. Even in the moment, I knew what I was doing was wrong. But a voice in my head convinced me it wasn't really stealing. *The money is just lying there*, it said. *You'd be crazy not to take it.*

What I didn't realize was that a recess aide witnessed my larceny. Sweat pooled on my skinny arms as a group of adults pulled me out of the afternoon writing session. Before I could make a full confession, however, something astonishing happened. The adults determined I shouldn't miss out on any of the remaining Authors Day activities, let alone face suspension or any other sanction that might mar my permanent record. You have a bright future, they told me. Don't screw it up. Then they told me discipline would be handled by my parents and ushered me back to the writing workshop.

At the time, the reprieve felt like a miracle, and my relief at my good fortune easily trumped the hollow feeling in my chest letting me know my pardon had been unearned. Before long, however, the whole thing started to just feel normal. Consequences and constant policing were for someone else; forgiveness and future opportunities were for me. By sixth grade, I was being tapped to help write a heartwarming front-page feature for my school's new newspaper, *The Dible Scoop*. By high school, I was getting showered with praise for my writing scores, which led to a spot on the Quiz Bowl team and the chance to take classes at a local university. And by graduation, I was being celebrated as one of the twenty-four covaledictorians of my class. All of us were white. Looking back, it's not hard to see how I bought into the third illusion upon which American suburbia is built; it was far easier to do nothing and accept the narrative that I'd earned such recognition solely by virtue of my own talent and hard work than it would've been to wade through the guilt, anxiety, and moral compromise lurking in the hollows inside me.

But reality couldn't be ignored forever. Less than a year after I left for college, the Penn Hills School District began showing signs of strain similar to those that had presaged the township's sewer system fiasco. In August 1995, the school board mulled a report from the district's architect. Dible and Shenandoah Elementary schools both needed new roofs. Linton Junior High needed new boilers. The high school needed to be rewired. All told, it was estimated that $10 million was necessary to renovate and repair the district's aging buildings. But such numbers didn't sit well with many Penn Hills taxpayers, especially the growing contingent of white seniors who increasingly valued property-tax relief over fresh rounds of public investment.

The truth was that my family had been part of the last generation of Penn Hills residents to receive the full fruits of suburbia's bounty. Opportunity had just been lying there on Princeton Drive, and my parents had taken it, because they would have been crazy not to. But many of the benefits we'd received were paid for by pushing the costs of maintaining the town's infrastructure off onto future generations. As a result, we had little frame of reference for understanding the changes that swept through the township when those bills started coming due. During the 1990s, for example, even as Penn Hills added more than 3,400 new Black residents, stalwart local institutions like the Penn Aqua Swim Club and Longvue Country Club began bleeding members, leading to tens of thousands of dollars in delinquent tax payments. Caught in a tightening vise, local leaders responded by doing what they'd always done. For five straight years, the Penn Hills school board voted to keep taxes flat. Only toward the end of the decade did they pass a modest bond measure, enough to only partially cover the district's capital needs.

"If we take on another major debt," board president Frank Grieco told the *Pittsburgh Post-Gazette* in September 1995, "we're going to be strapping the people."

"A GEOGRAPHIC TIME BOMB"

It was a quarter century later that I came across the work of a man named Charles Marohn. A moderate white conservative from Minnesota, he'd previously worked as a municipal engineer and planner. Then he'd reversed course, starting a nonprofit organization called Strong Towns, where he evangelized against the post–World War II suburban sprawl he'd once helped build. As we exchanged pleasantries during our first interview, Marohn's mild manner and wonky worldview were pretty much what I'd expected. Then I started telling him about Penn Hills.

"What you're describing is the development version of slash-and-burn agriculture," he interjected. "We build a place, we use up the resources, and when the returns start diminishing, we move on, leaving a geographic time bomb in our wake!"

That sounds a little extreme, I thought. *Thousands of suburban communities just like my hometown had been built after the war. They were now home to tens of millions of people. They couldn't all be sitting on ticking time bombs. Could they?*

But that was exactly the point, Marohn believed. America's postwar suburban experiment was so vast and had happened so quickly and rested on a mindset that had become so ingrained in the national psyche as "normal" that we still couldn't see it for what it was. In order to generate quick bursts of wealth and opportunity, good for maybe three or four generations, the federal government had radically distorted the housing market by offering huge subsidies for single-family suburban housing. To accommodate the explosive growth that ensued, suburb after suburb had taken on enormous long-term obligations and liabilities, in the form of roads, sewers, sidewalks, and public schools that all got built more or less overnight. But when all that infrastructure eventually needed repair, the revenue wasn't there, largely because those first generations of suburbanites had been conditioned to expect an unsustainable mix of abundant services and low taxes. The only way out was to double down, restarting the cycle over somewhere new and hoping not to be the one who got left behind when the music stopped.

There's a term for that kind of financial arrangement, Marohn said. It's called a Ponzi scheme. And in the case of mass suburbanization, it entails trading rapid short-term growth for massive intergenerational liabilities and a long-term loss of resilience and stability.

"The American pattern of development does not create real wealth. It creates the illusion of wealth," Marohn wrote in 2011. "We are in the process of seeing that illusion destroyed."

There are some American suburbs, of course, that live mostly outside this pattern. A few have been lucky enough to receive sustained reinvestment. Others are older and have a history of slower development, allowing for more gradual repair and renewal. Some experts also subscribe to a theory that Ohio State city and regional planning professor Bernadette Hanlon described to me as "the political and social stratification model," which holds that some suburbs are able to maintain their status and wealth across generations by retaining their racial and economic exclusivity, thus keeping home values artificially inflated. All three notions apply to Evanston.

But even those communities are now struggling to show they can deliver opportunity and a shared American dream to everyone, highlighting just how steep the challenge ahead will be. And in the meantime, outside Dallas, Atlanta, Pittsburgh, Los Angeles, and scores of other cities whose peripheries

were built out during the era of mass suburbanization, the Ponzi-scheme
pattern of development that Marohn describes has now had several decades
to gather its destructive momentum. To illustrate the havoc that awaits, Marohn points to Ferguson, Missouri, a fading inner-ring suburb just outside
St. Louis. During its heyday in the 1960s and '70s, the town was 99 percent
white. Back then, local leaders borrowed huge sums of money and accepted
massive state and federal subsidies in order to quickly build the infrastructure those residents demanded. Then, to keep taxes low, they put off budget-
ing for long-term maintenance. By 2013, however, the consequences of those
decisions were no longer avoidable. That year, Marohn said, Ferguson spent
$800,000 to pay down the interest on its debt, leaving just $25,000 for a basic
service like sidewalk improvement.

Race has never been central to Marohn's analysis, which focuses on the
economic dimensions of suburban decline. But it's impossible to ignore the
fact that Ferguson's population had since transitioned to two-thirds Black.
And sure enough, it was those residents who bore the brunt of the ensuing
crash. On the morning of August 9, 2014, eighteen-year-old Michael Brown,
Jr., and a friend, both Black, were strolling down the middle of Canfield
Drive, forgoing a sidewalk so narrow they would have had to walk single
file. Brown had just taken a box of cigarillos from a nearby convenience
store. Someone called 911. A Ferguson police officer stopped the two young
men in the street. An officer yelled at them to get on the sidewalk. Brown
and his friend refused. The ensuing confrontation ended with a white officer shooting Brown at least six times, then leaving his dead body in the
street for roughly four hours.

In the days that followed, Ferguson became the site of mass protests
against police violence, helping bring the Black Lives Matter movement to
national prominence. For a moment, a harsh spotlight fell on the forces that
had been quietly ravaging older suburbs for decades. Media outlets all over
the country reported with disbelief that more than 20 percent of Ferguson's
operating revenue came from fees, fines, and court summons costs aggressively collected from the town's mostly Black residents, often for minor infractions like not wearing a seat belt. Instead of lavishing families with

heavily subsidized opportunities, Ferguson had turned predatory, treating its residents first as vulnerable targets from whom desperately needed revenue could be extracted, then as dangerous threats if they resisted. It was a recipe for unrest and dislocation, Marohn argued. And all the ingredients were present in hundreds of other suburban communities across the country.

"I think we are going to see rioting in a lot of places as this stuff unwinds," he wrote three weeks after Ferguson police killed Brown. "How we respond to this is the social challenge of this generation."

His argument initially struck me as hyperbole. Then I realized that at precisely the same time Ferguson exploded, the decades' worth of duct tape the school district in my suburban hometown had been using to hide its massive structural problems suddenly gave way.

LIGHTING THE FUSE

The immediate chain of events that brought the Penn Hills School District's deep-seated problems to light started in summer 2014, when the school board there hired a pleasant white woman named Nancy Hines as its assistant superintendent. She was in her midforties, with short black hair that spiked up in the back. She'd first started working for the district as a teacher in the mid-1990s. Like everything else in Penn Hills, science classes were heavily tracked. Kids designated "promising," most of whom were white, took academic or Advanced Placement biology. The kids who weren't, mostly Black, took a less-rigorous version of the class with Hines. At the beginning of each year, she recalled, some of those students would tell her to just give them the D now. But she'd push and cajole, and in return, her students would insist on giving her free French fries and extra cheeseburgers when she hit the drive-thru of the McDonald's on Frankstown Road, where many of them worked evenings and weekends.

"It was a charming experience," Hines said.

Now, after working in two other school systems, she was excited to be back. The district had just built two new school buildings, a seemingly hopeful sign for the future. Hines also saw a clear path up the career ladder. Her boss announced he was leaving that November. Two months later, she was named acting superintendent.

Hines told me she was still settling into her new office chair when the Penn Hills school board asked her to call the Pennsylvania Department of Education to check out a rumor. When she finally got hold of someone, they told her to check the district's annual audit, which hadn't yet been made public. What Hines saw was so alarming she thought she must be reading the document wrong. Before accepting the assistant superintendency, Hines said, the board had told her that Penn Hills' fund balance (essentially, its emergency savings) totaled about $200,000, quite low for an organization with a $78 million annual operating budget. *I can build on this*, Hines thought. Now, though, she saw that the balance was in fact almost $9 million in the red, a number so bad she figured it must be linked to some deeper problem.

"I think of it like there was a piece of dirt on the ceiling tile, and it just didn't look right to me," Hines said in an interview several years later. "So I got up and scratched it with my fingernail, and the whole ceiling collapsed."

For years, it turned out, a recurring accounting error had obscured the dwindling fund balance. But now that someone was finally looking, it didn't take long to uncover deeper problems. The district's business manager had allegedly failed to make millions of dollars in annual debt-service payments. Then it came out that he'd also allegedly approved the use of district credit cards for a host of questionable purposes, including a residential hot-water heater, all while undercharging his daughter's youth soccer team by nearly $19,000 to rent Penn Hills athletic fields. And such apparent malfeasance, it turned out, was merely a symptom. For decades, district officials had been ignoring an increasingly toxic stew of declining enrollment, crumbling infrastructure, unfunded liabilities, and spiraling debt. In the early 2000s, the mess had started to metastasize. While the district was patching its deteriorating buildings, new charter schools began drawing families away, leading enrollment to plummet from more than six thousand students at the turn of the century to fewer than four thousand students when Hines took over. As a result, the district lost millions in per-pupil funding from the state, which should have triggered corresponding budget cuts. But the school board remained loath to lay off staff, consolidate buildings, or raise taxes on residents already unhappy with their sky-high sewage bills. By 2005, the district was running a $3.5 million operating deficit. The following year, that figure jumped to $7.5 million.

Finally spurred to action, the board only managed to make things worse. First, they attempted to paper over the shortfalls by approving a series of small municipal bonds. Then, they commissioned a series of studies of the district's finances and facilities, all of which recommended closing one or two of the district's most outdated elementary schools, renovating the buildings that remained, and either upgrading the 218,000-square-foot high school or replacing it with a smaller building. But in a move that was reminiscent of how the township had disregarded the recommendations of the Pittsburgh Regional Planning Association back in 1957, the school board ignored the advice it had sought out, pivoting instead to a disastrous plan to build two huge new school buildings from scratch.

In June 2008, the district issued a request for proposals for architectural services and construction management. Almost immediately, then school board president Erin Vecchio, a brash Irish American woman who favored heavy eyeliner and big costume jewelry, said she was contacted by Pennsylvania Turnpike Commissioner Joe Brimmeier, who would later plead guilty to felony conflict of interest charges over an unrelated pay-to-play scheme. At the time, Vecchio alleged, Brimmeier began talking up his sister Jan, who was the principal of a firm called Architectural Innovations.

"So Joe calls me up 'cause he finds out that the schools are being built," Vecchio told me in an interview. "He said, 'Hey, if you get my sister this contract, I can give jobs to Penn Hills.'"

Despite the alleged interference, Vecchio and the board voted in August 2008 to hire Architectural Innovations to assess the feasibility of building two new schools. The firm's plans were suspect from the jump. Despite Penn Hills' declining enrollment, AI said it wanted to make the new high school *bigger* than the building it would replace. The firm also claimed that consolidating the township's elementary schools into a single building would save the district upward of $8 million a year, a wildly optimistic figure that was twice what the district's own business manager projected. But the board embraced the magical thinking. Between new bonds, federal stimulus support, and state reimbursements, several members maintained the district could build both brand-new buildings, at a total cost of more than $130 million, without raising taxes or putting any of its own money down. They also insisted the new buildings would generate more than enough savings to cover the financing costs associated with the new debt. And as an added bonus, the board vowed, the plan would attract hundreds of new families and help the district lure back scores of others who'd already fled the Penn Hills public schools.

Based on that suspect logic, the board voted in February 2009 to approve a contract for AI to design the new high school. At the time, the firm called for the building to cover 239,400 square feet, 10 percent bigger than the old high school. But that turned out to just be an opening bid. Two months later, Architectural Innovations was saying the new school would now be 16 percent larger than the old building. Unfazed, the Penn Hills school board awarded the firm a contract for the $75 million construction project. Then it voted the following month to award AI a second contract, to design and develop the elementary school as well.

That October, the district closed on nearly $135 million in new bond debt to pay for the two new schools. The construction manager on the project, a company called Turner Construction, was already warning that the elementary school was $5 million over budget and that Architectural Innovations' proposed footprint for the new high school was still mysteriously growing. The board, however, didn't seem to care. At a public meeting in March 2010, AI proposed yet another expansion of the new high school, to 27 percent larger than the old building. No one at the meeting raised any objections. The board endorsed the plan.

In early 2011, Penn Hills officials realized the district's enrollment was going to plunge by three hundred or so students for the fifth consecutive year. Undeterred, Architectural Innovations announced that it was *again* expanding the new high school, to 303,000 square feet, or 39 percent larger than the old building. By then, it was apparent what was going on. The district had made the bewildering decision to tie the fee it paid Architectural Innovations to the total cost of construction for the two new schools, incentivizing the firm to continually make both projects more expensive. Then, when AI did just that, the board declined to crack down, instead greenlighting an extraordinary range of flourishes. At the new high school, for example, the firm proposed chandeliers, skylights, spiral staircases, curved hallways, two-story floor-to-ceiling glass windows, and a $1 million exterior canopy. At the new elementary school, they suggested the foyer be decorated with special tile imported from Italy. The board approved it all. Then, when they finally did ask Architectural Innovations to rein in the overruns, the firm responded by first removing from its list of deliverables $14.3 million worth of furniture, equipment, and fixtures, then by insisting its contract didn't cover new athletic fields—all of which the district would still have to pay someone else to provide.

In the spring of 2012, Turner Construction said another $17 million would be needed to finish the job. The Penn Hills school board responded by firing Turner, keeping AI, and approving $27 million in new bond debt. By 2014, the district's operating deficit had ballooned back up to $6.5 million. But instead of raising taxes or furloughing staff, the board hired several of their own friends and family members. One board member even got the district to add an entirely new bus route to accommodate a single child— one of her relatives.

By the time Nancy Hines saw that troublesome audit and began scratching at the metaphorical spot on the ceiling, it was far too late. In April 2015, she learned the district might not be able to make payroll. Its negative $9 million fund balance meant there were no emergency funds to cover the crisis. Forced to take out an emergency $12 million loan and approve $20 million more in bond debt, the Penn Hills school system went into financial free fall. Moody's downgraded the district's bond rating to junk status, signaling it was no longer a safe investment.

The problems now out in the open, Pennsylvania auditor general Eugene DePasquale launched a forensic audit. In May 2016, he announced that the Penn Hills School District's long-term debt burden, just $11 million in 2009, had grown to a whopping $167 million. Saying the district was "nearly broke" and that "everyone seems to have turned a blind eye as the district marched toward financial disaster," DePasquale referred the matter to the Allegheny County District Attorney's office, the U.S. Attorney's office, the Pennsylvania Department of Revenue, and the state ethics commission for investigations.

When we spoke a few years later, Hines tried to describe life in the Penn Hills School District during the months that followed. The board finally began cutting, laying off nonprofessional staff and sending out furlough notices to dozens of teachers. Convinced they were next, demoralized staff members began burning sick days. The resulting disarray left hundreds of students to spend long stretches in classrooms with unfamiliar teachers, substitutes, or no adults at all. On cue, the exodus of families out of the district intensified. Hines told me she would show up for work in the morning and immediately start scrambling to put out the day's fires, only to be interrupted by badge-wearing, gun-toting investigators who wheeled entire file cabinets out of the office, saying they might contain evidence.

"I mean, you just recover, [because] your ten o'clock appointment is here," she said.

Vecchio, meanwhile, continued lobbing alarming accusations around town. The school construction projects had been a vehicle for bribes and payoffs from the outset, the former school board president alleged, without providing hard evidence.

"The kickbacks that went on this school district were sickening," she told me in an interview, describing envelopes of cash being exchanged over the toilets of local restaurants. "I know what was happening, 'cause I witnessed it."

But after two and a half years of digging, the grand jury impaneled by the county DA's office declined to bring any criminal charges. Vecchio attributed this outcome (again, without hard evidence) to serious conflicts of interest and suggested I look into possible Mafia connections. She also began casting blame at the state education department for not stepping in. But it all amounted to tilting at windmills. In its final report, released in February 2019, the grand jury said the Penn Hills School District's long-term debt burden was now pushing $172 million. The system was just months away from another $6 million shortfall. Absent outside help, it would collapse. The state auditor general called a public forum to discuss the crisis. More than two hundred furious Penn Hills residents showed up.

"I need to put this out there," DePasquale began. "Penn Hills School District is in the worst financial shape of any school district I've seen."

Things went downhill from there.

"I will never be able to sell my house," an older white woman railed. "Stuff is going to start to look very bad in this community."

It already does, came a chorus of replies.

Some speakers urged the district to declare bankruptcy. Others proposed it merge with a neighboring school system. But most were focused on their property values. I've already sold my home in Penn Hills, an older white man said, and so should the rest of you. His suggestion was met with a bitter blow-by-blow from a white woman who said she'd recently attempted to do just that, but after her neighbors were raided by the Drug Enforcement Agency, it took fifty showings and a steep reduction in her asking price to find a buyer.

"Tell me, what is enticing people to move into Penn Hills?" the woman asked. "Is it the high tax bills? Is it the vacant homes? Is it the closed businesses?"

That same month, the Pennsylvania Department of Education appointed a veteran school administrator named Dan Matsook as the Penn Hills School District's new chief recovery officer, then charged him with overseeing the system's finances. By that point, the district had already furloughed roughly fifty teachers and eliminated dozens of other positions, from crossing guards to an assistant superintendent. Academics were suffering accordingly. At the high school, just 17 percent of Black students now passed the state biology exam.

Regardless, Matsook said, the district had to cut deeper. The district's annual debt-service payments were up to more than $12 million a year, with another spike looming. If the district stood pat, its operating deficit would explode, and its fund balance would nose-dive to an unimaginable negative $60 million. In response, the chief recovery officer proposed eliminating more than two dozen additional teachers. He also wanted to ax two school counselors, a social worker, a behavioral specialist, up to ten plant-services workers, and many of the district's paraprofessionals. Penn Hills would have to eliminate its pre-kindergarten program and abandon its Junior ROTC program, Matsook said. The athletics budget would also have to be slashed by up to 20 percent. So would school supply budgets. And even after all that, the district would still need a $3.3 million emergency loan from the state.

The first time I read through the litany of woe, I struggled to grasp the magnitude of the mess. It took a series of conversations with Vecchio, who returned to the school board as president in 2019, to help me assemble the broken pieces of my suburban hometown into a coherent picture.

"You know, I have such great feelings because of the fact that my kids did get a great education from Penn Hills," she began. "The three of them are doing great."

That part sounded very much like my own white family's story.

But "they don't care about Penn Hills anymore," the school board president continued, waving a hand to indicate all the politicians and state education officials who refused to bail the district out, and all the people who'd left the township behind but were now happy to point fingers from afar, myself presumably included.

Then Vecchio disputed my contention that the school district she now helped oversee was predominantly Black. Part of the problem, she said, was that some children now in the local public schools didn't have a legal right to be enrolled. Then she referenced the PAT bus line that ran out Frankstown Road past Lincoln Park and the predominantly Black neighborhoods of Homewood and Wilkinsburg on its way to downtown Pittsburgh.

"These kids are being bused in from different areas, you know, and we're paying for most of them," she said, tapping into the long history of local leaders treating the Black parts of Penn Hills as somehow separate from the rest of the township. "They have addresses that say they live in Penn Hills, but they actually don't. But every time we tried to take them to court to prove it, [the magistrate and judges] don't do anything."

Then Vecchio told me the most depressing thing of all. It was about the two new school buildings that were supposed to save Penn Hills. Both already needed millions of dollars in repairs.

"The boilers at the elementary and the high school are falling to shit. They put in windows you can't open. The roof is leaking. The air conditioner went in the first year. The brickwork's all falling apart," the school board president said. "If you want to know the God's honest truth, there's so many things in these schools that are falling apart, it's unbelievable."

STRANGERS NO MORE

It was January 2020 when I went back to Princeton Drive to confront the mess my family had left in our old backyard, then knocked unannounced on Bethany Smith's door. We had never met or spoken. She greeted me in a black-and-red sweater and wore braids in her hair. I introduced myself as a journalist working on a story about the Penn Hills public schools. Then I said I'd grown up in the house three doors down. At that, Bethany smiled wide and invited me in, apologizing for nonexistent clutter as I took off my shoes.

When I stepped into the small living room, my attention began skipping between my past and Bethany's present. Her small ranch house had the exact same floor plan as my childhood home and was uncannily familiar; three or four big steps to my right was the same impossibly small kitchen that had frustrated my mother for decades. But everything about the house was also strangely unfamiliar; instead of sagging blue fabric, Bethany's furniture was red and made of leather. The sound of a television emanated from what would've been my old bedroom, occupied here by her mother, who didn't come out to say hello. I was still trying to orient myself when Jackson vanished down the narrow hallway, then reappeared with a Nerf football that he kept throwing to himself, flooding me with memories of my brothers and me trying to score a touchdown by running through each other and diving onto the couch.

Bethany gestured for me to take a seat, then started looking over her son's second-grade homework as we began to talk. Although I was a stranger, she seemed preternaturally comfortable as she told me about her job as an aide at a center for adults with developmental disabilities, then about how a large snake had gotten stuck in one of the window screens shortly after she'd moved in. And almost immediately, Bethany began confounding my core assumptions about Penn Hills, telling me that she hadn't viewed relocating to the township as a step up, but as a pragmatic alternative to paying the skyrocketing rents in Pittsburgh's East End. Still blinded by my own history and expectations, I started throwing out follow-ups, quickly running into a wall I hadn't noticed.

"What did you see when you were there?" I asked Bethany of her time back in the city.

"I would say the people that lived in that area was changing," she said, choosing her words carefully.

"How so?" I pressed on.

"Ummm," Bethany began, now laughing nervously. "There's not really a way for me to say this."

"So it was gentrifying?" I guessed.

"Yes," Bethany replied, laughing a little more.

"So the white hipsters were moving in?"

"Yes," she said, putting her face in her hands.

"It was historically a Black neighborhood, but that was changing, and that was what was driving the prices up?"

Bethany peeked back over the wall.

"I believe so," she said. "Like with East Liberty. They call it East End now."

Her gentle chiding of my out-of-towner's choice of words briefly reminded me that I was now the interloper. But I ignored the feeling, plowing ahead as Bethany's mom turned up the volume on the television in the back room. "What was your reaction to these neighborhoods you knew so well suddenly flipping like that?" I asked. Bethany picked at one of her braids as she considered the question.

"I really didn't have a reaction," she finally replied. "I was going to school. I was working. I was a single mother. I was really involved in just getting through the day."

I'd assumed Bethany would see the unfolding disaster in Penn Hills the same way I did. Instead, she seemed to want exactly what my parents had wanted: a place where everything just worked. As we kept talking, I let my attention wander over the living-room walls, where tasteful reproductions of paintings by African American artists hung in spots we had left bare. The older white ladies across the street had invited Jackson over to play with their dog, I heard Bethany saying. Another neighbor had given him a set of encyclopedias. Penn Hills seemed like a pretty good community, she said. Sometimes, she'd just sit on the finished deck that ran along the rear of her house, feeling the sun on her skin and enjoying the sounds of birds singing in the woods below. I spoiled the moment by asking about Jackson's experience at school.

He'd been diagnosed ADHD and ODD just a few months before, Bethany told me. Things had fallen apart at the Black-run charter school shortly after.

"I felt like they gave up on him," she said, wiping her eyes. "It got to the point where I was second-guessing who my child was."

This was why she didn't like to talk about such things, Bethany told me. She wasn't some kind of activist. She just wanted her and her son to finally have the opportunity to *chill*. But the situation at the charter school had brought an old anxiety back. Eventually, Bethany had just gone ahead and enrolled Jackson at Penn Hills Elementary.

On his first day, she told me, she got a tour of the building. It felt cavernous and maybe a bit tacky. But everything still looked new. A recent round of furloughs had boosted class sizes to twenty-six or twenty-seven kids per room. But that didn't seem so bad. Bethany said she'd been worried the school would be scared off by her son's conditions. But the vice principal seemed to take the news in stride, saying a behavioral specialist was still on staff.

The real test, Bethany said, came when Jackson threw his first tantrum in his new classroom. Seeing the school's number pop up on her phone made her heart palpitate. But Jackson's teacher, a white woman named Ms. Levin who had been in the classroom for more than two decades, had been friendly and kind. After a moment of small talk, she calmly asked how Bethany dealt with her son's outbursts at home.

"I'd never been asked that before," Bethany told me in a soft voice. "It made me feel like, wow, we're in this together."

Once again, her words made me wonder if I was trying to force Penn Hills to be one thing, when it was really another. But before I could pursue the feeling, Jackson began shadow-boxing with the lamp and shooting imaginary free throws onto the coffee table, causing my heart to fill with a curious mix of affection, nostalgia, and dread. The golden era of his suburban childhood was just beginning. He deserved every opportunity, second chance, and invisible guardrail that Penn Hills had already given thousands of other kids, including me. Bethany seemed determined to believe that would happen. I wanted to think the same. But everything I knew about my hometown and its public schools suggested otherwise. I slipped in one more question as I slid on my shoes.

"Part of why I'm interested in Penn Hills is because of all the budget troubles in the school district," I said. "How worried about that stuff are you?"

Bethany paused again before responding.

"What I read," she said, "was they're not going to cut any of the programs at the school. They're just going to raise our taxes."

8

THE SUN'S HIGHEST POINT

THE BECKER FAMILY | LUCAS, TEXAS

> They just love what they have and they love the
> ability to do what they want.
>
> —Lucas mayor Jim Olk, 2019

The inky predawn sky over Lucas was still speckled with stars, the result of local ordinances that limited the use of lights in order to make the heavens a little more accessible here than everywhere else. It was October 2019. In an hour, Friday morning traffic would choke the intersection of Country Club and Stacy roads, leaving restless parents to inch SUV by SUV toward school drop-offs. For the moment, however, only the occasional pickup zipped by, leaving the yellow backhoes parked along the shoulder to finish their slumber undisturbed.

Because Lucas's zoning code also discouraged sidewalks, the Beckers' close-trimmed front lawn ran like a fairway from the rough of the street to their house's brick entryway, interrupted only by the culverts that took the place of storm sewers, which were also verboten. The three-car garage was tucked behind a stone privacy wall, against which a child's bike leaned carelessly. Nearby was a red lawn sign with the logo of the Foundation for Lovejoy Schools and "2019 DONOR" spelled out in big black letters.

Inside, Jim entered the kitchen shortly after 6:00 a.m. He wore cargo shorts, a Texas A&M T-shirt, and a Titleist cap. He'd gotten in late the night before from Orlando, where he was now serving as the acting chief financial officer of a restaurant chain hoping to avoid bankruptcy. He put on a pot of coffee and puttered around amiably, telling me how the new house in Lucas offered the thing he prized most.

"I like being able to step out in the yard and no one comes to talk to me," he said.

Susan emerged from the laundry room. It held two washers and two dryers. One of each was already running. So was the aromatherapy diffuser she'd set up on the long granite island in the kitchen. After rummaging through her sizable collection of vitamins and supplements, Susan created customized piles and put them in shot glasses at the spots where Jim and each of the kids liked to eat. Having recently landed on a regimen that seemed to limit the number of colds Jim caught while traveling, she was now working on a combination that might relieve the attention issues still keeping her daughter out of sync with the rhythms of the new school year.

"It's hard to get her up in the morning, and it's hard to get her to settle down at night," Susan sighed as she slid egg casserole leftovers into the oven.

On cue, Avery emerged from the back staircase. In her arms, she carried Astro, the family's fluffy white Coton de Tulear. She ignored the shot glass on her place mat, just as he ignored the anti-anxiety medication Susan had placed in his bowl. Instead, the happy pair lay down on the floor, where Astro could more easily lick Avery's face.

Noah came sliding down the main banister next. His shorts were on backward. He was still several inches shorter than his sister, so Susan had recently started him on growth hormones. She handed him a paper plate with eggs and blueberries.

"I wish these athletes would stay out of politics," said Jim, who was scrolling through alerts on his phone. Fox News host Tucker Carlson had recently made headlines by blasting NBA star LeBron James for his feeble response to communist China's crackdown on pro-democracy protesters.

"Don't tweet, just play sports," Susan concurred.

She had hoped the move to Lucas would put more distance between her family and such controversies. But the world and its problems were voracious. For weeks, Susan had tried to shield her children from the wall-to-wall news coverage of Amber Guyger, a white Dallas police officer who had come home to her apartment building after work, walked into the wrong unit, and shot and killed a Black man named Botham Jean as he sat on his couch eating ice cream. But then, at the sentencing hearing, something that Susan found remarkable had happened. Eighteen-year-old Brandt Jean had publicly forgiven his brother's killer. Then he'd asked the judge if he could give the tearful blond woman a hug. When the resulting video clip went viral, Susan rounded up the kids to watch. The country was increasingly fraught for people like them, she believed. Especially the boys, who would spend their lives walking on eggshells to avoid being labeled racist. Susan wanted them to know that even if they screwed up, they could still find forgiveness and grace.

"That's what's so lacking in our society right now," she said. "None of us are perfect."

Avery scooted back upstairs to brush her teeth, and Noah ran outside to play with Astro. Jim waded into the walk-in pantry in search of bagels. Susan opened a GPS-powered app that allowed her to monitor the progress of Lovejoy's school buses on her phone. Though Hart Elementary was only five hundred yards away, Noah couldn't walk to school on his own. All the roads in and out lacked sidewalks, and the campus was surrounded by a chain-link fence.

"Y'all need to get back here, it's almost at Harris," Susan called out when the dot on her phone was two blocks away. Then she hustled the kids out the door and followed them to the corner.

"Such a mom," Jim said.

Sean descended the stairs, barely making a ripple in the sudden quiet. Jim filled him in on the previous night's American League Championship Series game. Houston had won on the strength of a sixth-inning home run. Sean cursed his early bedtime and began searching for highlights on his phone. Jim finished making his son's lunch, then fumbled with the remote that controlled the blinds in the kitchen windows.

"Here, let me do that," Susan said as she swooped back into the kitchen. A few buttons, and sunlight came streaming in over the back lawn, now being watered by automatic sprinklers. Like all homeowners in Lucas, the Beckers were required to maintain their own septic system. It was supposed to feed treated water into the outdoor sprinklers. Back in August, though, the system had malfunctioned, apparently leading the sprinklers to spray untreated sewage all over the backyard. Susan reached for the planner where she kept her running to-do list. Scheduling a maintenance visit went near the bottom. All the highest-priority items were still related to the Beckers' ongoing effort to sell the old house back in Plano, which had been sitting empty for more than three months because many upwardly mobile young families around Dallas now tended to skip over such older communities altogether.

"What we're competing with is the new construction further out in Frisco and Prosper," Susan told me.

It was the kind of dilemma that made her anxiety spike. Fortunately, she now had a safety net of her own. In a couple of hours, she and Jim were heading over to Sloan Creek Intermediate for a parent coffee. Then they'd pick up tickets for the night's homecoming festivities. Before the game, they were having dinner with a few other families who were new to the Lovejoy Independent School District. Such routines reassured Susan, kept her grounded. And everyone involved with the district seemed to reinforce the feeling. Especially superintendent Michael Goddard.

"He's like the Energizer Bunny," Susan said. "He's everywhere."

THE PRICE OF SEPARATION

Lovejoy's previous superintendent had been forced out after a scandal involving inappropriate relationships with adult staffers. Goddard was hired a few months later. His first priority had been to neutralize the lingering odor of his predecessor's mess, a task that his deep connections to Lovejoy aided greatly. Goddard had grown up in the area, then gone on to become a star quarterback at neighboring Allen High. Two decades later, he'd come back home to serve as the very first principal of Lovejoy High. Even now, he was barrel-chested and charming, with a pale complexion still ruddy from the summer Texas sun, all of which helped put local parents at ease just as surely as his comfort reciting Scripture.

"I'm not even fifty yet, but I'm seen as an original and an old-timer," the superintendent told me as we sat down for an interview.

A firm believer in the power of branding, Goddard had already moved to make his own smiling mug the district's new calling card. In addition to posting an endless stream of selfies on social media, he'd recently agreed to sponsor a local bank, posing for pictures that were used in advertisements for a new Lovejoy Leopards debit card. Long-term, Goddard knew, satisfying the locals would require more than spreading positive vibes; many families longed for a return to the small-town values that often seemed under attack, but were just as adamant about maintaining the school system's reputation for exclusivity, which kept their home values high. The two desires were often at odds. Attracting the best teachers and building new school robotics labs took money. In the suburbs, that meant continual growth and new development. But in places like Lucas, that was exactly what the local zoning code was engineered to limit. Until the new superintendent could unlock that conundrum, his people skills would remain his most potent asset.

"It's four thousand, three hundred thirty-nine kids," Goddard told me. Before long, he'd be able to tell each of them "I know your brother and your sister, I know your dog's name, I know where you live, I know your parents and your grandparents."

That's how things had been in the 1980s. The area's main commercial strip was now packed tight with a Whole Foods and Cabela's and a hundred other stores. But back then it had been nothing more than a white-gravel country highway, and Lovejoy ISD had consisted of just a single K–6 school. Because the area had neither the population nor the tax base to support a secondary program, local kids were sent to neighboring Allen for middle and high school. And because Allen High had an excellent reputation, was still 90 percent white, and remained small enough that a kid like Goddard could letter in three separate varsity sports, everyone seemed happy with the arrangement.

But then Plano started filling up, and new development began spilling beyond its borders. By 1990, Allen's population had grown by 120 percent. Alarmed, the residents of neighboring Lucas and Fairview began insisting that the two towns be kept "country." The resulting rift was subtle at first. But during the 1990s, enrollment in Allen ISD more than doubled. Black enrollment went up 168 percent. Hispanic enrollment went up 281 percent. Asian enrollment went up 488 percent. All the while, the local elementary schools back in Lovejoy ISD continued to enroll fewer than seven hundred children, all but a few dozen of whom were white, and only a handful of whom were poor. Hoping to get a handle on the intentions and priorities of the community at the time, I reached out to Rich Hickman, who had served on the Lovejoy board from 1981 until 2011.

"Well, obviously it was a pro, because you didn't have the added expense," he said of the district's racial and economic homogeneity. "It wasn't anything that we tooted our horn about. It was a given fact. There are never going to be any apartments in our school district based on the land uses of both towns."

The benefits of such exclusion, however, were diluted by having to tell prospective homebuyers their kids would eventually attend Allen High. Money also became an issue after the Texas legislature closed a loophole that had long allowed Lovejoy to circumvent a "Robin Hood" provision in the state's education funding formula meant to redistribute property-tax revenue from wealthy districts to poor districts. Tensions came to a head in the late 1990s, when the Allen school board decided that instead of having two separate high schools, it would build a massive $45 million facility that everyone would attend together. Many Lovejoy parents grew worried that their well-to-do white children might soon get lost in a tidal wave of apartment dwellers, foreign-language speakers, and drug dealers.

"When they made the decision to keep one high school, you knew what was coming," Goddard said.

Lovejoy ISD leaders had considered seceding from the Allen school

system for years. The barrier had always been money. Any push to generate
the necessary revenue would require some combination of increased residential density, new commercial development, and higher taxes. But all three
strategies were nonstarters among local residents.

In early 2001, for example, the Lucas City Council and Planning and
Zoning Commission held hearings on a modest proposal that would reduce
the minimum lot size requirements in a few undeveloped plots of land and
allow new businesses to locate in a couple of others. The rationale was simple. When the town was eventually built out, revenue would plateau. But the
cost of maintaining existing services would keep rising by about 10 percent
per year. And that was before factoring in new expenses to keep up with already planned residential growth, including a new station for the fire department. The net result was that tiny Lucas, with its annual operating
budget of about $1.5 million, was looking at potential operating deficits of
more than $300,000 annually for the next decade. Failing to take action was
"impractical," and the status quo "does not contain a plan to make money to
support city services," an expert named Lawrence Redlinger from the University of Texas at Dallas told the Lucas council. Someone asked if any other
Texas jurisdictions had remained viable while maintaining Lucas's current
mix of large residential lots and limited commercial development. Redlinger
was unable to come up with an example.

Still, the town's residents viewed the proposed zoning changes as intolerable. So visceral was their reaction that public meetings on the topic had to
be moved from Lucas's City Hall into the existing fire station, where hundreds of extra folding chairs could be set up in the bay, a move that local
officials told me they could only remember happening a couple of other
times, including when the council was considering an ordinance that would
limit how many animals families could keep on their property. Confronted
with their constituents' outrage, Lucas officials backed down, leaving the
existing zoning code intact. The town issued $5.5 million in new debt in
2002, then added $5 million more a few years later. In the meantime, Lucas
voters spent the next two election cycles ousting every single council member who had originally supported the plan.

"They just love what they have and they love the ability to do what they want," Lucas mayor Jim Olk told me with a shrug in October 2019, by which point the town's debt burden had soared to $25 million, a figure that local officials downplayed because of substantial reserves and a still-rosy bond rating.

Lucas's decision to push the costs of its suburban lifestyle off into the future echoed the ways Compton, Penn Hills, and a host of older suburbs had chosen an unsustainable path that later proved disastrous. But the zoning-code fight was just the beginning. Less than two years later, residents in the areas served by Lovejoy ISD were asked to vote on pulling their high school students out of Allen. Secession would require the district to build new facilities, which in turn meant taking on mammoth new debts of the district's own, including a $61 million bond issue in 2003 and an even larger $78.5 million bond issue just four years later. But Lovejoy residents were undeterred.

To make the plan work, the school board decided they needed a leader who could create a secondary program so outstanding it would draw in wealthy families from across the region. They chose Goddard, then gave him an entire year to plan. He began traveling the country, visiting elite schools to learn their secrets, then returning home to press the same question on the Lovejoy community again and again.

What do we want to be famous for?

The answer turned out to be an intense focus on what officials sometimes referred to as the potential gap. It wasn't enough to help the affluent children of local families pass standardized tests. Instead, Goddard and his team wanted to help every child to realize at least a full year of academic growth, every single school year, no matter their aptitude or circumstances. Already advanced? Lovejoy High would offer you more AP classes, dual-enrollment courses, and independent study opportunities. Poor grades or special needs? The school would still expect you to take a full load of college-prep courses, and staff would do everything in their power to make sure you succeeded.

For the plan to work, the district would have to attract the right families into Lovejoy while keeping the wrong families out. Hoping to gauge the feasibility of threading that needle, the Lovejoy board hired a demographic firm to run some analyses. First, they took aerial photographs of the district's 17-square-mile attendance zone, counting the number of roofs versus available lots to ascertain likely development trends. Then, the firm analyzed census data and conducted interviews with local real estate agents, landowners, and developers to predict the household incomes and education levels of future residents. In their final report, the demographers projected that Lovejoy's enrollment would grow by 8 or 9 percent a year for the next decade, enough to support a midsize high school. And just as important, they expected that the local poverty rate would remain extremely low, allowing the towns to maintain what local leaders liked to call "quality growth." Elated, Lovejoy leaders began assuring prospective homeowners that their new high school would never look anything like its gargantuan counterpart in Allen.

When Lovejoy High opened in 2006, Goddard was its principal. He liked to joke that the first lesson he learned was to change up his morning routine every few weeks; otherwise, parents would stake out his parking spot in the morning to ask why their child had received a B in math or been cut from the cheerleading squad. Really, though, the district seemed to view such commitment as validation of its lofty standards, "advanced-only" curriculum, and abundant academic supports.

"It all turned out for the most part with a lot of smiles," said Hickman, the former school board member.

That was, until you looked at the bills Lovejoy was quietly racking up, just as places like Compton and Penn Hills had done in the same stages of their own development cycles. By the time Goddard returned as superintendent in 2019, the district's long-term debt burden had reached $166 million. Financing payments were almost $14 million per year and set to soon quadruple. Even more worrisome, the number of new kindergartners in the district was expected to keep dropping, and the district's chief financial officer was anticipating a significant operating deficit. But Goddard and the board professed not to be worried, touting instead their two secret weapons. The first was the Foundation for Lovejoy Schools, which raised about $500,000 a year in unrestricted funds. The second was Lovejoy Scholars, through which the district brought in another $1 million per year by charging families outside its attendance zone up to $11,000 per year to enroll their children in Love-joy schools.

Goddard cast the latter as a way of doing well by doing good, saying it allowed the district to close its budget gap while spreading opportunity. In reality, though, Lovejoy Scholars was constrained by that same tension—between maintaining exclusivity and generating revenue via new growth—that shaped everything else around Lovejoy ISD. The district wouldn't let just any family pay tuition to attend its public schools. Instead, it employed a host of admissions criteria, many of which were highly subjective. You couldn't enroll your kids in Lovejoy if they were going to "walk in ten steps behind," Goddard told me. Or if they were "going to come in and be so disruptive that they're going to hurt the learning of other kids." Or if they had done "something so egregious that I didn't want to take it on as a district." Despite facing a $1.1 million shortfall for 2019–20, the superintendent had already rejected at least two families, saying it was important to honor the Lovejoy community's standards.

"Otherwise, it gets a little willy-nilly," he said.

This was the system upon which the Beckers' well-being now depended. For the moment, they still enjoyed the very real benefits of being a Lovejoy family. But there was good reason for the disquiet at the edge of their days. Even the local hero turned superintendent whose job it was to be aggressively optimistic had started hedging his assessments of Lovejoy's future.

"If everything was to stay the same," Goddard told me, "I think it's highly sustainable."

"IF LOVEJOY TANKED TOMORROW"

Smiling photos of 356 children hung on the main wall inside the foyer of Sloan Creek Intermediate School. All were part of the school's leadership-development program, which taught them how to organize pep rallies, listen actively, and share their opinions without steamrolling other people.

"Usually, that's the coaching you get in your first year in a job," principal

Ray Winkler, a beefy middle-aged white man who favored red fleece vests and wore a panic button around his neck, told me. "We're giving that here in fifth grade."

Winkler had been an associate principal under Goddard back in the late 2000s. Then he'd gone on to work in the Dallas city schools. His own young son had attended Frisco ISD, another highly regarded suburban district.

"He wasn't considered behind according to Frisco standards because he wasn't setting fire to anything and he wasn't the bottom of the barrel," Winkler said. "Mediocre districts, or districts that have high poverty, tend to pitch it in the middle. Anybody that's on grade level, they kind of get a free pass. All the time and effort goes to working with kids who are below the line."

To really see the difference between that approach and Lovejoy's, he continued, you had to compare the type of work students did. Ask yourself a question, the principal urged me. Would you rather your child fill out worksheets on who did what at the Alamo? Or would you rather they write an argumentative essay about whether *Gone With the Wind* or *Pocahontas* presented a more sanitized version of American history?

Avery Becker's fifth-grade social studies class made clear where Sloan Creek stood. By mid-October, teacher Jake Vogel was two weeks into an immersive simulation of the Boston Tea Party and the "Intolerable Acts" enacted by Britain in its aftermath. Vogel relished playing the role of King George III, hamming it up as he imposed a series of increasingly harsh sanctions on his class; they'd eventually culminate with a "sugar tax" levied in the school cafeteria. Working against their teacher were two dozen students broken into small groups. Each represented a different colony. Avery was part of South Carolina. As her imperious teacher paced in front of the class, she chewed her gum vigorously, causing the freckles on her round cheeks to bob up and down.

"Hear ye, hear ye," Vogel-slash-King George said in a booming voice. "It's time to remind you that I'm king and you need to do what you're told."

The class groaned good-naturedly. Vogel told them Boston Harbor would be closed. Local colonists would be required to open empty buildings to

British soldiers. Those soldiers would be granted immunity from prosecution in local courts. Without missing a beat, Vogel then translated the significance of the acts into fifth-grade terms.

"Things are gonna change around here!" the teacher-king roared. "From now on, there will be no more talking! Your desks will be arranged in rows until I tell you otherwise! There's no water or bathroom breaks either!"

The class spent the rest of the period developing secret communications systems they could use to share information about how the Intolerable Acts were affecting daily life in their colonies. Next, Vogel told them, you'll be working together to craft responses to Britain's harsh dictates.

"This is due when you walk in the door tomorrow," he said just before the bell rang. "Oh, and remember, I have spies all over the school!"

The Sloan Creek parent coffee began not long after. Thirty or so people gathered in the school's black box theater. Jim had changed into jeans and a royal-blue fleece pullover bearing the logo of the company where he worked. Susan wore black jeans with a red, black, and leopard-print top. The digital smartboard at the front of the room showed the homepage of a drug-education program whose curriculum Lovejoy schools were about to adopt. Principal Winkler greeted everyone, then introduced the guest speaker he'd arranged.

Susan Hoemke had lost her son to substance abuse in 2014. He'd started drinking alcohol and smoking marijuana in ninth grade. After several unsuccessful rehab stints, Hoemke and her husband had moved from an ultra-wealthy enclave inside Dallas city limits out to the area served by Lovejoy ISD, where they hoped to find a fresh start. But it had taken only a few weeks for the police dogs inside Lovejoy High to sniff out Xanax in their son's pocket. After getting arrested, he'd started using harder drugs, then died of a heroin overdose at twenty-two. She and her husband initially hoped their son's drug use was a phase, Hoemke told the Sloan Creek parents.

"So here we are in our Highland Park bubble, off Route 75, and just on the other side, there's drug houses," she said. "They'd pop over there and get what they needed and come back."

When the problem didn't go away on its own, the Hoemkes took away first their son's phone, then his car. All manner of expensive therapy came next. But he kept stealing money from his mother's purse.

"It got to be where I could have a hundred dollars, and I'd go in my wallet and think, 'Did I spend twenty dollars somewhere? Because I only have eighty dollars now,'" she said. "But you know how it is. Money is like water."

Susan and Jim nodded knowingly. Hoemke handed out a timeline detailing her son's descent. Then she described the drug paraphernalia parents should look out for. Eyedrops, Bic lighters, glassine baggies, hollowed-out pens, empty cough syrup bottles, razor blades. A second handout listed the drugs that were now popular among teens. Her son had tried them all, Hoemke said. Even the anxiety medication she'd gotten for the family dog.

"I began finding packages that had cartoon pictures on them," she told the parents. "Synthetic drugs. They come from China, they come from Mexico, they can come from all over. He tried bath salts. He woke us up in the middle of the night, said people were watching him through his laptop. I thought he was having a psychotic breakdown."

The next step had been a residential treatment center in Montana. Boarding school would have been cheaper, Hoemke joked. Relocating the entire family out to the North Dallas exurbs had been their last hope.

"We decided to move out here to the country, because there's no drugs out here," Hoemke said ruefully. "The drugs were in the high school, the drugs were in the neighborhood, the drugs were everywhere. You cannot run from them."

By this point, Jim was stroking his goatee and rocking nervously in his red swivel chair. Susan had wrapped her arms around her rib cage. The screen on the smartboard had long since switched to blue.

"I'm watching your faces, and some of you are a little overwhelmed," Winkler said, stepping in.

Then he switched into principal mode. Every one of your kids will be offered drugs and alcohol at some point, he told the parents. You have to normalize talking about it. Practice being a good listener. Compress your emotional range. No screaming or freak-outs. And no over-the-top praise for simply doing the right thing.

"I want you to talk to your shoulder partner," Winkler said. "What new things have you learned today?"

When the Beckers finally retreated to their SUV, they looked shell-shocked.

"I always knew we're going to have to have these conversations at some point," Susan said. "But it's been kind of kicking the can down the road, we're not there yet."

Lovejoy High was just ten minutes away. The Beckers parked in the back of the giant lot, then signed in at the school's entrance. Teens in football jerseys, flannel shirts, and preppy sweaters mingled in a large commons. Susan headed for the school store, where she paid for the homecoming tickets and added a new black Lovejoy T-shirt for herself.

Afterward, she and Jim stopped for lunch at a roadside burger stand. They sat at an octagonal picnic table in a gravel lot beside an expanse of rolling pasture. Dragonflies buzzed contentedly over the high, dry grass. The midday traffic from the Walmart a half mile away was only a distant hum. The sun was headed to its highest point, and the day was as warm as it was going to get. The Beckers settled into a comfortable quiet as they ate.

At home, they had an hour before it was time to pick up the kids. Jim caught up on work emails. Susan moved another load of sheets through the laundry. Before heading out to dinner, he donned a Lovejoy baseball cap. She stayed with her black jeans, but pulled on the new black T-shirt she'd bought.

"You look like a ninja," Noah said helpfully.

The whole family climbed back into the Buick and drove over to the Italian place where they were meeting the other Lovejoy families. The kids crowded around their own table and played Candy Crush on their phones. The moms ordered glasses of red, and the couples began comparing notes on the Lovejoy schools. Lisa and Michael Stevick, whom Susan had gotten to know during the fifth-grade adventure camp trip, had recently moved from California. They still couldn't believe illegal immigrants were allowed to serve on public boards there. The schools, meanwhile, were so busted that their home district had taken to replacing broken locker doors with plywood.

"From a third-world country to 'This is our cello room,'" Lisa said of their move to Lovejoy.

Bells jingled as a police officer walked into the restaurant. No one seemed to notice. A dad named Brett arrived directly from the airport. He was the CEO of a tech firm that ran a business-to-business platform for hedge funds. He steered the conversation back to taxes. The group wondered whether theirs would eventually have to be raised in order to keep Lovejoy schools competitive.

"I could support doing a bond and upping my taxes, provided I really believed in the system," Brett's wife, Jamie, said.

"You've got to have that trust," Susan agreed. "There are communities where I wouldn't. But I completely have that trust in Lovejoy."

Where everyone drew the line, though, was any dramatic changes to the local zoning code. Yes, allowing apartments or reducing lot sizes would lead to more revenue, Brett allowed. But the families who moved in would ultimately strain the school system too much. You can't make people want to succeed, his wife interjected. No distant bureaucrat should have the power to make Lovejoy water down its standards in the name of diversity, Michael added. Why should I suffer to make sure everything is equal for everyone when certain disadvantages occur naturally in America, Brett asked the group as he leaned back in his chair.

The good news, Michael said, was that in Texas, you could always just buy a new home somewhere farther out.

"If Lovejoy tanked tomorrow, don't think for a second that I wouldn't move someplace else with a stronger school district," Brett agreed.

Everyone finished eating. The kids started to get fidgety. Outside, stars were starting to reappear in the darkening sky. Someone got a text saying traffic was already backing up outside the football stadium. I followed the Beckers out to the parking lot. Earlier in the day, I'd asked them the same question that had closed the dinner conversation. Would you move again if Lovejoy schools slipped?

Jim had taken a second to consider. Then his trademark grin reappeared.

"Well," he told me. "Noah is in fourth grade now. So I just need it to work for about eight more years."

9

COREY'S VILLAGE

THE ROBINSON FAMILY | GWINNETT COUNTY, GEORGIA

> They shit on anybody who said the emperor had no clothes.
>
> —MARLYN TILLMAN,
> Gwinnett SToPP, 2019

A few stretches of northern Gwinnett County remained country. Long-haired blond boys in Atlanta Braves baseball caps still rode shotgun in their fathers' pickups to packed Waffle Houses for postchurch brunches, and the occasional bear was still spotted patrolling the perimeter of a public school. By 2017, however, new houses starting in the mid-$200,000s were everywhere, and white students were now outnumbered inside Jones Middle.

There were a handful of other Black kids in Corey Robinson's seventh-grade social studies class, including a friend whom Corey considered his ride or die. Together, the pair found nameless satisfaction in tormenting their middle-aged white teacher. As soon as Mr. Keller turned his back at the whiteboard to write something about the Suez Canal or the partition of the Middle East, one of the boys would burp loudly or lift the bottom of his T-shirt up to his chin, exposing a childish belly. Keller would swivel on his heels, eyes already bulging. But Corey and his friend would meet their teacher's accusing questions with a chorus of yes-sirs and no-sirs and I-dunno-sirs, eventually forcing him to retreat back to his lesson.

The boys rarely pulled such crap in math. That class was taught by a no-nonsense Black woman who softened her strict classroom rules with a mother's touch during all the in-between moments in the day. But in social studies, Corey felt compelled to keep upping the ante. It was Halloween when he earned his first suspension. For whatever reason, Corey found Keller's manner especially grating. So he grabbed the small bottle of glue on his desk and silently squeezed its contents onto the head of the white boy who sat in front of him. When his unwitting classmate was called to the whiteboard, bedlam ensued.

After school, the Robinsons were waiting just inside the front door of their home. Keller had already emailed them about what happened. No no no, Corey said feebly, it wasn't me. But Anthony wasn't trying to hear it.

"His dad was furious, and Corey experienced that fury," was all Nika would say.

The first signs of trouble had popped up the previous year. Corey won most of his classmates over with his willingness to act the fool. To handle the rest, he leaned into his sledgehammer wit, sending any sorry soul who tried to match him insult for insult slinking down the mocking Jones hallways. There were some minor punishments that year, for things like cussing in the cafeteria. But it was the emerging perception that Corey might be a troublemaker that most worried the Robinsons. A few weeks before the end of school, for example, one of Corey's teachers called and left a message accusing him of academic dishonesty. Nika composed a response in her head during dinner, then fired off an email before bed.

"I received your disturbing voicemail this afternoon regarding unfounded, and quite frankly racist and insulting, allegations that Corey committed plagiarism on his make-up packet," her message read. "To be clear, this is not about a grade in a class that in the grand scheme of Corey's life had no bearing or relevance on his success, but rather your complete and utter lack of cultural competence and respect for us as parents and Corey as a student."

He'd finished the year with mostly As and Bs. Still, Corey limped into June feeling sour about himself.

"I just don't think they like me," he'd say. "I guess I'm just a bad kid."

That summer, the Robinsons had turned to a trusted ally to help revive their son's flagging spirit. The rules in Coach Russ's gym were simple and clear. No one cared if you busted on your friends or bounced around to the music in your head. Just don't let it interfere with drills. By the night of the seventh-grade open house, Corey was feeling almost like himself again.

"This is going to be a good year for me," he told his parents as they stepped out of the school's auditorium and into heavy August air.

Jones Middle, however, had habits of its own. The school's staff was proud of how they competed with the private schools and far-exurban districts out in Hall and Forsyth counties that were always trying to poach northern Gwinnett's whitest and wealthiest families, and administrators delighted in pointing out that Jones eighth graders scored seventy-five points better than the national average on the PSAT. But they were far less inclined to discuss the barrage of indicators showing that some students were relegated to the margins of their school's success. Black kids, for example, made up less than one fifth of Jones's total enrollment. But they received more than one third of all disciplinary actions at the school. On district surveys, they were also less likely than their white peers to say the adults at Jones treated them fairly.

The Robinsons had long responded to such tensions by using their odd-couple pairing to their advantage. Anthony's strength was putting other people at ease. It also helped that his inclination to give the benefit of the doubt went double for teachers; after nearly a decade in the classroom himself, he knew full well how middle schoolers could work on a man's nerves. To build relationships, he volunteered once a week in the Jones library, where he began chatting up staffers like the school police officer, a friendly young Black man who soon took an interest in Corey and began complimenting his sneakers in the hallway.

Nika, meanwhile, was excellent at locating the flaws in a system and the levers that might be pulled to fix them. This was partly a function of her work; now a manager at a consulting firm that had several large contracts with the National Institutes of Health and Centers for Disease Control and Prevention, she supervised junior staff, crafted budgets, and developed protocols to keep things running smoothly. So part of her parenting role was studying the Gwinnett County Public Schools' discipline policies. She also maintained a steady email correspondence with several Jones teachers, regularly sharing articles about how to engage kinesthetic learners like her son and offering tips on how to leverage the incentives the Robinsons offered Corey at home, including $100 for every A on his report card. Because Nika was also well aware that white women tended to interpret her exuberance as aggression, she spent considerable time preparing for any in-person meetings at her children's schools, both emotionally, by stripping her manner of anything that might be construed as threatening, locking those parts of herself temporarily away, and practically, by always having some piece of research or data she could use to steer a discussion back to neutral ground. And if a particular meeting seemed likely to grow contentious or venture into sensitive territory, she made sure Anthony was at her side.

"These people are still my child's teachers," she told me. "I don't want them to treat him unfairly because they don't like his mother."

Prior to Corey's seventh-grade year, such strategies had always worked well enough. But after his suspension over the glue incident, things had quickly spun out of control. Teachers began handing out regular detentions, describing in terse notes home how Corey was disrespectful and disruptive and took too long in the bathroom. Nika considered much of it to be nitpicking.

"I just couldn't understand what they were so anxious and upset about," she said. "Corey has documented GI issues. If he's in the bathroom for a long time, there's probably a reason."

Shortly before the end of the first marking period, Corey and Nika told me, Mr. Keller gave his social studies students a quiz. On the cusp of an A in the class and eager to claim his $100, Corey had studied hard. But his paper came back with an 88. Disappointed, he began comparing answers with his friends, discovering that he and another boy had put down the same response for one question, but Mr. Keller had marked it incorrect only for him. Corey told me he spent the rest of the class debating whether to just eat the B. He finally decided to approach his teacher after class.

I think I was supposed to get a 92 on this quiz, Corey remembered saying.

You made an 88 because that's what I put on the paper, he recalled Keller responding.

You just can't grade, Corey acknowledged shooting back.

That led to another write-up, for disrespect. After school, Nika and Anthony were again waiting inside the front door. This time, however, when Nika looked at the quiz, it appeared her son was right. Okay, she said. I'm sure Keller didn't mean to do you wrong. I'll send him an email tonight.

When forty-eight hours passed without a reply, Nika decided to put on her friendliest face and stop by the school. She reconstructed the exchange for me later.

Hey, I know this isn't really a big deal, she recalled telling Mr. Keller. Accidents happen all the time. I get it. But this is really important to Corey.

Keller responded by saying that Corey's constant goofing off regularly threw the whole class off track. *That's a lot of responsibility to put on a thirteen-year-old*, Nika remembered thinking. Eventually, Keller had relented and given Corey the 92. But Nika had walked away from the interaction feeling uneasy. Soon after, she decided to start popping by Jones on the days she worked from home so she could observe her son's behavior for herself.

Her chaperone was usually a white assistant principal named Kristi Lyons. Middle-aged, with shoulder-length auburn hair, she had the tightly controlled smile of a politician's wife; her husband was mayor in one of the exurban enclaves way out in Hall County that was still 80-plus percent white. Nika recalled the two of them walking the halls together, making small talk, Nika doing her best to mirror Lyons's affect and keep her tone nonconfrontational. Corey's dad used to be a teacher, she'd say breezily. Trust me, we know how hard it is. That's why we want to work together as a team. But the assistant principal mostly responded with noncommittal nods.

"She started off being fake nice," Nika said.

The friction became overt when the pair began peeking through the windows of Corey's classrooms. Nika would pull out a yellow legal pad to take notes. A pinched frown would form at the corners of Lyons's mouth. In her son's English class, Nika described watching large groups of students hold side conversations, wander around the room, and complain they needed to use the bathroom. She said Corey was usually near the center of the disorder, growing more boisterous as his teacher grew more flustered. She began making notes on the issues she intended to raise with her son that evening. But then, Nika said, she saw a white boy throw an empty water bottle across the room. Lyons and the teacher both remained silent. If that was Corey, Nika remembered saying, he'd have gotten written up for assault with a deadly weapon.

At that, Nika told me, the assistant principal rolled her eyes and claimed the teacher probably didn't see what happened. Nika felt a prisoner start banging on the inside of her rib cage.

No, the teacher definitely saw it, she remembered telling Lyons, an edge creeping into her voice. Listen, she continued. We've never said Corey is an angel. We're not opposed to consequences. We just want him to receive the same grace that your staff extends to white children. So what I'm asking you is to explain to me how your staff determines when misbehavior is just boys being boys and when it requires punishment.

When no answers were forthcoming, Nika and Anthony sat Corey down for a conversation they'd been holding off on for years. It's not right, Nika said. But in this country, there's one set of rules for the kids who look like you and another set for the kids who don't. I saw that little white boy getting crunk in your English class, Nika told her son. And I saw how no one said a thing to him. But if that had been you?

"Is that why I'm always getting a referral?" Corey asked.

"Yes," Nika said. "If you mess up even the slightest, they're going to give you a referral."

Corey sat in silence with this new information. Previous parental interventions had always focused on taking responsibility for his actions. Even more confusing was that he considered the white classmate who'd thrown the bottle a friend. In the moment, he'd been glad the boy didn't get in trouble. Corey realized his parents were waiting on a response.

"Yes, ma'am," he said, deciding to play it safe.

Parent-teacher conferences had seemed like an opportunity for a reset. Worried about her son's performance in English, Nika emailed his teacher in advance to ask if they could talk about extra credit. On the day of the meeting, she remembered sitting down at a semicircular table, then trying to make eye contact with her son's Black math teacher, who scribbled uncomfortably on a sheet of paper. *Oh no*, Nika recalled thinking, *math is Corey's best subject.*

It turned out that he had all Bs and Cs. But about ten minutes into the meeting, Assistant Principal Lyons cleared her throat. Nika remembered her saying something about wanting to help Corey be successful. *Maybe she's going to suggest tutoring*, Nika thought.

Instead, Lyons pulled out Corey's behavior record. We've seen that your son has trouble staying on task, Nika recalled the assistant principal saying. So we've referred him to the Student Support Team. We also want to have him evaluated. Nika felt the person locked inside her pull the fire alarm.

For what? she asked.

The SST process was supposed to prevent special education referrals whenever possible. In practice, however, it could just as easily turn into a paperwork exercise that school administrators viewed as a hoop to be jumped through before those placements were made. As the Jones assistant principal kept talking in circles, Nika began sensing the latter, which she found confusing because Corey's grades were solid. Ms. Lyons, she remembered saying, interrupting as gently as she could, please forgive me. But I am not picking up what you are trying to put down.

Your son's behavior is a significant problem, she recalled the assistant principal responding. We think it's ADHD. Children like him often do better on medication.

It was an ambush. All of Nika's internal sirens began to blare. She wished desperately that Anthony was there next to her. Her words came flying out like projectiles.

First of all, you're not a doctor, Nika remembered snapping. If your concern is that my son has a difficult time staying on task, fine, I can accept that as valid. But don't lie to me about what this meeting is for, then blindside me when I get here. And certainly do not sit here and try to diagnose my child.

Lying in bed that night, Nika replayed the incident for Anthony a fourth time, then a fifth. You may not like our kid, she fumed at her husband, who stood in gamely for the assistant principal, absorbing his wife's fury. But don't be so obvious that it impacts his ability to learn.

Thanksgiving and then Christmas had come soon after. Anthony's parents took the family to Disney World. By New Year's, the Robinsons were hoping the storm had blown over.

But when spring semester began, Corey was assigned to a class taught by the same teacher who'd accused him of plagiarism the previous year. Then he got into a verbal altercation with a white boy in the school cafeteria. Corey said the boy called him the n-word. Nika described being incredulous when the assistant principal told her that no disciplinary action could be taken because other students couldn't corroborate his account.

Then, on a Monday in mid-March, Corey had to serve an in-school suspension for disrupting class. The next day, he received another referral, for smacking a boy in the back of the head on a dare. Nika and Anthony were still trying to get to the bottom of that incident when their son got written up yet again on Wednesday. This time, it was for a collision during an outdoor game. Corey emerged unscathed, his parents said, but the other boy had the wind knocked out of him. When Jones staff coded the incidents as "Behav phys inj," Nika's mind filled with dark thoughts about the GIVE Center, which had once been housed in the old all-Black Hooper-Renwick school and was now located just up the road from a county jail. There was no way in hell she was going to let her son end up there.

But she and Anthony were also determined to remain clear-eyed about Corey's misbehavior. At home, they began deposing their oldest son like prosecutors. Under questioning, he revealed another brush with Jones administrators from several weeks earlier. The Backpack Incident. Nika hit the roof when she realized that no one from Jones had called to tell her a school police officer had searched her son. Sensing opportunity, Corey fudged the remaining details.

What actually happened, he told me during a later interview, was that he and a friend had been admiring the gold chain worn by an Asian American boy in their science class. Yo, that's a nice necklace, he remembered his friend saying. Can I hold it while you go to the bathroom? I guess, the boy had replied. Just don't lose it. But as soon as the boy stepped out of the classroom, Corey's friend stuffed the chain in his backpack. When the boy returned, Corey and his friend played dumb. What chain, they said. We don't know what you're talking about. But on the way to their next class, the pair got nervous and dumped the backpack with the chain in a hallway trash can. Mr. Keller was mid-lesson when the school police officer knocked on the door and pulled the two boys into the hall. Corey said the officer asked him to take off his shoes and empty the contents of his bag. Corey complied. The search came up empty, and nothing further happened.

Nika and Anthony, however, only got the broad strokes. A boy reported a stolen necklace. The school police officer searched the two Black kids. Neither had the necklace. For two consecutive nights, they stayed up until well past midnight, debating who to trust.

"Maybe Corey got it wrong," Anthony said. "You don't pull the two Black children in the classroom out to have them searched."

"What if he did steal the necklace," Nika replied. "He wasn't Mirandized. That is automatically putting him in a position where he's going to be entering the system."

Eventually, the Robinsons decided they had no choice but to set up yet another meeting at Jones. It didn't go well. Nika remembered a Jones administrator saying that maybe Corey would be better off in an alternative setting. Then she pulled out another thick stack of Corey's behavior reports. Nika started scanning the documents frantically. When she saw words like *bully* and *troublemaker*, all her alarms started going off again.

Later, Nika would tell me that a small part of her had entered the meeting still hoping she and Anthony might find a way to work together with Jones staff to figure out what their son had actually done wrong, hold him accountable, and get him back on track. But the gulf between her family and her child's school now felt uncrossable. Nika recognized the possibility that

Corey hadn't told her and Anthony the whole truth; he was, after all, a teen-ager. But forced to choose, it wasn't difficult to trust him over the Jones ad-ministrators.

No, no, no, no, Nika remembered erupting at the assistant principal during that final meeting of seventh grade. Let *me* explain something to *you*. I'm in management. So I understand exactly what you're doing. You're trying to document him to death. Get him labeled so he gets put out. I know, because I've done it myself. But there is no way we're going to let this stand.

The Robinsons pulled their son out of the Gwinnett County Public School the next day. Even Anthony had seen enough.

"Sometimes, it's hard to know how far to push the envelope," he told me. But ten years working in public schools had convinced him that the punish-ments handed out by Jones Middle were wildly out of proportion.

Nika, meanwhile, felt like she'd finally been set free.

"It was like, 'Okay, this is not a Corey issue. This is a systemic issue,'" she said. "And that's how I found Gwinnett SToPP."

"I-HAVE-ARRIVED SYNDROME"

Marlyn Tillman had silver hair, a dark complexion, and a wardrobe straight from Ann Taylor. She was no stranger to phone calls from worried parents like the Robinsons. After fighting her own battles with the Gwinnett County Public Schools, she'd cofounded a small nonprofit dedicated to ending the school-to-prison pipeline.

"Our issue all along has been that the district is overly punitive," she told me. "Black and Brown children were getting suspended for more subjective reasons and lower-level offenses than white students."

Tillman herself had grown up in a Black rowhome neighborhood of West Philadelphia back in the early 1960s, when doctors and lawyers lived a block over from hustlers and hairdressers. By the time Tillman was a teen, how-ever, most of the middle-class professionals had fled for the suburbs. She eventually joined them, moving to Silver Spring, Maryland, where the public schools had stable teaching staffs, Spanish immersion programs, and PTAs that raised six-figure sums each year. When Tillman's oldest started pre-K, she'd become a regular classroom volunteer, spending hours building personal relationships with school staff. At the same time, she also kept a constant eye out for something better, eventually upgrading to an elementary school that served the ritzy communities of Bethesda and Chevy Chase outside Washington, DC.

"My ex told me I'm the Blackest white woman in America," Tillman said jokingly the first time we met. "I was doing the things white mothers would do."

By 2001, she was ready to buy a home of her own. Because the DC suburbs were too expensive, she targeted Atlanta, quickly zeroing in on Gwinnett. But shortly after her family arrived, Tillman said, she found herself at odds with administrators at her sons' schools.

Her oldest boy was bright and creative, with good grades and a long list of extracurriculars. But he ran into trouble early, when the adults at his middle school determined that the pocket watch Tillman had given him as a gift was somehow gang related. By the time he'd made it to Brookwood High, administrators didn't seem to care that Tillman's son had always taken honors classes, or that he'd spent a summer at Howard University attending a camp for aspiring lawyers, or that his mother had gotten herself elected vice president of the school's PTA. They just kept writing him up in reports that used dangerously loaded terms to describe infractions that ranged from minor to nonexistent. The red polo shirt and matching wristband and do-rag he liked to wear, for example, were also deemed indicators of possible gang activity. The final straw had come when Tillman's son showed up to school wearing a homemade T-shirt that included a stylized rendering of his nickname, "KMATiKC," as well as a reference to his favorite basketball star. Again, he received an inflammatory write-up.

> [He] was wearing a gang-related shirt today. The back had the letters "K" and "C" whited out from the rest of the red lettering. This indicates "Crip Killer" according to the Gwinnett County

Gang Task Force. The front had the following letters whited out:
"IVRSIN." Allen Iverson is an icon to the Crip gang (GCGTF and
Internet sources).

Taken together, the accusations made little sense. But Tillman's son was suspended for three days and labeled a "chronic disciplinary problem" regardless. She responded with a lawsuit, eventually winning a partial victory. The Gwinnett school system formally acknowledged that her son—who later earned a master's degree and became a sociology professor, filmmaker, and entrepreneur—"is not now, nor ever has been, involved in gang activity," and Brookwood High tweaked its dress-code policy.

Unsatisfied, Tillman founded Gwinnett SToPP in 2007. During the group's early years, its work mostly involved helping parents understand their rights when their children got in trouble at school. SToPP also did some policy advocacy, much of which initially focused on trying to improve conditions at the GIVE Center. Tillman also helped organize direct actions, including a protest outside district headquarters when a school police officer was caught on camera knocking a student unconscious. SToPP won a few scattered victories, including getting the district to explicitly delineate what types of infractions justified police involvement. But Tillman began to see two big barriers to more systemic change.

The first was the way Gwinnett's history permeated its institutions. By 2017, the county school district was three-fourths Black, Hispanic, Asian, and multiracial. But its five-member governing board was all white and dominated by three women who'd held their seats for a combined total of nearly eighty years. Mary Kay Murphy had arrived in Gwinnett in 1992 and been elected to the school board four years later. Carole Boyce arrived in 1972 and sent her six children through the local schools before taking her seat on the board in 2005. And Louise Radloff had arrived in Gwinnett in 1970, back when the county was still so rural that school buses had to unload children before driving across a rickety wooden bridge. She'd won her seat in 1972, then held it for nearly half a century, making her the longest-serving public school board member in Georgia and possibly the country.

In an interview, I asked Radloff to describe her first couple of decades on the board, a period when hundreds of thousands of white families had fueled Gwinnett's first big wave of suburban development. Back then, Radloff told me, her core constituents were "standard families, three kids, a dog, and go to church on Sunday." They valued Little League games and neatly edged lawns. They did not want their children bused to faraway schools, and they didn't want kids from faraway places bused into Gwinnett. What they did want were good public schools in nice buildings that reflected their values.

"Bond issues and bond issues and bond issues," Radloff said of voters' priorities during that formative period. "Build what you need, and we'll pay the taxes."

The Gwinnett County school system would ultimately win approval for fourteen consecutive such measures without a defeat. By 1990, however, voters' enthusiasm for investment in public infrastructure was starting to falter. Perhaps Gwinnett's white residents could sense change on the horizon; over the next two decades, the county's Black population would grow by 938 percent. Whatever the reason, they started shooting down ballot measures for the first time in forever. The first would have extended the Metropolitan Atlanta Rapid Transit Authority out to the county's suburban neighborhoods. Racist jokes rebranding the system "Moving Africans Rapidly Through Atlanta" resurfaced, and the measure was defeated by a 2–1 margin. Then, that same year, the Gwinnett County Public Schools put a $75 million construction package on the ballot. Voters shocked everyone by rejecting it too.

Chastened, district leaders set to work developing a new strategy. This time, they tied money for new school construction to a series of far-reaching reforms. To reassure parents who worried that buying a home in Gwinnett might not guarantee their children access to desirable public schools, the district promised to realign its attendance zones and feeder patterns. To convince those same parents their children would still receive personalized attention, the district also promised to deemphasize testing. Most important of all, the school board also vowed to stop raising property taxes, suggesting that a special local sales tax be used to fund future school construction instead. The new proposal was a hit. Gwinnett voters approved a bond measure almost twice as large as the one they'd just rejected, and another two dozen–plus new schools would be built in the county before the decade was out.

It was during that period, however, that the complexion of the county and its public schools began to change dramatically. The shifts started with couples like the Blairs; he was a Black computer whiz from Kingston, Jamaica, and she was a Black medical student at Emory University. After marrying in 1990, the pair settled in DeKalb County. Two years later, however, the Supreme Court handed down its ruling in *Freeman v. Pitts*, setting the stage for a federal judge to release the DeKalb district from federal oversight of its desegregation effort several years later. As the school system became majority Black, the Blairs' neighbors began whispering about slipping test scores and wild fights. When Everton Blair, Jr., was ready to start kindergarten in 1997, his parents decided to move across the border into Gwinnett, buying a new home in the attendance zone of one of those recently built elementary schools.

Shiloh Elementary's student body was still 83 percent white when Blair started first grade. Five years later, when he moved on to nearby Shiloh Middle, his classmates were more or less evenly split between Black and white. And by the time Blair graduated from Shiloh High in 2009, the school was 75 percent Black and Brown.

From his vantage point, the shift was awesome, Blair told me years later, after he'd become the first person of color to win a seat on the Gwinnett County School Board. "I could bring my friends to church and it wouldn't require an explanation, like, 'Oh, yeah, people are going to be running up and down and speaking in tongues, because that's how we do things,'" he said.

He went on to earn a degree in applied mathematics from Harvard, then a master's in educational leadership from Stanford, then served a short stint as a fellow with the Obama White House's Initiative on Educational Excellence for African Americans. But even as he thrived, Blair said, he watched as experienced staff began leaving the Shiloh schools his younger siblings now attended, leading to a sharp decline in academic rigor. The county soon began to experience the same kind of northward exodus that had once destabilized DeKalb; between 2000 and 2017, the Gwinnett County Public Schools would lose more than 29,000 white students.

Through all the changes, though, Gwinnett's old guard maintained its iron grip on power. Now more than two decades into his tenure, a silver-haired white educator named J. Alvin Wilbanks remained entrenched as superintendent. Boyce, Murphy, and Radloff all still held their seats on the district's governing board. All of them believed stability at the top was the key to the Gwinnett County Public Schools' success, an argument that was backed up by considerable evidence. In 2005, Wilbanks was named Georgia Superintendent of the Year. In 2010, the district won the prestigious Broad Prize for outstanding academic achievement. Four years later, it won again.

All the while, though, Marlyn Tillman kept telling anyone who'd listen that such accolades amounted to lipstick on a pig. Yes, Black and Brown kids in Gwinnett were outperforming their peers in DeKalb and Atlanta. But they lagged the white and Asian kids who lived next door by twenty or thirty points. They also had to endure an endless series of egregious incidents, like the time in 2016 when administrators found swastikas, the words "Trump" and "Build the Wall," and a slew of homophobic slurs painted outside Collins Hill High. Fifty years after the ACLU documented in *Armour v. Nix* that the Gwinnett administrators hadn't identified a single Black child as gifted, Black and Brown children still accounted for just one third of those selected for the district's gifted and talented program, despite now accounting for nearly two thirds of the district's total enrollment. When I presented Murphy with that last data point, the longtime school board member's response was typical.

"Who would say they're to be equal?" she told me. "We don't operate by quotas."

Worst of all was the district's discipline system. Part of the problem, Tillman maintained, was that Wilbanks and the board were far more concerned with reputation than reality. Back in the early 2000s, for example, the district had been rocked by reports that it had failed to properly document thousands of fights, drug seizures, and weapons offenses; Wilbanks would eventually acknowledge underreporting serious disciplinary offenses by roughly 90 percent, attributing the problem to data-collection errors. But even as the district had been downplaying such significant problems, Tillman pointed out, it kept on aggressively punishing Black and Brown children for lower-level offenses. The pattern was difficult for individual families to identify and fight. Want to keep your child out of the GIVE Center after a referral from his principal? You first had to convince the district administrator serving as your hearing officer that your child hadn't done anything wrong—a task often made difficult because that hearing officer wanted to advance through the district's ranks and was thus loath to undermine a colleague. Fail at your hearing, and you could appeal to the school board, who would typically receive a recommendation on what to do from the district's executive director of academic support. But in Gwinnett, that position had long been filled by a Black man named Jim Taylor, who told me after he retired that the system was dramatically tilted in favor of administrators. He described being especially galled at how Superintendent Wilbanks sometimes overturned what Taylor considered to be cut-and-dried recommendations in favor of students. District leaders were "still operating as if it was a predominantly white school system," Taylor maintained. Then he referred to the whole setup as a "dog and pony show" in which all the key players were incentivized to ignore and deny the wild racial disparities the system produced.

"One thing about Gwinnett, everyone comes from within the organization. So they understand that you go along to get along," Taylor said. "The principals in no way, shape, or form are being held accountable for their actions," and no one was willing to admit any problems within the system.

Tillman put it even more bluntly.

"They shit on anybody who said the emperor has no clothes," she said.

Over time, however, Tillman had also concluded that a second factor also contributed to the relentlessness of Gwinnett's status quo. She called it "I-Have-Arrived Syndrome." Many parents of color didn't want to believe they were up against a larger structural problem, Tillman said, because doing so would mean accepting that their lifelong struggle to attain middle-class respectability hadn't insulated them from the effects of racism. Such denial often drove her crazy. But she also understood, Tillman told me, because she'd once suffered from the condition herself. Only after moving to Gwinnett had she seen that suburbia was just as hostile and racist as anywhere else. And in some ways, she believed, it was even worse, because in a place like Gwinnett County, you were on your own.

"That's the downside of integration," Tillman said. "Now our model is white America. And with white America, it's dog-eat-dog."

It wasn't exactly a hopeful take on the state of the post–civil rights dream that equal opportunity might finally be found in America's suburbs. But Tillman wasn't dismayed, because she'd recently been seeing signs of a shift. Partly it was demographics; people of color would soon be the majority in Gwinnett County, making it increasingly difficult for white administrators or elected officials to simply discount their experiences. But the real tipping point, Tillman said, was the 2016 election. Although Trump won Georgia handily, Hillary Clinton had surprised everyone by carrying the Atlanta suburbs, including Gwinnett. The results seemed to shake county Democrats out of their decades-long slumber. In the run-up to the 2018 midterms, a diverse slate of progressives whose roots ranged from Bangladesh to Jamaica lined up to run for the state legislature. A Black woman and a gay Asian American man were vying to become the first Democrats on the county commission since Reagan was president. Everton Blair, Jr., returned home to run for school board.

And increasingly, Tillman said, many of the Black parents calling Gwinnett SToPP were talking about the need for structural change. Including Nika Robinson. After her experience at Jones, she felt more compelled than ever to run for local office herself. She'd even signed up for candidate training with a group called Georgia Win. She was also seriously considering filing her own lawsuit against the Gwinnett County Public Schools.

"Not to be a jerk, but we're a family of means," Nika told me. "I'm fighting for all the other Coreys."

SCALED-BACK EXPECTATIONS

When Anthony first moved his young family out to the northern edge of Gwinnett County, his parents understood. After all, they'd made the same calculation nearly two decades earlier, when they'd bought the house out in DeKalb County's "New Frontier." Soon, though, it became difficult for Hank and Danielle to hold their tongues. Who wanted to drive forty-five minutes to watch their granddaughter's gymnastics recitals, only to see little white girls sniping when her back was turned? Or go shopping afterward, only to be made to feel unwelcome by everyone else there? Eventually, Danielle felt obliged to speak her piece.

"You guys are way out here in this pretty much all-white neighborhood. They can belittle you, and a child might not know it," she warned Anthony. "People have subtle ways of doing things."

But after things went south at Jones Middle, there was no time for I-told-you-sos. The elder Robinsons were happy to turn their house in its now-almost-entirely-Black subdivision into a safe harbor. Danielle in particular was thrilled to have her oldest grandson sleeping in Anthony's old bedroom. On the morning of his first day of school in DeKalb County, Danielle made Corey a fresh bacon, ham, and egg sandwich for breakfast and promised honey-barbecue ribs for dinner. Then she sent him off to Stephenson Middle. When he walked through the heavy double doors, the sights, sounds, and styles filled him with an entirely new sensation. Eight hundred seventy-six of the school's students were Black. Seven were white.

"It felt amazing," Corey said. "You don't got to worry about trying to impress white kids."

The good vibes, however, didn't last long. That first day, a brawl broke out in front of the cafeteria. This wasn't goofballs smacking each other in the back of the head. Mugs were full-out swinging on each other. Corey, who'd never before seen a serious fight, was shocked.

His own baptism came a few weeks later. Some boy in the hall said something smart. Corey pushed him. The kid threw a punch. Other students pulled out their phones and began recording. After a faceless adult pulled the boys apart, Corey braced for the call home and a summer spent on lockdown. But he needn't have worried.

"Not only did I not get called to the principal's office, but teachers saw the video and did nothing about it," he said. "At that moment, I really knew things were different in DeKalb."

Back in Gwinnett, meanwhile, life kept buzzing along. Nika had her hands full with yet another dispute involving the Gwinnett County Public Schools. This one involved her daughter. Cassidy earned straight As, had high test scores, and never got in trouble. But administrators at Ivy Creek Elementary had never followed up on her third-grade teacher's recommendation that she be considered for the gifted program. When Nika tried to press the issue, they insisted her daughter wasn't mature enough. *If this kind of bullshit is routine,* Nika began to wonder, *what would happen to my children if I sue the school district or run for school board?* Once again, she and Anthony had an impossible decision to make.

"What am I supposed to say?" Nika asked rhetorically after they decided gifted would have to wait another year. "Honey, I'm sorry, but we've got to put you on the back burner because we have a bigger fight on our hands"?

But the days just kept getting busier. Nika started a new job at a different consulting firm where she had even more responsibility. She was also preparing to start in the public health PhD program at the University of Georgia. By the time the Robinsons found out about Corey's fight at Stephenson, the lack of follow-up from the school seemed almost funny.

"He's not about that life," Nika joked. "He's just a coddled suburban kid."

Maybe it was all for the best, she sighed. She put her lawsuit and fledgling campaign on hold. Her nightly research into the area's private schools slowed. And when Corey said he wanted to return to Jones for eighth grade, Nika's resolve crumpled. *Is it really necessary to put my own family on the line?* she wondered. *Wouldn't becoming the person writing the rules make more of an impact? Isn't that what getting a doctorate is all about?*

That summer of 2018, Marlyn Tillman and Gwinnett SToPP joined a national effort to challenge the Trump administration's plans to stop examining how school discipline policies affected racial minorities. But Nika's focus was on getting Corey reinstated at Jones. The first step was filing a "parent concern form" with the district's Department of Equity and Compliance. When asked about their desired outcome, the Robinsons wrote:

> *We are seeking: 1) acknowledgment that implicit bias is impacting Corey's educational success at Jones Middle School 2) an acknowledgment from the administration that successive, punitive discipline measures are counter-productive and are not meeting Corey's (or the school's) needs 3) a collaborative planning meeting for school administration and Corey's parents to develop a success plan for 8th grade 4) removal of the SST from Corey's records.*

A meeting was set for late July. Every night for a week, Nika stayed up late to prepare. First, she developed a list of talking points that ran two pages long. Then she put together a PowerPoint deck and accompanying handouts that included twenty brightly colored charts and graphs. Next, she developed a list of supportive adults that included Corey's grandparents and godparents; Coach Russ; Nika's best friend, Imani; and their family minister. All were invited to join Nika and Anthony at Jones to show support for Corey.

On the day of the meeting, everyone who could make it gathered in the Jones lobby. Who are all these people, Nika and several others in attendance recalled the Gwinnett County Public Schools' director for equity and compliance demanding. You all have to wait outside, the woman said. That she was Black only made her attitude harder to swallow.

"She understood what we were doing," Nika told me later. "She knew we were showing that Corey comes from a good family."

The conflict was eventually defused by Jones's principal, a short-haired white woman named Memorie Reesman. It's okay, Nika and others remembered Reesman saying. Just give us a minute to find a room that can hold everyone. As the group headed back to the Jones counseling suite, however, the director of equity and compliance said the Robinsons' family, friends, coach, and minister would have to sit at a separate table and would not be allowed to speak.

Nika and Anthony found themselves at a U-shaped table opposite the Gwinnett administrators. Nika opened her laptop and distributed individual folders containing hard copies. The agenda she'd typed up included the URLs for six research studies she thought might be helpful. We're here to talk about Corey, Nika began. I'm hopeful we can come to some sort of agreement for him to return. Then she opened PowerPoint and clicked through to her second slide. The header said "Corey's Village." Underneath a talking point about the need to restore trust, Nika's first bullet read:

> *Primary goal is to encourage and support Jones in seeing Corey as a whole child and educating him as such—understand that his strengths are something to be celebrated and not demonized or attacked.*

Before she could get to bullet number two, however, the director of equity and compliance jumped in. Corey hadn't been kicked out of Jones, the woman pointedly reminded the group. The Robinsons had pulled him out. If he wanted to return, he'd first have to serve the two suspensions he'd earned back in March.

"Well, seems you want to start with the negative," Nika recalled responding.

She clicked to the next slide. It was titled "Implicit Bias and Impact on Student Learning/Development." The Jones administrators shifted in their seats.

"We don't always think it's malicious," Nika said, trying to rediscover a nonthreatening tone.

A second set of stapled handouts contained data Marlyn Tillman had showed her how to download from the website of the U.S. Department of Education's Office of Civil Rights. A series of charts showed that Black students made up 23 percent of all students at Jones. But they received nearly 38 percent of all out-of-school suspensions, almost 45 percent of all in-school suspensions, and half of all expulsions.

"We're not crazy parents, we understand that Corey is not perfect," Nika said. "But there's a systemic problem."

She remembered Reesman staring at the information in silence. When the principal finally spoke, Nika and others said, she didn't address the data before her or the patterns they described. Instead, she offered to forget the whole thing and wipe the slate clean. Let's figure out how can we move forward, they remembered Reesman saying.

At that, Nika felt her stomach settle back into its proper spot. When negotiations commenced, Jones administrators offered to let Corey return for eighth grade without first serving his two outstanding suspensions. They would not, however, remove the SST referral from his record. Nika tried to push for additional accommodations, asking that Corey be allowed to stand up during silent classroom reading and take regular bathroom and water breaks. The response from Jones administrators was less than definitive. After a brief consultation, the Robinsons decided to take the deal on the table.

"At that point," Anthony told me later, "we weren't necessarily trying to reform the school."

LIBERALS VS. PROGRESSIVES

THE ADESINA FAMILY | EVANSTON, ILLINOIS

> The work was too fast and too slow, too much and
> too little.
>
> —Decoteau J. Irby,
> *Stuck Improving*, 2021

Lauren Adesina still felt energized in the fall of 2018. As copresident of the Dewey Elementary PTA, she was a regular presence inside the school, planning fundraisers and peeking in on Chris's Spanish-immersion classroom. He was the only boy who presented as Black, which sometimes gave her pause, especially because he was so highly attuned to the shifting social allegiances of his classmates; when Lauren asked how his day went, her son usually zipped right past math and reading, diving instead into the details of how William or Avi had treated him at recess. Fortunately, principal Donna Sokolowski had made attending to the ways such experiences were often shaped by race a central part of her job. An older white woman with a background in special education, she'd already been through the district's SEED and Beyond Diversity trainings, read *Despite the Best Intentions* with her book club, and taken part in a study of *White Fragility* alongside her staff. She'd also applauded the diversification of the Dewey PTA and the changes the group's new board were making to school fundraisers. And one of her biggest priorities as principal was supporting a Dewey-wide push for "restorative" discipline intended as an antidote to the racialized suspensions and expulsions that defined school systems like Gwinnett's. Less than ten minutes into our first conversation, Sokolowski told me about her commitment to racial equity and social justice, then explained where that commitment had originated.

"My own lived experiences and my own passions," she said. "I was raised in Chicago in a very diverse community, so I grew up with a very diverse group of friends. I'm also married to a Black woman."

Chris's teacher, meanwhile, also had a reputation for turning classroom tiffs over things like sharing markers into broader discussions about what it means to care for your community. Mr. Abreu was an enthusiastic participant in Dewey's "Tiger Buddies" program, which paired younger children with upper-grade students in an informal mentoring program. He also delighted in working with his students to produce sweet little handmade books that featured the children's drawings of themselves sharing cookies and swinging together on the playground. Chris titled his *How to Keep All Your Frens.* It was one of the few books he never tired of rereading.

Room 103 embodied that same inviting warmth. Abreu had arranged the desks in tables that sat small groups of five or six. A bright carpet was covered with floor pillows and beanbag seats. In the back was a Treasure Box from which kids who'd helped a friend that day could pick a prize, a reward that motivated Chris tremendously. Eager to be as involved as possible, Lauren signed up to be a class parent, weaving herself into the daily life of Dewey by helping coordinate supply drives and lead read-alouds.

Given all the points of contact, she saw no reason to prepare for her first parent-teacher conference. Instead, she sat down, made a moment of small talk, and waited for Mr. Abreu to begin. Chris was doing well with his numbers but struggling to match some letters with the sounds they made, Lauren recalled the teacher saying when I asked her to reconstruct the meeting. Before she could voice her concern, however, Abreu was already putting her mind at ease, describing such early stumbles in two-way immersion class-rooms as common and not concerning, like a temporary backup at a traffic light. Once the light turns green, Lauren remembered him saying, kids start reading and writing up a storm in two languages at once. Chris will be fine, he said. Really. He's such a nice kid.

When we talked about such interactions later, Lauren told me she wasn't quite sure how to feel about them at the time. During her visits to Dewey, for example, she might see Sokolowski in the main office or at a meeting. The principal would flash a familiar smile and comment on what important work the PTA was doing. Mostly it felt grounding. But sometimes, Lauren maintained, Sokolowski would do something that just felt off, like making a not-so-subtle reference to her marriage.

"It was just annoying," Lauren said. "Like, every time you see me, you have to remind me that you have a Black partner?"

Sokolowski denied making such comments more than once or twice. And despite her annoyance, Lauren's life was too busy to register any deeper problem. The nonprofit where she worked had expanded its programming to dozens of new schools across Chicago. That meant more responsibility and a longer commute. There were also regular weeknight meetings of District 65's African American, Black, and Caribbean parent group, and Lauren had joined the planning committee of Next Steps and would soon take part in a panel discussion that also featured Kate Ellison, the progressive white principal at Washington Elementary who'd been working for years on ev-erything from encouraging cross-cultural playdates to keeping kids who needed specialized supports in their regular classrooms. Inspired, Lauren and the Dewey PTA's other copresidents had already canceled Pioneer Days and revamped the Fun Run. Now they set out to overhaul the school's second-largest fundraiser.

The event was called Dance for Dewey. In the past, students had asked for pledges from family members, then danced for an hour in the gymnasium during the school day. To open the event up to more parents from different backgrounds, the revamped Dewey PTA decided to book the DJ for a second evening performance and replace the entrance fee with a suggested donation. On the day of the dance, the walls and windows in Dewey's big multipurpose room were covered with construction-paper silhouettes of nighttime skyscrapers lit up with rectangular yellow windows. Above them, DEWEY CITY was spelled out in big block letters. As the music got louder, Chris turned up the enthusiasm on his version of the Orange Justice, bending over at the waist and twisting his hips side to side while turning his wrists and forearms inside out, leading his mother to break out in loving laughter.

"Even I was dancing," joked Lauren, now more than two decades removed from her days in Dance Troupe. "I thought I had forgotten how."

Beneath such joy and optimism, however, the discontent humming around Evanston had started growing into a rumble. A small but vocal minority of residents were starting to recoil at District 65's consuming focus on racial equity, questioning the need to spend $104,000 in a single school year on a consultant to lead equity audits and SEED trainings. Some teachers at Dewey and elsewhere were also less than thrilled about the prospect of reading books like *White Fragility* in study groups separated by race. Even on Dewey's PTA, some members of the leadership committee were getting antsy over the sudden, sweeping changes, including new bylaws requiring them to complete ten hours of equity training. Lauren struggled to contain her frustration when she overheard some of the Hispanic moms on the PTA complain about feeling invisible and white parents and faculty whisper that "the whole equity thing" was just another passing fad.

"Yes, things are changing," she told me later. "But every single thing in America is still for you. So I feel like you should just get over it."

Then came the racist slurs targeting her son. I asked Lauren to help me reconstruct the details of how she'd found out what happened. It was a Thursday evening in late October, she said. She had to work late. The golden leaves on the honey locust and elm trees surrounding the Dewey playground were shivering in the wind by the time she arrived to pick Chris up from his after-school program. He ran over for a hug, then started in on his usual list of updates, about things like picking a prize from the Treasure Box and playing a joke on William and a loud boy who scared the other kids in the after-school program. Lauren responded with the rhythmic mm-hmms of tired parents everywhere. And oh by the way, Chris added. Another boy told me that all Black people are monkeys.

I'm sorry, what did you say? Lauren remembered asking, suddenly at full attention.

This boy found me in line and leaned into my face and told me that all Black people are monkeys, Chris said. And that boy in the after-school program was bothering us again.

Lauren felt staggered, but tried to remain calm. She let her son talk for a minute about the bully in the after-school program, nodding along and acting unbothered. Then she circled back to the hand grenade between them. Tell me more about what happened with the other boy, she said in the most normal tone she could muster.

They'd been walking in line for drama class, Chris replied. The boy had gotten out of line to find him. Then he said what he said.

When did this happen? Lauren asked.

A couple weeks ago, Chris said.

He's been carrying this for weeks, Lauren thought. *And no one knew. Not even his mother.*

Then Chris said his drama teacher had overheard the boy's remark. He'd even talked to the class about it. Lauren dug her nails into the playground bench. The drama teacher was a white man, Lauren told me. Apparently, he'd heard her Black son get verbally assaulted with a vile racial slur, but didn't call home. Lauren wanted to scream. Chris looked worried he'd done something wrong.

I'm sorry, Lauren recalled telling her son. I'm not upset because of anything you did. I'm glad you told me. Are you okay?

It just hurt my feelings, Chris replied. Why would he say that?

Before Lauren could respond, her son answered his own question.

He's my friend, Chris said, suggesting that maybe the boy didn't intend his remarks to be mean.

There he goes again, thought Lauren, suddenly drowning in sadness. *Always searching for the good in every situation.* It was the quality about her son she most wanted to protect. At the same time, however, she didn't want him to think this other little boy's racist comments were acceptable.

You're dope just the way you are, she recalled saying.

Why is my skin different than his? Chris asked. Why is it darker than yours?

Lauren looked toward the sky. Dusk was swallowing the tops of the trees. She still didn't know what to make for dinner. The drive home took her past a soccer field and a community garden and fairy-tale houses with Black Lives Matter signs on their lawns. Lauren reminded her son that his grandparents came from different parts of the world and could speak lots of languages and cooked all kinds of wonderful foods. We're blessed to have all those cool backgrounds fused together inside us, she said, winning a satisfied nod.

But Lauren told me she had to attend a meeting of the African American, Black, and Caribbean parents' association later that night. By the time she arrived, her fury had returned twofold. What the other boy said was bad enough. But Lauren simply could not believe that no one from Dewey had called to let her know what happened. Maybe she could have been more thoughtful about tending to her young son's psyche. Maybe she could even have turned the whole thing into a teachable moment. Instead, she'd been forced to wing an impossible conversation on the fly. Unable to focus, Lauren pulled out her laptop and began composing the first of three momentous emails that would fundamentally alter the nature of her relationship to Evanston and District 65 during the 2018–19 school year. It began:

> *I'm not sure of another way to begin this email other than that I am livid and extremely disappointed.*

Then Lauren laid out for Mr. Abreu, Principal Sokolowski, and a couple of other Dewey staff members what Chris had told her and demanded to know what follow-up steps the school had taken.

> *What was said to Chris to reassure him that he is not a monkey? What were the consequences for the racist statement? How was*

*that student taught that Black people are not monkeys and should
never be referred to as monkeys?*

Then Lauren said she was sorry.

*I would like to apologize if this email comes off as brash, but I
have to be very honest when conveying my concerns.*

A flurry of messages among Dewey staff members ensued. Lauren and
Sokolowski agreed to meet the coming Monday afternoon. When we talked
later, the principal recalled one of her personal mottos at the time, about
choosing courage over comfort. It always comes down to what kind of personal work you're willing to do, she said. Lauren, meanwhile, recalled having
to leave work three and a half hours early. At the meeting, she said, everyone
from Dewey just kept saying they were sorry again and again. Although Sokolowski and the Dewey administrators encouraged further classroom discussions, consistent with the school's emphasis on restorative discipline,
Lauren told me it was largely left to her to actually propose tangible action
steps. She told the Dewey educators she wanted them to commit to reporting any racist incidents involving students to both administrators and parents. She also wanted Mr. Abreu to meet with her regularly to discuss her
son's well-being. The idea of pairing Chris with a Black Tiger Buddy also
came up. And Lauren asked Sokolowski to arrange a meeting with the parents of the boy who made the racist remark. The principal agreed to every
request but the last. *At least there's a plan in place*, Lauren recalled thinking
as she got up to leave.

The next three weeks were a blur. Out of nowhere, Chris would bust out
with a statement like, "I'm the darkest one in our family." *He's still holding
on to all that trauma*, Lauren would think as she brushed her teeth and
started to cry. Then she'd drop her son at school and go to work.

The rest of life didn't stop either. During this period, Lauren recalled, the
executive committee of the Dewey PTA gathered in the big, beautiful home
of a white family who lived near Lake Michigan. Her friend and copresident

Lila Anyango-Hill couldn't make it, Lauren said, so she was on her own when some of the other parents began complaining anew about the mandatory equity training. Lauren told me later that she'd held her tongue until one of the other PTA moms said she didn't have time to take part in such trainings. Y'all are giving me pushback about reading some articles while my son is in school experiencing racism? Lauren remembered responding. Then, she said, a white man interrupted her in a raised voice.

Yo, listen, Lauren remembered saying. I'm not the one. There's a whole other side of me that will come out. I let you say the nasty stuff you needed to say. Now you can sit there quietly and listen to me.

A week or so later, Lauren recalled, she arranged to talk with the mother of the boy who'd directed the slur at her son. They met at a coffeehouse with white Christmas lights hung in looping strings in its big picture window. Inside, the bulletin board was thick with ads for yoga lessons and a womyn's bike ride. We're handling this nicely because it's the first time, Lauren remembered telling the other mom. But your child better not talk to my kid like that ever again.

I am so, so sorry, she recalled the other mom responding. I have no idea where he got this from. That's not how we are. Our nanny is Belizean.

Not even a friend, Lauren thought. *The help.*

By late November, Lauren had quit her job so she could be more available to Chris. Around that time, he came home from school and started in on his usual update. Reading workshop was fine. Avi and William had played with him at recess. He'd met with his new Tiger Buddy.

What did the Tiger Buddy look like, Lauren remembered asking.

They're white, Chris responded.

Lauren told me she called the school looking for answers, but had to leave a message. While waiting for a response, she recalled, she got a call from another Black mom at Dewey. The woman said her Black daughter had been called a chimpanzee during art class, but no one from the school had notified her. When Dewey's assistant principal eventually called back, Lauren recalled receiving an update on the Tiger Buddy situation, then hearing the woman clear her throat and say she had something else to share.

I also wanted you to know that Chris just told me another student said they didn't want to play with him because they didn't like his skin color, Lauren remembered the assistant principal saying.

Lauren immediately burst into tears.

You're hurt, she recalled the assistant principal saying. I thought you'd be angry.

From the outset, Lauren told me, she'd bent over backward to avoid being labeled an angry Black woman. But this woman on the phone could still knee-cap her with a few careless words, leaving her with another impossible deci-sion to make. Call out the new microaggression? Or keep the conversation focused on Chris? Lauren swallowed something bitter and heavy, then asked the assistant principal for more information on the latest incident. By Sunday night, she was back at her laptop. Her second consequential email of the school year was addressed not only to Sokolowski and Dewey's assistant principal, but to superintendent Paul Goren and the entire District 65 board. It began:

> *After a couple of sleepless nights and determining whether speak-ing up would be detrimental to my son's experience at his school, I felt that it was imperative that I inform the D65 community of what is going on at Dewey.*

Lauren relayed the details of what happened to her son, then described the subsequent meeting.

> *I spoke with the teachers involved and principal to come up with a plan we all agreed on. Although not completely happy with the out-come, I left the meeting with a small feeling of hope.*

But it had all been a charade, Lauren wrote. Teachers still weren't tell-ing families about racist incidents affecting their children. Dewey staff hadn't followed through on their promises. She'd entrusted the school with her only child, then done everything she could to keep him safe, Lauren concluded. But it hadn't been enough.

> *The school did not hold up their end of the bargain.*

"THE OUTRAGE JUST WASN'T THERE"

Racial tensions inside District 65 were already running high when Lauren's email landed in the Joseph E. Hill Education Center. All school year, superintendent Paul Goren and his cabinet had been dealing with the fallout from racist incidents at Lincolnwood Elementary, where children had told Black classmates, "This isn't your school," and Willard Elementary, where someone had carved the n-word into a piece of playground equipment. Four years into his tenure, Goren was finally stumbling toward urgency.

"I think one of the lessons learned was that over time, the collective 'we,' including me, I'll own this as well, sort of brushed these kinds of incidents under the table," the superintendent said.

Bookish but charismatic, Goren had the manner of a popular professor who lived for office hours. Asked a question, he would often pause, look skyward as he organized his thoughts, then let loose a speeding torrent of words that swept up people's reactions, snippets of recent conversations, and ideas from old research articles as they gathered momentum. Then he'd stop midsentence and go back to the beginning, sharpening his original point with the new information he'd picked up as he was making it.

Goren was immensely proud of being featured in *Children of the Dream*, the Rucker Johnson book extolling the benefits of school integration. The section about him described three framed photos Goren hung on the walls of his office. The first, taken in 1964, featured his kindergarten class at Avalon Park Elementary on Chicago's South Side. The class was split roughly evenly between white and Black children. Chubby and pale, Goren stood smiling next to a dark-complexioned girl with pigtails. The other two class photos came from later years at the same school, when all the white kids but Goren and a couple others had disappeared.

"I think if you put me on the professional shrink's couch, you can see where my devotion to education comes from," the superintendent told me. "Some of this is about people who are moving because of the schools, so the question becomes, what about schools can we invest in?"

When it came to running a district, however, Goren's commitment to integrated schooling was tempered by a deep wariness of sudden change. As a doctoral student at Stanford, he'd studied alongside revered education historians David Tyack and Larry Cuban. At the time, they were working on a hugely influential book called *Tinkering Toward Utopia*. In it, the pair argued that Americans had a long history of demanding sweeping changes from their public schools, which they expected to serve as a panacea for a wide range of social ills. But while such urgency was understandable, Tyack and Cuban wrote, it was often counterproductive. The country's K–12 system was radically decentralized, school districts were extremely sensitive to the whims of local voters, and individual schools relied heavily on teachers who had near total control of their own classrooms. As a result, the historians suggested, dramatic top-down reforms rarely lasted. The better, more realistic path to progress was throwing everything you had into helping teachers gradually improve the nuts and bolts of their classroom practice.

Goren's belief in that philosophy had grown steadfast during his years working in school districts in Chicago and Minnesota, then at a variety of think tanks and foundations. Over time, he'd also come to admire the work of Richard Elmore, another legendary education researcher who focused on what he called schools' "instructional core" of teachers, students, and content. By the time Goren began interviewing for the District 65 superintendency, he was arguing that every investment a school district made should support such foundational goals as helping teachers get better, making the curriculum more rigorous, and creating safe and supportive learning environments for children. It was laborious and painstaking work, he told the District 65 board. But the path to justice and equity was paved brick by brick, with incremental improvements.

"Slow and steady and staying focused on instruction wins the race," Goren remembered saying.

Back in 2014, that message had resonated. Few Evanston residents wanted to blow District 65 up entirely, but the town was plagued by a nagging sense its public schools were leaking oil. Test scores were headed in the wrong direction. Some of the affluent white parents I spoke with were annoyed they had to invest in private French lessons if they wanted to keep up with the families who had moved to ritzier communities further north. Many families of color, meanwhile, had grown exasperated by watching their children's white classmates get ushered into opportunities like accelerated math classes through processes that remained mysterious to everyone else. The resulting feeling of losing ground was particularly pronounced for Black families, whose numbers were steadily declining as Evanston became more multicultural.

Two years earlier, the many-sided dissatisfaction had briefly bubbled to Evanston's surface. District 65 put forth a capital referendum intended to raise millions for a new elementary school in the Fifth Ward. Supporters pointed to history, stressing that Evanston's Black community had sacrificed its neighborhood school for the greater good back in 1967 and now deserved recompense. Goren, then just a regular Evanston resident, reacted in a way that was typical of the town's white liberal establishment. In theory, he told me later, he wanted to support the Black parents and activists. But he just didn't think the plan made financial sense. When the referendum was voted down, he figured the fight was over. Upon being hired as superintendent, he trained his attention on matters he considered more pressing.

"I landed in a district that had a foundation of quicksand. It was wobbly on the instructional side, with lots of people doing their own thing because that was what they had done for years," Goren said. "We were also facing some level of financial doom."

To address the first problem, he set out to improve Evanston's K–3 classrooms by clarifying what students were expected to learn, redesigning the district's literacy curriculum, and pushing school staff to take part in professional learning communities and make better use of data on students' academic performance. These were "mom and apple pie" reforms, Goren said. Who could be against better reading instruction?

Addressing District 65's structural budget deficit was more fraught. For the moment, its books were still balanced. But operating expenses were rising by roughly 3 percent a year, and the board was only allowed to raise property taxes by roughly 1.5 percent a year. Do nothing, and the problem would compound and spread. But start cutting, and Goren risked a popular uprising; the overwhelming majority of the district's costs were tied up in teachers' salaries and benefits, which couldn't be eliminated without sacrificing the small class sizes and specialized music and arts programs Evanston parents demanded.

Hoping to avoid both fates, Goren and the board decided to put forward a referendum of their own. This one was for $14.5 million a year in new operating revenue that could be stashed away in the short term, then used to paper over annual operating deficits when they began to appear. It wouldn't fix the structural problem. But the plan would buy District 65 about eight years to streamline its operations and ease into difficult decisions about layoffs and school closures. In April 2017, Evanston voters approved the operating referendum by a 4–1 margin. The measure won a majority of voters in every Evanston precinct, an outcome that Goren took as a sign he was successfully building cross-racial support.

"We as a community gave a clarion call on how much we care about public education," he said.

But the winds of change were already blowing. The whiplash of going from President Obama to President Trump had undercut many residents' faith in steady technocratic progress as the best path to social justice. And their shifting political calculus was reinforced by worrisome new trends in District 65. If anything, Goren's early reforms seemed to have made things worse; test scores were dipping, and the gap between Evanston's Black and white students now appeared to be even wider than it had been prior to desegregation a half century earlier.

The simmering discontent came to a boil when Stanford researcher Sean Reardon came to town to deliver a talk in spring 2017. He'd recently published a monumental analysis of the standardized test scores of more than 40 million American children. In the process, Reardon had determined that Evanston was home to one of the largest racial achievement gaps in the country. But nuances in the data turned his work into a political Rorschach test.

View Reardon's findings through a traditional liberal lens, and it appeared Black students in District 65 were doing rather well, outperforming their Black peers in three fourths of the nation's school systems and finishing middle school roughly on par with the typical American eighth grader.

View those same findings through a more progressive lens, however, and it appeared Black students in District 65 were struggling mightily. Most finished middle school lagging their white classmates by a whopping four grade levels. The reason, Reardon told the crowd, was that the average white student in District 65 finished eighth grade performing on par with the typical American twelfth grader. In other words, white kids in District 65 were scoring higher than students *in every other school district in the country.*

Reardon attributed the yawning disparity primarily to class differences. More than three fourths of Black District 65 students were eligible for a free or reduced-price lunch, he noted, compared to just 7 percent of white students. This line of thinking generally made sense to Evanston's liberal white establishment. In a column published that summer, the editor of a widely read local nonprofit news outlet called the *Evanston RoundTable* devoted nearly three thousand words to detailing the importance of socioeconomic status.

"It's clear that the gaps are already there at third grade" read one of the Reardon quotes the *RoundTable* highlighted. "Something is happening that is creating really different opportunities prior to that time."

Progressives, however, blanched at such arguments. They focused instead on one particularly significant scatterplot in Reardon's slide deck. It contained thousands of small white circles, each of which represented a U.S. school district. The farther to the right of the chart a circle appeared, the larger the gap in average incomes between the Black and white families that district served. The farther to the top, the larger the district's Black-white achievement gap. The circle representing District 65 was near the chart's center, indicating relatively modest income differences in Evanston. But that same circle was way up near the tippy-top of the chart, indicating that District 65's racial achievement gap was significantly larger than the gaps in other communities with similar economic profiles. Two years later, school board member Anya Tanyavutti told me that the scatterplot—and the faces in the mostly white audience for Reardon's talk, which beamed with pride upon being told their children were the top-performing students in the country—were still seared into her mind.

"What was hardest for me in that room was that inside, I felt like crying. But no one else did. The outrage just wasn't there," she said. "We have kids who sat next to each other in our schools for nine years in a row, getting vastly different results, and everyone's internalized it as 'I'm such a great parent, my kids are so wonderful, they're four grade levels ahead.'"

To underscore her point, Tanyavutti then posed a hypothetical. What if Reardon had told that same audience that boys in Evanston were outperforming girls by four grade levels?

"There's no way our community would say, 'That's okay with me. I'm real proud of our boys,'" she said. "It would be, 'What in this school system is doing this to our girls and how do we fix it immediately?'"

Such competing interpretations of Reardon's findings weren't just academic. Evanston's more-liberal establishment believed the solution to District 65's racial achievement gap was investing heavily in preschools and early childhood centers. The town's more-progressive leaders, on the other hand, believed the challenge was no longer "technical," requiring expert tinkering from on high, but "adaptive," requiring a radical, bottom-up rethinking of the system itself. This approach, progressive parents and activists believed, entailed changing people's hearts and minds, so they could see the ways racism really operated in District 65. It also meant changing policies, budgets, and personnel while calling out and disrupting all the invisible norms, routines, and assumptions that had allowed generations of white parents to hoard the opportunities available in District 65.

Evanston's community-wide shift toward the progressives' point of view was already evident in schools like Dewey; Principal Sokolowski later told me that it was the 2018–19 school year when she'd started to feel like the push for racial equity had started to switch from a feeling of "we're all in this together" to a pattern of "blame and shame." For his part, Superintendent Goren seemed to be caught in the middle. Like Coffin and Alson before him, he'd embraced the need for a public reckoning with Evanston's racial disparities; he'd already overseen the release of reports on Black and Hispanic

student achievement within District 65, both of which largely mirrored the
conclusions reached by the Educational Testing Service in 1971 and the Minority Student Achievement Network in 2002, inadvertently helping fuel
frustration at the glacial pace of change in Evanston. And when it came to
policy, Goren had been in charge when District 65 adopted its Racial and
Educational Equity Statement and created a new central-office position
known as the Director of Black Student Success. But he'd promptly followed
such steps to the left with attempts to circle back to the center.

The most prominent example of this dynamic involved District 65's racial literacy training, a key priority of Tanyavutti and activist groups like
Next Steps. Goren embraced the programs, even becoming one of the first
District 65 employees to complete Beyond Diversity. In a small room on
Northwestern's campus, the superintendent sat knee to knee with his co-
workers, recounting the moment he'd first become aware of his racial identity. He'd even taken part in a privilege walk, taking one step forward for
having grown up with both his parents, another for having inherited family
wealth, and a third for being born a white man. At the end of the exercise,
Goren had turned around and discovered he'd left all his colleagues of color
behind.

"It was really powerful," he told me later. "It made me physically see the difference in the room, rather than just being intellectual and reading about it."

The experience helped Goren realize it was no longer enough to trot out
his pat personal narrative about being the white kid whose family had stayed
in a Black neighborhood. He needed to be more intentional about not leaving
people of color to dismantle racism on their own. He tried to become a better
listener. And as District 65's superintendent, Goren came to believe, it was
his personal responsibility to bend the arc of the 7,500-student, $139 million
system toward equity.

Still, he was reluctant about moving too fast. There was scant empirical
evidence that racial literacy training shifted people's behavior or improved
educational outcomes for kids. Around the district, complaints about Beyond Diversity and SEED were starting to morph from mild concern about
rigid terminology to moral panic about Cultural Revolution–style brain-

washing. Inside individual classrooms, meanwhile, translating a teacher's newfound awareness of a concept like white privilege into better literacy instruction remained painstaking work. And District 65's other problems hadn't magically disappeared; in private, Goren was growing frustrated with the board, whose focus on advocating for racial equity seemed to be crowding out its other responsibilities and eroding its will for the budget cutbacks still needed to ensure the district's long-term solvency.

Such were the tensions swirling inside District 65 headquarters when Lauren Adesina's email showed up in the superintendent's inbox. Still determined to personally stitch up the wounds now being ripped open across Evanston, Goren decided the trouble at Dewey warranted a personal touch. As he picked up the phone and punched in Lauren's number, a fresh uncertainty hung in the highly charged air of one of suburbia's last best hopes for preserving the fading promise of integration. I'd originally decided to focus on Evanston because parents and educators there were already trying to address the problems that rapid demographic, economic, and cultural changes were exposing in other suburbs around the country. But those efforts were now sparking a new set of challenges and debates.

"Can a white person lead this work?" Goren would say several months later, repeating my question as he looked up to the ceiling and composed his thoughts. "I still think the answer is yes. But they have to jump right in."

OFF THE RAILS

The call from the superintendent started off smoothly enough. There's nothing more important than when a mom says her child has been called a name that has no place in school, Lauren heard Goren say over the phone. I'm the chief executive of this system, and I will be on this. Her first reaction was to feel thankful.

"I mean, he's a very nice, charismatic person. It was like a bubbly conversation," she said. "So it was kind of like, 'Okay, I appreciate the superintendent reaching out.'"

But then Goren kept talking. Part of the problem, he told Lauren, his words gathering momentum as they poured out of his mouth, was that District 65 didn't have established protocols for how to respond to racist speech by students. That put teachers in the unenviable position of being first responders without any backup. Asking them to carry the system's broader equity agenda alone was a tall order. The good news was that most District 65 teachers were sensitive and dedicated. Even so, improvements would take time.

Goren stopped himself midstream, then started over. Take the Dewey teacher who was involved in the incident with your son, he told Lauren. Mr. Abreu actually taught one of my own children. He's a wonderful teacher. Thoughtful, caring, deeply committed to equity. And I know personally how badly he wants to do right by families. When my son was in his class, the superintendent said, warming now to his own story, I went to New Zealand on a Fulbright fellowship. My family came too. My son grew very lonely. So my wife and I reached out to his school back in Evanston. And Mr. Abreu went well beyond the call of duty, even arranging a series of Skype calls. Such a simple act, Goren said. But it brought my kid so much joy.

That's great for your white son, Lauren thought as her earlier gratitude collapsed in a heap. *But why on earth do you think it's appropriate to tell this story to a Black mom whose son was just called a monkey at that same school?*

"He was just oblivious," she said when I asked her about the conversation later.

"I was trying to share that this is a reflective practitioner who cares deeply about kids," Goren tried to explain.

A week or so after the phone call, the superintendent sent a letter to all District 65 staff and families. The head—**D65 Stands Against Racism and Hate**—was bolded at the top. The message started by acknowledging the "hateful, racist, and sometimes violent language used by some students in District 65." It specifically referenced the recent incidents at Willard, Lincolnwood, and Dewey. Goren also sent a similar message to district staff, attaching a thirty-page guide on "Responding to Hate and Bias at School" from a group called Teaching Tolerance, and the district began the process of developing its own protocols for handling such incidents.

Lauren was mildly annoyed that Goren had shared the details of her family's experience at Dewey with all of Evanston without first seeking her permission. More important, she also believed that racist incidents were still clearly being mishandled by District 65 schools. How could she have faith in a system that was just now developing a policy to deal with entrenched racism that went back decades? And why on earth did Goren seem to think he should be congratulated for only responding now to a problem he and District 65 had been sweeping under the rug for years?

The sharing circles that followed only made things worse. The first was held at Dewey. Goren and District 65's new equity director joined about sixty parents around the same wooden tables in the library where the Racial Equity Impact Assessment Tool had filled Lauren with hope less than a year earlier. The district officials on hand tried to lay out ground rules stipulating that staff should listen silently as parents and family members shared their experience. Teachers promptly objected, saying they'd already been scapegoated enough. As ever, Goren saw both sides.

"My stance on that was as part of building a process, the adults in the building needed to put ourselves in the vulnerable position of hearing out those who had been pained," he said. "But we also have due process issues, which I have to pay attention to and respect."

Whatever patience Lauren still had for such moderation evaporated during a subsequent sharing circle later that school year. She remembered a bunch of white women starting to cry. She also remembered Principal Sokolowski talking about her Black partner again and the Belizean nanny coming back up. When several parents in attendance voiced concern that the Dewey students who'd made racist remarks—none of whom had been punished beyond being asked to apologize—were being "criminalized," Lauren again felt like screaming.

Then, in February, she had another parent-teacher conference with Mr. Abreu. When Lauren reconstructed the meeting for me later, she described a scene every bit as demoralizing as what the Robinsons experienced in Gwinnett and Bethany Smith would soon have to contend with in Penn Hills. The light hadn't turned green for Chris, who was still struggling with reading and writing. But before Lauren could demand that he be expected to write more than two complete sentences in a thirty-minute writing workshop, she told me, Mr. Abreu informed her that he'd started letting her son sit on a beanbag chair and play on an iPad when he felt sad. Lauren also recalled Abreu informing her that Chris had upped the frequency of his bathroom breaks from ten or so trips a day at the beginning of the school year to fifteen or more per day now. Lauren, who said it was the first she'd heard of the issue, knew immediately that her son was just trying to avoid unpleasant things; he was, after all, a seven-year-old. She remembered wondering why Mr. Abreu wasn't holding her son to higher standards.

I'm never going to tell a child they can't go to the bathroom, the teacher responded.

How that translates to me, Lauren thought, *is that you don't expect my child is going to learn.*

And all the while, new wounds kept ripping open around District 65. Before anyone could notice that Goren and his team had developed in record time their new protocols for responding to racist and discriminatory language, new student performance data from King Arts showed a 51-percentage-point gap between white and Black students in math and a 61-point gap in reading. Neither the magnitude nor the symbolism of those numbers were lost on the parents, activists, and PTA leaders who went ballistic, declaring a "state of emergency" over the "systematic neglect of Black children" in the same experimental elementary program that had once served as a shining beacon of Evanston's commitment to integrated public education.

The final straw came in March. Back at Dewey, Principal Sokolowski called for help responding to an incident involving a Black six-year-old at the school. From her perspective, she was following protocol, reaching out to a school resource officer who was an established part of the Dewey community and had a track record of helping deescalate difficult situations. Many progressives, however, saw a white school administrator calling a uniformed, gun-carrying police officer on a young Black child. The split left Sokolowski and others feeling like the push for justice and equity in Evanston schools was alienating the educators upon whom it depended.

"It became more difficult for staff to really want to continue the work and be open about it, because they saw how I was being viewed," she told me.

Tanyavutti, meanwhile, began publicly questioning the need for *any* ongoing relationship between Evanston's police and public schools, prompting intense discomfort among liberal parents far more worried about their children being hurt by school shooters than by local cops. Goren scrambled frantically for a solution that might satisfy everyone. But it was too late. In April 2019, the District 65 board gathered for a meeting. Unaware of what was coming, Goren began sifting through papers, then hit send on a text message. Tanyavutti opened her laptop and announced that she had a prepared statement to read.

"As a board, we can set our vision," Evanston's progressive champion said. "But the execution of that vision . . . is the responsibility of our one employee: the superintendent."

A look of surprise crept across Goren's face. Two months later, he'd offer his resignation. By then, Lauren Adesina had already sent her third and final major email of the 2018–19 school year. This time, she stated her request as a settled fact.

> *After much consideration, I have decided that a transfer to the two-way Spanish-immersion magnet program at Washington would be in my son's best interest.*

11

THE NEXT STEVE JOBS

THE HERNANDEZ FAMILY | COMPTON, CALIFORNIA

You never know what's inside of something.

—JACOB HERNANDEZ, 2019

The relentless routine of Alberto Hernandez's work as a welder scrubbed his weeks of most of their distinguishing details. But while the job left little room for personal growth, it was steady enough to offer something that many in his position struggled to find: a window of possibility for his children. Whether Marisol and Jacob made it to a better future would depend heavily on Compton's public schools, which were busy trying to create a twenty-first-century version of the promise they'd delivered back in the town's suburban heyday. In the meantime, Alberto had little choice but to content himself with punching the same codes into decade-old machines day after day, work that robots would likely take over once they found their way to the low-end furniture market in South Central Los Angeles.

"I've been doing it for sixteen years," he said with a shrug.

Fortunately, the Hernandezes still had weekends. And because the progressive California Assembly had made it possible for undocumented immigrants to obtain driver's licenses, lessening the fear of traffic stops, they were freer to roam and explore. So in the summer of 2019, Alberto and Cristina wrung a series of family outings from the family budget.

The first was to the ocean for the Fourth of July. As always, Cristina drove, steering the family minivan around the potholes that made so many Compton streets look like minefields from a long-ago war. Jacob stared out the window and read the names of all the exits. Their final destination felt like another country. Redondo County Beach was full of million-dollar condos and boasted a long wooden pier with a pick-your-own oyster jewelry store where $12 guaranteed you a pearl. The kids tumbled out of the van, then dodged bikes and scooters as they followed their father onto the sand. Jacob immediately began searching for shells. *Maybe I'll find something epic*, he thought. *Like the magic conch from that episode of* Sponge-Bob. The busy beach offered slim pickings, but he came away pleased, sliding into his pocket a pair of angel wings, the broken remains of a few ruffled butter clams, and part of an old sand dollar bleached white by the sun. Later, at home, Jacob would place the shells in a small wooden box he'd painted purple and blue. It held all the odds and ends he found during the sweet spots of his days, little time machines that could transport him backward, into a memory, or forward, into some brightly imagined future.

"I call it my found box," Jacob told me. "Sometimes, I hide it in my sister's drawer, all the way in the bottom. She's more likely to look in my stuff. She's capable of that."

Alberto knew about the box, but didn't let on. *Let the boy keep believing*, he figured. *Who knows? Maybe it will lead him to a job at NASA or Apple instead of some crummy furniture factory.*

The family's final adventure of that summer sprawled across Labor Day weekend. It began at Mona Park, a county rec center a few blocks from their home. Because it was in territory claimed by the Mona Park Compton Crips, the Hernandezes usually bypassed the center if too many people were around. By some miracle, however, the pool was mostly empty that Sunday, so Alberto and Cristina let the kids swim for an hour on their own while they ate lunch at a picnic table nearby. Jacob pressed his back against a low wall covered in a tiled mural, then let out a joyful yelp as he cannonballed into the clear blue water. That night, Alberto let him and Marisol each pick a movie, then folded them into his flanks as they sat on the sofa and watched *Titanic* and *Justice League*. The following day included a trip to Five Below for brush-tip drawing markers, then dinner at McDonald's. In the parking lot outside, Jacob noticed a handful of smooth gray and white stones. When he bent down for a closer look, he saw they were shot through with slim yellow seams. *Gold*, he thought. Later that night, he'd sneak one of his dad's hammers out into the backyard, then try to break his newest treasure open.

"You never know what's inside of something," he said.

By that point, fourth grade had already started. With its drop-tile ceilings and slits for windows, Mr. Moreno's classroom was hardly a picture of twenty-first-century modernity. But the teacher had personally fixed rain gutters to the walls, creating long shelves that were now loaded with books like *The Mouse and the Motorcycle* and *The House on Mango Street* and surrounded with student artwork modeled on the geometric abstractions of Piet Mondrian. One wall contained large posters extolling Jefferson's core values of communication, collaboration, critical thinking, and creativity. Another held whiteboards that showed each student's performance on key learning standards in long rows of numbers that were written in red if the student had come in below grade level and blue if they were above.

"So many tests," Moreno griped as he scanned through the ten open tabs in his browser during a weekday afternoon not long into the school year.

There was the ELPAC, used to determine if English learners were making adequate progress on their new language. There was also an endless stream of practice exams for the California Assessment of Student Performance and Progress (CAASPP), plus the software programs the district used to track what students were learning each week. Today's first order of business was reviewing the results of a recent iReady assessment of each child's reading level.

"Annabelle, grade one, okay. Josiah, grade three, you improved a lot, let's give a round of applause. Jacob, late fourth, excellent," Mr. Moreno said, using a laser pointer to cast a dot on each child's name.

Next up was a midunit checkpoint math test. Jacob talked himself through the word problems like a play-by-play announcer describing a Lakers' fast break. Tony had six times as many chips as Dana, Dana had nine chips, how many chips did Tony and Dana have all together? To solve the problem, he first underlined the words "all together." Then he drew a single box for Dana and six boxes for Tony. Next, he drew nine small circles in each of the boxes. Finally, he counted the total number of boxes.

"Seven. So seven times nine is sixty-three," Jacob said in a satisfied whisper. "These tests are easy."

The rest of the morning was devoted to blended learning. Moreno divided the students into small groups based on their iReady results. Kids reading below grade level received remedial instruction directly from their teacher. Middle-of-the-road kids worked on adaptive software programs that helped them practice specific skills. The handful of students left over headed to a long table at the perimeter of the classroom, where they were supposed to independently research a weird animal of their own choosing. Moreno had given the assignment a few weeks earlier. But ever since, his attention had been focused almost entirely on helping his struggling readers, leading some of the advanced students to wander off topic. I watched as a small boy named Adrian opened YouTube and became engrossed in a video about what happens when black holes collide ("I'm interested in space-time," he told me). A long-haired girl named Jocelyn was busy researching lesser-known U.S. presidents ("I want to do a presentation on Franklin Pierce," she said).

Jacob had stuck to the original assignment longer than most, completing seven separate slide decks, starting with the blobfish, then moving on to the naked mole rat, the lamprey, the baboon, the red-lipped batfish, the purple frog, and the sea pig. After running out of interesting animals to investigate, he'd gone back and added the Latin terms that described each animal's scientific classification, delighting in trying to pronounce words like *cephalaspidomorphi* as he typed them out. Then he'd started experimenting, teaching himself to add .gifs and hyperlinks and color-gradient backgrounds to his slides, then sharing the tricks with his friends.

"There are many secrets within the iPad," he said in a mock-serious voice while helping a boy named Kendall add smoke effects to a picture of a hog-nosed bumblebee bat.

Eventually, though, even Jacob's attention began to wander. He began telling me more about his plans for a class newspaper, which he hoped would include comic strips and events calendars and opinion polls. Then he peppered me with questions.

"So do you just, like, document everything?" he asked. "How many stories have you written? Which was the best?"

When my answers no longer held his interest, he turned back to his friends. The boys angled their screens out of Mr. Moreno's line of sight and began collecting power-ups in an online game called Ninja Action. Then they moved on to a clandestine Google Doc full of funny memes they'd been collecting together. When it *still* wasn't lunchtime, Jacob went back to looking up facts about weird animals, offering a stream-of-consciousness narration as he searched.

"Most people don't even know sea pigs live on the sea floor," he marveled. "Then they get caught in nets. I wonder if they're going to be endangered or extinct. Most people just think about the present. But I worry sometimes about the future. I would like to be tall, smart, with a good job. Maybe an artist or sculptor. I'd live in a big house and I'd have a small dog that could live inside. Maybe in Canada or China or Japan. Too many people in California live on the street and get into drugs or alcohol and don't even know what they're doing. I'd like to make a shelter for people like that."

When Mr. Moreno finally released the class, Jacob and his friends rushed to the lunchroom, where they inhaled their chicken nuggets and chocolate milk. Outside, they gathered with a few other kids under a mural of LeBron James, then launched into the latest installment of a playground game of their own design called "Zombie." It functioned as a cross between freeze tag, *Dungeons & Dragons*, and a futuristic sci-fi story the kids made up as they went; every rule was up for renegotiation, and no one's role was permanent. Jacob convinced the group to recognize him as a humanoid character he called the Killmaster. When a zombie froze another player in place, the Killmaster would try to finish them off with a make-believe sword or magic potion before a teammate could rescue them. Then the game would stop, and Kendall would make a show of spinning a big imaginary wheel like the one on *The Price Is Right*. When it stopped, he would invent a new weapon and award it to the Killmaster.

All the while, Mr. Moreno remained in his classroom, staring absentmindedly at his untied shoe and picking at the salad he'd packed in a thermos. He loved his students in the way only a teacher can love a child. Especially Jacob. He couldn't get enough of how the boy filled the smallest tasks with the biggest joy. How he slipped so easily into a kind of flow state, completely immersing himself in whatever he was doing. On those rare occasions when Moreno got a moment to reflect, his heart filled with worry he was failing him. Then he'd get interrupted by a colleague who needed a hand with a disruptive student, or a fourth grader who wanted to show off a loose tooth.

"I don't have the energy that I used to," Moreno told me. "I told Jacob when we start working on projects, we're going to make the newspaper happen. But I really don't know how to organize it myself."

Before he could finish the thought, his students came tumbling like dice back into the classroom. Moreno tied his shoe and corralled everyone into their seats. The afternoon would be spent finishing up narrative essays. The students had been asked to imagine their first day working at Lucasfilm. Jacob already had a strong first draft:

> *I will never forget the time I worked at Lucasfilm and created a new character for the new Star Wars movie. In the morning I got dressed made my coffee and took a granola bar. I got my keys to my Tesla . . . When I got there, the director was at the door. He said "Hello my name is Lucas Walker, you can call me Luke." . . . Then I got to meet the other stage crew and some of the actors. I even met the programmers of BB8 and R2-D2 . . . I made a couple designs and showed them to Luke and he said he liked them . . . I was sketching more ideas for other characters. I showed Luke and*

said "Maybe we can use them for a future movie." . . . I also tested
out the prototype light saber. It was like a retractable sword with
special effects. Then I went home and rested. I also ate because I
was STARVING.

Maybe, Moreno thought, all he and the other adults in Compton Unified really had to do was stay out of the boy's way.

REBUILDING FOR THE FUTURE

Darin Brawley was fifty-four, Black, with broad shoulders and short hair that faded to bare scalp well above his ears. He was also blunt, taciturn to the point of appearing disdainful, and entirely comfortable letting people squirm in the uncomfortable silences he unspooled the way others made small talk. But Compton Unified's leader did have a softer side; show him a muscle car, a programmable classroom robot, or the latest batch of test scores showing the progress of Compton Unified's twenty thousand students, and a warm smile would spread from one of his dimpled cheeks to the other. And when he made one of his regular visits to the headquarters of some high-flying company like Google or Boeing, Brawley often seemed to morph into an entirely different person.

One of his most compelling visits had been to Apple's futuristic new campus in Silicon Valley. The sprawling park was dominated by a sleek circular structure that ran like a supercollider around an orchard full of apple and apricot trees. Inside, open expanses of workspace were partitioned into pods for socializing, collaborative problem-solving, and focused individual work. Squint hard enough, and you could see what Mr. Moreno's blended-learning stations might look like if given a $5 billion facelift. This was no accident; from the start of his tenure, Brawley had been trying to take the busted pieces of the school system he'd walked into and transform them into a new bridge to the future, all so kids like Jacob Hernandez could find the networks and opportunities that might deliver them to positions with the world's leading companies, instead of getting inexorably drawn into the public sector, as had happened to him.

"This old ideology that certain jobs are for certain people, and some groups are relegated to just government jobs, that's nonsense," the superintendent told me.

That vision was embodied most clearly in Brawley's plans to transform Compton High. The school was still housed in a decrepit former junior college building that dated back to the mid-1930s. But four years earlier, the superintendent and the Compton Unified board had convinced local voters to approve a $350 million bond measure that would be used to raze the building and dozens of adjoining properties, then build a new information-age campus. Outside, Brawley wanted the new Compton High to feature a series of interconnected, ultramodern, steel-and-glass buildings. Inside, he wanted it to eschew traditional classrooms in favor of keystone-shaped "learning suites" with modular walls. Video renderings took viewers sweeping through the sun-drenched campus and high-tech collaboration hubs he imagined.

But while his tour of Apple Park had illuminated the possibilities, it also revealed challenges. Most notably, the company's workforce was 85 percent white and Asian. That was nearly the inverse of Compton Unified's student body, 96 percent Black and Hispanic. It was thanks to Brawley's own efforts that those kids now attended schools awash in iPads and other Apple products. But recruiters for the company weren't exactly lining up to hire Compton Unified graduates.

"The takeaway for me," the superintendent said, "is we've got to do everything for our kids at a much more rapid pace."

Before dismissing that as a pipe dream, you first had to consider how far Compton and its school district had come since Brawley took over in 2012. Back then, a mayoral race was gearing up. The candidates included Eric Perrodin, hoping to stretch his tenure into a fourth term; Omar Bradley, the former "gangster mayor" who had betrayed Compton's Latino community and briefly landed in prison for misusing public funds before his conviction was overturned; a struggling actor whose biggest claim to fame was starring in Jack in the Box commercials several decades earlier; an ex-organizer for

the Black Panthers; and the owner of a bail bond shop whose campaign platform boasted she was the "Moses that God sent to this community."

But it was Aja Brown, a thirtysomething Black woman with a master's
degree in urban planning, who had emerged victorious. She quickly began
talking up Compton as a place where the future was beckoning.

"I see it as a new Brooklyn," Brown said shortly after her 2013 win.

Still, the path forward had been treacherous. Decades of neglect had left
Compton's streets riddled with those tire-popping potholes. For years, trees
had gone untrimmed, graffiti unscrubbed. Corruption and fiscal mismanagement remained rampant, and years of overspending and using restricted
funds to cover general operating shortages had left the city on the edge of
bankruptcy. Also hanging around the city's neck like an albatross was
Compton Unified.

The district's test scores were still atrocious. Its four-year graduation had
sagged below 60 percent. Even those kids who did earn a diploma were rarely
prepared for college; fewer than one in five met the University of California's
minimum admissions requirements. And underlying all the academic problems was the putrid condition of the district's physical plant. At Compton
High, teachers and students frequently had to dodge drips from leaky ceilings, chunks of plaster that broke off from the crumbling hallway walls, and
floods caused by ruptures in ancient water mains barely held together by
decades' worth of patches. The rot extended deep into the bowels of the ancient building, where boxes of moldy textbooks lay scattered like offerings
around an ancient heating-oil tank that was no longer in use. Someone had
tagged the tank "DOOMS," and district engineers considered it a serious
environmental hazard.

And back then, Compton Unified's leadership wasn't faring much better.
The superintendent who preceded Brawley had been fired after an investigation found $14,000 in personal expenses on her district-issued credit card.
The two Mexican American candidates who had managed to win board
seats had both since been voted out, fueling a widespread belief that Compton's Black leaders were still conspiring to shut Latinos out of power, patronage jobs, and contracts. It didn't help when twenty-eight-year-old Black

school board member Skyy De'Anthony Fisher used a guest appearance on a local podcast to ridicule as "bullshit" the claims of a local Latino father who said his daughter had been sexually assaulted by a teacher, then ask the podcast hosts to let him know the next time they wanted to do lines of cocaine. Fisher was eventually convicted on charges of performing unwanted oral sex on an unconscious mentee with whom he'd been sharing both a hotel room and possibly the services of a sex worker.

The net result was that Brawley walked into a mess that had left thousands of parents feeling angry and aggrieved. Especially those who were Latino. A lawsuit the ACLU was preparing against the state of California revealed that Compton Unified wasn't providing any special services at all to nearly 1,700 English learners. Another legal effort sought to convert a local elementary school into a charter. And shortly after Brawley was hired, a group of Latino parents and activists filed a class-action suit against the district, alleging that in mid-2012, Compton school police had pepper-sprayed and put into illegal chokeholds a Latina mother and her teenage son and beat at least one bystander, then deleted videos of the incident from witnesses' phones and threatened anyone who spoke out with deportation. The plaintiffs sought $41.4 million in damages, an amount that threatened to recapsize a school system that had recently stared down a $30 million operating deficit. When I asked Brawley about the mess he'd inherited, the superintendent was matter of fact.

"We had no choice to get things in order, or we would've been taken over by the state again," he said.

The early years of his tenure were largely spent absorbing the ire of a particularly vehement faction of local Latino activists. Sometimes literally. In March 2015, the superintendent and several members of the Compton Unified board convened a special meeting to hear complaints about Dominguez High. The bleachers in the school's gym were extended to accommodate about 250 fed-up students and parents. The roof leaked, they said. The water fountains didn't work. Neither did the air conditioners. Wasp nests hung outside classroom windows. Homeless people sometimes wandered the campus. Some parents felt district leaders had shown a lack of concern over a Dominguez student who'd recently been killed. When some of the parents on hand began jeering and heckling, Brawley and the board responded by adjourning the meeting, prompting a petite middle-aged woman to stand up from her seat. *Robar esto*, she yelled out. Steal this. Then she threw a handful of coins, hitting Brawley in the face.

"There's no politics like Compton politics," the superintendent said dryly.

That was a big reason why he wielded his standoffish demeanor like a shield. Frustration among local Latino leaders about never winning district contracts? Brawley just shrugged. That class-action suit filed by Latino parents and activists, which was eventually settled for an amount the superintendent described as "nowhere near" what the plaintiffs were seeking? Brawley claimed it was Compton school police who got beat up, not the other way around. Ongoing complaints about underrepresentation of Latinos in various public offices and committees? Brawley would agree to a meeting, listen carefully, make few if any commitments, then usher people out the door as they wondered what the hell just happened.

"For me, it didn't matter one way or another," he said when I asked about the various controversies. "I didn't have a view on it."

Such deflection and reticence was the polar opposite of the "Shame on us if we are not open in having the discussion" approach favored in a place like Evanston. But America's competing suburban dreams had already collided in Compton. All the white families had already moved on, and the mess they'd left behind had already been compounded by decades of neglect, corruption, and denial. Because Compton had long since gone through all the ensuing pain and heartache, the challenge at hand wasn't maintaining exclusivity or trying to make white people share or even attempting to save a fading dream. It was to rebuild. Brawley believed that meant putting forth a new vision of the future that a divided community could rally around. And if he wanted to survive long enough to pull *that* off, he'd have to stay out of the Black-Brown fights that had riven Compton for decades.

"You can't *not* know about it. Who individuals support, who they like, who they don't like," Brawley eventually allowed when I kept asking about Compton's fault lines. "But I've tried to stay out of that drama."

That didn't mean the superintendent wasn't willing to pick fights. Early in his tenure, he'd shed teachers and central office staff, renegotiated contracts that had been rubber-stamped forever, and challenged Compton Unified's excessive use of budget workarounds like interdepartmental loans. In a subtle rebuke to the cynicism that still permeated the town, Brawley had also shown he wasn't too proud to search the sofa cushions for spare change, finding hundreds of thousands of dollars in annual savings through strategies like switching to energy-efficient lightbulbs. While effective, such strategies were hardly inspiring; even Brawley's supporters weren't exactly effusive in their praise.

"I'd almost liken him to a bean counter," bombastic Compton Unified school board leader Micah Ali told me.

But that was how Brawley wanted it. And his focus on building a sound financial foundation paid off when rivers of cash suddenly began flowing out of Sacramento. Under a progressive new school-funding formula approved by the California Assembly, every school district in the state began receiving extra dollars for each low-income student, English learner, and foster child they enrolled. In Compton Unified, that covered just about everyone. As a result, the district's annual per-pupil spending would jump from $9,804 in 2013, just as Brawley's tenure was beginning, to $14,707 seven years later. And crucially, the funds were unrestricted, opening the door for Brawley to start implementing his ambitious instructional vision.

The first pillar was data. Stealing a page from Silicon Valley product managers, Brawley and his team identified a set of key performance indicators, then built databases and dashboards that allowed them to track week-to-week fluctuations in data points like student attendance and school suspension rates. The effort was led by Jean-Jacques Francoisse, a Belgian national with a passion for advanced statistics who liked to describe his office as Compton Unified's "radar and compass." Inside a windowless pupil-records building, he sat at a desk covered with flash drives and aspirin bottles, building Tableau applications that allowed users to pull up every student in the district and the thousands of discrete standards and skills they were expected to learn, then analyze their results on various assessments by grade level, classroom, race, and dozens of other variables.

In its early days, this system had pointed to a glaring need: overhauling services and supports for English learners. Despite his shaky relationships with Compton Latinos and the potential backlash from their Black counterparts, Brawley began reallocating resources, hiring bilingual instructional assistants, establishing dual-language immersion programs, opening welcome programs for new immigrants, buying new classroom materials, and hiring community-relations specialists—all strategies that echoed the experimental bilingual program that had shown so much promise at Jefferson a half century earlier. By 2019, the impact was evident; when I asked Francoisse to pull up Mr. Moreno's class at Jefferson Elementary on his twin twenty-four-inch monitors, the data showed that 83 percent of the school's third graders had met or exceeded expectations on state math exams the previous year.

But that number was just a starting point, Francoisse said, opening another custom application he'd developed to let users crosswalk results from different assessments. That meant district officials could now model how next year's scores might look based on how students were performing in their classrooms right now. Francoisse again pulled up Jefferson.

"Their weakness this year is going to be in sixth and seventh grade," he said, already scribbling notes for that month's data chat with Principal Aquino. "Students have an issue with solving real problems and developing an understanding of statistics."

The second pillar of Brawley's instructional vision had first started to come together during a carpool. The superintendent lived in a community called Riverside. So did Alex Alvarez, the man he'd hired to be Compton Unified's director of business operations. To make the seventy-five-minutes-on-a-good-day commute more tolerable, the pair started driving together to the district's new administrative headquarters, now located on a site that had once housed a stretch of Santa Fe Gardens, the apartment complex that had gone from housing two future U.S. presidents to a squalid maze of crack dens. The irony was not lost on Brawley or Alvarez, whose car-ride discussions gradually expanded from policy debates and personnel decisions into more personal territory, including what it took to navigate their adopted town's many divisions and absurdities.

"We had a lot of conversations about culture, about our backgrounds and how they applied to Compton," Alvarez told me. "He has a good heart."

Usually, the unlikely duo drove straight home after work. In early 2013, however, they decided to take a detour. The University of Southern California had recently launched a PhD program for busy school district executives. After attending an orientation, Brawley and Alvarez decided to enroll together. Every Thursday night for nearly three years, they'd leave Compton at 5:30 p.m., then sit through classes on USC's campus until 10:00. When it came time to start planning his dissertation, Brawley wanted to research ways to get multinational corporations to take a more active role in America's public schools. It wasn't exactly a popular question among many of his progressive classmates. But in a place like Compton, Brawley believed, you could complain and change nothing, or you could prepare kids to compete and pressure companies to give them a chance.

He'd initially hoped to conduct his fieldwork in Cuba. His research group's adviser preferred Ireland. Brawley initially felt deflated. Then he learned that about one sixth of the country's population were migrants, the result of a quarter century of heavy immigration.

Brawley and Alvarez finally made it across the Atlantic in April 2016. Between observing schools, attending a national student science fair, and sneaking in visits to castles and pubs, they began visiting the Irish headquarters of several large corporations. Including Apple, which had turned a modest manufacturing center in Cork into its European headquarters and a buzzing hub for global logistics and technical support, largely on the strength of an influx of highly skilled immigrants. Inside a conference room, Brawley fired questions at company executives about the skills they valued most and how their hiring priorities might evolve over the next decade. What Apple wanted ended up being the same qualities that Compton Unified would soon begin trying to nurture in children like Jacob Hernandez.

"Success in the global market requires citizens and migrant workers to apply critical-thinking and problem-solving skills," Brawley had concluded in his dissertation. "Collaboration, leadership, adaptability, creativity, curiosity, oral communication, and written communication."

To help enact that vision in Compton, he hired away the San Francisco United School District's highly regarded director of educational technology. Robotics competitions, engineering challenges, and after-school app-development challenges soon followed. Several Compton Unified campuses were soon named Verizon Innovative Learning Schools, winning pallets full of new classroom technology and extensive coaching on how to best use it. The district also secured a ConnectED grant, bringing hundreds of iPads and more professional development into five additional Compton schools. Then Jefferson Elementary was named an Apple Distinguished School, an award that helped spur a quantum leap in the kind of technology-enabled, data-driven, real-world-problem-tackling education that many of its counterparts in wealthier communities like Lucas, Gwinnett County, and Evanston were still trying to get off the ground. Districtwide, the percentage of Compton students meeting or exceeding expectations on state tests went up fifteen points in both reading and math. The district's four-year graduation rate climbed to 84 percent. Nearly half of Compton Unified's Latino graduates now met the University of California's minimum admissions requirements, and by mid-2019, Brawley had settled on a label to describe the many threads of his agenda: inclusive innovation.

"Compton is never again going to be what it was in the past," the superintendent told me. "It's going to continue to change. And you've got to do everything you can do to prepare the citizenry and the students you have to excel. They're the ones that are going to be paying into your retirement, they're going to be paying into the infrastructure in your city, so you may as well do everything possible to make sure that you provide them with the best possible education."

POTENTIAL ENERGY

By early 2020, Compton Unified was preparing to host the annual summit of the League of Innovative Schools, a coalition of the most forward-looking school districts in the nation. Among the schools to be showcased was Jefferson Elementary, where Project Lead the Way National Teacher of the Year Mary Grace Santiago was leading Mr. Moreno's class through one of the hands-on engineering lessons that had everyone so excited.

"Who can tell me what potential energy is?" Santiago asked over the fourth graders' lively chatter.

Their task was to investigate how speed, direction, and force affect the transfer of energy between objects during a collision. Project Lead the Way had provided lesson plans and robotics kits. After letting the kids sift through gray plastic tubs full of pulleys, axles, and rubber wheels, Santiago divided them into teams of four. The children started with a test run, constructing long ramps that sloped down from opposing desks and met on the floor, then sending basic four-wheels-and-a-chassis Lego-style vehicles crashing into each other from a variety of heights and angles. After a brief discussion about what the class had noticed, Santiago revealed their real challenge: to design and build a more complex vehicle that could safely carry a raw egg down a ramp and keep it intact during a collision with the classroom wall. Before she was done talking, Jacob had already flung the ID card he wore in a lanyard around his neck over one shoulder and started hatching a plan.

"First, we're going to need a two-inch-by-eight-inch chassis and eight connectors," he said, digging into a supply kit.

Santiago smiled and held up a bright pinwheel flower. Its pink and yellow petals were labeled *manager, engineer, parts*, and *quality control*. Several spins later, each student had an assigned role. Jacob was tapped to be his team's engineer. After pumping his fist enthusiastically, he spent the next forty minutes completely absorbed in the experiment. He used his iPad to pull up a 3-D image of a sample vehicle, pinching and swiping to zoom and rotate it for closer inspection. He experimented with several different chassis designs of his own. He asked Ms. Santiago for help finding a part, assistance she wouldn't provide until he used the part's correct technical name, a 20-millimeter-diameter pulley. When his teammates started building a ramp out of poster board and two long foam pool noodles, Jacob stopped what he was doing and offered to help. And while a small girl in a Star Wars sweatshirt studied different ways to affix the wheels of their vehicle to its chassis, he rested his chin in his hand and watched intently, looking for all the world like a mix of his father and a young Steve Jobs.

"This is your two-minute warning," Santiago called out.

The students groaned. Some begged her to extend the period. Jacob said there was a problem his team was still trying to solve.

"It's okay," the teacher responded. "You'll get more time next Thursday. This kind of learning doesn't always fit into a single class period. Figuring out our own solutions to difficult problems is what school is all about. You have to trust the process."

The class began packing up.

"If you only followed the steps someone else laid out," Santiago finished as the bell rang, "how would you ever design something new?"

12

THINGS FALL APART

There are only the pursued, the pursuing, the busy and
the tired.

—F. Scott Fitzgerald,
The Great Gatsby, 1925

THE BECKER FAMILY │ LUCAS, TEXAS

Susan Becker raced the clock on the new Peloton she'd gotten for Christmas.
It was February 2020, a Thursday afternoon. Jim, off consulting with another company in trouble with its lenders, would be home that night. Avery
was having gum surgery tomorrow, a prelude to new braces later in the year.
And Saturday was Denim & Diamonds, one of the Foundation for Lovejoy
Schools' big annual fundraisers. *I still have to line up a babysitter*, Susan remembered. *After today's pickups.*

Noah was already home, sort of; after school, he'd flung his backpack
over the black iron gate surrounding the backyard, then headed down the
street to play. Sean was about to start swim practice. Avery had stayed late at
school to retake a math test. Susan said a silent thank-you to her daughter's
teacher, Ms. Kincel, a cheery white woman more than two decades into her
tenure with the Lovejoy schools. She was still meeting with Avery twice a
week for tutoring. For Susan, that meant no more Mathnasium, no more
being the mean mom, no more watching helplessly as her child lashed out

when asked to multiply fractions. But she had to pick up her daughter and a friend at Sloan Creek Intermediate in fifteen minutes.

Her workout done, Susan headed downstairs, then stepped around the 1,700-piece Lego set in the living room. Astro barked wildly when she grabbed her keys, then got hold of his tail and began running in circles, so Susan decided to take him along. Before she could back the SUV out of the garage, Avery called, asking to be dropped at the house of a friend whose parents were still at work.

"No . . ." Susan said into the car's speaker. "Here . . . You're coming here and then. . . . Well, no, we're not going to do that."

She pulled into the street. Astro placed his paws on the divider between the front seats and looked out the windshield expectantly. Several doors down, Noah stood astride his bike. An older boy on a dirt bike came sputtering up. Susan lowered her window.

"You're not getting on that," she said before her son could ask. "Where's your helmet?"

Sloan Creek was just ten minutes away. As Susan waited in the pickup line, Sean walked by on his way to the natatorium, appearing lost in thought. He'd befriended a few boys he texted with about baseball, but was still quiet and shy. Just that week, the family had attended a meeting at Willow Springs Middle to start mapping out his eighth-grade year. Sean's teachers and counselors suggested a double block of Pre-Algebra. That would mean losing an elective and falling behind many of his classmates, leading Sean and thus Susan to worry about a possible stigma.

"Because kids talk, right?" she said. "'That's for the dumb kids, that's the lowest class they have.'"

But the Lovejoy educators kept reminding her there was no "low" or "behind" in Lovejoy schools. An hour later, she and Sean had accepted their recommendation.

"All it means is he won't take calculus as a senior," Susan told me as we waited.

Containing all these little fires was just part of being a mom. But they seemed to be getting more frequent and unpredictable. In January, for example, Major League Baseball had released the results of an investigation into the Beckers' beloved Houston Astros. It turned out the team had been using an illegal sign-stealing scheme to cheat their way to victory for years. The ensuing furor led to calls for the team to forfeit its recent World Series title. Distraught, Sean started spending hours holed up in his room, investigating the team's winning percentage and run differential at home, where the alleged cheating took place, versus on the road, where it would have been impossible. His efforts had ultimately led to a family conversation. What the Astros had done was wrong, Susan and Jim said. But no one could erase all the team had achieved, all the joy they'd spread. It was Avery who finally gave voice to the kids' underlying fear.

"If the Astros get their World Series taken away, do we have to give him away?" she'd asked, looking at the dog.

Another problem was that Sean had grown fixated on global warming. It came out of the blue; he arrived home from school one day and started asking if the planet was really going to burn up and die during his lifetime. Susan figured his science teacher must have brought it up in class. A year ago, she wouldn't have thought much of it. Now, though, the accumulating incidents were starting to look like part of a pattern that showed how the globalist agenda and the groupthink it coerced were everywhere. Just that fall, the neighbors' twelve-year-old had announced she might be bisexual after watching some TikTok videos, and Susan found herself thinking back to the kids' old charter school, where a social studies teacher had taken to vocally criticizing Christopher Columbus.

"You start adjusting history a little bit here and little bit there, and you don't realize it because it's just baby steps, but then you get ten years down the road and you go, 'Whoa,'" Susan said, incredulous now at the memory.

In response, she and Jim had limited the kids' screen time and turned the news off again. They'd also arranged for the family to take part in a creek cleanup back in Plano. If protecting the environment is a passion of yours, they told Sean, we can do this every month.

"We try to turn it into a positive for him in that, look, is this something that's important? Absolutely," Susan said. "Especially with us being Christians, and having the faith that hey, we've got to do our part. But at the same time, we can't take this worry on for the whole world."

Now, though, a new danger loomed on the horizon. At the end of January, the World Health Organization had declared a strange new flu-like virus a global emergency. The federal government had already restricted travel from China. At least Donald Trump was in charge, Susan told me as Avery and her friend appeared in the school's parking lot. Not some establishment politician already in the pocket of Big Pharma.

At home, the girls made a silent beeline for Avery's room. Susan cut an apple into slices and followed them upstairs. Then she called the sitter for Denim & Diamonds. She'd already paid $135 apiece for her and Jim's tickets. She wanted to do whatever was needed to support Lovejoy schools, especially with the district now facing fresh budget challenges.

During his first six months on the job, Superintendent Goddard had embraced an "abundance mindset." I don't want to hear why we can't, he'd say. I want to hear how we will. But while local families loved that kind of talk, the district had entered the school year with a $1.1 million operating deficit. Then more bad news came in January. A fresh demographic study found that construction of new houses was down 30 percent inside the Lovejoy attendance zone, a sure sign the area would soon be built out. As a result, enrollment in the district was projected to stagnate, maybe even decline, threatening Lovejoy's bottom line even further. Feeling the squeeze, Goddard and the school board were looking to double down on the district's secret revenue-generating weapons. Especially the Foundation for Lovejoy Schools. This year, Denim & Diamonds was being held back in Plano, in a large Marriott hotel located in the heart of Legacy Town Center, a mixed-use development surrounded by a gargantuan business park.

On Saturday evening, parents pulled up their Escalades and Odysseys, then handed their keys to a valet before floating on the freedom of an evening with no kids. Inside the hotel lobby, a mechanical bull had been set up near some miniature bales of hay. Past them were several high-top bar tables topped with cardboard trifolds. Behind each stood a Lovejoy educator. Keenly aware of the disposable income that surrounded them, the teachers and principals were on hand to ask for donations that might cover the cost of wobble stools for fidgety children or a new iPad Pro to jazz up their lessons.

A spacious ballroom stood off to the right. Its large pillars were wrapped in fairy lights. Servers distributed shaved fennel salads to tables draped with white linens. The district's faculty-and-parent band occupied a stage fes- tooned with three-foot illuminated marquee letters spelling out LOVEJOY. Beside them, a bearded bartender in a vest staffed a bourbon-tasting bar provided courtesy of a local real estate agency that was among the groups that paid up to $15,000 to sponsor the event.

The Beckers arrived a little before seven, blending in seamlessly with the growing crowd, full of middle-aged white women in flowing red pantsuits and white men in crisply pressed blue jeans. Susan and Jim were sharing a table with the real estate agent and Foundation for Lovejoy Schools board member who'd helped steer them into Lucas less than a year earlier.

Revenue-generating contests and games were everywhere. For $75, moms and dads could try their hand at the Diamonds Direct Dig, sifting through a sand-filled tub and pulling out slips of numbered paper that would enter them into a drawing for a 4.5-carat diamond tennis bracelet. The event also featured both a silent auction and live auction. A custom mobile app de- tailed the items up for bid. At the low end was a month of free dog obedience training. Starting prices got significantly higher in the sports-memorabilia section, which featured one jersey signed by Dallas Mavericks star Luka Dončić and another by the entire 1980 gold-medal-winning Miracle on Ice U.S. national hockey team. Also up for auction were vacation packages to Cancún, Telluride, and a half dozen even more exotic locales, plus a custom- built backyard playhouse, a fully stocked wine cellar, and a complete course of vaginal rejuvenation therapy valued at $5,000. Interspersed with the lux- ury items were dozens of chances to purchase the time and attention of Lovejoy educators, including a swimming party at the home of a teacher at Noah's school, plus a private movie night hosted by Mr. Vogel and the other social studies teachers at Sloan Creek Intermediate.

Dinner was filet mignon, chicken Florentine, or gluten-free salmon. Con- versation focused on kids, property values, and current events. The day before, *The New York Times* had reported that the novel coronavirus was now raging on three continents. People were dying. Halfway around the world, feverish passengers on a luxury cruise liner had been forced into quarantine. But it was all noise from somewhere else. The band dived into a Lizzo cover, then a DJ spun Nelly and Vanilla Ice, drawing a group of women with frosted blond hair onto the dance floor, where they raised their arms and reeled each other into the blissful world behind the gates.

Then the lights went down. Superintendent Goddard took the stage in a dark suit and red necktie. Parents waved servers over for more cabernet as the live auction for the big-ticket items got under way. An all-expenses-paid trip to Reykjavík, Iceland, came up for bid. Dozens of parents raised their white paper paddles into the air, sending the price higher and higher. Susan and Jim laughed and cheered, then shared arched-eyebrow looks when the trip sold for $7,500. A private home dinner for fourteen prepared by Top Chef contestant Tre Wilcox fetched an even higher price. Then a six-night trip for four to the Dalmatian Coast of Croatia went for $10,000. Keys to a brand-new Audi every three months for a year went for $13,000. Then came the grand finale, with someone paying $14,000 for two tickets to the final round of the Masters golf tournament. All told, Denim & Diamonds would raise about $300,000, money Goddard and the Lovejoy board would use to help keep the wolves outside Lovejoy's borders at bay for another year.

Such extravagance made Susan and Jim blush; they weren't really that kind of family. When the auction wound down and the dessert plates were all empty, the couple strode out into the cool February night, arm in arm under a moon that had been full just the night before. They'd done their part, but in their own pragmatic way, paying $5,000 for a service they were soon going to need anyway.

"The kids' orthodontist had a package for braces," Susan said. "So we were like, 'All right, we know we need another set, let's see what we can get them for.' I think we ended up spending like maybe a thousand less than we would've paid."

THE ROBINSON FAMILY | GWINNETT COUNTY, GEORGIA

Radiant beams of midday sunlight streamed through the windows of the Robinsons' vaulted foyer, creating a checkerboard of light and shadow that crept slowly across the dining room wall, still plain beige save for those several squares of blue still awaiting a decision. It was Sunday afternoon. Anthony had already changed into his gray sweats. The Saints and Falcons were both on their bye week, so he'd pulled out one of his favorite slow-cooker recipes, then parked himself in the kitchen, where he tended to an enormous pot of black-eyed peas whose aroma drifted in piquant layers through the house.

"They're New Orleans style, Cajun spicy," Nika teased as she squeezed her husband's arm. "That's why I married him."

The homey comfort had long helped buffer the Robinsons against the outside world. But subtle tensions had begun worming their way into the couple's marriage during the back half of 2019. First, it was the decision about where to send their oldest son for ninth grade. At his mother's urging, Corey had applied to two of Gwinnett County's most prestigious private schools. But the Robinsons said Jones Middle had responded to her request for her son's academic records by sending them *and* his behavior records to both schools. The admissions officers at one decided Corey wouldn't be a good fit as soon as they saw the suspensions and the SST, leaving Nika outraged. Anthony was initially upset, too, but had since worked to put the episode in perspective.

"I tell her this all the time," he told me, gesturing with his head toward his wife, who was now in the other room. "She's always been a proponent of private school. I'm truly not. Even though I went to a private high school, I don't feel like I had to. It didn't matter where I went, I was going to do well."

The little rift had widened after the locker-room slap-boxing incident during Corey's first week at Mill Creek High. Administrators at the school initially coded the incident as a fight and suspended him for more than a week. Once again, Nika and Anthony had rallied for a series of meetings and phone conferences. In the face of their persistent badgering, the school had reduced the suspension to two days. Still, Nika told me, the principal had made a point of saying the altercation would still be taken into consideration if Corey ran into any more trouble.

"Again, very condescending," she said.

"See, here's where we have our dichotomy," Anthony countered. "I thought he was relatively receptive to where we were trying to come from."

Everyone had been walking on eggshells during the months that followed. Fourteen-year-old Corey bore the brunt of tension, drowning in a deluge of reminders from his parents to straighten his shirt and dial back his volume. You don't get to be rowdy anymore, his father said. Save it for the field, his mother added. Don't even put your hands *near* anyone, they both agreed. The constant vigilance seemed to be wearing him down. At the moment, he was supposed to be upstairs folding laundry. His parents suspected he'd fallen asleep. Their hunch was confirmed when he came yawning down the stairs, grabbed a plate of drumsticks from the kitchen counter, and sank into the overstuffed gray sofa to watch the early NFL games.

Anthony, who approached parenting like a grizzled bomb-disposal technician, decided to hold his tongue. The string of obstacles that confronted his family was never-ending. The only thing to do was pick each one up as it came, consider its weight and potential for damage, then defuse the crisis and move on.

"I can compartmentalize," he said when asked about his reaction to the events at Mill Creek High. "What happened with an administrator has nothing to do with what these teachers are trying to do."

"You can't tell me that administrators and faculty don't talk," Nika chimed in from the other room.

"Especially up there, it's too many kids," Anthony replied.

"I don't trust their intentions," Nika persisted. "I just think Corey has had so many challenges with faculty and administration that he's reticent to say, 'Hey, I don't understand something.'"

Anthony sighed and went back to his black-eyed peas. Even before this most recent round of drama, his wife had been overwhelmed with work and her PhD program; she'd recently backed out of her candidate training with Win Georgia, a sacrifice whose toll the entire family was still feeling. And he knew she wasn't entirely wrong about the Gwinnett County Public Schools, which were testing his patience too. Corey usually excelled in math, the family subject. This year, though, he'd started his ninth grade Geometry class by bombing a bunch of assignments and scoring a 30 on one of his first tests. Anthony could see his son's dismal grade posted in eCLASS, the district's online learning management system. But despite weeks of effort, he'd been unable to get a copy of his son's responses. Corey's teacher also declined to provide a road map of what the class would be covering during the coming weeks. As a result, Anthony had little insight into his son's strengths and weaknesses, and his attempts to introduce material himself amounted to shots in the dark. Unlike Lovejoy ISD, the Gwinnett district also didn't allow high school students to retake all their tests in order to correct their mistakes, a policy that annoyed Anthony to no end.

"As a teacher, why do I care how many times you take it before you demonstrate a functional knowledge and understanding of the material? Isn't that the ultimate goal?" he said. "What are we trying to do?"

Left to their own devices, the Robinsons had instituted regular tutoring sessions. A few nights every week, Anthony and Corey would start at the dinner table around 8:30 and work until after 10:00. Just part of being a dad, Anthony said. But that didn't leave much time for relaxing, he told me, signaling that our conversation was about to end. With dinner almost ready and the late games about to start, he wanted to gain some distance from the nagging fears that had long animated his wife and were now reaching out for him.

"If they just treated kids as if they were their own," he said, sharing a final thought, "that would solve a lot of the problems."

A day inside Mill Creek High later that week showed what he meant. Nearly 60 percent of ninth graders at the school were taking Geometry, but its freshman class was still intensely stratified. The most advanced kids took an accelerated version of the class that would put them on track to take AP Calculus junior year and something even more demanding as seniors. Although the class met in a creaky portable trailer in a lot outside the school, parents fought ferociously to enroll their children. The teacher was Charlene Sharp, a twenty-six-year veteran who wielded a software tool called Nearpod like a wizard. I watched as she sent a rapid-fire series of questions from her tablet directly to the students' laptops, then followed along on her screen as the class tried to solve the problems in real time. When they finished, Sharp chose one student's solution to highlight because it was particularly efficient, and another's to highlight because its errors reflected a common misunderstanding.

"It's constant formative assessment," she said as she teed up another problem on solving for an unknown variable. "Do you see it right away? This should take like fifteen seconds."

At the other end of the spectrum was college-prep Geometry, which moved more slowly. This was the class Corey had second period. Inside a regular Mill Creek classroom, he unzipped his red-and-black hoodie and plopped down noisily into a chair. His teacher was a white woman named Marybeth Coffey. She was in her fourth year out of college and still learning how to make strategic use of data. Instead of small groups based on ability, kids mostly sat with their friends; Corey was joined by two other Black students at a cluster of desks pushed together to form a small table. As latecomers straggled in, he tried to chat up the girl next to him, then frowned at the "Do Now" question written on the board:

> *What is the difference between the square root of 6 squared and the square root of 6 times the square root of 6?*

The day's focus was on simplifying radicals and rationalizing denominators. Both were building-block skills the students would need for the rest of their mathematical lives, including later in ninth grade, when the class would start calculating the lengths of the sides of right triangles. For now, though, Coffey expected her students to accept on faith that the lesson would someday be useful. The handout she distributed didn't exactly help; at the top, the academic standards she'd be covering that day were listed in untranslated text.

> *21.G.SRT.6—Understand that by similarity, side ratios in right triangles are properties of the angles in the triangle, leading to definitions of trigonometric ratios for acute angles.*

"This is like a foundation day," Coffey said as she took a sip from the yellow thermos on her desk. "Take out a sheet of paper."

She solved one problem on the board. The class watched. Corey copied her work down into his notebook.

"Okay, second question, what is the square root of seventy-two," Coffey said. "I don't care which way you choose, I just need to see some work."

Corey and a couple of other boys seized the opportunity to move, getting up and walking across the room to grab calculators from pocket sleeves hanging on a white cinderblock wall. For the rest of the fifty-two-minute period, they'd remain glued to their seats.

Much of the class was already familiar with the steps the class was now practicing. Because Corey had been assigned to regular Algebra at Jones Middle, however, the material was mostly new to him. When other students began heading to the board to show how they'd solved the problems, Coffey praised them, then zipped forward to the next stage of her lesson, on the procedural steps for rationalizing denominators.

"Be as detailed as possible," the teacher said. "You're baking a cake, this is your recipe."

Now flustered, Corey looked ready to bench-press his desk or run laps around the school. He checked the clock. He arched his back, stretched his arms to the ceiling, and yawned. He chewed on his pencil. He tried unsuccessfully to still his wayward leg bouncing frantically beneath the desk. When a few students raised their hands with questions, Coffey encouraged them to lean on their neighbors for help. Corey looked over at the girl next to him. No way he was going to tell her he didn't understand.

"On Monday, we'll start our new unit," Coffey said just before the bell.

While Corey went off to Chemistry, principal Jason Lane and assistant principal Melissa Nilsen escorted me to Mill Creek's third version of freshman Geometry. With his dark buzz cut and massive arms, Lane looked like he could've played right tackle for the Green Bay Packers in the 1960s. He loved Mill Creek, the principal told me as he dapped up the bearded white center from the football team. Though his own family lived in a different county, Lane said he was taking advantage of a Gwinnett County Public Schools policy that allowed administrators to enroll their own children in the feeder pattern where they worked. His younger son was still at Jones Middle. But in eighth grade, the principal told me proudly, he was going to come to Mill Creek for a few hours a day so he could get an early jump on Ms. Sharp's accelerated Geometry class.

Third period began, and I settled into a seat in the back of gifted Geometry. Next to me was Nilsen, whose faint blond eyebrows were barely visible against her translucent skin. She also lived well beyond Gwinnett's borders, and she was also taking advantage of the perk available to GCPS administrators. Two of her children were already enrolled at Mill Creek High, Nilsen told me as the class began.

"Are you ready to get cold?" teacher Linda Gates asked gaily, drawing her students' attention. "Because we're going to take a little trip outside."

Just like college-prep Geometry, the gifted students were learning how to simplify radicals and rationalize denominators. But the substance and tenor of the two classes were completely different. Gates was a ten-year classroom veteran and co-taught alongside a former engineer. Instead of having students practice disembodied procedural steps, they encouraged learning by doing. As students grabbed their coats and filed out of the classroom, Gates instructed them to grab a shiny metal tape measure from a green plastic basket.

Outside, the morning sun still hung low on the horizon, casting long shadows on the sidewalk that surrounded the school. Your mission, Gates said, is to figure out the angle at which sunlight is striking the ground. I watched as a team of three white girls huddled up and crafted a plan. The first girl stood with her back to the sun. The second held the end of the measuring tape against the back of her ankle. Then the third girl stretched the tape measure up, to measure the first girl's standing height, and then out along the ground, to measure how long her shadow extended. The resulting data allowed the group to calculate the length of the imaginary diagonal line running from the crown of the first girl's head down to the far end of her shadow. From there, they could easily calculate the angle at which the sun hit the ground.

"We were all measuring at the same time," Gates said after the class had reassembled inside the classroom. "What does that mean about the angles you just calculated?"

The students realized with delight that they'd all calculated the same angle. Still working in teams, they spent the rest of the period replicating the process with plastic spoons, cell-phone flashlights, and wooden yardsticks, moving around freely and adjusting their experiments just to see what happened. As they worked, I asked Nilsen what she made of the differences between the gifted class we were now observing and the college-prep class I had watched Corey muddle through the period before. The assistant principal told me she loved Gates's focus on "productive struggle" and real-world relevance. Then she smiled proudly.

"My daughter is in this class," Nilsen said, nodding in the direction of a tall girl in black yoga pants who wore her blond hair in a messy bun. "She was one of the students you were watching outside."

Such disparities in access to the most rigorous and engaging instruction were the norm in Gwinnett. Inside individual schools, the most highly regarded teachers tended to be concentrated in accelerated, gifted, International Baccalaureate, and Advanced Placement classrooms. And countywide, experience and innovation seemed to flow inexorably to the whitest and wealthiest communities. Such dynamics both reflected and reinforced the larger pattern of racialized development and decline that had started in suburban DeKalb County nearly a half century earlier, then gradually crept through successive rings of Altanta's suburbs in the years that followed. The resulting problems could be difficult to see day-to-day, and they certainly didn't receive as much attention as hate speech, unfair discipline, or the curdled vanilla homogeneity of the Gwinnett County school district's upper management. But the effects were serious, and they compounded over time, allowing some children to grow their academic advantages while others fell further behind.

That dynamic was one of the main reasons Everton Blair, Jr., had decided to come home and run for the Gwinnett County school board. On the campaign trail, he'd emphasized his local roots and his two years working as a math teacher at a charter high school in Atlanta. The intentionally nonconfrontational approach helped him win 57 percent of his district's vote. But when we talked after his election, Blair described the larger pattern he aimed to disrupt. No longer should suburban school districts like Gwinnett fixate on preventing white flight, he said, especially if that meant reserving the best instruction for a narrow handful of schools and classrooms.

"Offer a high-quality education to who's here, period," he said. "It should not be predicated on the retention of whiteness."

The same week I observed Corey at Mill Creek, Blair let me accompany him during classroom observations in the now heavily Black and Brown southern end of Gwinnett County that he'd grown up in and now represented. We met on Wednesday morning at his parents' McMansion, where he'd been living since returning home. The dining-room table was piled high with mail, magazines, and Bibles. A handwritten sticky note read "E.J. = Socialist." When I pointed it out, Blair laughed, saying it was a remnant of the previous evening's family debate, during which his mom had rejected his argument that billionaires were immoral in a country with rampant inequality. Then he began searching for the correct kind of milk for his morning protein shake, practically climbing into his parents' massive refrigerator.

"My mom likes the almond and coconut mix," he said with a tinge of annoyance. "I use the oat."

Out in the circular driveway, we bypassed a BMW and a Mercedes before settling into Blair's silver Tesla. Then he drove me to his alma mater. Shiloh High was now 89 percent Black and Hispanic. Sixty-seven percent of its students were considered poor. Just a third of the school's freshmen took Geometry, barely half the rate at Mill Creek. So Blair and I took up positions in the back of an Algebra 1 class. Twentysomething teacher Brent Witten and I were the only white people in the room. For a lesson on solving systems of linear equations, Witten narrated a word problem about a football player who ran for four times as many yards as his backup. Then he wrote the following on the whiteboard:

$$1550 = x + y$$
$$x = 4y$$

"What's going in for x?" Witten asked the class.

The students wrote on worksheets and asked questions. Witten responded earnestly, repeating the procedural steps they needed to understand, much the same as Coffey had done in Corey's class. My initial impression was of a perfectly decent high school math class. Then I noticed Blair muttering under his breath. What *he* saw was another example of nonwhite children being shuttled into the least rigorous classes, with the least experienced teachers, who were expected to use curriculum that reflected the least regard for their students' cognitive abilities.

"The teacher is doing all the work," Blair grumbled.

He got up and walked over to the desk of an uncertain-looking Black boy.

"What are you able to explain by solving that step?" he asked.

"How many yards the running back ran for," the boy replied.

"Okay, now what is the relationship between x and y?" Blair continued.

The ensuing silence lasted over a minute. Gwinnett's newest school board member wore it as comfortably as one of his tailored blazers.

"I don't know what you mean," the boy finally said.

"Go back to the word problem," Blair said in his same unruffled tone. "There's a relationship between these variables that's actually the important part of this problem. I know you know it."

By this point, a handful of other students had gathered around. Somebody reread the prompt for me, Blair suggested. One of the teens repeated Witten's initial instructions.

"One of those sentences gives you the relationship between the two players," Blair told the group.

"One rushed for four times as many yards as the other," a girl responded enthusiastically.

"Remember why you're doing these problems in the first place," Blair said, smiling wide.

While he moved on to another part of the classroom, I lingered behind. What just happened, I asked the students he'd been helping. Mr. Blair made solving the equation more of a critical-thinking moment, one of the teens responded. Instead of just giving us the answer or making it obvious, another added. He made us think instead of setting up a problem and we have to finish it, said a third. I asked the group which approach they preferred: Mr. Witten's or Mr. Blair's. After a quick conference, the students reached consensus. We really need both, they said. The how and the why. Blair smiled even wider when I later relayed the exchange.

"It just reinforces that kids know how to ascertain good instruction," he said.

For the time being, however, there wasn't much a lone school board member could do to make the best teaching more widely accessible. The same day he visited Shiloh, Blair was invited to a curriculum-review meeting at the district's relentlessly neutral administrative offices. We arrived twenty minutes late. The first third of every meeting is always a rehash of how great the district is, Blair told me with a shrug.

Inside, about sixty people were gathered in a large amphitheater-style meeting room. Their charge was to offer feedback and suggestions on the textbooks and other instructional materials used in Gwinnett classrooms. Such meetings had been taking place yearly for nearly a quarter century, and over time the format had evolved to minimize substantive engagement. District officials had already drafted the changes that superintendent J. Alvin

Wilbanks and his team wanted to see in 126 separate courses. Now, the district's associate superintendent for curriculum and instructional support explained, they were putting those changes out for validation.

Blair bowed only briefly to the kabuki rituals, clapping politely when the associate superintendent acknowledged Gwinnett's principal of the year. When he finally excused himself ninety minutes later, a staffer handed him a big brown legal folder full of files related to the district's pending expulsion hearings. The prospect of dragging reams of paper files around until the next board meeting annoyed the twenty-seven-year-old Blair to no end.

"There are so many ways to send digital files securely now," he complained as he dropped the folder into the front seat of his Tesla.

He was usually careful to prevent such frustrations from disturbing his unbothered manner. Just a few months into his tenure, for example, a group of high school students had showed up at a board meeting to protest what they viewed as the overuse of standardized tests. Blair voiced perfunctory support, asking Wilbanks and his cabinet if they could review the district's assessment calendar with an eye toward reducing the total number of days spent testing. The silver-haired superintendent claimed to welcome such questions. But at the next board meeting, he delivered an eight-and-a-half-minute soliloquy aimed squarely at Blair. The board's discussion of standardized testing had recently turned "toxic," Wilbanks said. Everyone who knew anything about education should know how important the exams were to Gwinnett County's continued success. He finished by directing his staff to produce a "historical reference piece" for new board members, saying they needed to learn more about the district's many accomplishments during his tenure. Sitting in the audience, Marlyn Tillman of Gwinnett SToPP had shaken her head in disgust.

"They'll always do it the Gwinnett way," she told me later.

Blair, however, just listened politely. His was the lone exception in an otherwise unbroken row of sagging white faces sitting up on the board's dais, and there was no benefit to starting a conversation that would amount to talking to a wall.

For now, his efforts would have to be focused outside the J. Alvin Wilbanks Instructional Support Center, where enthusiasm for the 2020 election was already running high. Three of Gwinnett's older white school board members—Carol Boyce, Mary Kay Murphy, and Louise Radloff—were up for reelection. Blair was already busy helping Gwinnett County Democrats line up young progressives of color to challenge them. One potential candidate was Tanisha Banks, a Black teacher whose years at GIVE Center East had made her a harsh critic of Gwinnett's approach to discipline. Another was Karen Watkins, a Black and Filipina woman in her midforties who worked in corporate supply-chain logistics and had a seven-year-old daughter who'd recently come home saying second grade felt like jail. That summer, Blair and Watkins both attended a Democratic fundraiser that coincided with Juneteenth. It was held at Edee's Place, a Black-run barbecue restaurant in a Dacula strip mall. Inside, a singer belted out Whitney Houston covers, then gave way to a parade of speakers who highlighted the ways frustration with the county's public schools was fueling rising political unrest.

Craig Newton was the recently elected African American mayor of Norcross, Georgia. He recounted the trauma he'd experienced as a child, when he was sent to desegregate one of Gwinnett's all-white schools, only to find himself side by side with hateful children who wiped their desks with a handkerchief if he happened to touch it. Brenda Lopez Romero, elected to the Georgia House in 2017, told the crowd how she'd been born in Mexico but never thought of herself as anything other than American, until she started high school in suburban Atlanta. When it was Blair's turn to speak, he jumped onstage and flashed his Instagram-perfect smile, then tapped directly into the mood of the moment. Yes, he'd gotten a good education in Gwinnett public schools, Blair said. But it had taken going off to the Ivy League for anyone to teach him about Juneteenth and its significance.

"I'm going to commit to making sure that's not a reality for the rest of our students in Gwinnett County," he vowed.

But the election was still more than a year off, and Blair had started

growing impatient. Driving away from the curriculum meeting, he continued to vent about the district's bureaucratic inertia. Then his Tesla got a flat.

"I really don't understand tires. How has there been no innovation in this
concept? Just inflate yourself!" he said while waiting for someone to pick up
at AAA. "These are the kinds of things that make my skin crawl, just having
to wait."

For better or worse, it was a skill that Anthony Robinson had already
learned. He wasn't an oat milk guy, and he didn't care much for politics. But
he'd made a habit of channeling whatever bitterness he felt back into the
things he could control, and he knew how to pace himself in order to get his
family through each week.

Thursday nights were usually the last big hurdle. Nika had one of her
doctoral classes. That meant he was on his own to make sure everyone got
picked up from school and made it to practice, ate dinner, and did their
homework. After wrapping up his own work, Anthony climbed into his
black Chevy Traverse and backed out of the driveway, willing himself to ignore the plastic ball still stuck in the gutter above the driveway. His first stop
was an after-school karate program. Inside the lobby of the makeshift dojo,
his younger son promptly declared he'd forgotten his jacket at school.

"Tell your mother," Anthony said as he signed the attendance sheet.

Inside the car, Carter asked if he could play Subway Surfers.

"Seat belts," his father responded.

The next stop was to pick up Corey. Along the way, Cassidy begged Anthony to come up with a math problem that could stump her. C'mon, she
said, give me any times-nine question. Out the window, old barns and battered RVs mingled with construction sites and white picket fences. Most of
the HOMES FOR SALE signs mentioned the Mill Creek Cluster right below
their listing prices. A phone call came in over the car's Bluetooth system.

"We're done," said Corey's disembodied voice.

"We're here," Anthony responded.

Back at the house, he laid out fruit cups and cereal bars on the kitchen
counter, then went upstairs to change. Corey put Cassidy in a playful head-
lock and held Nate off with his free arm. Anthony came back down in a

black fleece and white sneakers. He reminded his oldest son to finish his math homework, then draped a whistle around his neck. After a couple years on the sideline, he'd signed up to be the defensive coordinator for Carter's eight-year-old football team.

The field lights were already on when the Robinsons pulled into the parking lot of Duncan Creek Park. Cassidy ran off to find her friends and make TikTok videos. Carter squirmed into his shoulder pads and jogged down to the grass. Anthony followed at his own deliberate pace.

By the time scrimmages were over, a half-moon hung high in the sky. Players gathered around their coaches and dropped down to one knee. Someone led a prayer. Amen, dozens of tiny voices called out. It was almost 8:00 when Anthony pulled back into the driveway and hit the garage door opener.

"What's for dinner?" Cassidy asked.

"When will mom be home?" Carter followed.

Then Corey shuffled out to the garage. The hood of his sweatshirt was wrapped tightly around his head. His pencil was back in his mouth.

"Did you finish that math study guide?" Anthony asked.

"Nope," responded Corey, still unsure how to simplify radicals.

Anthony closed the garage door, headed to the kitchen to reheat some black-eyed peas, and nudged his oldest son toward the dinner table. His face betrayed no emotion.

"So we got some work to do," he said.

THE ADESINA FAMILY | EVANSTON, ILLINOIS

Before finalizing Chris's transfer into Washington Elementary for the start of the 2019–20 school year, Lauren Adesina asked the school's principal to discuss her lingering concerns from Dewey.

"Let's meet!" said Kate Ellison, now in her twelfth year at the school. "Those conversations are happening all the time here."

Approaching Washington, which many regarded as an exemplar of the

painstaking nuts-and-bolts reforms that might actually yield equitable outcomes for a diverse suburban student body, it was hard not to feel hopeful.
The school's original edifice was now 120 years old and featured a three-
story tower that was made of golden bricks and anchored by a spectacular
Palladian stained-glass window. Inside the main entrance, visitors were
greeted by a large rainbow-striped pride flag and hallway doors decorated
with social justice–themed collages. Classroom walls and bulletin boards
offered more of the same; one teacher had given her fourth graders black-
and-white worksheets with an outline of the American flag to color in however they chose, then hung up the resulting designs, which were white and
gold and black, pink and green, purple and yellow and blue, with some stars
left blank and some stripes filled with delicate crosshatch patterns or angry
scrawls that ran way outside the lines. *In my America*, one student had written on the side of her sheet, *red represents fun, green is life, purple is music,
pink is love.*

"The importance of cultural relevance was, like, smeared all over the
walls," said Lauren, who felt immediately at home.

Her talk with the principal only reinforced the feeling. Ellison favored
dangly round earrings, cashmere shawls, and lapel pins announcing her
pronouns. She'd started in District 65 as a social worker. Now, she told Lauren, her focus was on strong relationships and high expectations. Washington staff were deep into their study of Zaretta Hammond's book on culturally
responsive teaching, a development that set Lauren's heart aflutter. She
asked if all the school's teachers took part in District 65's Black Lives Matter
Week of Action.

"That's a nonnegotiable," Ellison responded, adding that she also expected staff to integrate such material into their lessons all year long.

Damn, Lauren thought. *I didn't know it went this deep.*

All she really wanted was a school with teachers who didn't punish Black
and Brown children for every little thing, but who also didn't let them get
away with going to the bathroom fifteen times a day. Ellison seemed to get
it. She told Lauren her goal was to build a staff that knew how to create inclusive environments while also challenging all kids academically. *Being a*

warm demander, the principal called it, lifting a phrase from Hammond's book. A precondition was that every adult in the school must be willing to continually reexamine their own practices, habits, assumptions, and biases.

"I'm very aware of needing to do my own work as a white leader in power," Ellison said. "If I'm doing the job well, then equity is a part of everything I'm doing. The budget is an equity document, the way I'm supporting kids socially and emotionally, this all has to be a part of that."

During her tenure, Washington had experienced its own series of racist incidents, including children using the n-word on the playground. In response, Ellison told me, she'd partnered with a college professor who was also the father of a Black Washington student to develop a training curriculum that was still in use. But she wasn't shy about acknowledging her own missteps, cringing openly at the naivete of the early racial equity work she'd led. Back then, Ellison said, her focus had been on "the visible stuff," like diversifying the artwork in Washington's hallways and adding more Spanish-language books to classroom libraries. And when Ellison had become the first principal to formally challenge District 65's traditional Pioneer Day celebration, some parents and staff had pushed back, so she initially agreed to a compromise. The name of the celebration was changed, lesson plans were tweaked to include a greater emphasis on the experiences of Indigenous people, and letters went home explaining why teachers would now be using the word "colonizer" instead of "pioneer." But when the celebration actually happened, it ended up feeling like the same old Pioneer Day.

"It just needed to end, you know?" Ellison said.

She'd also been heavily influenced by the parent activists involved with Next Steps, whose book studies and discussion series had helped Ellison rethink her interactions with white and affluent Washington families. Previously, the principal told me, she'd spend up to an hour on the phone with any parent who wanted their child to be assigned to a particular teacher, placed in accelerated courses, or given a spot in the school's dual-immersion language program. Now, she immediately drew a clear boundary and moved on. The shift had given Ellison precious time to focus on what she considered most important: improving classroom teaching. The ripple effects were significant. Washington staff meetings evolved from business updates and personal gripes to professional development related to key instructional strategies. Parent-teacher conferences were extended, especially for students who needed extra support. Ellison also began insisting that teachers maintain open lines of communication and track their interactions with Black and Brown parents, so that potential problems could be detected and addressed before they spiraled out of control.

The cumulative impact of such steps was evident during Chris's first few weeks of second grade at Washington. After some early academic struggles and several recesses spent alone on the playground, Lauren's son reverted to one of his most trusted avoidance strategies. This time, however, his teacher, a young woman named Ms. Reynolds, who was still relatively new to the classroom, quickly stepped in.

"She reached out to me and was like, 'Yeah, Chris goes to the bathroom every day during writing workshop,'" Lauren said. "And I'm like, 'Oh, I'm glad you noticed and someone is connecting with me.' And we immediately came up with this kind of star program for him. He gets like three or four stars a day, and those are the amount of times he can actually go to the bathroom. And there were parameters. Like, writing workshop isn't the time."

Reading was similar. Instead of giving Chris basic primers that would leave him ever further behind, Reynolds presented him with a series of books written on a second-grade level, then tried to make sure he received help navigating the more challenging material. It was an approach Ellison had been pushing hard.

"If we continually are only presenting easier content to some of our students, then who are we presenting the more complex content to?" she said. "Our high-performing white kids."

The early returns had been promising; half of Washington students now scored proficient or above on state English Language Arts exams, several points higher than in the early years of Ellison's tenure. But there were still challenges. Shortly before Christmas, for example, Chris began dragging his feet and complaining every time he was sent to work with the school's reading intervention specialist.

Again, Reynolds promptly tried to nip the problem in the bud. Upon being informed what was going on, Lauren requested another meeting. Ellison and Reynolds not only agreed, but roped in other adults Chris was fond of, including his former reading specialist and a school social worker. Before Lauren could get through her list of questions, the Washington educators were taking turns sharing all the little things they'd noticed about Chris, like how excited he got learning about dinosaurs, the topics he'd covered in his letters to a pen pal, and which letters he still wrote backward on his worksheets. Lauren was taken aback at how well these people seemed to know her child. Then Ellison stepped in and reminded the group to consider the big picture. We can try to impose a consequence on Chris, she said. Or we can try to make this a more positive experience for him.

I can get more books about dinosaurs, Reynolds suggested. He really responds well to jokes, the former reading specialist chimed in. I'll try to make him laugh at the start of each session, the current reading specialist responded. Together, everyone agreed to up the frequency of Chris's pen-pal correspondence, which he clearly enjoyed, and to pull together a special binder full of nonfiction Nat Geo Kids stories about animals that would be just for him. Lauren, eager to play her part, volunteered to reinforce to Chris how important it was to give his full attention to the reading specialist. And as the plan clicked into place, Ellison reminded her staff to make sure all the reading materials they pulled together were written at a second-grade level or above. Remember, she said. *Warm demanders.*

"She had a standard and expectation, she pushed him and saw that he is capable," Lauren said, elated.

By early 2020, however, such inch-by-inch efforts to make District 65 classrooms more equitable were getting overshadowed by the consuming ideological debates that had erupted the previous year, turning many of the complex, emotionally taxing issues at play in Evanston into political minefields. The City Council's Equity & Empowerment Committee, for example, was drawing national headlines for a groundbreaking proposal to provide up to $10 million in reparations to some of the town's Black residents. And Next Steps was running a second yearlong book study, this time focused on *How to Be an Antiracist* by Boston University professor Ibram X. Kendi. In early winter 2020, I sat in on one of the group's discussions. It took place in the basement of the old Foster school. While hot-water radiators clanged in the background and the lights on a small artificial Christmas tree flickered on and off, a multiracial group of fifteen people spent more than two hours considering Kendi's contention that the notion of "dangerous Black neighborhoods" was one of the most damaging racist ideas circulating in America.

"I know a lot of white families who have never gone into the Fifth Ward," the white mother of a fourth grader told the group.

A Black woman who wore a striped scarf pushed her glasses to the top of her head before responding.

"I had a very hard time with this chapter," she said. "When my family moved here from Detroit, I felt like the biggest sellout. Then I had a good night's sleep, and I was like, 'Why am I sleeping so well?' Because I felt safe."

All of District 65, meanwhile, seemed to be buzzing with progressive activity. Officials had moved to dramatically limit schools' contact with law enforcement. They'd also expanded the district's antidiscrimination policies to include gender and gender identity. Two school board members were pushing an initiative to create a shared citywide PTA fund so that money from wealthier school communities could be redistributed to schools in less affluent parts of town. And the most consuming issue of all was choosing a new superintendent. At one marathon school board meeting, dozens of local residents spent hours giving testimony on what they prioritized in a new leader, including turning District 65 into a carbon-neutral organization that ran entirely on renewable energy. Then the board spent hours more discussing the fine print of a 295-page report it had commissioned, including a debate on the difference between the "opportunity hoarding" practiced by privileged parents and the "opportunity prying" of their marginalized counterparts. All the while, the older Black woman the board had hired as its search consultant fiddled with her pink-and-green-monogrammed Alpha Kappa Alpha purse and tried not to suck her teeth.

Eventually, though, all the deliberation seemed to have paid off. In December 2019, the district announced its new superintendent: Devon Horton, a veteran Black educator who'd grown up in Chicago's Robert Taylor Homes housing projects, attended historically Black Jackson State University in Mississippi, and served as a deputy superintendent in East St. Louis, Illinois, and Jefferson County, Kentucky. At first, he hadn't even been sure whether to apply, Horton told me after he was hired.

"I had never seen myself working in a community like Evanston. I always felt like going into the 'hood was better suited for my skill set," he said. "But the board was really focused on racial equity and bringing in a really heavy social justice focus to the work. And I fell in love."

Lauren could feel herself healing. On a windy afternoon in February, we met at Washington Elementary's after-school basketball program. She took a seat on a long wooden bench that ran along the gymnasium's far wall, then pulled off the fur-lined hood of her coat, revealing a silver-bar piercing that now stretched across the top of one ear. We watched as Chris tried to dribble. He was slight and uncoordinated, but happy as could be, running around in silly circles and flashing a big smile when he came running over to take a long drink from his mom's water bottle.

"You're doing great, Chrissy," Lauren said, shooing him back toward the court.

But as ever, history lurked. For as long as Evanston had been around, progressive advances had always been followed by a pendulum swing in the other direction. Now a new backlash was gathering steam. A white drama teacher had filed a complaint with the U.S. Department of Education's Office of Civil Rights alleging that District 65's racial equity trainings, race-based staff affinity groups, and Black Lives Matter Week of Action curriculum reflected systemic discrimination against white people. ("When Plaintiff expressed these concerns, her colleagues interrupted her, rolled their eyes, and told Plaintiff she did not know what she was talking about," one of her complaints read.) On the District 65 board, meanwhile, former president Candance Chow was preparing to resign; she'd later tell me she felt like she didn't have a place in the emerging new order of Evanston, which was now racked by the same ambient urgency that had previously permeated places like Compton, suburban Atlanta, and North Dallas.

Angela Blaising felt it too. A white woman and lifelong Democrat, she worked in corporate finance and had two kids in District 65 schools. The last education issue she remembered paying much attention to was the 2017 operating referendum that Goren and Chow had shepherded; Blaising supported it because she didn't want to see her kids' class sizes go up. But after the measure passed, she'd retreated back into the routines of her daily life, missing years' worth of discussions, debates, and policy changes related to racial equity, including that District 65 board meeting in late 2018 when Lauren had publicly bared her racial trauma.

"I remember feeling like I *should* be more involved," Blaising would tell me later of this period before everything changed and she joined a slate of liberal challengers determined to regain control of the District 65 board. "But things were in good hands. Part of the reason I paid the taxes I paid was so that I could focus on working and send my kids to a school that was well run and I didn't need to be super involved."

THE SMITH FAMILY | PENN HILLS, PENNSYLVANIA

In early February 2020, Jackson Smith woke up under a dark cloud. His fury and frustration kept gathering as he pulled on his favorite Pikachu shirt, then noticed the hundred small absences that spoke to his failure. Books, homework assignments, permission slips, the conversation journal his mother and second-grade teacher shared—he'd lost half of them and kept forgetting the rest at school. His mother had responded with morning checklists, one of which she was running him through now.

"All right, all right!" Jackson snapped while searching for his backpack. "Will you just stop."

Bethany sucked in sour air and silently counted to three. Tell Mr. Ben what you got at the book fair, she finally said. And like that, the skies over her son brightened. Jackson found his bag, then pulled out two pens outfitted with ultraviolet lights you could use to write secret messages. I love detective stuff, he told me. Then he pulled on his winter coat and a pair of mismatched gloves and gave himself over to the routine of another school day.

Outside, crunchy white snow covered the Smiths' lawn. Bethany prodded her son down the gently curved sidewalk, silently widening her eyes and shaking her head as he ran toward the family's gray Nissan Rogue. A pink bumper sticker featured a smiling image of Mister Rogers and the words "Look for the good where you are and EMBRACE IT." We drove to the same parking lot of the same fading Lutheran church where I'd once waited on yellow buses of my own. When Jackson ran out into the cold to play, my attention was once again diverted by memories, this time of the snowball fights I used to take part in before school.

"... and everything is still going good," I heard Bethany say, interrupting my reverie. "Mr. Mastro is the behavior specialist at the school. He's been great. Jackson can go down to his office and take a break when he gets angry. And if he has five good days in a row, they have a snack together."

There was rapping at the window. Jackson asked his mom for a hug and kiss, then clambered aboard the bus. While Bethany headed back home to get ready for her day, I drove over to Penn Hills Elementary. The school's cavernous foyer made ants of the young children lined up against an incongruous wall covered in fancy Italian tile. My old school, Dible, had once been located on the same site, but all that remained was a few objects inside a red plastic time capsule. One of the other neighborhood elementary schools that had once dotted Penn Hills was now waiting to be converted into senior housing. A third was home to a charter school. And despite its financial woes, the school board had sold a fourth shuttered school for a bargain-basement price to the municipality, which had promptly torn down the building and built a gleaming new municipal building and police station. I headed to room 149, where a sign hanging in the front of the classroom said THE ONLY TIME YOU SHOULD EVER LOOK BACK IS TO SEE HOW FAR YOU HAVE COME. Below it was a long whiteboard and a string of green LED lights.

"Let me see whose desk is ready," said Ms. Levin, Jackson's teacher.

There were about twenty-five students in the class. Roughly a third were white. One of the other Black boys was also an expatriate from Urban Academy, the same charter school Jackson had attended. To keep him from getting up or moving around, Levin made the boy sit by himself at a semicircular table pushed against the room's back wall. Jackson took a seat in the front row, then waved as Mr. Mastro slipped into the room and unclipped a walkie-talkie from the waistband of his khakis. Levin switched the LED lights to red and told the class to stop talking.

The morning started with a game called Sparkle. All the children— except for the boy in the back, who stood behind his table—lined up side by side in a U. The first student in line started spelling a word. The next added the second letter, and so on down the line until the word was complete. If your turn came and you said the wrong letter, you had to sit. If the person before you successfully completed the word, you said "Sparkle" and took a seat too.

The boy in the back was the first to misspell a word. He sat down in a huff, stuck his red Jordans as far beyond the table as he could get them, then silently screamed into his fist. Ms. Levin issued a warning from the front of the room. The behavior specialist slid over and gave the boy his hand. "Squeeze," he said. The boy gripped his hand. "Squeeze harder," Mastro instructed. The boy put his full body into the effort until something inside let go. "I never win," he said quietly.

The game continued for several rounds. Most of the children who made mistakes smiled sheepishly and took their seats. When Jackson misspelled a word, however, the dark cloud from the morning reappeared. Instead of sitting down, he used his arm to sweep papers, books, and pencils from his desk onto the floor. Then he pounded the empty surface with his hand, buried his face in the crook of his arm, and stormed out of the room. Get back in your area, Ms. Levin said sharply when the boy in the back moved to follow him.

Mastro headed out into the hallway, then led Jackson to his office. The game of Sparkle ended shortly after. Levin sent the rest of the children for a bathroom break. When her classroom was empty, she brushed the hair back from her face and sighed deeply. Like every other teacher at Penn Hills Elementary, she was white. And like the school's entire second-grade team, she'd been teaching in Penn Hills for more than two decades. During that span, she'd developed a wide menu of tried-and-true strategies for redirecting students' frustration and disruptive behaviors. Now, though, all her established systems seemed to be breaking down. In private moments, some Penn Hills teachers confessed to feeling like many of their students—three fifths of whom were now Black, and more than one fourth of whom were now on individualized education plans, indicating special needs—were growing up amid circumstances they didn't understand.

"Did his mom tell you about his behavior?" Levin asked me in reference to Jackson. "The kids who come from the city, their behavior is just much worse."

Before she could elaborate, a group of girls came running down the hallway. Someone had locked a bathroom stall from the inside. Levin told the kids to wash up, then radioed the school custodian for help. Amid the clamor, Mastro marched a still-mopey Jackson back down the hall. Are you ready to go back in, he asked when they reached the classroom door. I want to go back to the book fair, Jackson responded. Then he threw his body into the wall and let it slide slowly to the floor, where he stayed for most of the next lesson.

That evening, the school hosted its annual Math and Reading Night. The Smiths arrived shortly before 7:00. Bethany wore gold earrings, buttery light-brown boots, and a long braid that circled her head like a crown. Jackson and the other children were shuttled to the cafeteria, where a magician was preparing to perform math tricks. Parents were herded off to classrooms, where teachers provided updates on what their children were supposed to be learning. I relayed to Bethany what I had witnessed in Jackson's class that morning.

"I still think Ms. Levin is great. She's pretty good," she responded. "She always was like, 'What can we try now?' Just trying to stay ahead of it. And I appreciated that. It wasn't like a them-against-me thing. It was, 'What are we going to do to make sure Jackson has a pleasant day in school and doesn't frustrate the hell out of his teacher?'"

Still unsettled by what I'd seen, I kept asking questions. How do you feel about him missing so much instructional time? What about the boy behind the table? Eventually, Bethany got annoyed. I don't need you to tell me to worry about my Black son, she said. On two separate occasions, she told me, the staff at Penn Hills Elementary had lost track of Jackson after he wandered out of his classroom. Both times, school security guards had to help locate him.

"And I'm like, that right there, that does not sound good," Bethany said. "Fast-forward, and I see a sixteen-year-old Black male—not a Black child, a Black male—being in a position where he's frustrated and the police are called. And how will that be handled?"

When the second-grade update was done, everyone headed to the cafeteria. A member of the Penn Hills school board was handing out gift cards to the winners of the Black History Month essay contest he and his fraternity brothers had sponsored. Then a school administrator directed families over to the gym for corn hole, ring tosses, and dancing. A smile returned to Bethany's face as she watched Jackson do 360-degree twirls down the hallway. I asked about her vision for the future. Bethany told me she'd been listening to financial self-help advisers. She was particularly enamored with a podcast called *Earn Your Leisure*. It was run by two hip young men who broke down the benefits of Roth IRAs, explained how to get started in the vending machine industry, and interviewed self-made real estate investors about how to flip distressed properties. Everyone involved was Black. Bethany told me she'd already signed up for a couple of webinars.

"My job gives me a purpose, but it's not getting me financially where I want to go," she said. "I'd love to be able to just chill. On an island somewhere, in the sand, watching the ocean."

To that end, she was forming an LLC and drafting plans to purchase several rental properties. Maybe someday my son will work alongside me, Bethany said. He could be a civil engineer, an architect, a construction manager. But then, just as quickly, she pulled the rug out from under her own fantasies. Knowing him, she laughed, he'd probably rather be a You-Tuber. Besides, she was already encountering other obstacles.

"I don't think it would be in Penn Hills," Bethany said of her investment plans. "The taxes and sewage and water are just so high."

I weighed whether to bring up the other problems I saw threatening her ambitions. Especially the other schools in Penn Hills. Linton Middle was a clear disaster; just that spring, social media had lit up with cell-phone videos of a brawl inside the school that ended with an eighth grader suffering a concussion after her head was smashed into a computer. And Penn Hills High was also in trouble. I'd recently visited a school counselor there named Janae Shaw. She was the 1,137-student school's only full-time Black profes-sional staffer. Thanks to the district's ongoing budget cuts, she was now re-sponsible for all the school's seniors and one third of its freshmen. She began to cry a few minutes into our conversation.

"They won't let go of the Native American thing," Shaw told me, referring to the school's "Indians" mascot. "Every day when I come here, I'm just like, *God*. There's a [bust] out here that the secretary of our office insists on hav-ing, which almost makes me physically sick."

As we talked, more stories came pouring out. How some members of the school's white staff resisted even the smallest efforts to celebrate diversity. How she'd been the only adult to speak up in support of Black students who didn't want to stand for the Pledge of Allegiance. How her colleagues still talked down to her, even though she was the only person in the building with the letters *P*, *H*, and *D* after her name.

"Remember Ferguson?" Shaw asked. "Okay, so I had this hashtag-Mike-Brown shirt, and I wore it to work on a dress-down day. And some mysterious citizen in Penn Hills thought they should go and talk to the superintendent. And so my principal came to talk to me, saying that people are concerned that it might cause a riot or something."

She'd responded by ordering the same shirt in a different color, then wearing it to the school the following Friday. Many students had responded appreciatively.

"It opened up a dialogue for them to express, 'I'm scared, I'm afraid.' And for me to say, 'It's not abnormal. There's something called proximal and distal trauma, right, that's akin to secondary trauma, where you don't have to be present in the space or even in the time that something happened. But it affects you,'" Shaw told me.

Then the bell rang. A parade of students—a Black boy with locs piled on top of his head, a Black girl with an armload of books, a white boy with a wispy mustache selling chocolate-covered pretzels to raise money for a school club—all came up to ask Shaw for a hug.

"Violence is actually more likely because you're keeping stuff inside you and it's building up and festering," she said when classes resumed.

Then Shaw took me on a tour of the new building. My first impression was of a relatively well-resourced school. The engineering studio was full of 3-D printers. The video production room featured a large green screen. The foyer was decked out with fancy chandeliers. A large display case outside the gym where I used to play basketball filled me with fresh nostalgia. But then Shaw began pointing out the problems.

Doors were missing handles. Sheetrock walls bowed if you leaned on them. A network of expensive security cameras was out of commission. The two-story media center with a spiral staircase was closed because there was no longer a librarian. A wing of the building was also blocked off; just as the construction manager had warned when the school was being built, the massive new facility didn't have nearly enough students to fill its classrooms. When we headed into the gym, Shaw directed my attention to a long crack snaking its way through one of the cinderblock walls; the rigging and safety straps holding a retractable basketball hoop to the ceiling had recently given way, causing $10,000 worth of damage. Shaw looked ready to cry again.

"At this point," she said, "what determines everything in this district is that money that was stolen from the people of Penn Hills."

But exactly who had ostensibly stolen that money remained unclear, and recovering it was now a pipe dream. As a result, the school board was stuck in a no-win situation that only seemed to be getting worse. At their Feb-

ruary 2020 meeting, I sat among thirty or so parents and residents who listened to a rundown of the district's worsening budget predicament. We can't
continue down this path, board president Erin Vecchio railed. Kids aren't
being educated. I'm not cutting another teacher. The fight is on.

But if there was some realistic way out, no one—including me—seemed
to know what it was. The board had only been able to balance its 2019–20
budget with $3 million that Vecchio wrangled from Pennsylvania state sen-
ator Jay Costa, who "recommended" that the board agree not to raise his
constituents' property taxes if they wanted the money. But at least $1 million
of the "gift" had never materialized, and accepting the rest had prevented
the district from opening a reliable new stream of recurring revenue by raising taxes. As a result, less than a year later, things were even more dire. A
mammoth 7 percent property-tax hike was now on the table. If the board
approved it, they'd risk a revolt among mostly white seniors, plus further
enrollment declines, and they'd still be facing a $3.2 million operating defi-
cit. Hold the line on taxes, on the other hand, and the district would be staring down a $6.1 million budget shortfall, a number so large it could trigger a
state takeover.

And all that was before you took into account snowballing issues with
the two new schools' HVAC systems, both of which were falling to shit, just
like Vecchio said, creating an eerie parallel to the conditions that had signaled Compton's impending collapse in the late 1960s and early '70s. Less
than a decade after the Penn Hills School District had mortgaged its future
to build new schools, three of the eight new boilers used to heat the two
buildings had failed. A chiller at the high school was also inoperable. Consultants hired to assess the damage uncovered staggering incompetence.
The problems were rooted in the design of the systems, which had been
unnecessarily expensive from the start, then made worse by a water treatment plan that had never been implemented and routine preventive maintenance steps, like changing filters, that had been largely ignored. Drafty
windows and exhaust fans that were installed without dampers had caused
added strain by allowing the weather outside to make its way into the
building.

"Validates staff reports of snow blowing into the corridors on winter days," the consultants concluded.

"Total clusterfuck, take-the-money-and-run job," added my dad, who I asked to review their report because his work at the University of Pittsburgh had entailed maintaining similar systems. "I'm just glad I got out of Penn Hills when I did."

I decided to share all that information with Bethany mostly because I thought she deserved to know what I was learning about Penn Hills. I also didn't want to contribute further to the thick fog of denial that still permeated the township. But there were less redeeming reasons as well. I remained blind to the depth of her desire to just lead a simple life, without having to spend her free time baring her soul at school board meetings or creating PowerPoint presentations in the hopes of convincing her child's teachers not to be racist. And I was also missing something deeper; consumed with making sense of all that I still carried from my time in Penn Hills, I couldn't see how Bethany and so many others kept finding the best in the township and trying to make it work. Regardless, when I finally stopped talking, it was clear something had shifted between us.

"You coming to me with statistics," Bethany told me. "Like, oh, this person said this, that, and the third about Penn Hills. But me personally? I'm thriving."

Math and Reading Night ended with a raffle. Jackson won an enormous gift basket stuffed with Judy Blume books and boxes of Swedish Fish. Exhilarated, he rushed over to show his grandmother, then made for the door. Bethany trailed behind, picking up the glove, water bottle, and sheets of loose paper her son left in his wake.

The next time we talked on the phone, our discussion was stilted. In an attempt to make sure I understood something Bethany had recently told me, I started asking questions. I want to get this correct, I said. I want to tell your story the right way. The ensuing silence seemed to stretch on forever.

"It just hit me when you said, 'tell your story,'" Bethany finally ventured.

Then, after some back-and-forth, she spoke to me more directly than she ever had before.

"All right, let me be transparent," Bethany began. "I enjoy talking to you, and I'm all for what you're doing. But there has been a long history of white people telling Black people's stories and profiting off of it. That right there is what I'm having an issue with."

Suddenly, the parts of myself I'd always struggled to see clearly—my whiteness, the history that came with it, the harms I caused without even noticing—were impossible to miss. As a result, I found myself face-to-face with suburbia's fourth big illusion: the false promise that white families like mine could live somehow outside of history, making personal decisions that didn't carry the weight of our past, then pretending those choices didn't add up to the larger forces now tearing at places like Penn Hills.

My initial response to Bethany was mostly hemming and hawing. But she kept pressing. Before I called, she told me, she'd been singing Whitney Houston songs, happy as could be. And now here I was bringing all my doom and gloom into her life. How did you even get to this point with the book, she asked. And what's your motivation for asking me all these questions about how I feel about Penn Hills?

I tried to answer honestly.

"So part of what I'm writing about and researching is what's been happening with the district. It's important to see the big-picture patterns," I offered. "But then we all live our lives within those patterns. That's how I'm approaching your story."

The line was quiet for a moment.

"Yeah, it just hit different today," Bethany said. "Let me think about this. And I will get back in touch with you."

THE HERNANDEZ FAMILY | COMPTON, CALIFORNIA

Jefferson Elementary's numbers could hardly have been better. With several months of the 2019–20 school year still to go, iReady data showed more than a third of the school's students had already mastered every grade-level standard. Fourth graders were on track for big performance gains in everything from comprehending literature to demonstrating algebraic thinking. Average daily attendance was over 97 percent. Thirty-four new students had been selected for the school's gifted program. Not a single student had been suspended so far that year. But Compton Unified superintendent Darin Brawley wasn't satisfied. Why were only five English learners reclassified last month? he asked Jefferson principal Salvador Aquino during their monthly data chat. What's going on with your first graders' vocabulary? What's your intervention plan?

"It's not a gotcha game," Brawley said for the thousandth time. "It's a reflective dialogue."

Aquino took the grilling in stride. Everyone needs feedback, the principal liked to say. It helped that he knew the shoe would be on the other foot later that week, when he'd hold similar conversations with each of Jefferson's teachers. That included Mr. Moreno, whom Aquino would push to develop a plan to provide extra supports for the dozen or so students in his class still struggling to comprehend informational texts.

"He was pretty cool about it," the teacher would say after. "Reasonable, in the sense that he knows what kids need and he understands that teachers know best."

Reasonable was good. Right before winter break, Moreno had felt himself wearing down. Normal classroom noise started grating on his nerves. He began raising his voice more than usual. He'd even taken to heading home right when the school day ended. Such developments were especially worrisome because they mirrored the pattern that had emerged just before his stroke two years earlier. Although things had been crazy at work back then, he'd taken on side jobs teaching night school and translating a math textbook to earn some extra money. He'd been sitting at his home computer when the vertigo hit. Then the entire left side of his body went numb. The next thing Moreno knew, he was on extended medical leave.

"I can't afford to forget," he said.

Fortunately, winter break had worked wonders. By mid-January, Moreno had reestablished his classroom's blended learning routine. With a two-week window before preparations for state tests consumed Jefferson, he figured it was time to make good on his promise.

"Let's start the class newspaper," he told Jacob on a Thursday afternoon. "You're going to be the chief editor, okay?"

Unsure where to begin, Moreno had gone to Ms. Santiago for advice. Open the door and point them in the right direction, she'd said. They'll figure it out from there. But there was one aspect of the project Moreno felt strongly about. The newspaper project couldn't be just for Jacob. A few other advanced students who didn't need more test prep could also benefit. So would a couple students who needed work on specific skills, like citing evidence. And a couple of other kids just needed a reason to come to school in the morning.

"We're also going to get an opinion writer, an informational writer, a book reviewer, and other components," Moreno told Jacob, laying out his plan.

Perhaps the most beautiful thing about Jefferson was that Jacob had never really doubted that his request to start the newspaper would eventually be honored. Beaming, he opened Google Docs, found the newsletter template Moraga had suggested, and shared it with his new team. Together, the fourth graders figured out how to add and scale pictures, then add captions and headlines. Watching from across the classroom, Moreno allowed himself a moment of satisfaction.

"These are the things that do not make me tired," he said.

The next item on the new editor in chief's agenda was organizing a staff photo. Everyone lined up in front of the Mondrian-inspired student artwork on the classroom's far wall. Adrian, the boy who'd been researching space-time before winter break, was tapped to be the science writer. Jocelyn, the girl who was obsessed with presidential history, would be the informational writer. At one end of the photo lineup was a boy wearing hipster glasses with thick dark frames who'd been tapped as the graphic designer-slash-comic artist. And at the other was Jacob, looking now like a young Dean Baquet or Marty Baron or Gregorio López, a pensive expression on his face and his hands stuffed deep into the pockets of his blue school-uniform pants.

That first week of work on the paper was glorious. Before school and at recess and during free time in the afternoons, the children organized page layouts and haggled over story placement. Jacob made the final call to lead with the piece he thought was strongest, an impassioned Op-Ed against homework. ("How are we supposed to relax?" the opinion writer wondered.) Moreno let forth a laugh that emanated from deep in his belly.

"I'm pretty sure he'll never forget this," the teacher said. "When he takes the state test and he's asked to write an opinion piece, he's going to do it flawlessly."

But an editor's duties were never done. Jacob had to talk Jocelyn out of the Franklin Pierce profile she was planning, suggesting instead a piece on Thomas Jefferson, whom everyone could relate to because he was their school's namesake. And when the calendar turned to February, he had to wrestle with another challenge involving his narrative fiction writer. The boy was one of the struggling students whose spirits Moreno had hoped to boost. That part had worked; he couldn't stop talking about his new role. But the copy he submitted amounted to several pages' worth of scribbled half sentences about video games.

"While he was explaining it to me, I could tell he was so excited," Jacob said.

Unsure what to do next, the editor in chief turned to his teacher. Moreno agreed it was important to validate the boy's effort. But he also passed on the same message that Brawley had given to Aquino and Aquino had given to him: we have to hold everybody to a high standard. Together, teacher, editor, and writer soon reached a compromise: The paper's inaugural edition would feature a one-page teaser that included a drawing of the story's main character and a paragraph on his background, including that he'd been forced to flee his home planet because it was getting sucked into a black hole, but had been gifted with the powers of teleportation and regeneration as recompense for his loss.

The newspaper was put on hold when testing season arrived. Students took the "common assessments" that Compton Unified used to get one last look at the skills and concepts teachers should review. Jacob and most of his friends did fine. But four students whose earlier scores suggested they should be in the 90th percentile or above bombed the practice exam because they were goofing off, and a handful of kids with limited English skills hadn't progressed as anticipated. As a result, Moreno's weekly data check-ins with Principal Aquino grew tense, sending the frustrated teacher's blood pressure soaring and leading him to start counting the days until his next break.

Relief seemed to come at the end of February, when the class took a field trip to the Cabrillo Marine Aquarium. Jacob was disappointed not to see any lampreys or sea pigs. But the entire class was rapt as a docent described a mystery that aquarium staff had recently unraveled. Fish began disappearing from their tanks overnight. No one could figure out why until security cameras were set up to run over the weekend, capturing footage of a hungry octopus escaping from its own tank, then raiding others for food.

"It was mind-boggling," Moreno said.

"I wasn't surprised," Jacob countered. "I had read that octopuses are really intelligent. They can climb anything."

After lunch came a free hour. That was when Moreno first noticed something was wrong. In years past, he'd used the time to play soccer with his students. Now, though, he wasn't feeling right, so he sat on a bench and waited. After getting everyone safely back to Jefferson, he went straight to an urgent care center. Concerned, they sent him to a hospital for a stress test. The good news, a doctor eventually told Moreno, is it's not another stroke. The bad news is you're suffering from exhaustion.

A parade of substitutes covered his class during the first week of March. Independent research, engineering experiments, and passion projects all fell by the wayside. The first edition of Jacob's class newspaper, still not quite finished, languished in his Google Drive.

Then, seemingly out of nowhere, Principal Aquino was promoted to Compton Unified's central office. A Latina woman named Bilma Bermudez was tapped to take over. Her first official day was set for Thursday, March

12, 2020. The afternoon before, she stopped by the school to connect with teachers and introduce herself to parents. By then COVID-19 was no longer a distant threat halfway across the world. More than a dozen Americans were already confirmed dead, and the country was starting to shut down. What's going to happen? anxious staff and parents demanded.

"There will be no gap in learning," Bermudez kept repeating. "As soon as we hear anything, I will notify you."

On Friday morning, word began circulating that the League of Innovative Schools summit the following week had been postponed. A few hours later, the Los Angeles Unified School District announced it was closing schools for two weeks. Long Beach Unified soon decided the same. Superintendent Brawley and the Compton Unified board had little choice but to follow suit.

Inside Jefferson, word came down from Bermudez not to alarm students. Mr. Moreno, still recovering, prepared packets of worksheets to send home. He wondered how he would keep doing his targeted interventions with struggling readers. He made a mental note not to forget about the class newspaper. Then, when 3:00 came, he sent his class out to their families like it was just another Friday. The Hernandezes wouldn't learn that schools had been closed until that weekend. Jacob's heart swelled with sadness when he heard.

"I didn't get a chance to say good-bye," he said.

PART IV

[NO MORE AWAY]

13

THE STORM ARRIVES

THE BECKER FAMILY | LUCAS, TEXAS

They fought all their lives to be there, and then all of a
sudden, something happened that changes their life.

—DONALD J. TRUMP, 2020

Donald Trump strode to a lectern facing the South Lawn of the White House. It was July 16, 2020. Sweating men in gray suits and sweltering women in sleeveless dresses sat in folding chairs spaced six feet apart. The president's speech about deregulation started off as expected, full of banal boasts about unburdening companies that produced everything from dishwashers to ventilators. Then, during a bit about unwinding water pressure limits for shower heads, Trump ad-libbed. "Because my hair, I don't know about you, but it has to be perfect," he said, earning laughs. Encouraged, he pivoted to an obscure Department of Housing and Urban Development regulation, then began railing about a supposed Democratic plot to "abolish our beautiful and successful suburbs."

"People have worked all their lives to get into a community, and now they're going to watch it go to hell? Not gonna happen. Not while I'm here," Trump thundered. "The suburb destruction will end with us."

Mainstream media figures subsequently derided the president as delusional,

snarking that if he hoped to preserve suburbia's racial and economic homogeneity, he was a half century too late. But millions of everyday Americans
got it. For decades, the country's national identity and collective sense of the
good life had been rooted in the suburbs and their promise that families
could always just move away from the nation's unresolved racial sins. In recent years, however, the combination of sweeping demographic changes, rising housing costs, and the vanishing heart of America's middle class had
disrupted that pattern, pushing the country's original postwar dream of
suburban safe havens into far-exurban enclaves accessible only to families
like the Beckers. In places like Evanston and Gwinnett County, meanwhile,
the country's civil-rights-era dreams of integration and equal opportunity
were running headlong into the pervasive need-not-to-know that still dominated suburbia, fueling increasingly fraught conflicts. In Penn Hills and
other suburbs on the brink, parents like Bethany Smith were still trying to
find a way out of the yawning traps that threatened their dreams. And in
Compton, schools like Jefferson Elementary and families like the Hernandezes were still trying to chart a new path out of the rubble of suburban
dreams that had already died. Even before 2020 announced itself, the ground
beneath everyone's feet had been unsteady, feeding a rising disillusionment
borne from the fear of ending up stuck. And now, the sudden emergence of
two forces well beyond anyone's control were illuminating and exacerbating
the trend.

Just weeks earlier, Minneapolis police had murdered a Black man named
George Floyd. Bystander video showed a white officer kneeling on Floyd's
neck for nearly nine minutes while horrified onlookers begged for mercy.
Furious demonstrations soon convulsed the nation, flooding American homes
with scenes of protesters being teargassed by black-clad riot police, anarchists setting fire to police stations, looters smashing the windows of Rite-
Aids, and troops on horseback clearing a park outside the White House as
flash-bang grenades boomed around them. And America's suburbs soon
found themselves at the center of the storm: In an unbroken line of more
than four thousand suburban communities stretching from Yarmouth,

Maine, to Orange County, California, soccer moms and softball dads took to the streets to proclaim Black Lives Matter or honk their horns in angry disagreement. One of the enduring images of discontent showed a Black first grader named Wynta-Amor Rogers chanting "No justice, no peace" as she and her mother marched through a well-heeled hamlet on suburban Long Island.

And all the while, COVID-19 kept throwing suburbia's fault lines into ever sharper relief. By the time Trump gave his July speech, more than 137,000 Americans were already dead. Nearly 70,000 had tested positive the previous day alone. The nation's 98,000 public schools had closed their doors. For families like the Beckers and the Robinsons, the Adesinas and Smiths and Hernandezes, the everyday routines of suburban life—tutoring sessions, family vacations, trips to the grocery store—had become tinder for a fire that roared from angry school board meetings through to impossible family decisions. Their traditional avenues of retreat cut off, millions of suburbanites suddenly found themselves face-to-face with the root causes of their disillusionment.

The resulting agita was particularly acute on the right, where many in the nation's resurgent conservative movement viewed the suburbs as a final bulwark against an existential threat to the nation. Trump's remarks on the South Lawn, for example, were rooted in the ideas of a conservative scholar named Stanley Kurtz, whose work had long drawn a straight line of quote-unquote real Americans that extended from "the Pilgrim Fathers to the frontier settlers to the post–World War II exodus to the suburbs." Just two weeks before Trump's speech, Kurtz had gone significantly further, writing in the *National Review* that Democratic plans to "abolish America's suburbs" would mean "the end of meaningful choices in how Americans can live."

> At the very moment when the pandemic has made people rethink the advantages of dense urban living, the choice of an alternative will be taken away. . . .

> *Suburbs as we know them will pass from the scene. With them*
> *will disappear the principle of local control that has been the key*
> *to American exceptionalism from the start.*

Suddenly, the tensions that had been building in suburbia for decades could no longer be denied.

"MUCH MORE UNKNOWNS"

The Beckers were at Disney World when everything went haywire. Susan and Jim had wanted to make use of their Marriott timeshare, and they wanted to enjoy another family trip before the kids grew uninterested in spending time together. Because the gravity of the threat posed by COVID-19 was still uncertain, Susan's travel preparations centered around going online to order multiple sets of matching T-shirts for the family.

They arrived in Orlando during the first full weekend in March. Susan soon came down with a scratchy throat and light cough. But her symptoms were mild, hardly enough to warrant disrupting their vacation. By Friday, the kids were riding a roller coaster on their own, and Susan and Jim settled into a table outside a restaurant. After ordering drinks, Susan pulled out her phone and scanned the news for the first time in days.

"What the heck?" she said.

"What?" Jim replied.

The National Basketball Association had suspended its season. School districts across North Texas were shutting down.

"No way," Susan said. "The world is losing its mind."

Within thirty-six hours, the virus and its effects were impossible to avoid. That Saturday morning, the family was enjoying a Bon Voyage Adventure Breakfast that Susan had arranged. Sean, Avery, and Noah grudgingly wore the "Disney 2020: #BestWeekEver" T-shirts their mother had picked out, but studiously avoided eye contact with the actors playing Rapunzel and Ariel who circulated around the restaurant. When Jim's phone buzzed, he got up to take the call outside, annoying Susan, who was already sad the trip was about to end.

Do you know how much I paid for this food you're just leaving here? she remembered thinking.

When Jim returned, however, it was clear something was amiss. The call had been from his newest client. They didn't want him traveling to see them in person. Oh my gosh, Susan said. This is serious.

By the time the Beckers made it back home to Texas, the Lovejoy Independent School District was preparing to announce an extended closure of its own. Susan, who by then had dived into the news coverage of the coronavirus and the limited scientific research that was starting to become available, thought the emerging national strategy of shutdowns, social distancing, and "flattening the curve" made sense. She and Jim began talking with the kids about keeping their immune systems strong so they could help prevent the nation's health-care system from being overrun.

"We don't want everybody getting sick all at once," she said.

It helped that Lovejoy schools' switch to remote learning was almost fun at first. Superintendent Goddard took to posting pictures of himself dressed up in Hawaiian shirts and magician's costumes while working from home. Teachers and administrators organized a virtual crazy hat day. Avery, now almost twelve, dyed the ends of her long hair green. Every morning, she and Susan would take Astro for a walk while Jim and Sean went for a run. The rest of each day's schedule—including regular "brain breaks" on the trampoline Susan bought for the backyard—ran according to an elaborate series of alarms and alerts that Susan had programmed into her phone. When it was time for Noah to log in to school, for example, he'd set up his laptop in Jim's office, listening to his teacher talk about Texas history while his dad took calls about a Japanese retail firm that was hemorrhaging cash. And when Sloan Creek began offering one-on-one virtual tutoring, Susan convinced Avery to sign up for a lunchtime slot she used to get help redoing a recent math assignment.

"You made an eighty-five, and you're coming back and doing it again to make a higher grade," said Ms. Kincel, now just a face on a screen. "I'm so proud of you."

Avery smiled and took the cap off her marker. Kincel talked through some of the grade-level questions she'd missed. Then she introduced some personalized Pre-Algebra problems she'd put together.

"So Avery and her family travel by car to visit Washington, DC," Kincel said, reading one of the problems aloud. "If the number of miles from Lucas, Texas, is 1,320, and Avery's parents drive 60 miles per hour, how many hours did it take them to get to Washington, DC?"

When Avery correctly solved the problem, her mother nodded proudly from the kitchen counter.

"Did I tell you she made the honor roll?" Susan asked me as I followed along over FaceTime.

But as the "temporary" switch to remote learning dragged on, the Beckers' patience and goodwill began wearing thin. It had taken Jim little more than a month to decide it was safe to go back into his Dallas office each morning.

"At this point, I think the government is all a bunch of bumbling boobs," he told me. "We have to reopen. At some point, it just becomes a matter of personal choice and personal responsibility."

Susan was growing agitated too. She hadn't anticipated being home alone with the kids all day again. And few of her connections to the wider world offered much in the way of relief. The parents association at Sloan Creek had to cancel its regular coffees. Cable news and her social media feeds were now overrun with images of antifa rioters trying to burn the country down. Even church had turned distant and fraught; during his Pentecostal prayer, the Beckers' pastor had encouraged the mostly white, mostly affluent congregation to ask the Lord's forgiveness for keeping people who looked and sounded different locked out of power.

"It's definitely been a shock to our system," Susan said as the school year limped to an end.

That summer, she found a dance studio that allowed in-person lessons for Avery, and Noah went back to his tennis lessons. But the pressure just kept building. Businesses remained closed. States began imposing mask mandates. The conventional wisdom was that such sacrifices were necessary steps on the road back to the way things were. To Susan, however, that argument increasingly felt like a bait and switch, especially when it was delivered by gazillionnaires like Bill Gates, now on the news seemingly every night to push for new COVID-19 vaccines. When I asked what she made of concerns on the left about rising right-wing extremism and the potential for a turn toward fascism if Trump was reelected, Susan turned the tables.

"I have had more and more friends have their accounts deleted from Facebook, simply for having a different opinion than what social media wants us to believe," she texted. "We are definitely seeing fascism, but it's coming from somewhere other than Trump and the right."

Why on earth should she and her family go along with that? Susan wondered. For the promise of a return to an old order that had produced teachers who denigrated Christopher Columbus, twelve-year-olds who thought they were bisexual, and a population that mindlessly handed control of their thoughts over to Big Tech? She didn't particularly care for Trump and his abrasive manner. But it sometimes seemed like the president was the only person in power willing to risk the fallout of naming the insanity spreading through the country.

"We haven't had an outsider in there since probably JFK," Susan told me as the COVID-related shutdowns stretched on. "And you know what happened to him."

Her research wasn't making her any more optimistic. She knew from her involvement in holistic health and wellness circles that even Fox News received 70 percent of its ad revenue from pharmaceutical companies. And those alarming spikes in local COVID-19 case counts? Susan now believed they were the result of Collin County commissioners changing their methodology in order to amplify public alarm. By the time Trump began talking about preserving the suburban lifestyle dream, Susan was staying up late to read epidemiological studies of transmission rates in Sweden, studying the correlations between rising unemployment rates and rising suicide rates, and scrolling through the feeds of social-media influencers like Bobby

Kennedy, Jr., once a prominent environmentalist, now a proponent of "vaccine safety." She also spent hours online, where she followed a virtual town hall hosted on Facebook Live by right-wing Texas state senator Bob Hall. The event featured six doctors, all of whom argued that strategies such as masks and social distancing were actually counterproductive. Instead, they said, the country should be aggressively pursuing treatment regimens involving drugs the federal Food and Drug Administration considered potentially harmful.

"We need to wake up and start going on the attack," said a doctor from nearby McKinney, Texas. "As far as opening schools, one idea would be to put high-risk teachers on hydroxychloroquine."

"We should be screaming this from the rooftops," Susan said after urging me to watch. "But my guess is you go to Google, they will show him as being a conspiracy theorist."

By midsummer 2020, the absurdity of the nation's COVID response seemed inescapable. In the grocery store, Susan would pack her cart full of organic fruits and vegetables, saying nothing as other parents loaded up with Doritos and Oreos. Then those same people would turn around and tell her to wear a mask if she wanted to keep her children healthy. It would have been funny if it wasn't so scary.

"You don't need a big government to tell you how to be safe," Susan began instructing the kids, who she told me had started to worry they would be forced to get vaccinated.

By August, the uncertainty around the coming school year was functioning as a force multiplier for such anxieties. Susan could plainly see how three months of virtual learning had stunted Sean's social development, Avery's grasp of new math concepts, and Noah's opportunities to work ahead of grade level. Another full year of online school seemed unthinkable. But she was also distraught over the prospect of her children being forced to wear a mask in order to return to a physical classroom.

She was hardly alone in such sentiments, which were putting the Lovejoy schools in a complicated bind. Thanks to both instructional cuts and fundraisers like Denim & Diamonds, the district's 2019–20 budget had been just about balanced when the pandemic hit. But two months later, Superintendent Goddard and his chief financial officer found themselves playing a daily game of whack-a-mole. Cafeteria staff, for example, were still being paid to make student lunches, many of which were now being delivered. But the district was no longer charging for the meals, opening up a $253,000 hole that had to be plugged with money from the district's fund balance. And the budget for the coming school year looked even more grim. By the Lovejoy board's May meeting, any talk of an "abundance mindset" had been tossed out the window.

"In 2020–21, we have much more unknowns," Goddard said over Zoom.

A series of slides laid out the grisly details. The starting point for discussion was a half-million-dollar operating deficit. That figure, however, assumed continued enrollment growth and strong daily attendance, both of which were being undermined by both the pandemic and parents' frustration with the district's response. It was also unclear whether families who lived outside Lovejoy's attendance zone would continue paying tuition if school remained online, raising the possibility of further declines in revenue from the Lovejoy Scholars program, one of the district's secret weapons. And it looked like the upcoming football season might also be canceled, which would cost the district hundreds of thousands in additional revenue from ticket sales, concessions, and scoreboard sponsorships. Suddenly, elective courses and other taken-for-granted amenities were on the chopping block.

"If we continue down this road," Goddard warned, "our programs seven through twelve are going to take a hit."

When the Lovejoy board eventually approved a $44.2 million budget, it eliminated free bus service for nearly six hundred students, sparking widespread outrage. The district's budget contingency was also trimmed from its normal 2 percent down to roughly 0.05 percent, leaving little wiggle room to cover unexpected expenses. The superintendent and board also embraced relatively rosy enrollment projections, banking on a total of 4,295 students the coming year. Among the few budget line items that went up was Goddard's annual salary, which the board raised from $240,000 to $270,000.

The plan began to look wobbly almost immediately. A district survey found that 62 percent of local parents wanted to start the coming school year as normally as possible. But the district was leaning toward a hybrid approach in which even limited in-person learning would be made unrecognizable by an extensive series of safety measures, including mandatory masks for all kids ten and up. Parents began inundating the district's online portal with questions and concerns. What was the plan for lunch? Recess? Speech therapy? Could kids use their own preferred brand of hand sanitizer? What about wearing face shields instead of masks? How on earth could one of the premier public school systems in Texas justify eliminating free busing?

"This area has too much money for this to happen," one angry parent wrote.

Facebook was even more heated. Some Lovejoy parents expressed support for the district, pointing out that paying taxes doesn't guarantee you will like every policy decision made on your behalf. But many others were less forgiving. Why were Goddard and the board denying kids full-time in-person schooling? Why wouldn't they let parents make their own decisions about masks? Why not ban driving and swimming, both of which had far higher mortality rates than COVID-19? One parent called for a mass bombardment of the district's phone line, email accounts, and social channels with demands to rescind the hybrid plan. Another suggested jumping straight to the "nuclear options," calling for parents to pull their kids from the district and hold recall elections for the board. Susan decided to voice her concerns directly to Goddard in a fifteen-hundred-word email. It began:

> I am writing to you as a concerned parent. I have watched our country go into what seems like the twilight zone since spring break. . . . One thing that has become increasingly clear to me is the panic that has been invoked amongst our entire population, and had been spread like gospel, was flat out wrong and unwarranted.

Yes, she continued, the virus had already killed a couple thousand Texans. But was that number really so bad in a state that was home to 29 million people? And did a statewide positivity rate of less than 1 percent really warrant keeping schools closed?

> *How can we be changing the utter fabric of how we educate our children? . . . Authoritarian-style guidelines are being handed down left and right, backed by little to no science.*

Then Susan closed with a direct plea:

> *It's time for someone to stand up and ask questions. It is time for someone to protect our children from the dehumanizing, fear mongering restrictions that are being suggested. The psychological impact on them from the types of restrictions being suggested will be far worse in the long term than any dangers from covid. We just cannot instill this constant sense of fear. . . . Our children need someone to stand for them. Please Dr. Goddard, I implore you to be that voice.*

When the superintendent sent a boilerplate reply, she felt her whole body deflate. Two hours later, she managed a terse response.

> *Thank you for the note back. . . . I feel we are in some serious spiritual warfare right now, but that also is a discussion for another time.*

Because Susan was far from alone in her concerns, Goddard and his cabinet were increasingly worried about a significant exodus of Lovejoy ISD families. The effects would be disastrous, especially because of the optimistic enrollment projections and razor-thin contingency upon which the 2020–21 budget now rested. Facing a brewing crisis, the superintendent began hosting live virtual town halls of his own. But Susan was already nearing the point of no return.

"The reason we moved out to Lovejoy was the community, and being able to go to school with the people you go to church with, and the good education," she explained. "But all that seemed to be crumbling."

Instead of following along with the superintendent's messages, Susan grew fixated on the work of a German neurologist who claimed masks limited the flow of oxygen to children's brains, inflicting damage that wouldn't become apparent for decades. She also became outraged when several of the wellness influencers she followed on social media were deplatformed over their views on vaccines. Then she and Sean decided to read *1984*, the dystopian novel about the rise of totalitarianism and the erosion of truth. Every page felt more relevant when Susan turned on the TV and saw the news media depicting anarchists and Black Lives Matters rioters as peaceful protesters.

"If you listen to what some of these radical antifa people say, just listen to them, they have said we're coming to the suburbs. I've seen videos from around the country," Susan said. "They tried to come to Weatherford, [just outside] Fort Worth. But the people that lived there had a heads-up, and so they got their own militia together."

The rightward turn soon began causing problems at home. Some of the friction was internal; Susan stopped identifying with the Republican Party, a touchstone in her life for as long as she could remember. There were also disagreements with the kids; mask or no mask, Sean desperately wanted to return to Willow Springs Middle in the fall. Even Jim started teasingly calling her a conspiracy theorist. You know what the difference between a conspiracy and real life is? Susan responded. Six months.

"It's about connecting a lot of different dots, among what's been happening over decades really," she told me. "I think we've seen a deterioration of the family unit. I think we've seen a lot of people move away from religion, whether it's Christianity or Judaism. And I think if the family unit deteriorates and religion goes away, you become more dependent on something else for your safety, to take care of you. That's where government can step in. And I think there are some who would like to have government controlling more. I think there is maybe a push to try to keep our population fearful. Because if they're fearful, they're willing to give up their liberties in order to be safe."

Then Willow Springs sent out its reading list for eighth graders. Susan told me it included a young adult novel called *Rumble*. She was stunned to see it promoted homosexuality, critically portrayed parents who push their local school board to ban controversial books, and included what Susan viewed as anti-Christian undertones.

"What people don't understand is that we don't want to go back to that," she said of the old order that allowed such material to flourish.

It was mid-August when she sent another email to Stacey Dillon, who had led her and Jim on their tour of Lovejoy schools just a year earlier. This time, Susan said she wanted to disenroll her children from the district.

All across the country, families were making similar choices. Between the fall of 2019 and the fall of 2020, enrollment in America's suburban public schools would fall by nearly 3 percent, a loss of nearly 400,000 students in the suburbs of America's twenty-five largest metro areas alone. And the trend was clearly being driven largely by white families; in a single year, white enrollment in suburban public schools would drop by an astonishing 5 percent. Lovejoy alone would lose more than 150 students, leaving Goddard and the board well short of the 4,295 students they'd banked on. I asked Susan if she felt any sense of obligation to help out the district by keeping her children enrolled.

"It's just like you do with a business that you may not agree with their policies," she responded. "You talk with your money. And that creates competition. And if enough people do that, then the business has to figure out, 'Okay, we need to change what we're doing.'"

The decision to leave Lovejoy had been easier after Susan found a new online private school built explicitly on Judeo-Christian values. Freedom Project Academy rejected revisionist history, left-wing indoctrination, and the vilification of white people. Its website featured cartoon depictions of George Washington, Thomas Jefferson, and Benjamin Franklin, all drawn to look like heavily muscled professional wrestlers, and class reading lists featured authors like Shakespeare and C. S. Lewis.

Susan later told me she wasn't aware the school was an offshoot of the John Birch Society, the same fringe right-wing group that had gained significant traction in America's newly developing white suburbs back in the late 1950s. After being labeled as too extreme by mainstream conservative leaders in the 1960s, the group had fallen dormant. But it had never entirely gone away. In the mid-2000s, Birch Society leaders had launched a spinoff nonprofit called the American Opinion Foundation, which in turn began publishing a magazine called *The New American.* Trump's election had fueled a surge of fresh interest. By 2019, the magazine's editors and regular contributors like Alex Newman and Duke Pesta were urging a return to a national system of homeschooling and private religious education. They also called for a Dunkirk-style mobilization of parents willing to abandon public schools they described as dedicated to promoting climate activism and the sexualization of children, "mass-producing uneducated people unable to resist planetary totalitarianism," and "preparing children not just to accept tyranny—but to love and demand it":

> *The American people, and parents in particular, are now faced with two stark choices: Withdraw from the public education system in massive numbers, or prepare for a future of planetary serfdom. It really is that simple.*

Pesta, it turned out, was also the executive director of the American Opinion Foundation and the director of Freedom Project Academy. The pandemic proved to be a boon for the school; after slouching along for years with just a few hundred students, enrollment soared to nearly a thousand kids in fall 2020. Among the newest Freedom Project Academy students were Sean, Avery, and Noah Becker.

As part of the switch to a new school, Susan upgraded from her old system of phone alarms to tracking everyone's classes and activities via a color-coded spreadsheet. Sean was blue. After 5:00 a.m. swim practices with his club team, he'd come home, eat breakfast, shower, and set up at the desk in his bedroom, now decorated with posters of Astros star Jose Altuve. Latin started at 8:00. From there, it was on to Earth Science and then English, where the teacher delivered lengthy lectures about *Cyrano de Bergerac* and the importance of placing eternal values over personal fulfillment.

"I like it," Sean told me. "It's kind of like a combination between a tragedy and a comedy."

With the entire family finally settled into the routines of the crazy new school year, Susan joined the rest of the country in obsessing over the looming presidential contest. The stakes seemed unbearably high. If Democrats took the White House, she believed, it wouldn't take long for the destructive forces already degrading America's coastal cities to breach the heartland.

"Look at Los Angeles. It's a complete dumpster fire," she told me. "Do we continue to be a constitutional republic, or do we go down the road of socialism and communism and let our lives be controlled? I really think that's where we are."

It was a message the kids quietly absorbed. That fall, Avery decided to write a long letter to President Trump. Then her voice teacher arranged for Avery to read the letter at a meeting of Collin County conservatives. A few weeks before election day, Avery stepped gingerly onto a low stage inside a hip new restaurant in McKinney. She wore a red dress, white sandals, and blue denim vest. *Dear President Trump*, she began:

> *I know 2020 has been rough. But without you, it would have been worse. I was never really into politics. Then you got elected and everything changed. . . .*
>
> *I was so happy the world was becoming a better place. Then coronavirus happened and the world started falling apart. My family and I were on Spring Break in Disney World when we learned schools were going to be closing. I was happy at first. I mean, what kid wouldn't be when they found out they got a longer Spring Break?*
>
> *But then it got worse, and we weren't able to go back to school. . . . The next thing I knew, BLM started rioting and destroying businesses. I started realizing the world will never be the same.*
>
> *So here's what I think. I was never racist. My family was never racist. My friends were never racist. And you, President Trump, were never racist. . . .*

I've been thinking about what 2020 would have been like if Hillary were president during coronavirus. It would have been so-cialist and next communist America. . . .

This next election year will be tough. But America needs you. Black, brown, white, we all need a free America. Make America Great Again. Keep America Great. America will be great forever.

P.S. I would really like to meet you one day.

When November 3 finally arrived, the Beckers gathered on the big comfy sofa in their family room. Jim, back from the road, wore a favorite gray T-shirt that read "Dadventure Awaits." Sean sat next to him with Astro on his lap. Avery had written "Trump 2020" up and down her forearm.

Susan tried to put up a happy front. But when closely contested states like Pennsylvania and Georgia indicated they might not finish counting votes that evening, it was clear where things were headed. Even Trump might not be able to stop Democrats and their allies in the mainstream media from stealing the election.

"If our democracy falls, I think everything else falls around the world pretty quickly," Susan said. "To me, we go down that road if we lose Trump."

A SUDDEN TRANSFORMATION

THE ROBINSON FAMILY | GWINNETT COUNTY, GEORGIA

> If we were white women, they probably wouldn't say
> we're going to bring down the school board.
>
> —TARECE JOHNSON, 2020

Nika Robinson's doctoral cohort in the public health program at the University of Georgia had always been close-knit, with people lifting one another's spirits anytime someone bombed an exam on biostatistics or an assignment on the economics of hospital administration. But just as everyone began steeling themselves for the grueling comprehensive exams they'd have to pass in order to advance in the program, COVID-19 shut Georgia down. Study dates that had once rotated between people's houses migrated to Zoom, then turned into awkward phone calls, then stopped altogether.

"I'm in extrovert hell," Nika said through gritted teeth.

And really, the feeling went deeper than that. As the pandemic began to rage, the people Nika trusted most were the public health professionals with PhDs whose ranks she hoped to join. But they were suddenly under attack. In late February, high-ranking officials at the Centers for Disease Control and Prevention had used a press briefing to warn that it was a matter of when, not if, the country was hit with mass sicknesses and severe disruptions to daily life. Nika had taken the message to heart, moving proactively to keep the kids home from school, a decision that seemed to be validated when the Gwinnett County Public Schools soon switched to digital learning. By then, however, President Trump was already threatening to have the CDC director fired. The agency's briefings were limited, and administration officials took to the airwaves to falsely assure the country that COVID would miraculously disappear.

Oh boy, Nika thought. *This isn't going to end well.*

Caught between feeling alarmed and helpless, she revisited her plans to run for public office. Gwinnett Democrats were trying to drum up a challenger to face David Clark, a white Republican state representative who would soon appear at an anti-lockdown rally where attendees vowed not to comply with government-initiated public health measures. But over the course of several calls, a friend and fellow moderate Black Democrat who was running for Georgia State Senate warned Nika about the threat of her family being doxxed, and the human resources officers at her job suggested she'd have to resign.

Then COVID killed one of her uncles. The father of a close friend died of complications from the virus shortly thereafter. Anthony was also starting to worry about the security of his IT job in the tanking hotel industry. And through it all, the grind of work and family continued unabated. By April, Nika was regularly staying up until two in the morning to finish a budget report or business development proposal, then waking up at eight to steer the kids through the confusion of online school.

It helped that Cassidy, now in fifth grade, was largely self-sufficient. Laptop in hand, she'd wander back and forth from the basement to her bedroom, never missing a class. But things were harder with Carter. Still just a third grader, he was struggling with English Language Arts and grew antsy after fifteen minutes in front of his screen. Unsure what else to do, Nika began sitting beside her younger son at the dining-room table from 10:00 a.m. until 2:00 p.m. each day, coaching him on reading comprehension with half her brain while reviewing contracts with the other. Just when things would start to feel almost manageable, the wi-fi would buckle under the strain of five simultaneous videoconferences. Then it would be 5:00, and Nika's work inbox would be a thicket of unread messages. Someone would still have to figure out dinner, and she'd have to choose between spending the evening studying for her comps and helping the kids with their homework.

"Just maintain what you know right now," Nika started saying. "If you don't really know the life cycle of a chicken, it's okay."

That message, however, didn't go over so well with several of her children's teachers.

"We got a few, uh, *nice-nasty* emails," Nika said.

Fortunately, there was a silver lining. Corey was undergoing a transformation that felt almost miraculous. Nika could barely believe her eyes when he developed his own system for keeping track of live synchronous sessions with his teachers, then established his own little homework routine, knocking out simple assignments first. Math became easy again when Anthony could coach Corey through questions in real time. The threat of detention no longer loomed over every trip to the bathroom, and he could grab an orange or bang out a beat on the table whenever he liked. Sometimes, Nika would just stand outside the home office and listen as her son switched between conjugating Spanish verbs and singing to himself in a silly voice.

"You're like my old Corey," she'd say when she finally poked her head in. "What's going on?"

"It's just nice," Corey would respond. "I can start my work when I want to."

Before long, though, the return of her oldest son's inner light was causing a painful reckoning.

"I knew he didn't like school. But I just didn't realize how much it was dragging him down," Nika told me that spring. "And as a mom, I'm like, 'How did we not see this?'"

Even worse was the dawning awareness that she and Anthony had been complicit in their son's withdrawal. Suddenly, Nika could see that even as she'd been fighting the local school system on her son's behalf, she'd been reinforcing the same damaging message it had been hammering him with: Who you are is not okay.

"That's a hard burden for any kid to have," Nika said. "As a parent, I was putting that on him too."

By mid-April, the Gwinnett County Public Schools was announcing it would finish out the 2019–20 school year remotely. Most of spring testing was canceled. So were high school proms, middle school soccer, and elementary school field trips. The county began splitting in two. One faction of its residents longed for a return to normal. Republican governor Brian Kemp stood squarely in their corner, making Georgia one of the first states in the country to lift its shelter-in-place order. But when Superintendent Wilbanks responded by calling Gwinnett educators back into school buildings to close out the year from their empty classrooms, another faction—teachers, nurses, bus drivers, grocery store workers, all disproportionately women or people of color, all suddenly deemed "essential" and expected to put themselves and their families at tremendous personal risk so the county could reopen— went ballistic. An online petition challenging the school district's return-to-work order, for example, quickly went viral:

> Gwinnett County alone has 1,934 confirmed cases, the third highest figure in the state. These are not the statistics of a crisis that has passed. Whatever the intentions of GCPS leadership, this new policy is too dangerous for our teachers, school personnel, and their families.

Sensing opportunity, the three progressive women of color that Everton Blair, Jr., and other Gwinnett Democrats had convinced to challenge for seats on the local school board began amplifying the message. Helping lead the charge was Karen Watkins, the Black and Filipina mom who'd decided to run after the Juneteenth fundraiser at Edee's Place and was now embroiled in a tight primary race for the right to challenge fifteen-year white Republican incumbent Carole Boyce.

"She has no clue what's going on," Watkins said of Boyce. "We see totally different worlds."

By June 1, Georgia was reporting seven hundred new COVID-19 cases a day. Gwinnett was a hot spot, with 27 percent of visitors at one county testing center testing positive for the virus in a single day. But the governor was steadfast in his refusal to impose a mask mandate or other restrictions. Nika increasingly believed the reason why wasn't a mystery.

"Kemp is trying to kill us," she said.

But the unleashing of so much emotion—fear about the pandemic, anger over the country's response, a mix of dread and pride in response to the protests still rocking the country, the countervailing pulls of happiness and self-flagellation over Corey's revival—was making her reflective. Since first hearing angels sing in Ted Brown's epidemiology class, Nika had moved to Atlanta and spent decades chasing the post–civil rights suburban dream of equal access, pursuing her master's and then her doctorate, all while trying to climb the public health professional ladder. And for what? It hardly seemed a coincidence that as soon as waves of Black professionals began taking seats at important tables and calling shots that mattered, large swaths of America had embraced ignorance and declared war on expertise. The crushing reality had been driven home when President Trump used one of the briefings his administration now gave instead of the CDC to raise a series of questions about killing the virus by injecting bleach or exposing yourself to ultraviolet light. Nor did it seem to Nika an accident that as soon as data began showing that COVID-19 was hitting Black and Brown and poor communities hardest, the country's "we're all in this together" mantra had quickly dissipated; she'd spent months listening in muted horror as her white neighbors minimized the suffering of people who were actually dying and losing family, only to freak out over the mild discomfort of wearing a mask. The hypocrisy would have made her laugh if it wasn't so scary. During one of our conversations that summer, I wondered aloud whether the discouragement and pessimism Nika now felt was new.

"It's funny you ask that, because I was just talking to a girlfriend of mine, and I was like, 'I used to be so hopeful,'" she responded. "But as I've really gotten deeper into public health and its ties to health policy and politics, I've really started to kind of see I've been fed some lies. All the hard work in the world isn't guaranteed to change your position in life."

Then the George Floyd demonstrations came to Gwinnett County. A group called the Alliance for Black Lives announced a rally and march on Sunday, June 7, 2020. One of the event's organizers was a Black and Jewish woman named Tarece Johnson. She'd once worked as a corporate diversity specialist, hoping to change institutions like JPMorgan Chase and the Fire Department of New York from within. Now, like Nika, she was in her mid-forties and running low on "Yes We Can" optimism. After moving to Gwinnett, Johnson had started her own school, but didn't have the money to move to a bigger space, so had opened a small day care in her home instead. The difference meant scrounging each semester to pay for her own children to attend private school, a step she'd deemed necessary after hearing all the whispers about how Gwinnett schools disciplined Black children. The pressures had gradually turned Johnson into an activist. But it was the pandemic that led her to start referring to herself as a revolutionary and announce a campaign to unseat Louise Radloff from the Gwinnett school board.

"I was the corporate girl, I was at the board room, I was wearing the suits, at the table. And I didn't see change," Johnson told me the first time we spoke. So now, she said, "I'm off the plantation."

The idea of successfully primarying an incumbent who'd held her seat for forty-seven years and had both a local middle school and a county health complex named after her seemed like a long shot. Johnson believed that voters in her part of Gwinnett, where immigrants and poor Black families tried to scrape their way from bleak extended-stay motels into aging subdivisions full of weathered single-family homes now available for rent, would be receptive to her message. But they had to learn her name first. And with door-to-door canvassing now a health risk, that meant mailers, which Johnson was dismayed to learn would cost roughly $4,000. That spring, she'd still been debating the ethics of asking her struggling neighbors to donate $5 to her campaign when she picked up her mail and saw a glossy flyer featuring Radloff's familiar white visage.

"My heart dropped," Johnson said.

The lone debate in which she'd square off directly with Radloff increasingly looked like her only real chance to make a mark. Nervous, Johnson called the Gwinnett school board's lone member of color.

"Just do you," Everton Blair, Jr., advised.

Johnson took the message to heart. The debate, held over Zoom, was hosted by the League of Women Voters and Gwinnett SToPP. Johnson surprised everyone by going on the offensive, pressing Radloff on everything from Superintendent Wilbanks's hefty compensation package to the district's resistance to racial-bias training. She landed her cleanest blows when the discussion turned to school police officers, whom Radloff vigorously supported.

"I do not support guns and tasers in the schools," Johnson declared, leaning into her laptop camera to emphasize the contrast. "I am a proponent of ending the school-to-prison pipeline."

Then, less than a week before primary day, Johnson became the local face of a larger national movement. The Justice for Black Lives rally she'd helped organize started at the now mostly vacant Gwinnett Place Mall. After once serving as a monument to the county's upward suburban trajectory, the sprawling site had deteriorated dramatically, eventually becoming a magnet for squatters and sex workers, then a set for the fictional "Starcourt Mall" in the 1980s-nostalgia show *Stranger Things*. Now, though, a large multiracial crowd showed up carrying signs that said SILENCE=COMPLICITY, HOW DO YOU SLEEP WITH ALL THE BLOOD ON YOUR UNIFORM, and KOREANS FOR BLACK LIVES MATTER. The throng marched past the Kia dealership on Satellite Boulevard, then took a knee in front of the Gwinnett Police Department's central precinct building. When it came time for speeches, a Black mother named Tynesha Tilson wept as she told the crowd how her twenty-two-year-old son had died in a county jail in suburban Rockdale, just twenty-five miles to the south, from blood clots resulting from severe dehydration following his arrest on a misdemeanor disorderly conduct charge. Johnson, wearing a patterned skirt accented by an oversize pink carnation in her hair, absorbed Tilson in a full-body embrace, then turned to address the crowd herself.

"The time has come when we say, 'Enough is enough,'" Johnson cried out. "The time has come to unpry the crippling fingers from around our necks and push the boot off our chests, so we can breathe."

Two days later, she beat Radloff by 33 points.

But for thousands of Gwinnett families, any excitement over the results was muted by a larger uncertainty about the looming 2020–21 school year. Since the start of summer, the Robinsons had been paying $600 a month for Cassidy and Carter to take part in a small learning pod at a local childcare center. Nika had also returned to researching alternatives to Mill Creek High. Homeschooling seemed like the most promising option, but only if Corey could still play for Mill Creek's football team, with whom he was now lifting weights each morning. But several calls to the district didn't yield any answers, and a fresh surge of COVID-19 infections and deaths was making a return to in-person instruction in August appear doubtful.

Hoping to find clarity, Nika logged in to Zoom to watch the July meeting of the Gwinnett school board. A parade of public speakers quickly began blasting Wilbanks and the board's Republican majority for broaching a plan to bring as many children and teachers as possible back into classrooms.

"It's simply not safe," one parent said.

"Our teachers are writing their wills," added another.

"Even before the pandemic, many were becoming disillusioned with being told they were getting world-class treatment when their experiences say otherwise," added a white high school social studies teacher. "Stop trying to manage our perceptions and start serving this community."

From his seat on the dais at the front of the room, Blair tried to nudge the conversation forward. Reopening is a complicated issue, he said diplomatically. Everyone is trying to make the best of a bad situation. Let's work together.

But Wilbanks and Radloff, still on the board until after the general election, moved to cut off discussion, even though no formal plan had yet been confirmed. Nika and many of the other parents following along were bewildered. Blair interjected, publicly challenging the superintendent to clarify his position. Stunned, Wilbanks pulled his face mask below his chin.

"Can I clarify what?" the seventy-eight-year-old white superintendent said sharply.

"Your recommendation for the school district right now," Blair responded evenly.

"I don't know that it does me any good to do that at this point," came Wilbanks's retort.

Finally, Blair had heard enough.

"I've been trying to respect the authority of our collective," he said. But "I cannot understand how we can lead in the number of cases in this state and choose to not do something else."

Applause rippled through the boardroom. Flustered and apparently unaware the proceedings were still being live streamed, Radloff adjourned the meeting and walked over to Wilbanks. When she leaned over and spoke into the superintendent's ear, a hot mic picked up her words.

"I could strangle him," the eighty-five-year-old white woman said of her twenty-eight-year-old Black colleague.

Nika felt the air rush from her lungs. The irony was that she actually sympathized with the stance of Wilbanks, Radloff, and the board's Republicans; she and Anthony were seriously considering sending Cassidy and Carter back to school for in-person learning. But the manner in which the district's leaders conducted themselves rendered such policy positions moot.

"It demonstrated the attitude you see in Gwinnett schools across the board," Nika said of Radloff's outburst. "If they don't agree with you, they'll cut you off or try to silence you or make demeaning remarks about you."

And the tensions just kept building. Johnson, running unopposed in the general election, began fundraising and phone banking for Watkins and Tanisha Banks, the Black teacher from GIVE East who was challenging Republican school board member Mary Kay Murphy. Everton and me are just two people, Johnson would say as she urged voters to back the now unified slate of progressive challengers. We won't have the majority. The message took on added heft as the Atlanta suburbs became the center of American politics. Mid-September polling showed Democratic challenger Jon Ossoff neck and neck with incumbent David Perdue in one U.S. Senate race, while

Democrat Raphael Warnock appeared likely to force a special-election run-off in the other. With the presidential race shaping up to be similarly tight, Trump redoubled his efforts to make suburban turmoil a defining issue, posting increasingly incendiary messages on Twitter.

> If I don't win, America's Suburbs will be OVERRUN with Low Income Projects, Anarchists, Agitators, Looters, and, of course, "Friendly Protestors."

Then Gwinnett police shot and killed a Black teenager from Stone Mountain. Democrats pushed for early-voting changes. Republicans resisted. Gwinnett's entire elections apparatus became bogged down in lawsuits. When the county's public schools settled on all-remote learning to start the school year, the already cantankerous school board race heated up even further, with the longtime Republican incumbents stoking fear that their sudden ouster would lead to the same kind of leadership turnover, financial instability, and declining academics that had ravaged neighboring DeKalb County a generation earlier.

"Quite frankly, the idea of tossing out three elected board members all at once does keep me up at night. We've seen here in metropolitan Atlanta some of the dysfunction that can happen," eighty-two-year-old Mary Kay Murphy told me.

Their Black and multiracial board challengers, meanwhile, denounced such concerns as racist.

"If we were white women, they probably wouldn't say we're going to bring down the school board," Johnson said.

Having let the filing deadline come and go without submitting her paperwork, Nika pitched in where she could, donating to Banks, Johnson, and Watkins while phone banking for their campaigns. None of it changed that she wasn't on the ballot herself, a fact that filled her with regret as Election Day neared.

"It just felt like giving up," she said. "That's really difficult for me to do."

But keeping up with the multiplying loose ends in her own life felt increasingly impossible. Cassidy was now a sixth grader at Jones Middle. She still hadn't been accepted into Gwinnett County's gifted program. Nika told me she swallowed her PTSD and called Jones's main office, but was told the pandemic meant all new placements were on hold.

"Maybe next semester we can push harder," she recalled having to tell her disappointed daughter.

In the meantime, there was a new learning pod with several other families from Girl Scouts to organize and maintain. Wednesday was Nika's day to host, which meant a black hole in the middle of each week. Even on good days, she was lucky to make it to lunch before she had to put her own work on hold to help Carter sign into one of the several different online learning programs that now constituted his classroom. The ripple effects included regular all-nighters and a nebulous guilt that often felt all-consuming. By October, Nika saw no choice but to take a week off from work to cram for her comps.

It was 12:01 a.m. the following Monday when the University of Georgia released its three questions for doctoral candidates in public health. The first asked for a breakdown of how a hypothetical change to the state's school nutrition program might impact different communities and families. The second required a detailed cost-benefit analysis of a proposal to change the officially recommended treatment for a particular disease. The third asked for an investigation into the root causes of the problems at a fictitious hospital that was losing money and had a higher-than-expected mortality rate. Nika got halfway through when her computer crashed. Frantic, she called a friend and began to bawl. Two minutes before the deadline, she finally managed to hit send and submit her responses.

She felt like a zombie the entire next week. All her fear and worry began to cluster around the pending election. Trump and Biden were in a dead heat. It was unclear whether Ossoff had enough in the tank to beat Perdue. No one had any idea about the Gwinnett school board. The only race on Nika's radar that wasn't a squeaker was in Georgia's 98th Congressional District, where the Republican she'd decided against challenging maintained a comfortable lead. On October 30, the Robinsons drove over to a local rec center to cast their early ballots. Still exhausted, Nika wore sneakers and gray sweats, but allowed herself an ounce of petty. In anticipation of the occasion, she'd ordered a new black T-shirt with "ANTI TRUMP AF" emblazoned across the front. After voting, she posed for a picture, stepping one foot forward and splashing a big cheesy grin across her face. Then it was time to go, and Nika felt the crushing weight of the past six months settle back onto her shoulders.

"I just don't understand how we got here so quickly," she said.

HATE IN HEAVEN

THE ADESINA FAMILY | EVANSTON, ILLINOIS

> Listen closely, tik tok, because something wicked is
> coming for you next.
>
> —CHRISTIAN EADES, email to District 65
> school board members, 2020

Two hundred fifty or so people gathered in the parking lot outside a small single-story strip mall in Evanston. It was late August 2020. Two days earlier, police in the blue-collar suburban town of Kenosha, Wisconsin, just fifty miles to the north, shot and seriously wounded a Black man named Jacob Blake. Now, Lauren Adesina, still terrified of COVID-19, clung to the far edges of the demonstration with her young son, Chris. After the owners of a takeout restaurant let organizers plug a portable PA system into their electricity, activists and parents and everyday citizens demanded justice, called for the defunding of police departments around the country, and lamented the violent reminder that racial diversity didn't mean that suburbia was integrated or safe.

"I don't know why I keep thinking about this, but the last shot, the officer wasn't even looking at him," said one of the speakers, Bobby Burns, a bald-headed Black man Lauren knew through the African American, Black, and

Caribbean parents group he'd helped found in District 65. "Our bodies don't mean nothing to these people."

Then he asked everyone to repeat Blake's name ten times. Lauren chanted along with the crowd. Because of work and parenting responsibilities, she'd reluctantly had to skip several recent protests. This one, however, was different.

"He's from Evanston," she said.

Indeed, the name Jacob Blake had rung out locally for generations. The rally was being held directly across the street from Jacob Blake Manor, a senior-housing complex named after the shooting victim's grandfather, the same pastor from Ebenezer AME Church who had helped lead Evanston's push for fair housing and integrated schools in the late 1960s. The younger Blake, now twenty-nine, had attended Evanston Township High a few years after Lauren graduated. She told me his godmother was the mother of the man she was currently dating.

Cell-phone video of the shooting had shown Blake walking from the sidewalk to the driver's-side door of an SUV parked on the street. At the time, he was wanted on a felony warrant after being accused of third-degree sexual assault (a charge that was later dropped), trespassing, and disorderly conduct. It was the mother of Blake's children who had called the police, telling a dispatcher that he was trying to take her car. On the street, officers with guns drawn began shouting. Blake, who was holding a knife, disregarded their orders. The officers twice tried to Taser him. He pressed forward, opening the door and leaning into the SUV. An officer grabbed his shirt, then opened fire. Seven shots could be heard. Blake was hit from behind. He ended up paralyzed from the waist down. Three of his children watched the whole scene unfold from the back seat of the car.

In the hours after the footage went viral, protesters had swarmed the streets of suburban Kenosha. For two nights, peaceful demonstrations were interspersed with arson, looting, and vandalism, sparking confrontations with riot police. The Wisconsin National Guard was called in to restore order. A former Kenosha alderman also issued a call for "patriots" willing to take up weapons in defense of local businesses. The latter message was picked up by conspiracist provocateur Alex Jones, whose InfoWars media empire quickly spread word around the nation. For Lauren and many other Evanston residents, the fact that the national tumult of 2020 was now hitting so close to home was unsurprising, but still devastating. At the rally, a woman who remembered meeting Blake in the eighth grade told the crowd he'd been her first boyfriend. They shot my son seven times, Blake's father said. Like he didn't matter. Fifth Ward alderman Robin Rue Simmons struggled to find words.

"We are exhausted," she eventually said. "We are functioning in trauma every day."

Chris, however, remained inquisitive as always. I thought we weren't supposed to be around lots of other people because of COVID, he said. I still don't understand why they shot that man. What's this march supposed to change? Why do bad things keep happening to Black people? And why would anyone want to be Black if this is what you have to deal with all the time?

Lauren dipped into her dwindling reserve of parental diplomacy.

We're staying back here so we can be safe, she said. What the police did was wrong. They need to be held accountable, just like kids who break the rules. Being Black is hard sometimes. But it's wonderful too.

"Well, the police should like me, because my aunt and uncle are police officers," Chris replied.

Yeah, Lauren said wearily. They should. But it doesn't always happen that way.

"But I thought the police are supposed to be good," Chris persisted, remembering an incident when a responding officer had aided his grandmother during a panic attack.

Lauren looked to the sky. Her son was supposed to start third grade in two days. She was still wondering if she should've registered him for summer camp. Yes, she said. That is the police officers' job. But you have to be careful. Because as we've been learning, their fear is more important than our lives.

When the speakers at the rally finished, the crowd began marching down

Emerson and up to Foster Street, past a purple mural that read "YOU ARE BRILLIANT" in wavy yellow letters. Kenosha exploded shortly afterward. Darkness fell, and angry protesters directed a hail of bottles and fireworks at police manning barricades outside the county courthouse. The officers responded with tear gas, sending hundreds of people scrambling out into suburban streets being patrolled by dozens of ad hoc vigilantes and militia members. Among them was Kyle Rittenhouse, a seventeen-year-old white male carrying a Smith & Wesson M&P 15 rifle. A protester threw a bag at Rittenhouse, then chased him through the parking lot of a nearby car dealership. Rittenhouse shot the man four times, killing him. As the angry crowd swarmed, someone then swung a skateboard at Rittenhouse. He shot and killed that man too. It wasn't long before President Trump began publicly defending Rittenhouse, erasing any lingering illusions that suburbia was somehow exempt from the strife consuming America.

And all the while, the duties of Lauren's daily life kept multiplying, even as the routines, supports, and connections that usually got her through the week kept disappearing. Playdates turned into elaborate logistical nightmares, then ceased altogether. Every Friday for almost a year, Lauren's father had been picking Chris up from school, then taking him to the park or library, but Grandpa Night was canceled too when her father was reassigned to the COVID ward at the hospital where he worked. Now, family visits were limited to waves through windows or a bag of pears dropped off on the stoop.

"I'm always freaking out," Lauren said. "I just randomly call him, like Dad, how was your day? Did you have your mask on? Do you have gloves?"

Because something had to go, Lauren began scaling back her activism. In its place, social media became the venue for her anger and frustration.

Dear non-black friends . . . I'm paying attention to your silence, she wrote on Instagram in May.

Y'all can understand a white kid shooting up a school cuz he was bullied after 4 months of school but don't understand why an oppressed group is compelled to burn shit down after 400 years read a tweet she reposted in June.

And *Ima just leave this right here*, she posted on August 30, alongside a message that highlighted the discrepancy between Kenosha police saying they'd felt threatened enough by Blake's knife to shoot him seven times in the back, but comfortable enough with Rittenhouse and his rifle to not shoot even though he was running toward them.

It didn't help that chaos had also begun to creep back into the rest of her life. For much of the spring, Lauren had been working in the development office of a Chicago private school. She'd wake up at 6:00 a.m. and spend a couple of hours composing letters to alumni before Chris needed breakfast. Then she'd try to log him into a different Zoom every twenty-five minutes while she sat through her own virtual staff meetings. And just before the pandemic hit, Lauren had also taken on a second job, as an aide for adults with special needs who lived in a residential treatment facility. That also turned into a disaster. Office staff, mostly white, were able to work from home. But caregivers, mostly Black and Brown, had to work inside the group homes where residents lived in close quarters. At least two COVID-19 outbreaks had already occurred. Then Chicago city officials imposed a 9:00 p.m. curfew, thrusting Lauren and the other caregivers whose shifts often lasted until 9:30 p.m. or later into the dangerous position of having to drive illegally through streets still patrolled by jittery police. When the higher-ups in the company added insult to injury by ending hazard pay, Lauren felt compelled to inform them how racist the policies were.

"They extended the hazard pay for another month or two after I sent the email," she told me several weeks later. "I just get frustrated that I always have to be the one making the noise."

Similar tensions were engulfing District 65. Lauren felt incoming superintendent Devon Horton had gotten off to a strong start; even before officially starting the job, he'd issued a lengthy statement titled "Racism in America," saying it was the district's moral imperative to "transcend equality and embrace equity." He'd gone on to quote the section of *Letter from Birmingham Jail* about moderate liberals:

> *Teacher, pastor, activist, and martyr, Dr. Martin Luther King, Jr. wrote, while in a cell advocating for an anti-racist America, that the barrier to that vision is, (the moderate) who is more devoted to "order" than to justice; who prefers a negative peace which is the absence of tension to a positive peace which is the presence of justice; who constantly says "I agree with you in the goal you seek, but I can't agree with your methods of direct action"; who paternalistically feels he can set the timetable for another man's freedom.*

By late summer, however, it was becoming apparent how fraught a position Horton had landed in. At the time, the district's revenues for the coming school year were expected to fall by about $3.4 million, the result of declining enrollment, a tanking economy, and troubles with tax collection. But fixed expenses for things like salaries and benefits were expected to keep rising, and COVID-19 was necessitating all sorts of new expenditures, causing costs to rise by more than $4 million. Horton and the board thought they could still balance the district's books in 2020–21. But after that, things would get dicey; before the school year was out, District 65 officials would be projecting a series of significant annual operating deficits that would start at $3.4 million in 2022–23 and balloon to more than $12 million by 2025–26, by which point the reserves generated by the operating referendum from several years earlier would already be exhausted. The only realistic solution was massive reductions in spending, starting with well over $1 million in cuts for 2021–22.

And even as District 65's financial picture worsened, the fight over whether and how to reopen school buildings kept escalating. Horton initially proposed all-remote learning through the end of September, suggesting parents could choose whether to send their kids back for in-person classes after that. The plan was met with a flood of questions and complaints. Some parents wanted the district to explore holding outdoor classes. Others wanted to know the consequences of disenrolling their children. Still more demanded to know why scientists, physicians, and "independent parents without a conflict of interest in the school system" hadn't been appointed to the district's return-to-school task force. For Lauren and many of the Evanston activists who'd been pushing on District 65 for years, the most outrageous part was that many of these newly engaged parents were couching *themselves* as the real proponents of racial justice.

"For a district that prides itself on its commitment to equity," testified one of more than a dozen speakers at District 65's July board meeting, "this one hundred percent remote plan would be a slap in the face to those who have worked so hard to improve said equity."

The same fight was unfolding in suburbs all across the country. *The New York Times* dubbed the phenomenon "rage moms" and said they were fueling a "political uprising." But the *Times* and much of the mainstream media missed the distinctly suburban nature of the turmoil. In many of the whiter and more affluent corners of America, the conflict over reopening schools was being driven by parents deeply unsettled by the prospect of their children "falling behind," casting a harsh light on the deeply ingrained belief that the suburbs and the public schools should provide their children with an advantage; in well-to-do enclaves like Scotch Plains, New Jersey, a critical mass of parents began treating pandemic-related disruptions to the established order as an existential threat that required drastic measures, including suing their local superintendent and school board. At the same time, however, many suburban families of color were wondering why other people seemed so eager to put their children in harm's way. And in the suburbs of Atlanta and Boston and countless other cities, thousands of families were experiencing an awakening similar to the Robinsons'. As they saw for themselves how teachers treated their children and how their children lit back up when not forced into a suffocating environment for seven hours a day, their demands for local education leaders to do more to address racism grew louder and more frequent.

Plunged into the center of these swirling tensions, Superintendent Horton and the District 65 board decided to explicitly prioritize the needs and concerns of families of color, even if it meant risking the wrath of other Evanstonians. When the state board of education recommended that districts place a "high priority" on bringing back students who needed the most support first, Horton folded the advice into his larger racial equity agenda. During an online town hall held in late July, District 65 deputy superintendent LaTarsha Green said priority access to in-person learning would be given to "students receiving free or reduced lunch, Black and Brown students, students who received an incomplete or less than 50 percent on their report cards, emerging bilinguals, and students with IEPs." Horton promptly reinforced that message with a statement of his own.

> We have to make sure that students who have been oppressed, that we don't continue to oppress them, and that we give them opportunity. I've heard for quite some time that this is a community that's about equity for Black and Brown students, for special education students, for LGBTQ students. We know that this is an important work, and we're going to prioritize that.

It took less than a week for Fox News to pick up the story, leading to widespread anger that Black and Brown students were ostensibly being given priority access to in-person learning at the expense of white and Asian children. District 65 headquarters was soon flooded with postcards, letters, and email messages full of offensive memes and screaming 24-point-font rants about Christ and pedophiles, Hitler and the Ku Klux Klan.

"What you're doing is a blessing for whatever white kids are still left in that shithole you run," read one email directed to Horton. "They're going to be graduating in half the time with remote learning while you're babysitting all the brown kids."

"I just read how you will be prioritizing 'blacks and browns' over whites for in person learning. TALK ABOUT RACISM!!" read another. "I'm so sick and tired of people like you talking about oppression when minorities have MORE OPPORTUNITIES than whites do any more."

"So now white kids will be segregated? Now white lives don't matter? Because we are white our kids can't get a good education?" said a third. "Your a total racist bigot."

Message after message also focused on the coming election, decrying the "fucking idiots" of the "Democrap Party" who catered to "people who want handouts." One meme that appeared repeatedly showed before-and-after images of Detroit and Hiroshima in 1945 and again in 2010. "It's easier to come back from a nuclear strike than 5 decades of Democrat control" read the caption. Demands and threats were also common:

> I hope that you will reply to this email and assuage my concerns. For if you are in fact deciding educational opportunities based on race, then I, and no doubt many other citizens, will do every legal thing to see that such a racist and discriminatory policy is put to an immediate stop as well as seeing you removed from your current position and prosecuted for Civil rights violations.

Inundated, Horton pivoted to damage control, attempting to walk back his earlier comments at the board's August 10 meeting.

"I just want to be clear that we are prioritizing in our design students who are free/reduced lunch, special education, emerging bilingual, [homeless], and any student who struggled during our spring learning," he said. "It just happens to be that the majority of our students who are in free/reduced lunch are Black and Brown."

The board also tried to turn the tables, making public one of the more stomach-churning messages they'd received. Its language had been directed specifically to the board's Asian and white members, calling them disgraces who did nothing to stop the district's "Black Supremacist" superintendent and school board president:

> Your failure to take them verbally, or via a lawsuit, by the collar and remind them of the black privilege emanating from ~15 trillion dollars in reparations paid to the black community since 1964 . . . means you should be removed yesterday because you said and did NOTHING as evil flourished, and kids who look like you were put at the back of the bus. Listen closely, tik tok, because something wicked is coming for you next.

Despite all the turmoil, though, Horton hardly backed away from his broader commitment to racial equity. In an interview, he told me he viewed the pandemic as an "opportunity to get into good trouble." That included launching a new effort to recruit teachers of color and train them to be anti-racist, plus planning a top-to-bottom review of the district's student assignment and bus routes, a step widely viewed as a precursor to District 65 closing a school or two in Evanston's wealthy white neighborhoods and constructing a new building in the Fifth Ward. Resistance would be a given, Horton told me, describing the blowback to his reopening policies as a "warm-up" for what was to come.

"The thing about change," the superintendent said, is that "it makes you feel like you're going to lose something. Especially if you've never had to lose in your life."

By early fall, the backlash that had been brewing for months finally boiled over. Evanston parents who'd long taken for granted that District 65 would prioritize their values and demands began finding one another on Facebook to strategize about how best to block Horton's plans. Two hundred twenty-seven fewer students than expected enrolled in the local public schools. National conservative leaders also began circling; legal strategist Edward Blum, who'd made a career of recruiting plaintiffs to lawsuits challenging affirmative action, and his group sent a letter to Horton and the board alleging massive violations of the Fourteenth Amendment's Equal Protection Clause. And inside the Trump administration, the U.S. Department of Education's Office of Civil Rights was wrapping up its review of the complaint filed against District 65 the summer before; federal officials would initially conclude that Evanston schools' creation of racial affinity groups, use of privilege walks, and explicit direction to consider students' race when meting out discipline were all unconstitutional.

As the turmoil mounted, Lauren's old fear of making a decision that might inadvertently harm her son returned. Though she was sure Chris had grown sick of spending all his time with his mother, she decided to keep him home for the 2020–21 school year. She also let her contract at the private school expire, then quit her second job, finding instead a part-time administrative position and moving into a less expensive apartment in South Evanston to cut costs. Where the Beckers had grown disillusioned because suburbia no longer reflected their values or gave them the benefits they felt they'd paid for, and the Robinsons had grown disillusioned because so many of their neighbors in Gwinnett County didn't want to be part of a public that included families like theirs, Lauren found herself wondering if the fight to make Evanston live up to its promise was worth it.

She still had faith in Horton, the District 65 board, and the growing network of racial equity advocates working in and around America's public schools. But the forces aligning against them were scary and overwhelming. In Southlake, Texas, conservative parents formed a political action committee to contest the district's plans for diversity training. Outside Phoenix, purple-clad conservative parents—some with gun holsters visible on their belts—flooded school board meetings to fight back against new equity trainings and sex-education programs. In Vermont, Pennsylvania, and Virginia, conservative parents began pressuring suburban school boards over their reading lists, curricula, and staff training they deemed "anti-white." In September, President Trump signed an executive order banning federal contractors and grant recipients—potentially including schools and universities—from providing training that might make white people feel "discomfort, guilt, anguish, or any other form of psychological distress on account of his or her race or sex." Within months, legislatures in dozens of states from Florida to Idaho were awash in related bills, many of which focused on sharply curtailing the ways K–12 teachers could talk about race and racism in their classrooms. And the front lines of the fight were suburban communities and schools undergoing the most sudden and significant racial changes, and where competing visions of the American dream were thus colliding; seemingly overnight, public education had become a hot-button political issue on a scale not seen since *Brown v. Board of Education* and the massive resistance to integration and busing that followed.

Despite the stakes, November 3 arrived almost by surprise. Lauren had the day off. She slept in until Chris began blasting the *Lion King* soundtrack in his bedroom. Then she got up, made breakfast, and sat down at her computer to research candidates for local judge. She'd voted for progressive Bernie Sanders in the primary. Now, though, she was preparing to hold her nose and vote for Joe Biden. And just in case, Lauren told me half jokingly as she pulled on a purple Fila hoodie and big aviator sunglasses and hustled Chris out to the car, she was also researching how to obtain citizenship in Ecuador or Nigeria.

"Did Mom go vote?" Lauren asked after picking up her younger sister outside their mother's house.

"Yeah," Amanda said. "But I still don't know who I'm going to vote for."

"Really?" Lauren replied, trying not to judge.

"What we have to do is get rid of Trump," Chris chimed in from the back seat.

Outside, it was a perfect autumn day. The trees lining Evanston's wide streets were still aflame. Bursts of brilliant sunlight filled the car at each intersection. Chris began belting out his favorite *Lion King* song. Lauren chewed on the string of her hoodie.

"But seriously," she said. "You saw what happened in Kentucky? Where Kanye West got all those wasted votes?"

"Why do we always have to vote for the lesser evil?" her sister responded.

Their polling place was a local elementary school. As they walked down the concrete sidewalk, Lauren handed her sister a copy of the cheat sheet she'd printed out on the judicial candidates. Inside the building, faded blue doors opened to a white-tiled lobby, then the polished hardwood floors of the gymnasium's basketball court. Poll workers sat behind folding tables set up on the free-throw line.

"Amanda, don't play with me," Lauren called from inside her voting booth.

They can't keep doing this to us, Lauren's sister said as the pair walked back to the car. People should have been looting even more. I don't even have health care. I know, Lauren responded. I don't think Biden is the gateway to everything we need. But electing him will stop the bleeding.

Except that it didn't. Though Biden won by 7 million votes, Trump and his supporters immediately contested the results, filing lawsuits, spreading conspiracy theories, and plotting to block certification of the Democrat's win. And all the while, the fights sweeping through suburban public schools kept growing more heated.

Within District 65, there were plenty of signs that remote learning was in fact somewhere between challenging and disastrous. Analytics showed that thousands of kids and dozens of teachers didn't appear to be logging in to some of the district's key learning-software programs. An internal analysis found that many elementary classrooms weren't on pace to cover anywhere near the full range of material kids were expected to learn. A district survey found that nearly 70 percent of parents and caregivers were concerned about their children's mental health.

As a result, Evanston's liberal establishment grew more vocal. At the district's December board meeting, a group of parents pleaded with Horton to immediately reopen schools and demanded that he disclose the names of the public health experts he was leaning on for guidance. The superintendent responded with a public letter saying he was looking at a shift to hybrid learning in mid-January. More threats began pouring into District 65 headquarters, and the board revealed that someone had broken into the car of one of its members and left a homophobic note. Then, in a series of emails directed to the superintendent, two local parents directly questioned Horton's competence.

"There is nothing more racist or divisive than keeping Evanston children out of school," wrote one. "You should feel ashamed for your continued lack of acts and appropriate choices."

"Please do not patronize us by pointing to stale information and saying it is new," wrote the other. "There is such a void of leadership from you and the school board."

Fed up and frazzled after having just lost a close friend, Horton sat down and pounded out a reply.

"If we are talking about the research, then you would know that COVID-19 has negatively impacted people of color at a much greater rate than others," the superintendent began.

Then he went for the throat.

"I'm sure that you have not had to reflect on your white supremist thinking and way of life," he wrote. "You make personal attacks toward me because we are not giving you what you want. I suggest you look in the mirror and reflect on who you are and how you are presenting yourself to an African American leader. I refuse to sit back and be assaulted about my decision-making to not return to in-person learning, especially when the undertone is outright racist."

News outlets quickly caught wind of the exchange.

"Parents who argue that schools should be opened for in-person learning are being attacked as racists and White Supremacists" read an article in the *Evanston RoundTable* that helped trigger a fresh round of outrage from right-wing commentators around the nation.

Amid the ensuing clash, a group of the Evanston parents involved in the fight to reopen schools decided it was time to take back control of the District 65 board. Helping lead the charge was Angela Blaising, the white mom who worked in corporate finance and generally ignored District 65's political and policy debates, at least before the pandemic. Feeling helpless after months of remote learning, Blaising had tuned in to her first District 65 board meeting in years that November. She couldn't believe what she was hearing. The board was engaged in a lengthy discussion of old data on racial disparities in suspensions and expulsions, not how to bring kids back into classrooms.

"I remember thinking all these people would be fired if we were working in corporate America," Blaising told me later.

Shortly before Christmas, she decided to run for a board seat herself. Chow, the recently resigned District 65 board member who'd clashed with Tanyavutti, reached out to offer help. By early 2021, the battle lines were drawn. Together with four other candidates, several of whom were being advised by Chow and sharing resources with one another, Blaising would try to unseat three of the District 65 board's most reliable progressives.

"Every time you work on one thing, you uncover something else," Lauren told me when she heard the news. "All of these institutions just need to be ripped down."

"DON'T FUCK WITH MY SHINE"

THE SMITH FAMILY | PENN HILLS, PENNSYLVANIA

> If white people only confront these issues on a cognitive basis, they will wind up hostages to political correctness.
>
> LILLIAN ROYBAL ROSE,
> "White Identity and Counseling White
> Allies About Racism," 1996

As COVID-19 illuminated and inflamed the long-standing tensions in places like Lucas, Gwinnett, and Evanston, I grew more confident in my view that the collision between the American dream and American history was at the center of suburbia's unraveling. But something was still missing. Back in my hometown, a host of barriers still seemed aligned against Bethany's hopes and ambitions. But she now had little inclination to indulge my questions about things like crumbling infrastructure and public school debt, choosing instead to keep me firmly on the other side of the wall she'd erected between herself and the world's problems following her spiritual epiphany fourteen years earlier.

And besides, since the start of the pandemic, life had been full of one impossible decision after another. The day Penn Hills Elementary closed its doors, Jackson had been home sick with a nasty stomach bug, causing him to fall immediately behind on the packet of worksheets Ms. Levin sent home.

To get through the following week, Bethany had taken off from work and put her entrepreneurial endeavors on hold, solutions that clearly weren't sustainable. Fortunately, her sister stepped into the breach, agreeing to host Jackson at her home from Sunday nights until Friday afternoons, an offer that initially felt like a blessing from above to her and Jackson alike.

"At first, he was like, 'Yay, vacation. Auntie's is always the fun house,'" Bethany said.

But that arrangement proved fragile too. During those early days of lockdowns and quarantines, Bethany would be at work, making dinner or trying to get the men she cared for through one of the thirteen-minute exercise videos she found on YouTube. Then an argument would break out over a coloring book, or one of the aging white residents would loudly complain about the "n----- station" that the Black caregivers liked to play on the radio. And in the middle of it all, Jackson would call, swearing he'd finished his remote schoolwork and begging Bethany to unlock the games on his phone, putting her in an impossible position; even if she could steal a minute to log in to Google Classroom and check her son's claims, any attempt to enforce her usual rules would ultimately just mean a heavier burden on her sister.

"I'm not trying to push it when I have a free babysitter," Bethany said.

Then Jackson intentionally broke the laptop she'd given him and announced he wanted to come home. Under mounting stress, Bethany redoubled her efforts to block out the world and its many threats, from my email messages to the TRUMP-PENCE 2020 signs she now saw starting to pop up on Penn Hills lawns. Instead, she focused on protecting and replenishing her own energy whenever and wherever possible, including the small break room in the back of the house where she worked. *Hey God*, she'd say in a spare moment. *It's me.* Then she'd let the words come tumbling out until she felt calm, pull up her favorite gospel song on her phone, and hum to herself while preparing to take a resident to the grocery store. *The world is ever-changing*, she'd sing. *But You are still the same.*

All the while, I was still stumbling in circles, returning again and again to the question that had prompted me to pursue this book in the first place:

How are the abundant opportunities my family extracted from
Penn Hills a generation earlier linked to the cratering fortunes of
the families who live there now?

For months, I'd been devoting considerable intellectual energy to the second half of that formulation, digging ever deeper into my hometown's problems, most of which seemed to be hitting Black residents like Bethany
especially hard. But that approach hadn't helped me get unstuck from suburbia's fifth big illusion: that white people are immune from the harms
caused by our own racism and racial ignorance.

It was an article by a woman named Lillian Roybal Rose that finally
helped me see a way out. A Latina woman who grew up in East Los Angeles,
Roybal Rose was a former school counselor who'd launched a consultancy
in cross-cultural leadership and communication. In 1996, an article of
hers was published in an edited volume titled *Impacts of Racism on White*
Americans. When I found a copy a quarter century later, I was struck by
Roybal Rose's point that white people must come to emotional grips with
how whiteness, white racism, and white racial ignorance have affected *us*
before we can make meaningful contributions to larger fights for a more just
world:

> *They see that they were misinformed by people they loved and*
> *trusted, and so they feel betrayed; they belong to a group that has*
> *dominance for generations, and so they feel guilt. If white people*
> *only confront these issues on a cognitive basis, they will wind up*
> *hostages to political correctness. . . .*
>
> *When the process is emotional as well as cognitive, the state of*
> *being an ally becomes a matter of reclaiming one's own humanity.*
> *Then there is no fear, because there is no image to tear down, no*
> *posture to correct. . . .*
>
> *I tell white people in my workshops that I expect them,*
> *as allies with power in the oppression of racism, to act justly*
> *and not dominate, regardless of the fact that we may never love*
> *them.*

The words transported me back to the final time I'd been with my father on Princeton Drive. It was December 2014. My dad was determined to leave Penn Hills altogether. By then, however, the house and yard had turned into a sprawling mess. We rented a 24-foot dumpster and parked it at the end of the driveway. I spent a couple of days emptying closets full of tattered Choose Your Own Adventure books and WWF wrestling dolls. But my nostalgia turned to dread when I made it to the garage. My dad's old radial-arm saw was still there. So was his mountain of scrap lumber. Though I was nearly forty at the time, I realized with surprise how deeply I still longed to know what was hiding below all the jagged ends of wood. But after hauling the final armload of scrap out to the dumpster, the spot on the concrete floor of the garage was just empty.

At the time, I'd done what I always did: push aside the hollow feeling in my chest, make a half-assed plan to come back at some unspecified future date, and run from Penn Hills as fast as I could. Now, though, Roybal Rose's essay helped me see that old pattern with fresh eyes. If I really wanted to bridge the distance between myself and Bethany, I had to start by filling in the blanks I still felt inside, many of which were a product of the racial denial I'd been internalizing for decades. That meant talking to my dad, who'd sold the house on Princeton Drive before I could return to help him clean up the hillside out back.

We sat together in the living room of his new home in a gated community thirty miles north of Dallas, in the attendance zone of the Lovejoy Independent School District. It was already just as cluttered as the one back on Princeton Drive. When we began talking, my dad remembered how much he loved working out West and how reluctant he'd been to take the union job at the University of Pittsburgh upon learning I was on the way. He also recalled one of his first big do-it-yourself projects, which involved pouring a block of cement in his work area, then using his finger to write the names of me and my brothers before it dried. The block must have still been there, maybe a yard from where my dad's scrap lumber pile had eventually formed in the garage.

"I spent all my time there and in the backyard trying to maintain my sanity," my dad responded when I asked what had motivated his efforts.

As we talked, his maze of walls and fences began to sound less like an effort to protect or hide something than an attempt to invent a way out of a trap he didn't want to pass on to his sons. But each year, my dad told me, he'd gotten a little more overwhelmed. And at some point, his piles of scrap and junk had started to feel intractable. It was a microcosm of the township's larger predicament, with one crucial difference: living in Penn Hills for forty years had allowed my dad to amass the resources he needed to move away from the mess his efforts had devolved into.

"I took a beating," he told me when I asked why he'd offloaded the house for a couple of thousand dollars *less* than he'd paid for it back in the late 1970s. "But to get it just so it would pass the requirement for habitation, I would have had to put thirty or forty grand into the place. And at that time, I wanted out as quick as possible."

I asked whether the changes in the township had influenced his decision to finally give up on Penn Hills.

"The color of the street was changing from white to Black," my dad replied. "The sewage bills, the property taxes. It was just like I was getting surrounded by problems."

I asked if he saw the Black families who'd started moving on to Princeton Drive as a problem.

"Not too much the Black adults," my dad said. "But having kids. I saw some of them. . . . They smoked, they kind of congregated a little bit in gangish type groups. I just didn't want to deal with kids, basically."

I thought of Jackson, and my heart filled with sadness. I told my father how a big part of my book was about how suburbs are getting more diverse and how white people who aren't happy about that often try to move somewhere farther out.

"Some of the best people I know are Black," my dad responded. "And the one or two times I've been back to Princeton Drive, they're taking care of the houses and making improvements much better than I ever did. So it's not like they're driving the neighborhood down or anything. I just wasn't interested in trying to be a good community person."

It was then that I finally began to grieve. For the spark my dad had gradually lost after moving to Penn Hills. For the realization that his loss was a by-product of the sacrifices he'd made to provide me with the suburban lifestyle dream. For all the years I'd been misinterpreting his cryptic message about not getting stuck like him, which I now recognized as the best way my dad knew how to express the enormity of his love for me. For my own complicity, and for how I'd continually repeated the patterns I wanted to disrupt. And most of all, for the hollow space inside I'd been carrying around since I was a child; my whole life had taken shape around absences and silences, like a vine spiraling around a tree that wasn't there.

It was late summer 2020 when I finally crafted a proposal I felt comfortable bringing to Bethany. I reached her by phone. She'd just gotten home from taking Jackson for a haircut. I know the concerns you raised are legitimate, I began, and I don't have any simple solutions. But I still believe there's an important story to be told about Penn Hills. And I think you are carrying a part of it that I cannot. So I have an invitation. How would you feel about contributing to this book directly, by writing something in your own words, for compensation, so that the two of us together can offer readers a more complete picture of what's happening here?

Once again, Bethany remained silent for what felt like forever.

"Yes, I'd be interested," she finally responded. "I've always wanted to write."

There was no quick reconciliation, no sudden creative outpouring. COVID-19 began surging again, and Bethany went back to fighting just to make it through her days. That fall, the Penn Hills School District transitioned to a hybrid schedule, offering most families the option of sending their children into physical classrooms two days a week. Bethany decided to keep her son home. But that meant more work for her.

To make sure Jackson understood he was still in school, she converted her finished basement into a makeshift elementary classroom. In one corner, a glass-topped desk held a Chromebook and a laminated sheet of multiplication tables. On the walls, Bethany hung a whiteboard calendar, a U.S. map, and posters featuring cartoon drawings of astronauts and doctors. Scattered around the space were a blue yoga ball and red punching bag that

Bethany had bought for her son to use when he got fidgety, a frequent occurrence that began turning hour-long math modules into grueling ordeals that lasted twice as long as scheduled. In an effort to keep things moving, Bethany spent much of September parked in a red camp chair, attending third grade over her son's shoulder. Then she decided to release herself from such hand-holding, telling Jackson that she'd graduated from school two years ago and it was time for him to take responsibility for his own learning.

The first parent-teacher conference of the new school year would provide an early verdict on her approach. Bethany settled into her old spot and logged into Microsoft Teams. Jackson's new teacher appeared on her screen. She was another middle-aged white woman. Your son is still struggling, she said. He hasn't been finishing assignments. As a result, he currently has a 52 in both English and Math. Upon hearing the numbers, Bethany felt a powerful current trying to sweep her out into the open seas of self-doubt. *You should have put him on medication a long time ago* came the voice in her head. *You should have sent him back into his classroom. You never should have let him work so independently.* But before the thoughts could spiral, her son's teacher promised to provide plenty of opportunities for him to bring his grades up. Then she and Bethany traded notes on different strategies they used to help Jackson focus and suggested they take a coordinated approach.

"I felt heard, and I felt the partnership," Bethany told me later, insisting again that Penn Hills was a place where she could thrive.

Inside the school district's central office, meanwhile, there were surprising new signs supporting that belief, asserting once more Penn Hills' character as a community forever on the brink. Near-zero interest rates had allowed the board to refinance a big chunk of the district's outstanding debt. Shuttering all its school buildings and shifting to all-remote learning had also led to significant savings on transportation and energy. And Congress was in the midst of allocating a total of almost $190 billion to the Elementary and Secondary School Emergency Relief fund, commonly known as ESSER. The money was distributed according to a progressive formula that tied aid levels to the number of poor students each district served. With 67 percent of its students now considered low income, Penn Hills ended up receiving a total of $18 million. A big chunk of that money would end up going to replacing the broken boilers at the district's two new school buildings, offering an unexpected glimpse into the kind of public investment it might take to bolster America's aging, diversifying suburbs.

"I think we have stabilized," superintendent Nancy Hines told me before offering a gentle rebuke of her own. "I see a lot of beauty here, and I think a lot of it is unrecognized and unappreciated."

Honestly, though, such optimism still felt flimsy. The ESSER funds would go away after three years, precluding the hiring of new permanent staff or the launch of any new long-term programs. The district's long-term debt was still more than $160 million and wouldn't be paid off until 2042. And most worrisome of all, the larger forces that had been squeezing my hometown for decades remained largely unchanged. Nearly 10 percent of the township's housing stock was already vacant, a trend that would only get worse if its population kept declining. Thousands of Penn Hills residents owned homes that were no longer vehicles for building intergenerational wealth; when you put everything into 2020 dollars for comparison's sake, the average house in the township was worth about $148,000 back around the time my parents moved to Princeton Drive, but the value of that same house had plummeted to less than $95,000 by the time Bethany and her mother followed suit. And the problem was particularly acute for homeowners in the Penn Hills neighborhoods with the most Black residents. At my request, a researcher named Andre Perry and his colleagues at the Brookings Institution took their groundbreaking national analysis comparing the values of homes in majority-Black neighborhoods with the values of similar homes in majority-white neighborhoods and applied it to Penn Hills. They found that houses in majority-Black sections of the township were undervalued by as much as 23 percent, likely as a result of discrimination in real estate appraisals and other aspects of the housing market. In the neighborhood around Princeton Drive, now roughly 35 percent Black, that meant outright structural racism was knocking thousands of dollars off the value of homes like Bethany's.

But she still wasn't interested in discussing such data points with me. When Election Day finally arrived, Bethany went to work, where CNN was blaring on the TV in the living room. She strolled right by and made a bee-line for the break room, where someone was watching *Martin* reruns instead.

Though she'd already voted by mail for Joe Biden, Bethany liked to joke that the only politics that would personally affect her was riots in the streets. Recently, however, that didn't seem so funny. Over the summer, downtown Pittsburgh had been rocked by violent demonstrations. The tumult had migrated up to the Hill District and out to the city's East End. Then, that July in Penn Hills, a sixty-three-year-old white man sped through a red light and drove his Hyundai into a crowd protesting the local police, then turned around and drove through the crowd again. One demonstrator was hit, and several others narrowly escaped injury. During the final debate of the presidential campaign, the potential for further violence had jarred even Bethany.

"Proud Boys, stand back and stand by," President Trump responded when asked to condemn the white supremacist and far-right militia groups now regularly showing up in places like Kenosha.

But the election came and went. And even as Trump and his supporters aggressively tried to overturn Biden's victory, specifically challenging the mail-in votes that she and thousands of other Pennsylvanians had cast, Bethany narrowed her focus back to what was right in front of her. Jackson was obsessed with a video game called Roblox and kept asking for five or ten dollars to upgrade his avatar. Bethany responded by passing on some of the financial literacy tips she'd been picking up, showing her son the statements for the savings account she'd opened in his name. The approach quickly yielded a few small victories; after coming home with four dollars he'd earned by helping his aunt with chores, for example, Jackson asked Bethany to put the money away so it would grow.

Smart idea, she said. Roblox ain't gonna feed you.

Then, a week before Christmas, the Pittsburgh area was blanketed with more than nine inches of snow. Bethany took Jackson outside to shovel. The two ended up in a snowball fight and rolled down the driveway together in a heap of laughter. Seeing her son so happy and carefree touched something deep inside Bethany. His ninth birthday was coming up. Now, she had an idea what to do. And this time, she had a careful plan for how to execute her vision.

Seven Springs was a ski resort about sixty miles southeast of the city. Bethany booked a three-night stay at a cabin for early January. Her mom, sister, aunt, a couple of nieces, and someone's boyfriend all came along. Outside, a long wooden deck offered gorgeous views of the snowy hillside below. Inside, exposed wooden beams ran the length of the ceiling, and a stone chimney surrounded a cozy fireplace. That first night, they threw a big birthday party for Jackson, filling the picture windows with Mylar balloons and hanging bright streamers from the ceiling. Laid out on the table were a Roblox-themed cake and dozens of matching cupcakes. Jackson promptly smooshed one into his mouth, leaving his nose dotted with turquoise frosting.

The next day, Bethany took her son for a hike, watching from a distance as he picked up huge mounds of snow and threw them into a stream rushing along the side of the trail. I love this trip, he said before heading off to search for branches big enough to break the ice on the lake. Back at the cabin, someone built a fire, and someone else broke out the cards and the board games, and the whole family stayed up until well past midnight playing spades and Scattergories. When he finally ran out of steam, Jackson fell asleep clutching a luxuriously soft pillow in a king-size bed. Then, on the last day, he stayed in his blue Snoopy pajamas for hours, reading and watching YouTube in a space he'd carved out between the sofa and window. The best trip ever, he kept saying as Bethany loaded up the car when it was time to leave the following morning. She couldn't remember the last time she'd felt so content.

By then, it was Wednesday, January 6, 2021. For weeks, the Proud Boys and another far-right extremist group called the Oath Keepers had been amassing weapons and tactical military gear and plotting to stop the transfer of presidential power. Bethany and Jackson were still on the Pennsylvania Turnpike when Trump began addressing an angry crowd of mostly white supporters who'd assembled on the Ellipse outside the White House. In a rambling speech, the president exhorted his followers to action:

> *We will never give up, we will never concede . . . Our country has had enough . . . We will not let them silence your voices . . . Because you'll never take back our country with weakness. You have to show strength . . . If you don't fight like hell, you're not going to have a country anymore.*

Within hours, the seat of American government was under attack. Among the angry mob storming the U.S. Capitol were a property manager from suburban Chicago, three real estate agents from the North Dallas suburbs, and at least half a dozen people from suburban Pittsburgh, including a twenty-six-year-old man who wielded a baseball bat and flagpole as weapons and a mother of eight who used a pipe as a battering ram. The throng erected a gallows outside, then surged forward, beating and overrunning security officers as they poured into the Capitol rotunda and vowed to hang Vice President Mike Pence and shoot Speaker of the House Nancy Pelosi.

By the time the insurrection was quelled, Bethany was back home. Instead of watching TV, she scrolled through Zillow, looking at properties for sale around Seven Springs. Her family's minivacation had cost almost $3,000. If someone could generate that kind of revenue from a quick rental, she figured, owning one of the cabins must be a golden ticket. In her notebook, Bethany began idly listing friends and family members who might be willing to join her nascent property-investment group. Then she began scratching out the names of anyone who was unreliable or had a penchant for drama or didn't share her focus on controlling what you could control, however limited that may be.

"Don't fuck with my shine," she said to no one in particular.

WHAT COMES AFTER

THE HERNANDEZ FAMILY | COMPTON, CALIFORNIA

> It's kind of like when you have a burnt forest and you
> start to see the flowers poke through.
>
> —Jefferson Elementary teacher
> Patricia Rivera, 2020

The lonely summer of 2020 wore on the Hernandezes' spirits. There were no trips to the beach. Mona Park was declared off-limits. With everyone at home all day, even the most basic daily routines felt dangerous, especially after the homeowner's elderly mother moved into their duplex, raising the stakes if someone did get sick. Alberto and Cristina again began looking to move, hopefully to a home of their own in a nearby community like Gardena or South Gate. But even with the free high-speed internet service they'd received at the start of the pandemic, it was still a challenge to cover monthly bills. When someone again broke the windshield on Alberto's truck, he found himself unable to make rent.

"We can't work like normal. Just maybe a couple days a week, to maintain the machines," he fretted. "I'm using a credit card to make payments."

By late June, all of Compton seemed to be on edge. Officers from the LA

County Sheriff's Department shot and killed an eighteen-year-old Salvadoran American man named Andrés Guardado, prompting large protests that police met with tear gas and rubber bullets. Soon after, a whistleblower alleged that a gang called the Compton Executioners was operating within the department and that Guardado's death was the result of an initiation ritual; officers who killed a civilian were said to receive a calf tattoo depicting a skeleton holding a Kalashnikov rifle with "XXVIII" written on the magazine, an apparent reference to Compton as the department's twenty-eighth substation. At least a dozen deputies were eventually found to have the tattoo.

The pandemic, meanwhile, continued to rage. By August, Los Angeles County was averaging more than three dozen new COVID-related deaths a day. Alberto and Cristina responded by forbidding the kids from even going inside the grocery store. Jacob did his best to occupy himself, first with long Minecraft sessions, then by creating his own trading-card game that functioned as a cross between Pokémon and Magic: The Gathering. But even after spending hours sitting cross-legged in the top bunk, filling in blank index cards with characters and spells of his own invention, he had no one to actually play with.

The start of fifth grade, then, arrived as an act of mercy. Jacob woke up disheveled and excited, then pulled a T-shirt from his drawer and grabbed his pencils, iPad, and a small box that drew a quizzical look from his sister. In the kitchen, he poured himself a bowl of Frosted Flakes. Then he situated his iPad on top of the box, creating an angle that would make him look better on Zoom. Other students soon popped into the square panels on his screen. Many of his friends were missing; by October, Compton Unified's total enrollment would be down roughly 1,750 students compared to pre-pandemic levels, thoroughly destabilizing the system just as it was poised for a big leap forward. But Jacob was just glad something different was finally happening. When his teacher turned her camera on, he was surprised to see she was inside a Jefferson classroom, sitting in front of a fancy new interactive whiteboard.

She's teaching into a screen, he thought. *So weird.*

Patricia Rivera was in her midthirties, with curly brown hair and carefully plucked eyebrows that arched gently over her eyes and the top of her KN95 mask. Born to Mexican and Portuguese parents, she'd grown up in a small Spanish-speaking agricultural community in Central California. After going off to Cal State, Long Beach, to study education, she'd fallen in love first with teaching, then with Compton, where she began finding small signs of beauty everywhere once she learned how to look beyond the town's history and reputation.

"It's kind of like when you have a burnt forest and you start to see the flowers poke through," Rivera told me the first time we talked. "The seeds are planted. They just need time to grow."

For more than five years, she'd approached her work at Jefferson with that mindset. One of Rivera's favorite projects involved breaking her fifth-grade classroom into teams and having the students work together to design and program robots that could collect waste while navigating a hazardous environment. The resulting class discussions might touch on everything from how to debug code to which jobs would get automated, leaving Rivera buzzing with excitement.

Since COVID, though, such hands-on activities were mostly a memory, and just getting to work had become an ordeal. Over the summer, Compton Unified had mandated that all teachers work from their physical classrooms during the coming school year, infuriating the local teachers' union. Rivera believed the plan was insane and was convinced Superintendent Brawley would eventually back down. But pickets and protests had a negligible impact, leaving Rivera to spend the last two weeks of summer scrambling to make remote-learning and day-care arrangements for her own young children. Her mother-in-law had eventually stepped up, retiring early from her own job so she could watch the kids, a major blessing. But her home didn't have internet access and she had no idea how to navigate Zoom. That morning, Rivera had to drive from Long Beach up to Downey, drop the kids off, then turn around and drive back down to Jefferson, stretching what had been a twenty-minute commute out to well over an hour. Then, when she'd arrived on campus, the weird emptiness of the new landscape had left her feeling almost helpless; the usual first-day scene of a community of colleagues reconnecting over coffee and donuts in the break room was replaced by individual teachers in face masks scurrying from the parking lot directly to their classrooms, where they were greeted by spray bottles of disinfectant. Rivera had decided to leave all her regular decorations stored in a closet, and all thirty-some students' desks in her room were shoved into a haphazard pile in the corner.

"I really focused my energy in my virtual classroom, which was very cute," she said. "But my physical classroom? It was kind of sad."

Her mood brightened when she logged in and saw Jacob's smiling face on her screen; she didn't yet know his name, but recognized him immediately as the well-mannered boy Mr. Moreno had always selected to accompany upset children sent out of his classroom for a timeout. Normally, she would have leveraged such little points of connection. But none of the relationship-building activities Rivera typically used to start off the year made sense over Zoom, so she'd decided to begin with a photography challenge. Each student was expected to take a portrait of themselves in profile, convert the image to black and white, and superimpose over the top of it a motivational quote that spoke to them. At his kitchen table, Jacob balanced his iPad and set the camera's timer. Then he turned toward the bright sunlight streaming through the window and held his chin between his thumb and forefinger.

"If you're offered a seat on a rocket ship, don't ask what seat! Just get on," he wrote over his selfie, quoting Facebook executive Sheryl Sandberg. The new school year was under way.

At stake was the fragile rebirth Superintendent Brawley had been nurturing in Compton for nearly a decade, but that a growing list of indicators suggested was now in danger. When it came to the school district's budget, for example, Brawley had spent the summer recording a series of increasingly dire warnings, saying revenue was expected to plunge by $23.4 million during the 2020–21 school year, then keep dropping from there, necessitating $8 million in cuts that had already been identified and layoffs likely to come.

Nearly a century earlier, Compton had faced a similar set of conjoined crises that included the Great Depression, a massive earthquake, and a tremendous influx of uneducated white migrants. Federal and state lawmakers had responded with massive public investments, subsidizing the affordable homes, new public schools, and readily accessible higher education that allowed the country's first truly suburban generation to flourish. The challenge now was to rally a similar level of support to refresh the aging housing stock and crumbling infrastructure in those same communities, even though their middle-class white families had been replaced by some of the nation's most vulnerable residents.

Remarkably, it looked for a moment like COVID-19 might actually spur just such a plan. An initial round of $24 million in ESSER funds allowed Brawley to start rolling back the cuts he'd warned of over the summer. Then, in December 2020, Congress and the Trump White House approved a second round of ESSER funds, $45.9 million of which went to Compton Unified. A few months later, President Biden and the new Democratic congressional majority green-lighted the American Rescue Plan, which included another $122 billion for public schools, $104 million of which would ultimately go to Compton Unified. In his public remarks, Biden put the package in the context of the New Deal of the 1930s and the Great Society initiatives of the 1960s.

"This is the first time we've been able to, since the Johnson Administration and maybe even before that, to begin to change the paradigm," the president said. "We have it within ourselves to come out of this moment more prosperous, more united, and stronger than we went in."

And a similar energy was bubbling up at the local level. That October, Compton mayor Aja Brown had unveiled the "Compton Pledge," a public-private partnership that promised to give 800 local residents no-strings-attached direct cash payments of between $300 and $600 per month. At the time, it represented the largest municipal experiment in guaranteed basic income in the nation's history. Critically, both Brown and outside advocates had pushed to make sure that *everyone*—including Compton's undocumented residents—was eligible.

"Sentiments are changing," said Martiza Agundez, the managing attorney for the Coalition for Humane Immigrant Rights of Los Angeles, who'd spent years fighting local government agencies, but was now on the Pledge's advisory board. "For the last three or four years, our Latino community has begun to mobilize ourselves, and we've been partnering up with our Black brothers and sisters as well."

In late January 2021, Brown announced she wouldn't seek a third term as mayor, placing that new spirit of Black-Brown unity on the ballot. Ten candidates lined up to run. One of the most prominent was Emma Sharif, a seventy-year-old Black woman who'd served on the Compton City Council since 2015 and on the board of Compton Unified for fourteen years before that. The other leading contender was Cristian Reynaga, a twenty-six-year-old Compton real estate agent whose family members had immigrated from Sinaloa, Mexico, in the 1970s, then opened a hair salon that for decades had been a community fixture for Compton Latinos. When Reynaga performed strongly in the primary, leading the field with 31 percent of the vote and landing a spot in a runoff election, local news outlets began forecasting that Compton would soon have its first Latino mayor. During an interview with Spectrum News 1, Reynaga stood before a Compton mural that featured Cesar Chavez and Martin Luther King, Jr., together against a garden backdrop. And in a twist that would have been unimaginable just a decade earlier, Brown gave him her full-throated endorsement.

"I've watched 'seasoned' 'politicians' vote against improvements, for years, not because they didn't know better—but their own selfish ambitions superseded the well-being of your children and our community," the outgoing mayor wrote on Instagram. "Cristian will be a mayor for ALL people. It's time to make room for the next generation."

Such surprising developments seemed to echo the multiracial, mestizaje vision upon which Los Angeles had been founded 240 years prior. A few scattered examples could already be found among the other aging bedroom communities south of downtown. University of Southern California Sociology and American Studies professor Manuel Pastor, for example, had spent years studying cross-racial cooperation in communities like Inglewood and Vermont Square, where longtime African American leaders had pursued an approach of "strategic inclusion," proactively looking for opportunities to share power with the growing Latino and Asian communities in their midst. The key, Pastor argued, was focusing on shared interests, long-term policy horizons, and cultivating future leaders from a variety of racial ethnic backgrounds.

"Building on the Blackness of the area . . . is a real possibility," the professor and his colleagues had written in a 2016 report titled *Roots/Raíces: Latino Engagement, Place Identities, and Shared Futures in South Los Angeles.* "Such an approach also avoids 'triumphalism'; rather than groups swapping influence, it points to building a more just world through the embrace of the sort of multiethnic model that is needed for our majority-minority region (and soon, nation)."

Even as the pandemic ground on, there were plenty of signs that Compton Unified and Jefferson Elementary were helping lay the groundwork for something similar. In September 2020, the district's board approved a plan to bring Compton's neediest students—foster children and students experiencing homelessness and housing instability, newcomers who'd been in the U.S. school system for three years or less, African American first and second graders who were reading below grade level—back into classrooms first. While some light grumbling could be heard around town, the resistance was mild compared to the freakouts that had occurred in suburbs like Evanston and Gwinnett County, which still had critical masses of middle-class white families resisting Black and Brown children being given priority access to educational opportunities. At Jefferson, meanwhile, Ms. Rivera led Friday afternoon cooking lessons over Zoom and gave her fifth graders the chance to program online animations about the water cycle and create digital art inspired by Joan Miró. She also had her class write autobiographical poems, one of which nearly melted her heart:

Jacob
Smart, creative, social
Who enjoys stroking a pencil on a
paper and creating a drawing
Who is able to express creativity
Who feels loved by his family
Who wonders about his future
Who fears disappointing people
When they need him
Who cares about his family and loved ones
Who dreams of a cleaner, safer, and equal earth.

Despite all the efforts to keep Compton growing, however, Alberto was unimpressed. My son is reading at a seventh-grade level, he told me that fall. But instead of pushing him to do more, his teacher gives him breaks so other students can catch up. Alberto's frustration worsened when he saw Jacob had joined the ranks of Jefferson students who no longer bothered to turn on their laptop cameras; by winter, he was visible to Ms. Rivera and his classmates only as a Bart Simpson avatar. And that disconnect was starting to show up on a larger scale; Jefferson's iReady data, for example, showed that only about 40 percent of students were working at or above grade level, more than ten points worse than had been typical at the same point during prepandemic school years.

Even for proponents, the prospect of turning Compton into a model of suburbia's multiracial future remained dicey. The town still lacked a strong civic and social service infrastructure, Pastor told me in an interview. Decades of scarcity had created conditions that still encouraged corruption. Burdensome rents and skyrocketing home prices were making it difficult for families like the Hernadezes to meet their monthly needs, let alone climb the social ladder. Tens of thousands of other Californians were fleeing the state, often for Texas. And the overlapping crises of 2020 threatened any progress that had been made; less than two months after Mayor Brown called for state and federal investigations into the LA County Sheriff's Department, saying deputies had unjustly stopped her the previous summer, then tried to search her car for drugs as her infant daughter watched from the back seat, a Black man ambushed two deputies as they sat in a patrol car, shooting one in the jaw and another in the forehead.

Add it up, and the Hernandezes were considering a return to Mexico.

"Right now, it is complicated. But later on, yes, we will have to," Alberto said of giving up on his American dreams. "My son asked me the other day if I had money saved for his college. I said, 'I'm waiting for you to receive scholarships. If you don't, then you go to Mexico and go to college there."

18

NO MORE AWAY

There is no "away" in the age of hyperobjects.

Timothy Morton,
Hyperobjects, 2011

THE BECKER FAMILY | LUCAS, TEXAS

By late January 2021, Susan Becker was feeling defeated. Months spent following election-related lawsuits and hearings in places like Arizona, Michigan, and Pennsylvania had gone to waste. Apparent January 6 false-flag operations that she initially thought had been orchestrated by antifa and later by the federal government had undermined the campaign to prevent the election from being stolen. Joe Biden was in the White House, half the country was intent on denying the purported evidence of fraud that got him there, and social media companies like Twitter were deplatforming any conservatives who dared speak out, up to and including the president of the United States.

"The corruption is everywhere," Susan told me, exasperated.

She didn't want to alarm the kids. But neither did she want to leave them unprepared for what was coming. So Susan settled on relaying the biblical story of Job, who developed a deep spiritual devotion during good times, then saw it tested when God visited a series of tragedies upon him and his family.

"I think honestly it helped to see that we've had it pretty good. Things have been pretty easy for us. We haven't really had anything that has significantly affected our way of life," she said of the family conversation. "But now, we don't know how all this is going to play out."

One thing was clear. Escape was no longer an option. I asked Susan if she and Jim had given any thought to moving somewhere farther outside Dallas and enrolling the kids in a new school system.

"It's not going to be any different," she said.

Still, Susan had to figure out where the kids would go for the 2021–22 school year. The boys in particular were antsy about spending a second year learning from their bedrooms at Freedom Project Academy. *She's gonna think I'm nuts*, Susan thought while composing yet another message to Stacey Dillon, this one asking to reenroll all three kids back in Lovejoy ISD.

Nearly as soon as she hit send, however, a series of worrisome signs affirmed her reluctance to return to the old normal.

The most ominous had to with the district's budget. To balance their book for 2020–21, Lovejoy officials had already drained their fund balance of $3.1 million. Heading into budget season for the upcoming year, things looked even bleaker. Enrollment was expected to come in at about two hundred lower-grades students fewer than even the district's lowest growth projections. The Texas state education department also determined that Lovejoy was no longer a "fast-growth" school system, costing the district another million per year in special allotments. Then state lawmakers began advancing legislation that would prohibit districts like Lovejoy from charging tuition to outside families, a move that could cause another million-dollar hit. And while other, more socioeconomically diverse school systems in places like Compton and Penn Hills were being propped up with millions of dollars in federal COVID relief dollars, Lovejoy was getting squeezed on that front too; because fewer than 2 percent of its students were considered low income, the district had received minimal ESSER funds.

As a result, Lovejoy ISD was staring down a $6 million budget hole. The district also faced a significant leadership void; just as the scope of the looming financial crisis was coming into view, Superintendent Goddard bailed, leaving the district for a position as the head of a local private school. With nothing else left to try, the officials who remained began cutting. Nearly three dozen teachers accepted early retirement buyouts. Positions in school security, libraries, and the district's communications, human resources, and business services departments were also eliminated.

Hoping to put the happiest possible face on the changes, the board used one of its spring meetings to announce they'd been recognized by the Texas Association of School Business Officials for sound financial management and that ten students from Lovejoy High's bass fishing team had placed in a state tournament. But then they announced a plan to take on more than $9 million in fresh bond debt to upgrade the district's athletic venues, a move that was intended to keep Lovejoy's facilities and amenities best in class but ended up bewildering many local parents. Tempers flared again when eleven additional resignations were announced, including the principal and librarian at Hart Elementary and two teachers at Sloan Creek Intermediate. District officials also expanded the fees families now had to pay to ride Lovejoy school buses, imposed across-the-board 15 percent spending cuts, and put the extra period for electives at Willow Springs Middle back on the chopping block. Then, in April, Lovejoy leaders dropped the biggest bombshell of all: Because of declining enrollment, Lovejoy Elementary would have to be closed.

Concerned parents quickly raised $175,000 in donations to the Foundation for Lovejoy Schools—but said the money was contingent on keeping the school open. Dozens of others flooded Lovejoy board meetings with complaints covering everything from the coming reduction in force to the district's mask policies. Susan was particularly focused on anything that suggested the district was promoting racial equity or social justice. One woman told her a story about her daughter being targeted by a Lovejoy teacher for expressing conservative views in class. Another said Lovejoy tenth graders had been subjected to a full day of indoctrination about systemic racism. Screenshots began circulating that appeared to show teachers in the district next door asking kids what pronouns they wanted to use. Then there was the brewing national fight over curriculum, which filtered down to Lovejoy even though the district hadn't made any significant changes to the material it taught.

"Take a word out here, a word out there, and before you know it, the next generation is convinced that we were founded by a bunch of racist white men and we all need to give up our property and land and repent," Susan said. "It gives them a reason to go, 'Yeah, our country sucks, let's burn it down.'"

Still, the decision at hand remained difficult. Sean had already attended six different schools and was adamant about wanting a normal high school experience; he'd even started reading Dale Carnegie's *How to Win Friends and Influence People* in preparation for starting ninth grade at Lovejoy High. Susan smiled along and resolved to play the long game.

That June, she and Jim took the family on an RV trip to New Braunfels, a South Texas town where Noah was attending a weeklong tennis camp. The long drive and open days provided ample opportunity to probe her older son's defenses. The first hint of a breakthrough came when the Beckers began chatting with the family one campsite over. The husband was a pilot with American Airlines. My older son has wanted to be a pilot since he was a little boy, Susan told him. The man asked if Sean had ever taken a discovery flight. It's where just you and a flight instructor go up in a little Cessna, he said. Your son is either going to love it and know he wants to be a pilot for sure, or he's going to hate it and decide to do something else.

Susan promptly began working the phones, arranging a discovery flight as a gift for Sean's birthday the following week. When he ate it up, she decided to play one of her strongest cards.

"Did you know you can get a pilot's license at seventeen?" Susan asked. "If we're homeschooling, it might give you the opportunity to start that process."

For weeks, it turned out, she'd been quietly researching a nonprofit called THEO Christian Solution. The group provided support to hundreds of homeschooling families in North Texas. Some classes were remote, which the Becker boys surely wouldn't be thrilled about. But THEO Christian also operated a meeting space where students could come for in-person teaching, tutoring, and socializing. Shortly after the RV trip and discovery flight, the boys grudgingly agreed to join Susan for a visit. It was a far cry from the tour they'd taken of Lovejoy's gleaming facilities just two years earlier; Sean was dismayed that the site resembled a telemarketing call center more than a school. But Susan held her tongue and remained upbeat, sidling over to THEO Christian's director as the tour wound down.

"I know this is a shot in the dark," she said. "But have you guys had any students come through that were aspiring pilots and maybe got their pilot's license while they were coming here? Just, you know, out of curiosity."

The director said a former student had started working for American at twenty-two. If Sean wanted to follow a similar path, he could take flying lessons for class credit. When her son still wasn't convinced, the family created a spreadsheet listing the pros and cons of the various options.

"And so that's how we kind of came to a conclusion," Susan told me.

Just before the 2021–22 school year started, she sent another message to Dillon, disenrolling her children from Lovejoy schools for the second time. If the decision felt kind of crazy, well, the world felt kind of crazy. Regular parents who spoke out against leftist indoctrination inside America's public schools were being labeled domestic terrorists. Inflation was sending the cost of everything from gas to bread skyrocketing. Some pharmacies wouldn't even fill prescriptions for hydroxychloroquine or ivermectin, an antiparasitic for horses that several of the wellness influencers Susan followed were now touting as a COVID treatment. I asked where she thought everything had gone off course. Susan told me it was the combination of the pandemic and the George Floyd protests that had inflamed the country's long-standing tensions and finally punctured the protective suburban shield that had been under attack for years.

"We're losing our country very quickly," she said.

On the first day of the 2021–22 school year, she loaded the kids back into the Buick. After pulling out of their still-sleepy subdivision in Lucas, she made for I-75, then merged into the traffic heading southbound. THEO Christian's meeting space was located back in Plano, just a few miles southeast of Daffron Elementary and the neighborhood the Beckers had recently fled. It was sandwiched between a dialysis center and a vacant storefront in a single-story strip mall. Ushering the kids out of the car, Susan felt a stab of regret that Lucas and Lovejoy ISD hadn't lived up to their promise. But she was confident she'd made the best decision current circumstances allowed.

"You can't run away from the problem," she said, waving her hand to indicate all the pressure she now felt to ignore her fears about individual liberty being sacrificed for some supposed greater good in which she didn't believe. "This has been in the making for a long time, and we happen to be the generation that's living through it."

THE ROBINSON FAMILY | GWINNETT COUNTY, GEORGIA

Throughout 2020, it had been clear Atlanta's multihued suburbs would play a pivotal role in deciding the presidency. But the results were still surprising. Biden won heavily Black DeKalb County by 67 percentage points. He also ran strong among college-educated whites living in the second- and third-ring suburban communities farther outside the city. And at the center of everything was Gwinnett: less than a decade after Republican Mitt Romney cruised to a 9-point victory, Biden wound up winning the county by 18.

"We were literally screaming in the house," Nika Robinson told me after Georgia was finally called for the Democrat. "It was amazing and very emotional. There was a sense of hope. Like, okay, maybe things can get back to normal."

The next few weeks had been full of "Thank God" texts from friends and knowing nods from strangers in the grocery store. The good vibes peaked shortly after New Year's, when Georgians went back to the polls for two runoff elections that would decide control of the U.S. Senate. Rev. Raphael Warnock won Gwinnett by 21 points, a margin that fellow Democrat Jon Ossoff nearly equaled. The key, analysts said, was a huge surge among Black voters; had Black turnout been more in line with typical runoff elections, *The Washington Post* reported, Ossoff would have lost by thirty thousand votes,

Warnock would have been mired in a recount, and Republicans would have retained control of the Senate.

We just saved the country, Nika thought when both races were finally called on January 6.

By that point, however, the insurrection at the U.S. Capitol had already started. The Robinsons sat glued to their television, watching in horror as hordes of angry Trump supporters paraded a Confederate flag through the building. Among the Georgians eventually arrested for their involvement was a forty-nine-year-old white construction worker named Verden Andrew Nalley, who lived in Buford, not far from the Robinsons' home. He'd illegally entered the Capitol's rotunda and crypt, then posted an alarming message on social media: "We took it with no weapons and we will be back with guns in two weeks if that's not fixed."

And the turmoil was just beginning. Even though Trump had tried to overturn the will of his state's voters and personally attacked him as "hapless," Georgia's Republican governor, Brian Kemp, took to Fox News to announce that he would absolutely support the now ex-president in 2024, insisting that his ideas "will be part of our party for a long time." Then, in late March, Kemp and Georgia's Republican-controlled state legislature passed sweeping new voting rules that critics blasted as a blatantly partisan attempt to make it harder for people in heavily Democratic areas to vote; suddenly, it was a crime to offer water to voters still waiting in line. Barely three months into a new year that had started off with such promise, Nika again felt exhausted, especially when she began receiving a fresh series of calls and Facebook messages urging her to run for office.

"Okay, we need to strike while the iron is hot," she said. "But realistically, is this going to work? I'm barely sleeping as it is."

Hanging over everything was her doctoral program. After passing her comprehensive exams, Nika had started planning a study of vaccine reluctance among rural Black families, even working with her dissertation committee to negotiate access to a trove of anonymized vaccine data from CVS. But the plan had fallen apart and the funding had evaporated, leading her to take the rest of the semester off and regroup.

"I kind of have to, not mourn, but let this idea go before I can really delve in again," she explained.

Then there was the constant jigsaw puzzle of the kids' schooling. Even after Mill Creek High reopened, Nika and Anthony decided to keep Corey home. But the younger kids were back to in-person learning. Nika was again going round and round with the staff at Jones Middle about getting her daughter into the school's gifted program. They'd finally agreed to test Cassidy that winter, but the results were slow to come.

"I just don't know how much more I have left," Nika said.

Then the politics around the Gwinnett County Public Schools turned even uglier. Shortly after Tarece Johnson and Karen Watkins won their elections and joined Everton Blair, Jr., on the five-member school board, the new progressives-of-color majority flexed its muscle, pushing through a 3–2 vote to oust superintendent J. Alvin Wilbanks a year before his contract was up.

"Ding Dong the witch is dead, the wicked witch is dead!!!!" Marlyn Tillman of Gwinnett SToPP texted me shortly after the news was official. "Peach martinis coming up!"

Elsewhere in Gwinnett, however, the reaction was more subdued.

"This is a detrimental change," octogenarian Republican board member Mary Kay Murphy, who'd narrowly beaten Democratic challenger Tanisha Banks to retain her seat, told *The Atlanta Journal-Constitution*. "It is counter to the world-class way the Gwinnett County public school system has operated over the last 25 years."

By May, conflicts over masks, vaccines, and racial equity were all raging anew. More than five thousand cases of COVID-19 had been reported among students and staff since the start of the school year, and the virus had already killed one beloved district employee and would soon claim more. Still, a boisterous crowd of roughly one hundred mostly white opponents of the district's new leadership showed up to the monthly meeting of the GCPS board. The fireworks began shortly after Blair called the meeting to order and reiterated the district's masking policy. The crowd responded with angry yells. When a brief recess failed to calm the unrest, Blair turned his microphone back on.

"Unfortunately, I'm looking at a lot of people who are not abiding by the county policy," he said. "So we're going to have to ask you to leave. And we'll stay recessed until you do."

A mix of cheers and boos erupted, then gave way to silence as dozens of people wearing T-shirts that said "UNMASK OUR CHILDREN" and "WE THE PEOPLE TAKE BACK OUR SCHOOLS" folded their arms in frustration. When the board finally reconvened, one of its two remaining white Republican members tried to play peacemaker, saying he didn't like wearing a mask either, but the policy was the policy. The crowd rained boos on him too. Watkins then called on security to start removing the maskless from the building. Heavily outnumbered, the officers on-site hesitated. Blair called another recess and directed a large group of staff and students to cross the hall and head into another room.

Dozens of Black and Brown and Asian and white and multiracial children were on hand to be recognized for designing sustainable development proposals, winning a national August Wilson Monologue Competition, and excelling in data science. The group bowed their heads and paraded mutely to the door as chants of "My body, my choice" broke out in the audience. They can't remove us all, someone in the crowd yelled out as security moved to break up a verbal altercation on the edge of turning physical.

Across the hall, the board handled its mundane business, approving old minutes and applauding the district's transportation department for getting students to school before the opening bell 99.6 percent of the time. But when it was time for public testimony to begin, everyone trudged wearily back into the main meeting area, where the angry crowd was still assembled. After a series of huddles and sidebar conferences, Watkins and Johnson left the room.

"Cowards!" came the yells from the audience.

"People were saying, 'stand your ground,'" Watkins later told NPR. "That's enough for me."

Nearly sixty speakers were still waiting to address the board. One of the first was a white woman named Wendy.

"We have been highly involved parents in Gwinnett County for the last seventeen years. But yet based on statements and posts made by the newest board members, we are now faced with a very different school environment," she began. "One that subscribes to critical race theory."

Her son had never before considered the races of his friends, the woman continued. But now he did, and it was breaking her heart.

"Therefore we are disenrolling our child," she concluded over whoops of encouragement from the crowd. "We refuse to leave him in an environment that tells him he is a racist merely based on the pigment of his skin and that attempts to shame him or make him feel guilty because he is white."

The next speaker was a bulky white man with a goatee and black baseball cap.

"For months, you've beaten the words 'equity,' 'diversity,' and 'inclusion' like they owe you money," he told the board. But that was just enforcing low expectations and ensuring mediocrity, he said. Maybe Blair, Johnson, and Watkins thought removing Wilbanks would allow them to hire someone more amenable to their divisive dogma. But every single candidate to replace him as superintendent should be forewarned.

"Anyone who supports this poisonous ideological cult, we the parents of Gwinnett County are coming for you," the man thundered.

The next hour-plus was more of the same. You will be held legally accountable for violating the Nuremberg code and the Universal Declaration of Human Rights, a white woman railed. This school board has been overtaken by a demon spirit, a white man preached. At the peak of the acrimony, a white mom with long blond hair issued a threat.

"You have woken a sleeping giant," she said, raising her voice to be heard over the roar of the audience behind her. "Every step you take, we are watching. We are going to come in like a stealth fighter jet, like a phoenix rising out of the ashes, because these schools belong to *us*."

During the weeks that followed, the agency responsible for accrediting Georgia school boards announced it was opening an investigation into

Gwinnett after receiving complaints that new board members didn't understand the roles, were using social media unethically, and were pushing racially discriminatory discipline policies. The state board of education also voted 11–2 in favor of a resolution declaring that neither Georgia nor the United States was racist and sharply limiting the way teachers were allowed to talk about race in their classrooms. Just months after tens of thousands of families like the Robinsons had finally asserted their claim to the Gwinnett school district's resources and policy agenda, their suburban dreams were running into a fierce backlash. A similar dynamic had reshaped Compton in the late 1960s and DeKalb County in the 1980s and '90s, leading to the white flight and capital disinvestment that eventually undercut those communities' visions of their future. Like those places before it, Gwinnett was now entering a crucial new stage in suburbia's cycle of racialized development and decline. And the view ahead wasn't pretty.

Take the warnings that filled the county's recently approved comprehensive plan. Gwinnett's poverty rate, barely 5 percent back in 2000, now hovered around 13 percent. At the same time, the county was home to a huge bubble of thirty- to fifty-five-year-olds who would soon need more senior housing, better public transit, and a wider variety of medical treatment facilities. And even larger problems loomed with Gwinnett's infrastructure. Half the county's 60 million square feet of retail space was at least a quarter century old, a number evident in the outdated malls and empty big-box stores that littered the landscape. Worse, 74,000 local households—representing roughly 30 percent of all the residential properties in the county—relied on aging septic systems that would eventually need to be replaced by new sewer lines, part of a larger set of wastewater upgrades that would eventually cost hundreds of millions of dollars. Roll it all up, and the plan's conclusions could have been taken straight from one of the broadsides Charles Marohn of Strong Towns regularly delivered against the mass-produced suburbs that proliferated across America after World War II.

"Much of [Gwinnett's] development at any given time was dominated by widespread construction of a single type of structure, built in a consistent configuration within a single geographic area, over a short period of time," the county's comprehensive plan read. "This has emerged as a major threat to our future success."

Given her druthers, Nika probably would've moved the family back to Chamblee, or maybe even into Atlanta proper; her bucket-list wish of living in a building with a doorman was still alive somewhere. Ever rational, however, Anthony pointed out that it was a terrible time to buy a house. And even if they did move, his preference was to head in the other direction, out into the country, where the family could find a larger piece of property and he could finally get his riding mower. Stuck, the Robinsons reluctantly turned their attention to the 2021–22 school year, already promising to start on a sour note.

"I got a letter saying they determined she didn't qualify," Nika replied when I checked in on her most recent effort to get Cassidy into Gwinnett's gifted program. "I don't know. I'm resigned. I can't express it. I think I'm just worn out."

Her attempts to figure out a homeschooling arrangement for Corey had fallen short, too, largely because she hadn't been able to ensure he would still be able to play for his high school football team. So on the next-to-last Saturday in August, the family headed to Mercedes-Benz Stadium, the 71,000-seat home of the Atlanta Falcons, where Mill Creek was facing rival Parkview. Still languishing near the bottom of the depth chart, Corey got just two carries for two yards, his only real highlight coming when he appeared on the stadium's massive Jumbotron long enough for Nika to snap a picture on her phone. Later, after sitting in traffic during the drive home, she found herself thinking back to the cascading series of disappointments that had followed her son's early troubles at Jones Middle.

"I just didn't have the wherewithal to realize, oh, this is just the beginning," she said.

Unsure what else to do, the couple decided to renovate their house in Buford. HGTV is a lie, Nika joked as the project evolved from installing new carpeting to remodeling the master bathroom to updating the home office. Then it came time to repaint the first floor. Even as she and Anthony were game-planning how to protect the furniture, they were still staring at the squares of color they'd applied to the dining room wall two years earlier. None of the options felt right. But fifteen minutes before the painters arrived for their consult, the Robinsons settled on Agreeable Gray.

THE ADESINA FAMILY | EVANSTON, ILLINOIS

By early 2021, Lauren Adesina was working at Evanston's public library, where she'd been hired to spur many of the same shifts already under way within District 65.

"They specifically invited me to be part of the strategic-planning process because of my equity background and blah, blah, blah," she told me. "But now I'm there, and they're doing racist shit, and I call out the racism, and they don't like that."

Lauren's mom, her mom's fiancé, her sister, and several members of Chris's father's family had come down with COVID-19 before winter break. As a result, she was determined to keep her son at home, even as local schools began reopening. But Chris's continued struggles with reading and writing were complicating the decision. He could sound out twelve-letter words, and he still loved to read dinosaur books. But asked to put pencil to page, his words were still missing vowels and full of backward letters. Hoping to protect her son's self-confidence, Lauren sat him down for a series of talks. There's nothing wrong with you, she'd explain. You just learn differently. So you deserve to be taught differently too. But it was unclear if the messages were getting through. When Chris began crying before every virtual meeting with his reading specialist, Lauren had no idea what to do.

"I didn't want to be the parent who always saves my kid from everything," she said. "Like, you're only in third grade. You have so many more years of education to go. Things aren't gonna work out with every single one of your teachers. Just go, learn how to read, and get out."

But her memories from Dewey still loomed. On the days she worked from home, Lauren began sitting nearby so she could listen in on Chris's sessions. One of the first things she noticed was a little white boy who liked to stick his face right into the laptop camera and scream. The reading specialist seemed patient and kind with him. But during a spelling test, Chris was supposed to write down a long list of words as the specialist read them aloud. He got to the end and was two words short. The specialist told him to turn his paper in as it was. Lauren chimed in from off-camera.

"So I say, 'Why don't you just explain to her that it's probably two words closer to the end and that it'd be real easy for y'all to figure it out,'" she recounted later. "And [the specialist] was like, 'You know what, sweetie, just hang back and we can figure this out together, don't worry.'"

The message Lauren took away was that the woman felt free to treat her son any kind of way when a parent wasn't watching.

Things briefly turned around after Principal Ellison got involved. But then Superintendent Horton, still face-to-face with District 65's severe budget problems, signaled he would eliminate the positions of more than twenty reading specialists and replace them with fewer staff members asked to provide more general academic intervention.

"I had like a minibreakdown with my dad last night," Lauren told me when I asked about the announcement. "I was torn between marching up there and demanding answers, and also kind of letting the new superintendent and his staff figure it out."

In the wake of the reopening fight and ensuing national attention, few others seemed inclined to extend similar grace. Lauren had been thrilled when District 65 held its third annual Black Lives Matter Week of Action. One day was devoted to appreciating Black family structures. ("There are lots of different kinds of families and what makes a family is how people care for and love each other," read the lesson guide for teachers.) Another was devoted to affirming transgender people. A third was devoted to class discussion of why the BLM movement was necessary. For Lauren, the highlight came on a hectic morning when she was trying to get Chris logged in to class while also getting ready for work. From the laundry room, she heard

Beyoncé playing on his computer. But when she headed into the kitchen ready to lay down the law, it turned out the song was a part of a class lesson on intersectionality and what it means to be unapologetically Black. Standing there watching her son bounce and smile, Lauren was transported back to her time choreographing dance routines to Destiny's Child hits for Dance Troupe.

"I was texting my friends like, yeah, Chris is in his class listening to *Brown Skin Girl*, what your kids doin'?" she said.

But as ever, a backlash soon followed. In mid-March 2021, *The Atlantic* published an article titled "What Happens When a Slogan Becomes the Curriculum." District 65 was introducing "children as young as 4 and 5 to some of America's most complex and controversial subjects," the article stated. Then it launched into a lengthy critique of a book Chris's third-grade class had read called *Not My Idea: A Book About Whiteness*. It included an illustration in which a devil offers a contract "binding you to whiteness" in exchange for your soul, stolen land, and the ability to tamper endlessly with the lives of people of color. "Jarringly didactic," *The Atlantic* concluded, quoting an anonymous parent upset that his daughter could make the case for defunding the police and thought anyone who disagreed was racist.

"To be this angry because now we get to learn about our history . . ." Lauren told me later, her voice trailing off.

Then Angela Blaising and the other liberals challenging for board seats began grumbling that Horton and the board were mismanaging District 65's finances. Board chair Anya Tanyavutti fired back, saying they'd been left holding a bag full of problems someone else had created. But Evanston's liberal establishment wasn't in a listening mood—especially when it became clear that Horton planned to redraw school attendance boundaries, overhaul the district's student-assignment system, and build a new school in the Fifth Ward. Taken together, the moves represented a dramatic retreat from District 65's half-century-long focus on maintaining racial balance in Evanston elementary schools. But with the backing of the board, the superintendent decided that continuing to chase Evanston's never-quite-realized dream of harmonious integration should no longer be the district's biggest priority.

"If you look at the research and data behind desegregation, what has that gotten our students? We still have one of the largest achievement gaps in the country," Horton said. "Desegregating for the sake of desegregating and having people feel good while students and families are struggling, that's not fair."

Lauren viewed such straight talk as evidence of the hard-won progress she and other Evanston parents of color had spurred. She was far less worried about any single policy disagreement than about the very real threat that District 65's progressive momentum might be rolled back entirely. Especially concerning was the looming school board election, in which a lineup of liberal challengers were trying to unseat three of the board's most reliable progressive incumbents.

Ndona Muboyayi was a Black woman whose family roots in Evanston went back five generations. She'd spoken at that same 2018 board meeting at which Lauren had shared her horror stories from Dewey Elementary. Back then, Muboyayi shared her frustrations about the ways families of color were being excluded from key decisions about their children's education. Now, though, she thought District 65's push for racial equity had gone too far.

"My son has wanted to be a lawyer since he was eleven," Muboyayi told the same *Atlantic* reporter who'd written the earlier piece. "Then one day he came home and told me, 'But Mommy, there are these systems put in place that prevent Black people from accomplishing anything.'"

Also running were Katie Magrino Voorhees, a white woman who worked in mental health and was distressed at the ways remote learning had affected the social and emotional well-being of Evanston's children, and Angela Blaising, the white Evanston mom who worked in corporate finance and had been stirred to action during the reopening fight.

In addition to blasting the District 65 board for giving Horton a "blank check," Blaising tried to make hay over the decision to eliminate accelerated math, the equity-related consulting work the superintendent and several board members were engaged in, and rumors that Horton wanted to close schools in Evanston's whitest and wealthiest neighborhoods—all positions popular with Evanston parents still outraged at having been called white supremacists because they wanted their kids back in school. As the campaign grew more contentious, Blaising agreed to do a remote interview with a local current-events program called "Evanston Live TV." The public was invited to log in to Zoom and follow along.

The discussion quickly grew heated, with host Meleika Gardner pushing the candidate to explain an earlier comment that it wasn't a good idea to have activists running the local school district.

"I think the most important thing a board can do is debate issues, and not have a viewpoint per se," Blaising said. "I think it's really dangerous when you have a very large school district being led by a common viewpoint."

"Is 'activist' a bad word to you?" Gardner asked.

"The reality is that we have a lot of activists on our board, and nothing has gotten done," Blaising responded.

When we sat down later, Blaising would tell me she and Gardner had mutually agreed the interview wouldn't be publicly posted because it had been so contentious. Unbeknownst to her, however, someone had recorded the discussion. Lauren obtained a copy and posted it to social media with the following message:

WE HAVE VIDEO FOOTAGE OF ANGELA BLAISING'S D65 CANDIDATE INTERVIEW WITH EVANSTON LIVE TV! YOU ALL HAVE TO WATCH THIS TRAINWRECK! THIS IS A MUST SEE! . . .

This interview only reaffirms her unchecked racism, anti-blackness, and her lack of understanding or care for, and frankly outright antagonism of the true meaning of equity.

Angela's campaign slogan is "The Change We Need" and her
slate's slogan is "Save Our Schools" . . . Save our schools from
what? From who? When these slogans are coupled with her hor-
rific comments and her suggested strategies, it reads "Make
America Great Again."

Blaising soon responded with a direct message of her own.

I am [not] sure what you think you are doing but you should
know you are violating the law by posting a video that is taped
by Evanston Live TV. So, you can take down your vile, hateful
post or you can get a letter from my attorney and I will see you
in court.

When I asked Lauren about the exchange, she could only shake her head.
"It's not even white fragility. It's white resistance," she told me. "We need
a whole new school board, a whole new administration, because there's a
thought that one of the predominantly white schools might shut down? It's
insane. No one cared for the last forty years. But then, oh my God, we may
have to close one of the schools in the rich white neighborhoods? We can't
let that happen, *our* kids can't be bused."

Still, the back-and-forth seemed to give her a second wind. In early April,
even as Chris was still struggling with his writing, COVID-19 raged on, and
she tried to settle into her new job, Lauren helped organize another rally
alongside Tanyavutti and other local education activists.

The event was dubbed the D65 Caregivers of Color and Our Village
March & Vote for Our Children's Lives. About fifty people gathered at a
park in South Evanston, grabbed cardboard and paint from a large folding table, and knelt on the sidewalk to make signs. As the crowd swelled,
people marched toward the local civic center, knocking on doors and distributing campaign literature. By midafternoon, the group had reassembled
at a second park. Campaign signs for the school board's incumbent progressives were stuck in the patchy grass. Behind them, a lone dogwood tree

offered a splash of purple against the gray sky. Tanyavutti was the featured speaker.

"So I'm going to start off with a land acknowledgment," the school board president began, naming several Indigenous tribes who'd inhabited the area. "Evanston and its founder John Evans are tied to the massacre of the Arapaho and Cheyenne for railroads and western expansion."

Later, I'd sit down with Tanyavutti too. She was proud of what District 65 had accomplished during her five years on the board. She believed the district was now operating in a state of productive discomfort, with people at all levels of the system forced to be more intentional about protecting and supporting children from marginalized backgrounds. But the changes the system needed were bigger and more far-reaching than even she had anticipated. So was the resistance. As a result, Tanyavutti had come to believe that suburbs like Evanston could only change if people—all people, including the white liberals leading the resistance to her agenda—were given the space to process what they were losing. She could relate personally, Tanyavutti told me as she relayed the story of a trip she'd taken to Africa as a college student.

"In the U.S., I was a poor Black girl. But in Senegal, I was an American. Period. And that meant power," she said. "And so I had to really grapple with what it meant to be privileged and about creating harm without intention. I humbled myself to learn how to create less harm, and also how to grieve the harms I embodied [and] the privileges I appreciated. So I can empathize with the discomfort folks are expressing."

But what she refused to do, Tanyavutti said, was accept the ways many white Evanstonians chose to express their discomfort and fought to put their feelings at the center of District 65's policy agenda. Back at the preelection rally, she laid out the stakes of the coming board election in even sharper terms than Lauren had used on Facebook.

"Now that we are being harassed, threatened, pathologized, and dehumanized by these candidates attempting to silence and marginalize our interests, through campaigns rooted in fear-mongering, lies, power-hoarding behaviors, and manipulation of the electorate, we must make it clear,"

Tanyavutti told the crowd. "We nor our children are your diversity accessories."

The several dozen people still on hand cheered. A dog began to bark. Later, Lauren would tell me that all the battles of the past three years had been worth the heartache they entailed. District 65 now had a Black superintendent and a Black school board president. More Black and Brown educators were being hired. Black and Brown students and children with special needs were no longer suspended at the first sign of trouble. The curriculum was becoming more inclusive. Evanston was now home to a critical mass of parents of all races who were willing to stick out their own necks to advance racial equity. And most significantly of all, Horton and the District 65 board were on their way to winning approval for a new $40 million school to be built on the playing fields outside the old Foster building, a vote that Horton would later describe as righting the wrongs that were done to the historically Black Fifth Ward in the name of desegregation.

The biggest problem, Lauren told me, was that it all still felt so fragile. Especially when Principal Ellison announced she was leaving Washington Elementary for another district, Tanyavutti began hinting she'd soon step down, and Horton began quietly contemplating leaving Evanston if the opposition slate took control of the District 65 board.

"It feels like all this work and effort can be taken away and just erased that easily," she said.

But for the moment, at least, Lauren was tired of fighting. Not because the battle was won, but because she had to wage it in the first place. The hardest thing to accept was that nothing could bring back what her family had already lost. Chris was about to turn nine. The best window to address his learning challenges was closing. Earlier that spring, during one of their sitdown conversations, Lauren had asked her son what *he* thought was the source of his troubles in school.

"Because I'm not trying hard enough," he'd responded.

THE HERNANDEZ FAMILY | COMPTON, CALIFORNIA

As the 2020–21 school year drew to a close, suburbia's past and future kept colliding in Compton.

The Hernandez family had finally relocated to an apartment three miles south of the house they'd been renting. But it was small and on the second floor and still within Compton's borders, all of which made the move a slog. Now it was the first of June. Vertical blinds cast alternating stripes of shadow and light across the kitchen. Jacob pulled big black headphones over his ears and sucked in his belly as he maneuvered around the table, still wedged between the fridge and a stack of unopened moving boxes. As he moved a small vase of yellow roses to make room for his iPad, Jacob told me he'd mostly made peace with remote learning extending into a second year.

"It's a little bit isolated," he said. "But it's more comfortable for me."

Roughly a quarter of the children in his class had elected to come back for in-person learning after Compton Unified reopened to everyone. To prepare for their arrival, Ms. Rivera and Jefferson administrators had tried to liven up the classroom with college pennants and star-shaped balloons. But the in-person kids still sat behind plexiglass shields at desks spaced six feet apart, and the rest of the class remained avatars on a screen. One boy had made his a picture of himself sleeping. Another's just said "BYE."

"Today you have your final project of the year," Rivera told the class as she sipped from a tall white Starbucks cup. "Get on the agenda and click on 'Future 5th Grader Letter.' Let's go ahead and do some prewrites."

The children fell silent. Rivera couldn't see what anyone was doing. Jacob stifled a yawn. He still missed his friends. He also missed Rebel, the dog his parents had been forced to give away when the family moved. And worst of all, he'd recently incurred his father's wrath for bringing home his first-ever B. After shaking out the rest of his morning cobwebs, he opened the instructions for the assignment and tried to focus on what next year's fifth graders needed to know.

"I'm thinking of adding a piece of advice, for them to not get frustrated so easily," he said after a few minutes of pondering. "That sometimes happens to me."

Despite everything, Jacob had remained a popular classroom leader. He regularly organized online Minecraft games among the boys in his class. He'd also developed his own little patter in the class chat, geeking out with his teacher over their shared fascination with ancient Egypt and typing in a prim and proper voice when the class read *The Lion, The Witch, and the Wardrobe.* And though Jacob's interest in journalism had waned after his fourth-grade class newspaper fell apart, a new interest had recently taken root. The annual mock-trial competition Rivera led had started a few weeks earlier. The class's fictional case, dubbed *The People v. Tracy Smith*, involved a teenager caught at an arcade with a loaded gun she'd intended to use to kill a school bully named C. J. Wilson. Jacob landed the role of Prosecutor 2.

The day's preparation began with a read-through of a prepared script. Determined to make sure her students were still learning, Rivera used the activity to focus on reading fluency. When the girl playing the part of the bailiff stumbled over the words "honorable" and "presiding," the teacher had her read the words again. And when Prosecutor 1 laid out the evidence against Smith in a sweet, mellifluous voice, Rivera instructed him to reread his part, too, with a focus on emphasizing words like "guilty."

When it was Jacob's turn to speak, he leaned forward and rocked gently as he questioned his friend Marques, who played the role of the responding police officer. Security guards at the Fun Dome Arcade had already apprehended Smith when he arrived, the officer said. He'd found a partially open backpack in a row of nearby bushes. Inside was a torn paper bag holding the gun. At this point, Jacob was supposed to go off script with a question he'd come up with on his own to bolster the prosecution's case.

"Did anyone else see it happen?" he asked.

"Wait, what do I say?" responded his stumped witness, unable to find the lines on the sheet in front of him.

When the read-through was complete, Rivera sent the prosecutors, defense team, and court officers into separate breakout rooms to work on their independent questions. Jacob quickly initiated a group chat.

"We need to prove two more things," he typed. "1. She knew the gun was there. 2. She intended to harm someone."

No one responded. Prosecutor 2 was undeterred.

"Marques, I have the question," he wrote to his friend. "The question is gonna be, 'What was Tracy's reaction when she saw the gun.' You need to answer something that demonstrates she wasn't surprised."

"All righty," Marques replied.

It was all preparation for the possibilities finally emerging in Compton. Even as the fifth graders imagined new futures for themselves, one of the most visible symbols of the town's past was about to come down; that same day, June 1, 2021, superintendent Darin Brawley and the Compton Unified school board kicked off in earnest the replacement of the old Compton High. The Art Deco–style facility at the center of campus had been built in the mid-1930s, back when the town's journey from farmland to "All-American" bedroom community to failed suburb was just beginning. Administrators at the time had placed a time capsule in the building's cornerstone. A letter from the president of the district's board read:

> *As we seal the cornerstone of this structure which so well expresses those desirable qualities of solidity and endurance, our thought turn to that more important process of building that is to take place within its walls, the shaping of the lives of our citizens of tomorrow. May those confronted with this task work so wisely and well that this material structure will be symbolic of the strength of character, the integrity and steadfastness of purpose that will characterize the students that pass through its halls.*

Ninety years later, things had come full circle. The campus would soon be dominated again by huge piles of dirt and rubble. The goal lines on the famed football field that had launched no fewer than twenty-three Compton High grads on to the NFL would soon be written over by the tracks of dump trucks. And a message that the current school board chair had streamed on Facebook Live during the demolition of an outlying building still hung in the air.

"We believe this community has a promised future. And that future re-
sides in those we educate today," Micah Ali had said into his phone as a huge
orange excavator rumbled to life in the background. "I always say, why
move, when you can stay and improve?"

Compton once again found itself in a kind of liminal space, a kaleidoscope of American change, its future dependent on the kind of cross-racial
cooperation upon which the Los Angeles region had been founded, but that
for centuries had seemed impossible to sustain. Even now, supply chain
problems were sending the already astronomical cost of the new high school
soaring. Many Compton Latinos were disappointed that Emma Sharif beat
Cristian Reynaga by just 218 votes during the runoff election for mayor—
and that Compton's lone Latino councilman was hit with felony vote-rigging
and bribery charges shortly thereafter. Even as the City Manager's office was
touting millions spent on street and sidewalk repairs, tree trimming, and
graffiti removal, the state Auditor's Office still believed Compton was at
higher risk of financial distress than any other jurisdiction in California.
And inside Compton Unified, Superintendent Brawley was doing his best to
temper expectations, pointing out that even the district's recent $350 mil-
lion bond measure and the $200 million it had received in COVID relief
funds were a drop in the bucket relative to what was needed.

"Truthfully, it would have to be about a $3 billion investment to bring
Compton [schools] up to par," he told me, highlighting the staggering scope
of the need throughout America's aging suburbs.

But having just watched one of the most challenging eras in the country's
recent memory through the eyes of the Hernandezes, it was difficult not to
feel like Compton Unified and Jefferson Elementary had already sparked
something significant. Together, Ali and Brawley and principals Salvador
Aquino and Bilma Bermudez and teachers Victor Moreno, Patricia Rivera,
and Mary Grace Santiago had joined scores of others in starting to op-
erationalize what a new social contract for America's suburbs might en-
tail. The basic contours still involved massive investment by every level of
government in the children who will shape the country's future. What was
new, however, was the determination to make those investments in a rising

generation that was mostly Black and Brown, often immigrants who were still learning English, sometimes poor and undocumented. For so long, so much of suburbia had been organized around trying first to keep those kids out, then treating them as a problem to be managed. But what I'd seen at Jefferson was the absolute conviction that Jacob and his classmates were all bursting with promise, and that nurturing their gifts was not a matter of charity, but a reflection of the belief that America's future depended on them thriving.

Take that mock trial in Jacob's class. A few days before school let out, teacher and students alike were on pins and needles for their final performance.

"Is my prosecution team ready?" Rivera asked.

The bailiff made it through her opening remarks without incident. Prosecutor 1 turned on his laptop camera, revealing a long-haired ten-year-old who had clearly been practicing his inflections and enunciations.

"Tracy must learn that a loaded gun is not a *toy*," he said, slowing for emphasis. "It is extremely *dangerous*."

Jacob followed along intently from his kitchen table, grilling his witness about the gun and the backpack, then giving a gentle nod when Marques gave a response indicating that Tracy hadn't been surprised when she saw the gun in the backpack. When the defendant was eventually found not guilty, the class group chat exploded.

"Yayyyyyyyyyyyyyyyyyyy!!!!" wrote a boy named Stephen.

"Bruhhhh" wrote a girl named Karina.

"C. J. Wilson sad" wrote a boy named Jaime.

Then the class ended and everyone else logged off. Jacob and I lingered on the Zoom. Despite everything, his spirit was still intact. I'd recently confessed to being a little disappointed that his dreams of becoming a newspaperman had dissipated. Don't worry, he'd responded. He had bigger plans now.

"I have a feeling that I want to be a lawyer, because I want to help people and make the world better," Jacob told me. "I don't know a lot of schools, but I've heard of Harvard, UCLA, and Yale."

THE SMITH FAMILY | PENN HILLS, PENNSYLVANIA

By summer 2021, the drumbeat of bad news befalling Penn Hills and its public schools felt maddeningly familiar. The local school board approved another property tax hike. District leaders again declined to change the team's "Indians" nickname and mascot. At the elementary school where Jackson Smith was getting ready to start fourth grade, the still-deficient HVAC system led to an "abnormal fungal ecology" growing in several classrooms and hallways, forcing the district to spend yet more money to install industrial dehumidifiers.

Bethany, meanwhile, had lost her W-2 job, a crushing financial development she was busy trying to turn into a positive. Most of her energy was going into the LLC she'd formed as a vehicle for her budding entrepreneurial endeavors, which now included services such as property management, grant writing, and data entry. In a related development, she'd begun cutting out much of the volunteer work, community service, and unpaid emotional labor she'd been doing since childhood.

"What did it do for me personally besides make me feel good? Did it help me get on a Disney cruise?" she asked over the phone one afternoon while watching her son's weekly karate lesson. "There's a point in life where you just get sick and tired of not doing the things you want to do."

It brought me considerable joy to have learned that writing was one of those things; only after Bethany agreed to contribute to this book did she tell me about her experiences in Helena Liddle's community college literature courses. I was also relieved that we were again talking regularly, trying to make sense of Penn Hills in a way that felt more reciprocal. But something stubborn and difficult remained lodged between us. And though we were now circling it together, neither of could name it, creating a block that prevented both of us from finding the words we still needed to write. Hoping some in-person time might help, I climbed back into my station wagon, hit the Pennsylvania Turnpike, and headed again for Princeton Drive.

The first time I'd knocked on Bethany's door felt like a lifetime ago. I'd since traveled the country, immersing myself in the lives of families on the front lines of suburban change. Their experiences and perspectives had helped me see a devastating cycle I'd been oblivious to for decades, even as it unfolded all around me, shaping my own trajectory and transforming the country with alarming speed. Exclusive enclaves in places like the North Dallas exurbs were now going from open ranchland to residential construction binges to public school enrollment declines and wicked budget crunches in the span of just twenty-five years. Racially diverse suburban communities like Evanston and Gwinnett County were being rocked by conflicts that exposed the hollowness of the country's post–civil rights promises. In older suburban communities, the unraveling seemed to have an unstoppable momentum, sucking places like Penn Hills into the same destructive spiral that had once decimated Compton. And in every corner of the country, the ensuing disillusionment was forcing families to reckon with an unsettling new question: What if the American dreams suburbia was built upon weren't enough to lead us out of the enormous problems that nearly a century of mass suburbanization had created?

Perhaps because answers still felt so out of reach, I found myself drawn to the work of a far-out philosopher named Timothy Morton. A professor at Rice University, they argue that humanity has entered a new era defined largely by the incomprehensible vastness of the messes we've created. Think global warming, or the quarter million metric tons of highly radioactive nuclear waste now scattered across the globe. Morton calls these "hyperobjects." They're so complex and so large and operate on such grand time scales that there's no possibility of escape. We can bury, deny, and outrun them for a while, sometimes even generations. But when there's no more *away*, we're forced to reckon with the illusions that led us astray in the first place.

Morton argues that there are no right answers when dealing with hyperobjects; we're all living inside patterns that completely surround and subsume us, regardless of our individual choices. This helped me better understand the Beckers' bewildered resignation after years of searching for some safe suburban haven in North Texas. Morton also contends that a defining feature of hyperobjects is how their scale and power shatter our sense of control and obliterate any fantasies that traditional authorities or smart policy solutions might save us, leaving us no choice but to live with constant threat. This helped me understand the quiet crisis that settled over the Robinson household in Gwinnett County. Learning to recognize the exhaustion of caring for one another through relentless crisis, even as we mourn all we're losing and reach for something new, likewise helped me grasp the weariness that had settled over Lauren Adesina and her fellow activists in Evanston. But none of that felt particularly uplifting. And while the Hernandez family and Jefferson Elementary in Compton raised the possibility of a new American dream that might someday bloom from the wreckage of what's now falling apart, I wasn't exactly eager to accept that entire generations of children—including my own—might be left to navigate the depths to which Compton had sunk before rebirth became possible. Three decades after fleeing suburbia, I was still desperately afraid of ending up stuck.

It was a Thursday afternoon when I arrived back in Pittsburgh. Since I wasn't scheduled to head to Princeton Drive until the following morning, I decided to spend a few hours wandering through Sugar Top, the Hill District neighborhood where Bethany had grown up.

My first stop was her alma mater. The gorgeous neoclassical limestone building that once housed Schenley High was now full of condominiums. A leasing agent greeted me in the lobby. We walked down a hallway whose marble floors had been buffed to a high shine, then peeked inside Schenley's legendary basketball gym, now an on-site fitness center populated by a dozen ponytailed white graduate students running in place on treadmills. Down a few stairs, the agent showed me into a model two-bedroom unit with an open floor plan that had been carved out of an old classroom. Rents started at around $2,000 a month, she told me in a cheery voice before asking when I might move in.

Back outside, I trudged up a steep cobblestone street toward the weathered golden bricks of Grace Memorial Presbyterian Church. The streets nearby were crowded with charming houses with steep lawns, plus the occasional low-rise housing project. Dozens of vacant buildings were scattered among them. Their windows and doors had been replaced with sheets of plywood, many of which had been spray-painted with the words "We Need More Black Love."

The house Bethany had grown up in had been demolished and was now just a narrow parcel of land with a few concrete slabs poking through thigh-high weeds. Across the street, a bright blue CONDEMNATION sign was stuck to the exterior of the superette where she and her fellow babysitters had once bought grape drink and freeze pops. Catty-corner across the intersection, Madison Elementary, shuttered for more than a decade, stood empty and silent.

I kept climbing, up to Williams Park, which spread out like a verdant green blanket around the reservoir at the top of the hill. There were no children playing kickball. But I found a seat on a comfortable bench and took in the stunning 360-degree view of the city below. I'd never realized such a vista existed.

At dusk, I got up and left along a different route, passing by beautiful three-story homes boasting carefully tended gardens and their original leaded windowpanes. A familiar voice piped up inside my head. *You could totally live here,* it said. *I bet these houses are still cheap.*

When it comes to hyperobjects, Timothy Morton had written, the most damaging thing of all is how they live inside us, leading us to constantly re-create, reinforce, and spread the messes we've made, even when doing so runs counter to our own interests and best intentions. It was the best definition of *stuck* I'd ever come across. Unfortunately, it resonated for a reason.

The next morning on Princeton Drive, Bethany greeted me again at her front door. We walked down to the finished basement Jackson had used for remote learning. When I pulled out my phone and hit record, a familiar heaviness filled the space between us. Bethany told me she still wasn't sure how her voice might fit into the larger book. I started talking about the hidden history of slash-and-burn suburbanization, about the millions of families like mine who had left aging communities like Penn Hills just before their debts came due, about all the problems that resulted. But I thought there was still a big unanswered question.

"Once you understand it, how do you be accountable to that?" I said. "That's the part I'm figuring out."

We spent a while discussing Bethany's views and ideas, then looked through old yearbooks and swapped parenting stories. For the hundredth time, I asked her what she wanted out of Penn Hills. And for the hundredth time, she considered the question warily.

We finally had a breakthrough several months later. Bethany had begun transforming the personal reflections she'd been writing into an essay that would serve as the epilogue to this book. But as we talked through a draft, something still wasn't clicking. I thought the problem was her reluctance to grapple with all the big forces I saw dragging Penn Hills down. Trying to be helpful, I offered to go back to my notes from our earlier conversation in her basement and pull out relevant snippets from what she'd already said on the topic. A few days later, I sent her an email that included the following:

> But when [Ben] told me about all the ideas in the book [he] was working on, the shit he was talking was all doom and gloom, you know? Stuff like that is big. And I never really wanted to be a part of it, because it takes a lot of work. When I did see something wrong, I'd be like, "Oh, I hope somebody do something about that one day." Because I didn't have the time or space mentally for thinking about the bigger picture. I was working on this right here. I owned a piece of real estate in Penn Hills. I made it my home. That's what was gonna take me and family to where we needed to go.

Bethany's response was swift and forceful:

> This paragraph right here is some bullshit and its offensive. For the past two years, I've been sharing details of my life with you. I've opened up my life and invited you into my world. . . . It hurt to read what was typed in that edit. Sound bites. Sensationalism . . .

Typical Black single mother struggling and too small-minded to think or contribute to the problems of society that white people created.

When we talked the following week, Bethany told me how profoundly I'd misinterpreted her. How deeply I'd hurt her. How white people like me were constantly doing things that seemed designed to put her back in her place.

"The way you put those words and statements together made me feel something I've been feeling this whole time but could never put into words," she said, explaining why she felt compelled to check me.

And with that, Bethany found the missing piece to her epilogue, and I found one more illusion I'd been carrying around since the beginning, leading me to hurt someone I'd grown to care for as a friend, a writing partner, and a kind of long-distance neighbor.

It was true that I'd relinquished my deep-rooted belief that I could always run away and start over somewhere new. I'd also learned how neglecting the Black and Brown parts of a community inevitably damages that community as a whole. I'd seen in the experiences of other people's children how my own comfortable middle-class life was built on a series of injustices large and small. And I'd accepted the need to emotionally process the ways that white racism and white racial denial had injured me too.

But somewhere beneath all that, I'd still assumed someone else would clean up the mess that my family had left behind, still assumed someone else would shoulder the burden of repairing America while I kept reaping its riches. And of all the ways this last illusion had caused harm, the worst was how it prevented me from seeing Bethany's true self and the gifts she had to offer.

Her Sugar Top, her skipping school, her Langston Hughes.

Her Jesus-Be-a-Fence-Around-Me, her knew-what-to-hold-on-to-because-it-was-already-there.

Her gotta-get-my-shit-together, her going back to college.

Her Earn Your Leisure and her LLC.

Her refusal to wear two faces, her resistance to my gloom.

Her island somewhere, in the sand, watching the ocean.

Her even-your-little-coup-attempt-can't-fuck-with-my-shine.

Her two flags flapping together furiously in the wind.

From the moment I'd walked up Bethany's sidewalk and knocked on her door, she'd been telling me how she rose every morning and remembered, imagined, prayed, strove, hustled, wrote, rested, and willed her way out of *stuck*. But my need-not-to-know kept getting in the way.

I had to own *that* before I could offer Bethany an apology proportionate to the injury I'd caused. And only then did I find what I'd been looking for since I first ran away from Penn Hills.

There has always been an American dream that refuses to get stuck, even when stuck is all there is.

There has always been an American dream that resists bleak visions of the future, despite all present evidence to the contrary.

There has always been an American dream that turns the fragments and shards of what came before into something beautiful and new.

And there has always been an American dream that seeks to preserve our very impulse to dream, for our children if not ourselves, regardless of the magnitude of the mess we find ourselves in.

That's an American dream that can carry us through the unraveling now at hand.

EPILOGUE

by Bethany Smith

This morning was Jackson's second day of fourth grade. I woke up around 6:30 a.m., walked through the house opening drapes and blinds to let in the dawn, then asked Google to play "Wake Up Everybody" by Harold Melvin and the Blue Notes. When I walked into my son's room and opened his blue ninja turtle curtains, he was still asleep. He looked so peaceful, calm, and handsome. I kissed his cheek, then nudged him a little. He opened his eyes and smiled at me, then stretched and kicked his covers off.

That little boy had been so excited about starting fourth grade. All the way up until the night before. Then he got nervous. He couldn't articulate what he was feeling inside. We stood there in the hallway for a moment. Then I asked him what he wanted to wear for his first day. Just like that, the tension melted away. He was focused on his swag: A gray T-shirt with characters from Roblox, black-on-black Nikes, a Pittsburgh Penguins hat turned to the back and side, and a book bag he'd picked out the day before. By day two, he couldn't wait to get to the bus stop. All that good shit I put out in the universe was playing out before my eyes. By the grace of God, the words that a high school mentor had shared with me twenty-plus years earlier were still keeping me going:

You are not where you want to be.
You are not where you are going to be.
You are not where you've been.

Since the day he knocked on my door, Ben has been asking me the same question: What do I want from the suburbs? Past experiences taught me not to expect much from society. And when I sat and thought about it, it brought depression and took me to a place I'd rather not visit. But until recently, I couldn't put into words why those feelings came over me when Ben asked that question.

Growing up, I didn't think about the suburbs. I was a proud resident of Sugar Top, as it is affectionately called by folks who are familiar with the Schenley Heights neighborhood of Pittsburgh's Hill District. The community had so much culture. We looked out for each other. I attended neighborhood public schools with administrators and teachers who exhibited good intentions toward all of us. It was safe. Some might even compare it to what the suburbs have to offer.

Still, when I think back to the day we closed on our home in Penn Hills in May 2018, a warm feeling comes over me. It was one of the proudest moments of my life. Until then, I knew the who and the why of my goals, but I couldn't decipher the what, when, where, and how. Not believing you are worthy? Losing hope because of your circumstances? Knowing you want better for yourself, but not knowing how to implement change? That shit is real. By the grace of God, though, I know I can accomplish whatever I put my energy into. And through His grace and mercy, I was blessed to make a home in a place where I can sit and be still.

Living in Penn Hills in the years since, I've noticed some things. One day, my mom, myself, and Jackson were making the five-minute drive to the grocery store. We counted no less than twelve FOR SALE signs in people's yards. I panicked for a moment. It was like when you see a group of birds fly away together, or mice running in unison in the opposite direction of danger.

There's also been a decline in the upkeep of some roads. On Old William

Penn Highway going eastbound, the left side of the road caved in. It's scary. My mom called the municipality to inform them. Now there are signs warning you to drive fifteen miles per hour through that stretch. But it's not fixed.

I worry about the rising taxes and the outrageous sewage bills as well. When we were living in a rental home in this area, the three-month water and sewage bill was close to $500. Word on the street was that there was some rule-breaking going on in the 1970s that we current residents are now paying the penalty for. I also heard talk about the school board mishandling funds and building a new elementary and high school that already has problems. But I didn't know for sure.

> *You are not where you want to be.*
> *You are not where you are going to be.*
> *You are not where you've been.*

It gets tough sometimes dealing with the shit life brings my way. The shit that comes from living in a municipality that isn't thriving due to mismanagement by the people in power and the horrible trickle-down effects. Or the shit that comes with just L-I-V-I-N. I am human. I hurt. I cry. I feel ashamed. Putting myself first and speaking up for myself is hard for me sometimes. The feeling of being left out haunts me. For a long time, too long, I just accepted what others wanted to give me. Adopting the habit of speaking up for myself wasn't easy. To be honest, it still isn't. I am smarter than I act. But even though it's necessary, standing up for myself still makes me uncomfortable.

In my late twenties, an incident at work led me to a therapist on the South Side of Pittsburgh. There I was introduced to an exercise that gave me some perspective on my life. Thirty little pieces of paper were set in front of me. Typed on the papers were words and phrases like "competence," "strength," "love," and "adequate resources." The idea was to remove those that were less important to me and narrow down the list to three. It was difficult at first. I started to set aside words like "control" and "order." Then I set aside words like "cooperation," "fairness," and "influence." Eventually, I was left sitting there with the three most important things in my life:

> *Financial security. Family, friends, and loved ones. Rest and relaxation.*

I was still on my journey in pursuit of those core values when I got a knock on my front door on a winter evening in early 2020. Me and Jackson had just finished dinner. I looked through the glass in the door and saw a white guy on the other side. Ben, standing there with a brown leather bag on his shoulder. I opened the door. He told me he was a journalist and he'd grown up on Princeton Drive a couple of doors down. He was interested in our experience as a Black family living in Penn Hills. I felt Ben was genuine in his approach. For some reason, I thought I could trust him. So I invited him in.

I still believe in what he is trying to do with this book.

But there came a point where I was uncomfortable sharing so much about myself. I started to notice what my perspective was bringing to Ben's project. American history kept flashing through my mind. Thoughts of white people not crediting or compensating Black people for their intellectual property or hard work. I kept thinking about how much I was giving. I wondered what I would get in return.

I prayed about my discomfort. I even talked about it with a confidant. I wasn't quite sure how to approach Ben with my concerns. I was always the type of person who thought I was strong enough to take whatever in order to make things better for everyone else. I found ways to maneuver around conflict, avoid things outside my control. But that way of living took a piece of me every time I did it. Conflict is guaranteed to show up one way or another. It has to be dealt with.

So I stepped out of my comfort zone and started a very difficult conversation. If Ben had replied, "You know what, Bethany, I hear you. But there's nothing I can do for you," I would have had some decisions to make.

We didn't talk for about a month. Ben sent me an email, and I didn't even open it. I thought I had scared him away and that I didn't have to worry about him anymore.

A while later, though, we spoke on the phone. Ben surprised me. I never thought he would ask me to write an essay as a contribution to his book. Let alone the fucking epilogue! He didn't even know I had experience writing. I accepted the task not knowing exactly what would come of it. Then my emotions went from honored and excited to dread. Life is funny like that. The stuff we encounter that makes us uncomfortable is usually what God sends our way to elevate us. But I put myself first, and an opportunity was born.

> *I am not where I want to be.*
> *I am not where I'm going to be.*
> *I am not where I've been.*

When Ben suggested I write about what I want from the suburbs, what I want from Penn Hills, it wasn't easy for me to answer. I didn't want to come off as a victim. I also didn't want to say what I feel and have it fall on deaf ears. Basically, I didn't want to get hurt.

He kept asking, though. And it reached a point where he really pissed me off. He seemed to see me as just another struggling single Black mother too small-minded to think about the societal problems that white people like him created. It was another reminder that even the most liberal white person will never see me, a Black woman, as an equal.

But I decided to tell him how I felt. This wasn't some kumbaya, let's be friends shit. Ben offended and hurt me. So I told him that in raw terms. And in the process, something surprising happened. I found the words to express how I feel about Penn Hills and the suburbs at large.

White people are always fucking some shit up, then expecting everybody else to go fix it. Why should Penn Hills be any different? White families lived here so they could have opportunities. They fucked things up. And now you have Black people like me expected to fix these problems that they didn't have a hand in creating.

That shit is tiring. Isn't that what I pay taxes for? So things get handled, and I can focus on doing what I have to do in my own life? Isn't that how the suburbs worked for families like Ben's? Why is it different for us?

Thinking about this stuff threatens to bring back that old feeling of not being good enough. That's what happens when I look at myself through the eyes of society instead of through my own eyes. Or better yet, through the eyes of God.

Now, though, as I sit on my deck writing, I feel something different. I have a path. Watching the sky and the trees, I hear birds chirping and bugs buzzing and a neighbor cutting his tree. It's actually kind of loud, lol. But I'm at peace.

I'm still focusing on the things I can control. I've been teaching Jackson about money, how to save and invest it. And as I sit back and think, I can appreciate the wins I've found in my own life. Last year, for example, my family received a letter informing us that we were behind on our mortgage escrow account due to rising taxes. We had two options: pay it all, or break the amount down to monthly payments, which would have added hundreds of dollars to our monthly mortgage payment. But I did my research, found out how low mortgage rates had dropped, and talked to my mom about refinancing our loan. We went from a 30-year to a 15-year mortgage, and our interest rate went down 1.5 points, saving us thousands.

I also decided that sitting on the sideline didn't sit right with me. In 2022, I was accepted into the Public Education Champion Fellowship. It's a program launched by Education Voters of Pennsylvania. I've already learned so much about state policy matters and how public education is funded, and I'll be educating other families in Penn Hills and beyond.

I now have a clearer idea about what I want from the suburbs too.

The space to be my true self. The opportunity to move past surviving and elevate to thriving. The chance to offer my gifts to this world. The chance to be heard, seen, and acknowledged as Bethany Smith. I want to play my part in showing what's really going on in places like Penn Hills, from my angle.

There are plenty of Black families who migrated here to find comfort and contentment. A lot of white folks still don't care for our presence. But we are here, buying homes and paying taxes and getting involved with politics, the school board, sports, and business.

We want to build good lives for ourselves. We want to raise our children in safe environments. We want to have them in schools where they are being taught and governed by folks who have their best interests at heart. We want the same deal that the suburbs gave white families like Ben's.

This time, though, we want it to last.

A NOTE ON SOURCING

I first met Nika Robinson at the Panera Bread in Lawrenceville, Georgia. She was one of six mothers who responded to a call from Marlyn Tillman of Gwinnett SToPP, an advocacy organization focused on ending the school-to-prison pipeline. One of the moms told me her eight-year-old Black son had been disciplined after getting jumped by three classmates. Another said her autistic thirteen-year-old, also Black, twice tried to commit suicide after being bullied at school. A third mom, who was Mexican American, said she didn't trust the administrators at her children's school not to report immigrant families for deportation. But there was something about the way Nika shared her experiences—her comfort acknowledging her own complicity, her determination to remain centered amid constant uncertainty—that I especially connected with.

Over the next three years, I would go on to interview her roughly twenty times. I also interviewed her husband and oldest son several times each; her in-laws; several family friends; Tillman; the chairpersons of the local Democratic and Republican parties; six current and former members of the Gwinnett school board; numerous students, teachers, administrators, and PTA leaders in the county; several professors and historians; two local journalists; the son of an influential former county commissioner; one of Nika's old college professors; a member of her doctoral cohort at the University of Georgia; and one of her husband's high school teachers. I also hung out with the Robinsons as they did things like prepare a Sunday dinner and coach football practice; observed multiple days of classes (both in-person and remotely) at the school Nika's oldest son attended; reviewed discipline reports, reams of data, and hundreds of documents obtained via open-records requests; and spent dozens of hours at the Gwinnett Historical Society and the National Archives at Atlanta.

I followed a similar process in getting to know the four other featured families, whom I met through a real estate agent, a network of parent activists, a cold call, and the staff at a local elementary school. Because they are all everyday people who were extraordinarily generous in sharing their experiences and perspectives, even when doing so was painful, unflattering, or involved sensitive material, I elected to use pseudonyms to protect their privacy. In a few instances, I also obscured or omitted details that risked putting someone in harm's way.

In tracing these families' journeys, I was also interested in how they made sense of incidents that occurred before we met. As a result, I often had to rely on the kind of memories that are malleable and sometimes shaky. Where possible, I took steps to corroborate, contextualize, and occasionally challenge recollections of events I didn't personally observe. That process was sometimes made difficult by public-school employees bound by privacy laws and their own reluctance to talk. I compensated by relying on documents, digital records such as emails and text messages, contemporaneous accounts shared with friends and family, photos and videos, recordings of public proceedings, and social media.

One example comes in Part II, when Nika describes her interactions with an assistant principal at Jones Middle School. Both an independent fact-checker and I attempted multiple times to talk with the assistant principal, other Jones staff, and administrators from the Gwinnett County Public Schools. Because those individuals all declined to participate, I was left to craft the scene largely on the basis of Nika's account, documents she provided, electronic records I obtained via records requests, and the recollections of family members and friends with whom Nika discussed the events as they happened. Because this process was imperfect, I've used both the text and endnotes to provide background on how such scenes were constructed.

I also used a handful of composite scenes, condensing multiple conversations or an incident that unfolded across multiple points in time into a single event to make the text more readable. In a few instances, composite scenes also reflect my efforts to retrace someone's steps during an event I did not directly witness. These examples are indicated in the endnotes.

In addition to personal stories, this book tells the histories of several communities and school systems. These accounts are drawn largely from interviews; archival materials and primary source documents; books and other historical accounts; newspaper and magazine stories; academic journal articles and dissertations; and various online materials. My use of these sources was reviewed by an independent fact-checker. Details can be found in the endnotes.

Last, this book includes a wealth of data, including several advanced analyses conducted at my request by school district staff, researchers whom I paid, and outside partners. The central office staff at Compton Unified School District were exceedingly gracious in providing student performance data far more granular than was available in public reports. Magdalena Bennett of the University of Texas at Austin conducted a brilliant analysis estimating the federal tax subsidies given to homeowners in a particular school district's attendance zone. Andre Perry, Jonathan Rothwell, and David Harshbarger of the Brookings Institution generously took their national research on the devaluation of homes in majority-Black neighborhoods and customized it to Penn Hills. And the incredible staff of the Ed-Week Research Center worked with me and Erica Frankenberg of Penn State University to update Frankenberg's groundbreaking 2012 analysis of the shifting demographics of suburban schools.

All told, this book involved nearly four years of reporting and research, writing and revision. My hope is that the result will not only explain the unraveling now at hand, but help us find a better path forward.

ACKNOWLEDGMENTS

To my parents, who reordered their entire lives around my future, starting before I had a name, thank you.

Thank you to the Adesina, Becker, Hernandez, Robinson, and Smith families, for sharing your lives and allowing this project to grow.

Thanks also to the leadership and staff of Compton Unified School District, Evanston/Skokie School District 65, Gwinnett County Public Schools, Lovejoy Independent School District, and Penn Hills School District, for returning (most of) my calls and doing the most important work in America.

Research on this book began with a Spencer Education Journalism Fellowship. Thank you to Daniel Alarcón, Samuel Freedman, LynNell Hancock, Dale Maharidge, and the Columbia University J-School for granting me the opportunity to become someone new.

To the Carnegie Mellon University Archives, the Gerth Archives & Special Collections at California State University Dominguez Hills, the Gwinnett Historical Society, the National Archives at Atlanta, the Northwestern University Archives, the Penn Hills Library, the Shorefront Legacy Center, and the Special Collections Libraries at the University of Georgia, thank you for building time machines and allowing me on board.

Thanks to the scholars and researchers whose brilliance lit my way. Special shout-outs to Linn Posey-Maddox, for her kindness when I knew nothing; to R. L'Heureux Lewis-McCoy, who helped put me on the right path, despite his Mets fandom; to Mary Barr, Albert M. Camarillo, Morris (Dino) Robinson, Jr., and Emily E. Straus, for the histories they documented; to Magdalena Bennett, Xinchun Chen, Erica Frankenberg, Yukiko Furuya, David Harshbarger, Alex Harwin, Andre Perry, and Jonathan Rothwell, for the original analyses that appear in this book; and to Alexandra Murphy, who pushed me to see the hope in my hometown, a gift for which I'll forever be grateful.

My gratitude extends also to the legion of journalists upon whose work, expertise, and encouragement I leaned, especially Eva-Marie Ayala, Howard Blume, Elliot Brack, Arlinda Smith Broady, Kevin Bushweller, Kavitha Cardoza, Eleanor Chute, Michael DiVittorio, Tyler Estep, Larry and Mary Gavin, Erica L. Green, Emily Hanford, Nikole Hannah-Jones, Samantha Hernandez, Linda Jacobson, Anya Kamenetz, Alia Malik, Casey Parks, David Pendered, Emily Richmond, Ty Tagami, Andrew Ujifusa, Paula Reed Ward, Teresa Watanabe, and Madeline Will. A special thanks to the bygone reporters, editors, and publishers of the *Atlanta Daily World*, the *Baltimore Afro-American*, the *California Eagle*, the *Cleveland Call and Post*, the *Los Angeles Sentinel*, and the *Pittsburgh Courier* and *New Pittsburgh Courier* for their talent and courage. Thank you to *Education Week*, where I learned to see America's schools in all their vast messiness and possibility, and to Dale Mezzacappa and Paul Socolar, from whom I learned how to know a place deeply.

Which brings me to Philadelphia. Thank you to my adopted home for teaching me to listen, to the world and to myself, during those wonder-filled days inside Sheppard Elementary and Ben Franklin High, outside 440 amid the shouting thousands, riding the 23 as SEPTA comedians rehearsed their routines over cries of *back door*, while working all those theater rushes at the Warsaw Café, all the mornings at the Melrose and B&B spent reading the *Daily News* back to front, reading the scoops Kristen Graham beat me to, reading the *Notebook* comments longer than my articles, reading Keith Pompey tweets and Ursula Rucker haikus, reading Buzz Bissinger and Steve Lopez and John Edgar Wideman, Lorene Cary, that Tara Murphy piece about Zoe Stauss's mattress flip photo that still haunts me, carrying whole armfuls of gold from Bookhaven and The Book Trader, Giovanni's Room and Uncle

Bobbie's, Harriett's and Wooden Shoe, all the treasure I collected from Spider, from Philly AIDS Thrift, from places too secret to share, bathing in the delirium of Maureece Rice crossing up LeBron at the Palestra, AI dropping 54 on Toronto, Sam Hinkie and his orchard, Joel THE PROCESS Embiid in my best Matty Cord, Harry and Whitey, Franzke and L.A., thank you to the complete canon of Eagles fans whose Action News clips went viral, Unlike Agholor and Big Dick Nick and Jeff Garcia Is Our Baby, Baby, learning to listen from Springsteen at the Spectrum, Hall & Oates at the Mann, Jilly at The Met, the Back to Basics Band at Silk City, from Black Thought freestyles, Kurt Vile mumbles, The Bridge on WRTI, school closings on KYW, Angry Al on WIP, "True Honey Buns" and "Dreams and Nightmares" on repeat as I wandered these streets, thank you to my First Person family, to Iris and her old squad at the Wayne Avenue Wendy's, to my neighbor Al, to my dads on the group chat, to the incredible family I married into, thanks to the shit talkers at 52nd and Parkside and to Bike Life Rex and Hey Pretty Pretty, all the people who never stop showing up, this entire city a glorious hoagiemouth choir, an orchestra of broken instruments, acres of diamonds determined to glisten and shine, never brighter than in the eyes of Michelle Schmitt, keeper of joy, who folded herself and this place around me like a map, impressing upon me the latitude and longitude of belonging, which is why any love letter I write to Philadelphia is also a love letter to her.

Thank you to my children, the sweetest and funniest songs I've heard. May there never be an April Fool's Day I don't get you good.

Thanks also to Aunt Peg, for seeing, naming, and believing in things that others don't.

A special thanks to everyone who contributed directly to this book. To Maya Riser-Kositsky and Hannah Murphy Winter, researchers and fact-checkers extraordinaire, thank you; I can sleep again. To Alex Brady, Daarel Burnette II, Sekou Campbell, Sonya Douglass, Luceth Escandell, Kristen Forbriger, Daniela Gerson, Mireille Harper, Glen Herold, Colin Hogan, Decoteau J. Irby, Gerry Krieg, Fabiola Perez Lopez, John McMurtrie, Beatrice Moyers, Katy O'Donnell, Lori Shorr, Renee Simms, and Steven Thrasher, thank you for getting me through my most doubt-filled days.

Thank you to Bethany Smith for being a real one.

From the part of me that used to imagine holding a book of my own, thank you to the entire team at Penguin Press, especially Mia Council and Scott Moyers, whose faith, patience, and vigor with editorial machetes allowed what's good in these pages to find the light of day.

And finally, thank you to my agent, Tanya McKinnon, who was the first to see what this book could be, and who demanded that I transform myself into a person who could write it, because she somehow saw the pieces of my heart I'd been protecting for so long. Any author out there who wants to dream a better dream, for yourself and for America, and don't have to worry about the executive producer trying to be all in the videos, come to McKinnon Literary.

NOTES

PREFACE

3 **"In the suburb":** Lewis Mumford, *The City in History: Its Origins, Its Transformations, and Its Prospects* (San Diego: Harcourt, Brace & Co., 1961), 494.

4 **a flood of devastating headlines:** Mary Niederberger, "State Auditor General Set to Examine Penn Hills Schools," *Pittsburgh Post-Gazette*, August 21, 2015, https://www.post-gazette.com/news/education/2015/08/21/State-audit-planned-for-financially-strapped-Penn-Hills-School-District/stories/201508210241.

4 **$172 million debt:** Sarah Schneider, "Penn Hills Residents Raise Concerns for Community as District Faces $172 Million Debt," WESA, February 28, 2019, https://www.wesa.fm/education/2019-02-28/penn-hills-residents-raise-concerns-for-community-as-district-faces-172-million-debt.

4 **services slashed, programs eliminated:** Daniel J. Matsook, "Financial Recovery Plan, Penn Hills School District, Allegheny County, Pennsylvania," May 20, 2019, 40, 46, https://resources.finalsite.net/images/v1687114682/phsdk12paus/z63yqhg7pip1hltekmjz/FinalPHSDFinancialRecoveryPlan52019.pdf.

4 **Home values stagnated:** U.S. Census Bureau, "Decennial Census Tables 1950–2000. American Community Survey Tables 2006–2010; 2012–2016; 2013–2017; 2016–2020 (5-Year Estimates). Prepared by Social Explorer" (accessed August 11, 2020).

4 **Property taxes skyrocketed:** Matsook, "Financial Recovery Plan, Penn Hills School District," 17.

4 **he'd ever seen:** Natasha Lindstrom, "Penn Hills School District Is in 'the Worst Financial Shape' in Pennsylvania, Auditor General Says," Trib Live, February 28, 2019, https://triblive.com/local/pittsburgh-allegheny/penn-hills-school-district-is-in-the-worst-financial-shape-in-pennsylvania-auditor-general-says/.

4 **"decades to come":** "Report One," "In Re: The 2017 Allegheny County Investigating Grand Jury: Case A," CP-02-MD-6182-2016, 4.

4 **63 percent Black:** All figures related to public school enrollments and racial/ethnic composition are drawn from the U.S. Department of Education, National Center for Education Statistics, Common Core of Data (CCD), unless otherwise noted.

4 **"good" public schools:** See, e.g., Raj Chetty, Nathaniel Hendren, and Lawrence Katz, "The Effects of Exposure to Better Neighborhoods on Children: New Evidence from the Moving to Opportunity Project," *American Economic Review* 106, no. 4 (2016), https://scholar.harvard.edu/files/hendren/files/mto_paper.pdf.

5 **a Ponzi scheme:** Special thanks to Charles Marohn, whose work and writing with the nonprofit advocacy group Strong Towns helped shape my understanding of suburban development and decline.

6 **"needed not to know":** Charles Mills, "White Ignorance," in *Race and Epistemologies of Ignorance*, eds. Shannon Sullivan and Nancy Tuana (Albany: State University of New York Press, 2007), 35. Eva Boodman's dissertation, "White Ignorance and Complicit Responsibility" (PhD diss., Stony Brook

University, 2017), which synthesizes decades of research and theory, also helped shape my understanding of white racial ignorance/denial and its implications.

6 **fled to suburbia:** See Douglas S. Massey and Nancy A. Denton, *American Apartheid: Segregation and the Making of the Underclass* (Cambridge, MA: Harvard University Press, 2003), 68, 71. By 1980, Massey and Denton found, the suburbs outside Atlanta were less than 15 percent Black, the suburbs outside Chicago were less than 6 percent Black, and the suburbs outside Dallas and Pittsburgh were barely 4 percent Black.

6 **to inherit money:** Richard Rothstein, *The Color of Law: A Forgotten History of How Our Government Segregated America* (New York: Liveright Publishing, 2018), 185–86.

6 **"has become permanent":** Rothstein, *The Color of Law*, 183.

7 **of youthful diversity:** William H. Frey, *Diversity Explosion: How New Racial Demographics Are Remaking America* (Washington, D.C.: Brookings Institution Press, 2018). For a deeper examination of the changing demographics of American suburbia, Frey's ongoing work is essential.

7 **three decades later:** William H. Frey, "Today's Suburbs Are Symbolic of America's Rising Diversity: A 2020 Census Portrait," Brookings Institution, June 15, 2022, https://www .brookings.edu/research/todays-suburbs-are -symbolic-of-americas-rising-diversity-a-2020 -census-portrait/.

7 **already a minority:** As of 2017–18, white children accounted for 48 percent of students in the suburbs of the nation's twenty-five largest metropolitan areas, according to a study of enrollment trends in roughly thirty thousand public schools conducted by Alex Harwin, Xinchun Chen, and Yukiko Furuya of the EdWeek Research Center. Their analysis updated the findings of Penn State University professor Erika Frankenberg, as published in the seminal 2012 book *The Resegregation of Suburban Schools*. For a full discussion, see: Benjamin Herold, "Suburban Public Schools Are Now Majority-Nonwhite. The Backlash Has Already Begun," *Education Week*, March 17, 2021, https://www.edweek.org/leadership /suburban-public-schools-are-now-majority -nonwhite-the-backlash-has-already-begun /2021/03.

7 **middle class kept disappearing:** Rakesh Kochhar and Stella Sechopoulos, "How the American Middle Class Has Changed in the Past Five Decades," Pew Research Center, April 20, 2022, https://www.pewresearch.org /fact-tank/2022/04/20/how-the-american -middle-class-has-changed-in-the-past-five -decades/.

7 **Home prices soared:** Jenny Schuetz, "Cost, Crowding, or Commuting? Housing Stress on the Middle Class," Brookings Institution, May 7, 2019, https://www.brookings.edu/research /cost-crowding-or-commuting-housing-stress -on-the-middle-class/.

7 **Water supplies dwindled:** Jack Healy, "Skipped Showers, Paper Plates: An Arizona Suburb's Water Is Cut Off," *New York Times*, January 16, 2023, https://www.nytimes.com /2023/01/16/us/arizona-water-rio-verde -scottsdale.html.

7 **Upper-middle-income families:** Richard V. Reeves, *Dream Hoarders: How the American Upper Middle Class Is Leaving Everyone Else in the Dust, Why That Is a Problem, and What to Do About It* (Washington, D.C.: Brookings Institution Press, 2018).

7 **than they'd enjoyed:** Kim Parker, Rich Morin, and Juliana Menasce Horowitz, "Looking to the Future, Public Sees an America in Decline on Many Fronts," Pew Research Center, March 21, 2019, https://www.pewresearch.org/social -trends/2019/03/21/public-sees-an-america -in-decline-on-many-fronts/.

8 **suburbs of Atlanta:** In Georgia, I focus on Gwinnett County as opposed to an individual municipality because Gwinnett County Public Schools is a countywide school system.

10 **Rather than punish me:** Ms. Bauman is the actual name of my third-grade teacher and is used here because she is no longer in the classroom. Unless otherwise noted, all other K–12 teachers described in this book are identified via pseudonyms in order to protect the anonymity of the children in their classrooms and to allow for unfiltered portraits.

10 **$27,000 in cash:** To protect the privacy of involved parties, sale prices, square footage, and related descriptions of the homes described in this book are drawn from Zillow.com but not cited, unless otherwise noted.

11 **poverty is rising:** Kim Parker, Juliana Menasce Horowitz, Anna Brown, Richard Fry, D'Vera Cohn, and Ruth Igielnik, "1. Demographic and Economic Trends in Urban, Suburban and Rural Communities," Pew Research Center, May 22, 2018, https://www.pewresearch.org /social-trends/2018/05/22/demographic-and -economic-trends-in-urban-suburban-and -rural-communities/.

12 **"let America be America":** Langston Hughes, "Let America Be America Again," *Esquire*, July 1, 1936, 92, https://classic.esquire.com/article /1936/7/1/let-america-be-america-again.

INTRODUCTION

15 **end-of-summer consignment sale:** The events and internal monologues described in this chapter are drawn from interviews with Nika Robinson and her family; subsequent field

reporting in which I retraced parts of Nika's day; and supporting documentation such as disciplinary reports, online photos and videos, and materials from the Georgia Department of Education. Officials from Mill Creek High and the Gwinnett County Public Schools declined multiple requests for comment.

17 **assault and battery:** Because officials from the Gwinnett County Public Schools declined to comment on the district's disciplinary policies, descriptions are drawn from interviews with former GCPS employees, advocates with experience navigating the district's discipline system, and families, plus documents including student handbooks and codes of conduct. See here, e.g., 2017–18 "Student/Parent Handbook Middle/High School," Gwinnett County Public Schools, 16–17, provided by Gwinnett County Public Schools in response to a records request, in the author's possession.

18 **reading and math:** Georgia Department of Education, 2019 College and Career Ready Performance Index (CCRPI), Gwinnett County District Mill Creek High School, http://ccrpi .gadoe.org/Reports/Views/Shared/_Layout.html.

18 **putting him ahead:** "Georgia Mathematics Graduation Requirement Guidance," Georgia Department of Education, June 2020, https:// www.gadoe.org/Curriculum-Instruction-and -Assessment/Curriculum-and-Instruction /Documents/Mathematics/GA-HS-Graduation -Requirement-Mathematics-Guidance.pdf.

20 **country's suburbs grew:** Attempts to compare the number of U.S. suburbanites in 1950 and 2020 are complicated by changes in the ways "suburbs" are defined. The rough figures presented here are drawn from two sources: S. Taylor Jarnagin, "Regional and Global Patterns of Population, Land Use, and Land Cover Change: An Overview of Stressors and Impacts," *GIScience & Remote Sensing* (2004): 207–27; and Kim Parker, Juliana Menasce Horowitz, Anna Brown, Richard Fry, D'Vera Cohn, and Ruth Igielnik, "1. Demographic and Economic Trends in Urban, Suburban and Rural Communities," Pew Research Center, May 22, 2018, https://www.pewresearch.org /social-trends/2018/05/22/demographic-and -economic-trends-in-urban-suburban-and -rural-communities/.

20 **remained deeply invested:** Polling by Gallup in 2018 found that 31 percent of Americans expressed a preference to live in the suburbs. See Frank Newport, "Americans Big on Idea of Living in the Country," Gallup, December 7, 2018, https://news.gallup.com/poll/245249 /americans-big-idea-living-country.aspx.

20 **work of scholars:** See, e.g., Amanda E. Lewis and John B. Diamond, *Despite the Best Intentions: How Racial Inequality Thrives in Good Schools* (Oxford: Oxford University Press, 2015); Linn Posey-Maddox, "Challenging

the Dichotomy Between 'Urban' and 'Suburban' in Educational Discourse and Policy," *The Educational Forum* 80, no. 2 (2016), http:// dx.doi.org/10.1080/00131725.2016.1135377; Sonya Douglass, *Learning in a Burning House: Educational Inequality, Ideology, and (Dis) Integration* (New York: Teachers College Press, 2011); Decoteau J. Irby, *Stuck Improving: Racial Equity and School Leadership* (Cambridge, MA: Harvard Education Press, 2021); and R. L'Heureux Lewis-McCoy, *Inequality in the Promised Land: Race, Resources, and Suburban Schooling* (Stanford, CA: Stanford University Press, 2014). Sonya Douglass previously published under the name Sonya Douglass-Horsford.

20 **suburbia's Generation Z:** Richard Fry and Kim Parker, "Early Benchmarks Show 'Post-Millennials' on Track to Be Most Diverse, Best -Educated Generation Yet," Pew Research Center, November 15, 2018, https://www .pewresearch.org/social-trends/2018/11/15 /early-benchmarks-show-post-millennials -on-track-to-be-most-diverse-best-educated -generation-yet/.

20 **90 percent white:** All figures relating to national, regional, and local demographic patterns are drawn from the U.S. Census Bureau, unless otherwise noted.

21 **$2.3 billion bureaucracy:** Gwinnett County Public Schools, FY2020 Public Budget Document July 1, 2019–June 30, 2020.

21 **dwindling tax base:** April Hunt, "One County Less Upbeat Up North," *Atlanta Journal-Constitution*, December 23, 2011, A1, A4.

21 **white population began to decline:** Special thanks to Michelle Schmitt for this custom analysis of changes in the racial composition of Plano between 2000 and 2020.

21 **with rising costs:** City of Plano, Comprehensive Plan: Public Services and Facilities Element (June 2006), https://planocompplan.org/259/The-Plan.

21 **prestigious national award:** "2017 Daniel Burnham Award for a Comprehensive Plan," American Planning Association, https://www .planning.org/awards/2017/planotomorrow/.

21 **"trying to turn Plano":** Peter Simek, "Inside the Legal Battle for Plano's Future," *D Magazine*, November 28, 2018, https://www.dmagazine .com/publications/d-magazine/2018/december /inside-the-legal-battle-for-planos-future/.

21 **"Keep Plano Suburban":** Emma Platoff, "Why Did the Texas AG Get into—and Then out of—a Controversial Lawsuit in His Home County?," *Texas Tribune*, December 4, 2018, https://www .texastribune.org/2018/12/04/texas-attorney -general-ken-paxton-reverses-course-plano -lawsuit/.

23 **passed the state tests:** Texas Education Agency, "2019 STAAR Performance Data Table LOVEJOY ISD (043919)," https://rptsvrl.tea .texas.gov/cgi/sas/broker?_service=marykay&

_debug=0&single=N&batch=N&app=
PUBLIC&ptype=H&_program=perfrept
.perfmast.sas&level=district&search=distnum
&namenum=043919&prgopt=2019/acct
/domain1a.sas.

23 **named Stacey Dillon:** All central office
administrators representing their K–12 school
districts before the public are identified by their
actual names, unless otherwise noted.

24 **met the Beckers:** This scene is a composite
drawn from interviews in which Susan and Jim
Becker described multiple visits to Lucas and
Lovejoy ISD, plus a similar tour of Lovejoy ISD
schools that I took on a separate date.

24 **Advanced Placement courses:** "Welcome to
Advanced Academics," Lovejoy Independent
School District, https://www.lovejoyisd.net
/apps/pages/index.jsp?uREC_ID=385829&
type=d&pREC_ID=877319.

25 **were considered poor:** Texas Education
Agency, "2018–19 School Report Card
WILLIAMS H S (043910003)," https://rptsvr1
.tea.texas.gov/cgi/sas/broker?_service=
marykay&_program=perfrept.perfmast.sas
&cyr=2019&level=campus.&search=district
&namenum=plano&district=043910&campus
=043910003&_debug=0&prgopt=2019%2Fsrc%
2Fsrc.sas. In America's K–12 schools, eligibility
for a free or reduced-price lunch under United
States Department of Agriculture guidelines is
frequently used as a proxy for poverty. During the
2019–20 school year, the criteria for eligibility
for a free lunch was living in a household with
an income below 130 percent of the federal
poverty line or receiving SNAP or TANF
benefits. The criteria for eligibility for a
reduced-price lunch was living in a household
with income between 130 and 185 percent of the
federal poverty line.

25 **Fewer than 4 percent:** Texas Education Agency,
"2018–19 School Report Card LOVEJOY H S
(043919001)," https://rptsvr1.tea.texas.gov/cgi
/sas/broker?_service=marykay&_program
=perfrept.perfmast.sas&cyr=2019&level=
campus.&search=district&namenum=lovejoy
&district=043919&campus=043919001&
_debug=0&prgopt=2019%2Fsrc%2Fsrc.sas.

25 **served parts of:** Population and Survey
Analysts, "2019–20 Demographic Update
Lovejoy Independent School District," January
2020, http://files.pasademographics.com:800
/Reports/2020/Demographic%20Update%20
-%20Lovejoy%20-%20Jan%202020.pdf.

25 **taken numerous steps:** See, e.g., "Zoning Map
2018," Lucas Official City Website, June 4, 2018,
https://www.lucastexas.us/documents/zoning
-map-2018/, and "City of Lucas Code of
Ordinances," May 19, 2022, https://z2codes
.franklinlegal.net/franklin/Z2Browser2.html
?showset=lucasset for examples of the relevant
zoning code provisions. Many suburbs embrace
one or two of these provisions, but the area

served by Lovejoy ISD is more typical of
suburbs from previous eras because of how the
various elements of local zoning codes interact
to foster socioeconomic exclusivity. The mayors
and city managers of both Fairview and Lucas
were also instrumental in helping me
understand the nature and practical impact of
these provisions.

25 **17-square-mile attendance zone:** "About LISD,"
Lovejoy Independent School District, https://
www.lovejoyisd.net/apps/pages/index.jsp?uREC
_ID=385786&type=d&pREC_ID=877229.

25 **in an apartment:** Special thanks to Edward G.
Goetz, Anthony Damiano, and Rashad A.
Williams, whose paper, "Racially Concentrated
Areas of Affluence: A Preliminary
Investigation," *Cityscape: A Journal of Policy
Development and Research* 21, no. 1 (2019),
makes a compelling argument for "equal
attention to the other end of the segregation
continuum, affluent White neighborhoods."

26 **as much as $50,000 more:** Figures on Lovejoy
ISD real estate market from Jeff Reinhard (real
estate agent), in conversation with the author,
July 2019.

26 **white families with the same income:** Special
thanks to Magdalena Bennett for her custom
analysis of racial disparities in mortgage
application and approval rates in the area
served by Lovejoy ISD, "Federal Subsidies,
Structural Racism, and the Housing Market in
an Affluent Suburban Dallas Community"
(memo, in the author's possession, 2019).

26 **more than $500,000:** "Financials," Foundation
for Lovejoy Schools, https://www.foundation
forlovejoyschools.org/financials-1.

26 **children with special needs:** "Invest in
Excellence Approved Grants, 2019–2020"
(spreadsheet, provided by Lovejoy ISD), 3;
Vikki Deerman (executive director of the
Foundation for Lovejoy Schools) in
conversation with the author, August 2019.

26 **$1,500 per household:** Bennett, "Federal
Subsidies, Structural Racism, and the Housing
Market."

26 **profit was tax-free:** "Topic No. 701 Sale of
Your Home," IRS, https://docs.google.com
/spreadsheets/d/1YZkFLbo_Qwfc_Hz6bPe
ZUqENKMZMgQ9NlzxY9ssXUWg/edit
#gid=2062823537.

27 **last white family leaving:** Sanford D. Horwitt,
*Let Them Call Me Rebel: Saul Alinsky, His Life and
Legacy* (New York: Vintage Books, 1992), 314.

28 **America's suburbs, however, vary:** Special
thanks to Penn State University professor Erica
Frankenberg, whose typology of suburban
school systems, found in Erica Frankenberg and
Gary Orfield, *The Resegregation of Suburban
Schools: A Hidden Crisis in American Education*
(Cambridge, MA: Harvard Education Press,
2012), 38–39, heavily influenced the locations I
selected to feature in this book.

28 **lovingly called "Heavenston":** Mary Barr, *Friends Disappear: The Battle for Racial Equality in Evanston* (Chicago: University of Chicago Press, 2014), 27.

28 **for 150 years:** Morris (Dino) Robinson, Jr., and Jenny Thompson, "Evanston Policies and Practices Directly Affecting the African American Community," November 2021, https://www.cityofevanston.org/home /showpublisheddocument/67191 /637715545144570000.

29 **several decades earlier:** Larry Gavin, "The Role of Foster School in the Implementation of School District 65's Desegregation Plan in 1967 and Its Closing in 1979," *Evanston RoundTable*, March 21, 2019, https://evanstonroundtable .com/2019/03/21/the-role-of-foster-school-in -the-implementation-of-school-district-65s -desegregation-plan-in-1967-and-its-closing -in-1979/.

29 **were getting under way:** Descriptions and quotations from the meeting described here derive from District 65, "School Board Meeting 12-17-2018," YouTube video, December 17, 2018, https://www.youtube.com/watch?v =BxkrcbBk4kU.

29 **recently been elevated:** Syd Stone, "District 65 Board Elects New President, Vice President," *Daily Northwestern*, May 2, 2017, https:// dailynorthwestern.com/2017/05/02/city /district-65-board-elects-new-president-vice -president/.

29 **how to desegregate:** Gregory C. Coffin, "How Evanston, Illinois Integrated All of Its Schools," paper presented at National Conference on Equal Educational Opportunity in American Cities, Washington, D.C., November 16–18, 1967, https://files.eric.ed.gov /fulltext/ED023740.pdf.

30 **racial equity statement:** "Racial & Educational Equity Statement," Evanston/Skokie School District 65, https://www.district65.net/Page /2395.

30 **racial equity policy:** "Racial and Educational Equity Policy," Evanston/Skokie School District 65.

30 **eighth-grade Algebra classes:** David Wartowski, "Algebra for All Update" (memo to District 65 School Board Policy Committee, in the author's possession, 2018).

31 **"Black Lives Matter":** "February 3–7: Black Lives Matter at School Week of Action," Evanston/Skokie School District 65, January 21, 2020, https://www.district65.net/site/default .aspx?PageType=3&DomainID=4&Module InstanceID=275&ViewID=6446EE88-D30C -497E-9316-3F8874B3E108&RenderLoc=0& FlexDataID=8892&PageID=1.

32 **was Heather Sweeney:** Sweeney and other activists described in this book who founded advocacy organizations and regularly spoke publicly on their behalf are identified by their actual names, unless otherwise noted.

34 **would be gone:** Bill Smith, "Goren Out as D65 Superintendent," Evanston Now, July 14, 2019, https://evanstonnow.com/goren-out-as-d65 -superintendent/.

35 **revenues kept falling:** "Municipality of Penn Hills 2016 Budget," December 31, 2015, https:// pennhillspa.gov/wp-content/uploads/2020/04 /2016Budget.pdf; "Municipality of Penn Hills 2020 Budget," December 30, 2019, https:// pennhillspa.gov/wp-content/uploads/2020/04 /2020-Adopted-Budget.pdf.

35 **infrastructure kept soaring:** "2022–2026 Penn Hills Capital Improvements Program," September 20, 2021, https://pennhillspa.gov /wp-content/uploads/2020/04/FY-Capital -Improvement-Program.pdf.

35 **38 percent Black:** U.S. Census Bureau; American Community Survey, 2018 American Community Survey 5-Year Estimates, Table DP05, generated by Maya Riser-Kositsky, using data.census.gov, https://data.census.gov/cedsci /table?q=Penn%20Hills%20township, %20Pennsylvania&y=2018.

35 **uniformly middle class:** U.S. Census Bureau; American Community Survey, 2010 American Community Survey 5-Year Estimates, Table S0601, generated by Maya Riser-Kositsky, using data.census.gov, https://data.census.gov/cedsci /table?q=Penn%20Hills%20township, %20Pennsylvania&y=2010&tid= ACSST5Y2010.S060; U.S. Census Bureau; American Community Survey, 2018 American Community Survey 5-Year Estimates, Table S0601, generated by Maya Riser-Kositsky, using data.census.gov, https://data.census.gov/cedsci /table?q=Penn%20Hills%20township, %20Pennsylvania&y=2018&tid= ACSST5Y2018.S060.

35 **a major problem:** "Municipality of Penn Hills 2015 Comprehensive Plan," https://pennhillspa .gov/wp-content/uploads/2020/04/2015comp _plan.pdf.

35 **unbuilt and unrepaired:** "2022–2026 Penn Hills Capital Improvements Program, Adopted September 20, 2021," https://pennhillspa.gov /wp-content/uploads/2020/04/FY-Capital -Improvement-Program.pdf.

36 **warmest childhood memories:** Descriptions throughout the book of the neighborhood where Bethany Smith grew up are drawn from interviews with her, local civic and religious leaders, neighborhood plans, church documents, media reports, and research studies.

36 **a new pastor:** "138th Anniversary Harvest Festival Celebration," Grace Memorial Presbyterian Church, November 19, 2006, provided by the Pittsburgh Presbytery.

37 **first charter school:** Deepak Karamcheti, "Urban League Makes History: Opens City's

First Charter School," *New Pittsburgh Courier*, August 26, 1998.

37 **called Bakery Square:** Christine H. O'Toole, "Slumbering Pittsburgh Neighborhood Reawakens," *New York Times*, March 2, 2010, https://www.nytimes.com/2010/03/03/realestate/03pittsburgh.html.

37 **leading rents to soar:** Bob Bauder, "Rising East Liberty Out of Reach for Pittsburgh's Poor," Trib Live, July 27, 2015, https://archive.triblive.com/local/pittsburgh-allegheny/rising-east-liberty-out-of-reach-for-pittsburghs-poor-2/.

37 **more than 40 percent:** "Profile of Change in the City of Pittsburgh," Program in Urban and Regional Analysis, University Center for Social and Urban Research, University of Pittsburgh, January 2020, https://www.ucsur.pitt.edu/files/census/ACS_Pgh_Profile_of_Change_2009 –2013_v_2014–2018.pdf, 45, 56, 94.

38 **in Urban Academy:** This account of the Smiths' experience at Urban Academy is drawn primarily from interviews with Bethany Smith. In a written response to questions, Urban Academy CEO Chase Patterson confirmed the school's history with Job Corps and AmeriCorps, Jackson Smith's enrollment, the occurrence of meetings between Smith and school officials, and Smith's volunteer service at the school. Mr. Patterson also described the meetings, parent communications, and punishments as generally plausible, but declined to confirm or comment upon specific incidents, assessments or diagnoses, or interactions involving individual parents or children.

38 **principal and CEO:** In written responses to questions, Urban Academy CEO Chase Patterson responded "no" when asked if he recalled this exchange.

39 **should work together:** Robert C. Johnston, "On a Mission," *Education Week*, March 28, 2001, https://www.edweek.org/leadership/on-a-mission/2001/03.

40 **the alfalfa fields:** Special thanks to Emily E. Straus, whose book *Death of a Suburban Dream: Race and Schools in Compton, California* (Philadelphia: University of Pennsylvania Press, 2014) served as an invaluable resource and is an essential read on the history of Compton (see p. 16).

40 **uneducated white migrants:** Manuel Pastor, *State of Resistance: What California's Dizzying Descent and Remarkable Resurgence Mean for America's Future* (New York: New Press, 2018).

40 **little as $200 down:** *Herald* classified ads, *Compton Herald American and the Compton Herald*, November 12, 1942, 15.

40 **largest Black-run community:** Dorothy Townsend, "Compton to Elect First Negro Mayor Tuesday," *Los Angeles Times*, June 1, 1969.

40 **real multiracial integration:** Special thanks to Stanford University historian Albert M. Camarillo, whose academic work and personal narrative were instrumental in helping me see Compton more fully. See, e.g., Albert M. Camarillo, "Black and Brown in Compton: Demographic Change, Suburban Decline, and Intergroup Relations in a South Central Los Angeles Community, 1950 to 2000," in *Not Just Black and White: Historical and Contemporary Perspectives on Immigration, Race, and Ethnicity in the United States*, eds. Nancy Foner and George M. Fredrickson (New York: Russell Sage Foundation, 2004), 368.

40 **its public schools:** Joe Mathews, "Compton Schools to Get Control in Steps; Education: Some Board Members Denounce Phased-In Plan, Want State to Relinquish Role at Once," *Los Angeles Times*, September 20, 2000.

41 **was shot at:** Deborah Belgum, "Snubbing the Schools; Compton Officials Who Are Angry with State Takeover of District Hail Defeat of Bond Issue After Urging Voters to Reject," *Los Angeles Times*, April 16, 1998.

41 **a casual suggestion:** Laura E. Gómez, *Manifest Destinies: The Making of the Mexican American Race* (New York: New York University Press, 2018), 146–47.

41 **militarized the border:** Douglas S. Massey and Karen A. Pren, "Origins of the New Latino Underclass," *Race and Social Problems* 4 (2012): 6.

41 **nation's changing identity:** Eric P. Kaufman, *Whiteshift: Populism, Immigration, and the Future of White Majorities* (New York: Abrams Press, 2019), 17.

41 **two-million-plus undocumented residents:** Joseph Hayes and Laura Hill, "Undocumented Immigrants in California," Public Policy Institute of California, March 2017, https://www.ppic.org/publication/undocumented-immigrants-in-california/.

42 **had nearly doubled:** "CAASPP Smarter Balanced 2014–2019 Longitudinal Visualization" (data file, in the author's possession).

42 **nearly thirty points:** "District Wide Historical Date for Grad Rate, A-G Completers & AP Scores * DATA from Calpads, DataQuest & C& C Dept" (data file, in the author's possession).

42 **$350 million construction bond:** Kevin Dayton, "Compton Unified School District Authorized by 3.1% of Its Registered Voters to Borrow $350 Million," FlashReport, November 5, 2015, http://www.flashreport.org/blog/2015/11/05/compton-unified-school-district-authorized-by-3-1-of-its-registered-voters-to-borrow-350-million/.

42 **a state-of-the-art campus:** DLR Group, "New Compton High School," YouTube video, 2:16, December 15, 2016, https://www.youtube.com/watch?v=4KTqiITTxjg.

42 **historic barrio neighborhood:** Alberto M. Camarillo, "Chicano Urban History: A Study of Compton's Barrio, 1936–1970," *Aztlan* 2, no. 2 (1971): 79–106.

43 **bilingual education program:** Frank M. Goodman, "Compton Bilingual Education Plan 1969–1970," Gerth Archives and Special Collections, California State University, Dominguez Hills.

43 **"There are indicators":** Donald Hodes, "Compton Unified School District Racial Imbalance Plan," December 1970, Gerth Archives and Special Collections, California State University, Dominguez Hills.

43 **began systematically excluding:** Camarillo, "Black and Brown in Compton," in *Not Just Black and White*, 368–70.

43 **on Piru Street:** Josh Sides, "Straight into Compton: American Dreams, Urban Nightmares, and the Metamorphosis of a Black Suburb," *American Quarterly* 56, no. 3 (2004): 593, https://www.jstor.org/stable /40068235.

43 **still learning English:** "2018–19 Enrollment by Subgroup Jefferson Elementary Report (19-73437-6012298)," DataQuest, https://data1.cde .ca.gov/dataquest/dqcensus/EnrCharterSub .aspx?cds=19734376012298&agglevel=school &year=2018-19.

43 **well over half:** "Thomas Jefferson Elementary School 2018–2019 School Accountability Report Card," January 2020, https://www .axiomanalytix.com/SARC/_SupportFiles/SAR CIndexPDFs/19734376012298_18-19_1.pdf.

44 **Black-Brown power struggle:** Darryl Fears, "Compton Latinos Still on Outside Looking In," *Los Angeles Times*, April 16, 1998, https://www .latimes.com/archives/la-xpm-1998-apr-16-mn -39881-story.html.

45 **the second volume:** Jacob Hernandez, "Captain Pumkin & Captain Max & the Cruel Dr. Crawbler."

45 **"the Compton turnaround":** "The Turnaround Story at Compton's Schools," *Los Angeles Sentinel*, October 15, 2015, https:// lasentinel.net/the-turnaround-story-at-comp tons-schools.html.

CHAPTER 1:
ONE RING FARTHER OUT

51 **"The shibboleth of newness":** Kenneth T. Jackson, *Crabgrass Frontier: The Suburbanization of America* (New York: Oxford University Press, 1985), 302.

51 **powerful Caddo Nation:** This and other details of the area's pre-twentieth-century history are drawn from Randolph W. Farmer, *From Blackland Prairie to Blacktop: A History of Collin County* (San Antonio, TX: Historical Pub. Network, 2011), unless otherwise noted.

51 **Spanish, then Mexican:** "Our Roots," Collin County, https://www.collincountytx.gov/living /pages/our_roots.aspx.

52 **small agricultural community:** Shirley Schell and Frances B. Wells, "Plano, TX," Texas State Historical Association, 1952, https://www .tshaonline.org/handbook/entries/plano-tx.

53 **the cotton harvest:** This and other details of presuburbanization Plano ISD are drawn from Sherrie S. McLeroy, *A Century of Excellence, Plano Independent School District: An Historical Perspective* (Plano, TX: Plano Futures Foundation, 1999), unless otherwise noted.

53 **Black families lived:** "The Plano Story," in Preservation Plan, November 2018, https:// content.civicplus.com/api/assets/d036db0d -afd2-4e72-b85d-2a1111cc335d?cache=1800.

53 **pushed to locate key plants:** Kevin Michael Kruse, *The New Suburban History* (Chicago: University of Chicago Press, 2007), 63–64.

53 **than thirty-five thousand workers:** Paul J. P. Sandul and M. Scott Sosebee, *Lone Star Suburbs: Life on Texas Metropolitan Frontier* (Norman: University of Oklahoma Press, 2019), 51.

53 **one million people:** For a comprehensive exploration of the forces driving U.S. suburbanization, see Kenneth T. Jackson, *Crabgrass Frontier: The Suburbanization of America* (New York: Oxford University Press, 1985), including discussion of "defense areas" on 232.

53 **created insurance maps:** All descriptions of HOLC insurance maps from Jackson, *Crabgrass Frontier*, unless otherwise noted.

53 **Dallas in 1937:** Alex Macon, "New Maps Show Consequences of Redlining in Dallas," *D Magazine*, August 16, 2017, https://www .dmagazine.com/frontburner/2017/08 /redlining-dallas-maps/.

54 **guarantees to developers:** Richard Rothstein, *The Color of Law: A Forgotten History of How Our Government Segregated America* (New York: Liveright Publishing Corporation, 2018), 64–67.

54 **poured into Dallas:** Andrew Wiese, *Places of Their Own: African American Suburbanization in the Twentieth Century* (Chicago: University of Chicago Press, 2009), 196.

54 **tried to move:** All descriptions of racial violence in Dallas in the 1940s and '50s from Stephen Grant Meyer, *As Long as They Don't Move Next Door: Segregation and Racial Conflict in American Neighborhoods* (Lanham, MD: Rowman & Littlefield, 2001), unless otherwise noted.

54 **from local construction sites:** "Dallas Residents Get 12th Bombing," *Baltimore Afro-American*, May 17, 1941, 2.

54 **razing a Black community:** Zac Crain, "In the Name of Progress: What Dallas Has Taken from the Black Community," *D Magazine*, November 12, 2021, https://www.dmagazine.com /publications/d-magazine/2021/november

/in-the-name-of-progress-what-dallas-has
-taken-from-the-black-community/.

55 **North Central Expressway:** Oscar Slotboom,
"Central Expressway, the Original," in *Dallas-
Fort Worth Freeways, Texas-Sized Ambition*
(self-pub, 2014), 77.

55 **Dallas planning director:** "Marvin Robert
Springer," *Dallas Morning News*, February 3,
2009, https://obits.dallasnews.com/obituaries
/dallasmorningnews/obituary.aspx?n=marvin
-robert-springer&pid=123687157.

55 **advise dozens of suburban communities:**
Margot Kristine Lystra, "Envisioning
Environments: Designs for Urban U.S.
Freeways, 1956–1968" (PhD diss., Cornell
University, 2017), 246.

55 **in August 1963:** This and other details of
Plano's first comprehensive plan are drawn
from Marvin R. Springer, "A Comprehensive
Plan Report City of Plano, Texas," 1963, unless
otherwise noted.

56 **lost 100,000 residents:** Michael Phillips, *White
Metropolis: Race, Ethnicity, and Religion in
Dallas, 1841–2001* (Austin: University of Texas
Press, 2006), 167.

56 **Midwest and the Rust Belt:** Keith Orejel,
"Political Power Keeps Shifting from the
Rust Belt to the Sun Belt. Here's Why,"
Washington Post, May 20, 2021, https://www
.washingtonpost.com/outlook/2021/05/20
/house-map-changes-geographical-pattern
-shaping-american-life-remains/; Associated
Press, "Houston Overtaken by Dallas in U.S.
Metropolitan Census," *New York Times*, July
24, 1987, https://www.nytimes.com/1987/07
/24/us/houston-overtaken-by-dallas-in-us
-metropolitan-census.html.

56 **shot and killed:** Phillips, *White Metropolis*, 164.

56 **prompted a spike:** Edward Herbert Miller,
"Mavericks of the Metroplex: Dallas
Republicans, the Southern Strategy, and the
American Right" (PhD diss., Boston College,
2013), 104–5. Competing interpretations of the
response to *Brown* in Texas abound, with
historians including Edward Miller and
Michael Phillips focusing on the rise of right-
wing extremism after the Court's decision and
others such as Sean P. Cunningham noting that
well over a hundred Texas school districts
voluntarily desegregated by 1957 and that most
of the state's prominent elected officials,
including then U.S. senator Lyndon Johnson
and U.S. Speaker of the House Sam Rayburn,
declined to sign the Southern Manifesto calling
for open defiance of *Brown*.

56 **slow-walking every desegregation:** Phillips,
White Metropolis, 156–58; "Background Info,"
DISD Desegregation Litigation Archives, SMU
Dedman School of Law, accessed March 18,
2023, https://www.smu.edu/Law/Library
/Collections/DISD-Desegregation-Litigation
-Archives/Background-Info.

56 **was gaining traction:** "Background Info," DISD
Desegregation Litigation Archives, https://
www.smu.edu/Law/Library/Collections/DISD
-Desegregation-Litigation-Archives
/Background-Info.

56 **52,000 white children:** Eric Nicholson, "In
Dallas, White Flight Never Ends," *Dallas
Observer*, May 3, 2016, https://www
.dallasobserver.com/news/in-dallas-white
-flight-never-ends-8265092.

56 **told** *D Magazine:* Tracy Curts, "Is White Flight
Ruining the Dallas Schools?," *D Magazine*,
August 1977, https://www.dmagazine.com
/publications/d-magazine/1977/august/is
-white-flight-ruining-the-dallas-schools/.

57 **reached 72,000 people:** "Land Use
Comprehensive Plan City of Plano," 1986, 2-2.

57 **of corporate relocations:** Douglas J. Watson
and Alicia C. Schortgen, "Guiding Change in a
First Ring Suburb: Plano, Texas," in *The
Facilitative Leader in City Hall: Reexamining
the Scope and Contributions*, ed. James H. Svara
(New York: Routledge, 2019), 126.

57 **nearly eighteen thousand acres:** "Land Use
Comprehensive Plan City of Plano," 1986, 2-2.

57 **to nearly $7 billion:** Plano Comprehensive
Plan Education Element, 1986, 8–4.

57 **described as "perfect":** Gregory Curtis, "Behind
the Lines," *Texas Monthly*, January 1982, 5.

57 **emerging racial politics:** This discussion of the
resurgent conservatism in mid-twentieth-
century Sunbelt suburbs draws from arguments
made by historian Kevin Michael Kruse (see,
e.g., *White Flight: Atlanta and the Making of
Modern Conservatism* [Princeton, NJ: Princeton
University Press, 2007]); historian Sean P.
Cunningham (see, e.g., *Cowboy Conservatism*
[Lexington: University Press of Kentucky,
2010]); historian and journalist Rick Perlstein
(see, e.g., *Before the Storm: Barry Goldwater
and the Unmaking of the American Consensus*
[New York: Nation Books, 2001], 76); and
Miller (see "Mavericks of the Metroplex").

57 **who reached millions:** This and subsequent
descriptions of right-wing suburban extremism
in the 1950s and '60s are drawn from Miller,
"Mavericks of the Metroplex," unless otherwise
noted.

58 **hanged for treason:** Donald Janson and
Bernard Eismann, *The Far Right* (New York:
McGraw-Hill, 1963), 113.

58 **more moderate agenda:** Perlstein, *Before the
Storm*, 76.

58 **to racial and ethnic minorities:** See, e.g.,
Matthew Lassiter and Kevin Kruse, "The
Bulldozer Revolution: Suburbs and Southern
History Since World War II," *Journal of
Southern History* 75, no. 3 (August 2009): 691–
706; and Glenn Feldman, *Painting Dixie Red:
When, Where, Why, and How the South Became
Republican* (Gainesville: University Press of
Florida, 2011), 16, 80, for the historical argument

that white suburban interests were central to the Republican Party's "Southern Strategy."

58 **newly ascendant GOP:** See, e.g., Everett Carll Ladd, "The '80s Generation Went Republican," *Christian Science Monitor,* October 13, 1989, https://www.csmonitor.com/1989/1013/elad d13.html.

58 **people and places:** See, e.g., Gillian Brockell, "She Was Stereotyped as 'the Welfare Queen.' The Truth Was More Disturbing, a New Book Says," *Washington Post,* May 21, 2019, https:// www.washingtonpost.com/history/2019/05/21 /she-was-stereotyped-welfare-queen-truth-was -more-disturbing-new-book-says/.

58 **by Satanic graffiti:** Mary Jacobs, Jeff Campbell, and Cheryl Smith, *Hidden History of Plano* (Charleston, SC: History Press, 2020), 111.

58 **rash of teen suicides:** "Number of Teen-Age Suicides Alarms Parents in Texas City," *New York Times,* September 4, 1983, https://www .nytimes.com/1983/09/04/us/number-of-teen -age-suicides-alarms-parents-in-texas-city.html.

58 **soaring divorce rate:** David Gelman, "Teen-Age Suicide in the Sun Belt," *Newsweek,* August 15, 1983.

58 **Young people were copping:** This and other details of Plano's heroin crisis during the 1990s are drawn from Matthew S. Durington, "Discourses of Racialized Moral Panic in a Suburban Community: Teenagers, Heroin and Media in Plano, Texas" (PhD diss., Temple University, 2003), unless otherwise noted.

59 **Nineteen local teens:** Cori Baker, "Addicted: Twenty Years Ago, a Heroin Crisis in Plano Left 19 Young People Dead; the Impact Is Still Felt Today," Collin County, Local Profile, May 11, 2017, https://localprofile.com/2017/05/11 /addicted-twenty-years-ago-a-heroin-crisis-in -plano-left-19-young-people-dead-the-impact -is-still-felt-today/.

59 **survived overdose scares:** T. Trent Gegax, "Heroin High," *Newsweek,* January 31, 1999, https://www.newsweek.com/heroin-high-165086.

59 **told her audience:** As quoted in Durington, "Discourses of Racialized Moral Panic in a Suburban Community: Teenagers," 141.

59 **yielded twenty-nine indictments:** Baker, "Addicted: Twenty Years Ago, a Heroin Crisis in Plano Left 19 Young People Dead."

60 **Enron was exposed:** Jack Beatty, "The Enron Ponzi Scheme," *The Atlantic,* March 2002, https://www.theatlantic.com/magazine/archive /2002/03/the-enron-ponzi-scheme/303156/.

60 **hide massive losses:** Troy Segal, "Enron Scandal: The Fall of a Wall Street Darling," Investopedia, May 4, 2020, https://www.investopedia.com /updates/enron-scandal-summary/.

60 **now eerily vacant:** David Barboza, "Enron's Collapse: The Office; Morale and Occupancy Are Low at the Headquarters in Houston," *New York Times,* January 24, 2002, https://www .nytimes.com/2002/01/24/business

/enron-s-collapse-office-morale-occupancy -are-low-headquarters-houston.html.

62 **than $60 billion:** Allan Sloan, "The Worst Thing about Enron: Checks and Balances Failed," *Washington Post,* January 15, 2002, https://www.washingtonpost.com/archive /business/2002/01/15/the-worst-thing-about -enron-checks-and-balances-failed/0d39ec64 -c100-449c-805a-fc24207520e4/.

62 **forty-five hundred lower-level workers:** Chris Woodyard and Martin Kasindorf, "Troubles Ripple Through Houston; From Residents to Local Businesses, Enron Affects Many," *USA Today,* January 21, 2002.

62 **stock also evaporated:** Rick Bragg, "Enron's Collapse: Workers Feel Pain of Layoffs and Added Sting of Betrayal," *New York Times,* January 20, 2002, https://www.nytimes.com/2002/01/20/us /enron-s-collapse-workers-workers-feel-pain -layoffs-added-sting-betrayal.html.

62 **1970s and '80s:** "City of Plano Comprehensive Plan Housing Element," March 2005, 5–8.

63 **Ninety percent of the school's students:** "Selected AEIS Campus Data, a Multi-Year History for 2003–2011: Daffron EL," Texas Education Agency, https://rptsvr1.tea.texas.gov /perfreport/aeis/hist/district.srch.html.

63 **department was concluding:** "Plano at Maturity, the Biggerstaff Report," October 2003, https://content.civicplus.com/api/assets /1cfe0b75-8d8e-4877-9d5e-ad00223666f5? cache=1800. Special thanks to Plano planning director Christina D. Day for helping me understand and contextualize the history of the city's comprehensive planning efforts.

64 **a new threat:** "Future Dimensions, Envisioning Plano's Future," Fall 2008, 5.

64 **typical household income:** Theodore Kim, "Plano Leaders Run from Census Bureau's 'Wealthiest' Designation," *McClatchy—Tribune Business News,* September 9, 2008.

64 **school construction bond:** "Plano ISD Facilities and Technology Task Force: Executive Summary Recommendations, 2004 Proposed Bond Program," 2004, https://www.pisd.edu /cms/lib/TX02215173/Centricity/domain/293 /2004%20bond%20pgm/bond.executive .summary.4.20.04.pdf.

64 **even had homes:** Terry Smith, "Celebrities Who Live in Plano," Plano Homes & Land, https:// planohomesandland.com/celebrities-who-live -in-plano/.

66 **One in four:** "Texas Academic Performance Report DAFFRON EL 2012–13 Campus Performance," https://rptsvr1.tea.texas.gov /perfreport/tapr/2013/static/campus /c043910124.pdf.

66 **bilingual Spanish program:** Plano ISD Curriculum and Student Records Departments records request response.

67 **major renovation project:** "Construction Projects to Update Older Plano ISD Buildings,

Other Facility Needs," *Dallas Morning News*, August 22, 2014, https://www.dallasnews.com /news/2014/08/22/construction-projects-to -update-older-plano-isd-buildings-other -facility-needs/.

CHAPTER 2: CHASING THE DREAM

69 **"Many middle-class blacks":** R. L'Heureux Lewis-McCoy, *Inequality in the Promised Land: Race, Resources, and Suburban Schooling* (Stanford, CA: Stanford University Press, 2014), x.

69 **the "velvet steamroller":** Michael Winerip, "School Integration in Buffalo Is Hailed as a Model for U.S.," *New York Times*, May 13, 1985, A1.

69 **60 percent Black and Brown:** School Enrollment—Race/Ethnicity data from 1976–77 and 1985–86, from "Enrollment Data Archive (1976–1994)," New York State Education Department, https://www.p12 .nysed.gov/irs/statistics/enroll-n-staff /ArchiveEnrollmentData1976-1994.html.

70 **slashed federal funding:** Robert Pear, "Desegration Plans in Peril," *New York Times*, September 7, 1982, https://www.nytimes.com /1982/09/07/gus/desegregation-plans-in-peril .html, A1.

70 **of people leaving:** Robert W. Crandall, "The Migration of U.S. Manufacturing and Its Impact on the Buffalo Metropolitan Area," June 6, 2002, https://www.brookings.edu/research /the-migration-of-u-s-manufacturing-and-its -impact-on-the-buffalo-metropolitan-area/.

70 **drank their alcohol:** In 2018, the board of the Nichols School released an eighty-five-page report detailing the results of an independent investigation into sexual and other misconduct by the school's faculty (see Laurel Pyke Malson, Esq., and Rebecca L. Springer, Esq., "Nichols School: Report of Independent Investigation of Certain Misconduct by Faculty with Students," https://s3.amazonaws.com/bncore/wp-content /uploads/2018/01/Nichols_Public_Report.pdf). In interviews, Nika Robinson described the findings as troubling but not surprising given the culture she'd experienced at Nichols and rumors that circulated during her time there.

71 **named Ted Brown:** All college and university professors are identified by their actual names, unless otherwise noted.

71 **persona of John Snow:** Details drawn from Ralph Frerichs, "John Snow, British Physician," *Britannica*, https://www.britannica.com /biography/John-Snow-British-physician.

71 **a leaking cesspit:** Michael Clarkson and Madeleine Udell, "Observation and Visualization: John Snow and the Broad Street Pump," Data Science for All Course Website, 2018, https://www.cs.cornell.edu/courses /cs1380/2018sp/textbook/chapters/02/1

/observation-and-visualization-john-snow-and -the-broad-street-pump.html.

72 **Club 112, made famous:** Joeff Davis, "That Was Then, This Is Now," Creative Loafing, June 18, 2015, https://creativeloafing.com/content -168411-that-was-then-this-is-now.

72 **singer Bobby Brown:** Richard L. Eldredge, "Party Time with Bobby Brown," *Atlanta Journal-Constitution*, February 12, 2003, E2.

73 **America's urban fringe:** Special thanks to historian Andrew Wiese, whose seminal work *Places of Their Own: African American Suburbanization in the Twentieth Century* (Chicago: University of Chicago Press, 2004) profoundly shaped my understanding of trends in U.S. suburbanization.

73 **"suburb sheds" outside:** Kenneth T. Jackson, *Crabgrass Frontier: The Suburbanization of America* (New York: Oxford University Press, 1985), 18.

73 **one in six:** Wiese, *Places of Their Own*, 5.

73 **20 percent of Black Americans:** Wiese, *Places of Their Own*, 5.

74 **began building homes:** Bob Williams, "Arrest Negro Homebuilder, Charge Violation of New Building Code in Woodmere, Village of Pioneers," *Cleveland Call and Post*, August 10, 1946, 1A.

74 **responded by incorporating:** Wiese, *Places of Their Own*, 96.

74 **"illegal use of used lumber":** Williams, "Arrest Negro Homebuilder," 1A.

74 **about 3.5 million:** Wiese, *Places of Their Own*, 211.

74 **forest and rolling farmland:** "Land Use Plan," DeKalb County, Georgia, April 20, 1964, 8, 45.

74 **smattering of Black families:** Joe Renfroe, *No Room for Compromise* (Glenview, IL: Scott, Foresman, 1974), 26.

74 **were often indistinguishable:** "DeKalb Officers Swoop Down on Negro Home, Shoot Mother, Son," *Atlanta Daily World*, May 25, 1940, 1; "Grand Dragon Denies Klan Part in Flogging, Killing," *Austin Statesman*, June 8, 1946, 1.

74 **remained rigidly segregated:** Jane Claire McKinzey, "In the Crossfire: A Case Study of Teachers and Racial Transition" (PhD diss., Georgia State University, 1999), 8–9.

74 **bent on maintaining:** While DeKalb school officials fought hard to preserve segregation through the late 1950s and early '60s, Joe Renfroe, Jane Claire McKinzey, and others point out that Jim Cherry was unusual among southern school superintendents in making significant investments in all-Black schools and resisting calls to shut down all of Georgia's public schools rather than integrate.

75 **busy breaking ground:** McKinzey, "In the Crossfire," 8–9.

75 **235,000 people in all:** Special thanks to Michelle Schmitt for preparing this custom analysis: "Table 42 General Characteristics of

the Population, for Counties 1950," *1950 Census of the Population: Volume 2. Characteristics of the Population, General Characteristics, Part 11: Georgia* (Washington, D.C.: US Government Printing Office, 1952), 11–118, https://www2 .census.gov/library/publications/decennial /1950/population-volume-2/37779083v2p11ch3 .pdf; "Table P-1: General Characteristics of the Population: 1970," *1970 Census of Population and Housing, Atlanta, GA, Standard Metropolitan Statistical Area (and Adjacent Area)* (Washington, D.C.: Government Printing Office, 1972), P-1, https://www2.census.gov /library/publications/decennial/1970/phc-1 /39204513p2ch02.pdf.

75 **"high-income white noose":** Nikole Hannah-Jones, "Living Apart: How the Government Betrayed a Landmark Civil Rights Law," *Pro Publica*, June 25, 2015, https://www.propublica .org/article/living-apart-how-the-government -betrayed-a-landmark-civil-rights-law.

75 **"Open Communities" program:** Hannah-Jones, "Living Apart: How the Government Betrayed a Landmark Civil Rights Law."

75 **were all integrated:** "*United States v. Jackson School Board*—Joint Motion for Declaration of Partial Unitary Status and for Approval of Consent Order," U.S. Department of Justice, May 29, 2018, https://www.justice.gov/crt/case -document/united-states-v-jackson-school -board-joint-motion-declaration-partial-unitary.

75 **six weeks later:** Daniel Amsterdam, "Toward the Resegregation of Southern Schools: African American Suburbanization and Historical Erasure in *Freeman v. Pitts*," *History of Education Quarterly* 57, no. 4 (November 2017): 460, doi:10.1017/heq.2017.28.

75 **because his surname:** Margo Schlanger, "*Freeman v. Pitts*, 112 S. Ct. 1430 (1992): The Travails of a 'Garden Variety Desegregation Case,'" for Professor Drew Days Constitutional Litigation, May 17, 1993, 5.

75 **Lynwood Park Elementary:** Defendant Exhibit 193: Historic Attendance Data 1954–1968, 1954–1968, RBRL/056/DCS, series 1, box 15, folder 26, DeKalb County School Desegregation Case Files, Richard B. Russell Library for Political Research and Studies, Athens, Georgia.

75 **still wholly segregated:** *Pitts v. Cherry*, Complaint, Filed July 5, 1968, in the U.S. District Court Northern District of Georgia, Atlanta Division, no. 11946, 4, RBRL/056/DCS, series 2, box 42, folder 4, DeKalb County School Desegregation Case Files, Richard B. Russell Library for Political Research and Studies, Athens, Georgia.

75 **"academic, disciplinary, and":** *Pitts v. Cherry*, Complaint.

75 **3,700 Black peers:** Margo Schlanger, "*Freeman v. Pitts*, 112 S. Ct. 1430 (1992)," 5.

76 **agreed in 1969:** McKinzey, "In the Crossfire," 13.

76 **only one school:** Amsterdam, "Toward the Resegregation of Southern Schools."

76 **94 percent white:** McKinzey, "In the Crossfire," 16.

76 **kept pouring millions:** Renfroe, *No Room for Compromise*, 84.

76 **thousands of newly middle-class Black:** See, e.g., B. Drummond Ayres, Jr., "Blacks Return to South in a Reverse Migration," *New York Times*, June 18, 1974, 81. As historian Andrew Wiese notes, this shift was spurred by the proportion of African American workers in newly open white-collar occupations nearly doubling during the 1960s, from 13 to 25 percent. See Wiese, *Places of Their Own*, 218.

76 **nearly 88,000 people:** McKinzey, "In the Crossfire," 17–18.

76 **16-mile commercial corridor:** Virginia Anderson, "Timeless Thoroughfares," *Atlanta Journal*, May 25, 1998, E01.

76 **first Home Depot:** Roger Thompson, "There's No Place Like Home Depot," *Nation's Business* 80, no. 2 (February 1992): 30.

76 **Bernie Marcus responded:** Sid Wrightsman, "A Renowned Trio Forges New-Twist Retail-Chain," *American Building Supplies*, August 1979, 12.

78 **trying to spur:** Special thanks to Ray White, the former director of economic development for DeKalb County, for helping to shape my understanding of DeKalb's history.

78 **"The buyer profile":** "The Secret Is Out: The New Frontier in DeKalb," Residential Development Group of the Economic Development Council of the DeKalb County Chamber of Commerce.

78 **white residents had begun moving:** Special thanks to Frances Abbott, whose dissertation "Black Migration to Atlanta: Metropolitan Spatial Patterns and Popular Representation, 1990–2012" (PhD diss. Emory University, 2012) proved enormously helpful in understanding the scale and nature of migration around Atlanta in the late twentieth century (see p. 30).

78 **newly suburbanizing areas:** See Kevin Michael Kruse, *White Flight: Atlanta and the Making of Modern Conservatism* (Princeton, NJ: Princeton University Press, 2007), 245, for a full discussion of the racial dynamics of suburbanization in metropolitan Atlanta during the 1970s.

78 **150 years earlier:** "Treaty with the Creeks, January 22, 1818," First Peoples, https://www .firstpeople.us/FP-Html-Treaties/Treaty WithTheCreeks1818.html.

78 **long been rural:** William Grady Holt, "Gwinnett Goes Global: The Changing Image of American Suburbia," *Research in Urban Sociology* 10 (2010): 51, doi:10.1108.

78 **turning the county even whiter:** See, e.g., "Growing Gwinnett: Changes and Challenges," University of Georgia Cooperative Extension Service, 11, which shows that Black residents' share of Gwinnett County's population fell

from nearly 12 percent in 1940 to less than 3 percent in 1980.

78 **called Research Atlanta:** Details regarding the state of desegregation in metropolitan Atlanta in the early 1970s are drawn from Paul West et al., "School Desegregation in Metro Atlanta, 1954–1973," Research Atlanta, Inc., February 1973, https://files.eric.ed.gov/fulltext /ED074204.pdf, unless otherwise noted.

79 **with the American Civil Liberties Union:** Tomiko Brown-Nagin, *Courage to Dissent: Atlanta and the Long History of the Civil Rights Movement* (Oxford: Oxford University Press, 2011), 409.

79 **fresh desegregation lawsuit:** *Armour v. Nix,* Complaint, filed June 7, 1972, in the U.S. District Court Northern District of Georgia, Atlanta Division, no. 16708.

79 **metro-wide desegregation order:** *Armour v. Nix,* Complaint, 9.

80 **avowed white segregationist:** *Armour v. Nix,* Plaintiff's Proposed Findings of Fact, filed October 25, 1977, in the U.S. District Court Northern District of Georgia, Atlanta Division, no. 16708, 105–6.

80 **built in Gwinnett:** *Armour v. Nix,* Plaintiff's Proffer of Proof (Public Housing), filed November 6, 1973, in the U.S. District Court Northern District of Georgia, Atlanta Division, no. 16708, 3383.

80 **nearly $200,000:** *Armour v. Nix,* Plaintiff's Proposed Findings of Fact, 127.

80 **"educable mentally retarded":** *Armour v. Nix,* Plaintiff's Proposed Findings of Fact, 145.

80 **as "monumental stupidity":** *Armour v. Nix,* Response of the State Defendents to the Proffers of Proof Submitted by the Various Plaintiffs, in the U.S. District Court Northern District of Georgia, Atlanta Division, 2745.

80 **"an educational viewpoint":** *Armour v. Nix,* Brief in Support of the Motions of the State Defendants, filed September 12, 1972, in the U.S. District Court Northern District of Georgia, Atlanta Division, no. 16708, 20.

80 **"Finally, we respectfully point out":** *Armour v. Nix,* Brief in Support of the Motions of the State Defendants, 28.

81 **the Reagan years:** Special thanks to Georgia Tech history professor Daniel Amsterdam, whose work tracing the history of *Freeman v. Pitts* and whose arguments about the case's significance to America's conservative establishment helped shape my understanding of the legal and political landscape around school desegregation in the Atlanta area and across the country.

81 **undermine the Fair Housing Act:** Hannah-Jones, "Living Apart: How the Government Betrayed a Landmark Civil Rights Law," *ProPublica.*

81 **appointing four new:** "Nixon and the Supreme Court," Richard Nixon Presidential Library and Museum, September 22, 2021, https://www .nixonlibrary.gov/news/nixon-and-supreme -court.

81 **former Goldwater confidant:** Rick Perlstein, *Before the Storm: Barry Goldwater and the Unmaking of the American Consensus* (New York: Nation Books, 2001), 76.

81 **school board member:** John Calvin Jeffries, *Justice Lewis F. Powell, Jr.* (New York: Charles Scribner's Sons, 1994), 2.

81 **slope toward communism:** Paul A. Sracic, *San Antonio v. Rodriguez and the Pursuit of Equal Education: The Debate over Discrimination and School Funding* (Lawrence: University Press of Kansas, 2006), 66.

81 **center of three decisions:** For a fuller discussion of these court cases and their significance, see Kruse, *White Flight: Atlanta and the Making of Modern Conservatism,* 257.

81 **for the majority:** Sracic, *San Antonio v. Rodriguez and the Pursuit of Equal Education,* 98.

81 **declining to hear:** *Warth v. Seldin,* 422 U.S. 490, 493 (1975).

81 ***Milliken v. Bradley:*** Joyce A. Baugh, *The Detroit School Busing Case: Milliken v. Bradley and the Controversy over Desegregation* (Lawrence: University Press of Kansas, 2011), 161.

81 **fifty-three school districts:** This and other details regarding *Milliken v. Bradley* are drawn from *Milliken v. Bradley,* Certiorari to the U.S. Court of Appeals for the Sixth Circuit, no. 73-434, decided July 25, 1974, unless otherwise noted.

82 **"sensitivity to individual needs":** *Armour v. Nix,* Brief in Support of the Motion to Dismiss, in the U.S. District Court Northern District of Georgia, Atlanta Division, no. 16708, 10201.

82 **dismissed in 1978:** *Armour v. Nix,* Order, filed March 2, 1978, in the U.S. District Court Northern District of Georgia, Atlanta Division, no. 16708.

82 **new single-family homes:** Gwinnett County Department of Planning & Development, "Gwinnett 2002: A Comprehensive Plan for Gwinnett County, Georgia," October 20, 1992, VII-3.

82 **whom were white:** "Gwinnett County—DP-1. General Population and Housing Characteristics: 1990," American Fact Finder, U.S. Census Bureau, https://www.gwinnettcounty.com /static/departments/planning/Census/gwinnett _county_1990_census_profile.pdf.

82 **up to fourteen:** Amsterdam, "Toward the Resegregation of Southern Schools,"

82 **back in court:** Schlanger, "*Freeman v. Pitts,* 112 S. Ct. 1430 (1992)," 10.

82 **a new question:** Amsterdam, "Toward the Resegregation of Southern Schools," 451.

82 **to provide buses:** Schlanger, "*Freeman v. Pitts,* 112 S. Ct. 1430 (1992)," 9.

82 **ninety-six students participated:** Amsterdam, "Toward the Resegregation of Southern Schools," 463.

82 **roughly three dozen:** Amsterdam, "Toward the Resegregation of Southern Schools."

82 **tens of thousands:** *Freeman v. Pitts*, 503 U.S. 467 (1992), 475,

82 **"Will the defendant":** Bill Torpy, "Bitter Lessons," *Atlanta Constitution*, September 30, 1999, A1.

83 **DeKalb schools altogether:** Schlanger, "*Freeman v. Pitts*, 112 S. Ct. 1430 (1992)," 21.

83 **the Supreme Court:** Amsterdam, "Toward the Resegregation of Southern Schools."

83 **by Reagan appointees:** "Supreme Court Justices During Reagan Administration,1981–1989," Ronald Reagan Presidential Libary and Museum, https://www.reaganlibrary.gov/reagans/reagan-administration/supreme-court-justices-during-reagan-administration1981-1989.

83 **turning their way:** *Board of Ed. of Oklahoma City v. Dowell*, 498 U.S. 237 (1991).

83 **top legal minds:** Amsterdam, "Toward the Resegregation of Southern Schools"; Schlanger, "*Freeman v. Pitts*, 112 S. Ct. 1430 (1992)," 33.

83 **ACLU's children's-rights project:** Schlanger, "*Freeman v. Pitts*, 112 S. Ct. 1430 (1992)," 36.

83 **Hansen argued gamely:** Details of oral arguments in this case are drawn from "*Freeman v. Pitts*," Oyez, https://www.oyez.org/cases/1991/89-1290, unless otherwise noted.

83 **"in good faith," contended Starr:** After serving as solicitor general, Ken Starr would later be named independent counsel to investigate Democratic president Bill Clinton, then help defend Republican president Donald Trump against impeachment charges. See, e.g., Peter Baker, "Ken Starr, Independent Counsel in Clinton Investigation, Dies at 76," *New York Times*, September 13, 2022, https://www.nytimes.com/2022/09/13/us/politics/ken-starr-dead.html.

84 **came down in 1992:** *Freeman v. Pitts*, 503 U.S. 467 (1992).

84 **"Though we cannot escape":** *Freeman v. Pitts*, 503 U.S. 467 (1992), 495–96.

84 **"specifics of desegregation cases":** Amsterdam, "Toward the Resegregation of Southern Schools," 472.

84 **more than two hundred:** Amsterdam, "Toward the Resegregation of Southern Schools," 476.

85 **Catholic boys' school:** Descriptions of St. Augustine's are drawn from Gwen Filosa, "50 Years of St. Aug Pride," *Times-Picayune*, August 26, 2001; Frank Donze, "Tradition-Rich School Faces Challenges of Changing City," *Times-Picayune*, April 2, 1989; Chris Adams, "St. Augustine Focused Early on Black Education," *Times-Picayune*, February 3, 1992; and Frank Donze, "St. Aug's Lessons Endure for Life," *Times-Picayune*, April 2, 1989.

85 **"Juilliard of the South":** Howard Reich, "The Long March Back," *Chicago Tribune*, November 23, 2006, 5.1.

86 **starting to teeter:** Virginia Anderson, "Timeless Thoroughfares: The Lessons of

Memorial Drive," *Atlanta Journal*, May 25, 1998, E01.

86 **slipped a smidge:** Betsy White, "Higher Test Scores Elude State's Pupils," *Atlanta Journal-Constitution*, June 3, 1995.

86 **recent budget shortfall:** Shelley Emling, "Falling Property Values Put a Drain on DeKalb," *Atlanta Constitution*, February 14, 1993, A1.

87 **their DeKalb operations:** Robert and Company, "DeKalb County Comprehensive Plan 1995–2015," April 1996, VI-95, https://www.dekalbcountyga.gov/sites/default/files/2020-02/Comprehensive%20Plan%20-%20Adopted%201995.pdf.

87 **with discount stores:** Ben Smith III, "South DeKalb Demanding More from Leaders Affluent African-Americans Are Frustrated by the Quality of Development Around Them," *Atlanta Journal Constitution*, February 25, 1996, C03.

87 **a flea market:** Anderson, "Timeless Thoroughfares: The Lessons of Memorial Drive."

CHAPTER 3:
A DOUBLE-SIDED LEGACY

89 **"There is, however, a striking":** Sonya Douglass, *Learning in a Burning House: Educational Inequality, Ideology, and (Dis)integration* (New York: Teachers College Press, 2011), 6.

89 **neighborhood was largely Hispanic:** Community Area 22—Logan Square, Community Area 2000 Census Profiles, City of Chicago Department of Planning and Development, 2003, https://www.chicago.gov/content/dam/city/depts/zlup/Zoning_Main_Page/Publications/Census_2000_Community_Area_Profiles/PDF_22.pdf.

89 **heavily Jewish community of Skokie:** "Skokie," WTTW, accessed March 31, 2023, https://interactive.wttw.com/chicago-by-l/neighborhoods/skokie.

90 **"You got to be one":** F. Gary Gray, *Friday* (Burbank, CA: New Line Cinema, 1995), https://www.imdb.com/title/tt0113118/.

90 **big hoop earrings:** Chute Middle School 1998–99, Evanston, Illinois, yearbook, http://chute50th.weebly.com/uploads/1/4/8/4/14849594/98-99.pdf.

92 **multistate shooting rampage:** All details of the shootings are drawn from Eric Ferkenhoff and Michael Ko, "Rampage Suspect Dead—North Shore Man Caught in Downstate Salem," *Chicago Tribune*, July 5, 1999, unless otherwise noted.

92 **was Ricky Byrdsong:** Dave Jackson and Neta Jackson, *No Random Act: Behind the Murder of Ricky Byrdsong* (Colorado Springs: Waterbrook Press, 2002), 7.

92 **from Walker Elementary:** "Former Coach Shot to Death Near Chicago; Others Injured," *New York Times*, July 4, 1999, https://www.nytimes

.com/1999/07/04/us/former-coach-shot-to
-death-near-chicago-others-injured.html.

92 **still sharp racial cleavages:** Details on the
social dynamics at Evanston Township High
School are drawn from Jodi S. Cohen,
"Celebrating Diversity, but Still Seeking Unity;
Despite Evanston High's Efforts, Integration
Faces Obstacles," *Chicago Tribune*, May 9, 2004,
https://www.chicagotribune.com/news/ct-xpm
-2004-05-09-0405080310-story.html, unless
otherwise noted.

92 **back to 1954:** Details about Cotillion and the
Ebony Ball drawn from Vikki Ortiz, "As
Evanston Students End 'Elitist' Cotillion, Other
Events Remain Strong," *Evanston Review*,
August 11, 2017, https://www
.chicagotribune.com/suburbs/evanston/ct
-evanston-cotillion-ends-20170809-story.html;
and Tracy Quattrocki, "End of an Era for
Evanston Cotillion Dance," *Evanston
RoundTable*, July 26, 2017, https://evanston
roundtable.com/2017/07/26/end-of-an-era
-for-evanston-cotillion-dance/, unless
otherwise noted.

93 **Minority Student Achievement Network:**
Details of the Minority Student Achievement
Network are drawn from Allan Alson, "The
Academic Achievement Gap: The Suburban
Challenge. CSR Connection," National
Clearinghouse for Comprehensive School
Reform, 2003, https://files.eric.ed.gov/fulltext
/ED482632.pdf; Cornelia Gruman, "Schools
Clamor to Join Evanston's Achiever Network,"
Chicago Tribune, September 3, 1999; and Debra
Nussbaum, "Making Money, but Not Grades.
The Next Step?," *New York Times*, September
12, 1999, 14NJ.1. Special thanks to Brown
University professor John Diamond for helping
to shape my understanding of the historical
context of racial-equity initiatives in Evanston.

93 **"The very first step":** Nussbaum, "Making
Money, but Not Grades. The Next Step?"

93 **began surveying 41,000:** Survey findings
drawn from Ronald F. Ferguson, "Ed-Excel
Assessment of Secondary School Student
Culture Tabulations by School District and
Race/Ethnicity: Responses from Middle
School, Junior High and High School Students
in Districts of the Minority Student
Achievement Network (MSAN), 2000–2001,"
November 18, 2002, https://eric.ed.gov/?id=
ED474667, 1.

93 **thirty- to forty-percentage-point:** Stephanie
Banchero, "Empowering Students to
Excel: Evanston School Works to Narrow
Achievement Gap," *Chicago Tribune*, June 3,
2001, 1.1.

93 **The superintendent changed:** Nora Ellin
O'Connor, "Evanston High's Desperate Need
for Reform," *Chicago Tribune*, May 16, 2004, 12.

94 **to more students:** Cohen, "Celebrating
Diversity, but Still Seeking Unity."

94 **Middle Eastern history:** "Global Thinking Has
Its Reward," *Chicago Tribune*, November 30,
2003, 2.

94 **into honors classes:** Cornelia Grumman, "Top
Black Students Prod Peers: They Will Challenge
Others to Achieve," *Chicago Tribune*, August
19, 1999, 1.

95 **living in the area:** Special thanks to Morris
(Dino) Robinson and the Shorefront Legacy
Center for their work preserving and
documenting the histories of African
Americans living on Chicago's North Shore.
See here Morris (Dino) Robinson, Jr., and
Jenny Thompson, "Evanston Policies and
Practices Directly Affecting the African
American Community," November 2021,
https://www.cityofevanston.org/home
/showpublisheddocument/67191/637715545
144570000, 4.

95 **infamous "Black Codes":** "Early Chicago:
Slavery in Illinois," WTTW, https://interactive
.wttw.com/dusable-to-obama/early-chicago
-slavery-illinois.

95 **north from Chicago:** Barr, *Friends
Disappear*, 30.

95 **downtown soon followed:** Evanston Small
Parks and Playgrounds Association, *Plan of
Evanston* (Evanston, IL: Bowman Publishing
Company, 1917), 28.

95 **approved $50,000:** Shorefront Legacy Center,
"Foster School Timeline of Events."

95 **Foster Elementary opened:** Shorefront Legacy
Center, "Foster School Timeline of Events."

95 **Jim Crow South:** Barr, *Friends Disappear*,
31–32.

95 **more than 2,500 people:** Robinson and
Thompson, "Evanston Policies and Practices
Directly Affecting the African American
Community," November 2021, https://www
.cityofevanston.org/home/showpublished
document/67191/637715545144570000, 20.

95 **white people's mansions:** Robinson and
Thompson, "Evanston Policies and
Practices Directly Affecting the African
American Community," November 2021,
https://www.cityofevanston.org/home
/showpublisheddocument/67191/637715545
144570000, 11–12.

95 **range of measures:** Details of the exclusionary
and restrictive steps taken by Evanston leaders
and institutions drawn from Morris (Dino)
Robinson, Jr., and Jenny Thompson, "Evanston
Policies and Practices Directly Affecting the
African American Community."

96 **residents banded together:** Barr, *Friends
Disappear*, 45.

96 **99 percent Black:** All details regarding
Evanston's Fifth Ward during the mid-
twentieth century are drawn from Robinson
and Thompson, "Evanston Policies and
Practices Directly Affecting the African
American Community."

97 **"Altho the area is unattractive"**: Robinson and Thompson, "Evanston Policies and Practices Directly Affecting the African American Community," 72.

97 **Black population kept growing**: Larry Gavin, "Developing a Segregated Town, 1900–1960," *Evanston RoundTable*, December 5, 2019, https://evanstonroundtable.com/2019/12/05/developing-a-segregated-town-1900-1960/.

97 **hallways grew busy**: Larry Gavin, "The Role of Foster School in the Implementation of School District 65's Desegregation Plan in 1967 and Its Closing in 1979," *Evanston RoundTable*, March 21, 2019, https://evanstonroundtable.com/2019/03/21/the-role-of-foster-school-in-the-implementation-of-school-district-65s-desegregation-plan-in-1967-and-its-closing-in-1979/, and "Foster School," photograph, 1948, from Priscilla Giles, Shorefront Legacy Center, Evanston, Illinois.

97 **at Foster since 1942**: Shorefront Legacy Center, "Foster School Timeline of Events."

97 **a fire devastated**: "$500,000 Evening Fire Sweeps Foster School; Thousands Jam Area to Watch 3-Hour Blaze," *Evanston Review*, October 30, 1958, 1.

97 **for fair-housing campaigns**: All details and quotations related to Evanston's fair housing campaign and the role of Martin Luther King, Jr., are drawn from Barr, *Friends Disappear*, 176–78, and Betsy Landes, "Martin Luther King, Jr. in Winnetka," *Winnetka Historical Society Gazette*, Spring/Summer 2006, https://www.winnetkahistory.org/gazette/martin-luther-king-jr-in-winnetka/, unless otherwise noted.

98 **parts of Evanston**: Gavin, "The Role of Foster School in the Implementation of School District 65's Desegregation Plan."

98 **Black and white**: Gregory C. Coffin, "How Evanston, Illinois Integrated All of Its Schools," presented at the National Conference on Equal Educational Opportunity in American Cities, Washington, D.C., November 16–18, 196, https://eric.ed.gov/?id=ED023740, 3, 5.

98 **started inside Foster**: David I. Bednarek, "Evanston Kindergarten Lab Integrates, Teaches Reading," *Milwaukee Journal*, June 2, 1967.

98 **schools in Harlem**: Barr, *Friends Disappear*, 76, 106.

98 **should shape society**: Barr, *Friends Disappear*, 76.

99 **bring about "psychological integration"**: Barr, *Friends Disappear*, 104; and Coffin, "How Evanston, Illinois Integrated All of Its Schools," 14.

99 **"All-white suburbia"**: Gregory C. Coffin, "A Rationale for School Integration: What Attitudes Are Being Developed in Our Children?" (speech, Lincolnwood, IL, May 4, 1967), 6–7, Shorefront Legacy Center, Evanston, Illinois.

99 **earned the new superintendent enemies**: Barr, *Friends Disappear*, 106–8.

99 **Evanston's open-housing movement**: John MacLean, "O.K. Stiffer Housing Law in Evanston," *Chicago Tribune*, April 30, 1968, 3.

99 **strident in their opposition**: Barr, *Friends Disappear*, 114, 121–22.

99 **"The destruction of our"**: Barr, *Friends Disappear*, 82.

99 **approach to policymaking**: Details of Coffin's strategy for desegregating District 65 schools are drawn from Coffin, "How Evanston, Illinois Integrated All of Its Schools."

99 **desegregate District 65 schools**: Gavin, "The Role of Foster School in the Implementation of School District 65's Desegregation Plan."

100 **first northern city**: Gavin, "The Role of Foster School in the Implementation of School District 65's Desegregation Plan."

100 **flyer began circulating**: "They Walked to a Better School," flyer, n.d., Shorefront Legacy Center, Evanston, Illinois.

101 **profiles in national newspapers**: Barr, *Friends Disappear*, 106.

101 **the new LAB School**: Details about the Foster Lab School are drawn from "Martin Luther King, Jr. Laboratory School," Spring 1973; "Laboratory School Plans Innovations," *School Outlook*, April 1967, 4; and "A Child Learns," Evanston, Illinois, public schools, District 65.

101 **short documentary film**: Lawrence B. Brooks, *The Integration of the Foster School* (1967), accessed at Shorefront Legacy Center; see https://shorefrontjournal.wordpress.com/2015/11/09/lawrence-b-brooks-filming-social-change/.

101 **three hundred Evanston educators**: All details regarding Integration Institute manuals are drawn from Evanston School District 65, "Black Power and Its Effect on Racial Interaction: Resource Manual," 1968, https://files.eric.ed.gov/fulltext/ED036568.pdf, unless otherwise noted. Special thanks to the Northwestern University Archives for preserving these materials.

101 **"the things that teachers do"**: Coffin, "How Evanston, Illinois Integrated All of Its Schools," 14.

102 **such as "I, Too"**: Langston Hughes, "I, Too," *Survey Graphic* 53, no. 11 (1925), 683, https://umedia.lib.umn.edu/item/p16022coll336:2133/p16022coll336:2089?child_index=60&query=sing%20america&sidebar_page=1.

102 **over sixty pages**: Evanston School District 65, "Grouping Children in Integrated Schools: Resource Manual," 1968, 21–86, https://files.eric.ed.gov/fulltext/ED041091.pdf.

102 **take self-administered surveys**: Evanston School District 65, "Discipline Standard in Integrated Schools: Resource Manual," 1968, 46, https://files.eric.ed.gov/fulltext/ED036570.pdf.

103 **end the superintendent's contract**: Barr, *Friends Disappear*, 109, 111.

103 **for one thousand supporters:** "'Back Coffin' Rally Draws 1,000 Persons," *Chicago Tribune*, June 28, 1969, S5.

103 **lead a petition drive:** "Evanston's Schools Will Open on Time," *Chicago Tribune*, September 3, 1969, 4.

103 **ten thousand signatures:** Charles Mount, "Board Studies Coffin Firing," *Chicago Tribune*, July 15, 1969, 1.

103 **the following spring:** Details and quotations related to the school board election that decided superintendent Gregory Coffin's fate are drawn from Barr, *Friends Disappear*.

104 **released a study:** All details and quotations related to ETS's 1971 evaluation of integration in District 65 schools are drawn from Jayjia, Hsia, "Integration in Evanston, 1967–71: A Longitudinal Evaluation," Educational Testing Service, https://files.eric.ed.gov/fulltext /ED054292.pdf.

104 *Children of the Dream:* Rucker C. Johnson and Alexander Nazaryan, *Children of the Dream: Why School Integration Works* (New York: Basic Books, 2019), 58, 60, 62, 64, 65.

105 **"come to believe":** Harry Belafonte with Michael Shnayerson, *My Song: A Memoir* (New York: Alfred A. Knopf, 2011), 329.

105 **Douglass would expand:** See, e.g., Sonya Douglass, *Learning in a Burning House: Educational Inequality, Ideology, and (Dis)Integration* (New York: Teachers College Press, 2011), and Sonya Douglass, "Whose School Integration?," *Voices in Urban Education* 49, no. 1 (Winter 2019–20), https://steinhardt.nyu .edu/metrocenter/vue/whose-school -integration-0.

105 **"hells where they are":** W. E. B. Du Bois, "Does the Negro Need Separate Schools?," *Journal of Negro Education* 4, no. 3 (1935): 328–35, https:// www.jstor.org/stable/2291871.

105 **tens of thousands:** Madeline Will, "65 Years After 'Brown v. Board,' Where Are All the Black Educators?," *Education Week*, May 14, 2019, https://www.edweek.org/policy-politics/65 -years-after-brown-v-board-where-are-all-the -black-educators/2019/05.

105 **shutter the old Foster building:** Gavin, "The Role of Foster School in the Implementation of School District 65's Desegregation Plan in 1967."

105 **filed a lawsuit:** Robinson and Thompson, "Evanston Policies and Practices Directly Affecting the African American Community," 26.

105 **named Delores Holmes:** Details about the Holmes family's experience with Foster and the condition of the building after it was purchased by Family Focus are drawn from interview by the author with Dolores Holmes, February 3, 2020.

107 **Christian private school:** "History," Kingsway Preparatory School, https://www.kingswayprep .org/about-us/.

107 **affordable place in Chicago:** Jonah Newman, "Half of Chicago Renters Can't Afford Their Housing," *Chicago Reporter*, June 1, 2015, https://www.chicagoreporter.com/half-of -chicago-renters-cant-afford-their-housing/.

108 **months of strike threats:** Kari Lydersen and Emma Brown, "Chicago Teachers Go on Strike, Shutting Down Nation's Third-Largest School System," *Washington Post*, April 1, 2016, https:// www.washingtonpost.com/news/education/wp /2016/04/01/chicago-teachers-to-strike-friday -shutting-down-nations-third-largest-school -system/.

108 **millions of dollars:** Juan Perez, Jr., "CPS Shortfall of $500 Million from Last Year Hangs over Current Budget Woes," *Chicago Tribune*, February 3, 2017, https://www.chicagotribune .com/politics/ct-chicago-schools-finance -trouble-met-20170203-story.html.

108 **"dumping ground for":** *Time* staff, "Here's Donald Trump's Presidential Announcement Speech," *Time*, June 16, 2015, https://time.com /3923128/donald-trump-announcement-speech/.

109 **sea of red:** Joseph Hewes, "Election Night Coverage: MSNBC—2016—Part Four," November 23, 2018, YouTube Video, 1:45:11, https://youtu.be/9FAOfsuwIKQ.

CHAPTER 4: AMBITION AND DISAPPOINTMENT

110 **I think, possibly:** Eleanor Chute, "Sewer System Drains Taxpayers," *Pittsburgh Post-Gazette*, August 20, 1995, C-1, C-6; Pamphlet File: Penn Hills—Sewage Disposal, 175780, Penn Hills Library.

111 **city's best-kept secrets:** Marc Hopkins, "Advocacy Group Wants Superintendent Who Will Help Blacks Achieve," *New Pittsburgh Courier*, July 25, 1992, A-1.

111 **Everything started with principal:** All descriptions of Madison Elementary are drawn from interviews with Bethany Smith and from Barbara A. Sizemore, "The Madison Elementary School: A Turnaround Case," *Journal of Negro Education* 57, no. 3 (Summer 1988), http://www.jstor.com/stable/2295423, unless otherwise noted.

111 **was 0.6 percent:** Andrew King, "Elementary School and Classroom Routines That Foster the Use of Achievement-Oriented Behavior in African American Male Student" (PhD diss., University of Pittsburgh, 1998), 70.

111 **out of vogue:** Emily Hanford, "At a Loss for Words," APM Reports, August 22, 2019, https:// www.apmreports.org/episode/2019/08/22 /whats-wrong-how-schools-teach-reading.

112 **have brown skin:** Ann Rodgers, "Hill District Pastor Who Fought Hockey Arena Retiring," *Pittsburgh Post-Gazette*, January 25, 2009, https://www.post-gazette.com/local /neighborhoods/2009/01/25/Hill-District -pastor-who-fought-hockey-arena-retiring /stories/200901250204.

113 **into the neighborhood:** Ervin Dyer, "Decades Haven't Dimmed the Allure of the Hill District's Sugar Top," *Pittsburgh Post-Gazette*, July 17, 2005, https://www.post-gazette.com /life/lifestyle/2005/07/17/Decades-haven -t-dimmed-the-allure-of-the-Hill-District -s-Sugar-Top/stories/200507170152; Eschaton, "Neighborhood of the Week: Upper Hill (Pittsburgh, Minersville: lawyers, houses, neighborhoods)" City-Data.com, March 5, 2018, www.city-data.com/forum/pittsburgh /2893537-neighborhood-week-upper-hill.html.

113 **more than 1,300 buildings:** Sasaki and Stull & Lee, "Greater Hill District Master Plan, Final Report," September 2011, https://apps .pittsburghpa.gov/redtail/images/10497_Greater _Hill_District_Master_Plan_2011.pdf, 142.

113 **thousands of families:** Robert Damewood and Bonnie Young-Laing, "Strategies to Prevent Displacement of Residents and Businesses in Pittsburgh's Hill District," September 2011, 2.

113 **Grace Memorial's membership:** "138th Anniversary Harvest Festival Celebration," Grace Memorial Presbyterian Church, November 19, 2006, provided by the Pittsburgh Presbytery.

113 **new integrated congregation:** "About Our Church," Community of Reconciliation Church, https://www.corchurchpgh.org/about.

113 **than 15,000 residents:** Kent MacIntyre James, "Public Policy and the Postwar Suburbanization of Pittsburgh, 1945–1990" (PhD diss., Carnegie Mellon University, 2005), 780, https://www .proquest.com/openview/c2f88e36c8be a1521fdf7b3535813f31/1?pq-origsite=gscholar &cbl=18750&diss=y.

114 **the neighborhood's king:** Special thanks to Mark Whitaker, whose book *Smoketown: The Untold Story of the Other Great Black Renaissance* (New York: Simon & Schuster, 2018) informed my understanding of Hill District history (see p. 13).

114 **the Pittsburgh Crawfords:** Euell A. Nielsen, "The Pittsburgh Crawfords (1931–1947)," Black Past, November 14, 2020, https://www .blackpast.org/african-american-history /groups-organizations-african-american-history/the-pittsburgh-crawfords-1931-1947/.

114 **7,500-seat brick stadium:** Geri Driscoll Strecker, "The Rise and Fall of Greenlee Field," Society for American Baseball Research, https:// sabr.org/journal/article/the-rise-and-fall-of -greenlee-field/.

114 **$25,000 a day:** Whitaker, *Smoketown*, 94.

114 **restrictive housing covenants:** James, "Public Policy and the Postwar Suburbanization of Pittsburgh, 1945–1990," 6.

114 **stately Tudor homes:** Whitaker, *Smoketown*, 94.

114 **posing for pictures:** "1938 Cadillac car parked in driveway of William 'Woogie' Harris' house with Charles 'Teenie' Harris and his son, Charles A. 'Little Teenie' Harris standing next to it, stork lawn ornament on right, Frankstown Road, Penn Hills," 1940, Teenie Harris Archive, Carnegie Museum of Art, Pittsburgh, https:// collection.cmoa.org/objects/037364a6-187c -4962-a960-789b2c6dfc6c.

115 **twenty square miles:** All descriptions of prewar Penn Township are drawn from Pittsburgh Regional Planning Association, "Master Plan for the Township of Penn, Allegheny County, Pennsylvania," January 1957, unless otherwise noted.

115 **to build 912:** All descriptions and quotations regarding Penn Township's postwar development boom are drawn from Pittsburgh Regional Planning Association.

116 **promptly required additions:** Jeffrey Alan Hinkelman, "Penn Hills: The Development of a Suburban Community," April 25, 1991, Joel Tarr Papers, Box 2, Carnegie Mellon University Archives, Pittsburgh, https://findingaids.library .cmu.edu/repositories/2/archival_objects/302, 5–6.

116 **voters shot down:** The League of Women Voters of the Pittsburgh Area, *Know Your Town: Penn Hills* (Pittsburgh: The League of Women Voters of the Pittsburgh Area, 1966), 27.

117 **The township rezoned:** All details and descriptions of the dumping-related sewage problems in Lincoln Park during the 1960s are drawn from Ralph E. Koger, "Charge 'Oust-Negroes' Trick," *Pittsburgh Courier*, October 23, 1965, 1, unless otherwise noted.

117 **influx of rats:** Ralph E. Koger, "Is Lincoln Park Doomed?," *Pittsburgh Courier*, October 30, 1965, 1.

118 **to fifty feet:** Koger, "Is Lincoln Park Doomed?," 1.

118 **Sewage Facilities Act:** "Lincoln Park May Get Aid," *Pittsburgh Courier*, February 5, 1966, 3A.

118 **a drainage plan:** Koger, "Is Lincoln Park Doomed?," 1.

118 **officials reportedly promised:** "$300,000 Sewage Plant Planned for Shades Run," *Pittsburgh Courier*, March 12, 1966, 1A, 4A.

118 **"an obvious absence":** Ralph E. Koger, "Poverty Visit Plan Spurs Leaders to Health Drive," *Pittsburgh Courier*, April 9, 1966, 1A, 4A.

119 **Lincoln Park Elementary:** "School Protest in Penn Hills," *Pittsburgh Courier*, September 15, 1962, 25.

119 **by local police:** "Penn Hills Police 'Mistreatment' Protested," *New Pittsburgh Courier*, April 15, 1967, 3.

119 **officers shot Arnold:** All descriptions of the police killing of Curtis Arnold are drawn from "Penn Hills Youth Slain by Police; Can't Find Bullet," *New Pittsburgh Courier*, February 13, 1971, unless otherwise noted.

119 **officers being suspended:** All descriptions of Penn Township's response to the police killing of Curtis Arnold are drawn from "Negroes Ask Justice in Death of Penn Hills Lad," *New Pittsburgh Courier*, March 6, 1971, unless otherwise noted.

119 **huge racial brawl:** All descriptions of racial violence in Penn Hills public schools in May 1971 are drawn from "Penn Hills School Gutted, $150,000 Damage," *New Pittsburgh Courier*, May 15, 1971, unless otherwise noted.

119 **fester for years:** Gene Reid, "Penn Hills Citizens Protest Police Act," *New Pittsburgh Courier*, November 30, 1974, 9; Lou Ransom, "Penn Hills Gets Multi-Purpose Center," *New Pittsburgh Courier*, August 9, 1980, 22; Diane R. Powell, "Lincoln Park Residents Air Health, Safety Gripes," *New Pittsburgh Courier*, May 12, 1984, 1.

120 **later, *Ebony* magazine:** Kevin Chappell, "Are These the 16 Best Communities for Blacks?," *Ebony* 51, no. 4, February 1966, 115.

120 **a pivotal scene:** August Wilson, *Jitney* (New York: Overlook Press, 2017), 84.

121 **Instead, every kindergartner:** Vicki Jarmulowski, "Penn Hills Schools Deficit up $700,000," *Pittsburgh Gazette East*, April 15, 1982, 1; "Kindergarten Helps Increase Penn Hills School Enrollment," *Pittsburgh Press Suburban East*, September 27, 1973, 13.

121 **began working together:** Richard Severo, "Kenneth Clark, Who Fought Segregation, Dies," *New York Times*, May 2, 2005, https://www.nytimes.com/2005/05/02/nyregion/kenneth-clark-whofought-segregation-dies.html.

122 *An American Dilemma*: Gunnar Myrdal and Sissela Bok, *An American Dilemma* (New Brunswick, NJ: Transaction Publishers, 1996).

122 **share of criticism:** See, e.g., Ibram X. Kendi, *Stamped from the Beginning: The Definitive History of Racist Ideas in America* (New York: Bold Type Books, 2017), 350–51.

122 **that Thurgood Marshall:** Severo, "Kenneth Clark, Who Fought Segregation, Dies," 1.

122 **find ourselves confronted:** Kenneth Bancroft Clark, *Prejudice and Your Child* (Middletown, CT: Wesleyan University Press, 1988), 78.

122 **We get confused:** Kenneth Bancroft Clark and Woody Klein, *Toward Humanity and Justice: The Writings of Kenneth B. Clark, Scholar of the 1954 Brown v. Board of Education Decision* (Westport, CT: Praeger, 2004), 34.

122 **be deeply invested:** Clark, *Prejudice and Your Child*, 78; Myrdal and Bok, *An American Dilemma*, lxxxi.

122 **a silent rupture:** Clark, *Prejudice and Your Child*, 78.

122 **"deep patterns of moral":** Clark, *Prejudice and Your Child*, 78.

122 **process unfolds unseen:** Myrdal and Bok, *An American Dilemma*, 30.

122 **"basement of man's soul":** Myrdal and Bok, *An American Dilemma*, lxxvii.

123 **about those feelings:** Clark, *Prejudice and Your Child*, 35.

123 **capacity for intimacy:** Lillian Roybal Rose, "White Identity and Counseling White Allies about Racism," in *Impacts of Racism on White Americans*, eds. Benjamin P. Bowser and Raymond G. Hunt (Beverly Hills, CA: Sage Publications, 1981).

123 **to accurately perceive:** Clark, *Prejudice and Your Child*, 81; Myrdal and Bok, *An American Dilemma*, lxxxi.

123 **won an injunction:** Chute, "Sewer System Drains Taxpayers."

123 **more than thirteen thousand violations:** *United States v. Municipality of Penn Hills*, 6 F. Supp. 2d 432 (W.D. Pa. 1998).

123 **the first municipality:** Chute, "Sewer System Drains Taxpayers."

123 **falsified treatment reports:** "PH Sewage Official Found Guilty," *The Progress*, February 10, 1993, Pamphlet File: Penn Hills—Sewage Disposal, 175780, Penn Hills Library.

124 **$675,000 in fines:** "U.S. and Pa. Settle Clean Water Lawsuit Against Penn Hills," United States Environmental Protection Agency, Region III—Office of External Affairs, July 8, 1998, Pamphlet File: Penn Hills—Sewage Disposal, 175780, Penn Hills Library.

124 **a consent decree:** *United States v. Municipality of Penn Hills*.

124 **more than $60 million:** Vera Miller, "Improved Penn Hills Sewer System in Compliance," *Pittsburgh Tribune-Review*, July 17, 2008.

124 **sewage bills skyrocket:** Christian Morrow, "Penn Hills Has Highest Sewage Rates in County: Municipality's Increased Rates the Result of EPA Fines for Dumping Untreated Sewage," *New Pittsburgh Courier*, December 25, 1999, A1.

124 **"Every politician, myself":** Chute, "Sewer System Drains Taxpayers."

124 **children to reproduce:** Josephine Gurch, "From the Archives: Dr. Kenneth Clark on Racism and Child Well-Being," Hogg Foundation for Mental Health, February 26, 2019, https://hogg.utexas.edu/podcast-dr-kenneth-clark-on-racism-and-child-well-being.

124 **of becoming complicit:** Myrdal and Bok, *An American Dilemma*, lxxxi.

124 **like an addiction:** James E. Dobbins and Judith H. Skillings, "Racism as a Clinical Syndrome," in *Social Work Diagnosis in Contemporary Practice*, ed. Francis J. Turner (New York: Oxford University Press, 2005), 560.

124 **"The escape mechanism":** Myrdal and Bok, *An American Dilemma*, 40.

125 **prestigious Schenley High:** All descriptions of Schenley High are drawn from interviews with Bethany Smith and others, and from Jake Oresick, *The Schenley Experiment* (University Park, PA: Pennsylvania State University Press, 2017), unless otherwise noted.

126 **closed both Madison:** "Board of Education Approves the Superintendent's Right-Sizing Plan," Pittsburgh Public Schools, February 28, 2006, https://www.pghschools.org/site/handlers/filedownload.ashx?moduleinstanceid=2254&dataid=3383&FileName=rsp.pdf.

126 **moved to shutter:** Bill Zlatos, "Schenley High School Shuttering on the Table Again," *Pittsburgh Tribune-Review*, November 2, 2007.

126 **over the objections:** Eleanor Chute, "Schenley High School Supporters Plot Strategy," *Pittsburgh Post-Gazette*, November 18, 2007, B.2.

CHAPTER 5:
HOW QUICKLY WE FORGET

129 **The fear and the silence:** David Franklin, *Compton: A Community in Transition* (Los Angeles: Welfare Planning Council, Los Angeles Region, 1962), 22–23.

129 **The founding families:** Pedro Castillo, *An Illustrated History of Mexican Los Angeles: 1781–1985* (Los Angeles, CA: Chicano Studies Research Center Publications, University of California, 1986), 33.

129 **the colonial genocide:** Erin Blakemore, "California Slaughtered 16,000 Native Americans. The State Finally Apologized for the Genocide," History.com, June 19, 2019, https://www.history.com/news/native -american-genocide-california-apology.

129 **Gabrielino Indians nearby:** Castillo, *An Illustrated History of Mexican Los Angeles*, 3, 53.

130 **Rancho San Pedro:** "History of Dominguez Rancho Adobe Museum," Dominguez Rancho Adobe Museum, https://dominguezrancho.org /domingo-rancho-history.

130 **all or parts:** Cristina Beltrán, *Cruelty as Citizenship: How Migrant Suffering Sustains White Democracy* (Minneapolis: University of Minnesota Press, 2020), 68.

130 **nation of Mexico:** All details regarding the Mexican American War, its aftermath, and the ensuring construction of racial and national identities are drawn from Laura E. Gómez, *Manifest Destinies: The Making of the Mexican American Race* (New York: New York University Press, 2018), unless otherwise noted (see p. 59).

130 **United States declared war:** "The Senate Votes for War against Mexico: May 12, 1846," United States Senate, https://www.senate.gov /artandhistory/history/minute/Senate_Votes _for_War_against_Mexico.htm.

130 **the ensuing invasion:** Castillo, *An Illustrated History of Mexican Los Angeles*, 90.

130 **signed in 1848:** Beltrán, *Cruelty as Citizenship*, 68.

130 **but socially second class:** Castillo, *An Illustrated History of Mexican Los Angeles*, 165.

130 **thirty-six cents an acre:** Special thanks to the Gerth Archives at California State University, Dominguez Hills, whose collections on Compton history opened whole new lines of inquiry. Here, see R. C. Gillingham, "Early Beginnings (Prior to Incorporation in 1888)," in *The Story of a City . . . Compton, California*

1888–1963, Gerth Archives and Special Collections, California State University, Dominguez Hills.

130 **five dollars an acre:** Emily E. Straus, *Death of a Suburban Dream: Race and Schools in Compton, California* (Philadelphia: University of Pennsylvania Press, 2014), 16.

130 **mix of people:** Alberto M. Camarillo, "Chicano Urban History: A Study of Compton's Barrio, 1936–1970," *Aztlan* 2, no. 2 (1971): 81–82; Shizue Seigel, *In Good Conscience: Supporting Japanese Americans During the Internment* (San Mateo, CA: AACP, 2006), 93.

131 **federal defense contracts:** Straus, *Death of a Suburban Dream*, 43.

131 **more than 45,000 people:** Straus, *Death of a Suburban Dream*, 46.

131 **Among the migrants:** John E. Yang, "For Bush, Compton Was Once Home," *Washington Post*, August 21, 1992, https://www.washingtonpost .com/archive/politics/1992/08/21/for-bush -compton-was-once-home/4efc00a2-c63d-4238 -90bd-8047c4b94951/.

132 **oil-field drilling equipment:** Emily Adams, "Bush's Compton Roots Raise Thorny Issue: Tribute: Some Criticize Landmark Quest for Apartment Where President Lived in 1949. Complex Is Now Plagued by Drugs," *Los Angeles Times*, August 3, 1992, https://www .latimes.com/archives/la-xpm-1992-08-03 -me-4550-story.html.

132 **included his father:** Steve Chawkins, "Two Future Presidents Slept Here," *Los Angeles Times*, October 11, 2005, https://www.latimes .com/archives/la-xpm-2005-oct-11-me-bush11 -story.html.

132 **Santa Fe Gardens:** Yang, "For Bush, Compton Was Once Home."

132 **most of whom:** Lloyd M. Morrisett and John A. Sexson, A *Report of a Survey of the Public Schools of the Compton Union High School and Junior College Districts, Los Angeles County, California*, 1949, 10–11; "Production of Industries at Compton Large," *Los Angeles Times*, February 14, 1926.

132 **racially restrictive covenants:** Straus, *Death of a Suburban Dream*, 28.

132 **opposing the families' release:** Straus, *Death of a Suburban Dream*, 246.

132 **Mexican American families:** Camarillo, "Chicano Urban History," 103.

132 **to a Spanish-speaking barrio:** Albert M. Camarillo, "Black and Brown in Compton: Demographic Change, Suburban Decline, and Intergroup Relations in a South Central Los Angeles Community, 1950 to 2000," in *Not Just Black and White: Historical and Contemporary Perspectives on Immigration, Race, and Ethnicity in the United States*, eds. Nancy Foner and George M. Fredrickson (New York: Russell Sage Foundation, 2004), 364; Camarillo, "Chicano Urban History."

132 **crackled with anxiety:** Straus, *Death of a Suburban Dream*, 74.

132 **HOLC had yellowlined:** Robert K. Nelson et al., "Mapping Inequality: Redlining in New Deal America," American Panorama, eds. Robert K. Nelson and Edward L. Ayers, https://dsl.richmond.edu/panorama/redlining/#loc=14/33.901/-118.208&city=los-angeles-ca.

132 **racial covenants unenforceable:** *Shelley v. Kraemer*, 334 U.S. 1 (1948).

132 **local elementary schools:** Straus, *Death of a Suburban Dream*, 60–61.

133 **named Vernon Whitley:** "Anti-Negro Signs in Compton: Owners Find Slurs Painted on House, Neighborly Greeting," *Los Angeles Sentinel*, September 2, 1948.

133 ***Los Angeles Sentinel* reported:** "New Terrorism in Compton Unchecked," *Los Angeles Sentinel*, October 28, 1948.

133 **the paper opined:** "Ku Klux Kompton," *Los Angeles Sentinel*, October 14, 1948.

133 **white families were vocal:** Straus, *Death of a Suburban Dream*, 47.

133 **stretched perilously thin:** Straus, *Death of a Suburban Dream*, 5.

133 **several distinct elementary districts:** Lloyd M. Morrisett and John A. Sexson, "A Report of a Survey of the Public Schools of the Compton Union High School and Junior College Districts," Los Angeles County, California, 1949, map 3.

133 **each was overcrowded:** Straus, *Death of a Suburban Dream*, 66.

133 **portable army barracks:** Morrisett and Sexson, "A Report of a Survey of the Public Schools of the Compton Union High School and Junior College Districts," 2.

133 **issuing more debt:** Straus, *Death of a Suburban Dream*, 67.

133 **Bush family left:** Adams, "Bush's Compton Roots Raise Thorny Issue."

134 **FOUR TEEN-AGERS SENTENCED:** "Four Teen-Agers Sentenced," *California Eagle*, February 26, 1953.

134 **SALE TO NEGROES:** Wendell Green, "Vigilantes Brutally Beat Man over Sale to Negroes," *California Eagle*, February 19, 1953.

134 **white vandals attacked:** "Compton Vandals Stage Sneak Attack," *California Eagle*, April 16, 1953.

134 **sixty small bungalows:** All details regarding racial violence on Reeve Street from Bob Ellis, "The Story of Reeve Street in Compton," *California Eagle*, May 14, 1953, unless otherwise noted.

134 **A front-page photo:** "Guard Homes as Pickets March," *California Eagle*, May 14, 1953, 1.

135 **"It is the story of men":** Bob Ellis, "Full Compton Story Told in Eagle Series," *California Eagle*, May 14, 1953, 8.

135 **fight for racial separation:** Straus, *Death of a Suburban Dream*, 83–89.

135 **the all-white board:** Details of Compton education leaders' strategies during this era all from Straus, *Death of a Suburban Dream*, 68–69, 84, unless otherwise noted.

135 **town's Maginot Line:** Franklin, *Compton: A Community in Transition*, 22–23.

135 **several Black students:** El Companile 1961 yearbook, 20–21.

135 **elected Douglas Dollarhide:** Straus, *Death of a Suburban Dream*, 101.

135 **would be mayor:** Straus, *Death of a Suburban Dream*, 119.

135 **first Black superintendent:** William J. Drummond, "Compton—A Self-Sufficiency Test for Black Leadership," *Los Angeles Times*, July 5, 1970, B2; Steven V. Roberts, "Compton, Calif., 65% Negro, Believes in Integration and in Peaceful Change," *New York Times*, June 8, 1969, 65; Chara Haeussler Bohan and Lauren Yarnell Bradshaw, "The Challenge to Create a 'Community of Believers': Civil Rights Superintendent Alonzo Crim and Atlanta's School Desegregation Compromise," *Vitae Scholasticae* 31, no. 1 (Spring 2014).

135 **a steady stream:** See, e.g., "Albert Camarillo," Stanford Department of History, https://history.stanford.edu/people/albert-camarillo; "Compton High School Hall of Fame," https://comptonhighalumni.org/hall-of-fame-2/; "Keb'Mo'," Grammy Awards, https://www.grammy.com/artists/kebmo/9850.

135 **town's first condominiums:** "Real Estate Development Big Success," *Los Angeles Sentinel*, April 29, 1971, B6.

136 **"We're not powerful enough":** William J. Drummond, "Compton—A Self-Sufficiency Test for Black Leadership," *Los Angeles Times*, July 5, 1970, B1.

136 **was Jefferson Elementary:** All details regarding Jefferson Elementary and its bilingual program during this era are drawn from Frank M. Goodman, "Compton Bilingual Education Plan 1969–1970," Gerth Archives and Special Collections, California State University, Dominguez Hills, unless otherwise noted.

136 **the newly consolidated:** Donald Hodes, "Compton Unified School District Racial Imbalance Plan," December 1970, Gerth Archives and Special Collections, California State University, Dominguez Hills.

136 **raise the alarm:** All details regarding Compton from the Welfare Planning Council report are drawn from Franklin, *Compton: Community in Transition*, unless otherwise noted.

137 **motorist in Watts:** All details regarding the Watts rebellion are drawn from "Watts Riots," Civil Rights Digital Library, http://crdl.usg.edu/events/watts_riots/?Welcome&Welcome, unless otherwise noted.

137 **residents stood together:** Josh Sides, "Straight into Compton: American Dreams, Urban Nightmares, and the Metamorphosis of a Black

Suburb," *American Quarterly* 56, no. 3 (September 2004): 591, https://www.jstor.org/stable/40068235.

137 **chaos at bay:** Steven V. Roberts, "Compton, California, 65% Negro, Believes in Integration and in Peaceful Change," *New York Times*, June 8, 1969.

137 **nineteen years old:** Earl Caldwell, "City in California, 72% Black, Looks to Future Despite Woes," *New York Times*, January 19, 1972, 18.

137 **Mexican American classmates bloody:** Details of racial violence and economic troubles in Compton schools in the early 1970s are drawn from Straus, *Death of a Suburban Dream*, unless otherwise noted.

137 **"after surviving Vietnam":** Straus, *Death of a Suburban Dream*, 129.

138 **Bloated and near broke:** Steven C. Smith, "Compton Schools: Is Unified Better?," *Los Angeles Times*, February 3, 1974, SE1.

138 **six-figure annual deficits:** Jack McCurdy, "Report Urges Closing of 5 Compton Schools," *Los Angeles Times*, December 19, 1973, A3.

138 **inside local schools:** See, e.g., Special Committee of the Los Angeles County Grand Jury, "Public Hearing City of Compton," January 14, 15, 16, 17, 20, 21, 22, 1975, 3, and Bob Allison, "Compton Schools: 'Tragic Decay,'" *Los Angeles Sentinel*, December 6, 1973, A1.

138 **running water or toilet paper:** Straus, *Death of a Suburban Dream*, 144.

138 **"What we're doing":** Straus, *Death of a Suburban Dream*, 122.

138 **in full-blown crisis:** Details regarding unemployment, murders, and community-police relations in Compton in the early 1970s are drawn from "An Open Letter to the Compton Community," Special Committee of the Los Angeles County Grand Jury, "Public Hearing City of Compton," January 14, 15, 16, 17, 20, 21, 22, 1975, unless otherwise noted.

138 **without proper documentation:** Straus, *Death of a Suburban Dream*, 146.

138 **a kickback scheme:** Straus, *Death of a Suburban Dream*, 145.

138 **fifteen family members:** Anne La Riviere and George Reasons, "Compton's Schools Sea of Troubles," *Los Angeles Times*, July 1, 1981, B1.

138 **conference in Honolulu:** Straus, *Death of a Suburban Dream*, 171.

138 **students with intellectual disabilities:** Tom Gorman, "Compton Trustees to Submit Bilingual Education Proposal to Federal Officials," *Los Angeles Times*, January 22, 1978, SE9.

139 **certified bilingual teachers:** Straus, *Death of a Suburban Dream*, 163.

139 **vandals did $750,000:** Straus, *Death of a Suburban Dream*, 155.

139 **accused of cheating:** All details regarding allegations of cheating in Compton Unified schools in 1980 are drawn from Mary Barber,

"Results of State Testing in Compton School Voided; Tampering Discovered," *Los Angeles Times*, October 17, 1980, 9, unless otherwise noted.

139 **suburban "disaster areas":** Judith Hernandez and John Pincus, *Troubled Suburbs: An Exploratory Study*, RAND, June 1982, N-1759-HUD, 78, 81.

139 **by 195 percent:** Straus, *Death of a Suburban Dream*, 154.

139 **slumlords ignored citations:** Adams, "Bush's Compton Roots Raise Thorny Issue," 1.

139 **and of the SWAT teams:** Bob Pool and Edward J. Boyer, "Area Closed Off in Search for Suspect in 2 Slayings," *Los Angeles Times*, April 20, 1988, https://www.latimes.com/archives/la-xpm-1988-04-20-me-1315-story.html.

139 **trash and feces:** Yang, "For Bush, Compton Was Once Home."

139 **to formally commemorate:** Walter R. Tucker III, "Landmark for Compton," *Los Angeles Times*, August 15, 1992, SDB9, https://www.latimes.com/archives/la-xpm-1992-08-15-me-4766-story.html.

140 **"I can't believe they want":** Adams, "Bush's Compton Roots Raise Thorny Issue," 1.

140 **motorist Rodney King:** History.com editors, "Riots Erupt in Los Angeles After Police Officers Are Acquitted in Rodney King Trial," History.com, March 3, 2010, https://www.history.com/this-day-in-history/riots-erupt-in-los-angeles.

140 **from inside Compton:** All details regarding Compton's involvement in the 1992 Los Angeles riots are drawn from Straus, *Death of a Suburban Dream*, 191, unless otherwise noted.

140 **when the violence erupted:** Jack Nelson, "Bush Denounces Rioting in L.A. as 'Purely Criminal,'" *Los Angeles Times*, May 1, 1992, https://www.latimes.com/archives/la-xpm-1992-05-01-mn-1416-story.html.

140 **"What we saw last night":** George H. W. Bush Presidential Library and Museum, "Address to the Nation Regarding the Riots in Los Angeles," May 1, 1992," YouTube video, 12:28, https://www.youtube.com/watch?v=ynoZY1npoYA.

140 **huge Volkswagen plant:** "Cuautlancingo," Wikipedia, https://en.wikipedia.org/wiki/Cuautlancingo.

140 **there since 1967:** "#TBT—The Rich History of Volkswagen's Puebla Plant," Volkswagen US Media Site, July 16, 2020, https://media.vw.com/en-us/releases/1354.

142 **to $4.75 an hour:** Mark Stevenson, "Mexico Labor Works Harder, Earns Less," UPI, October 24, 1996, https://www.upi.com/Archives/1996/10/24/Mexico-labor-works-harder-earns-less/1659846129600/.

142 **cut their workforces:** Martina Fuchs, "The Effects of the Crisis of 1994/95 on the Mexican Labour Market: The Case of the City of Puebla," *Urban Studies* 38, no. 10 (2001): 1808, 1814, https://www.jstor.org/stable/43196605.

143 **regular and predictable:** Douglas S. Massey and Karen A. Pren, "Origins of the New Latino Underclass," *Race and Social Problems* 4, no. 8 (2012), DOI 10.1007/s12552-012-9066-6.

143 **needs of U.S. employers:** Silvia E. Giorguli, Claudia Masferrer, and Victor M. García-Guerrero, "How Did We Get to the Current Mexico-US Migration System, and How Might It Look in the Near Future?," in *The Trump Paradox: Migration, Trade, and Racial Politics in US-Mexico Integration*, eds. Raúl Andrés Hinojosa Ojeda and Edward Eric Telles (Oakland, CA: University of California Press, 2021), 50.

143 **Mexico had been exempted:** Mae M. Ngai, *Impossible Subjects: Illegal Aliens and the Making of Modern America* (Princeton, NJ: Princeton University Press, 2014), 23.

143 **major repatriation campaign:** Massey and Pren, "Origins of the New Latino Underclass."

143 **more than 21 million:** Albert M. Camarillo, "Cities of Color: The New Racial Frontier in California's Minority-Majority Cities," *Pacific Historical Review*, 76, no. 1 (2007): 16.

143 **a new underclass:** Massey and Pren, "Origins of the New Latino Underclass."

143 **militarizing the border:** Douglas S. Massey, "What Were the Paradoxical Consequences of Militarizing the Border with Mexico?," in *The Trump Paradox*, 32.

143 **in the mid-1980s:** Hearing on "Role of Family-Based Immigration in the U.S. Immigration System, Before the House Judiciary Subcommittee on Immigration," 110th Cong., (2007) (Bill Ong Hing, Professor of Law and Asian American Studies, University of California, Davis).

143 **to more fear:** Massey and Pren, "Origins of the New Latino Underclass."

143 **little to impact:** Massey, "What Were the Paradoxical Consequences of Militarizing the Border with Mexico?," 43.

144 **beginning to gripe:** Michele Fuetsch, "Latino Aspirations on Rise in Compton," *Los Angeles Times*, May 7, 1990, B1, https://www.latimes.com/archives/la-xpm-1990-05-07-me-134-story.htm.

144 **Compton Unified's personnel commission:** Straus, *Death of a Suburban Dream*, 151.

144 **mixed xenophobia with accusations:** Fuetsch, "Latino Aspirations on Rise in Compton."

144 **"This is America":** Fuetsch, "Latino Aspirations on Rise in Compton."

144 **détente seemed possible:** All details of Compton's 1993 mayoral election are drawn from Darryl Fears, "Compton Latinos Still on Outside Looking In," *Los Angeles Times*, April 16, 1998, 1, https://www.latimes.com/archives/la-xpm-1998-apr-16-mn-39881-story.html, unless otherwise noted.

144 **soundly defeated Pallan:** "Bradley, Robbins Leading in Compton Council Vote," *Long Beach Press-Telegram*, June 5, 1991.

144 **teachers and security guards:** *Newsweek* staff, "'It's Our Turn Now,'" *Newsweek*, November 20, 1994, https://www.newsweek.com/its-our-turn-now-186396.

144 **called for boycotts:** Bryan Cotton, "Hispanics Boycott Compton School," *Los Angeles Sentinel*, September 22, 1994, A1.

145 **a false budget:** Straus, *Death of a Suburban Dream*, 188.

145 **defended Proposition 187:** Straus, *Death of a Suburban Dream*, 200.

145 **be ruled unconstitutional:** Patrick J. McDonnell, "Prop. 187 Found Unconstitutional by Federal Judge," *Los Angeles Times*, November 15, 1997, https://www.latimes.com/archives/la-xpm-1997-nov-15-mn-54053-story.html.

145 **seventeen-year-old Felipe Soltero:** "Officer Won't Be Tried in Boy's Beating," *Los Angeles Times*, February 10, 1995, https://www.latimes.com/archives/la-xpm-1995-02-10-me-30275-story.html.

145 **labeling them "agitators":** Fears, "Compton Latinos Still on Outside Looking In," 1.

145 **in South Africa:** *Newsweek* staff, "'It's Our Turn Now.'"

145 **well over half:** Camarillo, "Black and Brown in Compton," 366.

145 **nearly 80 percent:** Fuetsch, "Latino Aspirations on Rise in Compton."

145 **"Have the oppressed":** *Newsweek* staff, "'It's Our Turn Now.'"

CHAPTER 6: PROMISED LANDS

147 **"And the past is still":** John Koethe, "In the Park," in *North Point North: New and Selected Poems* (New York, HarperCollins: 2003).

148 **any homework at all:** "Trivium Academy Student Handbook," https://static1.squarespace.com/static/55e5dcdce4b0f13824a01109/t/630c2fa8d8bc46649ab99e5c/1661743018760/Student%2BHandbook.pdf.

148 **$25,000-a-year private school:** "Tuition & Fees," June Shelton School and Evaluation Center, https://web.archive.org/web/20171226053323/https://www.shelton.org/admission/tuition-fees.

149 **three-day team-building trip:** "SCIS Parent Message," Sloan Creek Intermediate School, August 23, 2019, https://myemail.constantcontact.com/SCIS-Principal-Message-8-23-19.html?soid=1114502746978&aid=d8rkcMZ3JT0.

149 **sent a message:** All descriptions of school and parent communications surrounding Sloan Creek Intermediate's fifth-grade camping trip are drawn from emails and other documents obtained via public-records requests to Lovejoy

Independent School District, unless otherwise noted.

150 **Monday in September:** This scene has been reconstructed based on interviews with Susan Becker, multiple other Sloan Creek parents, and staff of the Collin County Adventure Camp; a subsequent visit I made to the camp; documents provided by Collin County Adventure Camp and obtained via open-records requests; and photos and videos provided by Susan Becker.

152 **public address announcer cried:** YouthSportsRewind.com, http://ysrautoscalegroup1-loadbalancer-3568 48416.us-east-1.elb.amazonaws.com /NewSite/.

152 **an all-consuming experience:** All details about youth football in Gwinnett County are from former Gwinnett Football League president Erik Richard in discussion with the author, June 2021, unless otherwise noted.

152 **still heavily white:** "2040 Unified Plan," Gwinnett County Board of Commissioners, February 5, 2019, https://www.gwinnettcounty .com/web/gwinnett/departments/planning development/services/landuseplanning /2040unifiedplan.

152 **new academic clusters:** Keith Farner, "GCPS Redistricting Typically Brings Spirited Responses," *Gwinnett Daily Post*, November 28, 2015, https://www.gwinnettdailypost.com /local/education/gcps-redistricting-typically -brings-spirited-responses/article_05b1386c -297a-563f-b946-1e2cde97b70d.html; Laura Diamond, "School Lines to Be Redrawn; 'Complex' Redistricting Could Affect Thousands," *Atlanta Journal-Constitution*, September 18, 2007, 1J.

153 **a fantastic reputation:** D. Aileen Dodd, "Some Gwinnett Schools Still Grapple with Growth," *Atlanta Journal-Constitution*, September 8, 2010, B1, B4.

153 **police officers and firefighters:** "School History," Ivy Creek Elementary School, accessed November 7, 2022, https://www .gcpsk12.org/Page/26112.

155 **Every Sunday evening:** Descriptions of the Dacula youth football team coaches' meetings are drawn from interviews with Anthony Robinson and Russell Rhodes.

156 **was October 2017:** All descriptions of meetings of Lauren Adesina's SEED cohort are drawn from interviews with Lauren Adesina and fellow participant Katie Logan, as well as "SEED for Families," Evanston/Skokie School District 65, https://www.district65.net/site/Default .aspx?PageType=3&DomainID=4&PageID =1&ViewID=6446ee88-d30c-497e-9316 -3f8874b3e108&FlexDataID=8217, unless otherwise noted.

158 **local police alike:** Mary Gavin, "Walkout at ETHS in Protest of Trump," *Evanston RoundTable*, January 26, 2017, https://evanstonroundtable.com/2017/01/26/walkout -at-eths-in-protest-of-trump/.

158 **voted to create:** City of Evanston City Council Regular Meeting, October 16, 2017, Minutes, https://www.cityofevanston.org/home /showpublisheddocument/27857/636437 682263430000.

158 **services and programs:** "Equity and Empowerment Commission," City of Evanston, https://www.cityofevanston.org/government /equity-empowerment/equity-and- empowerment-commission.

158 **District 65 board:** Syd Stone, "District 65 Board Elects New President, Vice President," *Daily Northwestern*, May 2, 2017, https:// dailynorthwestern.com/2017/05/02/city/district -65-board-elects-new-president-vice-president/.

158 **Principal Kate Ellison:** Details about equity-related reforms at Washington Elementary are drawn from Kate Ellison in discussion with the author, February 2020, unless otherwise noted.

158 **equity freedom fighter Zaretta Hammond:** "About," Culturally Responsive Teaching and the Brain, https://crtandthebrain.com/about/.

160 **talk in Evanston:** Catherine Henderson, "Authors Evaluate Racial Inequities in Schools, Address District 65 Community Members," *Daily Northwestern*, March 7, 2018, https:// dailynorthwestern.com/2018/03/07/city /authors-evaluate-racial-inequities-schools -address-district-65-community-members/.

160 *Despite the Best Intentions:* Amanda E. Lewis and John B. Diamond, *Despite the Best Intentions: How Racial Inequality Thrives in Good Schools* (Oxford: Oxford University Press, 2015).

160 **Two hundred people:** Details of parent activism via the group that came to be known as Next Steps Evanston are drawn from interviews with members of the group's planning committee and documents such as promotional flyers, presentation materials, and meeting minutes.

160 **a vacant seat:** Mary Helt Gavin, "Anya Tanyavutti to Fill Phillips Vacancy on District 65 Board," *Evanston RoundTable*, October 19, 2016, https://evanstonroundtable.com/main .asp?SectionID=16&SubSectionID=27 &ArticleID=12664.

161 **person managing her campaign:** Keerti Gopal, "State Representative Candidate Candance Chow Faces Legal Scrutiny Days Before Election," *Daily Northwestern*, March 18, 2018, https:// dailynorthwestern.com/2018/03/18/city /state-representative-candidate-candance-chow -faces-legal-scrutiny-days-before-election/; and Ryan Wangman, "Candidate for State Representative Criticized by Challenger for Campaign Email," *Daily Northwestern*, March 8, 2018, https://dailynorthwestern.com/2018/03/08 /city/candidate-for-state-representative -criticized-by-challenger-for-campaign-email/.

161 **"Equity Impact Assessment Tool":** "Equity Impact Assessment Tool" file provided by Next

Steps Evanston planning committee member in email message to the author, June 10, 2021.

165 **"Mother to Son":** Langston Hughes, "Mother to Son," *The Crisis* 25, no. 2 (December 1922): 87.

166 **Hill District plays:** Charles Isherwood, "August Wilson, Theater's Poet of Black America, Is Dead at 60," *New York Times*, October 3, 2005, https://www.nytimes.com/2005/10/03/theater /newsandfeatures/august-wilson-theaters-poet -of-black-america-is-dead-at-60.html.

168 **about her reaction:** The Hernandez family's experience in Compton is told primarily from the perspectives of Alberto and Jacob. On the two occasions I was able to talk with Cristina, our focus was primarily on her recollections of growing up and attending university in Puebla. I did not interview Marisol.

169 **to Universal Studios:** All details regarding Universal Studios in 2003 are drawn from interviews with the Hernandez family and Bob Thomas, "Universal Studios Hollywood Celebrates Its 40th," Associated Press, July 25, 2004, unless otherwise noted.

170 **Led by Democrats:** Liz Halloran, "Gang of 8 Champion Plan, Declare 'Year of Immigration Reform,'" NPR, April 18, 2013, https://www.npr .org/sections/itsallpolitics/2013/04/18/1777806 65/bipartisan-senate-gang-prepares-to-sell -immigration-plan.

170 **path to citizenship:** "A Guide to S.744: Understanding the 2013 Senate Immigration Bill," American Immigration Council, July 10, 2013, https://www.americanimmigration council.org/research/guide-s744 -understanding-2013-senate-immigration-bill.

170 **roughly 11 million:** Michael D. Shear and Julia Preston, "Obama Pushed 'Fullest Extent' of His Powers on Immigration Plan," *New York Times*, November 28, 2014, https://www.nytimes.com /2014/11/29/us/white-house-tested-limits-of -powers-before-action-on-immigration.html.

170 **of legal challenges:** "Deferred Action for Childhood Arrivals. Federal Policy and Examples of State Actions," National Conference of State Legislatures, https://www.ncsl.org /research/immigration/deferred-action.aspx.

170 **roughly 3.7 million:** "MPI: As Many as 3.7 Million Unauthorized Immigrants Could Get Relief from Deportation Under Anticipated New Deferred Action Program," Migration Policy Institute, November 19, 2014, https:// www.migrationpolicy.org/news/mpi-many-37 -million-unauthorized-immigrants-could-get -relief-deportation-under-anticipated-new.

170 **red states sued:** Randy Capps, Michael Fix, and Jie Zong, "A Profile of U.S. Children with Unauthorized Immigrant Parents," Migration Policy Institute, January 2016, https://www .migrationpolicy.org/research/profile-us -children-unauthorized-immigrant-parents.

171 **effectively killing DAPA:** Adam Liptak and Michael D. Shear, "Supreme Court Tie Blocks Obama Immigration Plan," *New York Times*, June 23, 2016, https://www.nytimes.com/2016 /06/24/us/supreme-court-immigration-obama -dapa.html.

172 **Teachers of the Year:** "PLTW Names Educational Leader and Teacher of the Year," PLTW, February 18, 2019, https://www.pltw .org/news/project-lead-the-way-names-annual -educational-leader-and-teacher-of-the-year -recipients.

172 **third annual STEAMfest:** Compton Unified School District, "STEAMfest 2019," https:// drive.google.com/file/d/1HLqMjiUfQRb sL4GbkJtw3p5TypT8qmLy/view; ComptonSchools, "Compton STEAMfest 2019," YouTube video, 3:47, June 13, 2019, https:// youtu.be/PR74E2qAkuo.

CHAPTER 7: "GOD'S HONEST TRUTH"

177 **"I don't think history":** James Baldwin and Margaret Mead, *A Rap on Race* (New York: Dell Publishing, 1974), 188.

178 **"Up to Date with Room 38":** Special thanks to my mother for saving every issue of "Up to Date with Room 38" (in the author's possession, undated).

179 *The Dible Scoop:* Kim Glasser, Susie Gray, and Ben Herold, "Student Teachers Come to Dible," *Dible Scoop*, January 1988, 1 (in the author's possession).

179 **the twenty-four covaledictorians:** Penn Hills High School, *Ahead of Our Time* (Penn Hills, Pennsylvania, 1994), 54–55, yearbook in the author's possession.

179 **mulled a report:** Official Minutes, Penn Hills Board of School Directors, August 30, 1995.

179 **to renovate and repair:** Eleanor Chute, "Bond Not Likely to Fund School District Wish List," *Pittsburgh Post-Gazette*, September 3, 1995, EW-2.

179 **didn't sit well:** Michelle Camp, "Penn Hills Taxpayers Seek Relief," *Pittsburgh Post-Gazette*, March 10, 1994, E-2.

180 **Penn Aqua Swim Club:** "Staying Afloat: Swim Clubs Hoping to Pay Up on Taxes," *Pittsburgh Post-Gazette*, September 8, 1996, EW-2.

180 **Longvue Country Club:** "Point Park College President Stepping Down," *Pittsburgh Post-Gazette*, January 11, 1995, B-5.

180 **keep taxes flat:** *Pittsburgh Post-Gazette*, May 8, 1996, B-3; Official Minutes, Penn Hills Board of School Directors, May 7, 1996; Official Minutes, Penn Hills Board of School Directors, April 8, 1997.

180 **modest bond measure:** "Minutes of the Regular Board Workshop," Penn Hills Board of School Directors, August 6, 1996.

180 **"If we take on another":** Chute, "Bond Not Likely to Fund School District Wish List."

180 **called Strong Towns:** "Charles Marohn," Strong Towns, https://www.strongtowns.org /contributors-journal/charles-marohn.

181 **for what it was:** Charles Marohn, "The Growth Ponzi Scheme," Strong Towns, https://www .strongtowns.org/the-growth-ponzi-scheme.

181 **single-family suburban housing:** Charles Marohn, "It's Time to Abolish Single-Family Zoning," *American Conservative*, July 3, 2020, https://www.theamericanconservative.com/its -time-to-abolish-single-family-zoning/.

181 **a Ponzi scheme:** Charles Marohn, "The Growth Ponzi Scheme."

181 **"We are in the process":** Charles Marohn, "The Growth Ponzi Scheme."

181 **professor Bernadette Hanlon:** See, e.g., Bernadette Hanlon, *Once the American Dream: Inner-Ring Suburbs of the Metropolitan United States* (Philadelphia: Temple University Press, 2010).

182 **points to Ferguson:** This argument about Ferguson's history is drawn from Charles Marohn, "Stroad Nation," Strong Towns, August 25, 2014, https://www.strongtowns.org /journal/2014/8/25/stroad-nation.html, unless otherwise noted.

182 **99 percent white:** Paulina Firozi, "5 Things to Know about Ferguson Police Department," *USA Today*, August 14, 2014, https://www.usatoday .com/story/news/nation-now/2014/08/14/ ferguson-police-department-details/14064451/.

182 **to two-thirds Black:** Elizabeth Kneebone, "Ferguson, Mo. Emblematic of Growing Suburban Poverty," Brookings, August 15, 2014, https://www.brookings.edu/blog/the-avenue /2014/08/15/ferguson-mo-emblematic-of -growing-suburban-poverty/.

182 **middle of Canfield Drive:** Details of the killing of Michael Brown are drawn from Emily Wax-Thibodeaux, "Ferguson Timeline: What's Happened Since the Aug. 9 Shooting of Michael Brown," *Washington Post*, November 21, 2014, https://www.washingtonpost.com/news/post -nation/wp/2014/11/21/ferguson-timeline-whats -happened-since-the-aug-9-shooting-of -michael-brown/, unless otherwise noted.

182 **to walk single file:** Marohn, "Stroad Nation."

182 **on the sidewalk:** "Department of Justice Report Regarding the Criminal Investigation into the Shooting Death of Michael Brown by Ferguson, Missouri Police Officer Darren Wilson," Department of Justice, March 5, 2015, https:// www.justice.gov/sites/default/files/opa/press -releases/attachments/2015/03/04/doj_report _on_shooting_of_michael_brown_1.pdf.

182 **against police violence:** "Timeline of Events in Shooting of Michael Brown in Ferguson," AP News, April 8, 2019, https://apnews.com/article /shootings-police-us-news-st-louis-michael -brown-9aa32033692547699a3b61da8fd1fc62.

182 **to national prominence:** Shannon Luibrand, "How a Death in Ferguson Sparked a Movement in America," CBS News, August 7, 2015, https:// www.cbsnews.com/news/how-the-black-lives -matter-movement-changed-america-one-year -later/.

182 **than 20 percent:** Wilson Andrews, Alicia DeSantis, and Josh Keller, "Justice Department's Report on the Ferguson Police Department," *New York Times*, March 4, 2015, https://www .nytimes.com/interactive/2015/03/04/us /ferguson-police-racial-discrimination.html.

182 **wearing a seat belt:** "Investigation of the Ferguson Police Department," United States Department of Justice Civil Rights Division, March 4, 2015, 4, https://www.justice.gov/sites /default/files/opa/press-releases/attachments/2015 /03/04/ferguson_police_department_report.pdf.

183 **"I think we are going to see":** Marohn, "Stroad Nation."

184 **named acting superintendent:** Tim Means, "Penn Hills School Board Appoints Superintendent," *Pittsburgh Post-Gazette*, June 29, 2015, https://www.post-gazette.com/news /education/2015/06/29/Penn-Hills-school-board -appoints-superintendent/stories/201506290194.

184 **annual operating budget:** Patrick Varine, "Penn Hills School Budget for 2014–15 Totals $77.94 Million," Trib Live, June 30, 2014, https:// archive.triblive.com/news/penn-hills-school -budget-for-2014-15-totals-77-94-million/.

184 **recurring accounting error:** "In Re: The 2017 Allegheny County Investigating Grand Jury: Case A," CP-02-MD-6182-2016, Report one, 37.

184 **annual debt-service payments:** This and other details regarding alleged malfeasance by the Penn Hills School District's former business manager are drawn from "Before the Board of School Directors of Penn Hills School District in the Matter of Richard E. Liberto," unless otherwise noted. A lawyer for the former business manager did not respond to a request for comment.

185 **district lost millions:** U.S. Department of Education, National Center for Education Statistics, Common Core of Data (CCD), "School District Finance Survey (F-33)," 2014–15 (FY 2015), v.1a.

185 **make things worse:** All details regarding the Penn Hills School District's finances and decision-making around the construction of two new schools between 2005 and 2019 are drawn from "In Re: The 2017 Allegheny County Investigating Grand Jury: Case A," unless otherwise noted.

185 **series of studies:** Phillip Foreman, "Capital Needs Assessment Study Penn Hills School District," Foreman Group Architects, April 20, 2006.

185 **unrelated pay-to-play scheme:** Kate Giammarise, "Pa. Turnpike Corruption Case Ends with Former Officials Avoiding Jail," *Pittsburgh Post-Gazette*, November 20, 2014, https://www.mcall.com /news/pennsylvania/mc-pa-turnpike-pay-to-play -scandal-20141120-story.html.

186 **nearly $135 million:** "Penn Hills School District Transcript of Settlement," September 22, 2009; "In Re: The 2017 Allegheny County Investigating Grand Jury: Case A," 22.

187 **fifth consecutive year:** "Report One," "In Re: The 2017 Allegheny County Investigating Grand Jury: Case A," CP-02-MD-6182-2016, 27-28; U.S. Department of Education, National Center for Education Statistics, Common Core of Data (CCD), "Local Education Agency (School District) Universe Survey," 2006–07 v.1c, 2007–08 v.1b, 2008–09 v.1a, 2009–10 v.2a, 2010–11 v.2a, 2011–12 v.1a, 2012–13 v.1a, 2021–22 v.1a.

188 **to junk status:** Orlie Prince to Lori McKay, August 24, 2015; Will Kenton, "B3/B-," Investopedia, June 15, 2022, https://www.investopedia.com/terms/b/b3-b.asp.

188 **a forensic audit:** Mary Niederberger, "State Auditor General Set to Examine Penn Hills Schools," *Pittsburgh Post-Gazette*, August 21, 2015, https://www.post-gazette.com/news/education/2015/08/21/State-audit-planned-for-financially-strapped-Penn-Hills-School-District/stories/201508210241.

188 **whopping $167 million:** Commonwealth of Pennsylvania Department of the Auditor General, "Performance Audit, Penn Hills School District, Allegheny County, Pennsylvania," May 2016, 18.

188 **referred the matter:** Pennsylvania Department of the Auditor General, "Auditor General DePasquale Says Dereliction of Duties Pushed Penn Hills School District to Edge of Financial Cliff," May 18, 2016, https://www.paauditor.gov/press-releases/auditor-general-depasquale-says-dereliction-of-duties-pushed-penn-hills-school-district-to-edge-of-financial-cliff.

188 **any criminal charges:** Matt McKinney, "Penn Hills School District: Massive Debt Long Road to Recovery," *Pittsburgh Post-Gazette*, June 24, 2019.

189 **possible Mafia connections:** I did not pursue Ms. Vecchio's suggestion that I look into possible Mafia connections within the Allegheny County District Attorney's Office.

189 **pushing $172 million:** Matt McKinney, "Grand Jury Report on Penn Hills School District: 'Catastrophic Financial Condition,'" *Pittsburgh Post-Gazette*, February 5, 2019, https://www.post-gazette.com/news/education/2019/02/05/Penn-Hills-School-District-Grand-Jury-report-budget-mismanagement/stories/201902040125.

189 **residents showed up:** Natasha Lindstrom, "Penn Hills School District Is in 'the Worst Financial Shape' in Pennsylvania, Auditor General Says," Trib Live, February 28, 2019, https://triblive.com/local/pittsburgh-allegheny/penn-hills-school-district-is-in-the-worst-financial-shape-in-pennsylvania-auditor-general-says/.

189 **"I need to put this":** Author's notes from recording of meeting, February 28, 2019.

189 **downhill from there:** All details regarding the auditor general forum to discuss the financial crisis in the Penn Hills School District are drawn from author's notes from recording of meeting, February 28, 2019, unless otherwise noted.

189 **the system's finances:** Matt McKinney, "Penn Hills School District: Massive Debt Long Road to Recovery."

189 **roughly fifty teachers:** All details regarding the condition of the Penn Hills School District following revelations of its massive debt and the actual and proposed cuts that followed are drawn from Daniel J. Matsook, "Financial Recovery Plan, Penn Hills School District," June 29, 2019, https://4.files.edl.io/4b6c/07/18/19/134133-2ad34a90-9221-48e7-95d3-f681ee39287f.pdf, unless otherwise noted.

CHAPTER 8: THE SUN'S HIGHEST POINT

195 **than everywhere else:** City of Lucas Ordinance §14.04.251, accessed November 26, 2022, https://ecode360.com/39199477?highlight=lighting&searchId=29537591074760146#39199477.

196 **on pro-democracy protesters:** Fox News, *Tucker Carlson Tonight*, "LeBron Sides with China, Not Free Speech," uploaded on October 15, 2019, YouTube video, 5:51 min, https://youtu.be/vVHPseUiz0E.

197 **coverage of Amber Guyger:** Stacy Fernández and Juan Pablo Garnham, "Former Dallas Police Officer Amber Guyger Found Guilty of Murder in Shooting of Botham Jean," *Texas Tribune*, October 1, 2019, https://www.texastribune.org/2019/10/01/amber-guyger-verdict-former-dallas-police-officer-found-guilty-murder/.

197 **woman a hug:** Hannah Knowles, "Amber Guyger Was Hugged by Her Victim's Brother and a Judge, Igniting a Debate about Forgiveness and Race," *Washington Post*, October 3, 2019, https://www.washingtonpost.com/nation/2019/10/03/judge-botham-jeans-brother-hugged-amber-guyger-igniting-debate-about-forgiveness-race/.

197 **sixth-inning home run:** Astros vs. Yankees, ESPN, October 17, 2019, https://www.espn.com/mlb/game/_/gameId/401169102.

198 **with adult staffers:** Dave Lieber, "Lovejoy ISD Chief Ousted After 'Inappropriate Conduct' Was a Master Manipulator," *Dallas Morning News*, February 21, 2019, https://www.dallasnews.com/news/watchdog/2019/02/22/lovejoy-isd-chief-ousted-after-inappropriate-conduct-was-a-master-manipulator/.

199 **single K–6 school:** U.S. Department of Education, National Center for Education Statistics, Common Core of Data (CCD), "Local Education Agency (School District) Universe Survey,"

1989–90 v.1a; "Public Elementary/Secondary School Universe Survey," 1989–90 v.1a.

199 **to neighboring Allen:** "Frequently Asked Questions & Answers," Lovejoy Independent School District, August 22, 2002.

200 **started filling up:** "Plano at Maturity, The Biggerstaff Report," October 2003, https://planotomorrow.org/231/Past-Plans-and-Studies.

200 **beyond its borders:** M/PF Research, Inc., "Allen Independent School District Student Enrollment Projections," November 2001, 9.

200 **be kept "country":** Minutes of Joint Comprehensive Plan Meeting #4, Lucas City Council and Planning & Zoning, February 13, 2001.

200 **became an issue:** Moak, Casey & Associates, LLP, "Allen ISD and Lovejoy ISD Options for the Future, Final Report," August 2002, 1.

200 **$45 million facility:** Mary Doclar, "Highest Security: Allen School Has Extensive Precautions," *Fort Worth Star-Telegram*, August 4, 1999, 11B.

200 **had considered seceding:** Rich Hickman in discussion with the author, October 2019.

201 **Zoning Commission held hearings:** All details and quotations regarding zoning-code proposals in Lucas, Texas, in 2001 are drawn from minutes of the town's Joint Comprehensive Plan Meetings held between February 13 and July 10, 2001.

201 **in new debt:** "Bond and Debt Issue History," City of Lucas, February 25, 2020, https://www.lucastexas.us/documents/debt-issue-history/.

202 **to $25 million:** "Total Debt Outstanding per Year," City of Lucas, March 9, 2022, https://www.lucastexas.us/documents/total-debt-outstanding-per-year/.

202 **asked to vote:** "Combined Election Day & Early Ballots, Special Elections, Collin County, Texas," February 1, 2003, https://www.collincountytx.gov/elections/election_results/Archive/2003/020103/February%201,%202003%20Combined%20Election%20Day%20and%20Early%20Ballots%20-%20Statement%20of%20Votes%20Cast.TXT.

202 **four years later:** "Debt Transparency Report," Lovejoy Independent School District, June 30, 2020.

202 **They chose Goddard:** Jim Kilpatrick, "Goddard Accepts Position at Prosper ISD," *Allen American*, April 22, 2010, https://starlocalmedia.com/allenamerican/news/goddard-accepts-position-at-prosper-isd/article_94ea735a-28e0-5751-a91d-a377342158b8.html.

202 *What do we want:* Michael Goddard in discussion with the author, October 2019.

202 **aptitude or circumstances:** Ray Winkler in discussion with the author, October 2019.

203 **run some analyses:** Population and Survey Analysts, "Demographic Update for Lovejoy

I.S.D.: Projections of Housing Occupancies by Planning Unit, Ratios of Students per Household, Districtwide Projections, and Long-Range Planning," April 2004.

203 **call "quality growth":** Then Fairview mayor Henry Lessner in discussion with the author, May 2019.

203 **liked to joke:** Michael Goddard in discussion with the author, October 2019.

203 **quietly racking up:** In early 2023, Lovejoy ISD officials declined to review or comment on the details of the district's finances described in this chapter, citing recent changes in the district's leadership.

203 **reached $166 million:** "Debt Transparency Report," Lovejoy Independent School District, June 30, 2019, https://4.files.edl.io/a0d9/01/07/20/173351-bbd2cdad-709b-47c0-869e-485ac9ddfde6.pdf.

203 **almost $14 million:** "2019–2020 Proposed Budget," Lovejoy ISD, https://www.lovejoyisd.net/apps/pages/index.jsp?uREC_ID=385835&type=d&pREC_ID=1067095.

203 **to soon quadruple:** "Notes to the Basic Financial Statements for the Year Ended June 30, 2020," Lovejoy ISD, accessed December 2, 2022, https://4.files.edl.io/d636/02/08/21/152608-4e2a8e7d-7603-481d-a6e3-d5e5818995a9.pdf.

203 **to keep dropping:** "2019–20 Demographic Update, Lovejoy Independent School District," Population and Survey Analysts, January 2020, 131, http://files.pasademographics.com:800/Reports/2020/Demographic%20Update%20-%20Lovejoy%20-%20Jan%202020.pdf.

203 **significant operating deficit:** "2019–2020 Proposed Budget," Lovejoy ISD, https://www.lovejoyisd.net/apps/pages/index.jsp?uREC_ID=385835&type=d&pREC_ID=1067095.

203 **$500,000 a year:** "Financials," Foundation for Lovejoy Schools, https://www.foundationforlovejoyschools.org/financials-1.

204 **in Lovejoy schools:** "Lovejoy Scholars: Tuition-Based Enrollment for Families Residing Outside of District Boundaries," presentation slides shown to Lovejoy ISD school board, February 2021, 11–12.

204 **$1.1 million shortfall:** "2019–2020 Proposed Budget," Lovejoy ISD.

204 **at least two families:** Michael Goddard in discussion with the author, October 2019.

206 **in local courts:** "The Coercive Acts (Intolerable Acts)," classroom handout, Lovejoy ISD.

206 **not long after:** This description of Sloan Creek Intermediate School is a composite scene covering events that were spread over two days.

206 **lost her son:** "Susan Hoemke, CLC," I Make a Plan (IMAP), accessed December 2, 2022, https://www.addictionimpacts.com/pages/about.

206 **in ninth grade:** "Timeline of Hayden's Actions and Drug Use," I Make a Plan (IMAP), handout at October 18, 2019, Sloan Creek parents coffee.

207 **A second handout:** "Reading the Signs of Substance Abuse," I Make a Plan (IMAP), handout at October 18, 2019, Sloan Creek parents coffee.

CHAPTER 9: COREY'S VILLAGE

211 **the occasional bear:** "Bear Sighting at Jones Middle School Brings Students Inside for the Day," *Gwinnett Daily Post*, October 20, 2017, https://www.gwinnettdailypost.com/local /bear-sighting-at-jones-middle-school-brings -students-inside-for-the-day/article_caee906a -b5a7-11e7-9325-371c83871299.html.

211 **their middle-aged white teacher:** The Jones Middle School teacher and assistant principal identified pseudonymously in this chapter did not respond to multiple requests for comment made over the course of several years. The Gwinnett County Public Schools also declined multiple requests for comment on the disciplinary incidents described. In January 2023, GCPS chief engagement officer Melissa Laramie's responded to the final such request with a message that read in part: "In Gwinnett County Public Schools, we believe open, ongoing, two-way communication is critical. . . . We certainly honor and respect the [Robinson] family's right to make a decision to share their student's information with you, including their personal experiences and perspectives of our district. As public school employees, legally, we are not able to use our time, paid for by public funds, to fact-check your book."

211 **the Middle East:** Gwinnett County Public Schools Social Studies: 7th Grade— Instructional Calendar 2017–2018, revised 2017.

212 **to his lesson:** Because the Gwinnett County Public Schools and individual educators declined to comment, all descriptions of incidents and meetings in this chapter are by necessity based on the accounts of multiple members of the Robinson family, friends, and associates who were either physically present at or heard contemporaneous accounts of the events described; and/or on documents including discipline reports, curriculum guides, email messages and other correspondence, and meeting notes and materials.

212 **earned his first suspension:** The description of this incident is based primarily on Corey's recollections.

212 **her message read:** Email from Nika Robinson to redacted, May 24, 2017, received by the author as part of a records request.

213 **seventy-five points better:** *Jones Middle School Results-Based Evaluation System Accountability Report*, Issued 2017–18, Gwinnett County Public Schools, accessed November 30, 2022, https://www.gcpsk12.org/site/handlers /filedownload.ashx?moduleinstanceid=15739 &dataid=43764&FileName=2017%202018%20 Accountability%20report%20JonesMS.pdf.

213 **more than one third:** "Discipline Rate by Subgroup," Georgia Department of Education, received by the author as part of a records request.

213 **treated them fairly:** "GA DOE Student Health Survey 2.0, subgroup data," Georgia Department of Education, received by the author as part of a records request.

217 **The SST process:** "Student Support Teams (SST) Structure and Process," Georgia Department of Education, June 1, 2019, provided by Gwinnett County Public Schools in response to a records request, in the author's possession.

218 **for disrupting class:** Corey Robinson Jones Middle School Student Discipline Profile, 2018–19 year, received by the author from the Robinson family.

219 **he and a friend:** The family of Corey's friend declined to corroborate Corey's account of the "Backpack Incident."

220 **the school-to-prison pipeline:** "History," Gwinnett SToPP, https://www.gwinnettstopp .org/about-us/history/.

221 **was somehow gang related:** Kesler T. Roberts et al., "MARLYN TILLMAN, individually and as next friend of her minor son JOHN DOE, Plaintiffs, v. GWINNETT COUNTY SCHOOL DISTRICT d/b/a GWINNETT COUNTY PUBLIC SCHOOLS, and J. ALVIN WILBANKS, as Superintendent of Gwinnett County Board of Education, and JANE STEGALL, as Principal of Brookwood High School, in their individual and official capacities, Defendants" (Verified Complaint, in the United States District Court for the Northern District of Georgia Atlanta Division, 2004), 7.

221 **minor to nonexistent:** All details regarding Marlyn Tillman's complaints about the Gwinnett County Public Schools' treatment of her sons and subsequent lawsuit are drawn from Beverly B. Martin, "MARLYN TILLMAN, individually and as next friend of her minor son JOHN DOE, Plaintiffs, v. GWINNETT COUNTY SCHOOL DISTRICT d/b/a GWINNETT COUNTY PUBLIC SCHOOLS, and J. ALVIN WILBANKS, Superintendent of Gwinnett County Board of Education, and JANE STEGALL, Principal of Brookwood High School, in their individual and official capacities, Defendants" (Civil Action File No. 1:04-CV-1180-BBM In the United States District Court for the Northern District of Georgia Atlanta Division, 2005), 1– 10, unless otherwise noted.

222 **a student unconscious:** Eric Stirgus, "Group Demands Gwinnett County School Officers Be Fired," ajc.com, *Atlanta Journal-Constitution*,

April 20, 2017, https://drive.google.com/file/d
/18DHG-iyiyV-F_i-SYQatgJqqIuLUdl8M/view.

222 **the way Gwinnett's history:** Special thanks to
journalist and publisher Elliott Brack and
sociologist William Grady Holt, whose
respective works *Gwinnett: A Little Above
Atlanta* (Norcross, GA: Gwinnett Forum 2008)
and "Gwinnett Goes Global," a research article
published in *Sububanization in Global Society,
Research in Urban Society* 10 (2020): 51–73,
helped shape my understanding of Gwinnett
history.

222 **on the board in 2005:** Taylor Denman, "Carole
Boyce Announces She Will Run for the
Board of Education Again in 2020," *Gwinnett
Daily Post*, February 11, 2020, https://www
.gwinnettdailypost.com/local/carole-boyce
-announces-she-will-run-for-the-board-of
-education-again-in-2020/article_bfcffc9c-4cf3
-11ea-9022-23043b4b3478.html.

222 **school board member in Georgia:** Curt
Yeomans, "Longest Serving School Board
Member in Georgia, Louise Radloff, Likely
Ousted from Gwinnett Board of Education
Seat," *Gwinnett Daily Post*, June 10, 2020,
https://www.gwinnettdailypost.com/local
/longest-serving-school-board-member-in
-georgia-louise-radloff-likely-ousted-from
-gwinnett-board-of/article_5266d494-aace
-11ea-b3ef-ebc1123a7232.html.

223 **thousands of white families:** "Growing
Gwinnett: Changes and Challenges" (University
of Georgia Cooperative Extension Service,
1990), 4, 11.

223 **without a defeat:** Linda Jacobson, "Schools
Have Laid Groundwork for Improvements
Inside and Out," *Gwinnett Extra*, *Atlanta
Journal-Constitution*, December 24, 1990.

223 **by 938 percent:** Frances Abbott, "Black
Migration to Atlanta: Metropolitan Spatial
Patterns and Popular Representation, 1990–
2012" (PhD diss., James T. Laney School of
Graduate Studies, Emory University, 2012), 38.

223 **"Moving Africans Rapidly":** Laura Bliss,
"Atlanta's Big Transit Vote Is a Referendum on
Race," Bloomberg, March 15, 2019, https://
www.bloomberg.com/news/articles/2019
-03-15/gwinnett-county-will-decide-atlanta
-s-transit-future.

223 **a 2–1 margin:** Frances Schwartzkopff, David
Beasley, and Bill Rankin, "Gwinnett Is
Anti-MARTA, for School Bond: By 2–1
Margin, Voters Reject Transit System,"
Atlanta Journal-Constitution, November 7,
1990, A10.

223 **Voters shocked everyone:** David Pendered,
"Gwinnett Voters Kill Bond Issue," *Atlanta
Journal-Constitution*, February 14, 1990, 27.

223 **attendance zones and feeder patterns:** David
Pendered, "School Board Likely to Back
Attendance Plan," *Gwinnett Extra*, *Atlanta
Journal-Constitution*, July 9, 1990, 73.

223 **to deemphasize testing:** David Pendered,
"Schools Begin Writing a Lesson Plan for the
Future," *Atlanta Journal-Constitution*, January
17, 1991, 124.

224 **Gwinnett voters approved:** Linda Jacobson,
"Schools Scouting New Sources of Funds,"
Gwinnett Extra, *Atlanta Journal-Constitution*,
November 20, 1990, 69.

224 **before the decade was out:** "Gwinnett County
Public Schools Square Footage Report by School
Type" (spreadsheet, Gwinnett County, Georgia,
2020), 1–30.

224 **release the DeKalb district:** Gary Sams,
"DeKalb County School Desegregation Case
Files," Special Collections Libraries, University
of Georgia, https://sclfind.libs.uga.edu/sclfind
/view/docId=ead/RBRL056DCS.xml#:~:text
=In%201996%20the%20case%20was,no
%20longer%20required%20judicial%20
supervision.

224 **first person of color:** Martha Dalton,
"Gwinnett School Board Gets Its First
Member of Color," WABE 90.1, November 7,
2018, https://drive.google.com/file
/d/1RzQn_zCXHARIbH7A43sDX-
KbzcuaRDD9/view.

224 **Excellence for African Americans:** "Meet
Everton," Everton Blair for Georgia, https://
evertonblair.com/.

225 **same kind of northward exodus:** "2040
Unified Plan," Gwinnett County Board of
Commissioners, February 5, 2019, https://
www.gwinnettcounty.com/web/gwinnett
/departments/planningdevelopment/services
/landuseplanning/2040unifiedplan.

225 **Superintendent of the Year:** "J. Alvin
Wilbanks, CEO/Superintendent," Gwinnett
County Public Schools, https://publish
.gwinnett.k12.ga.us/gcps/home/public/about
/ceo/content/bio#:~:text=Wilbanks%20is
%20the%20founding%20president,finalists
%20for%20the%20national%20title.

225 **prestigious Broad Prize:** Maureen Downey,
"Gwinnett Public Schools Wins Broad Prize
Again. Recognized for 'Steady, Sustainable
Gains,'" *Atlanta Journal-Constitution*,
September 22, 2014, https://www.ajc.com/blog
/get-schooled/gwinnett-public-schools-wins
-broad-prize-again-recognized-for-steady
-sustainable-gains/4inhoeyBPHQeDVDn
LjeuzO/#:~:text=Broad%20Prize%20again
.-,Recognized%20for%20%27steady%2C
%20sustainable%20gains.,%27&text
=Congratulations%20to%20Gwinnett
%20County%20Schools,but%20for%20the
%20entire%20nation.&text=Gwinnett
%20won%20the%20prestigious
%20Broad,Orange%20County%20
Schools%20in%20Florida.

225 **peers in DeKalb and Atlanta:** Georgia
Department of Education, 2019 College and
Career Ready Performance Index.

225 **twenty or thirty points:** Georgia Department of Education, 2019 College and Career Ready Performance Index.

225 **Collins Hill High:** Tyler Estep, "Gwinnett Principal: Racist Graffiti 'Does Not Define Our School,'" *Atlanta Journal-Constitution*, November 22, 2016, https://www.ajc.com/news /local/gwinnett-principal-racist-graffiti-does -not-define-our-school/Q55OoqyPha4Z18 AhMiNI1J/.

225 **just one third:** Georgia Department of Education, records request, in the author's possession.

226 **roughly 90 percent:** Aileen Dodd, "Gwinnett Officials Won't Be Charged School Discipline Underreported," *Atlanta Journal-Constitution*, October 21, 2003, B1.

226 **had to convince:** This description of the Gwinnett County Public Schools disciplinary appeals process is based on interviews with Jim Taylor and Marlyn Tillman, as well as the 2017–18 Student/Parent Handbook Middle/High School, Gwinnett County Public Schools, 22–23, provided by Gwinnett County Public Schools in response to a records request.

227 **be the majority:** "QuickFacts Gwinnett County, Georgia," U.S. Census Bureau, accessed December 5, 2022, https://www.census.gov /quickfacts/gwinnettcountygeorgia; Tyler Estep, "In 2040, Gwinnett Will Have More Hispanics Than Whites, Forecast Says," *Atlanta Journal-Constitution*, October 11, 2016, https://www.ajc .com/news/local/2040-gwinnett-will-have -more-hispanics-than-whites-forecast-says /aGgZpByhj8pGSAn86VkfpK/.

227 **Atlanta suburbs, including Gwinnett:** Tyler Estep, "Hillary Clinton Won Gwinnett. "How Did Your Neighbors Vote?," *Atlanta Journal-Constitution*, November 6, 2016, https://www .ajc.com/news/local/hillary-clinton-won -gwinnett-how-did-your-neighbors-vote /fOHTJLXj0UcLw4iiyKfctO/.

227 **run for school board:** Trevor McNaboe, "Eight Candidates Vying for Two Open Gwinnett Board of Education Seats," *Gwinnett Daily Post*, May 11, 2018, https://www.gwinnettdailypost.com/local /eight-candidates-vying-for-two-open-gwinnett -board-of-education-seats/article_b1ecf983 -341e-5a70-9367-6ce70bba5ca0.html.

230 **affected racial minorities:** Marlyn Tillman, "Keep Guidelines in Place That Work to Ensure Fair Discipline for Black, Brown Students," *USA Today*, January 6, 2018, https://www.usatoday .com/story/opinion/policing/spotlight/2018/01 /06/keep-guidelines-place-work-ensure -fair-discipline-black-brown-students /998684001/.

230 **"parent concern form":** Descriptions of all materials related to the Robinsons' meeting to have Corey reinstated at Jones Middle School are drawn from interviews with the Robinson family and others who attended the meeting, as well as files and documents provided by Nika

Robinson. Neither then Jones principal Memorie Reesman nor the Gwinnett County Public Schools' director of equity and compliance agreed to be interviewed.

231 **half of all expulsions:** "Glenn C. Jones Middle School Discipline Report," Civil Rights Data Collection, 2015, https://ocrdata.ed.gov/profile /8/school/236856/summary.

CHAPTER 10: LIBERALS VS. PROGRESSIVES

233 **"The work was too fast":** Decoteau J. Irby, *Stuck Improving: Racial Equity and School Leadership* (Cambridge, MA: Harvard Education Press, 2021), 84.

233 **principal Donna Sokolowski:** Former Dewey Elementary principal Donna Sokolowski agreed to two interviews about the events described in this chapter, but declined to comment on any interactions involving specific students, parents, or Dewey staff members, citing privacy concerns.

234 **Chris's teacher, meanwhile:** Chris Adesina's first-grade teacher at Dewey Elementary, identified pseudonymously, declined to be interviewed about the events described in this chapter, but responded in writing to a fact-checking request covering several relevant details.

235 **a traffic light:** In response to written questions, a district spokesperson indicated that such a response would be consistent with District 65's overall approach to instruction in a two-way immersion classroom, writing that "dual language research does indicate that language and literacy development occurs more slowly at first due to learning two languages but accelerates as the student learns to lift strengths in both language and literacy domains."

238 **three momentous emails:** All descriptions and excerpts from the three email messages described in this chapter are drawn from electronic copies provided by Lauren Adesina; interviews about their contents and impact with Lauren and other involved parties, including principal Donna Sokolowski and superintendent Paul Goren, and/or related documents obtained via public-records requests made to District 65.

239 **Dewey PTA gathered:** Multiple members of the Dewey PTA board at the time recalled meetings at the house on Lake Michigan, and one of those members recalled tensions between Lauren and her counterparts, but those individuals did not recall this specific exchange.

242 **at Lincolnwood Elementary:** Larry Gavin, "Racial Slurs at Lincolnwood School," *Evanston RoundTable*, November 14, 2018, https:// evanstonroundtable.com/2018/11/14/racial -slurs-at-lincolnwood-school/.

242 **piece of playground equipment:** Charles Bartling, "Racial Epithet Found on Wilard Playground," Evanston Now, March 12, 2018,

https://evanstonnow.com/racial-epithet-found
-on-willard-playground/.

242 *Children of the Dream:* Rucker Johnson and
Alexander Nazaryan, *Children of the Dream:
Why School Integration Works* (New York:
Basic Books, 2019), 45–49.

243 **hugely influential book:** Beth Holland,
"Reflecting on Tinkering Toward Utopia,"
Education Week, September 16, 2015, https://
www.edweek.org/leadership/opinion
-reflecting-on-tinkering-toward-utopia/2015/09.

243 **their classroom practice:** David Tyack and
Larry Cuban, *Tinkering Toward Utopia: A
Century of Public School Reform* (Cambridge,
MA: Harvard University Press, 1997).

243 **think tanks and foundations:** "Paul Goren,"
Spencer Fellows, Spencer Education Journalism
Fellowships, accessed December 5, 2022, https://
spencerfellows.org/board/paul-goren/. During
his time working at the Spencer Foundation,
Goren helped start the Spencer Education
Journalism Fellowship program. Several years
after Goren left the foundation, I participated in
the fellowship program and received financial
and other support from Columbia University by
way of the Spencer Foundation.

243 **schools' "instructional core":** Elizabeth City,
Richard Elmore, Sarah Fiarman, and Lee Teitel,
*Instructional Rounds in Education: A Newtork
Approach to Improving Teaching and Learning*
(Cambridge, MA: Harvard Education Press,
2009).

243 **the wrong direction:** "2015 Achievement &
Accountability Report: Evanston/Skokie
District 65," Public Document, Evanston,
Illinois, 2016, 1–3.

244 **mysterious to everyone else:** Ben Pope, "D65
Board Approves Consolidation of 8th Grade
Algebra Courses," *Daily Northwestern*
(Evanston, Illinois), June 13, 2017, https://
dailynorthwestern.com/2017/06/13/city/d65
-board-approves-consolidation-of-8th-grade
-algebra-courses/.

244 **was voted down:** Larry Gavin, "School District
65's Referendum Defeated, Board Reactions,"
Evanston RoundTable, March 21, 2012, https://
evanstonroundtable.com/2012/03/21/school
-district-65s-referendum-defeated-board
-reactions.

244 **students' academic performance:** Evanston
/Skokie School District 65, "Strategic Plan
2015–2020," 10–11.

244 **roughly 1.5 percent:** "Evanston/Skokie School
District 65 Budget-at-a-Glance, 2016–2017
Fiscal Year," Public Document, Evanston,
Illinois, 2017, 8.

245 **for $14.5 million:** "District 65 to Seek
Operating Referendum," Evanston/Skokie
School District 65, https://www.district65.net
/site/Default.aspx?PageType=3&DomainID=4
&PageID=1&ViewID=6446ee88-d30c-497e
-9316-3f8874b3e108&FlexDataID=4117.

245 **a 4–1 margin:** "D65 Operating Referendum
Passes," Evanston/Skokie School District 65,
2022, https://www.district65.net/site/Default
.aspx?PageType=3&DomainID=4&PageID
=1&ViewID=6446ee88-d30c-497e-9316-3f887
4b3e108&FlexDataID=440.

245 **every Evanston precinct:** "April 04, 2017,
Consolidated General Election: School District
65, Increase Limiting Rate Township & Precinct
Results," Cook County Clerk's Office, https://
results417.cookcountyclerkil.gov/Detail
.aspx?eid=40417&rid=1067&vfor=1&twp
ftr=0.

245 **scores were dipping:** Evanston CCSD 65,
PARCC (2016–2018), Illinois Report Card 2021
–2022, https://www.illinoisreportcard.com
/District.aspx?source=retiredtests&source2
=parcc&Districtid=05016065004.

245 **appeared to be even wider:** While an apples-to-
apples comparison of student test scores in 1967
and 2017 was not possible, see, e.g., Jayjia Hsia,
"Integration in Evanston, 1967–71: A
Longitudinal Evaluation," Educational Testing
Service, https://files.eric.ed.gov/fulltext
/ED054292.pdf, 48; and 2017 "Achievement &
Accountability Report," Evanston/Skokie School
District 65, Office of Research, Accountability,
and Data, accessed March 23, 2023, https://
www.district65.net/cms/lib/IL01906289
/Centricity/Domain/59/AchievementReport
_2017_Final.pdf, 25.

245 **deliver a talk:** Larry Gavin, "Study Finds
Achievement/Opportunity Gaps Are Due
Primarily to Differences That Occur Before
Third Grade," *Evanston RoundTable*, May 17,
2017, https://evanstonroundtable.com/2017/05
/17/study-finds-achievement-opportunity-gaps
-are-due-primarily-to-differences-that-occur
-before-third-grade/.

245 **a monumental analysis:** Sean Reardon,
Demetra Kalogrides, and Ken Shores, "The
Geography of Racial/Ethnic Test Score Gaps"
(CEPA Working Paper No. 16-10, Stanford
Center for Education Policy Analysis: http://
cepa.stanford.edu/wp16-10, 2017).

246 *school district in the country:* Gavin, "Study
Finds Achievement/Opportunity Gaps Are Due
Primarily to Differences That Occur Before
Third Grade."

246 **nearly three thousand words:** Larry Gavin,
"The Nature of the Achievement Gap at District
65, and the Scope of the Opportunity Gap,"
Evanston RoundTable, August 9, 2017, https://
evanstonroundtable.com/2017/08/09/the
-nature-of-the-achievement-gap-at-district
-65-and-the-scope-of-the-opportunity-gap/.

246 **particularly significant scatterplot:** Gavin,
"The Nature of the Achievement Gap at
District 65, and the Scope of the Opportunity
Gap."

247 **the release of reports:** Office of Research,
Accountability, and Data, "Report on Black

Student Achievement in District 65," Public Document, Evanston, Illinois, 2017, and "Report on Hispanic Student Achievement, Evanston/Skokie School District 65," Public Document, Evanston, Illinois, 2017.

248 **Black Student Success:** Catherine Henderson, "District 65 to Create New Positions Addressing Black Student Success, Racial Achievement Gap," *Daily Northwestern*, January 23, 2018, https://dailynorthwestern.com/2018/01/23/city /district-65-create-new-positions-addressing- black-student-success-racial-achievement-gap/.

248 **$139 million system:** "Evanston/Skokie School District 65 Budget-at-a-Glance, 2017–2018 Fiscal Year," 6.

248 **scant empirical evidence:** Sarah Sparks, "Training Bias out of Teachers: Research Shows Little Promise So Far," *Education Week*, November 17, 2020, https://www.edweek.org /leadership/training-bias-out-of-teachers -research-shows-little-promise-so-far/2020/11.

250 **sent a letter:** Paul Goren, "D65 Stands Against Racism and Hate," letter, December 13, 2018, in the author's possession.

250 **a thirty-page guide:** "A Guide for Administrators, Counselors and Teachers: Responding to Hate and Bias at School," Teaching Tolerance, 2017, in the author's possession.

251 **handling such incidents:** Joaquin Stephenson, email to Paul Goren, April 5, 2019, in the author's possession.

252 **their new protocols:** "Responding to Racism, Discriminatory Language, and Hateful Acts," Evanston/Skokie School District 65, in the author's possession.

252 **"state of emergency":** Larry Gavin, "'Black Parents of King Arts' Host Town Hall Meeting on Test Scores," *Evanston RoundTable*, March 20, 2019, https://evanstonroundtable.com/2019 /03/20/black-parents-of-king-arts-hosts-town -hall-meeting-on-test-scores/.

252 **called for help:** Genevieve Bookwalter, "After Incident with 6-Year-Old Student, Evanston /Skokie District 65 Evaluating Use of Police Officers in Schools," *Evanston Review*, https:// www.chicagotribune.com/suburbs/evanston /ct-evr-district-65-school-threats-police -tl-0523-story.html.

253 **for a meeting:** District 65, "Re-organization Meeting 4-22-2019," YouTube video, 29:44, April 24, 2019, https://youtu.be/vYWu4h0oIZ0.

253 **offer his resignation:** Genevieve Bookwalter, "Evanston/Skokie Dist. 65 Superintendent Announces Resignation Effective July 1," *Chicago Tribune*, June 14, 2019.

CHAPTER II: THE NEXT STEVE JOBS

254 **obtain driver's licenses:** An act to amend, repeal, and add Sections 1653.5, 12800, 12801, and 12801.5 of, and to add Sections 12801.9, 12801.10, and 12801.11 to, the Vehicle Code,

relating to driver's licenses, Chapter 524, Statutes of 2013 (2013), www.leginfo.ca.gov /pub/13-14/bill/asm/ab_0051-0100/ab_60_bill _20131003_chaptered.html.

255 **around the potholes:** Jovana Lara, "Compton Residents Still Dealing with Pothole-Filled Streets as City Makes Progress," ABC7 Eyewitness News, December 4, 2019, https:// abc7.com/compton-pot-holes-los-angeles -family-fills-potholes/5732497/.

255 **Mona Park Compton Crips:** "Mona Parcc Compton Crips in Willowbrook / Compton," streetgangs.com, https://www.streetgangs.com /crips/compton/mpcc/.

257 **to blended learning:** "Elevate Academics," Compton Unified School District, https://www .compton.k12.ca.us/others/home/elevate -spotlights/elevate-academics.

260 **Google or Boeing:** Matt Zalaznick, "How Early Coding Gives Students a Jumpstart," District Administration, August 27, 2020, https:// districtadministration.com/how-early-coding -gives-students-a-jumpstart/.

260 **futuristic new campus:** All descriptions and details regarding Apple Park are drawn from "Inside Apple's Massive $5 Billion 'Spaceship' Headquarters," Snaptrude, June 16, 2022, https://www.snaptrude.com/blog/inside -apples-massive-5-billion-spaceship -headquarters; Steven Levy, "Apple Park's Tree Whisperer," *Wired*, June 1, 2017, https://www .wired.com/story/apple-parks-tree-whisperer/; and Abigail Johnson Hess, "The Science and Design Behind Apple's Innovation-Obsessed New Workspace," CNBC.com, September 14, 2017, https://www.cnbc.com/2017/09/13/the -science-and-design-behind-apples-innovation -obsessed-new-workspace.html.

261 **to the mid-1930s:** "Our History," Compton High School, https://chs-compton-ca .schoolloop.com/history.

261 **$350 million bond:** "Compton Unified School District Bond Issue, Measure S (November 2015)," Ballotpedia, https://ballotpedia.org /Compton_Unified_School_District _Bond_Issue,_Measure_S _(November_2015).

261 **new information-age campus:** DLR Group, "New Compton High School," December 15, 2016, https://www.youtube.com/watch?v =4KTqiITTxjg&t=3s.

261 **white and Asian:** Sara Harrison, "Five Years of Tech Diversity Reports—and Little Progress," October 1, 2019, *Wired*, https://www.wired .com/story/five-years-tech-diversity-reports -little-progress/.

261 **mayoral race was gearing up:** All details regarding Compton's 2013 mayoral race are drawn from Abby Sewell and Angel Jennings, "Compton's Pivot Point; In a City at a Crossroads, a Former Mayor Who Still Faces Trial Is Among a Crowded Field Challenging

Incumbent Eric Perrodin," *Los Angeles Times,* April 6, 2013, A.1, unless otherwise noted.

261 **included Eric Perrodin:** Kenneth Miller, "Compton's Own Eric Perrodin Is First Three Term Mayor in 100 Years," *Los Angeles Sentinel,* April 30, 2009, https://lasentinel.net/compton -s-own-eric-perrodin-is-first-three-term -mayor-in-100-years.html.

262 **"I see it as a new Brooklyn":** Rory Carrol, "Aja Brown, Compton's New Mayor: 'I See It as a New Brooklyn,'" *Guardian,* October 15, 2013, https:// www.theguardian.com/world/2013/oct/15/aja -brown-compton-new-mayor-sees-brooklyn.

262 **mismanagement remained rampant:** Marc Joffe, "California's Most Financially Stressed Cities and Counties," California Policy Center, November 5, 2014, https:// californiapolicycenter.org/californias-most -financially-stressed-cities-and-counties/.

262 **test scores were still atrocious:** "CAASPP Smarter Balanced 2014–2019 Longitudinal Visualization," in author's possession.

262 **below 60 percent:** "District Wide Historical Data for Grade Rate, A-G Completers & AP Scores," data from Calpads, DataQuest & C&C Dept., in author's possession.

262 **minimum admissions requirements:** "District Wide Historical Data for Grade Rate, A-G Completers & AP Scores."

262 **district-issued credit card:** Abby Sewell, "Compton Schools Chief Is Fired; She'd Been on Leave over Use of District Credit Cards. Now She Is Threatening to Sue," *Los Angeles Times,* October 14, 2010, AA.3.

262 **conspiring to shut Latinos:** Jim Newton, "Compton's Racial Divide," *Los Angeles Times,* May 16, 2011, A.13.

263 **a guest appearance:** Simone Wilson, "Skyy Fisher, Compton School Board Member, Calls Superintendent a 'Bitch' and Trayvon Martin a 'Faggot' (VIDEO)," *LA Weekly,* May 2, 2012, https://www.laweekly.com/skyy-fisher-compton -school-board-member-calls-superintendent-a -bitch-and-trayvon-martin-a-faggot-video/.

263 **was eventually convicted:** Kelly Wheeler, "Former Compton School Trustee Gets Six-Year Term for Sexual Assault in Hotel Room," City News Service, July 14, 2016.

263 **who were Latino:** Rebekah Kearn, "Latino-Black Relations on Edge in Compton," Courthouse News Service, May 20, 2013, https://www.courthousenews.com/latino-black -relations-on-edge-in-compton/.

263 **lawsuit the ACLU:** Howard Blume, "Lawsuit: State Fails Some English Learners," *Los Angeles Times,* April 25, 2013, AA.4.

263 **1,700 English learners:** John Festernwald, "ACLU Warns It Will Sue State over 20,000 Unserved English Learners," EdSource, January 24, 2013, https://edsource.org/2013/aclu-warns -it-will-sue-state-over-2000-unserved-english -learners/25965.

263 **convert a local elementary:** Howard Blume and Teresa Watanabe, "Parents Use New Law to Remake Compton School; Activists Force District to Turn Over Operation of Mckinley Campus to a Charter Company," *Los Angeles Times,* December 8, 2010, AA.1.

263 **a class-action suit:** *Raquel Espinoza et al. v. Compton Unified School District,* Case 2:13-cv -03519-GW-JCG, District Court for the Central District of California, Western Division—Los Angeles.

263 **$30 million operating deficit:** "The Turnaround Story at Compton's Schools," *Los Angeles Sentinel,* October 15, 2015, A4.

263 **complaints about Dominguez High:** All details of the 2015 meeting at Dominguez High are drawn from an interview with Darin Brawley; "Incident Report Form, Log Number PD-15-01568, File Number CD-15-11703" (Compton School Police Incident Report Form, Compton, CA, 2015); and "Minutes of the Special Meeting of the Compton Unified School District Board of Trustees, Tuesday March 27, 2015" (Public Minutes, San Jose, Compton, CA, 2015). I use the term "homeless" in my description of the complaints that arose during the meeting because that is the term used in the meeting minutes.

264 **which was eventually settled:** *Espinoza et al. v. Compton Unified Sch. Dist. Police Dep't, et al.,* Case No. CV-13-3519 GW (JCGx), 33.

265 **to energy-efficient lightbulbs:** Nadra Nittle, "Compton Unified to Save $370K Yearly with Energy Efficiency Program," *Press-Telegram* (Long Beach, CA), January 25, 2015, https:// www.presstelegram.com/2015/01/25/compton -unified-to-save-370k-yearly-with-energy -efficiency-program/.

265 **new school-funding formula:** Rucker Johnson, Paul Bruno, and Sean Tanner, "Effects of the Local Control Funding Formula on Revenues, Expenditures, and Student Outcomes," research brief, Stanford University and PACE, 2018, 2.

265 **just about everyone:** Mario Marcos, "Local Control Accountability Plan and Annual Update (LCAP) Template," Public Document, Compton Unified, 2020.

265 **to $14,707 seven years later:** 2013–14 Current Expense per Average Daily Attendance (ADA), California Department of Education—School Fiscal Services Division, as of February 2, 2015, downloaded from https://www.cde.ca.gov/ds /fd/ec/currentexpense.asp; 2020–21 Current Expense Per Average Daily Attendance (ADA), California Department of Education—School Fiscal Services Division, as of February 8, 2022, downloaded from https://www.cde.ca.gov/ds /fd/ec/currentexpense.asp.

265 **by Jean-Jacques Francoisse:** All descriptions of the Compton Unified School District's internal data systems in this chapter are drawn from a visit and interview with Francoisse in 2019.

266 **new administrative headquarters:** Fiscal Crisis & Management Assistance Team (FCMAT), "Compton Unified School District," Public Report, California School Information Services, 2007, 12.

267 **planning his dissertation:** All details and descriptions regarding Darin Brawley's doctoral studies and dissertation are drawn from interviews with Brawley, and from Alex Alvarez and Darin Brawley, "Impact of Globalization on Education in Ireland" (PhD diss., University of Southern California, Rossier School of Education, 2017).

267 **about one sixth:** Brawley, "Impact of Globalization on Education in Ireland."

267 **logistics and technical support:** "Apple's Cork Campus Celebrates 40 Years of Community and Looks to the Future," Apple, November 17, 2020, https://www.apple.com/newsroom/2020/11/apples-cork-campus-celebrates-40-years-of-community-and-looks-to-the-future/.

268 **additional Compton schools:** "Elevate Academics," Compton Unified School District, https://www.compton.k12.ca.us/others/home/elevate-spotlights/elevate-academics.

268 **Apple Distinguished School:** "Thomas Jefferson Elementary Named Apple Distinguished School," Compton Unified School District, February 6, 2019, https://www.compton.k12.ca.us/news-release/news/2019/february/apple-distinguished-school.

268 **up fifteen points:** "CAASPP Smarter Balanced 2014–2019 Longitudinal Visualization."

268 **to 84 percent:** "District Wide Historical Data for Grade Rate, A-G Completers & AP Scores."

268 **Compton Unified's Latino graduates:** "District Wide Historical Data for Grade Rate, A-G Completers & AP Scores."

268 **his agenda: inclusive innovation:** Colin Angevine et al., "Designing a Process for Inclusive Innovation: A Radical Commitment to Equity," Digital Promise, November 2019, https://digitalpromise.org/wp-content/uploads/2019/11/Designing-a-Process-for-Inclusive-Innovation.pdf.

269 **preparing to host:** "League of Innovative Schools Fall 2020 Meeting," Digital Promise, https://docs.google.com/document/d/1qAdbx6KQ1gIxKzps6f0oD_iSn47fZzYx943pt9HXpIQ/edit?usp=sharing.

269 **hands-on engineering lessons:** Descriptions of this lesson are drawn from remote classroom observations conducted via FaceTime; "PLTW Launch Module Descriptions," Project Lead the Way, https://www.pltw.org/pltw-launch-module-descriptions; and "Energy: Collisions Teacher Resources," Project Lead the Way, https://www.pltw.org/our-programs/pltw-launch-curriculum#aligned-to-fourth-grade-standards-curriculum-1.

CHAPTER 12: THINGS FALL APART

271 **"There are only the pursued":** F. Scott Fitzgerald, *The Great Gatsby* (New York: Charles Scribner's Sons, 1925), 50.

273 **beloved Houston Astros:** "MLB Completes Astros' Investigation," MLB, January 13, 2020, https://www.mlb.com/press-release/press-release-mlb-completes-astros-investigation.

274 **a global emergency:** "Coronavirus Declared Global Health Emergency by WHO," BBC, January 31, 2020, https://www.bbc.com/news/world-51318246.

274 **travel from China:** "Proclamation on Suspension of Entry as Immigrants and Nonimmigrants of Persons Who Pose a Risk of Transmitting 2019 Novel Coronavirus," Federal Register, January 31, 2020, https://www.federalregister.gov/documents/2020/02/05/2020-02424/suspension-of-entry-as-immigrants-and-nonimmigrants-of-persons-who-pose-a-risk-of-transmitting-2019.

274 **$1.1 million operating deficit:** "Lovejoy I.S.D. 2019–2020 Approved Budget Summary of Revenues & Expenditures General Funds (includes funds 183 & 199)," Lovejoy ISD, October 14, 2019, https://www.lovejoyisd.net/apps/pages/index.jsp?uREC_ID=385835&type=d&pREC_ID=1067095.

274 **fresh demographic study:** Population and Survey Analysts, "2019–20 Demographic Update Lovejoy Independent School District," January 2020, http://files.pasademographics.com:800/Reports/2020/Demographic%20Update%20-%20Lovejoy%20-%20Jan%202020.pdf.

274 **On Saturday evening:** Because Lovejoy ISD and the Foundation for Lovejoy Schools rejected my request to attend the 2020 Denim & Diamonds fundraiser, all descriptions of the event are drawn from interviews with the Beckers and other participants; social media posts; photos and videos provided by Lovejoy ISD; and records from the mobile app used to run auctions, to which I had access.

276 **on three continents:** Vivian Wang et al., "With 4 Deaths in Iran and More Cases on 3 Continents, Fears of Coronavirus Pandemic Rise," *New York Times*, February 21, 2020, https://www.nytimes.com/2020/02/21/world/asia/china-coronavirus-iran.html.

276 **forced into quarantine:** Ben Dooley and Motoko Rich, "Cruise Ship's Coronavirus Outbreak Leaves Crew Nowhere to Hide," *New York Times*, February 10, 2020, https://www.nytimes.com/2020/02/10/business/coronavirus-japan-cruise-ship.html.

276 **raise about $300,000:** Laurie Vondersaar, email to the author, April 3, 2020, in the author's possession.

279 **Unlike Lovejoy ISD:** "Student Handbook, Lovejoy High School, 2017–18," Lovejoy ISD,

https://1.cdn.edl.io/KBuX40yo0Gj7Ssfh7i
GokLGdAVOiOKF6gWDKpP2nEpD
pauAh.pdf, 79.

279 **Nearly 60 percent:** Data provided by Gwinnett
County Public Schools in response to a records
request, in the author's possession.

280 **software tool called Nearpod:** Nearpod Team,
"10 Ways to Use Nearpod in the Classroom,"
Nearpodblog, November 8, 2022, https://
nearpod.com/blog/nearpod-in-the-classroom/.

281 **the fifty-two-minute period:** "Bell Schedules,"
Mill Creek High School, https://www.gcpsk12
.org/domain/2971.

284 **win 57 percent:** "Everton Blair Jr.," Ballotpedia,
https://ballotpedia.org/Everton_Blair_Jr.

284 **now heavily Black and Brown southern end:**
"Chapter 1 Overview," Gwinnett 2040 Unified
Plan, accessed March 22, 2023, https://www
.gwinnettcounty.com/static/departments
/planning/unified_plan/2040_Plan/Chapter
_1-Overview.pdf, 16.

285 **were considered poor:** U.S. Department
of Education, National Center for
Education Statistics, Common Core of
Data (CCD), "Public Elementary/Secondary
School Universe Survey," 2019–20 v.1a,
2020–21 v.1a.

285 **Just a third:** Data provided by Gwinnett
County Public Schools in response to a records
request, in the author's possession.

287 **overuse of standardized tests:** Arlinda Smith
Broady, "Gwinnett Students Ask Board to Ease
Test Load," *Atlanta Journal-Constitution*,
April 17, 2019, B1, B8.

287 **welcome such questions:** Sloan Roach, email to
the author, October 22, 2020, in the author's
possession.

288 **to challenge them:** Benjamin Herold, "How the
Fight for America's Suburbs Started in Public
Schools," *Education Week*, October 26, 2020,
https://www.edweek.org/leadership/how-the
-fight-for-americas-suburbs-started-in-public
-schools/2020/10.

288 **mayor of Norcross, Georgia:** "Craig L.
Newton," https://www.norcrossga.net
/DocumentCenter/View/2785/Craig-L-Newton
-Short-version-1.

288 **Georgia House in 2017:** "Brenda Lopez
Romero," Ballotpedia, https://ballotpedia.org
/Brenda_Lopez_Romero.

290 **into Washington Elementary:** Because District
65 would not grant access to directly observe
classrooms during the 2019–20 school year, the
descriptions of Washington Elementary,
principal Kate Ellison's approach to school
leadership and promoting racial equity, and
Lauren Adesina's reactions that are included in
this chapter are composites drawn from
interviews with Ellison, Lauren, and others; a
later tour I took of Washington; and news
accounts, district and school documents, and
social media postings regarding the school.

291 **120 years old:** "914 Ashland Avenue,
Washington School," City of Evanston
Landmarks, https://www.sitevistamaps.com
/evanston/index.php?showonlyp=yes&project
=yes&c=6&p=121.

291 **on culturally responsive teaching:** Zaretta
Hammond, *Culturally Responsive Teaching and
the Brain* (Thousand Oaks, CA: Corwin, 2015),
97–99.

292 **from Hammond's book:** Hammond, *Culturally
Responsive Teaching and the Brain*. The notion
of the "warm demander" and its connection to
culturally responsive teaching dates back
decades. See, e.g., James A. Vasquez, "Contexts
of Learning for Minority Students," *Educational
Forum* 52, no. 3 (1988): 243–53, https://www
.tandfonline.com/doi/epdf/10.1080
/00131728809335490; and Gloria Ladson-
Billings, *The Dreamkeepers: Successful Teachers
of African American Children* (San Francisco:
Jossey-Bass, 2009).

293 **half of Washington students:** "Washington
Elementary School," Illinois Report Card,
2018–2019, IllinoisReportCard.com.

293 **several points higher:** "Washington
Elementary School," Illinois Report Card,
2014–2015, illinoisreportcard.com.

294 **drawing national headlines:** Eric Lutz, "One
City's Reparations Program That Could Offer a
Blueprint for the Nation," *Guardian*, January
19, 2020, https://www.theguardian.com/us
-news/2020/jan/19/reparations-program
-evanston-illinois-african-americans
-slavery.

294 **yearlong book study:** "Learn to Be an
Antiracist," Next Steps, https://www
.nextstepsevanston.com/series.

295 **"dangerous Black neighborhoods":** Ibram X.
Kendi, *How to Be an Antiracist* (New York: One
World, 2019).

295 **contact with law enforcement:** Larry Gavin,
"District 65 Committee Considers Revised Role
for School Resource Officers, Increasing
School's Capacity to De-escalate Situations,"
Evanston RoundTable, October 16, 2019, https://
evanstonroundtable.com/2019/10/16/district
-65-committee-considers-revised-role-for
-school-resource-officers-increasing-schools
-capacity-to-de-escalate-situations/.

295 **gender and gender identity:** "Support for
Transgender & Gender Expansive Students,"
Evanston/Skokie School District 65, https://
www.district65.net/Page/23966.

295 **citywide PTA fund:** "Our Work," PTA Equity
Project, https://ptaequityproject.com/our-work;
"About," PTA Equity Project, https://
ptaequityproject.com/about.

295 **school board meeting:** District 65, "School
Board Meeting 9-23-2019," YouTube video,
3:42:31, https://youtu.be/90f2KwNYjaE.

295 **a 295-page report:** Dr. Debra Hill, Dr. Mark
Friedman, and Dr. Anne Noland, "Evanston

/Skokie School District 65 2019 Superintendent Search Community Engagement and Profile Report," September 23, 2019, https://www .district65.net/cms/lib/IL01906289/Centricity /Domain/60/2019%20Leadership%20Profile %20and%20Survey%20Results.pdf.

296 **its new superintendent:** "District 65 Announces New Superintendent," Evanston /Skokie School District 65, https://www .district65.net/site/Default.aspx?PageType=3 &DomainID=4&PageID=1&ViewID =6446ee88-d30c-497e-9316-3f8874b3e108 &FlexDataID=8815.

296 **and Jefferson County, Kentucky:** "Devon Q. Horton Ed.D," https://www.district65.net/cms /lib/IL01906289/Centricity/Domain/60/Horton %20resume.pdf.

296 **filed a complaint:** "Complaint for Declaratory and Injunctive Relief," Civil Action File No. 1:21-CV-03466 in the United States District Court for the Northern District of Illinois Eastern Division, 2021, 7.

296 **preparing to resign:** Larry Gavin, "Candance Chow Resigns from District 65 School Board," *Evanston RoundTable*, February 11, 2020, https://evanstonroundtable.com/2020/02/11 /candance-chow-resigns-from-district-65 -school-board/.

298 **into senior housing:** Dillon Carr, "Plans to Turn Former Forbes Elementary Site into Senior Housing Move Forward," Trib Live, February 19, 2019, https://triblive.com/local/penn-hills /plans-to-turn-former-forbes-elementary-Site -into-senior-housing-move-forward/.

298 **a charter school:** Michael DiVittorio, "Penn Hills School District Sells Former Elementary Building to Charter School," Trib Live, May 22, 2018, https://archive.triblive.com/local/penn -hills/penn-hills-school-district-sells-former -elementary-building-to-charter-school/.

298 **to the municipality:** Tim Means, "Sale of Vacant Penn Hills School Criticized," *Pittsburgh Post-Gazette*, May 27, 2015, https:// www.post-gazette.com/local/east/2015/05/27 /Sale-of-vacant-Penn-Hills-school-criticized /stories/201505270261.

298 **municipal building and police station:** Dillon Carr, "Penn Hills Weeks Away from Opening First New Municipal Building in 50 Years," Trib Live, May 30, 2018, https://www.triblive.com /local/penn-hills/penn-hills-weeks-away-from -opening-first-new-municipal-building-in-50 -years/.

300 **indicating special needs:** U.S. Department of Education, National Center for Education Statistics, Common Core of Data (CCD), "Local Education Agency (School District) Universe Survey."

301 **kept asking questions:** My conversation with Bethany described here occurred across Math and Reading Night and a subsequent phone call and has been condensed here for readability.

301 *Earn Your Leisure:* "Our Story," *Earn Your Leisure*, https://www.earnyourleisure.com /pages/about-2022.

302 **with cell-phone videos:** Michael DiVittorio, "Penn Hills Parent Seeks Crackdown on Fighting, Cyber Bullying at Linton," *Pittsburgh Tribune-Review*, March 25, 2019, https://triblive .com/local/pittsburgh-allegheny/penn-hills -parent-seeks-crack-down-on-fighting-cyber -bullying-at-linton/.

303 **out of commission:** "Agenda Proposal 123 Security Products," Penn Hills School District, May 5, 2020, https://go.boarddocs.com/pa /phsd/Board.nsf/files/BPSQAG680913/$file /123%20Security%20Products%20Budget%20 Proposal.pdf; Russell Seibert, email message to Nancy Hines and Dayne Dice, March 11, 2020.

303 **causing $10,000 worth:** Insurance claim payment, November 15, 2019, in the author's possession.

304 **state senator Jay Costa:** Michael DiVittorio, "Penn Hills School District's Preliminary Budget Adopted, Tax Increase Likely," TCA Regional News, January 30, 2020; Jay Costa in discussion with the author, June 2020.

304 **if they wanted the money:** Jay Costa in discussion with the author, June 2020. School board president Erin Vecchio, Chief Recovery Officer Daniel J. Matsook, and others in the Penn Hills School District said they understood Costa's recommendation not to raise taxes to be a condition for receiving the money.

304 **had never materialized:** Michael DiVittorio, "Penn Hills School District Officials Hope to Hold the Line on Taxes with State Help," Penn Hills Progress, Trib Live, May 26, 2020, https:// neighborhoods.triblive.com/pennhillsprogress /penn%20hills%20school%20district %20officials%20hope%20to%20hold%20the %20line%20on%20taxes%20with%20state%20 help/bid870e6563494342074a791dce974be31b.

304 **by raising taxes:** Daniel J. Matsook in discussion with the author, February 2020.

304 **7 percent property-tax hike:** DiVittorio, "Penn Hills School District's Preliminary Budget Adopted, Tax Increase Likely."

304 **risk a revolt:** Erin Vecchio in discussion with the author, February 2020.

304 **$3.2 million operating deficit:** "Proposed 2020– 2021 Preliminary Budget," Penn Hills School District, presented January 9, 2020, 5, https:// www.phsd.k12.pa.us/apps/pages/index.jsp?uREC _ID=1328043&type=d&pREC_ID=1822260.

304 **a state takeover:** Daniel J. Matsook in discussion with the author, February 2020.

304 **heat the two buildings:** All details regarding the HVAC system failures in Penn Hills schools are drawn from Reynolds, "Penn Hills School District Board Update," March 16, 2020, in the author's possession, unless otherwise noted.

304 **design of the systems:** "Safety/Buildings and Grounds Committee Minutes," Penn Hills School District, March 16, 2020, 3, https://4.files.edl.io/3362/03/20/20/181459-41bc6edf-8784-4124-994e-e8928be2ae21.pdf.

304 **been largely ignored:** "Safety/Buildings and Grounds Committee Minutes."

304 **Jefferson Elementary's numbers:** All information regarding academic performance at Jefferson Elementary midway through the 2019–20 school year are drawn from data provided by Compton Unified in response to a records request, in the author's possession, unless otherwise noted.

306 **iReady data showed:** Data provided by Compton Unified in response to a records request, in the author's possession.

309 **Op-Ed against homework:** "Is Homework a Good Thing?," in the author's possession.

311 **already confirmed dead:** All figures regarding COVID-19 deaths and case counts are from the Centers for Disease Control and Prevention, unless otherwise noted.

311 **starting to shut down:** "Americans Face Dramatic Limits on Public Life as Schools, Theme Parks, Events Shut Down," NBC News, https://www.nbcnews.com/health/health-news/live-blog/2020-03-12-coronavirus-news-n1156266.

311 **closing schools for two weeks:** Howard Blume et al., "Los Angeles Unified District to Close All Schools," *Los Angeles Times*, March 13, 2020, https://www.latimes.com/california/story/2020-03-13/los-angeles-schools-closure-possible-cornavirus.

311 **decided the same:** "All Long Beach Unified Schools to Close March 16," Long Beach Local News, March 13, 2020, https://www.longbeachlocalnews.com/2020/03/13/all-long-beach-unified-schools-to-close-march-16/.

311 **to follow suit:** "Update Regarding Close of Compton Schools March 16–30," Compton Unified School District, March 14, 2020, https://www.compton.k12.ca.us/news-release/news/2020/march/closing-of-schools.

CHAPTER 13: THE STORM ARRIVES

315 **"They fought all their lives":** The White House, "Remarks by President Trump in Press Briefing," August 13, 2020, https://trumpwhitehouse.archives.gov/briefings-statements/remarks-president-trump-press-briefing-081320/.

315 **the White House:** All descriptions and quotations regarding President Donald Trump's speech on the South Lawn are drawn from Donald Trump, "President Trump Remarks on Rolling Back Regulations," July 16, 2020, White House, C-SPAN video recording, 47:55, https://www.c-span.org/video/?473927-1/president-trump-comments-protesters-removal-statues, unless otherwise noted.

316 **half century too late:** Karen Tumulty, "What Century Does Trump Think American Women Are Living In?," *Washington Post*, July 24, 2020, https://www.washingtonpost.com/opinions/2020/07/24/what-century-does-trump-think-american-women-are-living/.

316 **police had murdered:** All descriptions of the police murder of George Floyd and subsequent protests are drawn from Giulia McDonnell Nieto del Rio, John Eligon, Adeel Hassan, "A Timeline of What Happened in the Year Since George Floyd's Death," *New York Times*, May 25, 2021, https://www.nytimes.com/2021/05/25/us/george-floyd-protests-unrest-events-timeline.html, unless otherwise noted.

316 **protesters being teargassed:** Christie Ileto, "Philadelphia Protesters Gassed, Maced on I-676 Taking Legal Action," ABC6, June 19, 2020, https://6abc.com/philadelphia-protest-philly-news-in/6255083/.

316 **setting fire to police stations:** "Police Precinct Set on Fire During Portland Protest; Authorities Declare Riot," Associated Press, August 24, 2020, https://www.usatoday.com/story/news/nation/2020/08/24/portland-protests-police-precinct-set-fire/3427950001/.

316 **windows of Rite-Aids:** "Vandalism Damage Closes Rochester Pharmacies," WXXI News, June 3, 2020, https://www.wxxinews.org/health/2020-06-03/vandalism-damage-closes-rochester-pharmacies.

316 **as flash-bang grenades boomed around them:** Philip Bump, "Timeline: The Clearing of Lafayette Square," *Washington Post*, June 5, 2020, https://www.washingtonpost.com/politics/2020/06/02/timeline-clearing-lafayette-square/.

316 **four thousand suburban communities:** Dan Reed, "Protests: A Racial Reckoning in Suburbia," NRDC, July 9, 2020, https://www.nrdc.org/stories/protests-racial-reckoning-suburbia.

317 **to Orange County:** Dave Murphy and Alex Smith, "Black Lives Matter Protests 2020," cresotemaps.com, https://www.creosotemaps.com/blm2020/index.html.

317 **suburban Long Island:** Scott Brinton, "The Girl Who Lit Up the Twittersphere," LIHerald.com, June 15, 2020, https://www.liherald.com/stories/the-girl-who-lit-up-the-twittersphere,125911; and "Mother of 7-Year-Old LI Girl Seen Marching, Chanting with Protesters in Viral Video Says She Wants to Teach Her She Can Make a Difference," CBS New York, June 4, 2020, https://www.cbsnews.com/newyork/news/little-girl-protesting-long-island/.

317 **tested positive the previous:** "Coronavirus in the U.S.: Latest Map and Case Count," *New York Times*, https://www.nytimes.com/interactive/2021/us/covid-cases.html.

317 **closed their doors:** "Data: Coronavirus and School Closures in 2019–2020," *Education Week*, December 3, 2021, https://www.edweek .org/data-coronavirus-and-school-closures -in-2019-2020/2021/12#:~:text=The% 20coronavirus%20pandemic%20forced% 20a,6%20to%20May%2015%2C%202020.

317 **Kurtz, whose work:** Special thanks to Stanley N. Kurtz, whose work helped shape my understanding of conservative attempts to make suburban change a major issue during the 2020 presidential campaign. See, e.g., Stanley Kurtz, *Spreading the Wealth: How Obama Is Robbing the Suburbs to Pay for the Cities* (New York: Sentinel, 2012).

317 **"exodus to the suburbs":** Kurtz, *Spreading the Wealth*, xiii.

317 **the *National Review*:** Stanley N. Kurtz, "Biden and Dems Are Set to Abolish the Suburbs," *National Review*, June 30, 2020, https://www .nationalreview.com/corner/biden-and-dems -are-set-to-abolish-the-suburbs/.

318 **suspended its season:** Steve Aschburner, "Coronavirus Pandemic Causes NBA to Suspend Season After Player Tests Positive," NBA.com, March 12, 2020, https://www.nba .com/news/coronavirus-pandemic-causes-nba -suspend-season.

318 **were shutting down:** Lana Duran, "List of DFW Schools That Closed or Cancelled Classes Due to Coronavirus (COVID-19)," Metroplex Social, March 12, 2020, https://metroplexsocial.com /universities-and-school-districts-in-dfw-that -have-cancelled-class-due-to-coronavirus/.

319 **announce an extended closure:** Michael Goddard, "Message from District: Health Information, March 18, 2020," email message to Lovejoy ISD parents, March 18, 2020.

319 **crazy hat day:** Michael Goddard, "Message from Mike, April 3, 2020," email message to Lovejoy ISD parents, April 3, 2020.

319 **about Texas history:** "Texas Essential Knowledge and Skills for Grade 4," Texas Education Agency, revised August 2019, https:// tea.texas.gov/sites/default/files/Grade4_TEKS _0819.pdf.

320 **his Pentecostal prayer:** David Lessner, May 31, 2020, Creekwood United Methodist Church, livestream video, 1:09:58, https://www .facebook.com/creekwoodumc/videos /718802392268707.

321 **Businesses remained closed:** Nate Chute, "When Texas Closed, Reopened and Closed Again During COVID-19," *El Paso Times*, July 3, 2020, https://www.elpasotimes.com/story /news/2020/07/03/covid-texas-coronavirus -timeline-greg-abbott-close-reopen/536889 4002/.

321 **imposing mask mandates:** "State-Level Mask Requirements in Response to the Coronavirus (Covid-19) Pandemic, 2020–2022," Ballotpedia, https://ballotpedia.org/State-level_mask _requirements_in_response_to_the _coronavirus_(COVID-19)_pandemic, _2020-2022.

321 **from pharmaceutical companies:** Justin Baragona, "How Vaccine Companies Have Bankrolled Fox News' Anti-Vaxx Insanity," *Daily Beast*, July 22, 2021, https://www .thedailybeast.com/how-vaccine-companies -have-bankrolled-fox-news-anti-vaxx-insanity.

321 **And those alarming spikes:** "Tracking Coronavirus in Collin County, Texas: Latest Map and Case Count," *New York Times*, https:// www.nytimes.com/interactive/2021/us/collin -texas-covid-cases.html.

321 **changing their methodology:** Erin Anderson, "Texas' New Coronavirus Criteria Could Artificially Spike Collin County Cases," Texas Scorecard, May 26, 2020, https://texasscorecard .com/local/texas-new-coronavirus-criteria -could-artificially-spike-collin-county-cases/.

322 **proponent of "vaccine safety":** Michelle Smith, "How a Kennedy Built an Anti-Vaccine Juggernaut amid COVID-19," AP News, December 15, 2021, https://apnews.com/article /how-rfk-jr-built-anti-vaccine-juggernaut -amid-covid-4997be1bcf591fe8b7f1f90d 16c9321e.

322 **state senator Bob Hall:** "WATCH: Senator Bob Hall Hosts Town Hall with Medical Experts," Blue Ribbon News, July 16, 2020, https:// blueribbonnews.com/2020/07/watch-senator -bob-hall-hosts-town-hall-with-medical -experts/.

322 **considered potentially harmful:** "FDA Cautions Against Use of Hydroxychloroquine or Chloroquine for COVID-19 Outside of the Hospital Setting or a Clinical Trial Due to Risk of Heart Rhythm Problems," Food and Drug Administration, https://www.fda.gov/drugs/drug -safety-and-availability/fda-cautions-against-use -hydroxychloroquine-or-chloroquine-covid -19-outside-hospital-setting-or.

323 **a $253,000 hole:** All details of Lovejoy ISD's budget predicament in spring 2020 are drawn from Shay Adams, "Lovejoy ISD 2019–2020 Budget Update," video conference presentation, Lovejoy ISD Board Meeting, May 11, 2020, unless otherwise noted.

323 **$44.2 million budget:** "2020–2021 Approved Budget," school budget, Board of Trustees of the Lovejoy Independent School District, 2020, https://www.lovejoyisd.net/apps/pages/index .jsp?uREC_ID=385835&type=d&pREC_ID =1067095.

323 **nearly six hundred students:** Shay Adams, "Transportation," video conference presentation, Lovejoy ISD Board Meeting, June 22, 2020.

324 **Goddard's annual salary:** "Superintendent's Employment Contract," contract of employment, Board of Trustees of the Lovejoy Independent School District, 2020, in possession of the author.

324 **that 62 percent:** "2020–2021 Parent Survey Results," survey results, Lovejoy ISD, June 2020, 1, in possession of author.

324 **a hybrid approach:** Michael Goddard, "Superintendent's Update," video conference presentation, Lovejoy ISD Board Meeting, June 22, 2020.

324 **ten and up:** "Executive Order GA 29 of July 2, 2020, Relating to the Use of Face Coverings During the COVID-19 Disaster," filed in the Office of the Secretary of State, Austin, Texas, https://gov.texas.gov/uploads/files/press /EO-GA-29-use-of-face-coverings-during -COVID-19-IMAGE-07-02-2020.pdf.

324 **questions and concerns:** "COVID-19 Questionnaire Concern: Redacted Responses," survey responses, Lovejoy ISD, 2020, in possession of author.

324 **a fifteen-hundred-word email:** Susan Becker's email message and Superintendent Goddard's response were provided by Lovejoy ISD in response to a request for all electronic records of parental questions and complaints during spring 2020.

326 **"their own militia":** Eric Griffey, "A Weatherford, Texas Protest Turned Violent," Spectrum News 1, July 29, 2020, https:// spectrumlocalnews.com/tx/south-texas-el -paso/news/2020/07/28/a-weatherford-protest -turned-violent-.

327 **novel called *Rumble*:** Ellen Hopkins, *Rumble* (New York: Margaret K. McElderry Books, 2014).

327 **nearly 400,000 students:** Benjamin Herold and Xinchun Chen, "Suburban Schools Saw Huge Drops in White Enrollment During the Pandemic," *Education Week*, August 29, 2022, https://www.edweek.org/leadership/suburban -schools-saw-huge-drops-in-white-enrollment -during-the-pandemic/2022/08.

327 **vilification of white people:** Dave Harper, principal at Freedom Project Academy, in discussion with the author, August, 20, 2020.

327 **was an offshoot:** "Form 990: American Opinion Foundation Inc., doing business as Freedom Project," public tax documents, Internal Revenue Service, 2019.

327 **newly developing white suburbs:** Benjamin Epstein and Arnold Forster, *The Radical Right: Report on the John Birch Society and Its Allies* (New York: Random House, 1967), 3.

328 **as too extreme:** Alvin Felzenberg, "The Inside Story of William F. Buckley Jr.'s Crusade Against the John Birch Society," *National Review*, June 20, 2017, https://www .nationalreview.com/2017/06/william-f -buckley-john-birch-society-history -conflict-robert-welch/.

328 **entirely gone away:** John Savage, "The John Birch Society Is Back," *Politico*, July 16, 2017, https://www.politico.com/magazine/story/2017 /07/16/the-john-birch-society-is-alive-and-well -in-the-lone-star-state-215377.

328 **American Opinion Foundation:** "Form 990: American Opinion Foundation Inc., doing business as Freedom Project," public tax documents, Internal Revenue Service, 2019, Schedule O.

328 **urging a return:** Gary Benoit, "Battle Over Education," *New American* 35, no. 3, February 4, 2019, https://thenewamerican.com/magazine /tna3503/page/55986.

328 **private religious education:** Alex Newman, "Insanity in the Classroom: Government Schools Today," *New American*, February 4, 2019, https://thenewamerican.com /magazine/tna3503/page/55986.

328 **a Dunkirk-style mobilization:** Duke Pesta, "Get Them Out (of Public Schools)!," *New American*, February 8, 2019, https://thenewamerican.com /magazine/tna3503/page/56068.

328 **"mass-producing uneducated":** Alex Newman, "Education's Future: Globalization of Indoctrination," *New American*, February 4, 2019, https://thenewamerican.com/magazine /tna3503/page/56030.

328 **"and parents in particular":** Duke Pesta, "Get Them Out (of Public Schools)!," *New American*, February 8, 2019, https://thenewamerican.com /magazine/tna3503/page/56068.

328 **the executive director:** "Form 990: American Opinion Foundation Inc., doing business as Freedom Project," public tax documents, Internal Revenue Service, 2019, 7.

328 **nearly a thousand kids:** Dave Harper, principal at Freedom Project Academy, in discussion with the author, February 9, 2021.

329 **to read the letter:** All descriptions and quotations from Avery Becker's reading to Collin County conservatives are drawn from videos provided by Susan Becker.

330 **finish counting votes:** Tom McCarthy and Joan E. Greve, "Race Too Close to Call after Polls Close—As It Happened," *Guardian*, November 4, 2020, https://www.theguardian.com/us -news/live/2020/nov/03/us-election-2020 -live-updates-president-donald-trump-joe -biden-latest-presidential-election-news-polls -update.

CHAPTER 14: A SUDDEN TRANSFORMATION

331 **pass in order to advance:** "DrPH Requirements," Graduate School University of Georgia, https://grad.uga.edu/graduate -bulletin/doctoral-degree-requirements /drph-requirements/.

331 **shut Georgia down:** Arielle Kass, "COVID-19: Gwinnett County, Cities, Close Restaurants, Gathering Places," TCA Regional News, March 25, 2020; Lois Norder, "Detailed COVID timeline," *Atlanta Journal-Constitution*, December 23, 2020, https://www.ajc.com/news /coronavirus/a-covid-timeline-how-the

-coronavirus-swallowed-2020/USUE2
HXXQBD2TB4A3J7UW3DQO4/.

331 **used a press briefing:** "Transcript for the
CDC Telebriefing Update on COVID-19,"
Centers for Disease Control and Prevention,
February 26, 2020, https://www.cdc.gov/media
/releases/2020/t0225-cdc-telebriefing-covid-19
.html.

332 **switched to digital learning:** Arlinda Smith
Broady, "Gwinnett County Public Schools
Implement 'Digital Learning Days,'" *Atlanta
Journal-Constitution*, March 12, 2020, https://
www.ajc.com/news/local-education/gwinnett
-county-public-schools-implement-digital
-learning-days/uwvhOGNfGDtcvgrIv0fnXO/.

332 **CDC director fired:** Rebecca Ballhaus and
Stephanie Armour, "Health Chief's Early
Missteps Set Back Coronavirus Response,"
April 22, 2020, *Wall Street Journal*, https://
www.wsj.com/articles/health-chiefs-early
-missteps-set-back-coronavirus-response
-11587570514.

332 **briefings were limited:** Kristen Holmes and
Veronica Stracqualursi, "CDC to Resume Regular
Coronavirus Briefings After Being Sidelined by
White House," CNN, May 30, 2020, https://
www.cnn.com/2020/05/30/politics/cdc
-coronavirus-briefings-resume/index.html.

332 **would miraculously disappear:** Juana
Summers, "Timeline: How Trump Has
Downplayed the Coronavirus Pandemic,"
NPR, October 2, 2020, https://www.npr.org
/sections/latest-updates-trump-covid-19
-results/2020/10/02/919432383/how-trump
-has-downplayed-the-coronavirus-pandemic.

332 **public health measures:** J. D. Capelouto,
"Group Protests Georgia's Coronavirus-Related
Closures," TCA Regional News, April 20, 2020.

332 **tanking hotel industry:** Jared Mandell, "Covid
Hit the Hotel Industry Hard. Data Shows It's
Still Missing a Key Part of Its Business," NBC
News, September 24, 2021, https://www
.nbcnews.com/news/us-news/covid-hit-hotel
-industry-hard-data-shows-it-s-still-n1280061.

334 **2019–20 school year remotely:** Arlinda Smith
Broady, "Gwinnett Announces End-of-Year
Plan: Seniors Will Have Virtual Graduation
Ceremony in May," *Atlanta Journal-
Constitution*, April 13, 2020, B.4.

334 **spring testing was canceled:** "Gwinnett County
Public Schools Digital Learning Update,"
Gwinnett County Public Schools, April 13,
2020, http://gcps-communique.com
/archive/2020/4/13/gwinnett-county-public
-schools-digital-learning-update; Arlinda
Smith Broady, "Gwinnett Announces End-of
-Year Plan," 4.

334 **splitting in two:** Jim Galloway, Greg Bluestein,
and Tia Mitchell, "The Jolt: Georgia Mayors
Blindsided by Brian Kemp's Decision to Let
Businesses Reopen," TCA Regional News, April
21, 2020.

334 **their empty classrooms:** Arlinda Smith Broady,
"Gwinnett Schools Staff Among First to Return
to On-Site Duties," TCA Regional News, May 1,
2020.

334 **"Gwinnett County alone":** "GCPS School Board,
Don't Put Our Heroes at Risk!," Change.org,
https://www.change.org/p/gwinnett-county
-public-school-gcps-school-board-don-t-put
-our-heroes-at-risk?recruiter=1084896511&
utm_source=share_petition&utm_.

334 **amplifying the message:** Karen Watkins, email
to Gwinnett elected officials and community
leaders, May 5, 2020, in the author's possession.

335 **reporting seven hundred new:** "Tracking
Coronavirus in Georgia: Latest Map and Case
Count," *New York Times*, https://www.nytimes
.com/interactive/2021/us/georgia-covid-cases
.html.

335 **a single day:** Arielle Kass, "TESTING:
Gwinnett Tops Fulton, Has More Cases Than
Anywhere Else in State: At One Testing Center
Recently, 27% Had COVID-19," *Atlanta
Journal-Constitution*, June 14, 2020, A.3.

335 **refusal to impose:** Johnny Edwards, "A Look at
Major Coronavirus Developments During the
Past Week," *Atlanta Journal-Constitution*, June
27, 2020.

335 **a series of questions:** Daniel Funke, "In
Context: What Donald Trump Said about
Disinfectant, Sun and Coronavirus," PolitiFact,
April 24, 2020, https://www.politifact.com
/article/2020/apr/24/context-what-donald
-trump-said-about-disinfectant-/.

336 **announced a rally:** "Justice for Black Lives,"
Facebook, accessed December 16, 2022, https://
www.facebook.com/events/836685630156919
/?active_tab=about.

336 **for forty-seven years:** "Louise Radloff Loses
Re-Election After Nearly 50 Years on the
Gwinnett School Board," *Gwinnett Daily
Post*, January 2, 2021, https://www
.gwinnettdailypost.com/louise-radloff
-looses-re-election-after-nearly-50-years-on
-the-gwinnett-school-board/image_5a98f5fc
-4d12-11eb-a0c5-dfe90a56b48b.html.

336 **bleak extended-stay motels:** Michael E. Kanell,
"Working but Poor, Many Families Are
Trapped in Extended-Stay Hotels," *Atlanta
Journal-Constitution*, April 5, 2020, https://
www.detroitnews.com/story/business/personal
-finance/2020/04/05/working-but-poor-many-
families-trapped-extended-stay-hotels
/2943123001/.

336 **available for rent:** Alana Semuels, "Suburbs
and the New American Poverty," *Atlantic*,
January 5, 2015, https://www.theatlantic.com
/business/archive/2015/01/suburbs-and-the
-new-american-poverty/384259/.

337 **directly with Radloff:** All descriptions and
quotations from the 2020 Gwinnett County
School Board District 5 candidate forum are
drawn from GwinnettSTOP, "Gwinnett County

Board of Education District 5 Candidate Forum," YouTube video, 1:00:07, May 14, 2020, https://youtu.be/FEzhqMDmyOw, unless otherwise noted.

337 **Gwinnett Place Mall:** Asia Simone Burns, Greg Bluestein, J. Scott Trubey, Ernie Suggs, "Atlanta Protests: No Arrests Made During 10th Straight Day of Demonstrations," *Atlanta Journal -Constitution*, June 7, 2020, https://www.ajc.com /news/breaking-news/atlanta-protests-another -round-demonstrations-planned-across-metro -atlanta/11MY8Ldt6gKwjaazx2pVkK/.

337 **KOREANS FOR BLACK LIVES MATTER:** All descriptions of the Justice for Black Lives rally are drawn from "PHOTOS: Protesters March in Gwinnett County," *Atlanta Journal -Constitution*, June 7, 2020, https://www .ajc.com/news/photos-demonstrations-held -gwinnett-county/dnl73ockqye3as K81Oa1TM /?fbclid=IwAR2wI-DemmedhFArH4gCG-wxU _1NvKx8tmWP9LzcaX1MGy3eXYupyYSJgEY, unless otherwise noted.

337 **disorderly conduct charge:** Larry Stanford, "Grand Jury Releases Presentment in Death of Shali Tilson at Rockdale County Jail," *Citizens*, September 25, 2019, https://www.rockdale newtoncitizen.com/news/grand-jury-releases -presentment-in-death-of-shali-tilson-at -rockdale-county-jail/article_5a18d1ac-dfda -11e9-ab41-a315488e60c8.html.

338 **by 33 points:** "Tarece Johnson," Ballotpedia, accessed December 16, 2022, https:// ballotpedia.org/Tarece_Johnson.

338 **infections and deaths:** "Tracking Coronavirus in Georgia: Latest Map and Case Count," *New York Times*, updated January 2, 2023, https:// www.nytimes.com/interactive/2021/us/georgia -covid-cases.html.

338 **back into classrooms:** Gwinnett County Public Schools, email, June 25, 2020, in the author's possession.

339 **"I could strangle him":** Curt Yeomans, "Gwinnett School Board Chair Louise Radloff: Remark about Strangling Board Member Everton Blair Was 'Out of Order,'" *Gwinnett Daily Post*, July 18, 2020, https://www .gwinnettdailypost.com/local/gwinnett-school -board-chair-louise-radloff-remark-about -strangling-board-member-everton-blair-was -out/article_2ce8693c-c7e6-11ea-8c52-5bc1 3a22a192.html.

339 **became the center:** Jordan Smith, "Georgia Is in Play in the 2020 Election, and It's Not Just the White House Up for Grabs," Fox 5 Atlanta, October 27, 2020, https://www.fox5atlanta.com /news/georgia-is-in-play-in-the-2020-election -and-its-not-just-the-white-house-up-for-grabs.

339 **Mid-September polling showed:** "Georgia Presidential and Senate Contests Are Tight, Quinnipiac University Poll Finds," Targeted News Service, September 30, 2020; Greg Bluestein, "AJC Poll: Race for President, Senate

Contests in Georgia 'Too Close to Call,'" *Atlanta Journal-Constitution*, September 22, 2020.

340 **likely to force:** Greg Bluestein, "AJC Poll: Race for President, Senate Contests in Georgia 'Too Close to Call.'"

340 **"If I don't win":** Donald Trump (@realDonaldTrump), Donald Trump Twitter post, September 10, 2020, 10:14 a.m.

340 **shot and killed:** Alexis Stevens, "Gwinnett County Police Shooting: Teen Killed by Officers Was on Probation: He Was Arrested at a School Last Year for Carrying a Gun," *Atlanta Journal-Constitution*, September 16, 2020, B.8.

340 **down in lawsuits:** "Activist Lawsuit Undermines Election Administration in Gwinnett County in Weeks Before Election," U.S. Federal News Service, October 2, 2020.

340 **on all-remote learning:** Alia Malik, "In-Person or Remote? Gwinnett Schools Deadline Nears for Next Semester," *Atlanta Journal-Constitution*, November 12, 2020, https://www .ajc.com/news/in-person-or-remote-gwinnett -schools-deadline-nears-for-next-semester /BI2HQTYCRBGMBNZAJCLXSSPK5M/.

340 **Murphy told me:** Benjamin Herold, "How the Fight for America's Suburbs Started in Public Schools," *Education Week*, October 26, 2020, https://www.edweek.org/leadership/how-the -fight-for-americas-suburbs-started-in-public -schools/2020/10.

341 **a dead heat:** Quint Forgey, "Poll: Democrats Even with Republicans in Georgia Senate Races," *Politico*, October 20, 2020, https://www .politico.com/news/2020/10/20/georgia-senate -races-polls-430344.

341 **a comfortable lead:** "David Clark (Georgia)," Ballotpedia, https://ballotpedia.org/David _Clark_(Georgia).

CHAPTER 15: HATE IN HEAVEN

343 **Two hundred fifty:** Bill Smith, "Evanstonians Protest Police Shooting in Kenosha," Evanston Now, August 25, 2020, https://evanstonnow .com/evanstonians-protest-police-shooting-in -kenosha/.

343 **named Jacob Blake:** Christina Morales, "What We Know about the Shooting of Jacob Blake," *New York Times*, November 16, 2021, https:// www.nytimes.com/article/jacob-blake -shooting-kenosha.html.

343 **into their electricity:** William Phitness Eason, Facebook, August 26, 2020, https://www .facebook.com/permalink.php?story_fbid =2466624936970061&id=100008677365626.

343 **defunding of police departments:** Madeline Kenney (@madkenney), Twitter post, August 25, 2020, 7:01 p.m., https://twitter.com /madkenney/status/1298395177317523464?s =20&t=tk74tF6A4jW7yK85fIJEZw.

344 **had rung out:** Tammy Gibson, "Jacob Blake's Family Has a History of Activism," *Chicago*

Defender, September 10, 2020, https://chicagodefender.com/jacob-blake-family-has-a-history-of-activism/.

344 **Evanston Township High:** Genevieve Bookwalter, "Jacob Blake, Shot by POLICE OFFICER in Kenosha, Part of Evanston Family Long Associated with Community Activism," *Evanston Review*, August 25, 2020, https://www.chicagotribune.com/suburbs/evanston/ct-evr-jacob-blake-kenosha-police-shooting-evanston-tl-0827-20200824-h63o7uquo5esnf7lnv23njzrx4-story.html.

344 **video of the shooting:** All descriptions of the police shooting of Jacob Blake are drawn from Michael D. Graveley, "Report on the Officer Involved Shooting of Jacob Blake Synopsis," County of Kenosha District Attorney, January 5, 2021, 7, https://www.kenoshacounty.org/DocumentCenter/View/11827/Report-on-the-Officer-Involved-Shooting-of-Jacob-Blake; Morales, "What We Know about the Shooting of Jacob Blake," unless otherwise noted.

344 **For two nights:** Julie Bosman, "A Timeline of the Kyle Rittenhouse Shootings and His Trial," *New York Times*, November 19, 2021, https://www.nytimes.com/article/kyle-rittenhouse-shooting-timeline.html.

344 **Wisconsin National Guard:** Brakkton Booker and Emma Bowman, "Wisconsin Deploys National Guard After Shooting of Black Man Sparks Protests," NPR, August 24, 2020, https://www.npr.org/sections/live-updates-protests-for-racial-justice/2020/08/24/905316709/wisconsin-police-shooting-leaves-black-man-in-serious-condition.

344 **call for "patriots":** Erik Gunn, "A 'Call to Arms' That Filled Kenosha with Combat Weapons," *Wisconsin Examiner*, August 27, 2020, https://wisconsinexaminer.com/2020/08/27/a-call-to-arms-that-filled-kenosha-with-combat-weapons/.

345 **quickly spread word:** Neil MacFarquhar, "When Armed Vigilantes Are Summoned with a Few Keystrokes," *New York Times*, October 16, 2020, https://www.nytimes.com/2020/10/16/us/kenosha-guard-militia-kevin-mathewson.html.

345 **At the rally:** Kaitlin Edquist, "Rally Held in Evanston as Show of Support for Jacob Blake and Family: 'We Cry Together,'" *Chicago Tribune*, August 25, 2020, https://www.chicagotribune.com/suburbs/evanston/ct-evr-evanston-jacob-blake-kenosha-shooting-rally-tl-0827-20200826-u3twv6tztjasnbchbpvpodkpky-story.html.

345 **"We are exhausted":** "Evanston rally held for Jacob Blake and his family," Dear Evanston, August 26, 2020, https://www.dearevanston.org/post/evanston-rally-held-for-jacob-blake-and-his-family.

346 **Kenosha exploded shortly afterward:** All descriptions of protests and violence in Kenosha are drawn from Julie Bosman, "A Timeline of the Kyle Rittenhouse Shootings and His Trial," *New York Times*, November 19, 2021, https://www.nytimes.com/article/kyle-rittenhouse-shooting-timeline.html, unless otherwise noted.

346 **hundreds of people scrambling:** Leah Watson, "Kyle Rittenhouse Didn't Act Alone: Law Enforcement Must Be Held Accountable," ACLU, November 19, 2021, https://www.aclu.org/news/criminal-law-reform/kyle-rittenhouse-didnt-act-alone-law-enforcement-must-be-held-accountable.

346 **seventeen-year-old white male:** "Key Events in the Kenosha Shootings Case of Kyle Rittenhouse," AP News, November 19, 2021, https://apnews.com/article/kyle-rittenhouse-police-shootings-wisconsin-kenosha-5e4f6bdf938fc42baea5bc648d9829df.

346 **Smith & Wesson M&P 15 rifle:** Neil Vigdor, "Rifle Used by Kyle Rittenhouse in Kenosha Shootings Will Be Destroyed," *New York Times*, January 28, 2022, https://www.nytimes.com/2022/01/28/us/kyle-rittenhouse-ar15-gun.html.

346 **four times, killing him:** "How Kyle Rittenhouse Went from Cleaning Graffiti to Shooting 3 People," Reuters, November 19, 2021, https://www.reuters.com/world/us/how-kyle-rittenhouse-went-cleaning-graffiti-shooting-3-people-2021-11-11/.

346 **swung a skateboard:** Vanessa Romo and Sharon Pruitt-Young, "What We Know about the 3 Men Who Were Shot by Kyle Rittenhouse," NPR, November 20, 2021, https://www.npr.org/2021/11/20/1057571558/what-we-know-3-men-kyle-rittenhouse-victims-rosenbaum-huber-grosskreutz.

346 **publicly defending Rittenhouse:** Alana Wise, "Trump Defends Kenosha Shooting Suspect," NPR, August 31, 2020, https://www.npr.org/sections/live-updates-protests-for-racial-justice/2020/08/31/908137377/trump-defends-kenosha-shooting-suspect.

347 **a 9:00 p.m. curfew:** Alison Martin and Mitchell Armentrout, "Lightfoot Imposes Curfew Starting at 9 P.M. Saturday," *Chicago Sun-Times*, May 30, 2020, https://chicago.suntimes.com/news/2020/5/30/21275833/lightfoot-chicago-curfew-george-floyd-protests.

347 **"Racism in America":** "Racism in America: A Statement from Dr. Horton," Evanston/Skokie School District 65, May 31, 2020, https://www.district65.net/site/Default.aspx?PageType=3&DomainID=4&PageID=1&ViewID=6446ee88-d30c-497e-9316-3f8874b3e108&FlexDataID=9457.

348 **the district's revenues:** All details regarding District 65's 2020–21 budget are drawn from Evanston/Skokie School District 65, FY21 Tentative Budget board presentation, August 10, 2020, 28, https://meetings.boardbook.org/Documents/WebViewer/1247?file=e2426c92

-6840-4b14-bdce-d2abd9014b8b, unless otherwise noted.

348 **annual operating deficits:** Larry Gavin, "District 65 Finance Committee Tentatively Aims at Cutting About $10 Million in Expenses over Next Four Years," *Evanston RoundTable*, December 14, 2020, https://evanstonroundtable .com/2020/12/14/district-65-finance -committee-tentatively-aims-at-cutting-about -10-million-in-expenses-over-next-four-years/.

348 **would already be exhausted:** In a written response to questions, a District 65 spokesperson emphasized that these were best available projections at the time, but that the district's financial position subsequently changed as more information became available.

348 **cuts for 2021–22:** "District 65 Financial Facts," Evanston/Skokie School District 65, December 2, 2020.

348 **proposed all-remote learning:** "Return to School Update & 2020–2021 Learning Pathways," Evanston/Skokie School District 65, July 22, 2020.

348 **questions and complaints:** School Board Public Comment, Evanston/Skokie School District 65, board meeting July 22, 2020, https://meetings .boardbook.org/Documents/WebViewer/1247 ?file=d5748b0e-8f14-4f09-9e55-0ffc3f094c65.

349 **a "political uprising":** Lisa Lerer and Jennifer Medina, "The 'Rage Moms' Democrats Are Counting On," *New York Times*, August 18, 2020, https://www.nytimes.com/2020/08/17/us /politics/democrats-women-voters-anger.html.

349 **the conflict over reopening:** Benjamin Herold, "How Schools Survived Two Years of COVID-19," *Education Week*, March 15, 2022, https://www .edweek.org/teaching-learning/how-schools -survived-two-years-of-covid-19/2022/03.

349 **drastic measures, including suing:** John Mooney, "Scotch Plains-Fanwood Parents Filed Lawsuit vs. School District, BOE, and Superintendent to Open Schools," TAPinto Scotch Plains/Fanwood, December 23, 2020, https://www.tapinto.net /towns/scotch-plains-slash-fanwood/sections /education/articles/scotch-plains-fanwood -parents-filed-lawsuit-vs-school-district-boe-and -superintendent-to-open-schools.

349 **in harm's way:** Lauren Camera, "Reopening America's Schools and the Privilege of Opting Out," *U.S. News & World Report*, May 22, 2020, https://www.usnews.com/news/the-report /articles/2020-05-22/reopening-americas -schools-and-the-privilege-of-opting-out.

349 **louder and more frequent:** Jenna Russell, "In Arlington, Black Voices Challenge a White Suburban School District to Do Better," *Boston Globe*, https://www.bostonglobe.com/2020/07 /11/metro/amid-national-reckoning-black -voices-challenge-white-suburban-school -district-do-better/; Rafael Garcia, "More Than Half of Seaman High's Students of Color Say They Experience Racism," *Topeka Capital-*

Journal, December 7, 2020, https://www .cjonline.com/story/news/local/2020/12/08 /more-than-half-of-seaman-highrsquos -students-of-color-say-they-experience-racism /115117234/.

349 **a "high priority":** Illinois State Board of Education and Illinois Department of Public Health, "Starting the 2020–21 School Year: Part 3-Transition Joint Guidance," June 23, 2020, https://www.isbe.net/Documents/Part-3 -Transition-Planning-Phase-4.pdf.

350 **with a statement:** Larry Gavin, "What Will Remote Learning Look Like in the 2020–2021 School Year?," *Evanston RoundTable*, August 1, 2020, https://evanstonroundtable.com/2020/08 /01/what-will-remote-learning-look-like-in-the -2020-2021-school-year/.

350 **for Fox News:** Sam Dorman, "Illinois District Includes Students of Color in Groups with First Chance at In-Person Learning: Report," Fox News, August 6, 2020, https://www.foxnews .com/us/illinois-schools-black-brown-students -in-person-learning.

350 **was soon flooded:** All descriptions of and quotations from letters and emails sent to District 65 following Fox News's coverage of the reopening fight in Evanston are drawn from a FOIA request response, records provided by Evanston/Skokie School District 65, unless otherwise noted.

351 **"I hope that you will reply":** Email to Devon Horton and John Cabello, August 7, 2020, a FOIA request response, records provided by Evanston/Skokie School District 65.

351 **attempting to walk back:** Larry Gavin, "District 65 Superintendent and Board Members Defend Priorities for Admission to In-Person Learning," *Evanston RoundTable*, August 11, 2020, https://evanstonroundtable .com/2020/08/11/district-65-superintendent -and-board-members-defend-priorities-for -admission-to-in-person-learning/.

351 **"during our spring learning":** In this quote from District 65 superintendent Devon Horton, I substitute "[homeless]" for Horton's actual words, "McKinney Vento," which is a reference to the federal McKinney-Vento Homeless Assistance Act guaranteeing rights and services to K–12 students experiencing homelessness.

351 **"Your failure to take them":** Email from Christian Eades to Evanston/Skokie School District 65 board members, August 6, 2020.

352 **to be antiracist:** Benjamin Herold, "A New Teacher at 50: Inside the Struggle to Rebuild America's Black Teaching Workforce," *Education Week*, October 11, 2022, https:// www.edweek.org/leadership/a-teacher-at-50 -inside-the-struggle-to-rebuild-americas-black -teaching-workforce/2022/10.

352 **a top-to-bottom review:** Larry Gavin, "School District 65 to Consider New Assignment System, New School Boundaries, New School in

Fifth Ward," *Evanston RoundTable*, February 12, 2021, https://evanstonroundtable.com/2021/02/12/school-district-65-to-consider-new-assignment-system-new-school-boundaries-new-school-in-fifth-ward/.

352 **one another on Facebook:** "Kids First Evanston," Facebook, accessed January 14, 2023, https://www.facebook.com/groups/2422730608021076/.

352 **Two hundred twenty-seven:** Memorandum from Sarita Smith to Evanston/Skokie School District 65 Board of Education, "Re: Opening of Schools Enrollment Update for 2020–21," September 15, 2020, https://meetings.boardbook.org/Documents/WebViewer/1247?file=363af55d-2125-41d8-af72-96372c7ba7e8.

352 **strategist Edward Blum:** Anemona Hartocollis, "He Took On the Voting Rights Act and Won. Now He's Taking On Harvard," *New York Times*, November 19, 2017, https://www.nytimes.com/2017/11/19/us/affirmative-action-lawsuits.html.

352 **alleging massive violations:** Letter from Daniel Woodring to Devon Horton and District 65 school board members, October 19, 2020, https://mma.prnewswire.com/media/1315446/SFFA_Evanston__Final_Letter_to_Illinois_School_Board__signed.pdf?p=pdf.

352 **were all unconstitutional:** Carl Campanile, "US Dept. of Education Curbs Decision on Race-Based 'Affinity Groups,'" *New York Post*, March 7, 2021, https://nypost.com/2021/03/07/education-dept-curbs-decision-on-race-based-affinity-groups/.

353 **political action committee:** "About Us," Southlake Families, accessed December 18, 2022, https://www.southlakefamilies.org/about-us.

353 **purple-clad conservative parents:** Benjamin Herold, "Suburban Public Schools Are Now Majority-Nonwhite. The Backlash Has Already Begun," *Education Week*, March 17, 2021, https://www.edweek.org/leadership/suburban-public-schools-are-now-majority-nonwhite-the-backlash-has-already-begun/2021/03.

353 **they deemed "anti-white":** Jordan J. Phelan, "Complaint over Book, Instruction Sparks Community Conversation on Race," *Eagle Times*, August 19, 2020, https://www.eagletimes.com/community/complaint-over-book-instruction-sparks-community-conversation-on-race/article_b7c7ee4c-a81f-5e57-9a2c-9408ec4dec0f.html; Michael Torres, "Main Line Madness," City Journal, September 1, 2021, https://www.city-journal.org/philly-suburbs-schools-adopt-critical-race-theory?wallit_nosession=1; James Oliphant and Gabriella Borter, "Partisan War over Teaching History and Racism Stokes Tensions in U.S. Schools," Reuters, June 23, 2021, https://www.reuters.com/world/us/partisan-war-over-teaching-history-racism-stokes-tensions-us-schools-2021-06-23/.

353 **an executive order:** Donald J. Trump, "Executive Order on Combating Race and Sex Stereotyping," September 22, 2020, https://trumpwhitehouse.archives.gov/presidential-actions/executive-order-combating-race-sex-stereotyping/.

353 **Florida to Idaho:** Sarah Schwartz, "Map: Where Critical Race Theory Is Under Attack," *Education Week*, June 11, 2021, https://www.edweek.org/policy-politics/map-where-critical-race-theory-is-under-attack/2021/06.

354 **7 million votes:** "Presidential Election, 2020," Ballotpedia, https://ballotpedia.org/Presidential_election,_2020.

354 **contested the results:** Alan Feuer, Luke Broadwater, Maggie Haberman, Katie Benner, and Michael S. Schmidt, "Jan. 6: The Story So Far," *New York Times*, https://www.nytimes.com/interactive/2022/us/politics/jan-6-timeline.html.

355 **didn't appear to be logging in:** Memorandum from Stacey Beardsley, Andalib Khelghati, and Terrance Little to Devon Horton, "Re: Remote Learning Update," October 26, 2020, https://meetings.boardbook.org/Documents/WebViewer/1247?file=9c51cb40-7a90-4665-843b-416539206dc9.

355 **An internal analysis:** Memorandum from Stacey Beardsley, Andalib Khelghati, and Terrance Little to Devon Horton, "Re: Remote Learning Update," November 16, 2020, 2–4, https://meetings.boardbook.org/Documents/WebViewer/1247?file=daf949e9-f166-4378-aafb-882acc0dce3e.

355 **children's mental health:** "Remote Learning Update," Evanston/Skokie School District 65, November 16, 2020, 18, https://meetings.boardbook.org/Public/Agenda/1247?meeting=440642.

355 **disclose the names:** Larry Gavin, "District 65 Parents Call for the District to Implement In-Person Learning, Question Metrics," *Evanston RoundTable*, December 19, 2020, https://evanstonroundtable.com/2020/12/19/district-65-parents-call-for-the-district-to-implement-in-person-learning-question-metrics/.

355 **series of emails:** All descriptions of and quotations from the emails exchanged between Devon Horton and Evanston parents in January 2021 are drawn from Larry Gavin, "District 65 School Board Holds Meeting to Discuss Safety; Claim Parents Pushing to Open Schools for In-Person Learning Are 'White Supremacists,'" *Evanston RoundTable*, January 14, 2021, https://evanstonroundtable.com/2021/01/14/district-65-school-board-holds-meeting-to-discuss-safety-claim-parents-pushing-to-open-schools-for-in-person-learning-are-white-supremacists/, unless otherwise noted.

355 **lost a close friend:** "Evanston/Skokie Superintendent Apologizes for White Supremacist Comments," *North Cook News*,

January 26, 2021, https://northcooknews.com/stories/573003183-evanston-skokie-superintendent-apologizes-for-white-supremacist-comments.

356 **fresh round of outrage:** Emails to Evanston/Skokie School District 65 board members, January 14, 2021, FOIA request response, records provided by Evanston/Skokie School District 65.

CHAPTER 16: "DON'T FUCK WITH MY SHINE"

357 **"If white people only":** Lillian Roybal Rose, "White Identity and Counseling White Allies about Racism," in *Impacts of Racism on White Americans*, eds. Benjamin P. Bowser and Raymond G. Hunt (Thousand Oaks, CA: Sage Publications, 1996).

359 **East Los Angeles:** "Lillian Roybal Rose," https://www.lillianroybalrose.com/.

359 **former school counselor:** "Lillian's Legacy," Luna Jiménez Institute for Social Transformation, February 15, 2018, https://ljist.com/featured/lillians-legacy/.

359 **"They see that they were misinformed":** Lillian Roybal Rose, "White Identity and Counseling White Allies about Racism," in *Impacts of Racism on White Americans*.

362 **a hybrid schedule:** "Update from the Superintendent-October 5, 2020," Penn Hills School District, October 5, 2020, https://www.phsd.k12.pa.us/apps/news/article/1310813.

363 **district's outstanding debt:** Michael DiVittorio, "Audit: Penn Hills School District Closing Reserve Fund Deficit," Trib Live, March 31, 2021, https://triblive.com/local/penn-hills/audit-penn-hills-school-district-closing-reserve-fund-deficit/.

363 **transportation and energy:** Daniel J. Matsook, "Financial Recovery Plan Second Amendment," Penn Hills School District, April 21, 2021, 5, https://4.files.edl.io/4a76/10/25/21/182501-25e1ebda-3233-4203-ba6b-2599a3df5654.pdf.

363 **almost $190 billion:** "Elementary and Secondary School Emergency Relief Fund," Office of Elementary & Secondary Education, https://oese.ed.gov/offices/education-stabilization-fund/elementary-secondary-school-emergency-relief-fund/.

363 **a progressive formula:** Mark Lieberman and Andrew Ujifusa, "Everything You Need to Know about Schools and COVID Relief Funds," *Education Week*, September 10, 2021, https://www.edweek.org/policy-politics/everything-you-need-to-know-about-schools-and-covid-relief-funds/2021/09.

364 **With 67 percent:** "2021 Low Income Percentage by LEA and School," Pennsylvania Department of Education, https://www.education.pa.gov/DataAndReporting/LoanCanLowIncome/Pages/PublicSchools.aspx.

364 **a total of $18 million:** Daniel J. Matsook, "Financial Recovery Plan Second Amendment," 5.

364 **more than $160 million:** "Penn Hills School District Financial Statements for the Year Ended June 30, 2021," xiii, https://4.files.edl.io/6081/11/04/22/114900-077d630d-7e20-4a14-a3d9-bbc01e4384b8.pdf.

364 **Nearly 10 percent:** U.S. Census Bureau (2017–2021), Occupancy Status American Community Survey 5-Year Estimates.

364 **the average house:** U.S. Census Bureau, Decennial Census Tables 1950–2000. American Community Survey Tables 2006–2010; 2012–2016; 2013–2017; 2016–2020 (5-Year Estimates), prepared by Social Explorer, accessed August 11, 2020.

364 **groundbreaking national analysis:** Andre Perry, Jonathan Rothwell, and David Harshbarger, "The Devaluation of Assets in Black Neighborhoods: The Case of Residential Property," Metropolitan Policy Program at Brookings Institution, November 2018, https://www.brookings.edu/wp-content/uploads/2018/11/2018.11_Brookings-Metro_Devaluation-Assets-Black-Neighborhoods_final.pdf.

364 **as much as 23 percent:** Jonathan Rothwell, email message to the author, December 16, 2019.

364 **roughly 35 percent Black:** "How Many People Live in Census Tract 5236, Allegheny County, Pennsylvania," *Courier Journal*, accessed December 20, 2022, https://data.courier-journal.com/census/total-population/diversity-index/census-tract-5236-allegheny-county-pennsylvania/140-42003523600/.

365 **rocked by violent demonstrations:** Jamie Martines, Dillon Carr, and Natasha Lindstrom, "Pittsburgh Erupts in Violence as George Floyd Protests Spin Out of Control," Trib Live, May 30, 2020, https://triblive.com/local/pittsburgh-allegheny/pittsburgh-erupts-in-violence-as-george-floyd-protests-spin-out-of-control/.

365 **the Hill District:** "Group Protesting over George Floyd's Death Gathers in East Liberty," CBS Pittsburgh, June 1, 2020, https://www.cbsnews.com/pittsburgh/news/east-liberty-george-floyd-protest-monday/.

365 **drove through the crowd again:** Mick Stinelli, "Penn Hills Man, 63, Charged for Driving into Protest Crowd," *Pittsburgh Post-Gazette*, July 17, 2020, C-7.

365 **"Proud Boys, stand back":** Kathleen Ronayne and Michael Kunzelman, "Trump to Far-Right Extremists: 'Stand Back and Stand By,'" AP News, September 30, 2020, https://apnews.com/article/election-2020-joe-biden-race-and-ethnicity-donald-trump-chris-wallace-0b32339da25fbc9e8b7c7c7066a1db0f.

365 **Pennsylvanians had cast:** Jeremy Roebuck and Jonathan Lai, "Trump and His Allies Tried to Overturn Pennsylvania's Election Results for Two Months. Here Are the Highlights,"

Philadelphia Inquirer, January 7, 2021, https://www.inquirer.com/politics/election/pennsylvania-2020-election-lawsuits-timeline-20210107.html.

366 **at a cabin:** Descriptions of the Smith family's vacation in Seven Springs are drawn from interviews, photos, and videos provided by Bethany Smith.

367 **transfer of presidential power:** Sergio Olmos, "Guns, Ammo . . . Even a Boat: How Oath Keepers Plotted an Armed Coup," *Guardian*, January 14, 2022, https://www.theguardian.com/us-news/2022/jan/14/oath-keepers-leader-charges-armed-plot-us-capitol-attack.

367 **"have a country anymore":** Brian Naylor, "Read Trump's Jan. 6 Speech, a Key Part of Impeachment Trial," NPR, February 10, 2021, https://www.npr.org/2021/02/10/966396848/read-trumps-jan-6-speech-a-key-part-of-impeachment-trial.

367 **was under attack:** Kat Lonsdorf, Courtney Doring, Amy Isackson, Mary Louise Kelly, and Ailsa Chang, "A Timeline of How the Jan. 6 Attack Unfolded—Including Who Said What and When," NPR, https://www.npr.org/2022/01/05/1069977469/a-timeline-of-how-the-jan-6-attack-unfolded-including-who-said-what-and-when.

367 **from suburban Chicago:** Chuck Goudie and Barb Markoff, Christine Tressel and Ross Weidner, "Suburban Chicago Women Charged in Jan. 6 Attack on US Capitol Expected to Plead Guilty," ABC 7, August 16, 2022, https://abc7chicago.com/january-6-2021-capitol-riot-arrest-trudy-castle-kimberly-difrancesco/12131684/; Jason Meisner, "Chicago Woman Arrested for Breaching US Capitol During Jan. 6 Riot," Yahoo Finance, June 2, 2022, https://finance.yahoo.com/news/chicago-woman-arrested-breaching-us-174300205.html.

367 **North Dallas suburbs:** Annie Gowen, "The Rioter Next Door: How the Dallas Suburbs Spawned Domestic Extremists," *Washington Post*, March 21, 2021, https://www.washingtonpost.com/national/dallas-suburbs-capitol-riot/2021/03/21/468646f2-8299-11eb-ac37-4383f7709abe_story.html.

367 **from suburban Pittsburgh:** Paula Reed Ward, "17 from Western Pa. Charged So Far in Connection with Capitol Riot," Trib Live, January 5, 2022, https://triblive.com/local/regional/17-from-western-pa-charged-so-far-in-connection-with-capitol-riot/.

367 **flagpole as weapons:** Paula Reed Ward, "Judge Orders Detention for South Fayette Man Accused in Capitol Riot," Trib Live, January 29, 2021, https://triblive.com/local/judge-orders-detention-for-oakdale-man-accused-in-capitol-riot/.

367 **erected a gallows:** Catie Edmondson, "'So the Traitors Know the Stakes': The Meaning of the Jan. 6 Gallows," *New York Times*, June 16, 2022, https://www.nytimes.com/2022/06/16/us/politics/jan-6-gallows.html.

367 **Speaker of the House Nancy Pelosi:** Spencer S. Hsu, "Man Who Drove from Colo. to D.C. on Jan. 6 Pleads Guilty to Threatening to Shoot Pelosi in Head on Live TV," *Washington Post*, September 10, 2021, https://www.washingtonpost.com/local/legal-issues/pelosi-threat-guilty-plea/2021/09/10/e43066ae-1262-11ec-bc8a-8d9a5b534194_story.html.

CHAPTER 17: WHAT COMES AFTER

369 **a whistleblower alleged:** "Whistleblower: California Deputy Killed Teen to Join Department's 'Gang,'" Spectrum News 9, August 31, 2020, https://www.baynews9.com/fl/tampa/news/2020/08/31/whistleblower—deputy-killed-teen-to-join-department-s—gang—.

369 **to have the tattoo:** By 2022, widespread allegations of criminal gangs operating within L.A. County Sheriff's offices had prompted a series of local and federal investigations. See, e.g., Alene Tchekmedyian and Maya Lau, "L.A. County Deputy Alleges 'Executioner' Gang Dominates Compton Sheriff Station," *Los Angeles Times*, July 30, 2020, https://www.latimes.com/california/story/2020-07-30/sheriff-clique-compton-station-executioners and Ethan Brown, "The Man Who Cracked the Code of L.A.'s Notorious Sheriff Gangs," *New York*, February 2, 2022, https://nymag.com/intelligencer/2022/02/the-man-who-brought-down-l-a-s-notorious-police-gangs.html.

369 **more than three dozen:** "Tracking Coronavirus in Los Angeles County, CA: Latest Maps and Case Count," *New York Times*, https://www.nytimes.com/interactive/2021/us/los-angeles-california-covid-cases.html.

370 **their physical classrooms:** Emily Sanchez, "Compton Teachers Forced to Teach in Empty Classrooms," Annenberg Media, November 6, 2020, https://www.uscannenbergmedia.com/2020/11/06/compton-teachers-forced-to-teach-in-an-empty-classroom/.

370 **pickets and protests:** Howard Blume, "L.A. School Board Approves Deal on Remote Learning; Critics Say It Falls Short on Teaching," *Los Angeles Times*, August 11, 2020, https://www.latimes.com/california/story/2020-08-11/lausd-approves-teaching-agreement-over-critics-objections.

371 **executive Sheryl Sandberg:** Kashmir Hill, "Sheryl Sandberg to Harvard Biz Grads: 'Find a Rocket Ship,'" *Forbes*, May 24, 2012, https://www.forbes.com/sites/kashmirhill/2012/05/24/sheryl-sandberg-to-harvard-biz-grads-find-a-rocket-ship/?sh=2974fdda3b37.

371 **increasingly dire warnings:** Darin Brawley, "Compton Unified School District 2020 Budget Update 1," ComptonSchools, June 16, 2020,

Eyg==

https://www.youtube.com/watch?v
=Tf4T2S0MVrg; Darin Brawley, "Compton
Unified School District 2020 Budget Update 2,"
ComptonSchools, June 23, 2020, https://www
.youtube.com/watch?v=65ngweLe4Z4; Darin
Brawley, "Compton Unified School District
2020 Budget Update 3," ComptonSchools, June
23, 2020, https://www.youtube.com/watch?v
=jueHL9bbzjg.

372 **round of $24 million:** Shannon Soto in
discussion with the author, May 2021.

372 **ESSER funds, $45.9 million:** Shannon Soto in
discussion with the author, May 2021.

372 **another $122 billion:** "Elementary and
Secondary School Emergency Relief Fund,"
Office of Elementary & Secondary Education,
https://oese.ed.gov/offices/education
-stabilization-fund/elementary-secondary-
school-emergency-relief-fund/.

372 **$104 million of which:** "ESSER III Expenditure
Plan," Compton Unified School District,
California Department of Education, July 2021,
https://www.compton.k12.ca.us/media/7410
/cusd-esser-iii-expenditure-plan.pdf.

372 **his public remarks:** "Remarks by President
Biden on the American Rescue Plan," White
House, March 12, 2021, https://www
.whitehouse.gov/briefing-room/speeches
-remarks/2021/03/12/remarks-by-president
-biden-on-the-american-rescue-plan-2/.

372 **the "Compton Pledge":** All details regarding
the Compton Pledge are drawn from N'dea
Yancey-Bragg, "California City to Give 800
Residents Free Cash in the Country's Largest
Guaranteed Income Program," USA Today,
October 20, 2020, https://www.usatoday.com
/story/news/nation/2020/10/20/compton
-california-launches-universal-basic-income
-program/5993508002/; "Compton Pledge Fact
Sheet," Compton Pledge, https://
comptonpledge.org/wp-content/uploads/2020
/12/Compton-Pledge-Factsheet_Final_3.pdf,
unless otherwise noted.

373 **the Pledge's advisory board:** "Compton Pledge
Fact Sheet."

373 **third term as mayor:** Brittany Martin,
"Compton Mayor Aja Brown Will Not Seek
Reelection," Los Angeles magazine, January 26,
2021, https://www.lamag.com/citythinkblog
/compton-mayor-aja-brown-will-not-seek
-reelection/.

373 **most prominent was Emma Sharif:** "Emma
Sharif, Mayor," Compton, California, https://
www.comptoncity.org/our-city/elected
-officials/mayor-emma-sharif.

373 **fixture for Compton Latinos:** Marjorie Miller,
"Column One; Roots Show at This Salon;
Adults Who First Came to Pueblos Unidos
for Haircuts as Children Still Patronize
the Compton Shop, with New Generations
in Tow," Los Angeles Times, September 5,
2008, A.1.

373 **first Latino mayor:** Aziza Shuler, "Compton
Close to Electing First Latino Mayor, Endorsed
by Mayor Brown," Spectrum News 1, April 30,
2021, https://spectrumnews1.com/ca/la-west
/politics/2021/04/30/compton-close-to
-electing-first-latino-mayor—endorsed-by
-mayor-brown.

373 **her full-throated endorsement:** Kailyn Brown
and Ruben Vives, "Compton Could Make
History by Electing Its First Latino Mayor,
Marking a Milestone for the City and Region,"
Los Angeles Times, May 29, 2021, https://www
.latimes.com/california/story/2021-05-29
/compton-could-make-history-by-electing-its
-first-latino-mayor.

373 **wrote on Instagram:** Aja Brown (@ajalbrown),
"Hello Compton Family . . . ," Instagram post,
March 23, 2021, https://drive.google.com/file/d
/1t-DgCbC-UUUyIiQedho1k7MKNuIq7aiz
/view. Deleted post.

374 **studying cross-racial cooperation:** Special
thanks to Manuel Pastor, whose work helped
shape my understanding of Black-Brown
relations in Compton and throughout South
Los Angeles.

374 **a 2016 report:** Manuel Pastor et al.,
"Roots|Raíces: Latino Engagement, Place
Identities, and Shared Futures in South Los
Angeles: Executive Summary," USC Center for
the Study of Immigrant Integration, July 2016,
https://dornsife.usc.edu/assets/sites/731/docs
/Roots_Raices_CSII_Final_WebVersion.pdf.

374 **back into classrooms first:** "Learning
Continuity and Attendance Plan Template
(2020–21)," Compton Unified School District,
July 2020, accessed March 23, 2023,
downloaded from https://elcap.lacoe.edu
/approvedlearningcontinuity and "Reopening—
Elementary Small Cohort Criteria," Compton
Unified School District, July 2020, in the
author's possession.

375 **Jefferson's iReady data:** Data provided by
Compton Unified in response to a records
request, in the author's possession.

375 **Burdensome rents and:** Jenesse Miller, "Even
Before the Pandemic, Struggling L.A. Renters
Cut Back on Food, Clothes and Transportation,"
USC News, December 15, 2020, https://news.usc
.edu/179928/los-angeles-rent-burdened
-households-basic-needs-usc-research/.

375 **skyrocketing home prices:** William Fulton, "It
Seems Like All of California Is Moving to
Texas. Is That True?," Kinder Institute for Urban
Research, March 2, 2021, https://kinder.rice
.edu/urbanedge/it-seems-all-california-moving
-texas-true.

375 **often for Texas:** Fulton, "It Seems Like All of
California Is Moving to Texas. Is That True?"

375 **less than two months:** Natalie Brunell,
"Compton Mayor Aja Brown Accuses LASD of
Misconduct, Sheriff Responds," Spectrum News
1, August 7, 2020, https://spectrumnews1.com

/ca/la-west/news/2020/08/08/compton-mayor
-aja-brown-accuses-of-lasd-misconduct—
sheriff-responds.

376 **ambushed two deputies:** Leanne Suter and
Marc Cota-Robles, "2 LA County Deputies in
Stable Condition After Being Shot in Compton;
Search for Gunman Continues," ABC 7,
September 14, 2020, https://abc7.com/la
-deputies-shot-los-angeles-shooting-compton
-ambush/6421149/.

CHAPTER 18: NO MORE AWAY

377 **"There is no 'away'":** Timothy Morton,
*Hyperobjects: Philosophy and Ecology after the
End of the World* (Minneapolis: University of
Minnesota Press, 2013), 112.

377 **lawsuits and hearings:** Maryclaire Dale,
"Trump's Legal Team Cried Vote Fraud, but
Courts Found None," Associated Press,
November 22, 2020, https://apnews.com/article
/election-2020-donald-trump-pennsylvania
-elections-talk-radio-433b6efe72720d8648
221f405c2111f9.

378 **balance of $3.1 million**: All details regarding
Lovejoy ISD's spring 2021 budget discussions
are drawn from "Pathway to a Balanced
Budget," school board presentation, Lovejoy
Independent School District, March 25, 2021,
in author's possession, unless otherwise
noted.

378 **two hundred lower-grades students:**
"Elementary Program Structure," school board
presentation, Lovejoy Independent School
District, April 19, 2021, 1, in author's
possession.

378 **fewer than 2 percent:** Corbett Smith and Emily
Donaldson, "Wealthy Texas Schools Didn't
Receive Much Federal Pandemic Aid. But Costs
Are Mounting, Causing Tight Budgets," *Dallas
Morning News*, May 17, 2021, https://www
.dallasnews.com/news/education/2021/05/17
/wealthy-texas-schools-didnt-receive-much
-federal-pandemic-aid-but-costs-are
-mounting-causing-tight-budgets/.

378 **$6 million budget hole:** Corbett Smith,
"Lovejoy to Vote on Closing an Elementary
Campus, as Challenges Brought on by
Enrollment, COVID-19 Mount," *Dallas
Morning News*, April 23, 2021, https://www
.dallasnews.com/news/education/2021/04/23
/lovejoy-to-vote-on-closing-an-elementary
-campus-as-challenges-brought-on-by
-enrollment-covid-mount/.

379 **leaving the district:** Laurie Vondersaar,
"Lovejoy ISD Superintendent Dr. Michael
Goddard Leaving to Assume New Role,"
press release, Lovejoy Independent
School District, 2021, in author's
possession.

379 **local private school:** Michael Goddard, "Letter
to the board," public letter, Lovejoy

Independent School District, February 22, 2021,
in author's possession.

379 **three dozen teachers:** Chloe Bennett, "Lovejoy
ISD Closing Flagship Elementary School to
Combat Projected Multimillion Dollar
Shortfall," *Dallas Morning News*, June 4, 2021,
https://www.dallasnews.com/news/education
/2021/06/04/lovejoy-isd-closing-flagship
-elementary-school-to-combat-projected
-multimillion-dollar-shortfall/.

379 **Positions in school security:** "Reduction in
Force," school board presentation, Lovejoy
Independent School District, April 19, 2021, 1,
in author's possession.

379 **sound financial management:** Tracy Ginsburg,
"Lovejoy ISD Earns the Excellence in Financial
Management Award," press release, Texas
Association of School Business Officials,
March 25, 2021, in author's possession.

379 **more than $9 million:** "Athletic Improvement
Bond Projects," school board presentation,
Lovejoy Independent School District, May 10,
2021, 1–3, in author's possession.

379 **eleven additional resignations:** "Personnel
Sheet—Resignations," school board
presentation, Lovejoy Independent School
District, May 10, 2021, 1, in author's possession.

379 **expanded the fees:** "Student Fees for 2021–
2022," school board presentation, Lovejoy Independent School District, May 24, 2021, 1–3, in
author's possession.

379 **Because of declining enrollment:** Bennett,
"Lovejoy ISD Closing Flagship Elementary
School to Combat Projected Multimillion
Dollar Shortfall."

379 **$175,000 in donations:** Smith, "Lovejoy to
Vote on Closing an Elementary Campus, as
Challenges Brought on by Enrollment,
COVID-19 Mount."

379 **to the district's:** "April 19, 2021, Board Brief,"
Lovejoy Independent School District, April 19,
2021, https://myemail.constantcontact.com
/Lovejoy-ISD——April-19–2021-Board-Brief
.html?soid=1114502746978&aid=EE6DQ
7UGJkc.

380 **THEO Christian Solution:** "Theo Christian
Solution Inc.," Charity Navigator, https://www
.charitynavigator.org/ein/813992485.

381 **labeled domestic terrorists:** Andrew Ujifusa,
"National School Board Group's Apology for
'Domestic Terrorism' Letter May Not Quell
Uproar," *Education Week*, October 24, 2021,
https://www.edweek.org/policy-politics
/national-school-board-groups-apology
-for-domestic-terrorism-letter-may-not
-quell-uproar/2021/10.

381 **Inflation was sending:** "Consumer Price
Index—June 2021," news release—
USDL-21-1313, Bureau of Labor Statistics,
2021), 1–9.

381 **pharmacies wouldn't even fill:** Yasmin Tayag,
"How Pharmacists Are Dealing with the Surge

of Shady Ivermectin Prescriptions," *Slate*, September 9, 2021, https://slate.com/technology /2021/09/pharmacists-ivermectin-prescriptions .html.

382 **play a pivotal role**: Robert Costa, "'They're Afraid': Suburban Voters in Red States Threaten GOP's Grip on Power,' *Washington Post*, August 9, 2019, https://www.washingtonpost.com /politics/theyre-afraid-suburban-voters-in-red -states-threaten-gops-grip-on-power/2019/08 /08/86b12410-b868-11e9-bad6-609f75bfd97f _story.html.

382 **by 67 percentage points**: Perry Bacon, Jr., "How Georgia Turned Blue," FiveThirtyEight, November 18, 2020, https://fivethirtyeight.com /features/how-georgia-turned-blue/.

382 **among college-educated whites**: Nate Cohn, Matthew Conlen, and Charlie Smart, "Detailed Turnout Data Shows How Georgia Turned Blue," *New York Times*, November 17, 2020, https://www.nytimes.com/interactive/2020/11 /17/upshot/georgia-precinct-shift-suburbs. html.

382 **county by 18**: Bacon, Jr., "How Georgia Turned Blue."

382 **won Gwinnett by 21 points**: "Georgia Runoff Results: Loeffler vs. Warnock," *New York Times*, January 15, 2021, https://www.nytimes.com /interactive/2021/01/05/us/elections/results - georgia-senate-runoff-loeffler-warnock .html.

382 *Washington Post* **reported**: Bernard L. Fraga, Zachary Peskowitz, and James Szewcyzk, "New Georgia Runoffs Data Finds That More Black Voters Than Usual Came Out. Trump Voters Stayed Home," *Washington Post*, January 29, 2021, https://www.washingtonpost.com /politics/2021/01/29/new-georgia -runoffs-data-finds-that-more-black-voters -than-usual-came-out-trump-voters-stayed -home/.

383 **were finally called**: Brian Slodysko, "Explainer: How Democrats Won Georgia's 2 Senate Runoffs," Associated Press, January 6, 2021, https:// apnews.com/article/associated-press -georgia-election-result-60954fd7d3d3 b6b49a8884c0c026247d.

383 **a Confederate flag**: Javonte Anderson, "Capitol Riot Images Showing Confederate Flag a Reminder of Country's Darkest Past," *USA Today*, January 7, 2021, https://www.usatoday.com /story/news/2021/01/07/capitol-riot-images -confederate-flag-terror/6588104002/.

383 **Georgians eventually arrested**: Chris Joyner, "Georgia Couple Arrested in Jan. 6 Capitol Riot," *Atlanta Journal-Constitution*, March 14, 2022, https://www.ajc.com/news/georgia -couple-arrested-in-jan-6-capitol-riot/PGF MCZ4UE5HZTKPABYARMZIH7E/.

383 **Verden Andrew Nalley**: "Buford Man Arrested for Role in Riots at U.S. Capitol, FBI Says," *Gwinnett Daily Post*, February 18, 2021, https://

www.gwinnettdailypost.com/local/buford -man-arrested-for-role-in-riots-at-u-s-capitol -fbi- says/article_73d7409a-7243-11eb-b0e2 -cb4615cd5689.html.

383 **an alarming message**: Chris Joyner, "Buford Man Pleads Guilty to Jan. 6 Charge," *Atlanta Journal-Constitution*, December 2, 2021, https://www.ajc.com/news/buford-man-pleads -guilty-to-jan-6-charge/7Q4RVVQU6VHSLA 3OKF4WKRFG6U/.

383 **attacked him as "hapless"**: Paul Conner, "Trump Presses 'Hapless' Georgia Governor to Overrule Secretary of State on Signature Matching," Fox News, November 30, 2020, https://www.foxnews.com/politics/trump -georgia-governor-brian-kemp-overrule- secretary-of-state-signature-matching- recount.

383 **for a long time**: Aris Folley, "Georgia Gov. Kemp Says He'd 'Absolutely' Back Trump as 2024 Nominee," The Hill, March 3, 2021, https://thehill.com/homenews/state-watch /541539-georgia-gov-kemp-says-hed -absolutely-back-trump-as-2024-nominee/.

383 **new voting rules**: Rich McKay, "Georgia Bans Giving Water to Voters in Line under Sweeping Restrictions," Reuters, March 25, 2021, https:// www.reuters.com/article/us-usa-georgia -voting/georgia-bans-giving-water-to -voters-in-line-under-sweeping-restrictions -idUSKBN2BH2TC.

384 **won their elections**: "Karen Watkins (Georgia)," Ballotpedia, https://ballotpedia.org /Karen_Watkins_(Georgia), and "Tarece Johnson," Ballotpedia, https://ballotpedia.org /Tarece_Johnson.

384 **vote to oust**: Alia Malik, "Gwinnett Superintendent's Legacy Confronts Increased Diversity," *Atlanta Journal-Constitution*, April 7, 2021, https://www.ajc.com/news/gwinnett -superintendents-legacy-confronts-increased -diversity/FUEK7QAABBBAVADMEG75S WKIYY/.

384 **"This is a detrimental change"**: Alia Malik, "Gwinnett School Board Ends Superintendent Wilbanks' Contract Early," *Atlanta Journal- Constitution*, March 19, 2021, https://www.ajc .com/news/gwinnett-school-board-ends -superintendents-wilbanks-contract-early /FGJNBMTNOZDN7C5AQUFYM7 O52Y/.

384 **beaten Democratic challenger**: "Mary Kay Murphy," Ballotpedia, https://ballotpedia.org /Mary_Kay_Murphy.

384 **than five thousand cases**: Alia Malik, "Anti-Mask Crowd Disrupts Gwinnett School Board Meeting," *Atlanta Journal-Constitution*, May 21, 2021, https://www.ajc.com/news/anti-mask -crowd-disrupts-gwinnett-school-board-meet ing/IYO7R6GHJ5DTLEFCQHER7V3GBA/.

384 **soon claim more**: Allie Goolrick, "More Than 60 Georgia Teachers, Staff Lost to COVID-19

Since July 2021," WSBTV.com, February 20, 2022, https://www.wgauradio.com/news/local/atlanta/more-than-60-georgia-teachers-staff-lost-covid-19-since-july-2021/SFURXQOXAJH25E3VGVZGTEU3HI/.

384 **the monthly meeting:** All descriptions and quotations from the Gwinnett County Public Schools' May 2021 board meeting are drawn from "Business Meeting May 20, 2021," Gwinnett County Public Schools, https://publish.gwinnett.k12.ga.us/gcps/home/gcpstv/videos/gcps/boe-meetings/553117126?WCM_PAGE.gcpstv-episodes=1; and "May 20, 2021—Monthly Business Meeting 7 p.m.," school board meeting agenda, Gwinnett County Public Schools, May 2021, 4.03, https://go.boarddocs.com/ga/gcps/Board.nsf/Public, unless otherwise noted.

385 **can't remove us all:** Anya Kamenetz, "What It's Like to Be on the Front Lines of the School Board Culture War," NPR, October 21, 2021, https://www.npr.org/2021/10/21/1047334766/school-board-threats-race-masks-vaccines-protests-harassment.

385 **later told NPR:** Kamenetz, "What It's Like to Be on the Front Lines of the School Board Culture War."

386 **opening an investigation:** Alia Malik, "School Board's Behavior Questioned: Written Complaints of Code of Ethics Concerns Prompt Accreditation Study, Training Sessions," *Atlanta Journal-Constitution*, June 7, 2021.

387 **11–2 in favor:** Ty Tagami, "Board: Limit Race Lessons in Ga. Schools: Resolution Comes amid Emotional Debate over Curriculum Changes," *Atlanta Journal-Constitution*, June 4, 2021, https://www.ajc.com/education/state-board-passes-resolution-to-limit-classroom-discussions-of-race/L4HYBED74BBFLEYTK5JSNDTK44/.

387 **approved comprehensive plan:** All details and descriptions regarding Gwinnett County's comprehensive plan are drawn from "Gwinnett 2040 Unified Plan," Gwinnett County Board of Commissioners, September 27, 2022, https://www.gwinnettcounty.com/web/gwinnett/departments/planningdevelopment/services/landuseplanning/2040unifiedplan, unless otherwise noted.

388 **the 71,000-seat home:** "Stadium Fast Facts," Mercedes-Benz Stadium, https://mercedesbenzstadium.com/stadium-fast-facts/.

389 **schools began reopening:** Bill Smith, "In-Person Schools Finally Reopen in District 65," Evanston Now, February 18, 2021, https://evanstonnow.com/in-person-schools-finally-reopen-in-district-65/.

390 **more than twenty reading specialists:** Mary Gavin, "District 65 Replaces 22 Reading Specialists with 18 Interventionists," *Evanston RoundTable*, March 16, 2021, https://evanstonroundtable.com/2021/03/16/district-65-replaces-22-reading-specialists-with-18-interventionists/.

390 **"There are lots of different":** "Thursday—Intergenerational, Black Families and Black Villages," lesson plan, District 65, 2021, 1–3, in author's possession.

390 **affirming transgender people:** "Wednesday—Queer-Affirming, Trans-Affirming and Collective Value," lesson plan, District 65, 2021, 1–2, in author's possession.

390 **BLM movement was necessary:** "Monday—Restorative Justice, Empathy and Loving Engagement," lesson plan, District 65, 2021, 1–3, in author's possession.

391 **to be unapologetically Black:** "Friday—Black Women and Unapologetically Black," lesson plan, District 65, 2021, 1–3, in author's possession.

391 **"What Happens When a Slogan":** Conor Friedersdorf, "What Happens When a Slogan Becomes the Curriculum," *Atlantic*, March 14, 2021, https://www.theatlantic.com/ideas/archive/2021/03/should-black-lives-matter-agenda-be-taught-school/618277/.

391 *Not My Idea:* Anastasia Higginbotham, *Not My Idea: A Book about Whiteness* (New York: Dottir Press, 2018).

391 **that Horton planned:** Jeff Hirsch, "D65 Citizen Panel to Advise on Redistricting, 5th Ward School," Evanston Now, February 25, 2021, https://evanstonnow.com/d65-citizen-panel-to-advise-on-redistricting-5th-ward-school/.

392 **lineup of liberal challengers:** Jordan Mangi, "Here's Who's Running for D65, D202 School Boards This April," *Daily Northwestern*, January 18, 2021, https://dailynorthwestern.com/2021/01/18/city/heres-whos-running-for-d65-d202-school-boards-this-april/.

392 **a Black woman:** "Ndona Muboyayi, Candidate for District 65 School Board," *Evanston RoundTable*, March 15, 2021, https://evanstonroundtable.com/2021/03/15/ndona-muboyayi-candidate-for-district-65-school-board/.

392 **a white woman:** "Katie Voorhees, Candidate for District 65 School Board," *Evanston RoundTable*, March 14, 2021, https://evanstonroundtable.com/2021/03/14/katie-magrino-candidate-for-district-65-school-board/.

394 **local education activists:** All descriptions and quotations from the D65 Caregivers of Color and Our Village March & Vote for Our Children's Lives are drawn from Nick Francis, Delaney Nelson, and Jorja Siemons, "District 65 Parents of Color Lead March to Cast Ballots for Equity-Focused School Board Amid Contentious Election Season," *Daily Northwestern*, April 5, 2021, https://dailynorthwestern.com/2021/04/05/city/district-65-parents-of-color-lead-march-to-cast-ballots-for-equity-focused

-school-board-amid-contentious-election
-season/; Heidi Randhava, "District 65
Caregivers of Color & Our Village Lead March
and Press Conference in Support of the
District's Efforts to Put Equity at the Forefront,"
Evanston RoundTable, April 5, 2021, https://
evanstonroundtable.com/2021/04/05/district
-65-caregivers-of-color-our-village-lead-march
-and-press-conference-in-support-of-the
-districts-efforts-to-put-equity-at-the-
forefront/; and "Parents of Color March—
District 65 Evanston Rally—Karla Thomas,
Melissa Blount, Atena Danner," Karla Thomas,
April 4, 2021, https://www.youtube.com/watch
?v=O97Lm09JdeA, unless otherwise noted.

396 **$40 million school:** Adina Keeling, "Plans for
Fifth Ward School Approved in Historic 7–0
Vote," *Evanston RoundTable*, March 15, 2022,
https://evanstonroundtable.com/2022/03/15
/fifth-ward-school-approved-in-historic-vote/.

396 **outside the old Foster building:** Bob
Seidenberg, "Possible New Piece to Fifth Ward
School Campus Puzzle—a Library?," *Evanston
RoundTable*, December 17, 2022, https://
evanstonroundtable.com/2022/12/17/possible
-new-piece-to-fifth-ward-school-puzzle
-a-library/.

396 **soon step down:** Duncan Agnew, "Tanyavutti
Resigns from District 65 School Board After 6
Years," *Evanston RoundTable*, September 20,
2022, https://evanstonroundtable.com/2022/09
/20/tanyavutti-resigns-from-district-65-school
-board-after-6-years/.

397 **reopened to everyone:** Melissa Gomez, "More
Los Angeles School Districts Are Moving to
Reopen," *Los Angeles Times*, March 5, 2021,
https://www.latimes.com/california/story/2021
-03-05/schools-in-los-angles-county-are
-making-swift-plans-to-reopen.

397 **and star-shaped balloons:** All descriptions and
quotations from Patricia Rivera's fifth-grade
classroom during the 2020–21 school year are
drawn from remote observations conducted
over Zoom, unless otherwise noted.

399 **old Compton High:** Kimberly Morris,
Facebook, June 1, 2021, https://www.facebook
.com/kimberly.morris.94402/posts/pfbid0V7
GkfD7M8Qtx2KsTkj29MvJTb2a2Hn
DbhAzD8epXK4DWAasiDm1rrjMDmp1mFm
gYl?__cft__[0]=AZU0vHW_ti5S_lboIBq
chRud0x9mIqBCjCm1h5eYorhTwrG5hb
wrc4XGH1xHsRrdOY_1dlOoptS-9qklXhC
OEBWEiy_0ohUiwIWqCfrpJxek7G6hT34eH
1V1CIX9HBFWP1Q&__tn__=%2CO%2CP-R.

399 **"All-American" bedroom community:**
"All-America City Winners," National Civic
League, January 30, 2023, https://www
.nationalcivicleague.org/america-city-award
/past-winners/.

399 **a time capsule:** A. P. Mattier, "Record of
Contents Placed in the Corner Stone Repository
of the Compton Junior College Administration

Building," October 29, 1935, SPC.2005.001, box
5, folder 21, Compton History Collection, Gerth
Archives and Special Collections, California
State University, Dominguez Hills, Carson,
California.

399 **"As we seal the cornerstone":** Letter from H. J.
Mayo to Compton Union Secondary Schools,
in A. P. Mattier, "Record of Contents Placed in
the Corner Stone Repository of the
Compton Junior College Administration
Building."

399 **dirt and rubble:** Charles Davis, photo,
Facebook, June 4, 2021, https://www
.facebook.com/photo?fbid=4043466312408
466&set=pcb.1197066960730516; WJOYPro
ductions, "Compton High School Rebuild,"
YouTube video, 1:24 min.,
https://www.youtube.com/watch?v
=5wRVj44E2bU.

399 **to the NFL:** Ryan Brennan, "25 High Schools
with the Most NFL Players," At the Buzzer,
October 15, 2021, https://at-the-buzzer
.com/high-schools-with-the-most-nfl
-players/.

399 **of dump trucks:** West Coast Footage,
"Compton High School 8/26/21," YouTube
video, 2:09 min., https://www.youtube.com
/watch?v=nB8E8bqKqDg.

399 **on Facebook Live:** Micah Ali, "Compton High
School Ceremony—Demolition," Facebook,
March 31, 2020, https://www.facebook.com
/micah.ali.1/videos/10219710748832684
/?__tn__=%2CO-R.

400 **high school soaring:** Shannon Soto in
discussion with the author, May 2021.

400 **just 218 votes:** "Election Results," Compton
California, https://www.comptoncity.org
/departments/city-clerk/elections/election
-results.

400 **felony vote-rigging:** James Queally and Ruben
Vives, "Compton City Councilman Charged
with Election Rigging, Bribery in Race Decided
by One Vote," *Los Angeles Times*, August 13,
2021, https://www.latimes.com/california
/story/2021-08-13/compton-city-councilman
-charged-with-election-rigging-bribery-in
-race-decided-by-one-vote.

400 **at higher risk:** "Local Government High Risk,"
Auditor of the State of California, https://www
.auditor.ca.gov/local_high_risk/at-a-glance
-csa.

402 **property tax hike:** Michael DiVittorio, "Penn
Hills School District Officials Approve 1.3%
Tax Hike as Part of 2021–22 Budget," Trib Live,
June 30, 2021, https://triblive.com
/local/penn-hills/penn-hills-school-district
-officials-approve-1-3-tax-hike-as
-part-of-2021-22-budget/.

402 **"abnormal fungal ecology":** Herbert Layman,
"Report on Mold Investigation of Penn Hills
Elementary," September 7, 2021, 5, Penn Hills
School District records request response.

402 **install industrial dehumidifiers:** Michael
DiVittorio, "Penn Hills School District Officials
Address Reports of Mold at Elementary School;
Building Deemed Safe," Trib Live,
August 26, 2021, https://triblive.com/local
/penn-hills/penn-hills-school
-district-officials-address-reports-of-mold
-at-the-elementary-school
-building-deemed-to-be-safe/.

403 **named Timothy Morton:** All descriptions of
Timothy Morton's philosophy of hyperobjects
are drawn from Timothy Morton, *Hyperobjects:
Philosophy and Ecology After the End of the*

World (Minneapolis: University of Minnesota
Press, 2013), unless otherwise noted.

403 **radioactive nuclear waste:** Mitch Jacoby, "As
Nuclear Waste Piles Up, Scientists Seek the
Best Long-Term Storage Solutions," *Chemical
& Engineering News*, March 30, 2020,
https://cen.acs.org/environment/pollution
/nuclear-waste-piles-scientists-seek-best
/98/i12.

404 **$2,000 a month:** "Schenley Apartments,"
PMC Property Group, https://www
.pmcpropertygroup.com/properties/schenley
-apartments.

INDEX

Italicized page numbers indicate material in maps.